德古意特认知语言学应用丛书

# COGNITIVE LINGUISTICS

## CURRENT APPLICATIONS AND FUTURE PERSPECTIVES

# 认知语言学：
## 应用与展望

Gitte Kristiansen, Michel Achard, René Dirven,
Francisco J. Ruiz de Mendoza Ibáñez 编

上海外语教育出版社
外教社 SHANGHAI FOREIGN LANGUAGE EDUCATION PRESS
www.sflep.com

De Gruyter Mouton

# 图书在版编目（CIP）数据

认知语言学：应用与展望 ／（西）吉特·克里斯蒂安森等编.
—上海：上海外语教育出版社，2017
（德古意特认知语言学应用丛书）
ISBN 978-7-5446-5030-4

I. ①认… II. ①吉… III. ①认知语言学—研究—英文 IV. ①H0-06

中国版本图书馆CIP数据核字（2017）第249808号

*Cognitive Linguistics: Current Applications and Future Perspectives* edited by
Gitte Kristiansen, Michel Achard, René Dirven, Francisco J. Ruiz de Mendoza
Ibáñez
© Walter de Gruyter GmbH Berlin Boston. All rights reserved.
This work is a reprint edition of the original work from De Gruyter, *Cognitive
Linguistics: Current Applications and Future Perspectives* edited by Gitte
Kristiansen, Michel Achard, René Dirven, Francisco J. Ruiz de Mendoza
Ibáñez and is only intended for sale throughout the People's Republic of China,
excluding the territories of Hong Kong, Macau and Taiwan. The work may not
be translated or copied in whole or part without the written permission of the
publisher (Walter de Gruyter GmbH, Genthiner Straße 13, 10785 Berlin,
Germany).
本书由德古意特出版社授权上海外语教育出版社有限公司出版。
仅供在中华人民共和国境内（香港、澳门、台湾除外）销售。

图字：09–2017–666号

**出版发行：上海外语教育出版社**
（上海外国语大学内） 邮编：200083
电　　话：021-65425300（总机）
电子邮箱：bookinfo@sflep.com.cn
网　　址：http://www.sflep.com
责任编辑：苗　杨

印　　刷：上海叶大印务发展有限公司
开　　本：700×1000　1/16　印张 32.25　字数 652千字
版　　次：2018 年 5 月第 1 版　2018 年 5 月第 1 次印刷
印　　数：1 500 册

书　　号：ISBN 978-7-5446-5030-4 / H
定　　价：100.00 元

本版图书如有印装质量问题，可向本社调换
质量服务热线：4008-213-263　电子邮箱：editorial@sflep.com

# 出版说明

　　认知语言学是语言学的一门重要分支学科，自20世纪80年代诞生以来，受到了国际和国内学界的广泛关注。近年来，外教社陆续推出了一系列相关丛书，集中体现了国际、国内的优质研究成果。其中"国际认知语言学经典论丛"收入了Ronald Langacker、Leonard Talmy、Dirk Geeraerts等国际认知语言学领域顶尖学者的经典作品；"外教社认知语言学丛书·普及系列"、"外教社认知语言学丛书·应用系列"则体现了国内学界的最新研究成果。这些丛书因内容权威、见解独到受到了外语界的广泛好评。

　　认知语言学作为一门新兴的跨领域学科，与多种学科有密切的联系，具有很强的应用意义。因此，我们又从德古意特出版社近年来推出的相关学术图书中精选了6种，组成"德古意特认知语言学应用丛书"，引进出版。丛书反映了近十几年来认知语言学应用领域的前沿成果，集中体现了该学科的理论与实践、应用与展望，及其与人工智能、诗学、语言教学等领域的联系和互动，信息量大，时效性强，代表了国际认知语言学应用研究方面的最高水准。丛书作者汇集了Gitte Kristiansen、Francisco J. Ruiz de Mendoza Ibáñez、René Dirven等国际认知语言学界领军人物，以及欧美相关领域的优秀学者，体现了国际认知语言学应用研究方面的最强阵容。

　　相信丛书的引进可进一步帮助国内读者了解这一领域的研究热点和最新成果，为国内研究者带来新的启示。

# Cognitive Linguistics: Current Applications and Future Perspectives

*edited by*
Gitte Kristiansen
Michel Achard
René Dirven
Francisco J. Ruiz de Mendoza Ibáñez

# Acknowledgements

The editors of this volume would like to thank those who made this publication possible.

First and foremost we are deeply grateful to Anke Beck for her interest in this project.

We also wish to express our gratitude to all the contributors for their insights and professionalism – and for complying with strict deadlines in spite of their many other commitments.

Finally, a sincere thanks goes to Birgit Sievert, Wolfgang Konwitschny, Monika Wendland, Julia Ulrich, Ursula Kleinhenz, Jennifer Mand and Kirstin Börgen at Mouton de Gruyter for their efficient help and fruitful cooperation.

# Table of contents

# List of contributors

*Michel Achard*
Department of Linguistics
Rice University
Houston, TX
USA
e-mail: achard@rice.edu

*John A. Barnden*
School of Computer Science
University of Birmingham
U. K.
e-mail: J.A.Barnden@
cs.bham.ac.uk

*Frank Boers*
Department of Applied
Linguistics
Erasmushogeschool
Brussels
Belgium
e-mail: frank.boers@docent.
ehb.be
Institute of Education
University of Antwerp
e-mail: Frank.Boers@ua.ac.be

*Cristiano Broccias*
Department of Linguistic
and Cultural Communication
Università di Genova
Italy
e-mail: Cristiano.Broccias@
unige.it

*Seana Coulson*
Department of Cognitive Science
University of California
San Diego, CA
USA
e-mail: coulson@cogsci.ucsd.edu

*René Dirven*
Mechelen
Belgium
e-mail: rene.dirven@pandora.be

*Charles Forceville*
Department of Media Studies
Universiteit van Amsterdam
The Netherlands
e-mail: c.j.forceville@uva.nl

*Margaret H. Freeman*
Myrifield Institute for Cognition
and the Arts
Heath, MA
USA
e-mail: freemamh@lavc.edu

*Dirk Geeraerts*
Department of Linguistics
University of Leuven
Belgium
e-mail: dirk.geeraerts@arts.
kuleuven.be

*Raymond W. Gibbs, Jr.*
Department of Psychology
University of California
Santa Cruz, CA
USA
e-mail: gibbs@ucsc.edu

*Susan Goldin-Meadow*
Department of Psychology
University of Chicago, IL
USA
e-mail: sgm@uchicago.edu

*Terry Janzen*
Department of Linguistics
University of Manitoba
Canada
e-mail: janzent@cc.umanitoba.ca

*Gitte Kristiansen*
Department of English Language
and Linguistics
Universidad Complutense
de Madrid
Madrid
Spain
e-mail: gkristia@filol.ucm.es

*Seth Lindstromberg*
Hilderstone College
Kent
U.K.
e-mail: TessanSeth@aol.com

*Şeyda Özçalışkan*
Department of Psychology
University of Chicago, IL
USA
e-mail: seyda@uchicago.edu

*Gary B. Palmer*
Department of Anthropology
and Ethnic Studies
University of Nevada
Las Vegas, NV
USA
e-mail: gary.palmer@unlv.edu

*Klaus-Uwe Panther*
Department of English
and American Studies
Universität Hamburg
Germany
e-mail: Panther@uni-hamburg.de

*Marcus Perlman*
Department of Psychology
University of California
Santa Cruz, CA
USA
e-mail: mperlman@ucsc.edu

*Tim Rohrer*
Colorado Advanced Research
Institute
Boulder, CO
USA
e-mail: rohrer@cogsci.ucsd.edu

*Francisco J. Ruiz de Mendoza
Ibáñez*
Department of Modern
Languages
Universidad de La Rioja
Logrono, La Rioja
Spain
e-mail: ruizdemendoza@
reterioja.com

*John R. Taylor*
Department of English
University of Otago
New Zealand
e-mail: john.taylor@stonebow.
otago.ac.nz

*Tony Veale*
School of Computer Science
and Informatics
University College Dublin
Ireland
e-mail: tony.veale@ucd.ie

# Introduction
# Cognitive Linguistics: Current applications and future perspectives

*Gitte Kristiansen, Michel Achard, René Dirven and Francisco J. Ruiz de Mendoza Ibáñez*

## 1. General orientation of the volume: towards an empirical revolution

The collective volume *Cognitive Linguistics: Current Applications and Future Perspectives* brings together specific case studies and critical overviews of work in a variety of CL strands. Written by prominent researchers, the chapters of the volume thus provide the scientific community with an updated survey of recent research in Cognitive Linguistics. Most authors furthermore go beyond the more immediate scope of describing or exemplifying state-of-the-art research (e.g. by providing the reader with a generally accessible synthesis or a specialized case study) and explicitly address a number of pressing questions pertaining to future perspectives and future research agendas.

Together with its companion volume *Cognitive Linguistics: Basic Readings* (Cognitive Linguistics Research 34, edited by Dirk Geeraerts), it constitutes a highly informative resource for linguists and scholars in neighbouring disciplines, and in general for any scholar wishing to become familiar with what Cognitive Linguistics is all about. Whereas *Cognitive Linguistics: Basic Readings* offers an introductory survey of the foundational concepts of Cognitive Linguistics, the present volume focuses on more recent theoretical developments, illustrates the many fields of application that CL already covers (both within linguistics and in an interdisciplinary environment), and identifies the future research trends that CL is now heading for.

At the same time, the present volume is the very first issue in the new book series *Applications of Cognitive Linguistics* (ACL). In collaboration with its sister series *Cognitive Linguistics Research*, ACL offers a platform for high quality work which applies the rich framework developed in Cognitive Linguistics to a wide range of different fields of application. These fields include descriptive linguistics, cultural linguistics, language acquisition, discourse studies, sociolinguistics, visual communication, stylistics, poetics, pedagogical linguistics, computational linguistics, signed language and still many other fields, often within an interdisciplinary framework. The goals of ACL will be summarised in section 3 of this introduction.

First and foremost, however, as the subtitle suggests, the volume overviews and explores the major avenues of the cognitive linguistic enterprise at present and towards the future. Over the last two, perhaps even three, decades, Cognitive Linguistics has gradually but firmly established itself as a complete and innovating discipline, but certainly not one which for these reasons has ceased to evolve, nor to expand. The contributions in this volume testify to the existence of a number of different strands, the most important of which may be summarised as follows. First, a number of basic concepts (cf. the twelve cornerstones of Cognitive Linguistics described and exemplified in *Cognitive Linguistics: Basic Readings*) are currently being critically refined or even challenged. Second, the fact that Cognitive Linguistics is fully committed to the analysis of meaning in all its various facets naturally lends itself to multiple applications in all those areas of human communication where meaningfulness is relevant. Hence, the range of applications is expanding, not only across disciplines, but also within linguistics itself. This volume is a representative, but necessarily non-exhaustive illustration of this trend: while it covers a broader perspective than most other "readers" or "introductions" to Cognitive Linguistics, it obviously cannot reflect all of the many burgeoning applications. And last, but not least, there is a call for increasing methodological depth, to ensure a firm position for CL within Cognitive Science at large.

The volume is structured in six main sections. While the first three sections (chapters 1–8) focus on fundamental theoretical and methodological issues, the last sections (chapters 9–15) either discuss or exemplify the extent to which the cognitive linguistic framework can be applied in a variety of neighbouring disciplines (i.e. interdisciplinary or transdisciplinary applications) or to a wide range of practical language-related phenomena (applied linguistics). The distinction between these two main areas (theory and method vs. interdisciplinary applications and applied linguistics) is not, however, meant as a strictly separated one. On the contrary, application perspectives are legion in the first part, and basic theoretical issues naturally pervade the more application-oriented sections of the second part.

The first section, 'The cognitive base', addresses issues which in various ways relate to the basic tenet that Cognitive Linguistics is fundamentally usage-based. The section opens with a chapter on linguistic methodology and emphasizes the necessity of an empirical revolution. In the rest of section 1, the mental lexicon is seen as the highly flexible result of numerous usage events, and the various grammar models such as cognitive grammar, construction grammar, and radical construction grammar are revisited in terms of notational variants. The second section, 'The conceptual leap', looks into the embodied basis and nature of conceptual metaphor, the semiotic and indexical basis of conceptual metonymy, and the rhetorical potential of conceptual blending. The third section, 'The psychological basis', exhibits a possible implementation of the empirical revolution advocated in chapter 1 to the area of metaphor research.

Sections 4 to 6 exemplify a representative selection of fields of application. The first comes to the fore in section 4, 'Go tell it on the mountain,' which focuses on language, culture and thought. It opens with a dialogue between cognitive linguistics and anthropological linguistics, thus emphasizing the cultural core of language and the linguistic core of culture. Another long-established field is second and foreign language education (or 'pedagogical linguistics'), which can boast of a long tradition of empirical research, but which is still in the process of discovering the "motivational" potential of a cognition- and usage-based approach to foreign language teaching and learning. Section 5, 'The verbal and beyond', extends the research on verbal modes of expression to other modes of conceptual self-expression. The cognitive-linguistic approach is applied to the visual modes of expression as exploited in signed languages and in the manipulation of visual metaphors in the media-dominated communication landscape. Similarly, the imaginative realities of poetic text worlds are explored in a cognitive analysis of Robert Frost's poem "Mending Wall", a choice that serves as a symbol and pun for the wall between linguistics and literary studies. In section 6, 'Virtual reality', computer linguistics is looking at cognitive linguistics and lays down the conditions that have to be fulfilled in order to make it testable for computational experimentation.

It must be clear that these fields of application do not exhaust the possibilities for interdisciplinary cognitively inspired explorations. To name just one area, cognitive sociolinguistics is only indirectly represented in the context of cultural linguistics. This issue will be taken up in the last part of this introduction. Let us begin, however, by introducing the fifteen chapters in slightly further detail.

## 2.    The various contributions: foundations, applications and future perspectives

### 2.1. The cognitive base

This opening section critically surveys the groundwork of Cognitive Linguistics, whose main ambition it is to be a fully usage-based theory of language. In his chapter entitled "Methodology in Cognitive Linguistics", **Dirk Geeraerts** examines the methodological consequences of this tenet and weighs the validity of various linguistic research methods leading to the realisation of this ambition. Geeraerts first assesses the actual situation in Cognitive Linguistics and concludes that it is a mixed picture, with a clearly growing interest in empirical methods on the one hand, but still a dominance of traditionally analytic approaches on the other. Adopting a constructive approach, he foresees a growing increase in the empirical demands on linguistics: corpus research, experimental designs, surveys, and the accompanying forms of quantitative data analysis are likely to occupy a more central position than it currently does, gradually raising the standards of scholarship in linguistics in general and in Cognitive Linguistics in particular to such a level that unsubstantiated claims will become unfashionable. Linguistics needs an empirical revolution, and empirical research, Geeraerts argues, does not involve abandoning theory formation in favor of purely descriptive research, but rather trying to provide proof for theories, and from there, refining the theories. Interpretation is thus viewed as but one step within a cycle of empirical and successful research, which, crucially, requires the operationalization of hypotheses.

Many traditional dichotomies such as competence versus performance, or lexicon versus grammar are irreconcilable with a usage-based description of language. In the chapter "Polysemy and the lexicon", **John R. Taylor** looks at this continuum from the lexicon perspective, and revisits several questions which earlier CL models have treated in the form of radial networks (the extreme polysemy of 'over', for example). In the case of 'over', Taylor argues that attempts to determine just how many meanings a word has, and what these meanings might be are ultimately based on a particular model, viz. the "dictionary+grammar book" conception of language. Taylor argues that such a conception is undermined by the pervasiveness of the idiomatic and illustrates his claim with an easily repeatable, small-sized corpus-based study of some uses of the expression *all over*. He shows that the expression has a range of uses which cannot be derived on the basis of independently identifiable meanings of its parts, and concludes that knowing a word proceeds through knowledge of the highly flexible usage range of the word, rather than through the association of the word with a fixed number of determinate meanings.

One major application of CL is likely to be in the area of linguistic descriptions of parts or even the whole of grammar, of single languages or, contrastively, across different languages. The third chapter in this section, "Cognitive approaches to grammar", by **Cristiano Broccias**, outlines the development of CL grammar models and compares three CL grammar models: Langacker's cognitive grammar (Langacker 2005), and Goldberg's (Goldberg 1995) and Croft's (Croft 2001) avenues into construction grammar. Finally, the chapter explores the descriptive complementary potential of mental space theory and blending theory for the representation of conceptual links in grammatical complexity. As Broccias points out, the similarities between the models described are so fundamental that they can be called "notational variants": they all share the assumption that language must be studied in relation to other cognitive abilities and agree on the fact that language consists of far more than just a syntax plus a lexicon. Rather, language is viewed as a taxonomic hierarchy, where sharp distinctions should not be assumed; language is a "diffuse" network since much in language is a matter of degree.

## 2.2. The conceptual leap

This section surveys the various ways in which human thought manages to explore and conceptually structure the experiential world of man by means of mainly three cognitive operations: conceptual metaphor, conceptual metonymy, and conceptual integration or blending, probably based to different degrees on underlying pre-conceptual building stones such as image schemas. The chapter by **Tim Rohrer**, "Three dogmas of embodiment: Cognitive linguistics as a cognitive science" critically reviews a series of recent approaches to another fundamental cornerstone in Cognitive Linguistics, namely the assumption that conceptual structure is "embodied". Rohrer argues against any non-socially and non-culturally based conception of embodiment which envisages it as if it were (a) an eliminativist project (i.e. one which places the main or sole emphasis on brain structures and neurons, to the detriment of the role of sociocultural factors), (b) a static or fixed model (as opposed to a temporally flexible and dynamic model, as well in ontogenetic, in historical as in phylogenetic terms), and (c) ultimately compatible with methods of conscious introspection. In this respect, Rohrer highlights the importance of findings resulting from cross-disciplinary empirical and experimental methods, and, like most contributors to the volume calls for empirical methodological approaches which will place Cognitive Linguistics more firmly within the broader experimentally-oriented community of Cognitive Science.

In his chapter, entitled "Metonymy as a usage event", **Klaus-Uwe Panther** examines the interrelation between metonymy and metaphor, arguing that the hardly distinguishable notions of 'domain', 'subdomain', 'single domain', and 'separate domains', which since 1980 have often been used as definitional criteria for differentiating metonymy from metaphor, are unclear and unreliable because they are cover terms for heterogeneous concepts and conceptual relations. Instead, Panther returns to the semiotic approach advocated by C. S. Peirce according to which the difference between metaphor and metonymy resides in the type of semiotic relation between their respective source and target: metaphor is an *iconic* relation and metonymy an *indexical* relation. In consonance with this idea, metonymy is a kind of meaning elaboration whose result is a conceptually prominent target meaning, an integrated whole that contains the backgrounded source meaning and novel meaning components resulting from the process of elaboration. Panther explores the role of context in the interpretation of metonymy in usage events in two detailed case studies and concludes that one important function of metonymy is to provide generic prompts, serving as inputs for additional pragmatic inferences that flesh out the specifics of the intended utterance meaning.

How do the cognitive operations of metaphor, metonymy and blending relate to each other and to the world of thought? In her chapter entitled "Conceptual blending in thought, rhetoric and ideology", **Seana Coulson** first introduces the reader to the framework of conceptual blending theory and provides an example of a rhetorically motivated blend. Then she goes on to describe the commonalities and differences of conceptual blending and conceptual metaphor. Coulson exemplifies these by means of humorous blends and suggests that processes of conceptual blending mediate the exploitation of stable conventional mapping schemes in order to adapt shared cultural models to the idiosyncratic needs of individuals. In her section on "Persuasive absurdity," a number of examples of persuasive texts and discourse are analyzed to highlight the point that the creative elaboration and accommodation of cultural models relies heavily on conventionalized mapping and blending schemes. In the concluding section, Coulson briefly also touches on the relationship between the meaning of sentences and the meaning of utterances, i.e. between the standard default meanings explored by linguists and the idiosyncratic meanings speakers derive in situated instances of language use.

## 2.3. The psychological basis

Research into the psychological basis of linguistic processing is the proper field of psycholinguistics, a vast area from which two domains are represented: metaphor processing and language acquisition. In their chapter "The contested impact of cognitive linguistic research on the psycholinguistics of metaphor understanding", **Raymond W. Gibbs Jr.** and **Marcus Perlman** discuss some of the most important criticisms of cognitive linguistic studies on metaphor. The authors argue that linguistic analyses alone are unable to determine what putative conceptual metaphors underlie the use of particular linguistic expressions and call for experimental research providing independent evidence for such structures. They question CL assumptions that (a) there should be a direct, or motivated, relationship between systematicity in language and people's underlying cognitive functions (including their unconscious mental representations and brain structures, cf. Dodge and Lakoff 2005), and (b) that the complexity of metaphorical meanings requires equally complex cognitive processes to create or understand these meanings by ordinary language users, as in conceptual blending theory (Fauconnier and Turner 2002). According to Gibbs and Perlman, the challenge for cognitive linguistic research is to frame hypotheses in a falsifiable way, and in this respect they briefly outline a number of steps that cognitive linguists could adopt to deal with some of these problems. The authors conclude that despite its success, cognitive linguistic research will continue to be contested by scholars in different neighbouring disciplines until it addresses some of its methodological weaknesses in a systematic way.

The second chapter in this section, entitled "X is like Y: The emergence of similarity mappings in children's early speech and gesture" also examines the psychological reality of basic constructs. **Şeyda Özçalışkan** and **Susan Goldin-Meadow** first discuss simple analogical mappings in terms of one of the earliest metalinguistic abilities which children master and which thus constitute the stepping-stones for the development of metaphorical thinking. The authors then present the results of research which investigated the emergence and later development of similarity mapping abilities (X is like Y) in spontaneous speech and gesture, using longitudinal observations of English-speaking children from ages 1;2 to 2;10. The results show that the children began to produce similarity mappings routinely by age 2;2, initially conveying only the source domain of the mapping in their speech and relying on nonverbal modalities (i.e., gesture and communicative context) to convey the target domain. The onset of 'X IS LIKE Y' constructions was furthermore preceded by the onset of gesture-speech combinations expressing similarity relations without the word *like*. Özçalışkan and Goldin-Meadow conclude that gesture is at the cutting edge of early language development, as it both predates and serves as the supporting context for oncoming changes in speech.

## 2.4. Go tell it on the mountain

Section four explores cognitive approaches in the field of anthropological linguistics, now conceived as cultural linguistics, and in language pedagogy, also conceivable as pedagogical linguistics. These two fields both highlight the construal of the world according to multiple cognitive cultural models internalised in childhood and subsequently lived by or learned as new assets of cross-cultural understanding in a given cultural community. The acquisition of language and culture and the interplay between both dimensions thus constitute the main topics of this section. **Gary B. Palmer**'s chapter, entitled "Energy through fusion at last: Synergies in cognitive anthropology and cognitive linguistics", focuses on the positive results of interdisciplinary research and fruitful dialogue: Palmer reviews a series of topics to which both cognitive linguists and cognitive anthropologists have made significant research contributions, namely "language as culture", "psychological unity vs. cultural diversity", "distributed knowledge versus consensus in language communities", "complex categories (reduplication and noun classifiers)", "the new relativity in spatial orientation" and "the origins of language". He concludes that Cognitive Linguistics is proving its value by producing insightful applications to the descriptions, analyses, and comparisons of both western and non-western languages and that a version of Cognitive Linguistics that emphasizes the cultural origins of linguistic categories enables cross-linguistic comparisons and insights into both grammar and world view that were unavailable to other paradigms in anthropology or linguistics. Conversely, cognitive linguists could do more to incorporate the frameworks of cognitive anthropology to discover cultural schemas and scenarios and provide additional evidence for proposed cognitive linguistic models.

In their chapter "Cognitive linguistic applications in second or foreign language instruction: Rationale, proposals and evaluation", **Frank Boers** and **Seth Lindstromberg** point out that insights from Cognitive Linguistics have been taken up by education-oriented applied linguistics at a relatively slow pace in spite of the fact that a number of CL premises seem well-suited to complement current language pedagogy research. According to Boers and Lindstromberg, the CL view that appears to have the greatest potential for language pedagogy is its quest for the conceptual motivation of linguistic structures, since the presentation of segments of language as motivated is likely to enhance comprehension, retention, cultural awareness and positive learning effects. The authors survey work based on cognitive insights in second or foreign language teaching and contend that although most controlled experiments reported so far tend to be small-scale ones, taken collectively they begin to constitute a fairly robust body of evidence in favour of a CL-inspired pedagogy. Boers and Lindstromberg conclude by proposing a research agenda consisting of expanding the scope of linguistic motivation, measuring the impact of learner-connected variables on its pedagogical effectiveness and fine-tuning its implementations so as to maximise the pedagogical benefits.

## 2.5. The verbal and beyond: Vision and imagination

Verbal expression merely represents one means of conceptual self-expression. Similar means of expression include visual, pictorial, and/or rhythmic systems that can be interwoven with it, or operate in parallel or as complete alternatives. While verbal communication cannot do without its para-verbal and non-verbal support, signed language is equally composed of conceptual-content gestures and other accompanying meta-gestures signalling how the message is to be interpreted. In his chapter entitled "Visual communication: Signed language and cognition", **Terry Janzen** argues that a cognitively oriented approach to signed languages allows us to gain an insight into human conceptual structures, as the mapping between conceptual space and articulation space is often expressly iconic. Janzen first provides the reader with a survey of some of the current research and findings in the area of CL and signed languages and dedicates the rest of the chapter to accounts of specific theoretical questions: what visual perception of language means for an articulation system, the relation between gesture and signs with focus on a discontinuous versus a continuous view of such domains, iconic representations (including a proposal for cognitive iconicity grounded in the theory of cognitive grammar), metaphor and metonymy, body partitioning, blended spaces and the embodied expression of point of view. Like other contributors, Janzen also addresses the issue of future directions for cognitive linguistic research on signed language.

In far more general terms and outside the domain of signed language, the visual mode, or rather multimodal systems, have now come to largely dominate Western and global communication systems, as **Charles Forceville**'s cognitive rhetoric studies have shown for the world of advertising. In the chapter "Non-verbal and multimodal metaphor in a cognitivist framework: Agendas for research," Forceville pursues the thesis that if conceptual metaphor theory is right in assuming that humans pervasively use verbal metaphor because they largely think metaphorically, then metaphorical thought should manifest itself not just in language, but also via all other modes of communication, such as pictures, music, sounds, and gestures. Forceville offers a review of work done in this area and focuses on a series of theoretical issues that require further research, including the distinction between monomodal and multimodal metaphor, the difference between structural and creative metaphor, the question of how verbalizations of non-verbal or conceptual metaphors may affect their possible interpretation, the intriguing problem how exactly similarity between target and source is created, and the importance of genre for the construal and interpretation of metaphor.

Due to its full exploitation of the visual and the imaginative potential in poetry, narrative and drama, literature by far transcends the monomodal constraints of verbal expression. It does not come as a surprise that CL has also given rise to a cognitive approach to literature, known as cognitive poetics (or cognitive stylistics), which employs cognitive tools to interpret the imaginative depths of literary text worlds. In her chapter entitled "The fall of the wall between literary studies and linguistics: Cognitive poetics", **Margaret H. Freeman** first presents a brief overview of the cognitive poetics enterprise. To Freeman, cognitive poetics is essentially an exploration into poetic iconicity, and one which links the literary text to the cognitive processes of the human mind, providing a theoretical cognitive linguistic basis for literary intuition. Next, Freeman exemplifies the field by means of a case study, analysing Robert Frost's poem "Mending Wall." Here she applies the theoretical framework pertaining to blending theory, metaphor theory, deixis, and image schemas, among others, to show how cognitive poetics, by exploring the iconic functions that create literature as the semblance of felt life contributes to our understanding of the embodied mind. The effect of "poetic iconicity" is to create sensations, feelings, and images in language that enable the mind to encounter them as phenomenally real. The choice of "Mending Wall" as a case study undoubtedly contributes to rendering the "fall of the wall" an even more symbolic and entertaining process.

## 2.6. Virtual reality as a new experience

The study of the computational applications to CL is a comparatively new area of enquiry which poses a challenge both for CL, which needs to be tested in terms of its adaptability to computational requirements, and for computer science, which needs to assess its own ability to cope with the descriptive and explanatory richness of an approach to language that explicitly ties together body, mind, thinking and language.

In this context of mutual challenges, **John Barnden**'s chapter, entitled "Artificial intelligence, figurative language and cognitive linguistics", discusses the relationship between CL and Artificial Intelligence. The chapter is focused on Barnden's well-known ATT-Meta project, which is both an explanatory approach and a computer program capable of performing reasoning tasks involved in metaphorical utterances. The overall project is related to but at the same time challenges some of the central assumptions in Lakoff's (1993) conceptual metaphor theory. However, as Barnden himself remarks, ATT-Meta is in some respects fairly close to Grady's theory of primary metaphor (Grady 2005). Thus, rather than a mapping from machines to minds, ATT-Meta prefers to postulate transfer rules from 'physical operation' to 'mental operation'. Also significantly, the ATT-Meta approach questions the usefulness of the notion of domain in computational implementations because of the high degree of arbitrariness involved in determining domain boundaries. This leads Barnden – together with other AI theorists – to disregard domain mappings and see metaphor as a matter of transferring from a pretence to reality. This move has implications for the traditional distinction between metaphor and metonymy in terms of domain-external versus domain-internal mappings. For Barnden, metaphor and metonymy are merely vague notions playing a heuristic role, while the real phenomena lie at a deeper level involving conceptual distance, similarity, contiguity, and connections between source and target, an approach which thus ties in with Panther's criticism of the unreliability of the notion of 'domain'.

Unlike Barnden's contribution, the chapter by **Tony Veale**, entitled "Computability as a test on linguistics theories", focuses more on computational assessment than on mutual feedback between CL and AI. The chapter explores the explanatory power of three CL models of language processing – Attardo's general theory of verbal humor (Attardo et al. 2002), Fauconnier and Turner's blending theory (Fauconnier and Turner 2002) and Croft's Radical Construction Grammar (Croft 2001) – in terms of several computational criteria, among them specificity, efficiency, and tractability. Computational specificity is a test of explicitness whereby every step and every data element in a process must be clearly specified. Efficiency is measured against the ability of a theory to avoid unnecessary proliferation of representations, constraints, and processes. Tractability reflects the ability to run sufficiently explicit computer specifications in a "reasonable" amount of time. The exploration allows Veale to show how the computational perspective brings to the fore a number of strengths and weaknesses in each approach. For example, while the multiple-input account provided by blending theory fares poorly in terms of efficiency, the general theory of verbal humor is more constrained in this respect. However, Attardo's theory falls short of providing a sufficiently explanatory account of processing. The chapter ends by discussing, together with a number of structure-mapping issues, the computational feasibility of Radical Construction Grammar (RCG). All in all, Veale's chapter suggests that computationalism can not only assess the explanatory power of a linguistic theory but also allow researchers to gain a clearer understanding of linguistic phenomena by making sure that terms and their corresponding notions have a precise theoretical meaning from the perspective of computational sufficiency.

### 3.    Aims and scope of "Applications of Cognitive Linguistics" (ACL)

The series *Applications of Cognitive Linguistics* (ACL) aims at providing a platform for high quality research applying the theoretical framework developed in Cognitive Linguistics to a variety of different fields. While the *Cognitive Linguistics Research* series focuses on theoretical and descriptive aspects and on the cognitive, cultural and usage-based foundations of the facts of language, ACL explores the effect of these theoretical insights when applied in various linguistic sub-disciplines, in interdisciplinary research fields, and in the practice-oriented domain of applied linguistics. Furthermore, as illustrated by many contributions in this volume, not only is there a route from CL theory to a range of applications to explore, but also one which goes back from the application to the theoretical foundations and to possible implications for CL theory.

The available CL theoretical know-how, constructs and general characterisations of language are well-suited for explorative applications in the research areas traditionally known as descriptive linguistics, text linguistics, psycholinguistics, applied linguistics, sociolinguistics, anthropological linguistics, etc. It is indeed the case that such applications are currently in fast expansion in many fields, as the chapters just surveyed in this introduction amply show. The CL usage-based approach furthermore naturally calls for a non-restrictive interpretation of the term 'application': one of the main assumptions of ACL is that linguistic research must be firmly grounded in usage-based, descriptive data, which may, more often than not, imply an interdisciplinary approach to the object under scrutiny. In language pedagogy, for instance, linguistics meets with psycholinguistics and educational psychology to study the combined processes of natural and conducted acquisition of second and/or foreign languages; hence the label 'pedagogical linguistics' is out of place. In cultural linguistics, the deeper relation between language and culture is explored, which covers and overlaps with various scientific disciplines or fields such as (cognitive) anthropology, cross-cultural semantics, intercultural pragmatics, cross-cultural communication, social psychology and still other disciplines. In computational linguistics, amongst many other possibilities, theoretical models such as cognitive grammar, conceptual metaphor theory, blending theory, etc. are caught in self-monitoring artificial intelligence programs to test the viability of the constructs used.

As to the scope of ACL the following may serve as an attempt to spell out some examples of ACL's orientations, at best signposting some major areas on the map, but certainly not laying out a complete map.

One major application of CL is the area of *descriptive linguistics* covering either the description of parts or the whole of the grammar of given languages, or else the description of language as used in given domains of human experience. The grammatical descriptions can focus on any level of linguistic organization, including syntax (e.g. Cornillie fc.), lexis, morphology and phonology, and thereby concentrate on one language in particular or be conceived cross-linguistically as contrastive studies. Descriptive applications can also focus on the exploration of theoretical models in actual language use: for example, on views of mental motion and summary scanning, on prototype theory, on construction grammar, on conceptual metaphor or metonymy (as already practiced in the many discourse studies of political (e.g. Musolff 2004), economic (e.g. Koller 2004) and even architectural communication (e.g. Caballero 2006) or on conceptual blending (as illustrated by Coulson's chapter in this volume and in various other studies). Further burgeoning fields in descriptive applications of CL are cognitive discourse studies, either in the tradition of blending theory or in the search for coherence relations (e.g. Sanders and Gernsbacher, eds. 2004). As shown in Freeman's chapter in this volume, highly interesting developments are also taking place at the interface of literary studies and cognitive linguistics, known as cognitive poetics or stylistics, thereby offering many bridges to both disciplines.

Another major field is constituted by the *pedagogical application* of CL, which is now becoming a novel area of research in the cognitive-linguistic world (e.g. Achard and Niemeier, eds. 2004), and one which naturally finds an interdisciplinary basis in psycholinguistics, educational psychology, theoretical and descriptive linguistics, also pointed out by Boers and Lindstromberg in this volume. It is probably because of their inherently interdisciplinary orientation that pedagogical applications of linguistics, or the somewhat all-encompassing and hence misleading term 'applied linguistics,' has seldom (except by Pütz et al., eds. 2001) been brought together with descriptive linguistics in one organizational framework, be it journals, series of volumes, or conferences. Still, since Cognitive Linguistics offers such a strong conceptual unity in its approach to language and linguistics, it is entitled to accept the challenge of rallying such seemingly diverse applications of Cognitive Linguistics into one conceptual organic whole. The interdisciplinary character of pedagogical linguistics, or 'language pedagogy' – to use a more generally accepted and less misleading label – may necessitate a multi-layered foundation, but in a sense this equally applies to several other applications, such as cognitive sociolinguistics and cultural linguistics, two other fields we still want to go into.

In cognitive sociolinguistics (e.g. Kristiansen and Dirven fc.) several branches of traditional sociolinguistics are redefined from a cognitive perspective. Cognitive sociolinguistics combines the usage-based CL tenet with fine-grained research on language variation and examines the correlations with cognitive models, now widened as cultural models (e.g. Dirven et al., eds.). Sociolinguistic research which at one end tends to overlap with cultural linguistics further includes work on language policy, global language variation and ideology in socio-politico-economic areas such as political, educational, and corporate-culture frameworks.

Cultural linguistics is, as just stated, a close neighbour of cognitive sociolinguistics. Cultural linguistics makes use of the analytical tools developed within the framework of CL in order to explain many aspects of human languages in their cultural contexts, thereby exhibiting clear ties with work in cognitive anthropology, where much emphasis is being put

on the cognitive grounding of social structure and on how cultural schemas relate to action. In spatial and social cognition, on the other hand,
cross-cultural studies with an emphasis on language acquisition have provided us with evidence for the social grounding of cognitive structure.
Studies on cultural beliefs, values and norms (e.g. Holland and Quinn
1987; Goddard, ed. 2006) likewise constitute an interesting area of research in constant evolution. It may also be interesting to note that proponents of cultural linguistics have recently begun to explore the way their
theoretical persuasion applies to language learning, language teaching
and cross-cultural communication. Relevant issues in this applied perspective are the study of meaning negotiation as adjustment of cultural
schemas, the analysis of the impact of conceptual metaphor and metonymy in misinterpretation in cross-cultural encounters, the study of cultural models, cultural keywords and culture-specific collocations in L2
varieties of English.

   In conclusion, it should be emphasised that, in spite of the great diversity of research fields, one central cohesive factor remains and binds all
strands and models within CL together: the ubiquity of the link between
language in use and other cognitive faculties. Descriptive applications use
the research tools of CL and explore their validity in the description of
single languages or in cross-linguistic explorations. Language pedagogy
may be as diversified as the functions of language in usage events, but language learning is probably the most spectacular place to look for the integration of all cognitive faculties, a new nascent set of schemas derived
from language usage events and social interaction. Cultural-specific categories and models not only necessitate the adoption of psychologically
real constructs, but also – and far beyond that – the adoption of models
capable of accounting for culturally distributed knowledge, that is, common cultural knowledge that is not necessarily possessed by all single
members of a community, but only possessed by the collectivity of the cultural community.

   Although this aspect has not been restated in this final section on the
new series ACL, it must be clear that – in line with the whole orientation
of this volume – only empirical research, possibly including computational verification of any linguistic or cultural model, is the pre-condition
and the ultimate test guaranteeing that the constructs work and can sur-
vive in the long-term future both of cognitive linguistics and its diverse
fields of application.

## References

Achard, Michel, and Susanne Niemeier (eds.)
2004    *Cognitive Linguistics, Second Language Acquisition, and Foreign Language Teaching.* Studies on Language Acquisition 18. Berlin/New York: Mouton de Gruyter.
Attardo, Salvatore, Christian F. Hempelmann, and Sara Di Maio
2002    Script oppositions and logical mechanisms: Modeling incongruities and their resolutions. *Humor: International Journal of Humor Research* 15 (1): 3–46.
Caballero, Rosario
2006    *Re-Viewing Space: Figurative Language in Architects' Assessment of Built Space.* Applications of Cognitive Linguistics 2. Berlin/New York: Mouton de Gruyter.
Cornillie, Bert
Forth-    *Evidentiality and Epistemic Modality in Spanish (Semi-) Auxiliaries: A*
coming    *Cognitive-Functional Approach.* Berlin/New York: Mouton de Gruyter.
Croft, William
2001    *Radical Construction Grammar: Syntactic Theory from a Typological Perspective.* Oxford: Oxford University Press.
Dirven, René, Roslyn Frank, and Martin Pütz (eds.)
2003    *Cognitive Models in Language and Thought: Ideology, Metaphors and Meanings.* Cognitive Linguistics Research 24. Berlin/New York: Mouton de Gruyter.
Dodge, Ellen, and George Lakoff
2005    Image schemas: From linguistic analysis to neural grounding. In *From Perception to Meaning: Image Schemas in Cognitive Linguistics,* Hampe, Beate (ed.), 57–91. Cognitive Linguistics Research 29. Berlin/New York: Mouton de Gruyter.
Fauconnier, Gilles, and Mark Turner
2002    *The Way We Think: Conceptual Blending and the Mind's Hidden Complexities.* New York: Basic Books.
Geeraerts, Dirk (ed.)
2006    *Cognitive Linguistics: Basic Readings.* Cognitive Linguistics Research 34. Berlin/New York: Mouton de Gruyter.
Goddard, Cliff (ed.)
2006    *Ethnopragmatics: Understanding Discourse in Cultural Context.* Applications of Cognitive Linguistics 3. Berlin/New York: Mouton de Gruyter.
Goldberg, Adele E.
1995    *Constructions: A Construction Grammar Approach to Argument Structure.* Chicago: University of Chicago Press.
Grady, Joseph
2005    Primary metaphors as inputs to conceptual integration. *Journal of Pragmatics* 37 (10): 1595–1614.

Holland, Dorothy, and Naomi Quinn (eds.)
1987    *Cultural Models in Language and Thought*. Cambridge: Cambridge
        University Press.
Koller, Veronika
2004    *Metaphor and Gender in Business Media Discourse. A Critical Cognitive
        Study.* Basingstoke, U.K.: Palgrave Macmillan.
Kristiansen, Gitte, and René Dirven (eds.)
Forth-  *Cognitive Sociolinguistics: Language Variation, Cultural Models, Social
coming  Systems.* Cognitive Linguistics Research. Berlin/New York: Mouton de
        Gruyter.
Lakoff, George
1993    The contemporary theory of metaphor. In *Metaphor and Thought*, Or-
        tony, Andrew (ed.), 202–251. Cambridge: Cambridge University Press.
Langacker, Ronald W.
2005    Construction grammars: Cognitive, radical, and less so. In *Cognitive
        Linguistics: Internal Dynamics and Interdisciplinary Interaction*, Ruiz
        de Mendoza, Francisco J., and Sandra Peña Cervel (eds.). Cognitive
        Linguistics Research 32. Berlin/New York: Mouton de Gruyter.
Musolff, Andreas
2004    *Metaphor and Political Discourse: Analogical Reasoning in Debates
        about Europe.* Houndsmills, Basingstoke, U.K.: Palgrave Macmillan.
Pütz, Martin, Susanne Niemeier, and René Dirven (eds.)
2001    *Applied Cognitive Linguistics I: Theory and Language Acquisition. II:
        Language Pedagogy.* Cognitive Linguistics Research 19. Berlin/New
        York: Mouton de Gruyter.
Sanders, Ted J.M., and Morton Ann Gernsbacher
2004    Discourse Processes. *Discourse Processes* 37: 79–186

# Part one: The cognitive base

# Methodology in Cognitive Linguistics

## Dirk Geeraerts

*Abstract*
The future of linguistics is likely to be determined by methodological issues: whether linguistics will be able to turn its current theoretical chaos (however creative it may be) into a situation of cumulative development will crucially depend on the possibility of finding a common ground that allows competing accounts to be compared in an objective way. This chapter explores the position of Cognitive Linguistics vis à vis the methodological evolution of linguistics: what is the current state of affairs in Cognitive Linguistics, and in what direction could the cognitive approach contribute to the methodological progress of linguistics? The first section introduces the concept of empirical research, using a non-linguistic example. The second section sketches a scenario for the evolution of linguistics at large, highlighting the specific role of method as a safeguard of theoretical comparability. The third section describes the particularly advantageous position of Cognitive Linguistics, i.e. the fact that a number of theoretical features of Cognitive Linguistics seem to be specifically favorable to the methodological development that is meant here. The fourth section takes into account the other side of the coin: if we consider the actual state of affairs in Cognitive Linguistics, the situation is definitely a mixed one, with a growing concern for empirical method on the one hand and waving of hands at the other. If this heterogeneous situation is not accidental, we should be able to identify theoretical features that have exactly the opposite effect of the ones discussed in the third section – features, that is, that go against the tendency towards well-grounded empirical research. The overall future of Cognitive Linguistics, needless to say, will then be determined by the extent to which it can resolve the methodological tensions that seem to derive from its theoretical assumptions.

*Keywords*: methodology; empirical research; experimentation; corpus linguistics; introspection; future developments; cognitive science; psychology; statistics

## 1.  What empirical research involves

Suppose for a moment that you are a professor of linguistics teaching an introductory course to a large audience of a few hundreds of students. You hardly know them personally, but when you grade their exams, there's a funny thing that catches your attention: over the years, you notice that the students' first names come in clusters. In one year, your attention is caught by a frequent group of *Heleen*'s or *Ineke*'s, in another, by a conspicuous cluster of *Ron*'s or *Len*'s or *George*'s. As a professor of linguistics, you're an inquisitive type of person, so you wonder whether this is a coincidence. What could be the case? One possibility would be that the clustering of proper names in your class is a faithful reflection of what is happening in the population at large: there are fashions in giving first names that change over the years, and the sample of the population that attends your class reproduces the overall tendencies. In that case, there is something specific about the age of your students: they were born in a period in which a particular name was trendy. But there is at least one other possibility to consider: it could be that the frequency of specific names in your class differs from what you could expect given the distribution of names in the population as a whole. In that case, there would be something specific about your class: for one reason or another, it attracts people with a certain name.

How could you decide between the two options? You would want to make a number of comparisons: on the one hand, you would compare the distribution of names in your class with the distribution of names in the entire population of the same age group, and on the other, you would compare the distribution of names in one year or one period with the distribution of names in another year or period. In both comparisons, you would not just want to know whether the distributions differ, but specifically also whether the differences you observe are a coincidence or not. That is, of course, where statistics will help you: a statistical test will allow you to see whether a difference you detect is due to chance or not.

If it is due to chance, you will leave the matter for what it is, but if it is not, your curiosity will get the better of you, and you will start wondering about an explanation. For instance, if there are fashions that change through time (as there would be), what is it that determines them? What is it that makes *Heleen* popular in a particular period? A hypothesis that you are likely to come up with is that naming fashions of this kind are determined by the degree of exposure certain names get in the media and in popular culture: popular sports people or popular characters from television fiction – people "whose name gets around" – may well provide a model for naming new-borns. Again, you would want to put the hypothesis to the test: you may have to put in a considerable effort to find the right kind of data, but you would want to find out whether one or another *Heleen* was popular some twenty years before you noticed all those *Heleen*'s in your class. Or rather, you would not want to do this for just one of the names, but you would want to reach a general conclusion: if a certain name is popular in the media in a certain period, does that lead to an increase in the number of babies receiving that name in the following years? And again, you would need some statistics to ascertain whether the influence you think you see might not just be a coincidence.

We could go on like this, surely, investigating explanatory questions and research techniques for our hypothetical Christian Name Conundrum, but that is not the point of the exercise. The point is this: the procedure illustrated in the previous pages is typical of what we call *empirical research*, and it involves a way of thinking that we all understand – and that we all recognize as being superior to an attitude in which you would simply say: "I notice these clusters of names in my classes. I conclude that they are due to fashion". Before you can *really* conclude that, you have to take a number of steps, steps of the type that we explored above.

This chapter, then, is all about the position of empirical research in Cognitive Linguistics. It will argue, first, that linguistics in general would benefit from more research of this type; second, that Cognitive Linguistics has an excellent starting-point to contribute to such an increase in the use of empirical studies; and third, that in spite of that advantageous basis, Cognitive Linguistics has not yet fully realized the breakthrough towards the massive use of empirical methods. What the chapter will *not* do, by the way, is discuss the practicalities of doing empirical research in linguistics. Although, in terms of boosting empirical studies, it would be extremely useful to do so, it is simply beyond the scope of the present text to offer a practically oriented primer in experimental or corpus-based studies in linguistics. It is hoped that the references to empirical studies scattered throughout the text will help the reader to get started. Further, see Gonzalez, Mittelberg, Coulson, and Spivey (forthcoming) for a book-length introduction to different empirical methods for Cognitive Linguistics.

As a crucial backdrop for the following discussion, let us now summarize the main features of empirical research that we can derive from our simple example.

1. Empirical research is *data-driven*. You cannot easily draw conclusions from single cases and isolated observations, and the more data you can collect to study a particular phenomenon, the better your conclusions will get. The observations could come from many sources, by the way: you could collect them as they exist (as in our Christian Name Conundrum), but you could also elicit them by doing experimental research, or by doing survey research – we will come back to that.

2. Empirical research involves *quantitative methods*. In order to get a good grip on the broad observational basis that you will start from, you need techniques to come to terms with the amount of material involved. Specifically, you need statistical tests to determine whether your observations might be due to chance or not.

3. Empirical research is all about asking the right questions – the *formulation of hypotheses*, in other words. No perception could be more misguided than to think that once you have your database of elicited or non-elicited observations, the conclusions will arise automatically and purely inductively from the data. On the contrary, the only conclusions you will be able to draw are the ones that relate to hypotheses you have formulated and tested – so that will be your first task. In our example, you have to think creatively and inventively about the possible background of the clusters of names that catch your attention, and it is only when you have arrived at such a hypothesis that you can start thinking about testing it. Another way of saying this is that empirical research necessarily combines inductive and deductive reasoning: on the one hand, you work in a bottom-up way from data to hypotheses, but on the other hand, those hypotheses will also be derived top-down from the theoretical perspective you adopt in thinking about your data.

4. Empirical research requires the *operationalization of hypotheses*. It is not sufficient to think up a plausible and intriguing hypothesis: you also have to formulate it in such a way that it can be put to the test. That is what is meant by "operationalization": turning your hypothesis into concrete data. For instance, it is fine to conjecture that media exposure could have an influence on proper name fashions, but how do you measure the popularity of a name in the media? It's not just a question of finding the relevant data that allow you to measure the popularity of a name (like maybe broadcasting schedules), but also of settling on a method of measurement. Would you just measure the number of times a name is broadcast, or would you take into account the ratings of the programs in which it appears? And how would you deal with the existence of different television channels, or the simultaneous effect of television, radio, and the written press? In most empirical research in linguistics, it is questions of operationalization that require all the ingenuity of the researcher – and most of his or her time, because getting the relevant data and measurements is not an automatic process.

5. Empirical research involves an *empirical cycle* in which several rounds of data gathering, testing of hypotheses, and interpretation of the results follow each other. In the (fictitious) example, we started with an

anecdotal observation, tried to interpret it, turned the possible interpretations into alternative hypotheses, tested the hypotheses, and so arrived at a new, more secure and better established observation. But this observation was only the starting-point for a new attempt at interpretation, which led to a new hypothesis about media influence, which led to new research efforts. Just like it is misguided to think that empirical, data-driven research automatically gives you all the answers, it is misguided to think that it *immediately* gives you the final answer.

## 2. Why linguistic needs an empirical revolution

Let us now turn to linguistics: why could we say that more empirical research of the type illustrated and demarcated above would be beneficial for the development of linguistics? Theoretical linguistics is characterized by the existence of a multitude of theories: Universal Grammar in the generativist sense, a family of models claiming the label of Functional Grammar, smaller trends like Role and Reference Grammar or HPSG – and of course Cognitive Linguistics, in a number of versions that may each branch off into subversions, and then into alternative realizations of subversions. There is Cognitive Linguistics Langacker-style (Cognitive Grammar in the narrow sense), and there is Cognitive Linguistics Talmy-style – to some extent using the same vocabulary, involving notions like the figure/ground opposition, but still sufficiently different to be easily recognizable by anyone familiar with the relevant literature. And then there is Construction Grammar, which may or may not include Cognitive Grammar (Langacker-style), but which certainly encompasses different approaches like Fillmore and Goldberg-style Construction Grammar, Radical Construction Grammar, and even Embodied Construction Grammar.

Superficially, it might seem that the existence of different "theories" is not really typical of linguistics, as the foregoing passage may seem to suggest. In psychology (to take a discipline that is not too far removed from linguistics), one may come across different theories about how categories are stored in the mind: you get exemplar models that assume that the bulk of the work is done via the knowledge we have of typical members of a category, and you get concept-based models that rather start from the assumption that there is an abstract, schematic definition of a concept, and then you get mixed models that explore different combinations of exemplar- and concept-based models. Is there no difference with linguistics, then?

The difference seems to be that there is a common, commonly accepted way in psycholinguistics of settling theoretical disputes: experimentation. Given a number of conditions, experimental results decide between competing analyses, and psycholinguists predominantly accept the experimental paradigm as the cornerstone of their discipline. The conditions that need to be fulfilled to make the paradigm work are in principle simple: the experiment has to be adequately carried out, and it has to be properly designed in order to be distinctive with regard to the competing theories. That is to say, you need good experimental training (knowledge of techniques and analytical tools), and you need the ability to define a relevant experimental design. The bulk of the effort in psycholinguistic research, in other words, involves attending to these two conditions: setting up adequate designs, and carrying out the design while paying due caution to experimental validity. The contrast with linguistics will be clear: theoretical multiplicity in linguistics is only weakly constrained by a common methodological basis. This observation may be specified in various ways.

First, systematic theory comparison focusing on specific empirical phenomena is not a dominant activity in linguistics. Even within the realm of Cognitive Linguistics, for instance, an analytical and critical comparison of different approaches (as in Langacker 2005, Nuyts 2005 or Croft and Wood 2000) is exceptional.

Second, as a sociological corollary, linguists flock together with their own theoretical crowd. Each of the approaches has a number of founding fathers and leading figures, of the Chomsky, Halliday, Labov type, and these authorities are the core members of sociological networks that include specialized journals, conferences with a specific orientation, and local curricula that determine how a novice learns to do the job (which would probably mean: learn to work within a given theoretical framework). Breaking through the boundaries of a given approach is not obvious.

And third, linguistics at large does not possess a common empirical ground, in the form of a set of observations derived through a generally accepted method, that plays the same role that experimentation does in psycholinguistics. The latter factor is the crucial one: attempts to compare theories (the first point) require data with regard to which to compare them, and bridging distances between theories (the second point) would have to be built on a systematic comparison of theories. Referring to the terminology introduced in the first section, it is probably justified to say that linguistics does not invest a lot in the empirical operationalization of its hypotheses. For instance, in the domain of Cognitive Linguistics, what exactly would it mean that a certain construction is a "reference point construction" in the terms of Langacker (1999)? What are the measurable correlates of analyzing a particular construction in such terms? As it stands, a concept like "reference point construction" is primarily a concept that makes sense (and probably good sense at that) of a number of grammatical phenomena. That is to say, it provides an interpretation for those phenomena, but as we have seen in the first section, such an interpretation is merely a hypothesis from the point of view of empirical research, and what we would really like to see are operationalizations of such interpretative hypotheses that allow for testing of the kind discussed before. (Incidentally, readers who might be interested in ways of operationalizing the notion of reference point might have a look at Grondelaers, Speelman, and Geeraerts 2002.)

It would seem, then, that (to use the terminology of a traditional theory of science, see Nagel 1961), linguistics should primarily develop an independent *observational language* that the different *theoretical languages* of linguistics can be mapped onto: in the same way in which a psychological theory is translated into a set of statements about the behavior of test subjects under certain experimental circumstances, linguistic theories should be translatable into statements about linguistic behavior that are independent of the theory. Even if we take into account that the demarcation between theoretical and observational languages may not be totally rigid (this is a point made by the theory of science that developed in the wake of Kuhn 1962: observational statements may themselves be couched in a theoretical vocabulary), a lot of progress is possible in the operationalization of linguistics, i.e. in the attempt to turn theoretical concepts and statements into independently testable and theoretically distinctive empirical statements.

Such a systematic attempt at operationalization of linguistic hypotheses would indeed constitute an empirical revolution in linguistics. The observational basis for such a revolution would to some extent overlap with that of psychology: experimental methods and neurophysiological evidence would obviously be part of it. But so would a number of other approaches: survey techniques as used in sociolinguistic research, and corpus linguistics. Generalizing somewhat, one might say that a truly empirical form of linguistics would share experimental techniques with psychology, and survey and field techniques with sociology, whereas corpus analysis would be the most typically linguistic method.

## 3.    Why Cognitive Linguistics could (easily) be an empirical science

If we assume that linguistics is indeed in need of an empirical revolution that will eventually bring about an intertheoretical level of comparability that is similar to what we find in experimental psychology, what are the chances for Cognitive Linguistics of being part of this methodological transformation of linguistics? Before we look at the actual state of affairs, we should establish whether the specific theoretical stance of Cognitive Linguistics is conducive to the empirical turn that was introduced in the previous section. If we look at the way in which Cognitive Linguistics describes and defines itself, does its specific form of linguistics have features that would either encourage or impede an empirical approach?

Both are in fact the case. On the one hand, at least three features of Cognitive Linguistics would seem to create favorable circumstances for an empirical approach: its very *cognitive* nature, the *usage-based* perspective it takes, and the importance it attaches to *contextualizing* linguistic structures. Conversely, on the other hand, there is one dominant feature of Cognitive Linguistics that could work in the other direction: the emphasis on the analysis of linguistic meaning over linguistic form might go hand in hand with the view that only introspection is a reliable method of direct access to semantic phenomena. Let us now have a closer look (in this and the following sections) at each of these factors.

Cognitive Linguistics, if we may believe the name, is *a cognitive science*, i.e. it is one of those scientific disciplines that study the mind (which, by the way, includes the totality of the mental life of human beings, and not just knowledge in the restricted sense). It would seem obvious then, that the methods that have proved their value in the cognitive sciences at large have a strong position in Cognitive Linguistics: the experimental techniques of psychology, computer modelling, and neurophysiologic research.

We will discuss below whether this is indeed the actual state of affairs (it is not entirely, as will become clear), but let us perhaps establish first that the conclusion as such is not unproblematic: a self-conception as a cognitive science does not necessarily entail the application of an empirical methodology. Generative grammar, in fact, is a clear case in point: as part of the so-called cognitive revolution of the 1950s, its mentalist self-conception definitely means that it considers itself to be a cognitive science – but the methodology of generative grammar is predominantly introspective. The argumentation is well-known: the grammaticality of sentences is determined by (or at least restricted by) innate principles of grammar, and native speakers have immediate access to the relevant grammaticality judgements. Given the assumption of a completely homogeneous language community, this epistemological starting-point does not invite empirical research. (When the assumption of a completely homogeneous community is relaxed, attempts at statistical analysis of grammaticality judgements may enter the picture. This is a recent, albeit marginal trend in generative grammar: see e.g. Keller and Sorace 2003.)

But if, then, generative grammar is both a cognitive form of linguistics and a largely introspective one, why would Cognitive Linguistics be more prone to empirical research than generative grammar? Is there a sense in which Cognitive Linguistics is a different type of cognitive enterprise than generative grammar? And does this difference suggest a different attitude with regard to empirical research? The specific way in which Cognitive Linguistics conceives of its "cognitive" character would indeed seem to favor a more empirical approach to linguistic methodology. In generative grammar, the ultimate foundation for an introspective methodology is the autonomy of language and linguistics, whereas Cognitive Linguistics conceives of language as integrated with the other cognitive capacities of man: giving up the autonomy assumption motivates a broader range of methodological techniques, in line with the practice used by the cognitive sciences.

Turning to a second relevant feature of Cognitive Linguistics, the appeal of empirical methods within the cognitive approach is boosted by the growing tendency of Cognitive Linguistics to stress its essential nature as *a usage-based linguistics* – a form of linguistic analysis, that is, that takes into account not just grammatical structure, but that sees this structure as arising from and interacting with actual language use. The central notions of usage-based linguistics have been programmatically outlined in different publications (specifically, see Barlow and Kemmer 2000), and an increasing number of recent volumes show how the program can be put into practice. The link between the self-awareness of Cognitive Linguistics as a usage-based form of linguistic investigation and the deployment of empirical methods is straightforward: you cannot have a usage-based linguistics unless you study actual usage – as it appears in corpora in the form of spontaneous, non-elicited language data, or as it appears in an online and elicited form in experimental settings.

As a third theoretical feature of Cognitive Linguistics promoting an empirical methodology, we may again point to its *contextualized conception of language*. The relevant context, however, does not just consist of the other human cognitive capacities (everything that links up with the embodied nature of the mind), it also involves society and culture. In this sense, an interest in language variation forms an integral part of Cognitive Linguistics. Now, language variation has been studied in Cognitive Linguistics and adjacent approaches primarily from three points of view: from a diachronic perspective, including grammaticalization research (see e.g. Geeraerts 1997; Bybee 2001; Hopper and Traugott 1993; Heine 1991), from a comparative and anthropological point of view (see e.g. Pederson 1998; Kövecses 2000; Levinson 2003), and from a developmental point of view (see e.g. Tomasello 2003). Language-internal variation and sociolinguistic diversity has been much less studied, but still, we may note a number of developments within Cognitive Linguistics that are likely to contribute to an increased interest in sociolinguistic research.

First, there is the interest in cultural models and the way in which they may compete within a community: see e.g. many of the papers collected in Dirven, Frank, and Pütz (2003). Specifically, it has been pointed out (Geeraerts 2003) that such models may also characterize the beliefs that language users entertain regarding language and language varieties. In this way, Cognitive Linguistics may link up with existing sociolinguistic research about language attitudes.

Second, there is a growing tendency in the theoretical conception of language entertained by Cognitive Linguistics to stress the social nature of language. A number of researchers have started to investigate social variation from the perspective of Cognitive Linguistics: see e.g. the work by Kristiansen on phonetic variation (2003). In the realm of lexicological investigations, the research tradition started in Geeraerts, Grondelaers, and Bakema (1994) and continued in works such as Geeraerts, Grondelaers, and Speelman (1999), or Speelman, Grondelaers, and Geeraerts (2003), integrates theoretical ideas from Cognitive Linguistics with a variational perspective and a corpus-based methodology.

Third, the usage data that Cognitive Linguistics, as a self-styled usage-based approach, is confronted with, automatically include sociolinguistic variation. Assuming that the primary empirical source for a usage-based approach to linguistics consists of corpus materials, then more often than not, the corpus will not be internally homogeneous: because the texts collected for the corpus come from various sources, it will not be known in advance whether the variation that may be observed in the corpus is due to lectal factors or not. (The term *lectal* is used here to refer to all types of language varieties or *lects*: dialects, regiolects, national varieties, registers, styles, idiolects, whatever). As such, filtering out the effects of such factors will be necessary for any cognitive linguistic attempt to analyse the usage data – even if the analysis is not a priori interested in lectal variation.

The importance of socially and culturally determined variation for Cognitive Linguistics has an obvious methodological correlate: these socially oriented forms of Cognitive Linguistics would naturally support the adoption of the quantitative, empirical methodology that is dominant in sociolinguistic research at large.

We may conclude, in short, that using the main types of empirical methodology that were mentioned in the first section is motivated by the theoretical stance of Cognitive Linguistics: its very *cognitive* nature, its *usage-based* perspective, and its *contextualizing* approach may lead in various ways to the use of experimental data, corpus material, survey techniques, and advanced quantitative analysis.

## 4.   What Cognitive Linguistics actually does

So how exactly does Cognitive Linguistics fare? Three points should be made to get an adequate and nuanced picture of the situation. First, from very early on, there has been a permanent presence in Cognitive Linguistics of the major forms of empirical methodology. Second, there is a growing interest in such an approach. But third, the move towards a large-scale application of empirical methods is far from completed. The overall picture, then, will have to be a mixed one: Cognitive Linguistics has a promising theoretical background that is conducive to empirical research, and it broadly seems to have the intention to live up to that promise, but it still has quite a way to go before it entirely fulfills it. Whether that is seen as the glass being half full or rather as it being half empty, is probably just a matter of mood and mentality. However, if we can agree on the importance of introducing empirical methods in Cognitive Linguistics, we should not just identify what has already been achieved and what contributes positively to the desired developments, but we should also pinpoint the possible impediments to a further evolution in the direction of empirical methods. – But that is what we will do in the next section.

### 4.1. Long-standing presence of an empirical methodology

To begin with, we may indeed notice that the empirical methods mentioned above are to a greater or smaller extent present in the field of Cognitive Linguistics, and have been so for quite a while. The following observations are not meant as a systematic overview, but merely as a set of examples establishing the long-standing presence of the various approaches in Cognitive Linguistics. To keep matters simple, let us distinguish between two groups: elicitation and experimentation on the one hand, corpus-based observation on the other.

With regard to the use of *elicitation and experimentation,* psycholinguistic work has since long been part of Cognitive Linguistics in the work of Gibbs (1994 and many more). Another influential early example is Sandra and Rice (1995). The related use of neurolinguistic evidence, which is now most conspicuously associated with George Lakoff's Neural Theory of Language group, may be noted as early as Deane (1992). Elicitation techniques have also been used in anthropological and comparative research. For instance, to get an independent assessment of the relation between language and cognition, non-linguistic tests are used, such as problem solving tasks (Pederson 1995). Production tasks are also used in language acquisition research: Berman and Slobin (1994) use pictures to elicit stories from children.

*Corpus data* too were used early on in the history of Cognitive Linguistics. The methodology of European studies in Cognitive Linguistics in particular has tended to be more corpus-based than the early American studies, which were predominantly introspective. The use of corpus materials (which seems to have come to the attention of the broader community of Cognitive Linguistics only since Barlow and Kemmer 2000) was already part of early European studies like Dirven, Goossens, Putseys and Vorlat (1982), Dirven and Taylor (1988), Rudzka-Ostyn (1988), Schulze (1988), Geeraerts, Grondelaers, and Bakema (1994).

## 4.2. Growing interest in an empirical methodology

Now, this initial overview only establishes that the relevant empirical methods do indeed appear in the context of Cognitive Linguistics, and that most of them have in fact been around for quite a while. However, the overview does not say much about the impact they have: what is the position of these forms of research within Cognitive Linguistics as a whole? If one compares the impact of data-oriented studies in the total field of Cognitive Linguistics over a number years, a steady increase in the importance of empirical research may be noticed. In Table 1, the presence of a number of relevant keywords in the Cognitive Linguistics Bibliography is broken down over four periods in time. The terms (whose presence in any field in the bibliographical entries is counted) relate to empirical methods of research: the general terms *data* and *empirical* on the one hand, and the methodologically more specific terms *corpus* and *experiment(al)* on the other. The Cognitive Linguistics Bibliography is a magnificent research instrument compiled predominantly by René Dirven; it is included in the subscription to the journal Cognitive Linguistics. The version of the bibliography used for Table 1 is the version of September 2005, which includes a total of 7000 entries.

*Table 1.* Presence of terms related to empirical methods in the Cognitive Linguistics Bibliography, divided over five-year periods

|  | 1985–1989 n=766 | | 1990–1994 n=1140 | | 1995–1999 n=1881 | | 2000–2004 n=2314 | |
|---|---|---|---|---|---|---|---|---|
| *corpus* | 4 | 0.5% | 18 | 1.6% | 68 | 3.6% | 215 | 9.3% |
| *experiment(al)* | 15 | 2.0% | 46 | 4.0% | 119 | 6.3% | 214 | 9.2% |
| *empirical* | 24 | 3.1% | 59 | 5.2% | 116 | 6.2% | 213 | 9.2% |
| *data* | 21 | 2.7% | 69 | 6.0% | 151 | 8.0% | 249 | 10.8% |
| total | 64 | 8.3% | 151 | 13.2% | 357 | 19.0% | 648 | 28.0% |

Coarse though the calculation may be, the table does show that there is a continuous increase in the number of books and articles that refer to empirical approaches: the number of bibliographical entries that cites either of the four terms (the row labeled TOTAL) rises steadily to 28% in the final period, and the growth occurs with each of the four terms separately. The separate growth curves for the individual terms are fairly even, except in the case of *corpus*, where the line shows a marked increase from the penultimate to the last period. This is not altogether surprising: the massive availability of corpus materials is a relatively recent phenomenon, specifically if we take into account the use of the internet as a corpus.

The impression we get from Table 1 is strengthened by further indications of an intensification of the appeal of empirical methods within Cognitive Linguistics. It suffices to have a look at some of the thematic symposia organized over the last few years: the Empirical Methods in Cognitive Linguistics workshop held at Cornell University in May 2003, the theme session on the use of corpora in Cognitive Linguistics organized during the ICLC8 in Logrono, July 2003, the workshop on the necessity of experimental methods in semantics organized during the 20th Scandinavian Conference in Linguistics at the University of Helsinki in January 2004, the choice of experimental and empirical methods as the focus theme of the 7th Conference on Conceptual Structure, Discourse, and Language at the University of Alberta in October 2004, and the corpus-based theme session Language System and Language Use at the ICLC9 in Seoul, July 2005 – all of these testify to the growing importance that the Cognitive Linguistics community attaches to an empirical methodology.

## 4.3. Room for expansion in the use of an empirical methodology

Table 1 also suggests that the empirical approach, although on the rise, does not yet dominate the methodological landscape in Cognitive Linguistics. This impression may be further supported if we have a look at the program of the ICLC9 conference in Seoul, July 2005. Table 2 gives the distribution of the talks over three methodological classes: experimental research (which in this case is intended to include the use of all elicitation techniques, neurological evidence, and survey methods), corpus-based research, and traditional research. In terms of data gathering, the latter approach basically uses examples drawn from the linguistic knowledge of the researcher. The figures involve the plenary talks at the conference, and the talks from the general session, i.e. posters and theme session papers have not been included. Since the data are predominantly based on the abstracts of the talks (attending all of them would have been impossible), a certain degree of caution is necessary: it need not be the case that the actual method of research is well described in the abstract (and actual talks may differ somewhat from what is announced in the abstracts). Given this proviso, a number of interesting conclusions present themselves.

*Table 2.*  Methodological breakdown of plenary and general session talks at the ICLC9, Seoul, July 2005

|  | EXPERIMENTAL | | CORPUS-BASED | | TRADITIONAL | |
|---|---|---|---|---|---|---|
| General Session | 31 | 17.6% | 50 | 28.4% | 95 | 53.9% |
| Plenary Session | 2 | 20.0% | 1 | 10.0% | 7 | 70.0% |

First, the figures confirm the conclusion drawn from Table 1 with regard to the dominance of the traditional method: there is an outspoken interest in empirical methods, but they do not yet represent the majority of cases. Admittedly, it would be wrong to expect a 100% presence of empirical research: theory formation *does* require pure conceptual analysis, internal and external comparison of results, meta-reflection on methods and terminology, or synthetic overviews that do not immediately involve new research – and there will always be talks of that kind at conferences. There should be no empirical imperialism, then: one of the great things about Cognitive Linguistics is the room it has always left for creativity and the bold development of novel ideas, and it should remain that way if the approach is to keep its dynamism. However, at least half of the talks in the category labeled TRADITIONAL are not of that kind. They are descriptive talks that lend themselves to the use of an empirical methodology. In this sense, a further growth of the empirical trend in Cognitive Linguistics is definitely possible.

Second, the picture emanating from the plenaries is more conservative than that from the general session papers. The majority of the plenary talks, i.e. those of Eve Sweetser, Gilles Fauconnier, Ron Langacker, Len Talmy, Keedong Lee and Günther Radden were based on a traditional methodology of conceptual analysis, without much explicit attention for empirical data of the type discussed here. The plenary talks by Melissa Bowerman and Seana Coulson, by contrast, were firmly placed within the experimental tradition, while Suzanne Kemmer's talk used state of the art corpus methods. Despite its promising title, John Taylor's paper on "The mental corpus" basically used the corpus idea as a metaphor for the organization of knowledge in the mind but did not provide systematic indications how this metaphor could be linked to actual corpus research. As such, it is here counted with the traditional category.

Third, if we look more closely at the disciplines and domains of research covered by the different methodologies, we may note that experimental methods and corpus research are more firmly entrenched in some fields than in others. In foreign language learning, language acquisition research, and sign language and gesture research, for instance, experimental methods are well entrenched. This is a reflection of the importance of such methods in the fields in question at large: if experimental testing of the efficiency of a given teaching method is a standard practice in second language learning research generally, it is no surprise that cognitive linguists working in that domain will adopt an experimental methodology. Similarly, using corpora is normal in historical linguistics, language acquisition research, and text linguistics and discourse analysis. If we take this skewed distribution over disciplines into account, we may again conclude that there is room for a further expansion of an empirical methodology in what is usually thought of as the core area of linguistics, i.e. synchronic grammar.

Fourth, an analysis of the two empirical classes in Table 2 in terms of substance rather than frequency further supports the idea that an expansion of the methodological repertoire of Cognitive Linguistics is possible. To begin with, we may note that some methodological formats are relatively underrepresented. The experimental techniques that are being used predominantly involve elicitation in the form of production and comprehension tasks, plus some decision, association, and categorization tasks. Sophisticated methods like eye tracking or FMRI and other neurological imaging techniques are used only occasionally. This also holds for survey techniques in the form of interviews and questionnaires, or for direct observation as usual in some forms of sociolinguistics and anthropological linguistics. The corpora of observed language use that are being investigated are very often existing corpora like the British National Corpus, or readily available data like the ones you can get by googling, but compiling corpora with a specific purpose (like a corpus of advertisements or newspaper headlines) does occur. At this point, the borderline between elicitation and observation tends to fade a little. When a writing task takes the form of writing whole texts or narratives, the production task borders on "corpus elicitation": pooled together, the stories of the participants constitute a mini-corpus. Overall, then, the range of empirical methods in Cognitive Linguistics is broad but rather skewed: a further expansion of the spectrum of available methods may be envisaged.

Fifth, and finally, that there is an opportunity for further progression along the empirical path also becomes apparent if we zoom in on the type of corpus analysis that we find in the CORPUS-BASED category in Table 2. The question that concerns us here relates directly to section 1 of the present chapter: there may be a lot of corpus use around, but does it live up to the general criteria for empirical research that we formulated at the end of section 1? (Incidentally, the present paper tends to pay more attention to corpus-based approaches in empirical linguistics than to experimentation and the other relevant techniques, but that is a question of convenience rather than principle: more about experimentation may be found in Gibbs, this volume.)

In general, corpora appear to be often used as a simple data gathering technique and not as a empirical testing ground for operationalized hypotheses, that is to say, in a large part of the cases in the CORPUS-BASED category in Table 2, the corpus is primarily a repository of examples that are then analysed in a traditional way. The examples you analyze are no longer derived from your own knowledge of the language, but the way in which you analyze them is still a predominantly intuitive one. This is the type of corpus use that Tummers, Heylen and Geeraerts (2005) call *corpus-illustrated* research. In a sense, it considers usage events as a data set for the selection of examples. The presence of an expected pattern in the corpus data is then so to speak interpreted as a grammaticality judgment, albeit to some extent a more reliable one than the usual, introspectively derived ones. Although corpus-illustrated work constitutes a big step forward in comparison with introspective work, there are two points with regard to which a more advanced way of dealing with corpus materials is possible, and indeed necessary. Both points, needless to say, link up with the basic characteristics of an empirical approach as identified in section 1.

A first point concerns the systematicity with which the data are gathered and/or analyzed. Typically, the argumentation in corpus-illustrated research takes one of two forms. When a theory predicts a phenomenon, the corpus presence of the phenomenon is taken as a confirmation of the theory. When a theory excludes a phenomenon, the corpus presence of the phenomenon is taken as a falsification of the theory. In both cases, however, a problem arises when the frequency of the selected corpus data is low: what if the confirming or falsifying data are marginal with regard to the alternatives? Because corpus evidence is seldom a question of black or white (of one hundred percent versus zero percent of occurrences), a proper analysis of corpus materials requires that alternative patterns are systematically explored and that their frequencies are statistically evaluated. Grammatical models like Cognitive Linguistics and Construction Grammar in particular, which accept the existence of networks in which elements or levels may have different degrees of salience, should be particularly sensitive to differences in the frequency of alternative expressions. That is to say, a *usage-based linguistics needs quantification and statistical analysis*.

A second point with regard to which a more advanced form of corpus analysis may be envisaged is the interpretation of the corpus data. In a corpus-illustrated approach, the corpus data are used to restrict a process of intuitive interpretation: examples of a linguistic phenomenon (say, a construction) are retrieved from the corpus, and the set of examples is then analyzed largely intuitively. The availability of large corpora may allow for a more advanced approach. A given interpretation may be turned into a set of expectations with regard to the behavior of the entity under investigation, and these expectations may then be tested against the corpus. That is to say, *advanced corpus research needs to pay specific attention to the operationalization of hypotheses*. If we interpretatively assume that a linguistic entity has this meaning or that function, what can we expect about its observable behavior in actual language use? The further steps for a corpus approach follow logically: how can we identify that behavior in the corpus data, and when can we say that the initial hypothesis is correct?

Within the broad domain of Cognitive Linguistics, a corpus-based methodology as meant here may be found in various fields (the references are exemplary, not exhaustive): in language acquisition research (Tomasello 2003); in language change research (Bybee 2001; Krug 2000); in language variation research (Grondelaers, Speelman and Geeraerts 2002; Speelman, Grondelaers and Geeraerts 2003); in functional discourse analysis (Sanders and Gernsbacher 2004), and in quantitative construction grammar (Gries 2003; Stefanowitsch 2003; Stefanowitsch and Gries 2003; Tummers, Speelman and Geeraerts 2005).

But if we take the Seoul conference as representative for Cognitive Linguistics as a whole, this type of advanced corpus research represents only a small minority of the CORPUS-BASED category in Table 2: not more than 10 or 15% of the corpus-based papers in the General Session would seem to move beyond the corpus-illustrated level as defined above. It is here in particular that the raw figures in Table 2 appear to be somewhat deceptive: yes, corpus materials are being widely used, but from the point of view of an "empirical revolution" in linguistics and the characteristics of genuinely empirical research as identified in section 1, the sophistication with which they are being analyzed could still be improved.

In addition, note that the dichotomy between corpus-illustrated and more advanced forms of corpus-based linguistics obviously only defines the endpoints of a continuum. A lot of case studies occupy an intermediary position between both extremes. In particular, studies that do not yet use quantitative forms of analysis may display a lot of variation with respect to the systematicity with which the empirical data are collected and scrutinized, ranging from an anecdotal selection of examples from a corpus to a systematic scanning of a corpus to uncover the patterns and uses of a linguistic phenomenon. Good examples of what may be achieved with a thorough but not specifically quantified examination of corpus materials include Deignan and Potter (2004), Heyvaert (2003), Maldonado (2002) – and of course, there are traditional branches of linguistics, like historical lexicography, that testify to the value of in-depth qualitative analyses of large-scale corpus data (cp. Geeraerts 1997). But just like lexicography has, in recent decades, fruitfully enriched its traditional corpus-based approach with quantitative methods of information retrieval, it is to be expected that theoretical linguistics too might profit from further sophistication in the analysis of corpus data. The existence of a continuum, then, should not surprise us. If the spread of empirical methods in Cognitive Linguistics is a gradual process, it is normal that there will be researchers, and areas of research, that have progressed further in the empirical cycle than others.

## 5. Why Cognitive Linguistics is not yet as empirical as might be

Empirical methods, even though they are receiving an unquestionably rising amount of attention, do not yet constitute the dominant tendency in Cognitive Linguistics, and considerable progress can still be made in the direction of a full-fledged implementation of the empirical research program. What could be the reasons for this situation – a situation that contrasts somewhat with the expectations that follow from the theoretical self-conception of Cognitive Linguistics? Two fundamentally different groups of reasons have to be brought into the picture. One has to do with rather more mundane, practical reasons, with the way, that is, in which Cognitive Linguistics is actually being practised and the way it presents itself to young researchers. The other group concerns reasons of principle: could there be fundamental features of Cognitive Linguistics that slow down the introduction of empirical methods? In particular, couldn't we say that the emphasis on meaning in Cognitive Linguistics would naturally favor the use of introspection, as the only reliable method of direct access to semantic phenomena? If this is correct, there would be a methodological tension at the heart of Cognitive Linguistics, because we established in section 3 that a number of other characteristics of Cognitive Linguistics are particularly favorable towards the adoption of empirical methods. We will argue, however, that the theoretical reasons in favor of an introspective methodology are not compelling.

### 5.1. Reasons of practice

Two practical factors may be invoked to explain why Cognitive Linguistics has not yet progressed in the direction of empirical research to the full extent that might perhaps be expected on the basis of its theoretical position: the fact that training in experimental techniques or corpus research is not a standard part of curricula in linguistics, and the recognition that the "public image" that Cognitive Linguistics presents to young researchers and newcomers does not contain a commitment to empirical research as a conspicuous feature.

The first factor is undoubtedly the major one: coming from traditional curricula in language and linguistics, many cognitive linguists are simply at a loss on how to get started on empirical research of an experimental or a corpus-based kind. (And, to repeat, the present paper will not immediately help them, because it was conceived as a metatheoretical overview and not as a practical guide.) The practical steps to be taken are indeed numerous and often cumbersome. In the case of corpus research, you need to collect appropriate corpus materials, retrieve the relevant observations from the corpus, code the observations for all the features that you think might be relevant in the analysis, perform the right quantitative analysis – and then start your second round in the empirical cycle with an interpretative effort. In the case of experimental research, the practical difficulties are similar: you need to set up an experimental design with the right stimuli (something which you may achieve only after an initial pilot study), find an appropriate set of experimental subjects, carry out the actual experiments, analyze them with the relevant techniques – and then start your second round in the empirical cycle with an interpretative effort.

It is no surprise then, that linguists trained in a more purely analytic paradigm need time and help to get acquainted with this form of doing research. At the same time, there are clear indications that many within the Cognitive Linguistics community are willing and waiting to receive such an initiation. A good example is the appeal of the "collostructional" approach introduced by Stefanowitsch and Gries (2003). It applies existing methods of statistical collocation analysis (i.e. methods that measure the strength of association that exists between two elements) to the relationship between the lexical items that occupy the slots in a construction and the construction as such. Cast in a readily applicable format, the method has soon attracted a number of scholars working within Construction Grammar: see Gries and Stefanowitsch (2006) for a sample. From the perspective of the present chapter, the appeal of the collostructional method shows that there is indeed a demand for the adoption of empirical techniques – thus strengthening the assumption that a lack of familiarity is one of the main explanations for the situation sketched in the previous section.

At the same time, the collostructional example reveals a potential danger: not much would be achieved if cognitive linguists, out of ignorance of alternatives, would simply equate empirical research with readily available specific techniques like the collostructional analysis. What we should achieve, in the long run, is for cognitive linguists to be aware of the full range of empirical techniques, experimental as well as corpus-based. But that will require a reorganization of the average curriculum and a long-term investment in empirical training.

A second practical factor that should be mentioned involves the example provided by the leading authorities in Cognitive Linguistics: what is the image that newcomers and young researchers get when they are confronted with the work of the most highly valued researchers in the field? What methodological impression does a novice get from Cognitive Linguistics if he or she looks at the current work of the founding fathers? Their work, in fact, is to a large extent of an analytical, theory-building kind that does not go, in terms of methodological procedure, beyond the traditional methodology of contemporary linguistics: remember that Table 2 showed a more conservative picture for the plenary talks at ICLC9 than for the general session talks. Let's assume that we restrict the set of founding fathers of Cognitive Linguistics to Langacker, Lakoff, Talmy, and Fillmore. (The position of Fillmore may need some explanation, because sociologically speaking, he never identified very strongly with Cognitive Linguistics as a movement. His ideas about frame semantics and construction grammar constitute an integral part of the foundational concepts of Cognitive Linguistics, however.)

Now, in their work on grammatical phenomena and linguistic theory, Langacker (in spite of the fact that he is the person who coined the phrase "usage-based model": Langacker 1988), Talmy, and Fauconnier are highly traditional linguists in terms of data gathering and data analysis: no systematic corpus analysis or ingenious experimentation in this line of research. Fillmore is a notable exception, to the extent that the FrameNet project that pursues a large-scale application of frame semantics to the English lexicon is definitely and deliberately corpus-based.

Lakoff too occupies a specific position, to the extent that the "cognitive commitment" that he formulated in Lakoff (1990) has led him to numerous forms of interdisciplinary collaborations with philosophers, literary scholars, and other cognitive scientists. In particular, he lies at the basis of a neural theory of language that looks at the neurophysiological basis of his Conceptual Metaphor Theory. However, the way in which Conceptual Metaphor Theory is usually practised is largely an introspective matter (see Haser 2005, and Gibbs, this volume, for a critical assessment). It is, in fact, possibly the easiest form of linguistics that you can do in the domain of Cognitive Linguistics: collect a number of expressions for an arbitrary target field in a given language, identify a common semantic denominator for them, and conclude that thàt is the way the target field is conceptualized in the language, in other words, that thàt is the way people think in that language.

The picture is perhaps slightly caricatural, but the restrictions on this type of work will be clear. To really establish the conclusion, one would first have to assess the importance of the expression in the language: what other expressions are there, how often are they used, and what factors actually determine the choice between the alternatives? Such questions

require a thorough investigation of actual usage, and in any case a methodology that goes beyond just enumerating examples. Next, concluding
from the mere presence of a form in the language to a certain way of
thinking requires at least that the productivity of the image inherent in the
message is established, i.e. that it is made clear that the metaphor is not a
dead one but actually influences or reflects, to a greater or a lesser extent,
thinking. To be explicit, the point made here is not that attempts to establish an effect of language on thinking by means of adequate techniques do
not exist, but rather that such an approach is far from dominant in research in the realm of Conceptual Metaphor Theory.

In other words, what is probably the most broadly attractive and most
widely known form of research in Cognitive Linguistics is at the same
time one of the most facile ones in methodological terms, in spite of the
long-standing efforts of people like Ray Gibbs (and more recently, researchers like Lera Boroditsky, 2001) to provide empirical underpinnings
for Conceptual Metaphor Theory. To the extent that this contributes to a
certain image of what it involves to do interesting work in Cognitive Linguistics, this is not advantageous for the expansion of empirical methods
in Cognitive Linguistics.

## 5.2. Reasons of principle

In addition to this absence of empirical tendencies in the dominant public
image of Cognitive Linguistics – both in terms of the attitude of its leading figures and in terms of its best known fields of application – there
might be a more principled reluctance with regard to cutting edge empirical work. Cognitive Linguistics considers itself to be a non-objectivist theory of language, whereas the use of corpus materials involves an attempt
to maximalize the objective basis of linguistic descriptions. Is an objectivist methodology compatible with a non-objectivist theory? Isn't any attempt to reduce the role of introspection and intuition in linguistic research
contrary to the spirit of Cognitive Linguistics, which stresses the semantic
aspects of the language – and the meaning of linguistic expressions is the
least tangible of linguistic phenomena. Because meanings do not present
themselves directly in the corpus data, will introspection not always be
used in any cognitive analysis of language? (For an explicit defense of
such a position, albeit in terms of 'intuition' rather than 'introspection',
see Itkonen 2003.)

There seems to exist a tension, in other words, between a broad methodological tendency in Cognitive Linguistics that considers introspection

the most or perhaps the only appropriate method for studying meaning, and a marginal but increasing tendency to apply empirical methods that are customary in the other cognitive sciences.

To summarize: the dissemination of empirical methods in Cognitive Linguistics is far from complete, because some of the leading figures adhere (if not in principle, at least in practice) to a more traditional linguistic methodology; because the most broadly appealing branches of Cognitive Linguistics tend to be the methodologically least constrained ones; because the use of empirical methods is insufficiently incorporated in Cognitive Linguistics programs; and maybe also because there is a certain degree of theoretical skepticism with regard to empirical methods.

Because the latter argument is clearly the most fundamental one (it is the only one that could not be countered on a very practical level), let us try to assess its weight. Just how essential is a principled skepticism with regard to empirical methods? The argument may in fact be construed in two ways, a minimalist and a maximalist one. The *minimalist* position entails that empirical methods may never completely replace a more interpretative approach: even though it is granted that empirical methods yield highly valuable circumstantial evidence with regard to the semantics of natural language, there is an irreducible core to meaning that cannot be accessed from the outside, with the indirect evidence provided by objective methods, but that necessarily has to be experienced subjectively. The *maximalist* position involves the view that a hermeneutic, interpretative methodology is not only inevitable but also vastly superior when it comes to the study of meaning, and that the addition of empirical evidence is basically superfluous. The minimalist reading of the skeptical argument, in short, implies that empirical evidence is not sufficient for a proper study of meaning, while the maximalist reading implies that it is not necessary.

Both arguments can be easily countered. The minimalist reading of the skeptical argument will not stand in the way of an attempt to maximize the benefit that one can get from empirical evidence. Even if you accept that subjectivity cannot be reduced for a 100%, the practical imperative for research will be to push the employment of methods aspiring to objectivity as far as it can gets – that is to say, the practical consequences of the minimalist position will be virtually non-existent: you would still try to pursue the empirical line of research as far as you can take it.

The maximalist reading of the skeptical argument, on the other hand, will have difficulty to stand up against the line of reasoning developed in the second section of this paper. If it is indeed important for the further progress of linguistics to achieve a higher degree of intertheoretical comparability, staying with highly subjective methods of research would simply be counterproductive. How could a maximalist interpretation be superior if it does not increase objectivity and comparability? A shift towards a minimalist reading of the skeptical stance – "let's try to reduce subjectivity to the maximal extent, even if we may not be able to do so in any absolute sense" – would then be inevitable.

In addition, there is compelling evidence that introspective evidence is *not* a superior method of linguistic description. In general terms, this was established by Labov in his seminal 1972 article, in which he clearly identifies the dangers of "armchair linguistics". More specifically with regard to the description of meaning in the context of Cognitive Linguistics, Geeraerts, Grondelaers and Bakema (1994) compare the results of an introspective analysis of Wierzbicka's with a data-based description, concluding that the analysis presented by Wierzbicka (who is one of the most explicit defendants of an introspective approach) is either plainly inadequate, or formulated in such a way that it is immune to criticism.

## 6.    What needs to be done

The argument developed in the previous pages may be summarized in three steps. First, a growing increase in the empirical demands on linguistics is to be expected: corpus research, experimental designs, surveys, and the accompanying forms of quantitative data analysis are likely to occupy a more important position in linguistics than they have so far done. Even if they will not penetrate massively in linguistics in the short run, they will probably determine what is methodological cutting-edge research in languages studies. Second, the theoretical make-up of Cognitive Linguistics provides an excellent basis for participating in this empirical revolution: its theoretical principles are generally advantageous for the incorporation of empirical methods, even though the primary interest of Cognitive Linguistics in semantics might favor an opposite methodological orientation. Third, the actual situation in Cognitive Linguistics is a mixed one, with a clearly growing interest in empirical methods on the one hand, but a lingering dominance of traditionally analytic approaches on the other.

What needs to be done, then? The primary step will be for Cognitive Linguistics to make its mind up: in which direction is it going to develop? Will it wholeheartedly embrace the empirical turn, or will it stay with a predominantly traditional approach? Assuming that only the former option is fruitful in the long run, a number of recommendations for the future development of Cognitive Linguistics may be spelled out.

First, if it is correct that the spread of empirical methods is hampered by insufficient knowledge of approaches and techniques, didactic efforts are necessary to make cognitive linguists acquainted with corpus analysis, experimental design, survey techniques, and statistical processing of data. A program in Cognitive Linguistics worthy of that name should resolutely opt for advanced training in empirical linguistics. In the process, it will have to be made clear what the essence of empirical research really is, so that the misconceptions that now sometimes mar the debate may be avoided. No, empirical research does not involve abandoning theory formation in favor of purely descriptive research: rather, it involves trying to provide proof for theories, and from there, refining the theories. No, empirical research does not imply that intuition and interpretation have no role to play in linguistic research: rather, it implies that interpretation is but one step in the empirical cycle of successful research. And no, empirical research is not about restricting the investigation to one kind of method or technique: rather, it is about using experimental, and corpus-based, and other empirical approaches in combination to achieve maximally reliable results.

Second, the standards of scholarship in Cognitive Linguistics will gradually have to be raised to such a level that unsubstantiated claims will become unfashionable. This is not to say that the bold and inspired analytical and theoretical work that sparked off Cognitive Linguistics to begin with, should be ruled out: that would be a counterproductive check on the creativity of the community of cognitive linguists (and if there is one thing you cannot deny them, it's creativity). Nor is this to say that the desired level should be achieved in one go and simultaneously by all: what we are talking about is a medium-term development that leaves room for different paces of development, just like it is in theory development. But even if the speed with which Cognitive Linguistics will get there may be moderate and variable according to the circumstances, the direction of the development should be clear, and all those who have responsible positions in Cognitive Linguistics – leading authors, editors of journals and books, referees, conference organizers – should consciously and consistently pay more attention to empirical grounding, to keep that development going.

And third, Cognitive Linguistics (and linguistics at large, for that matter) will have to learn how to live with a slower pace of development. Empirical thoroughness and reproducibility come at a price: that of painstaking and time-consuming effort. While the late 20th century in linguistics may have had a tendency to prefer conceptual audacity and the construction of grand theories, these are values that we associate primarily with 19th century philological accuracy and meticulousness. Perhaps, then, the early 21st century may profit from a return of some the 19th century spirit ...

## References

Barlow, Michael, and Suzanne Kemmer (eds.)
2000    *Usage-based Models of Language.* Stanford: CSLI.
Berman, Ruth A., and Dan I. Slobin
1994    *Relating Events in Narrative: A Crosslinguistic Developmental Study.* Hillsdale: Lawrence Erlbaum Associates.
Boroditsky, Lera
2001    Does language shape thought? Mandarin and English speakers' conceptions of time. *Cognitive Psychology* 43: 1–22.
Bybee, Joan
2001    *Phonology and Language Use.* Cambridge: Cambridge University Press.
Croft, William, and Esther J. Wood
2000    Construal operations in linguistics and artificial intelligence. In *Meaning and Cognition,* Liliana Albertazzi (ed.), 51–78. Amsterdam/Philadelphia: Benjamins.
Deane, Paul D.
1992    *Grammar in Mind and Brain: Explorations in Cognitive Syntax.* Berlin/New York: Mouton de Gruyter.
Deignan, Alice, and Liz Potter
2004    A corpus study of metaphors and metonyms in English and Italian. *Journal of Pragmatics* 36: 1231–1252.
Dirven, René, Louis Goossens, Yvan Putseys, and Emma Vorlat
1982    *The Scene of Linguistic Action and its Perspectivization by* Speak, Talk, Say, *and* Tell. Amsterdam/Philadelphia: Benjamins.
Dirven, René, Roslyn Frank, and Martin Pütz (eds.)
2003    *Cognitive Models in Language and Thought. Ideology, Metaphors and Meanings.* Berlin/New York: Mouton de Gruyter.
Dirven, René, and John Taylor
1988    The conceptualisation of vertical space in English: the case of *tall.* In *Topics in Cognitive Linguistics,* Brygida Rudzka-Ostyn (ed.), 379–402. Amsterdam/Philadelphia: Benjamins.
Geeraerts, Dirk
1997    *Diachronic Prototype Semantics.* Oxford: The Clarendon Press.
2003    Cultural models of linguistic standardization. In *Cognitive Models in Language and Thought. Ideology, Metaphors and Meanings,* René

Dirven, Roslyn Frank, and Martin Pütz (eds.), 25–68. Berlin/New York: Mouton de Gruyter.

Geeraerts, Dirk, Stefan Grondelaers, and Peter Bakema
1994 *The Structure of Lexical Variation. Meaning, Naming, and Context.* Berlin/New York: Mouton de Gruyter.

Geeraerts, Dirk, Stefan Grondelaers, and Dirk Speelman
1999 *Convergentie en divergentie in de Nederlandse woordenschat.* Amsterdam: Meertens Instituut.

Gibbs, Raymond W.
1994 *The Poetics of Mind. Figurative Thought, Language, and Understanding.* Cambridge: Cambridge University Press.

Gonzalez-Marquez, Monica, Irene Mittelberg, Seana Coulson, and Michael J. Spivey (eds.)
Forthc. *Methods in Cognitive Linguistics.* Amsterdam/Philadelphia: Benjamins.

Gries, Stefan Th.
2003 *Multifactorial Analysis in Corpus Linguistics: A Study of Particle Placement.* London: Continuum Press.

Gries, Stefan Th., and Anatol Stefanowitsch (eds.)
2006 *Corpora in Cognitive Linguistics. Corpus-based Approaches to Syntax and Lexis.* Berlin/New York: Mouton de Gruyter.

Grondelaers, Stefan, Dirk Speelman, and Dirk Geeraerts
2002 Regressing on *er*. Statistical analysis of texts and language variation. In *6th International Conference on the Statistical Analysis of Textual Data,* Anne Morin and Pascal Sébillot (eds.), 335–346. Rennes: Institut National de Recherche en Informatique et en Automatique.

Haser, Verena
2005 *Metaphor, Metonymy, and Experientialist Philosophy: Challenging Cognitive Semantics.* Berlin/New York: Mouton de Gruyter.

Heine, Bernd
1991 *Grammaticalization: A Conceptual Framework.* Chicago: University of Chicago Press.

Heyvaert, Liesbet
2003 *A Cognitive-Functional Approach to Nominalization in English.* Berlin/ New York: Mouton de Gruyter.

Hopper, Paul J., and Elizabeth Closs Traugott
1993 *Grammaticalization.* Cambridge: Cambridge University Press.

Itkonen, Esa
2003 *What is Language? A Study in the Philosophy of Linguistics.* Turku: Åbo Akademis tryckeri

Keller, Frank, and Antonella Sorace
2003 Gradient auxiliary selection and impersonal passivization in German: An experimental investigation. *Journal of Linguistics* 39: 57–108.

Kövecses, Zoltán
2001 *Metaphor and Emotion: Language, Culture, and Body in Human Feeling.* Cambridge: Cambridge University Press.

Kristiansen, Gitte
2003    How to do things with allophones: linguistic stereotypes as cognitive reference points in social cognition. In *Cognitive Models in Language and Thought: Ideologies, Metaphors, and Meanings*, René Dirven, Roslyn Frank, and Martin Pütz (eds.), 69–120. Berlin/New York: Mouton de Gruyter.

Krug, Manfred
2000    *Emerging English Modals: A Corpus-Based Study of Grammaticalization*. Berlin/New York: Mouton de Gruyter.

Kuhn, Thomas S.
1962    *The Structure of Scientific Revolutions*. Chicago: The University of Chicago Press.

Labov, William
1972    Some principles of linguistic methodology. *Language in Society* 1: 97–120.

Lakoff, George
1990    The Invariance Hypothesis. *Cognitive Linguistics* 1: 39–74.

Langacker, Ronald W.
1988    A usage-based model. In *Topics in Cognitive Linguistics*, Brygida Rudzka-Ostyn (ed.), 127–161. Amsterdam/Philadelphia: Benjamins.
1999    Reference point constructions. In *Grammar and Conceptualization,* Ronald W. Langacker, 171–202. Berlin/New York: Mouton de Gruyter.
2005    Construction Grammars: cognitive, radical, and less so. In *Cognitive Linguistics. Internal Dynamics and Interdisciplinary Interaction,* Francisco J. Ruiz de Mendoza Ibáñez, and M. Sandra Peña Cervel (eds.), 101–159. Berlin/New York: Mouton de Gruyter.

Levinson, Stephen
2003    *Space in Language and Cognition*. Cambridge: Cambridge University Press.

Maldonado, Ricardo
2002    Objective and subjective datives. *Cognitive Linguistics* 13: 1–65.

Nagel, Ernst
1961    *The Structure of Science*. London: Routledge and Kegan Paul.

Nuyts, Jan
2005    Brothers in arms? On the relations between Cognitive and Functional Linguistics. In *Cognitive Linguistics. Internal Dynamics and Interdisciplinary Interaction,* Francisco J. Ruiz de Mendoza Ibáñez, and M. Sandra Peña Cervel (eds.), 69–100. Berlin: Mouton de Gruyter.

Pederson, Eric
1995    Language as context, language as means: Spatial cognition and habitual language use. *Cognitive Linguistics* 6: 33–62.
1998    Spatial language, reasoning, and variation across Tamil communities. In *Language and Location in Space and Time*, Petr Zima, and Vladimír Tax (eds.), 111–119. München: Lincom Europa.

Rudzka-Ostyn, Brygida
  1988    Semantic extensions into the domain of verbal communication. In
          *Topics in Cognitive Linguistics*, Brygida Rudzka-Ostyn (ed.), 507–554.
          Amsterdam/Philadelphia: Benjamins.
Sanders, Ted J. M., and Morton Ann Gernsbacher
  2004    Accessibility in text and discourse processing. *Discourse Processes* 37:
          79–89
Sandra, Dominiek, and Sally Rice
  1995    Network analyses of prepositional meaning: Mirroring whose mind –
          the linguist's or the language user's? *Cognitive Linguistics* 6: 89–130.
Schulze, Rainer
  1988    A short story of *down*. In *Understanding the Lexicon: Meaning, Sense
          and World Knowledge in Lexical Semantics,* Werner Hülllen, and Rainer
          Schulze (eds.), 394–410. Tübingen: Max Niemeyer Verlag.
Speelman, Dirk, Stefan Grondelaers, and Dirk Geeraerts
  2003    Profile-based linguistic uniformity as a generic method for comparing
          language varieties. *Computers and the Humanities* 37: 317–337.
Stefanowitsch, Anatol
  2003    Constructional semantics as a limit to grammatical alternation: The
          two genitives of English. In *Determinants of Grammatical Variation*,
          Günter Rohdenburg, and Britta Mondorf (eds.), 413–444. Berlin/New
          York: Mouton de Gruyter.
Stefanowitsch, Anatol, and Stefan Th. Gries
  2003    Collostructions: Investigating the interaction between words and con-
          structions. *International Journal of Corpus Linguistics* 8: 209–243.
Tomasello, Michael
  2003    *Constructing a Language. A Usage-based Theory of Language Acquisi-
          tion*. Harvard: Harvard University Press.
Tummers, José, Kris Heylen, and Dirk Geeraerts
  2005    Usage-based approaches in Cognitive Linguistics: A technical state of
          the art. *Corpus Linguistics and Linguistic Theory* 1: 225–261.
Tummers, José, Dirk Speelman, and Dirk Geeraerts
  2005    Inflectional variation in Belgian and Netherlandic Dutch: A usage-
          based account of the adjectival inflection. In *Perspectives on Variation.
          Sociolinguistic, Historical, Comparative*, Nicole Delbecque, Johan van
          der Auwera, and Dirk Geeraerts (eds.), 93–110. Berlin/New York:
          Mouton de Gruyter.

# Polysemy and the lexicon

*John R. Taylor*

*Abstract*

In this paper I take issue with the standard view of polysemy as the association of a single word-form with a multitude of distinct meanings. First, I review different approaches to polysemy, concluding that it may not be legitimate to attempt to determine just how many meanings a word has, and what these meanings might be. I suggest that such a programme may be the outgrowth of a particular conception of language, which I characterize as the "dictionary+grammar book" model. This model is undermined by the pervasiveness of the idiomatic in language. The matter is illustrated by a corpus-based study of (some uses of) the expression *all over*. The expression has a range of uses which cannot be derived on the basis of independently identifiable meanings of its parts. *All over*, in turn, participates in larger expressions whose semantic values likewise cannot be compositionally derived. The "creative" extension of these idiomatic uses is also documented. These findings lend support to the view that knowing a word involves knowing the usage range of the word, rather than through the association of the word with a fixed number of determinate meanings.

*Keywords*: polysemy; lexicon; polyseme; metonymy; idiom; construction; creativity; compositionality; network

## 1. How many meanings?

Some years ago I wrote a paper entitled "How many meanings does a word have?" (Taylor 1992). I began by juxtaposing some remarks by John Searle on the verb *to open* and observations by George Lakoff on the word *window*.

- Lakoff (1987: 416) pointed out that *window* can be used to refer to different categories of things. If someone throws a rock and breaks a window, what is broken is (most probably) a glass panel, whereas if someone paints a window, what they paint is (most probably) the wooden structure encasing the glass panels. *Deliver the window, brick up the window, sit in the window* again refer to different kinds of entity. For Lakoff, this was evidence that the word was polysemous, that is, it had distinct, though closely related meanings.

- Searle (1983: 145–8), discussing the verb *open*, noted that a person who opens a door and a surgeon who opens a wound do very different things to the entities in question. You would not, for example, open a door by making incisions in it with a surgical scalpel. The truth conditions for "open a door" and "open a wound" – the kinds of things that a person would have to do in order for the expressions to properly apply to their actions – are therefore different in the two cases. Searle, however, does not draw the conclusion that *open* is polysemous. Rather, he claims that the verb has a fixed and constant value. Truth conditions emerge as a consequence of the way in which we interpret the expressions, relative to what he calls "the Background", that is, our knowledge of cultural practices, how we interact with the world, and how the world is constituted. Searle illustrates the role of interpretation relative to the Background on the example *Sam opened the Sun*. We can, Searle claims, readily understand this expression on the basis of the semantic content of the component words, but we cannot generate a set of truth conditions for it. Opening the Sun is not an established practice, and we have no idea what a person who "opened the Sun" is supposed to have done.

Lakoff and Searle exemplify two radically different approaches to the issue of word meaning. Each approach is problematic. Let us begin with Lakoff's approach. Lakoff seems inclined to recognize a distinct meaning whenever a difference in the reference of a word can be detected. There are several problems with this approach:

- The number of distinct meanings which would have to be assigned to words such as *window* and *open* (and no doubt to many others), even in their literal, non-metaphorical uses, is going to be very large indeed. Given that the referents of *window* in *paint the window, break the window, open the window, install a window, look through the window, brick up the window, sit in the window*, and so on, are identifiably different, we should have to say that *window* is many-ways polysemous. Such "rampant polysemy" (Cuyckens & Zawada 2001: xvii) would make enormous demands on the storage capacity of the language user.
- Polysemy generates ambiguity, and ambiguity has to be resolved, presumably at a cost in cognitive processing. If a word is *n*-ways polysemous, any sentence containing that word is in principle *n*-ways ambiguous. As more and more polysemous words come together in a sentence, the ambiguity increases exponentially. Concretely: If *open* is $n_1$-ways polysemous, and *window* is $n_2$-ways polysemous, the expression

*open the window* would have $n_1 \times n_2$ possible readings, and could only be understood as the result of a complex process of disambiguation. This conclusion is patently counterintuitive. If anything, the more context that is added to a word, the less likely it is to be perceived as ambiguous.
- The number of distinct polysemes of a word is not only likely to be very large, it may well be indefinitely large. For example, the number of different things that can be opened, and the different sets of truth conditions associated with these various opening activities, is in principle open-ended. Tolerating large-scale polysemy is one thing, admitting indefinitely large polysemy would border on the absurd (Searle 1983: 146).

Searle's position, which assumes a single semantic value for a word, is also not without its problems.

- If we wish to maintain that a word has a constant semantic value, we are under the obligation to spell out exactly what that meaning is. Searle's discussion of *open* is instructive in this respect. Although Searle insisted that *open* has but a single meaning (at least, in the non-metaphorical examples which he cites), Searle nowhere states what this meaning is. Perhaps Searle considered that the meaning of *open* was so self-evident that it was not necessary to spell it out. But the task is anything but trivial. It is, of course, not at all difficult to state what it means to "open the door", "open the curtains", "open a book", and so on. We can demonstrate these activities (given appropriate props), we can mime them, we can describe quite precisely how the patient entities (the door, curtains, etc.) are affected by the process. The difficulty is to state the meaning of *open* abstracting away from the particularities of these various expressions and the activities which they designate. Moreover, the proposed meaning will have to be sufficiently specific so as to differentiate the word from words of similar, though contrasting meaning. For example, it would not do to define *open* as involving the creation of a gap in an entity through the separation of its parts. Such a definition would also be valid for *cut*, in some of its uses. Neither would it do to define *open* in terms of gaining access to the interior of an entity. Such a definition would predict that *open* would be used to describe the peeling of an orange, or the cracking of nut.
- Let us assume, for the sake of argument, that a unitary meaning of a word can be identified, and has been satisfactorily characterized. We now need to state the mechanisms which give rise to the various interpretations which the word can have, in the different contexts in which it

can appear. These mechanisms will need to be of a very general nature, in the sense that they are not specific to a particular lexical item as used in a particular context – otherwise, we will run the risk of introducing polysemy by the back door, as it were.

• On Searle's account, the truth conditions of a word pertain to its contextualized interpretation, not to its unitary meaning. Presumably, other logical properties of an expression, such as its entailments and presuppositions, would also be attributes of an interpretation, it would not be possible to read them off from the (unitary) linguistic meanings of the component items and their manner of combination. This raises questions about the usefulness of unitary representations. If they are not involved in determining truth conditions or entailments, what are they for, and why should we be bothered by them?

The above remarks suggest that tolerance for extreme polysemy on the one hand, and attempts to eliminate polysemy on the other, are both seriously flawed. Both, it will be noted, raise questions of psychological plausibility. Can we reasonably suppose that speakers of a language have stored, and access, and make choices between large numbers of polysemes, and that the understanding of even very banal expressions requires a massive amount of disambiguation? Can we, on the other hand, suppose that speakers have stored schematic meanings for each lexical item (meanings which may actually be quite difficult to articulate) and that they really do apply to these all manner of elaboration strategies? Observe that the question of cognitive economy cuts both ways. Unitary meanings economize on storage but necessitate the computation of contextual interpretations. Polysemy economizes on the computation of contextual variants but increases storage demands; it also requires disambiguation procedures. We should also bear in mind that while a streamlined lexicon might appeal to some theorists on account of its "elegance", or "parsimony", there are no principled grounds for setting an upper limit on the amount of polysemy that the lexicon can tolerate, or for deciding, a priori, what an "optimal" amount of polysemy might be.

Given the problems associated with rampant polysemy on the one hand and unitary abstract senses on the other, a reasonable approach would be to seek a compromise. We can imagine two kinds of compromise:

• Going half-way. We try to reduce polysemy by abstracting as much as possible over individual meaning nuances of the different uses of a word. At the same time we allow polysemy where unifying abstract

senses are not feasible. In other words, we strive for as little polysemy as possible, but permit as much as necessary, arriving at an account which eschews both rampant polysemy and strict monosemy.
• Having it both ways. We allow *both* fine-grained semantic distinctions *and* more general, schematic meanings which capture the commonality amongst groups of specific meanings. The meanings, at various levels of schematicity, would be typically displayed in a network format, with more specific meanings standing as elaborations of more schematic meanings.

I consider these two approaches below, and some of the issues that they raise.

## 2.   Compromise #1: Going half-way

According to the first compromise, we strive to eliminate from the lexicon those meaning nuances which can plausibly be derived, and predicted, on general principles, while admitting polysemy in cases where the meaning differences cannot be so derived. This approach has been cogently presented by Tyler and Evans (2001), in their analysis of the polysemy of *over*; for a discussion of the methodological issues, see Croft (1998).

### 2.1. As little polysemy as possible

Rampant polysemy might be reduced to the extent that small differences in meaning might be attributable to the meanings of surrounding words, in association with general conceptual knowledge of how the world works; the meaning differences would therefore not need to be enshrined in the mental lexicon as distinct polysemes. Consider, as an example, the properties of the path followed by the trajector when you "walk over a field", "fly over the ocean", or "jump over the wall", with respect to such matters as whether the trajector is in contact with the landmark entity, or whether the path has a (roughly) rectilinear or a curved shape. It could be argued that these aspects follow from what we know about the situations involved. Walking involves contact with a surface, flying involves lack of contact, jumping involves an up-down path. It would follow, therefore, that we need to recognize, for these examples, only one sense of *over*, namely, as designating a path which goes from one side of a landmark to the other, in a configuration which is appropriate for the kind of trajector, its manner of motion, and the kind of landmark entity, in question.

Take, as another example, the variable reference of the word *window*, cited above. This might be handled in terms of the active zone phenomenon (Langacker 1990). Whenever an entity is involved in a predication, typically only some facet, or facets, of the entity will participate in the predication, whereby the relevant active zone can be inferred on the basis of general conceptual knowledge of the entity and of the kind of predication that it participates in. Given what we know about windows, and about what it means to paint something, we can reasonably infer that "paint a window" implicates only the "paintable" facets of the window, namely, its wooden frame. Likewise, when we "brick up a window", we can infer that the reference of *window* has got to be a vacant gap in a wall, not a wooden frame, or a pane of glass.

Appeal to the active zone phenomenon begs the question of what the basic, or "real" meaning of a word is. What kind of thing does *window* – before the active zone phenomenon kicks in – refer to? It cannot be the sum of its active zones – wood, glass, and a hole in a wall do not add up to a coherent category. Rather, we want to say that the word *window* provides access to a body of conceptual knowledge, concerning the typical location, the typical function, and the typical manner of construction of the things in question. It would follow that *window,* as a decontextualized word, does not actually refer to a thing at all, but rather stands at the hub of a conceptual network; for contextualized uses, the relevant concept would be conjured up in accordance with the specifications of a particular scene (cf. Barsalou 1987). Our impression that the word *does* have a determinate reference would be due to the fact that certain contextualized uses – such as *open the window* – frequently re-occur, thereby entrenching the relevant conceptualization.

As Langacker noted, the active zone phenomenon gradually shades into the more general process of metonymy (see also Taylor 2003b: 127). The named entity functions as a reference point for accessing the intended referent. The intended referent may be a part of the named entity, or it may be something that is closely associated with it within a given knowledge configuration. Interestingly, processes of metonymic extension typically apply across the board to words of a certain semantic category. A well-known example concerns the names of institutions. *University* can be used to refer to the institution, to the building which houses the institution, and even to a person who acts on behalf of the institution. Compare: *The University was founded in the 19th century, I parked near the University,* and *The University just telephoned.* Similar metonymies can be observed with institution-type words in general: *school, museum, institute,* etc. For another example, consider the fact that path prepositions in English can in general be used to designate a place at the end-point of a real or imaginary path. Compare: *walk round the corner* vs. *live round the corner; run up the hill* vs. *be standing up the hill* (for further polysemization patterns of the English prepositions, see Taylor 1993). To the extent that we can identify processes which apply across the board to sets of words, the different senses that are thereby generated may not need to be separately listed. This kind of "generative" approach to polysemy has been pursued by, amongst others, Pustejovsky (1991), as well as by Bierwisch and the "two-level" theorists (Bierwisch 1981; Wunderlich 1993).[1]

## 2.2. As much polysemy as necessary

Polysemy would have to be recognized just in case the special properties of a word's use cannot be predicted from associated words, from general background knowledge, or from general principles of polysemization. For example, one use of the preposition *round* is to designate a path defined by the perimeter of a landmark entity, as when you "walk round the lake", "swim round the lake", "sail round the island", and such like. To "go round the guests" would mean, then, to trace a path defined by the perimeter of a group of assembled guests. But the expression would most likely refer to a situation in which the trajector traces a random path amongst the guests, going from one guest to another. This special "random path" sense cannot plausibly be derived, by any process of conceptual elaboration, from the perimeter-following sense; it would need to be separately listed.

Sometimes, a word fails to participate in what is otherwise a productive polysemization process. We can readily use *museum, school,* and *university* to refer both to the institutions and to the buildings which house them. The same, however, does not apply to *government* and *parliament.* These words may refer to the institutions, and to the people who work in them, but they cannot readily refer to the buildings which house them: ?*The parliament was built in 1980,* ?*The government burnt down.* (In these cases, we should probably specify the entity explicitly as *the government building,* or *the parliament building.*[2]) Likewise, polysemy between the path sense of a preposition and the use designating the end-point of a path is not fully productive. You can "walk towards the back of the room" (path) and "stand towards to the back of the room" (place as end-point of a fictitious path). But while you can "walk towards the sea" or "drive towards the mountains", but it would be odd to say of someone that they "live towards the sea", or "live towards the mountains".[3]

These latter cases would be particularly problematic for attempts to systemically regulate the incidence of polysemy. They concern, not so much the availability of different senses on the basis of general polysemization processes, but the non-occurrence of otherwise expected senses. To the extent that the different senses of *museum*, etc., are predictable from general processes at work in English, we could reduce the amount of polysemy in the lexicon by not separately listing the different senses. But in the case of *government* and *parliament*, we would need to flag these words as not undergoing the polysemization process. Paradoxically, the words with fewer different uses would need a more complex representation than the ones which undergo regular polysemization. But even flagging a word as an "exception" might not be fully adequate in the case of *towards*. It is not that *towards* does not allow the "place as end-point" reading; what are odd, are some specific examples which invoke this reading, such as its occurrence with *live* in connection with a geophysical landmark.

### 3.    Compromise #2: Having it both ways

There is a second kind of compromise between rampant polysemy and austere monosemy and it is one which has been particularly favoured in cognitive linguistic accounts. We allow *both* fine-grained semantic distinctions *and* more general, schematic meanings which capture the commonality amongst groups of specific meanings. The different meanings, at various levels of schematicity, are typically displayed in a network. A particularly fine illustration of the methodology is provided by Tuggy's (2003) analysis of the Nawatl verb *kīsa* (though many other examples, to be sure, could also be cited; see Palmer, this volume, Figure 2). The network model is clearly an advance on the "half-way" solution, in that the analyst is not forced to choose between an array of distinct senses and an overarching schematic sense, but simply incorporates both. Note, for example, that the network model can easily handle cases of less than fully productive polysemization. Specific senses, even when predictable from general principles, would be included in the network representation; the fact that an otherwise expected sense is not attested would be captured, quite simply, by the absence of the relevant sense.

I have characterized and presented arguments for the network approach to polysemy elsewhere (Taylor 1995). The network model cannot, however, be regarded as the last word on polysemy. In recent years, the model has in fact come in for some substantial criticism. These are both methodological and conceptual in nature:

(i) Methodological problems. Suppose two linguists are working independently on the same word and each makes a proposal for a polysemy network. Suppose, furthermore, that the proposed networks differ in important respects. One linguist identifies a large number of highly specific senses which the other ignores, or there is disagreement about how particularized senses are to be allocated to more schematic senses and how these schematic senses are to be characterized. What criteria do we apply for evaluating the two accounts? The example is by no means hypothetical. Consider, for example, the still ongoing story of *over*.[4] What has driven the discussion of this word, for more than two decades since Brugman's (1981) pioneering dissertation, is disagreement over these methodological questions. How many different senses does the word really have and how are we to decide the matter? What is the content of these different senses? Should we accord representational status to highly particularized senses? To what extent is it feasible to collapse different uses under more schematic representations and what is the content of the proposed schemas? Further questions have been, how these different sense clusters relate to each other, and which, if any, of the proposed senses can be regarded as the most central.

(ii) The second issue concerns the ontological status of networks. Is a network supposed to have psychological reality? Are networks meant as hypotheses about speakers' knowledge of words? If so, how can the psychological reality of a proposed network be tested? If not, what is a network supposed to be representing? What is the relevance of the networks in language acquisition? At what point in the network is a word accessed in production and reception? These are still very much open questions (Sandra & Rice 1995; Hallan 2001; Rice 2003; Langacker 2006).

## 4. Alternative perspectives on word meaning

In view of the kinds of problems that arise when one attempts to give a detailed semantic description of a word, it comes as no surprise that different scholars (and lexicographers) often fail to converge on a common answer to the question of just how many different meanings a word has and what these meanings are supposed to be (Fillmore & Atkins 2000). Given this state of affairs, there are, broadly speaking, two approaches that an analyst might take. One would be to continue refining the criteria by which two uses are to be regarded as elaborations of the same meaning or representative of distinct polysemes. But given the less than unanimous outcomes of research to date, it is not surprising that a number of scholars have recently come to question the traditional notion of polysemy (namely, as the association of a single word-form with more than one distinct meaning), and the reification of meaning which the notion entails (Allwood 2003; Geeraerts 1993; Zlatev 2003; Langacker 2006). It may be well to stand back a little from the discussion and consider the theoretical issues that drive it.

Elsewhere (Taylor 2003a, c) I have suggested that a desire to associate a word with a fixed number of distinct meanings derives from a specific conceptualization of the object of investigation. I have referred to this (Taylor, in press, a) as the "generative" model of language, or, more colloquially, as the "dictionary+grammar book" model. According to this model, knowledge of a language resides in two components. One component is the dictionary, or lexicon, which lists the basic meaning-bearing units of the language (prototypically, the words). The other component is the syntax, which lists the rules whereby smaller elements can be combined. The rationale for this view of linguistic knowledge is explained in the following remarks by Jackendoff:

> Since the number of possible utterances in a human language is unlimited, language users cannot store them all in their heads. Rather, ... knowledge of language requires two components. One is a finite list of structural elements that are available to be combined. This list is traditionally called the "lexicon," and its elements are called "lexical items". ... The other component is a finite set of combinatorial principles, or a *grammar*. To the extent that speakers of a language (or a dialect) are consistent with one another ... we can speak of the "grammar of a language" as a useful approximation to what all its speakers have in their heads. (Jackendoff 2002: 39)
> For a first approximation, the lexicon is the store of words in long-term memory from which the grammar constructs phrases and sentences. (Jackendoff 2002: 130)

Baker is even more explicit in his presentation of the model:

> Suppose someone were to ask you what English is. ... You might say that English is the set of sentences that are constructed by combining the following ingredients (you hand her a massive dictionary that lists all the English words)

according to the following rules of grammar (you hand her an equally massive English grammar). ... [B]etween them they would tell the reader how to make any conceivable English sentence. (Baker 2001: 53–4)

There are several corollaries to the dictionary+grammar book model. One is the expectation that complex expressions exhibit compositionality. According to the compositionality principle, complex expressions are formed by the assembly of smaller units, such that the properties of the whole can be predicted from the properties of the parts and the manner of their combination. Now, for compositionality to go through, it is necessary that each of the constituent parts has a set of fixed properties which it is able to contribute to the whole. This, in turn, requires that words have fixed meanings. Moreover, since it is manifestly the case that some words can make different semantic contributions depending on the context of their use, the postulation of polysemy becomes imperative. Concretely: the normal interpretation of *I went round the guests, introducing myself*, if it is to be derived compositionally, must make reference to a meaning of *round* which is different from the meaning that is accessed in the compositionally derived reading of *I walked round the lake*.

The compositionality principle is deeply ingrained in our thinking about language. Indeed, compositionality is accorded the status of an axiom, needed in order to account for our ability to produce (and readily understand) novel combinations of words. This, indeed, is the point which Jackendoff makes, at the beginning of the above citation. Three considerations, however, weaken the compositionality imperative (and the generative model of language with which it is associated):

(i) Full compositionality is rarely the case. There is a sense in which every expression, even the most banal, when used in a specific situation to symbolize the speaker's momentaneous conceptualization, will inevitably take on properties that go beyond, or which may be at variance with, its strictly compositional value. This would be the case even if highly specific senses were attributed to a word. The point was recognized by the two-level theorists, and, indeed, was one of their motivations for recognizing a "conceptual" (or situation-specific) level of representation, as distinct from a "semantic" level. The point has also been made by Langacker (though within a different theoretical framework). See, for example, his remarks on the expression *the football under the table* (Langacker 1987: 279–82), as the expression would be understood in different utterance contexts, and the more extended discussion of the example in Taylor (2002: 106–109).

(ii) In spite of the pre-eminence of the compositionality principle, it is generally acknowledged that compositionality fails to apply in the case of idiomatic expressions. In fact, idioms are commonly defined against the backdrop of compositionality – an idiom, namely, is an expression whose (conventionalized) meaning is *not* compositional (see, e.g., Chomsky 1980: 149, cited in Nunberg et al. 1994: 498). *Let the cat out of the bag* ('reveal the secret') is an idiom, since the meaning of the expression cannot be worked out on the basis of the meanings which *cat* and *bag* have elsewhere in the language (more precisely: from the meanings which *cat* and *bag* have, when they are not being used idiomatically). The approach, needless to say, presupposes that one can determine, for any use of a word, whether its use is idiomatic or non-idiomatic. This is a requirement which falls out, once again, from the dictionary+grammar book model, and its various entailments.

(iii) The distinction between the idiomatic and the non-idiomatic may not be so clear-cut, however. Interestingly, much of the relevant research has been conducted, not so much by linguistic theoreticians, but by scholars with a more practical orientation – second language acquisition researchers and lexicographers (see, e.g., Moon 1998; Wray 2002). The emerging view is that a very great deal of a person's knowledge of a language may consist in knowledge of multi-word expressions – not only idioms as such, but phraseologies, formulaic phrases, collocations, clichés, quotations, catch phrases, and such like. At the same time, the scope of the idiomatic has been extended to include not only the prototypical "non-compositional" idioms, of the kind *let the cat out of the bag*, but all manner of expressions which, by dint of their frequent use, have become entrenched in the minds of language users and which are not plausibly assembled afresh on each occasion of their use. Even expressions whose semantics are not at all remarkable (e.g. *I wouldn't do that if I were you*) may still be regarded as "idiomatic", to the extent that they are learned, and used, as pre-formed chunks. A particularly fruitful line of study has centred on constructions, specifically, so-called constructional idioms, and the predisposition of certain words to occur in certain constructions, together with the tendency for constructions to select the words which instantiate them (Stefanowitsch & Gries 2003; Goldberg 2006). On this approach, one facet of knowing a word would be knowing the word's distribution within constructions. Knowing the word *dint*, for example, involves knowing that the word occurs almost exclusively in the complex preposition *by dint of* (Taylor, in press, b).

In the remaining part of this chapter I wish to demonstrate that searching for "the meaning of a word" may be a futile exercise, once we take account of the contexts in which the word is used. This is because contextualized uses may take on semantic values that cannot be compositionally derived. The process, moreover, can be recursive, in that a contextualized use may itself have contextual variants. As we consider the properties of ever larger configurations, the semantic contribution of component words will become less and less of a concern.

## 5. Encroaching idiomaticity: over again

If it is true that language use is riddled with idioms, of various kinds, the question of how many different meanings a word has may not be a legitimate thing to ask. What we should be concerned with is not the meanings of a word as such, but the uses of a word, in various kinds of linguistic context. For an illustration of this, we need go no further than the example of *over*.

There is general agreement that, of the various senses of *over*, one has to do with a trajector covering, or occluding, a landmark. Lakoff cites the following examples:

(1)  a.  She spread the tablecloth over the table. (Lakoff 1987: 419)
  b.  The board is over the hole. (Lakoff 1987: 427)

Here, the trajector is "at least two-dimensional and extends across the boundaries of the [landmark]" (p. 426), a view endorsed by Tyler and Evans (2001), who note that the trajector is "larger, or perceived to be larger than the [landmark]", such that the trajector "physically intervene[s] between the viewer and the [landmark]", thereby obscuring the landmark from view (p. 752).

Here are some examples of the covering sense of *over*, taken from the British National Corpus (BNC):[5]

(2)  a.  I held my hand *over* my face for a few moments before speaking.
  b.  His black trousers were held together by safety-pins, paperclips and needles. *Over* this he had a black mackintosh; there were five belts strapped around his waist and a sort of grey linen nappy attached to the back of his trousers.
  c.  Tugging her jeans *over* her thighs, she said: " ...
  d.  She folded her scarf *over* her blonde hair.

It will be noted, to begin with, that none of these examples exhibits the covering sense with the pristine clarity of Lakoff's (invented) examples (nor, it might be added, of the invented examples which other scholars, such as Tyler and Evans 2001, and Deane 2005, have cited in this connection). There are, moreover, some subtle differences between the uses in (2). In (a) the idea seems to be that the trajector (a hand) partially obscures the landmark (a face) – partially, because a hand is smaller than a face and cannot fully obscure the face from view. In (b), the mackintosh is a large, outer garment, which wraps around other clothing, such as the trousers and the belts, and hides them from view. In (c), the trajector is moved into a position which covers the landmark, though not with the idea of obscuring it, but rather of enclosing it, and adapting to its shape. In (d), the relevant point seems to be the positioning of the scarf, rather than the obscuring of the hair.

Rather than dwelling on the covering sense of *over* – which, to be sure, would merit a much closer examination than what it has been accorded in the already voluminous literature on the word – I want to move on to the use of *over* in a larger expression. Some 4.2% of all uses of *over* in the BNC occur in the phrase *all over*. Here are some examples:

(3)  a.  More often because of his impatience, it blew back in his face, dusting him *all over*.
     b.  Lamarr jumped back dropping the broken pieces and with blood *all over* his hand and face.
     c.  She's got the dress on and she's taken her hat off so her hair's *all over* her shoulders.
     d.  I still weigh 66 kilos and still have a galaxy of spots around my nose and *all over* my chin.
     e.  Oh, God, I thought, she can see the lipstick *all over* me.
     f.  She was trembling *all over*, holding on to the car door for support, despising herself for her own weakness.

*All over* is commonly analyzed as a variant of "covering" *over*. Here, I want to raise the question of the contribution of *all*. An obvious answer, and one consistent with the compositionality principle, would be that *all* has a quantificational sense, in that the coverage, or occlusion, is total. The meaning of *all over*, therefore, would be a function of the covering meaning of *over* in combination with the quantifying meaning of *all* (Lakoff 1987: 428). There are several problems with this account.

(i) *All* is not readily omitted in some of the examples with *all over*, suggesting that *all over* functions as a unit:

(4)  a. *It blew back in his face, dusting him *over*.
     b. *Oh, God, I thought, she can see the lipstick *over* me.

(ii) Equally, *over*, in (2), can often not be quantified with *all*:

(5)  a. * I held my hand *all over* my face for a few moments before speaking.
     b. *Tugging her jeans *all over* her thighs, she said: " ...
     c. *She folded her scarf *all over* her blonde hair.

Note, in connection with (5a), that the strangeness of the sentence is not due to the factual impossibility of a hand covering all of a person's face. *I held both my hands all over my face* (thereby totally obscuring my face) is equally bizarre.

(iii) *All* does not readily contrast with other quantifying expressions, such as *half, partly, somewhat, mostly*, etc.

(6)  *Oh, God, I thought, she can see the lipstick {*half, partly, somewhat, mostly*} over me.

The oddness of *half over*, in this example, in not due to the impossibility of the expression *per se*. There are 32 occurrences of *half over* in the BNC (as against 5479 occurrences of *all over*). Here are some examples:

(7)  a. She pulled the sheet *half over* her head, to be ready to jump out, and she waited.
     b. Maggie looked up, peering at him, the towel like a white tent over her head, her long hair *half over* his face.
     c. Meredith, stranded inelegantly with a foot on the wooden step and the other leg *half over* the topmost bar, said crossly, "I can't see it."
     d. Allain moved until his body was *half over* her.

Here, some notion of quantification does seem to be involved. *Half* can be replaced by *partly*, it can be omitted without too much of a strain on acceptability, and even, in the case of (7b), it might be replaced by *all*. But if quantification is involved – and to this extent, *half over* displays a greater degree of compositionality than *all over* – the question arises as to what, exactly, is being quantified. In (7a) it is presumably the head which is only half obscured by the sheet, rather than half of the sheet covering (all of) the head. In (7c), however, it is presumably only half the leg which is over the bar, rather than the whole leg being over half the bar. (The example, of course, invokes, not the covering sense of *over*, but has to do with the trajector being positioned on the topmost part of the landmark.) The vagueness with respect to what is being quantified is apparent in (8), which is based in (3c):

(8)  She's got the dress on and she's taken her hat off so her hair's {*all* / *half* / *partly* / *somewhat*} over her shoulders.

Consider, in this light, example (3d), repeated below as (9):

(9)  I still weigh 66 kilos and still have a galaxy of spots around my nose and *all over* my chin.

Is it the case that all of the trajector is over the landmark, or that the trajector covers all of the landmark? The context in (9) makes it clear that at least some of the spots are around the nose, so it cannot be the case that all of the spots are on the chin. We would have to assume that there are spots on all of the chin. But what does this relation between spots and chin involve? It is not a relation of "covering", in the sense that the two-dimensional extension of the trajectory ("the spots") exceeds that of the landmark ("the chin"), such that the chin is obscured from view. Rather, it has to do with the dense distribution of a large number of spots on the chin, such that an observer can see the chin, with a large number of spots on it.

(iv) If we accept Lakoff's characterization of the covering sense of *over*, namely, as involving a trajector which extends across the boundaries of the landmark (Lakoff 1987: 426), *all* in its quantifying sense would be redundant, since, on its covering sense, *over* clearly requires that *all* of the landmark is fully "covered" by the trajector. Neither would it make much sense to claim that it is the trajector that is being quantified. If the trajector fully "covers" the landmark, it would be irrelevant whether all, or only part, of the trajector is in the covering relation.

(v) The major objection to the compositional account of *all over*, however, is that "covering", whether quantified or not, is hardly the appropriate way to characterize the examples in (3). In fact, the examples in (3) do not exhibit a covering relation at all, in the strict sense that the trajector occludes the landmark. Rather, as suggested above, what unifies the examples is some notion of the distribution, or dispersal of the trajector entity within the boundary of the landmark, or, in the case of (3f), with the manifestation of a process at different places on the landmark. The point has been developed by Queller (2001: 58), who drew attention to the following contrast:

(10) a. This tablecloth has got bloodstains *all over* it.
   b. ?? This tablecloth has got red squares *all over* it.

According to Queller, example (10b) is unacceptable because the red squares are a design feature of the tablecloth. Sentence (10a), in contrast, is fine, and has to do with the random dispersal of the stains on the surface of the cloth, whereby, as noted above, the stains, as a mass, do not strictly "cover" the landmark – a point also acknowledged by Lakoff (1987: 428). Moreover, the stains are perceived as being an unwanted imperfection on the cloth, or, at least, a temporary blemish. If we now go back to examine the examples in (3), we note that the idea of random distribution, in association with temporary blemish or dishevelment, applies in all cases.

What this means, I think, is that the semantic value of *all over* cannot be computed compositionally, from one of the meanings (the covering meaning) of *over*, in association with *all*. *All over* would have the status of an idiomatic expression. As such, it has its own specific conditions of use. In this connection, it is interesting to take note of a property which is shared by all of the BNC examples with *all over* cited above and which distinguishes these examples from the invented sentences in (1). This is, that the attested examples all make reference to the human body, or parts of it, either as trajector or as landmark, or as both, or, in the case of (2b), to an article of clothing located on a human body. As far as I am aware, this distinctive feature of the "dispersal" sense of *all over* has not previously been commented upon, and further corpus research would be needed in order to substantiate the association. If substantiated, this property would contribute to what Stubbs (1995) has referred to as the "semantic profile" of the expression. The expression, to be sure, has other semantic profiles. Particularly prominent are uses of *all over* which have a geopolitical entity as the landmark.

(11) a. Why are managers from *all over Britain* and sometimes even from abroad, even from Japan, attracted to start industries on these trading estates?
   b. People must be hunting *all over the country* for him.
   c. Police *all over the country* are known to want the DNA register.
   d. Pietro Metastasio (whose texts were set to music *all over Europe* by the best composers of the time)
   e. The worship of, of professed belief in, a god of some kind is to be found in varying degrees of sincerity *all over the world.*

The discovery that *all over* functions as a unit, with its own distinctive semantic value(s), may not, in itself, be all that remarkable. The matter becomes more interesting, however, when we realize that this process of "idiomaticization" is recursive. Just as *over* combines with *all* to give an expression with its own distinctive and idiomatic value(s), so *all over* can combine with other items to produce expressions which also have their distinctive values.

As many as 8.6% of all occurrences of *all over* in the BNC are in the context *all over the place*. The "place" in question is not specified precisely.

(12) a. Why somebody's left an old choc-ice on the floor, and it's run *all over the place.*
   b. Although Shaker has become fashionable and "Shaker style" furniture is appearing *all over the place*, very little of it bears much relation to the real thing.
   c. We started using it and interestingly enough that typeface is really popular now, you see it in the United States everywhere, it's *all over the place.*
   d. There is no way that a farrier can shoe a horse that is so angry or frightened that it is rearing and leaping *all over the place.*

In (12a-c), *all over the place* conveys that the designated process is manifested at numerous places (within a contextually defined region); *everywhere* (= 'at all places within the defined region') offers itself as a suitable (though perhaps hyperbolic) paraphrase. Substitution with *everywhere* would not be possible in (12d), however. Here, the idea is that the activity ("rearing and leaping") is taking place in a random and unpredictable manner. This notion is exploited in the following:

(13) Yesterday's polls looked much of a muchness – they were not *"all over the place"* – but concealed politically crucial variations.

If the results of an opinion poll – or any other set of data, for that matter – are "all over the place", the idea is that there is no obvious trend; that data points appear to be random and show no clear pattern. A specialization of this idea is exemplified by the following (from Queller 2001: 62):

(14) a. This paper is *all over the place.*
     b. You are *all over* the place.

In saying (14a) to a student, the instructor conveys that the essay lacks structure; it jumps, seemingly at random, from one point to another, without an overall plan. If the student is said to be "all over the place" (14b), the idea, again, is that the student's work, or thought processes, lack direction and coherence.

At this point, it may be well to recall the earlier citation from Jackendoff. Jackendoff presented the standard argument for the dictionary+grammar book model of language. This has to do with the fact of linguistic creativity. The fact that speakers are constantly creating novel sentences means that speakers do not learn sentences, they learn the principles by which sentences can be generated. It follows – so the argument goes – that speakers need to learn a (finite) set of meaning-bearing units (the words) and a finite set of rules for combining the words. Idioms, being non-compositional, would constitute a non-essential supplement to the lexicon and the syntax. This view, however, ignores the fact that idioms can also be used "creatively". The usage range of an idiom can be extended to new contexts (as when *all over the place* is extended from its more basic meaning "everywhere" to conveying random distribution or directionless behaviour). Alternatively, the "slots" in an idiom can be filled by different lexical items. And, indeed, there exist a number of variants of *all over the place*; these include *all over the show*, *all over the shop*, and *all over the map*.

*All over the show* occurs three times in the BNC; in none of these is a "show" (in the "basic", literal sense of the word) implicated:

(15) a. Squealing and squawking and leaving its dirty nappies *all over the show.*
     b. Speaking of Deano – everyone I talked felt that as we had paid £2.7 million for a centre forward wouldn't it be nice if hung around near the goal or in the box for that matter instead of running *all*

*over the show* and when we finally get the ball in the box there's no-body there.

c. My legs were *all over the show* and I've got to stand tall tomorrow.

The first example can be paraphrased by *everywhere*, while the second conveys running in random directions, without purpose. The third elaborates on a specific case of random behaviour, namely, that the person did not have control over the movements of his/her legs.

*All over the shop* is attested 9 times. The first example below aligns itself with those uses of *all over* which take a geopolitical entity as its landmark, while the second is a variation on the theme of random, directionless activity. Neither of the examples involves reference to "a shop".

(16) a. Wisely cautious at first –; awed, probably, by sheer numbers (because they were coming in, now, from *all over the shop*, from Canada, from Palestine) –; German society duly broadened itself to let the newcomers in

b. The movie's dilemma is that its luxurious pace ambles *all over the shop*, never really getting anywhere or bringing any of the characters to a satisfying conclusion

*All over the map* is attested only twice in the BNC. The first example involves, literally, places on "a map" of a terrain. The second, however, refers again to the random distribution of data.

(17) a. In the east and centre of the county we find a close network of narrow, winding lanes, wandering from hamlet to hamlet and farm to farm, churches standing alone, isolated houses dotted *all over the map*, many of them called Hall or Old Hall –; significant names

b. Er what I have chosen to do is to do what we were doing in the nineteen eighties, which is to take the simplest measure of the maximum flow and the detrusor pressure at that volume and when we do that, you can see that these patients, instead of being a single group of patients with a single kind of bladder pressure and flow, these patients are *all over the map*.

Google returned over 1.3 million hits for *all over the map* – the figure no doubt inflated by the existence of an atlas of that name. The following, however, clearly elaborate on the idea of random distribution, or directionless behaviour.

(18) a. When it comes to "interests," I am *all over the map*. I read and enjoy all genres of novels, but most of my reading is nonfiction.
   b. I am *all over the map* these days. I can't seem to settle into one project.
   c. Bond Yields in the Euro Zone Are *All Over the Map*.
   d. The next largest group comes from what he called "New Age" cults, whose belief systems are *all over the map*.

A particularly interesting variant is *all over the paddock* (not attested in the BNC). This appears to be a peculiarly Australasian expression, *paddock*, in Australian and New Zealand English, corresponding to standard English *field, meadow*. Google searching suggests that the expression may be (or may have been) specifically associated with the behaviour of players on a rugby field:

(19) a. This set the tone for the rest of the game with tries being ran in from *all over the paddock* against a side which battled bravely.
   b. It was the sort of thing the big men hate to see and no one was bigger on the night than Springbok lock Botha who was *all over the paddock*.
   c. The determined and dogged Irish weren't giving up and had the Aussies running ragged *all over the paddock*
   d. We had them *all over the paddock*, particularly our ruckman LS Craig ... We had winners like LSPT Robert Tarjani *all over the paddock*.
   e. The Welsh scrum didn't push the Wallabies *all over the paddock* because they were a set of England-style behemoths, it was because they were better coached.

Not surprisingly, *all over the paddock* has uses which have nothing to do with a "paddock", or rugby field. In fact, I first noticed this expression in a commentary on the 2005 general election in New Zealand, where it was stated that the initial election results were "all over the paddock". This usage is clearly a variation on the one cited in (13). In contrast, the following, from a New Zealand politician's weblog, retains the image of the paddock (or rugby field), fusing it with the notion of the Prime Minister randomly changing her account in response to the news channel's persistent questioning.

(20) I remember when TV One chased Prime Minister Jenny Shipley *all over the paddock* over whether she had discussed politics when having dinner with Saatchi chief Kevin Roberts.

*All over* enters into another set of idiomatic expressions. About 1 % of all uses of *all over* in the BNC occur in the context *written all over*. Consider, first, the following example.

(21) My partner for the event was the marvellous American player Muffin Spencer-Devlin, who turned up with a bag which had "Save the Whales" *written all over* it.

There is no suggestion, here, that all of the bag's (outer) surface was covered by the inscription (this would be a nonsense, anyway), nor that the lettering was randomly displayed on the bag's surface (though it could be the case that "Save the Whales" was inscribed more than once on the bag). The idea, instead, is that the wording "Save the Whales" was prominently displayed on the bag, visible to any observer.

Of special interest are cases in which there is no literal "writing" on a surface; rather, what seems to be involved are certain features of an entity which are salient to any observer. The following (BNC) examples elaborate on the idea that the prominent feature is (literally) "inscribed" on the entity.

(22) a. Glazed, red-rimmed, they stare off into some distant past that has mid-1980s *written all over* it.
  b. And it's got faulty *written all over* the box, you know.

In the following, the entity bears the name of its author (or instigator):

(23) a. Dave's rhythm work has got his name *written all over* it.
  b. This has Paul *written all over* it.

Zooming in still further on the idiomatic, we find expressions in which the "writing" is located on a person's face, this making the person's thoughts or emotional state apparent to an observer. The inscription may even take the form of a quoted expression (24b):

(24) a. He shook his head, doubt *written all over his face*
  b. "Mr Kopek, I didn't know you had it in you", was the phrase I could see *written all over her expression*.

Queller proposes that *written all over (one's face)* is associated with the unintentional expression of emotion, pointing out that the phrase is more likely to be used of guilt and disappointment, which a person might prefer to keep hidden, than of rage or pleasure, which a person freely expresses. He (2002: 57) glosses the phrase as "someone's attempt to present a 'front' of composure or nonchalance is being 'messed up' by an unconscious or reflexive dispersal of emotion over his/her face". While some BNC examples, such as (25a), might conform with this account, others, e.g. (25b), don't.

(25) a. Though Jackson was the first to congratulate Olympic champion McKoy, the disappointment was *written all over his face.*
   b. As William and Harry boarded the 10.30am BA flight, excitement was *written all over their faces.*

There is no reason to suppose, in (25b), that William and Harry would want to hide their excitement behind an expression of composure or non-chalance. These examples, rather, all elaborate on the notion of THE FACE AS INTERFACE. A person's face is where emotions and intentions are made manifest, and where they can be "read" by others. This conceptualization of the face is prominent in the following (Googled) examples:

(26) a. He approaches slowly, anxiety *visible all over his face.*
   b. The Conductor was sitting with satisfaction *clearly visible all over his face*
   c. Connor peers at him, disgust *legible all over his face.*
   d. the agony was *prominent all over his face* as was the disappointment.

I mentioned above the possibility of the idioms being creatively extended. Google searching discovered numerous variations on the expression *written all over (one's) face*. Here is a small sample:

(27) a. Frustration was *scrawled all over his face.*
   b. This is a comic, then, who walks on stage with "please like me" *scrawled all over his face.*
   c. Mr Eun glanced at the half-empty classroom, and then back at me, the usual "kids these-days" look *scribbled all over his face.*
   d. He leant over with compassion *printed all over his face in italic type.*

e. The man has "rising star" *printed all over his face.*
f. arrogance *inscribed all over his face*
g. "I can't believe it," he moaned, betrayal *stamped all over his face.*
h. His love of life was *stamped all over his face.*
i. Selariu dragged himself up to complete his routine but his disappointment was *etched all over his face.*
j. The delight is visibly *etched all over his face.*
k. Gourry looks down at me, confusion *etched all over his face.*
l. Simon looked up from his computer screen, irritation *engraved all over his face.*
m. The Source? Simple. It's Dan Rather's daughter. It was *typed all over his face* when he "defended" the story Friday.
n. Zainab looked up at her mother, helplessness *portrayed all over her face.*
o. with a terrifying earnestness *pictured all over my face*
p. Contempt was *depicted all over his face.*

It would, I think, be futile to approach these examples enquiring which sense of *over* (or, indeed, which sense of *all over*) is being exemplified. The examples play on the FACE AS INTERFACE metaphor, in association with the entrenched expression *(have something) written all over one's face.*[6]

# 6.    Concluding remarks

In my 1992 paper, I suggested that a search for *the* meaning, or meanings, of a word, such as *open* or *window*, may be ill-conceived. Speakers acquiring English do not acquire the lexicon word by word, nor, for any given word, do they acquire a finite number of discrete meaning packages. Neither, a fortiori, do they understand complex expressions by making choices amongst the various meanings supposedly associated with the words in question. They do not, for example, understand the expressions *open a book, open your eyes, open the door, open the box, open a wound,* and so on, by combining a meaning of *open* that they have acquired with a meaning of the direct object nominal; this is irrespective of whether the word meanings are presumed to be schematic or highly particularized. It is more plausible to assume that speakers understand these expressions because they have learned them as such. They have encountered the verb *open* in association with actions performed on various basic-level kinds of objects, such as doors, books, and eyes. If asked to state the meaning of *open a book*, speakers are readily able to describe the action, they can perform it, and mime it. But to state the meaning of *open*, abstracting away from the action performed on the book, is not only a difficult task, it is also an artificial one. Speakers may, no doubt, perceive some commonality between the different kinds of opening events. However, this perception of commonality is by no means necessary to guarantee mastery of the word – speakers merely need to have learned the relevant collocations. Appeal to established usage patterns and their associated practices readily resolves the disambiguation problem (or, rather, non-problem) that was raised in opening sections of the present chapter. *Open the window* is not perceived as being ambiguous, and no choices amongst the various senses of *open* and *window* are involved. This by no means entails that *open* and *window* have fixed invariant senses, merely that *open the window* has a learned sense, it is associated with an "embodied" practice, and, as Searle pointed out, it comes with easily statable truth-conditions. New uses, when encountered, will be interpreted on the basis of their similarity with already familiar uses. In the case of Searle's example *open the Sun*, speakers would need to determine which of the established uses of *open* is to be taken as a model for interpreting the expression. They might construct some fantastic science-fiction scenario, in which opening the Sun would be analogous to, say, opening a wound. Or they might well conclude that the expression is simply nonsense.

In this paper I have focussed on corpus evidence for the reality of usage patterns, showing that at least some uses of *over* resist a compositional analysis. This casts doubt on the idea that the word might have a finite number of discrete meanings. What was true of *over*, is no less true of *all over*. This expression also has a number of particularized uses, with their own distinctive semantic values, which, once again, resist a strict compositional analysis.

Wittgenstein's *Blue Book* opens with the question: "What is the meaning of a word?" (Wittgenstein 1958: 1). Wittgenstein proposed to bring this rather abstract question – a question which, as he put it, is liable to induce in us a kind of "mental cramp" – "down to earth" by operationalizing it, that is, by replacing it with a more practical question, concerning how one might set about determining the meaning of a word. His answer, as is well-known, was that meaning was to be studied by examining how language is used: to say that a word has a meaning is to say that it has "a use in our language" (p. 69). The aphorism, to be sure, begs the question of what "use in [a] language" entails, and how it is to be characterized. This chapter can be read as an attempt to come to grips with this issue, with respect to a (very) limited range of uses of *over*, and of *all over*. The picture that emerges is that a speaker of a language does not learn a list of words (with their meanings) and a list of rules for combining words, as proposed in the earlier citations from Jackendoff and Baker. A speaker has learned a vast number of word uses, some more frequent than others, to be sure, and some more "idiomatic" than others. This approach need not be in conflict with the argument from linguistic creativity, which is standardly put forward in support of the dictionary+grammar book model of language. On the contrary. Idiomatic expressions can themselves be creatively extended to new usage situations, and are subject to creative modification. Creativity need not be the bogey of a non-generative, usage-based linguistics.

## Notes

1. The "two-level" approach is of interest, in that it attempted to address some of the problems raised above in connection with Searle's proposal for unitary word meanings. The two-level theorists did make proposals for unitary "semantic representations" for a selected number of words, above all, the prepositions, and for a few other examples, such as institution-type words. In addition, mechanisms were proposed for explicitly deriving "conceptual" (that is, contextualized) interpretations from these semantic representations. I have critically reviewed the two-level approach elsewhere (Taylor 1994, 1995, 2003b). One of my criticisms was that the mechanisms for conceptual elaboration often failed to predict the sometimes quite specific properties of the words in context. These specific properties could only be derived by appeal to ad hoc principles of conceptual interpretation. Appeal to such ad hoc principles, however, would be tantamount to recognizing the distinctiveness and independence of the different readings of the words in question, that is, that the words were indeed polysemous.
2. René Dirven (personal communication) has suggested that *government* and *parliament* behave differently from *museum, university*, etc., because they focus on the "body politic" rather than on the institutions *per se*.
3. A Google search (April 14, 2006) conformed these intuitions. The phrase *stand towards the back* scored 213 hits (alongside 410 hits for *stand toward the back*), as against no hits for *live toward(s) the sea/mountains*.
4. The literature on *over* is vast. For some recent contributions, see Tyler and Evans (2001), Queller (2001), and Deane (2005), and the references cited therein.
5. The examples were generated using the "Simple Search" facility of the British National Corpus at *http://sara.natcorp.ox.ac.uk/*. This facility returns a maximum of 50 randomly selected instances of the search item.

6. The examples in (27), as well as earlier examples with *written all over*, would profit from an analysis in terms of conceptual blending (Fauconnier & Turner 2003). This is not explored here, for lack of space.

## References

Allwood, Jens
2003 Meaning potentials and context: Some consequences for the analysis of variation in meaning. In *Cognitive Approaches to Lexical Semantics*, Hubert Cuyckens, René Dirven, and John R Taylor (eds.), 29–65. Berlin/New York: Mouton de Gruyter.
Baker, Mark
2001 *The Atoms of Language: The Mind's Hidden Rules of Grammar.* Oxford: Oxford University Press.
Barsalou, Lawrence
1987 The instability of graded structure: Implications for the nature of concepts. In *Concepts and Conceptual Development: Ecological and Intellectual Factors in Categorization*, Ulrich Neisser (ed.), 101–140. Cambridge: Cambridge University Press.
Bierwisch, Manfred
1981 Semantische und konzeptuelle Repräsentation lexikalischer Einheiten. In *Untersuchungen zur Semantik ( = Studia Grammatica XXII)*, R. Růžička, and Wolfgang Motsch (eds.), 61–99. Berlin: Akademiie-Verklag.
Brugman, Claudia
1981 Story of OVER. MA thesis, University of California, Berkeley.
Chomsky, Noam
1980 *Rules and Representations.* New York: Columbia University Press.
Croft, William
1998 Linguistic evidence and mental representations. *Cognitive Linguistics* 9: 151–173.
Cuyckens, Hubert, and Britta Zawada
2001 Introduction. In *Polysemy in Cognitive Linguistics*, Hubert Cuyckens, and Britta Zawada (eds.), ix-xxvii. Amsterdam/Philadelphia: Benjamins.
Deane, Paul
2005 Multimodal spatial representations: On the semantic unity of *over*. In *From Perception or Meaning: Image Schemas in Cognitive Linguistics*, Beate Hampe (ed.), 235–82. Berlin: Mouton de Gruyter.
Fauconnier, Gilles, and Mark Turner
2003 *The Way We Think.* New York: Basic Books.
Fillmore, Charles, and Beryl Atkins
2000 Describing polysemy: The case of *crawl*. In *Polysemy: Theoretical and Computational Approaches*, Yael Ravin, and Claudia Leacock (eds.), 91–10. Oxford: Oxford University Press.

Geeraerts, Dirk
   1993   Vagueness's puzzles, polysemy's vagaries. *Cognitive Linguistics* 4: 223–272.
Goldberg, Adele
   2006   *Constructions at Work: The Nature of Generalization in Grammar.* Oxford: Oxford University Press.
Hallan, Naomi
   2001   Paths to prepositions? A corpus-based study of the acquisition of a lexico-grammatical category. In *Frequency and the Emergence of Linguistic Structure*, Joan Bybee, and Paul Hopper (eds.), 91–120. Amsterdam/Philadelphia: Benjamins.
Jackendoff, Ray
   2002   *Foundations of Language.* Oxford: Oxford University Press.
Lakoff, George
   1987   *Women, Fire, and Dangerous Things: What Categories Reveal about the Mind.* Chicago: University of Chicago Press.
Langacker, Ronald W.
   1987   *Foundations of Cognitive Grammar. Vol. I: Theoretical Prerequisites.* Stanford: Stanford University Press.
   1990   Active zones. In *Concept, Image, and Symbol: The Cognitive Basis of Grammar*, Ronald W. Langacker, 177–88. Berlin: Mouton de Gruyter.
   2006   On the continuous debate about discreteness. *Cognitive Linguistics* 17: 107–151.
Moon, Rosamund
   1998   *Fixed Expressions and Idioms in English: A Corpus-based Approach.* Oxford: Oxford University Press.
Nunberg, Geoffrey, Ivan Sag, and Thomas Wasow
   1994   Idioms. *Language* 70: 491–538.
Pustejovsky, James
   1991   The generative lexicon. *Computational Linguistics* 17: 409–441.
Queller, Kurt
   2001   A usage-based approach to modeling and teaching the phrasal lexicon. In *Applied Cognitive Linguistics II: Language Pedagogy*, Martin Pütz, Susanne Niemeyer, and René Dirven (eds.), 55–83. Berlin/New York: Mouton de Gruyter.
Rice, Sally
   2003   Growth of a lexical network: Nine English prepositions in acquisition. In *Cognitive Approaches to Lexical Semantics*, Hubert Cuyckens, René Dirven, and John R Taylor (eds.), 243–280. Berlin/New York: Mouton de Gruyter.
Sandra, Dominiek, and Sally Rice
   1995   Network analyses of prepositional meaning: Mirroring whose mind – the linguist's or the language user's? *Cognitive Linguistics* 6: 89–130.
Searle, John
   1983   *Intentionality: An Essay in the Philosophy of Mind.* Cambridge: Cambridge University Press.

Stefanowitsch Anatol, and Stefan Gries
2003    Collostructions: Investigating the interaction of words and constructions. *International Journal of Corpus Linguistics* 8 209–243.
Stubbs, Michael
1995    Collocations and semantic profiles: On the cause of the trouble with quantitative studies. *Functions of Language* 2: 23–55.
Taylor, John R.
1992    How many meanings does a word have? *SPIL (= Stellenbosch Papers in Linguistics)* 25: 133–168.
1993    Prepositions: Patterns of polysemization and strategies of disambiguation. In *The Semantics of Prepositions*, Cornelia Zelinsky-Wibbelt (ed.), 151–175. Berlin/New York: Mouton de Gruyter.
1994    The two-level approach to meaning. *Linguistische Berichte* 149: 3–26.
1995    Models of word meaning in comparison: The two-level model (Manfred Bierwisch) and the network model (Ronald Langacker). In *Current Approaches to the Lexicon*, Johan Vanparys, and René Dirven (eds.), 3–26. Frankfurt: Lang.
2002    *Cognitive Grammar.* Oxford: Oxford University Press.
2003a   Cognitive models of polysemy. In *Polysemy: Flexible Patterns of Meaning in Mind and Language.* Brigitte Nerlich, Zazie Todd, Vimala Herman, and David D. Clarke (eds.), 31–47. Berlin/New York: Mouton de Gruyter.
2003b   *Linguistic Categorization.* Oxford: Oxford University Press. First edition, 1989.
2003c   Polysemy's paradoxes. *Language Sciences* 25: 637–655.
in press, a Metaphors of linguistic knowledge: The generative metaphor vs. the mental corpus. To appear in *Language, Mind and the Lexicon*, Iraide Ibarretxe-Antuñano, Carlos Inchaurralde, and Jesús Sánchez (eds.), Frankfurt: Lang.
in press, b Prototypes in cognitive linguistics. To appear in: Peter Robinson & Nick Ellis (eds.), *Handbook of Cognitive Linguistics and Second Language Acquisition.* Elsevier.
Tuggy, David
2003    The Nawatl verb *kīsa*: A case study in polysemy. In *Cognitive Approaches to Lexical Semantics*, Hubert Cuyckens, René Dirven, and John R Taylor (eds.), 323–362. Berlin/New York: Mouton de Gruyter.
Tyler, Andrea, and Vyvyan Evans
2001    Reconsidering prepositional polysemy networks: The case of *over*. *Language* 77: 724–765. Reprinted in *Polysemy: Flexible Patterns of Meaning in Mind and Language.* Brigitte Nerlich, Zazie Todd, Vimala Herman, and David D. Clarke (eds.), 95–159. Berlin/New York: Mouton de Gruyter.
Wittgenstein, Ludwig
1958    *The Blue and Brown Books.* New York: Harper and Row.

Wray, Alison
  2002    *Formulaic Language and the Lexicon*. Cambridge: Cambridge University Press.
Wunderlich, Dietrich
  1993    On German *um*: Semantic and conceptual aspects. *Linguistics* 31: 111–133.
Zlatev, Jordan
  2003    Polysemy or generality? Mu. In *Cognitive Approaches to Lexical Semantics*, Hubert Cuyckens, René Dirven, and John R Taylor (eds.), 447–494. Berlin/New York: Mouton de Gruyter.

# Cognitive approaches to grammar

## Cristiano Broccias

*Abstract*
This paper offers a short description and critical appraisal of four cognitive approaches to grammar, Langacker's Cognitive Grammar, Goldberg's Construction Grammar, Croft's Radical Construction Grammar and Fauconnier and Turner's Blending Theory. It first points out that the term "grammar" is polysemous, having both a narrow/traditional/descriptive sense (grammar as syntax plus morphology) and a broad/generative/cognitive sense (grammar as a theory of language). Both interpretations are taken into account. In a narrow sense, the present paper tries to evaluate how the four models define word classes and syntactic functions and how they handle specific constructions such as change constructions and noun phrases. In a broad sense, this contribution argues that Cognitive Grammar remains the most innovative and comprehensive cognitive theory of grammar and that the other models can, to some extent, be regarded as notational variants. They highlight different (though related) facets of the shared conceptualization of language as a taxonomic and diffuse network, i.e. of language as a structured inventory of conventional linguistic units where much is a matter of degree.

*Keywords*: grammar; construction; Cognitive Grammar; Construction Grammar; Radical Construction Grammar; Blending Theory; network; syntax-lexicon continuum; grammatical function; word class; polysemy; usage-based model; change construction; noun phrase; resultative construction; caused motion construction

## 1. Introduction

The term *grammar* is polysemous. In **descriptive** approaches, grammar is usually taken to include both syntax (i.e. word order patterns) and (inflectional) morphology (see e.g. Quirk *et al.* 1985: 12). Within the **generative** tradition, grammar is viewed as the set of principles by which a language works (see Radford 1997: 2–4 for discussion). This definition is based on the conceptualization (or construal) of language as a system made up of unpredictable forms (i.e. the lexicon) and productive rules (i.e. syntax). Syntactic rules specify how lexical items can be combined in a principled and regular way. **Cognitive** linguistics does not accept the sharp distinction made in generative grammar between syntax and the lexicon. In fact, it does not subscribe to the existence of generative rules either. Rather, it contends that syntax and the lexicon form a continuum of constructions ranging from very specific elements (e.g. *cat, kick the bucket*) to increasingly more general patterns (e.g. noun, transitive construction). General patterns (or schemas) capture the commonality of various specific instantiations (e.g. *kick the bucket* and *stroke the cat* are both instantiations of the transitive construction) and thus serve the same purpose as rules in generative grammars, i.e. they account for our ability to combine linguistic elements in a regular way. Despite the agreement on the non-derivational (or monostratal) nature of grammar – since rules are not posited, constructions are not taken to be derived by manipulating underlying forms – cognitive linguists do not always view *grammar* identically, as will be shown below.

The present overview begins by presenting some of the core notions of Cognitive Grammar (see Langacker 1987, 1990, 1991, 1999), which offers the clearest definition of what is meant by *grammar* within a cognitive theory of language (see section 2). It should become apparent from the discussion that grammar can (and will) be used in two main senses: a **narrow** sense, corresponding to the descriptive definition (i.e. syntax plus morphology), and a **broad** sense, as in generative and cognitive approaches. In the latter sense, grammar refers generally to how language works and is not restricted to syntax and morphology (so one can speak of a Cognitive Grammar approach to English phonology, for example). The reader should also be aware that a similar distinction applies to the notion of *construction*, which will figure prominently in this paper. In a narrow (or traditional) sense, a *construction* refers to the combination of syntactic phrases but, in a broad (or cognitive) sense, construction is a synonym of (any kind of) linguistic unit, as will be explained in section 2.

The title (and hence the topic) of the present paper refers mainly to grammar in the narrow sense. That is, my primary concern will be problems which are part and parcel of traditional grammar, e.g. the definition of word classes and grammatical functions, noun phrases and change constructions (i.e. caused motion constructions and resultative constructions). Nevertheless, in order to deal with such problems in a principled way, I will of course have to discuss cognitive approaches to grammar in the broad sense, i.e. grammar as a theory of language. But I will do so only insofar as they are relevant to the problems discussed here.

After having examined Cognitive Grammar, I will illustrate and discuss in section 3 the basic tenets of Goldberg's Construction Grammar (see Goldberg 1995). Section 4 will summarize the fundamental assumptions behind Croft's Radical Construction Grammar (see Croft 2001). Section 5 will briefly review how grammar (in the traditional sense) is handled in Fauconnier and Turner's Blending Theory (see Fauconnier and Turner 2002). Section 6 will draw the main conclusions. In particular, I will point out that, despite some (important) differences, a coherent picture emerges from the various cognitive approaches examined. The importance of the various theories lies in the fact that they tend to highlight different (although related) facets of the shared conceptualization of language as a **taxonomic** and **diffuse network**.

## 2.   Cognitive Grammar

### 2.1  The symbolic alternative to traditional concepts of grammar

Cognitive Grammar dispenses with both the descriptive and the generative definitions of *grammar* and views grammar as "a structured inventory of conventional linguistic units" (Langacker 1987: 37). This construal of the term *grammar* is also known as the **symbolic alternative** (to traditional/structural/generative grammar) because it rests on the assumption that any linguistic expression is an association between a semantic and a phonological structure, i.e. any linguistic expression is a symbol. For example, the lexical item *cat* is regarded as consisting of a semantic pole (i.e. what would traditionally be called both its denotative and its connotative meaning, abbreviated as [CAT]) and a phonological pole (abbreviated as [kæt]). Apart from the two poles and the details concerning how they are linked (i.e. their symbolic links), no other entities (e.g. traces, empty elements, etc.), (independent) levels/modules (e.g. syntax, logical form, etc.), or principles (e.g. the projection principle) are recognized in Cognitive Grammar. Further, a linguistic unit is a symbolic structure which has unit status, i.e. it is accessed in largely automatic fashion or, to put it differently, is entrenched. A linguistic unit is conventional if it is shared by a substantial number of individuals. Further, by the term "inventory" in his definition of grammar, Langacker means that a grammar is not a generative algorithm but, rather, a collection of conventional symbolic units. Crucially, such an inventory is not a list, but is structured because symbolic units, as schemas abstracted from usage events, are related by way of **categorizing relationships**. For example, the clause *I love you* is an instantiation or elaboration of the transitive construction; *hot* meaning "spicy", as in *hot mustard*, is a metaphorical extension of *hot* from the domain of temperature to that of taste.

The Cognitive Grammar definition of grammar has important consequences. First, linguistic units can be of any length. Grammar includes symbolic assemblies of any internal **complexity** rather than just atomic units like *cat*. Complex constructions like the ditransitive construction (e.g. *He gave her a present*) are part and parcel of grammar and are not taken to be projected from a verb's argument structure (as in generative grammar). Second, linguistic units can be of any degree of **specificity**. Grammar includes both very specific patterns (e.g. *I love you*, which can be considered an entrenched unit in the English language although its meaning is transparent, unlike idioms such as *kick the bucket, give up the ghost*, etc.) and general schemas that may subsume them (e.g. grammar includes the transitive construction, of which *I love you* is an elaboration or instantiation). From these two observations regarding complexity and specificity, it follows that there are no clear boundaries between what are traditionally referred to as the lexicon, morphology and syntax (this is known as the **syntax-lexicon continuum** hypothesis). These labels refer to symbolic assemblies differing from one another only in terms of structural complexity and schematicity (or specificity), as is illustrated in Table 1 below (adapted from Croft 2001: 17). Indeed, any entrenched symbolic assembly is regarded as a **construction** in Cognitive Grammar (as well as in Radical Construction Grammar, see below) irrespective of either its internal complexity or its specificity. More generally, Cognitive Grammar constantly underlines that much in language is a **matter of degree**. Since grammar is an integral part of human cognition and since human cognition rests, among other abilities, on categorization (which operates by way of instantiation and extension relations rather than feature-listing), sharp boundaries should not be expected in grammar.

*Table 1.* The syntax-lexicon continuum.

| Construction type | Traditional name | Examples |
|---|---|---|
| Complex and (mostly) schematic | syntax | noun verb noun (i.e. transitive construction), adjective noun (i.e. noun phrase) |
| Complex and (mostly) specific | idiom | *I love you*, *black cat* |
| Complex but bound | morphology | noun-*s* |
| Atomic and schematic | word class | verb, adjective, noun, pronoun |
| Atomic and specific | word/lexicon | *love, black, cat, I, you* |

The Cognitive Grammar definition of grammar also implies that linguistic analyses should always be checked against two omnipresent fallacies in linguistic argumentation, namely the **exclusionary fallacy** and the **rule/list** fallacy. The gist of the former is that "one analysis [...] for a linguistic phenomenon necessarily precludes another" (Langacker 1987: 28). For example, if we take the noun *computer* and say that this word is derived by rule (i.e. the suffix *-er* is added to the verb base *compute*), we cannot account for the fact that *computer* means more than "something that computes". By contrast, if we regard it as an item listed in the lexicon (on the assumption that the lexicon is an independent level of the linguistic system corresponding to an unstructured inventory of linguistic forms), we fail to capture the productivity of the verb + *-er* derivational pattern.

The rule/list fallacy is the assumption that "particular statements (i.e. lists) must be excised from the grammar of a language if general statements (i.e. rules) that subsume them can be established" (Langacker 1987: 29). For example, the fact that most plural nouns can be derived from the corresponding singular forms by adding *-s* does not necessarily imply that specific plural forms like *cats*, *dogs*, etc. are not listed in the grammar. In other words, the best grammar is not the shortest grammar according to Cognitive Grammar since redundancies are an integral feature of the Cognitive Grammar model. Both *computer* and *cats* are analysed as linguistic units in Cognitive Grammar since they are probably accessed automatically or, at least, without much constructive effort. Further, they are regarded as instantiations of (i.e. are categorized by) two other linguistics units, namely the verb + *-er* schema and the noun-*s* schema, respectively. This also means, incidentally, that what are traditionally called morphemes (see also Table 1) are in fact schemas which involve at least one more (phonologically unspecified) element, e.g. a verb in the case of *-er* and a noun in the case of *-s*.

Although the symbolic links between the semantic pole and the phonological pole of a construction may often be regarded as arbitrary (e.g. it is arbitrary that a doer is often signalled morphologically by way of the *-er* morpheme), Cognitive Grammar does not neglect the issue of **motivation** behind symbolic links. For example, the form of the prepositional dative construction (e.g. *He sent a letter to Susan*) is not arbitrary but emphasizes "the path traversed by the letter with Susan as a goal" (Langacker 1987: 39), as is signalled by the motion preposition *to*. Conversely, the double object construction (e.g. *He sent Susan a letter*) is said to emphasize the possessive relation between Susan and the letter by way of their "juxtaposition and linear order" (Langacker 1987: 39). Cognitive Grammar claims that the meaning of these two constructions is not necessarily identical because, among other things, they impose different **construals** (i.e. "views") on a common conceptual content. The prepositional dative construction construes transfer of possession in motion terms while the double object construction construes transfer of possession in terms of its outcome, i.e. the establishment of a relation of possession (or, more generally, control) between the indirect object and the direct object.

## 2.1. Word classes and grammatical functions in Cognitive Grammar

The view of language as an integral part of human cognition rather than as an independent module has also important repercussions for the analysis of traditional notions such as **grammatical** (or syntactic) **functions** (also known as grammatical/syntactic relations or roles) and **word classes** (also known as parts-of-speech or lexical categories). In particular, Cognitive Grammar, adopts (at least, in some cases) a universalist stance towards both grammatical functions and word classes (but not in the same sense as in Radical Construction Grammar, as will be pointed out below).

In Cognitive Grammar, "subject" for example is regarded as a universal notion ultimately based on the (perceptual) distinction between figure and ground, viz. trajector and landmark, configurations in a scene. As is well-known from Gestalt psychology (see Ungerer and Schmid 1996: Ch. 4 for an overview), certain objects function as primary foci of attention (e.g. smaller and/or moving objects as opposed to larger, static objects). A sentence like *The table is under the book* (employed to convey the scene depicted by *The book is on the table*) is felt to be deviant because it reflects a non-canonical perception of the intended spatial configuration. A smaller object like a book is usually chosen as the primary focus of attention (or trajector, in Cognitive Grammar terminology) whereas a larger object like a table functions as a secondary focus of attention (or landmark, in Cognitive Grammar terminology).

Cognitive Grammar proposes that subject is a universal category in that it can be defined **schematically** by characterizing it as a clause-level trajector. Similarly, object can be defined schematically as a clause-level secondary figure or landmark.

In addition to its schematic conception of grammatical relations, Cognitive Grammar also provides a schematic characterization of word classes. Cognitive Grammar contends that parts-of-speech can not only be defined prototypically (e.g. a noun prototypically refers to a physical object) but can also be described in a manner which is valid for all its other instantiations (i.e. a noun describes a "thing", see below). In other words, an "invariant" can be found for all major lexical categories. The Cognitive Grammar analysis of (the semantic pole of) word classes is summarized diagrammatically in Figure 1 (shaded boxes indicate concepts that are possible semantic poles for words; for example, the higher category of entities, unlike that of things, does not correspond to any particular word class). We start with the very general category of **entities**, which can be divided into **things** and **relations**. A "thing", a technical term in Cognitive Grammar, is a set of interconnected entities and is the semantic pole of the noun class. For example, the noun *team* (see Langacker 1987: 197) profiles a set of entities (represented in Figure 2a as the dashed boxes connected to each other) rather than singling out any constitutive member. The bold circle visually represents such a set in Figure 2a. "Relations", by contrast, profile connections between entities (as well as the entities themselves), as is shown for two arbitrary entities $e_1$ and $e_2$ in Figure 2b. Relations can be either **processes** (or temporal relations) or **atemporal relations**. In order to distinguish between the two, Cognitive Grammar contends that we can process complex scenes in two different ways. The different facets of a scene (e.g. the constitutive parts of a kissing event) are conceptualized either successively (as in a motion picture) or as a single Gestalt (as in a photo with multiple exposures, where the various parts are all made available simultaneously). The former mode of cognitive processing is called *sequential scanning* while the latter is referred to as *summary scanning*. Processes are said to involve sequential scanning: the different facets of a process are accessed sequentially, one after the other. Processes, depicted schematically in Figure 2c, constitute the semantic pole of verbs (e.g. *kiss*). The bold (temporal) line in Figure 2c represents the fact that the relation in question has a positive temporal profile, i.e. is scanned sequentially. By contrast, atemporal relations have a "null" temporal profile. This means that they are scanned summarily. Atemporal relations come in two types: *stative relations* and *complex atemporal relations*. Stative relations involve a single, stable configuration through time and correspond to the semantic pole of adjectives (i.e. stative relations whose trajector is a noun and whose landmark is a region on a scale), adverbs (i.e. stative relations whose trajector is a process and whose landmark is a region along a scale), and static prepositions (such as *in*, as opposed to *into*). Complex atemporal relations (e.g. *into*) are made up of more than one configuration over time and such configurations or facets are scanned in summary fashion.

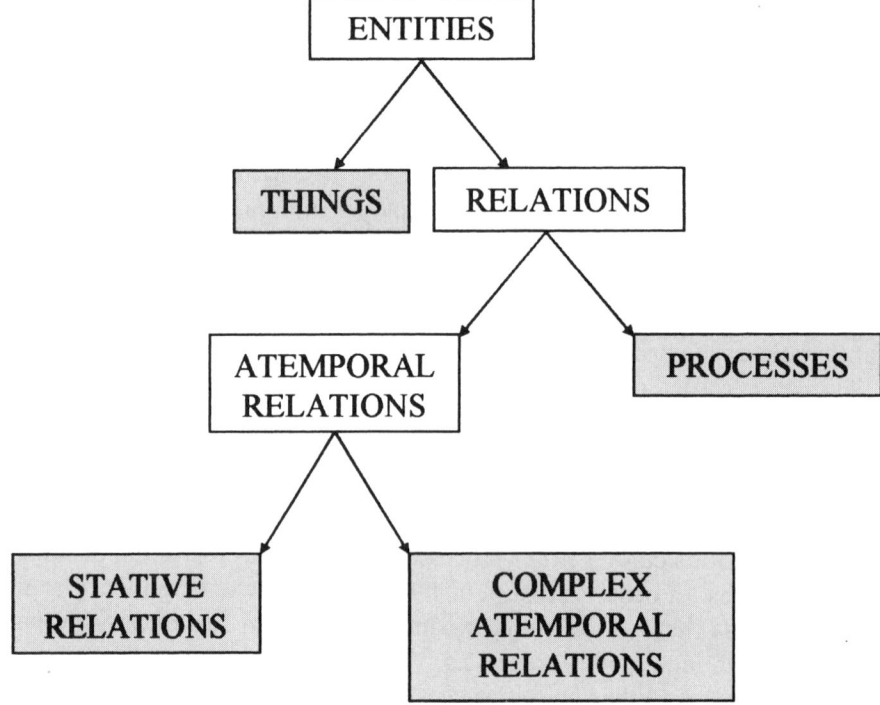

*Figure 1.* The Cognitive Grammar analysis of word classes

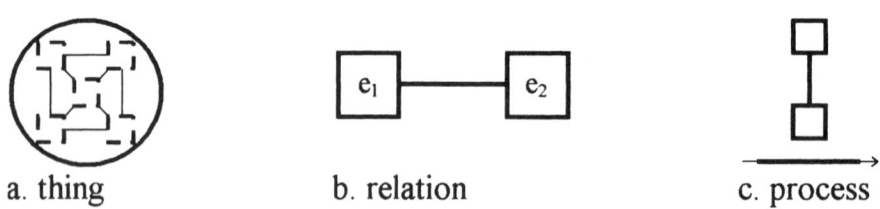

a. thing                  b. relation                  c. process

*Figure 2.* Schematic representations of things (a), relations (b) and processes (c)

## 2.2. Discussion

One of the features setting Cognitive Grammar apart from other cognitive models is the contention that notions such as "subject" and "object" can be defined schematically, i.e. independently of specific forms (or realizations) in a way that encompasses all their uses across all languages. Indeed, such a position may appear controversial (especially in the light of typologically-oriented research, see the discussion of Radical Construction Grammar below). Cognitive Grammar claims for example that *there* should be analyzed as a subject in a sentence like *There are a lot of people in the lift* (i.e. a presentational *there*-construction). *There*, in the case at hand, is categorized as a subject because it refers to an abstract setting which is used as a first trajector, i.e. an initial reference point for accessing the described situation, or a spotlight of prominence (see also Langacker's 2005b analysis of *it*-subjects). Observe that, under this analysis, the trajector (*there*) refers to an entity larger than that evoked by the landmark (*a lot of people*). That is, the schematic definition of subject does not necessarily pick out smaller entities as trajectors (cf. also the setting-subject construction *The garden is swarming with bees*, where the trajector *the garden* refers to a location and the smaller and moving entities, *the bees*, are the clause-level landmark). Related to this is the question of whether the analysis of presentational *there* constructions poses any problems for a sentence such as *Down the hill came a strange procession* (an inversion construction, see Chen 2003). Is *down the hill* also to be categorized as a subject? *Down the hill*, like *there*, refers to a setting, although a concrete one, and, like *there*, can be taken to be the starting point for accessing the configuration depicted by the clause (see Langacker 2005b). Still, *down the hill* is categorized as a landmark in Cognitive Grammar.

To be sure, the Cognitive Grammar analysis of the notion of *subject* defies traditional analyses. Traditionally, subject identification is based on morphological and/or syntactic criteria (e.g. verb-agreement and word-order, respectively, in English). Consequently, distributional facts point to both *there* and the postcopular noun phrase (e.g. *a lot of people*) as having subject status. The morphological criterion (at least in Standard English, cf. colloquial *There's a lot of people in the lift* where *a lot of people* does not agree with the copula) identifies *a lot of people* as a subject. The syntactic criterion (cf. *Are there a lot of people in the lift?*) forces us to conclude that *there* is also a subject. In the case of the inversion construction, by contrast, distributional facts would lead us to identify *a strange procession* as the subject.

At the very least, one can conclude that the Cognitive Grammar analysis is conceptual, not grammatical (in the traditional sense). That is, the Cognitive Grammar analysis is not necessarily meant to pick out those "subjects" identified by formal criteria. After all, distributional evidence simply points to the fact that some elements have a special status compared to others. The deeper and more interesting question is why this is so. Cognitive Grammar contends that such special (formal) behaviour is symptomatic of a specific cognitive ability (i.e. trajector/landmark alignment).

The word class analysis proposed by Cognitive Grammar may also appear controversial. As is pointed out by Taylor (2002: 563), (acquisitionally) word classes emerge as abstractions out of specific constructions (see also Tomasello 2003). The question is: is it possible to reconcile a usage-based perspective (see also section 4.1 below) with the construction-independent characterization summarized in Figure 1? At present, the question cannot be answered satisfactorily because, among other things, the psychological reality of some of the notions invoked by the Cognitive Grammar analysis has not been proved. This is the case of summary and sequential scanning, whose existence (and relevance to word class categorization) has not been validated experimentally yet (see e.g. Broccias and Hollmann 2005, Duffley 2005; but see also Matlock 2004 and Matlock *et al.* 2005 for some psycholinguistic experiments involving the notion of scanning).

Nevertheless, the Cognitive Grammar approach remains very innovative because it strives to link (traditional) grammatical categories with cognitive processes. The fact that certain schemas (e.g. noun, adjective, subject, etc.) emerge out of specific usage events at all should ultimately be related to our cognitive abilities. Of course, the details of what abilities are involved, how they interact with one another and the extent to which they define cross-linguistically valid schemas remain to be established.

## 3.    Construction Grammar

### 3.1. Predictability and polysemy

The reference work for the framework labelled Construction Grammar is usually taken to be Goldberg (1995). In what follows the label "Construction Grammar" is taken to refer to Goldberg's version. Originally (i.e. in Goldberg 1995 as well as in Fillmore's work, from which Goldberg's model derives, see e.g. Fillmore 1988 and Fillmore and Kay 1996), constructions were posited in grammar if and only if some aspect of their meaning was regarded as "not strictly predictable from [the construction's] component parts or from other previously established constructions" (Goldberg 1995: 4). For example, a sentence like *Sam slept the whole trip away* is said to be unaccounted for by the syntactic rules of English (e.g. *sleep a trip* is not a possible string in English) and, hence, a construction with the syntax "Subject Verb Object (referring to time) *away*" and the meaning (roughly) "to spend the specified amount of time by being constantly engaged in the activity denoted by the verb" should be recognized as a unit in the grammar of English. Further, the term construction was usually taken to exclude combinations of two or more morphemes, that is, it covered only combinations of syntactic phrases (cf. syntax and idioms in Table 1 above). More recently, however, Goldberg (e.g. Goldberg and Casenhiser 2006) seems to have opted for (or at least to have taken an agnostic stance on) a more comprehensive definition of construction, i.e. one along the lines of both Cognitive Grammar and Radical Construction Grammar. Constructions should be posited in grammar even if they are fully **predictable** (e.g. *I love you* vs. *kick the bucket*) and all the types listed in Table 1 should be categorized as constructions. This in turn implies that, as in Cognitive Grammar and Radical Construction Grammar, no strict separation is postulated between what are traditionally called the lexicon and syntax. Rather, they are taken to form a continuum.

Despite the use of a more inclusive notion of construction in recent work, Construction Grammar still draws a sharp distinction between constructional meaning and word meaning. As is pointed out by Langacker (2005a), Construction Grammar aims at **minimizing lexical polysemy** in favour of constructional polysemy. Consider the verb *slice*, which can be used in a variety of constructions, as shown in (1) (from Goldberg and Casenhiser 2006):

(1)  a. He sliced the bread. (transitive)
     b. Pat sliced the carrots into the salad. (caused motion)
     c. Pat sliced Chris a piece of pie. (ditransitive)
     d. Emeril sliced and diced his way to stardom. (*way*-construction)
     e. Pat sliced the box open. (resultative)

Construction Grammar argues against postulating five different senses for *slice* (as would be done in traditional generative approaches, where constructions are projected from a verb's argument structure). Rather, *slice*, meaning simply "cut with a sharp instrument", is claimed to combine with five different constructions (or argument structures), all of which are independently stored in the grammar of English. The interaction between constructional meaning and verbal meaning in the case of (1b) is illustrated in a Construction Grammar format in Figure 3.

CAUSED MOTION CONSTRUCTION

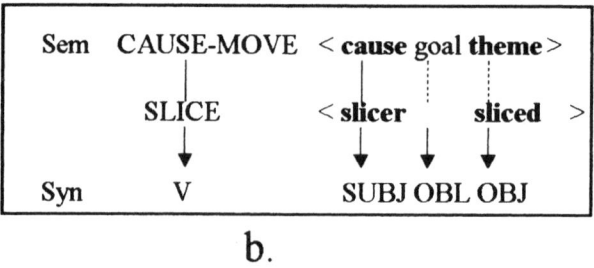

a.

b.

*Figure 3.* The caused motion construction in Construction Grammar

Figure 3a depicts the schema for the caused motion construction. Construction Grammar distinguishes between the semantics (*Sem*) and the syntax (*Syn*) of a given construction. The exact details of the representational conventions used in Construction Grammar are not our concern here. It will suffice to point out that the semantics of the caused motion construction indicates that an argument (*cause*) causes another entity (*theme*) to move towards a certain position (i.e. *goal*). The causal relation and the ensuing movement, i.e. the overall caused motion predicate, are abbreviated as CAUSE-MOVE. *Cause* is realized syntactically as a subject (SUBJ), *goal* as an oblique (OBL, that is, an adjective phrase or a prepositional phrase), and *theme* as a direct object (OBJ). The construction also specifies (by way of the middle tier) that specific instantiations of the construction are obtained by merging the schematic caused motion predicate (CAUSE-MOVE) with a specific predicate (PRED), which corresponds syntactically to a verb (V), e.g. *slice* in our example. This is shown in Figure 3b. *Slice* (as well as making reference to a sharp instrument as part of its semantic base) takes two arguments, a "slicer" argument (i.e. the cause argument), *Pat*, and a "sliced" argument (the theme argument), *the carrots*. The merger between the caused motion construction and *slice* results in the specific construction *Pat sliced the carrots into the salad*.

## 3.2. Networks

As in Cognitive Grammar, grammatical knowledge is represented in networks. Instead of categorizing relations, Construction Grammar makes use of **inheritance links** (as in computer science) to relate constructions to one another. Four major types of inheritance links are recognized: polysemy links, metaphorical extension links, subparts links and instance links (see Goldberg 1995: 74–81). Before briefly illustrating them, it should be observed that inheritance links are treated as objects in Construction Grammar (see Goldberg 1995: 74–75). This differs from Cognitive Grammar (and Radical Construction Grammar), where the only elements postulated in grammar are the semantic and phonological poles of a construction plus their symbolic links. Like other cognitive models, however, Construction Grammar allows for multiple inheritance, i.e. a construction can be categorized by two (or more) independently established constructions. For example, the intransitive motion construction (e.g. *The car screeched around the corner*) inherits from both the intransitive construction (since the intransitive motion construction is quite trivially intransitive) and the motion construction (since motion is predicated of one of the constructional elements, i.e. the subject, via an oblique phrase).

Polysemy links and metaphorical links roughly correspond to extension relations in Cognitive Grammar. Construction Grammar claims for example that the double object construction has a variety of senses which can be viewed as extensions (via polysemy links) from the central sense "[a]gent successfully causes recipient to receive patient" (see Goldberg 1995: Fig. 2.2). A metaphorical link connects the caused motion construction and the resultative construction (see (1d) and (1e) above) in that the latter is said to have originated from the former via the metaphorical construal of states (e.g. *crazy* in *Chris drove Pat crazy*) as locations. A subpart link is posited when a construction is "a proper subpart of another construction" (Goldberg 1995: 78). The intransitive motion construction is linked to the caused-motion construction via such a link since the former is a proper subpart of the latter (the only missing element in the intransitive motion construction is the "cause" argument; for a different view see Broccias 2003: Ch.5). Finally, instance links correspond to elaborative categorization in Cognitive Grammar. This obtains when a construction specifies another construction in more detail (e.g. *Chris drove Pat crazy* instantiates the schematic resultative construction).

It should be pointed out that Construction Grammar, at least in its 1995 version, also makes use of constraints to motivate the (alleged) impossibility of some patterns. Among them is the constraint (see Broccias 2003: 213–218 for a review of Goldberg's 1995 constraints) that states that no intermediary time intervals are possible between the causing event and the resultant event in a resultative construction (as in *Chris shot Pat dead*, where death is said to necessarily occur immediately after the shooting event). Even if we accepted the descriptive correctness of this and other proposed constraints (but see Broccias 2003: Ch. 6), it remains to be established how they are represented in the grammar. One might claim that, in a truly cognitive model of grammar, constraints cannot be independent objects in the grammatical system. Constraints should simply amount to paraphrases of schemas which subsume a large amount of specific instances (see e.g. Taylor's 2002: Ch. 5 discussion of phonological constraints as phonological schemas).[1] Broccias (2003) argues, for example, that Goldberg's (1995) constraints for the caused motion construction and the (transitive) resultative construction are just paraphrases of the conceptual import of the schema to which both construction types can be related, i.e. the billiard-ball schema.[2]

## 3.3. Discussion

There are various differences between Construction Grammar, on the one hand, and other cognitive models like Cognitive Grammar and Radical Construction Grammar, on the other. The previous subsection has already pointed out the possibly problematic postulation of constraints or generalizations, which cannot be assumed as independent objects in Cognitive Grammar, for example. Similarly, the fact that constructions are related to one another does not rest in Cognitive Grammar on the postulation of links as objects as is the case in Construction Grammar. Relatedness in Cognitive Grammar is a necessary corollary of the language-independent cognitive ability of categorization, which structures any type of information in terms of a standard (of comparison) and a target (of conceptualization), i.e. all information is stored in networks by default. There is no need to postulate links as independent objects in Cognitive Grammar.

Construction Grammar also makes use of abstract predicates (e.g. CAUSE, MOVE, see Figure 3 above) and roles (both semantic, e.g. *theme*, and syntactic, e.g. SUBJ) but their nature is not detailed any further. That is, Construction Grammar, unlike Cognitive Grammar and Radical Construction Grammar, does not take a stance on their universality (or lack thereof).

Even more importantly, although constructions (like linguistic symbols in Cognitive Grammar) are defined as pairs of form and meaning, form is equated with syntax in Construction Grammar. That is, syntax is taken to symbolize (i.e. express) the semantic level, see Figure 3 above. Langacker (2005a) objects to this analysis because it implies that syntax is treated as a level independent of semantics (as in modular approaches). In Cognitive Grammar what is (traditionally) called syntax simply amounts to a collection of (sufficiently) abstract schemas, i.e. assemblies of semantic and phonological structure. A pattern like SUBJ VERB OBJ OBL (instantiated for example by *Pat sliced the carrots into the salad*) cannot be taken as pure form in Cognitive Grammar. "Subject" and "object", for example, refer to, respectively, the trajector and landmark of the relation designated by the verb and hence they profile concepts (although their phonological pole is maximally non-specific). Similarly, "verb" stands for a pairing of meaning and form. Its semantic pole designates a sequentially scanned relation and its phonological pole is non-specific (although we know, among other things, that most verbs usually take a final alveolar plosive segment when used to refer to the past, etc.). In sum, in Cognitive Grammar what symbolizes the semantic pole is the phonological pole, not syntax, because syntax in Cognitive Grammar is not pure form.

We can now turn to the issue of lexical (vs. constructional) polysemy, which also sets Construction Grammar apart from other cognitive models. As was pointed out in section 3.1, Construction Grammar aims to minimize lexical polysemy. *Slice* in (1) is analysed as having only one meaning, roughly "cut with a sharp instrument". The fact that *slice* can be used with a caused motion meaning, see (1b), is attributed to the interaction between the verb and the caused motion construction. Construction Grammar does not assume that this type of interaction results in the verb's acquiring a new meaning (i.e. in the verb being polysemous). More generally, such an analysis implies that Construction Grammar subscribes to a parsimonious view of grammar (i.e. "the best grammar is the shortest grammar"). A new (e.g. caused motion meaning) for *slice* is not postulated because this meaning can be retrieved from our knowledge that *slice* can be used in a caused motion construction. Even if we accepted this position as correct (i.e. cognitively plausible), at closer inspection there seems to be no clear theoretical advantage (in terms of parsimony) by reducing the number of word meanings. Such a move automatically implies an increase in the number of postulated constructions, whose inventory is potentially infinite. This is exactly analogous to what happens in lexicalist approaches, where the number of word meanings is potentially endless while the number of constructions is minimized. Further, Construction Grammar faces the same problem as do lexicalist approaches: how can we distinguish between constructions (i.e. word meanings in lexicalist approaches)? Are, for example, the prepositional dative construction (e.g. *Sally sent a present to Chris*) and the caused motion construction (see (1b)) truly two different constructions?

Be that as it may, the more general point is that the parsimonious view of grammar is not necessarily descriptively, i.e. cognitively, adequate (i.e. it does not necessarily reflect how our mind works) and, hence, questions such as those concerning the distinction between constructions and lexemes may turn out to be vacuous. There is no compelling reason, within a cognitive model of language, to assume (a) that word meanings (vs. constructions) should be kept at a minimum (or vice versa), (b) that word meanings can neatly be separated from constructional meanings and (c) that (allegedly) different lexical meanings, or (allegedly) different constructional meanings for that matter, can be isolated from one another in clear-cut fashion.

In sum, the treatment of the relation between word meanings and constructions in Construction Grammar differs greatly from the one offered in Cognitive Grammar. Langacker (2005a) claims that in the case of the caused motion construction, which he incidentally conflates with the prepositional dative construction, a continuum should be recognized. Langacker states that the verb *send* (as in *Sally sent a present to Chris*) should be regarded as coinciding with the caused motion construction itself. In other words, *send* is regarded as having a caused motion meaning by default: the constructional meaning and the verbal meaning overlap completely. By contrast, in Goldberg's (1995) famous example *Sally sneezed the napkin off the table* (i.e. Sally caused the napkin to fall off the table by sneezing), *sneeze* is not analysed by Langacker (2005a) as a caused motion verb. Rather, as in Goldberg's approach, the caused motion meaning is viewed as emerging from the merger of the verb *sneeze* with the caused motion construction: the caused motion meaning is imposed upon the verb by the construction and the verb has not (at least yet) developed a caused motion meaning. Between *send* and *sneeze* lies the verb *kick* (as in *John kicked the football into the stadium*): speakers may have difficulty in deciding whether it has a caused motion meaning or not.[3]

All in all, the Cognitive Grammar analysis of verbal vs. constructional meaning seems more consonant with truly cognitive assumptions about language. If one accepts that much in language is a matter of degree, then there is no a priori reason to assume the need for minimizing lexical polysemy, as does Construction Grammar. Still, the importance of Construction Grammar resides, among other things, in having brought to the fore the treatment of constructions (in the traditional sense, i.e. assemblies of two or more units) as "objects" of the linguistic system in their own right and in having stressed that they, like lexical items, can be polysemous. Of course, it remains to be seen to what extent analyses based on constructional polysemy networks (see section 3.2 on the dative construction) can be regarded as psychologically plausible (cf. Langacker's 2005b claim that networks may be more "diffuse" than is usually assumed; see also Sandra and Rice's 1995 seminal paper on the psychological reality of network mapping and Broccias's 2005a critique of network approaches like Evans and Tyler's 2004).

## 4.   Radical Construction Grammar

### 4.1. Why Radical Construction Grammar is radical

In contrast to Goldberg's Construction Grammar, which is partly indebted to Fillmore's non-commitment to a fully cognitive linguistic model, Croft's (2001) Radical Construction Grammar is claimed to be radical for four reasons. Firstly, grammatical categories (i.e. words classes and syntactic roles) are not viewed as primitives but are argued to be **construction-specific**. One of the greatest merits of Radical Construction Grammar is to have exposed the circularity inherent in much of modern syntactic argumentation. Constructions are used to define categories (this is known as the distributional method) and then the categories so established are used to define (or categorize) other constructions. As a matter of illustration, consider how direct object status is evaluated in English (see Croft 2001: 35–45). Croft points out that, traditionally, passivizability – the fact that the alleged direct object in an active sentence can become the subject of the corresponding passive sentence, see (2a) vs. (2a') – is taken to be the defining criterion for direct object status. Consequently, *80 kg* in (2b) may not be categorized as a direct object by some linguists: no corresponding passive sentence is possible, see (2b'). By contrast, objects of prepositions may sometimes be passivized, see (2c'). This would lead us to classify such objects as direct objects. The problem here is that the choice of passiviz-ation (over, for example, obligatory presence vs. absence of a preposition after the verb) as the defining criterion for direct object status is not the-oretically motivated. Further, there is no a priori reason why we should group different cases into the same category. In fact, a Radical Construc-tion Grammar analysis would claim that the three sentences at hand con-tain three different types of "objects" whose properties overlap only par-tially: *John* immediately follows the verb and can become the subject of a passive sentence; *80 kg* cannot become the subject of a passive sentence but, like *John*, occurs immediately after the verb; *this house*, like *John*, can become the subject of a passive sentence but, unlike *John* and *80 kg*, is sep-arated from the verb by a preposition.

(2)  a.  A mule kicked John.
     a'. John was kicked by a mule
     b.  John weighs 80 kg.
     b'. *80 kg are weighed by John.
     c.  Hemingway lived in this house.
     c'. This house was lived in by Hemingway.

The second reason why Radical Construction Grammar is radical is be-cause constructions are taken to be the **basic units** of syntactic represen-tation. This assumption is also shared by Cognitive Grammar and Con-struction Grammar (at least in its latest implementations) and was illustrated in Table 1 above.

Thirdly, Radical Construction Grammar is radical because syntactic **relations** are claimed not to exist. Croft argues that the term syntactic **role** should be used instead. He points out that the term "subject", for example, can be used in two different ways (see e.g. Croft 2001: 24 and Croft and Cruse 2004: 285–286). "Subject" can be used to refer to the syn-tactic relation between an element of a construction and another element (the verb), e.g. we say that *Heather* is the subject of *sings* in *Heather sings*. "Subject" can also be used to refer to the role that an element has in a con-struction, i.e. the part-whole (or meronomic) relation of an element with the whole construction. For example, we say that *Heather* has the role subject in the intransitive construction *Heather sings*. The crucial point here is that Croft uses the term syntactic relation in a traditional (formal) sense, whereby a syntactic relation like subject is taken to be construction-independent by definition – cf. the Government and Binding Theory con-figurational definition of subject as the Specifier of an Inflectional Phrase or [Spec, IP] – and does not necessarily symbolize any semantic content. Since the only entities which should be posited in grammar according to Croft are constructions (as well as relations among them), it follows that syntactic relations (as construction-independent objects) must be dispensed with. Accordingly, Radical Construction Grammar only uses the term role, which refers to the relation between an element and the whole construction rather than the relation between an element and another element within the same construction.

Finally, constructions are said to be **language-specific**: no two constructions can be assumed to be identical across languages. This assumption is also shared by Construction Grammar and Cognitive Grammar.

In sum, Radical Construction Grammar can be described as a **usage-based model**: grammar is maximalist and bottom-up, rather than minimalist and top-down (like formal approaches). It consists of taxonomic hierarchies of constructions which include very specific constructions (e.g. *kick the bucket*, *kick the habit*) as well as more general schemas abstracting away their commonalities (e.g. a transitive schema for *kick*, a general transitive schema, etc.). A self-explanatory example of the kind of taxonomy assumed in Radical Construction Grammar is offered in Figure 4 below (adapted from Croft 2001: Figure 1.15, p.56).

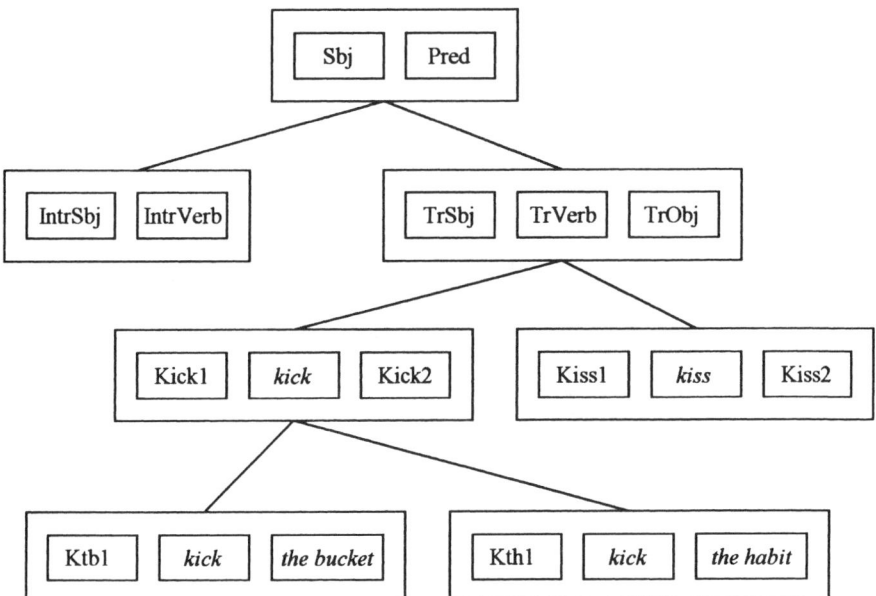

*Figure 4.* A construction taxonomy in Radical Construction Grammar

Although Radical Construction Grammar claims that grammatical categories are construction and language-specific, Croft (2001) shows that syntactic roles can be compared across languages once semantic notions (e.g. actor event, undergoer event, etc.) are appealed to. In a similar vein, he argues that a **universal** characterization of parts of speech is possible. (For reasons of space, I will only discuss parts-of-speech here.) Croft's analysis is based on the interaction between **discourse functions** and **semantic classes**. Croft recognizes three discourse (or pragmatic/communicative) functions (see Croft 2001: 66), namely the propositional acts of predication (e.g. *This intelligent detective is young*, where *young* is predicated of *this intelligent detective*), reference (e.g. *this intelligent detective*, which picks out a certain referent) and modification (e.g. *intelligent detective*, where *intelligent* modifies our "cognitive file" for the detective in question, i.e. it enriches the detective's identity by adding a property to the "features" already stored in our mind concerning the detective). As these examples illustrate, we tend to use certain constructions to code such discourse functions (the constructions in question are called propositional act constructions). Croft hypothesizes that the typological prototypes of the referring, attributive, and predicating constructions are the semantic classes of objects, properties and actions, respectively, i.e. we prototypically refer to objects, modify cognitive files by attributing properties to entities and predicate actions of entities. It should be observed that these semantic classes are only a small subset of the semantic classes of words found in human languages (and are defined in terms of four semantic properties, namely relationality, stativity, transitoriness, gradability, see Croft 2001: 87). Parts-of-speech in a given language can therefore be represented onto a bi-dimensional space (a semantic map) defined by the dimensions "discourse functions" and "semantic classes". Nouns, adjectives and verbs are viewed as the (prototypical) pairings of reference/object, modification/property and predication/action, respectively. This is shown in Table 2 (adapted from Croft 2001: Table 2.3, p.88. "Unmarked" means that no derivational morphemes are employed, e.g. *cat* is an unmarked noun while *happiness* is a marked, deadjectival noun).[4]

*Table 2.* The two-dimensional space for English parts-of-speech

| | | discourse function | | |
|---|---|---|---|---|
| | | *reference* | *modification* | *predication* |
| semantic class | *objects* | UNMARKED NOUNS | genitive, adjectivalizations, PPs on nouns | predicate nominals, copulas |
| | *properties* | deadjectival nouns | UNMARKED ADJECTIVES | predicate adjectives, copulas |
| | *actions* | action nominals, complements, infinitives, gerunds | participles, relative clauses | UNMARKED VERBS |

## 4.2. Discussion

Radical Construction Grammar's assumptions are very similar to those made in Cognitive Grammar. Indeed, they are radical especially if compared to Goldberg's Construction Grammar, rather than Cognitive Grammar. Construction Grammar, unlike Cognitive Grammar, does not seem to take a stand on the first three reasons mentioned in the previous subsection. This observation may lead us to view Radical Construction Grammar as a notational variant of Cognitive Grammar applied to typological research (since the main focus of Croft 2001 is typology). Nevertheless, Langacker (2005a) argues that there are some substantive differences between the two models.

The main difference between the two grammars (see also Broccias 2003) resides in the fact that grammatical categories are given a **schematic** characterization in Cognitive Grammar whereas they are claimed to be construction and language-specific in Radical Construction Grammar. Radical Construction Grammar, at most, offers a prototype description of parts of speech. By contrast, Cognitive Grammar claims that a schematic definition (hence, a definition valid for all cases) can be offered for both parts of speech (see Figure 1) and (at least some) grammatical relations (i.e. in terms of trajector/landmark alignment, see section 2.2). As was pointed out in section 2.3, the schematic characterization provided in Cognitive Grammar is not usage-driven but is advanced as a matter of conceptual necessity, i.e. it stems from our cognitive abilities. This amounts to saying that Cognitive Grammar, unlike Radical Construction Grammar, is, at the same time, a usage-based or bottom-up model and a universalist or top-down model. Like Radical Construction Grammar,

Langacker views grammar as including constructions of varying degrees of specificity and complexity (see section 2.1). But, as in non-cognitive models, universal categories are assumed to exist.

If the universalist stance adopted in Cognitive Grammar may be reminiscent of traditional and formal treatments in scope (but not in its implementation, since universal or schematic categories are based on cognitive processing in Cognitive Grammar), Radical Construction Grammar prototypical approach to words classes is not "immune" from "traditional" influences either. As was pointed out in the previous subsection, the Radical Construction Grammar analysis rests on the interaction between propositional acts and semantic classes. Crucially, propositional acts seem to involve a rather objectivist view of semantics/pragmatics. For example, the act of predication is defined, quite traditionally, as the ascription of something to a referent (Croft 2001: 66) and the verb is taken to prototypically code such a role. However, the view that verbs prototypically code acts of predication may be debatable.[5] It remains to be demonstrated quantitatively and cognitively that this is indeed the case. Lambrecht (1994), for example, reminds us that a sentence like *The children went to school* does not necessarily predicate the event of going to the school of the subject (i.e. this is what he calls a topic-comment sentence or predicate-focus structure) but has a variety of different uses. It can also identify who did the action of going to school (if it is used as an identificational sentence or argument-focus structure, i.e. to answer the question *Who went to school?*) and, more generally, what happened (if it is used as an event-reporting or argument-focus structure, i.e. to answer the question *What happened?*).

Langacker's Cognitive Grammar dispenses with the traditional analysis of verbs as involving the act of predication and views verbs (see section 2.2) as relations (scanned sequentially). In this way, he can capture the intuition that the human ability to establish links between entities (i.e. what relations are about) is shared by verbs and (Croft's unmarked) adjectives (see section 2.2). The two only differ in their temporal profile: the former designate temporal relations; the latter profile atemporal relations. By contrast, (unmarked) adjectives are linked to a different propositional function in Croft's theory. In fact, the very distinction between predication and modification (within a Croftian view) may be an intricate affair (see Broccias 2003).[6] Nevertheless, it was pointed out earlier that Langacker's analysis is also open to debate since it involves the controversial notion of scanning. Further, Langacker's view that verbs always activate a relational content should also be the matter of empirical investigation (is for example an action verb like *sleep* (always) represented in our mind as a relation, akin, one may speculate, to "to be asleep"?).

Alongside grammatical categories, a further difference between Radical Construction Grammar and Cognitive Grammar involves the use of the term "syntactic representation", which seems to be employed in Croft's theory quite similarly to Construction Grammar. Croft subscribes to the Cognitive Grammar and Construction Grammar view of constructions as (partially arbitrary) symbolic units (or pairings of form and meaning). Rather controversially, however (see also Broccias 2003), he views form as including syntactic, morphological and phonological properties. This, as was pointed out in section 3.3 for Construction Grammar, is potentially problematic because syntax in a cognitively oriented theory of language does not exist as an independent grammatical level. (Remember that Croft himself denies the existence of syntactic relations because they are taken to be independent of meaning.) Nevertheless, since the formal pole of constructions is said to include syntactic, morphological and phonological properties (and not only syntactic properties as in Construction Grammar), one may speculate that Croft's use of the term "syntax" may just be a convenient label to refer to word order patterns in a construction.

All in all, a fundamental contribution of Radical Construction Grammar has not only been to have shifted the focus of scholarly research from lexemes to constructions (in the traditional sense) but, most of all, to have underlined the need for a truly usage-based or bottom-up model in language description.

## 5. Blending Theory

### 5.1. Conceptual and formal integration

Fauconnier and Turner's (2002) Blending Theory is not a theory of grammar as such. Rather, Fauconnier and Turner show that the basic conceptual operation of blending should be invoked to account for a variety of grammatical constructions, including "simple" syntactic patterns like adjective-noun combinations (e.g. *red ball*, *safe beach*) and noun-noun combinations (e.g. *land yacht*). Structure from two (or more) input mental spaces is projected into a separate space, the blend, where it is integrated into a single conceptual unit. Crucially, the blend can develop structure of its own (i.e. structure which was not present in either input), known as emergent structure. Blending Theory points out that both in supposedly (semantically) simple cases like *red ball* and more exotic cases like *land yacht* (used to refer to a large, luxurious car) we resort to identical complex mental operations.

Consider the noun-noun combination *land yacht*. The conceptual pole of this noun phrase results from the blending of two input spaces, as is shown in Figure 5 (adapted from Fauconnier and Turner 2002: Fig.17.1, p. 357). One input involves water, a skipper, a course, a yacht and a tycoon; the other space includes land, a driver, a road, a car and an owner. These elements from the two inputs are put into correspondence with one another (so that water corresponds to land, skipper to driver, etc.) and some of them (e.g. tycoon/owner and car/yacht) are projected into the blend so as to create emergent structure: a *land yacht* names a new object, which is neither a generic car nor a yacht. (Cases like *computer* mentioned in section 2.1 above would be handled similarly. *Computer* involves the blending of an input space referring to the activity of computation, symbolized by the verb *compute*, and an input space referring abstractly to an entity performing an action, symbolized by *-er*. Crucially, the blended noun, *computer*, has features which are not inherited by either input because a computer is more than something that computes. In other words, the blend contains emergent structure.)

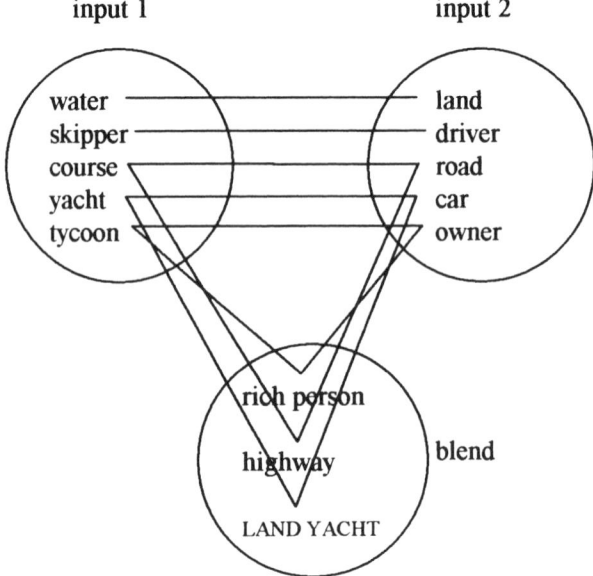

*Figure 5. Land yacht* in Blending Theory

Let us now analyse the adjective-noun combination *red ball*. This noun phrase is deceptively simple. It could mean a pen whose case is red, a pen whose ink is red, a pen whose cap is red, a pen "used to record the activities of a team dressed in red" (see Fauconnier and Turner 2002: 355) and so on. In other words, we integrate (as was the case with *land yacht*) two input spaces, one containing the colour red and the other containing the pen plus, if necessary, relevant frames (i.e. scenarios) in which the pen plays some role (e.g. a frame describing the use of the pen to record the activities of a team). The operation of conceptual integration takes place by virtue of the correspondences established between the two inputs (e.g. between the colour of the pen cap and the colour red) and by projecting the pen and the colour red into the blend. The fact that certain interpretations seem to be simpler and more accessible than others is simply due to the existence of strong defaults: "[...] simplicity of form, conventionality of vocabulary, and frequency of use [do not] indicate simplicity of underlying conceptual organization" (Fauconnier and Turner 2002: 365).

More generally, Fauconnier and Turner demonstrate that the elements within any construction should be taken as prompts for the activation of complex blending operations. One more example will suffice. Consider copular constructions like *The child is safe*, *The beach is safe*, and *The shovel is safe*. Blending Theory contends that it is not strictly speaking correct to say that *safe* attributes a property to the subject referent (cf. the Radical Construction Grammar characterization of predication in the previous section). After all, the first example means that the child is not likely to be harmed (i.e. the child is a potential victim), while the second and third examples mean that the beach and the shovel are not likely to cause harm (but observe that beach refers to a location while shovel refers to an instrument). In Fauconnier and Turner's analysis (see Fauconnier and Turner 2002: 25–26 and 354) *safe* is a prompt for evoking an abstract frame of danger (i.e. an input space containing, among other things, a victim, a location and an instrument) which is blended with the current situation of the child playing on the beach (i.e. another input space) so as to obtain a *counterfactual* blend (where the child is harmed while playing on the beach). To put it differently, the counterfactual blend is *disanalogous* to the current situation since the child is not harmed in the "real world". The counterfactual blend is blended, in its turn, with the current situation into a new blend where *safe* signals the compression of the relation of disanalogy between the counterfactual blend and the current situation: the child is not harmed while playing on the beach.

Conceptual integration can go hand in hand with formal integration. This is the case, for example, of the word *Chunnel*, which is used to refer to the underwater tunnel connecting England and France. Morphologically, *tunnel* and *Channel* (i.e. the English Channel) are blended into a single word by substituting the phoneme /æ/ of *Channel* with /ʌ/ from *tunnel*. The formal integration mirrors the conceptual integration whereby the frame of a tunnel is put into correspondence with the frame of the specific stretch of water separating England and France.

Fauconnier and Turner claim that blending can also occur between a construction and a diffuse (or unintegrated) input. They illustrate this point by analyzing the resultative construction (e.g. *I boiled the pan dry*) and the caused motion construction (e.g. *He sneezed the napkin off the table*). They regard specific instantiations of these two constructions as originating from the blending of an input space which contains the schematic construction (represented in a Goldbergian format as a pairing of semantics and syntax) and an input containing the actual event sequence of e.g. sneezing and the napkin's falling off the table. *He sneezed the napkin off the table* is illustrated diagramatically in Figure 6 below, adapted from Fauconnier and Turner 1996 (the generic space captures what is common across the input spaces; the syntax of the construction is represented purely for graphic reasons outside Input 1 and the Blend).

Importantly, in the blend it is as if the subject referent acted directly on the napkin (or, in the resultative example, the pan), see Fauconnier and Turner (2002: 178–179). We compress the diffuse event sequence into a scenario where an agent acts on object thus causing its displacement (or change of state in a resultative example).

## 5.2. Discussion

One of the major contributions of Blending Theory is to have successfully shown that the meaning of any complex expression is not the sum of the meanings of its parts. Its constitutive elements are better regarded as prompts for the construction of the overall meaning. More often than not, new structure emerges from the fusion of two (or more) elements which was not present in either.[7]

Further, it should be pointed out that the analysis of specific cases like the resultative and caused motion constructions provided by Blending Theory is superior to approaches like Goldberg's and Langacker's. Fauconnier and Turner's analysis implies that we should distinguish between two event levels when dealing with sentences like *I boiled the pan dry* and

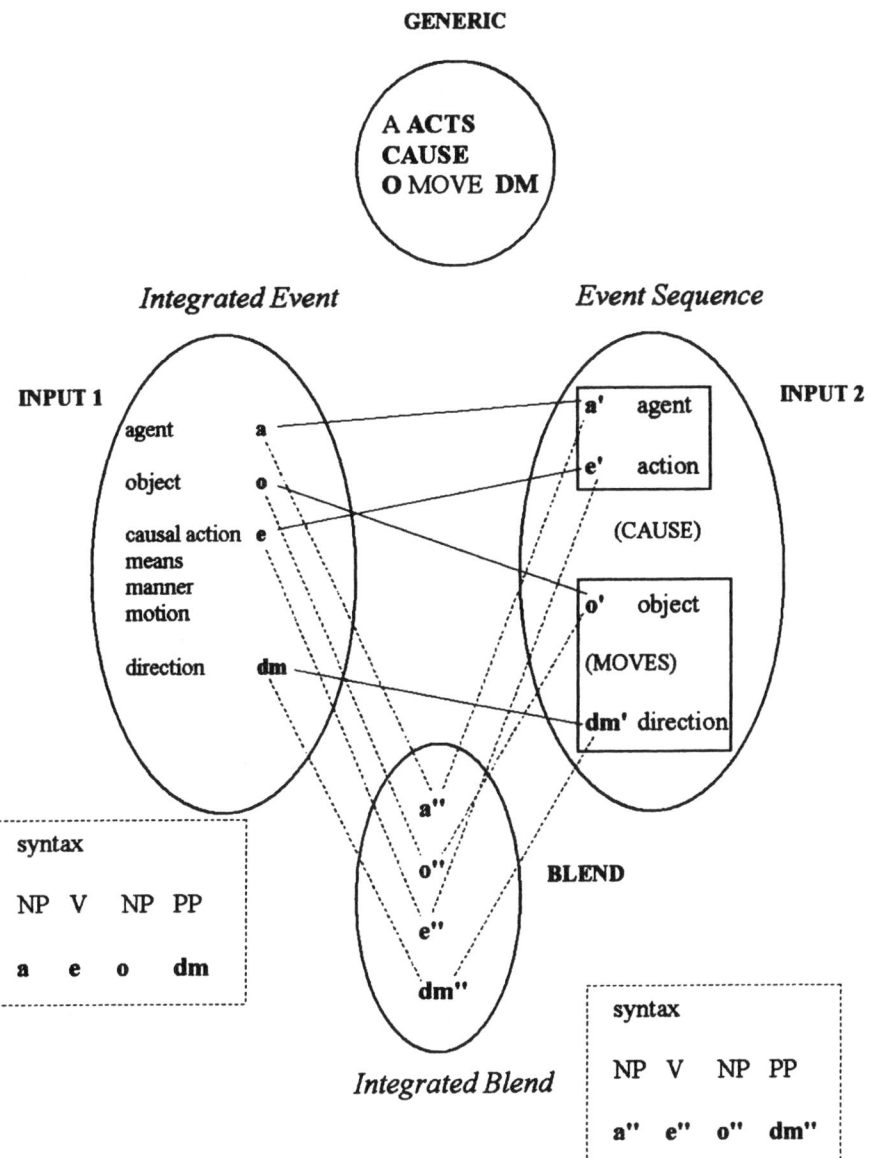

*Figure 6.* A blending analysis of *He sneezed the napkin off the table*

*He sneezed the napkin off the table.* The former sentence does not mean literally that I performed any action on the pan (I could have forgotten about the pan and let the water in it evaporate). However, in the blend we construe the real world event sequence in terms of the subject's acting on the pan itself. It is not simply a matter of the construction's imposing a causal interpretation on the specific verb being used (as Goldberg claims) or of categorizing the event referred to by the verb as a force-dynamic event (as Langacker claims, see also Broccias 2003). We also construe the whole unintegrated event sequence as a very compact event, where results are construed as obtaining immediately because some force-dynamic action is being carried out on a manipulable entity.

There is, however, a potential problem with Fauconnier and Turner's approach (see Broccias 2003: Ch.5 and Broccias 2004). It is not clear why the parts in the event sequence represented as input 2 in Figure 6 are not treated individually as input spaces which are blended into the force-dynamic scenario represented as an input in Figure 6. In fact, this alternative analysis would be consonant with the Blending Theory analysis of, for example, noun phrases such as *red ball*, where *red* and *ball* are viewed as belonging to two different input spaces. By the same token, the verbal event and the change event (i.e. the change of state or place of the affected entity) could be treated as two different inputs. The relation of causation existing between the two is compressed into a force-dynamic interaction in the blend (the reader is referred to Broccias 2003 for an analysis along these lines).

Be that as it may, Blending Theory is a powerful tool for the detailed description of the conceptual operations underlying the construction and interpretations of both simple and complex expressions. Nevertheless, a more detailed discussion of the limits and implementation of Blending Theory should be the focus of future research (see e.g. Ruiz de Mendoza Ibáñez's critique of the idea of emergent structure: Ruiz de Mendoza Ibáñez 1998, 2002, Ruiz de Mendoza Ibáñez and Peña Cervel 2005).

## 6. Conclusion

Although the present overview could not obviously do justice to its complex articulation, Langacker's theory is by far the most comprehensive theory of grammar available in the cognitive linguistic camp. To some extent, other cognitive models such as Goldberg's Construction Grammar, Radical Construction Grammar and Blending Theory (as applied to the investigation of linguistic structures) can be seen as notational variants of Cognitive Grammar. The similarities are numerous. They all share, among other things, the assumption that language must not be studied independently of general cognitive abilities. In fact, general cognitive abilities are taken to shape language. They also agree on the fact that language does not merely consist of a syntax plus a lexicon. Rather, language is viewed as a taxonomic hierarchy, where sharp distinctions should not be assumed; language is a "diffuse" network since much in language is a matter of degree. This means that linguistic units (or constructions) can be of any length and of any degree of complexity. Further, cognitive theories subscribe to the view that constructions are often ready-made pairings of form and meaning. We do not need to "generate" all their various parts every time we want to use them but they may be available to us automatically, as gestalts (i.e. we are often unaware of the contribution of their constitutive parts).

Still, important differences exist among the various theories. I have tried to point out that the nature of word classes and grammatical relations is still a matter of controversy. Similarly, the relation between constructional meaning and lexical meaning is still the topic of heated debate. Nevertheless, the theories briefly illustrated in this paper alongside Cognitive Grammar serve a very important purpose if they are all given due consideration (especially) when specific phenomena are studied. They highlight certain facets of grammar (in the Langackerian sense) that may not have been worked out fully in the Cognitive Grammar model. This is most evident in the case of change constructions.

Blending Theory reminds us that when we examine complex expressions we should distinguish between two conceptual levels, the unblended (or unintegrated) level and the blended (or integrated) level. The latter can convey new meaning (with respect to the input spaces, cf. Langacker's scaffolding metaphor mentioned in note 7), as is indeed the case with change constructions. An unintegrated, complex sequence of events is conceptualized as (or categorized by) a force-dynamic event. Thus, we construe the unintegrated causal sequence as implying instantaneous causation (cf. the discussion of *I boiled the pan dry* above).[8]

Goldberg's analysis brings two important points to the fore. We should investigate the relation between the meaning of a construction and the meanings of its parts, e.g. the verb's meaning in a change construction. In this respect, Langacker urges us to be cautious. The overlap between constructional and verbal meaning may be a matter of degree and, ultimately, we may add, the issue should be the object of psycholinguistic investigation. To be sure, in some cases, even if a verb is entrenched in a specific construction, this does not (at least intuitively) result in the verb's acquiring a new sense.[9] For example, if we consider the two constructions *I laughed him out of patience* and *I laughed him into patience*, we may find it intuitively odd to claim that *laugh* should be categorized as a verb of "removal" in the former case (since the object referent, metaphorically speaking, moved out of patience) and as a verb of "creation" in the latter case (since the object referent, metaphorically speaking, moved into a region of patience). Rather, we categorize *laugh* as a force-dynamic process by virtue of our knowledge that laughing can affect people surrounding us.

Goldberg's other important point is that constructions can be polysemous. This is indeed the case with change constructions. Consider the examples in (3).

(3)  a. She kissed the anxiety out of him.
     b. The fans booed the team off the pitch at the interval.
     c. The river froze solid.
     d. She lifted the parcel up.

In (3a), *kiss* receives a force-construal. It is categorized as a force (because we know that kissing engenders some emotional response) causing anxiety to be removed from someone. Hence, (3a) is a prototypical example of a change construction.[10] By contrast, (3b) shares its form with prototypical change constructions (cf. *He was booed off the podium*, which may have a causal interpretation) but only has a temporal interpretation, as the prepositional phrase at the end makes clear (see Broccias 2005b). The team would have abandoned the pitch even if the fans had not booed at them because it was half-time. The fans' booing simply unfolded as the team left the pitch. Hence, (3b) shares with prototypical change constructions only unity of time, not (immediate) causation. (Remember that, at the blended level, change constructions construe the causing event and the caused event as obtaining one immediately after the other even if this is not the case in the "real world".) (3c) can be analysed as a change construction (i.e. the river became solid because it froze) but also shows that certain change phrases (e.g. *solid*) may be better analysed as intensifiers. After all, if speakers understand *freeze* as "to become solid", to say that "the river became solid because it froze (i.e. became solid)" is a tautology. Hence, *solid* may be interpreted as meaning something akin to "completely", i.e. it intensifies the event denoted by the verb by specifying that the freezing affected all parts of the river. (3d) also illustrates redundancy of the change phrase (i.e. *up*) with respect to the verbal meaning. After all, *lift* already means to "move up". But *up* does not obviously have an intensifying function. Rather, it seems to be used to make the spatial component implicit in *lift* explicit (since *up* explicitly refers to a spatial configuration, or at least this is taken to be the schematic meaning of *up*).

Croft's approach is also of crucial importance. It stresses that grammar (hence constructions) should be studied using a bottom-up approach. In the specific case of change constructions, this means, for example, that it may be immaterial to try to distinguish sharply between caused motion constructions, on the one hand, and resultative constructions, on the other (hence the label "change construction" introduced by Broccias 2003). It may not be important to decide whether a construction like *He opened the window wide* is a caused motion construction (i.e. *wide* refers to a position) or a resultative construction (i.e. *wide* refers to a state). It may simply be an instantiation of either (cf. the idea of multiple inheritance, or multiple categorization, in section 3.2). Indeed, it is a fallacy to assume that binary-categorization is always possible in the first place (or even useful, for that matter).

Further, Croft's insistence on taxonomic hierarchies highlights the importance of specific (i.e. lexically-filled or lower-level) patterns for speakers. Nevertheless, I would like to add that the importance of higher-level schemas should not be discounted. They capture regularities across constructions (i.e. they allow us to orientate ourselves among specific linguistic instantiations) and are also important in language learning/acquisition (see also Tomasello 2003).

In sum, despite some (of course important) differences, the models illustrated in this overview shape a view of grammar that is largely unanimous. Grammar (in a broad sense) is best viewed as a structured inventory of conventional linguistic units. One of the next challenges for cognitive linguistics is to see how we can put this view into effect by relating it to the realm of applied linguistics.

## Notes

1. Taylor (2002) stresses that phonology is autonomous, i.e. it does not necessarily symbolize the semantic pole and it obeys constraints of its own. Despite this, phonological constraints are analysed as phonological schemas. Their nature, therefore, is in no way different from that of constraints pertaining to symbolic units: both are schemas abstracted away from specific instances.
2. The billiard-ball model captures our conceptualization of events in terms of

energetic interactions between two entities resulting in some change (of either state or location) of the affected entity, see Langacker (1991: 13).

3. The idea that the degree of overlap between verbal meaning and constructional meaning is a matter of degree is expanded on in Langacker (2005b). In this paper, he claims that "an element which regularly fills the verb position in a construction tends to develop a meaning congruent with that position".

4. Table 2 is not the complete map of English part of speech constructions (see Croft 2001: Fig.2.3, p.99). But it will suffice for our present purposes.

5. Such a view derives from the Aristotelian analysis of copular sentences like *Socrates is mortal* as involving the ascription of a quality (e.g. that of being mortal) to the subject referent. This analysis is then extended to non-copular sentences (e.g. *The children went to school*). But observe (see Table 2) that, paradoxically (with respect to the history of the notion of predication), non-copular sentences are not treated as the prototypical constructions coding the propositional act of predication in Croft's theory.

6. My understanding of Croft's analysis is that a clear-cut distinction between the three types of discourse functions and the three types of semantic classes is possible. Indeed, the distinction between predication and modification may seem intuitively straightforward. Consider, however, a sentence like *John lives poorly*: what is the function of *poorly* in this sentence? Is it predicating or modifying?

7. The view that the overall meaning of a construction is obtained by summing "arithmetically" the meanings of its constitutive parts is known as compositionality and is expressed by the *building-block metaphor* in Langacker's analysis. He dubs the view that constitutive parts are just prompts the *scaffolding metaphor*.

8. The reader should observe that the present formulation is meant to be noncommittal about the issue of whether the integrated sequence should be viewed as input 1 or just as a blend.

9. I am not suggesting that this is Langacker's position (cf. especially Langacker 2005b). Rather, I am making a more general point concerning the usefulness of Goldberg's view that a construction can impose a meaning (or construal) on a verb used in it (without the verb's acquiring this meaning).

10. Incidentally, (3a) also shows that the "subcategorized" object of the verb (i.e. *him*, cf. *She kissed him*) is not always inherited as an object in the construction (although it shows up in the construction as the object of the complex preposition *out of*). The constructional object *anxiety* is not a possible object for the verb in isolation (cf. *\*She kissed the anxiety*). This type of change construction is called an asymmetric construction by Broccias (2003).

## References

Broccias, Cristiano
2003 *The English Change Network. Forcing Changes into Schemas.* Berlin/ New York: Mouton de Gruyter.
2004 Review of Gilles Fauconnier and Mark Turner. 2002. *Cognitive Linguistics* 15(4): 575–588.
2005a Review of Günter Radden and Klaus-Uwe Panther (eds.) 2004. *Studies in Linguistic Motivation.* Berlin/New York: Mouton de Gruyter. In: LINGUIST List: Vol-16–872. Tue Mar 22 2005.
2005b Non-causal change constructions. In *Modelling Thought and Constructing Meaning: Cognitive Models in Interaction,* Annalisa Baicchi, Cristiano Broccias, Andrea Sansò (eds.), 76–88. Milano: FrancoAngeli.

Broccias, Cristiano, and Willem Hollmann
2005 Do we need summary and sequential scanning in (Cognitive) grammar? Ms., Università di Genova/Lancaster University.

Chen, Rong
2003 *Inversion. A Ground-before-Figure Construction.* Berlin/New York: Mouton de Gruyter.

Croft, William
2001 *Radical Construction Grammar. Syntactic Theory in Typological Perspective.* Oxford: Oxford University Press.

Croft, William, and D. Alan Cruse
2004 *Cognitive Linguistics* Cambridge: Cambridge University Press.

Duffley, Patrick J.
2005 The English gerund-participle in Cognitive Grammar. Paper presented at the 32rd LACUS Forum, Dartmouth College, Hanover.

Evans, Vyvyan, and Andrea Tyler
2004 Spatial experience, lexical structure and motivation: the case of *in.* In *Studies in Linguistic Motivation,* Günter Radden, and Klaus-Uwe Panther (eds.), 157–192. Berlin/New York: Mouton de Gruyter

Fauconnier, Gilles, and Mark Turner
1996 Blending as a central process of grammar. In *Conceptual Structure, Discourse and Language,* Adele Goldberg (ed.), 113–130. Stanford: Center for the Study of Language and Information.
2002 *The Way We Think. Conceptual Blending and the Mind's Hidden Complexities.* New York: Basic Books.

Fillmore, Charles
1988 The mechanisms of 'Construction Grammar'. *Berkeley Linguistics Society* 14: 35–55.

Fillmore, Charles, and Paul Kay
1996 Construction Grammar. Ms., University of California at Berkeley, Department of Linguistics.

Goldberg, Adele
1995 *Constructions. A Construction Grammar Approach to Argument Structure.* Chicago: University of Chicago Press.

Goldberg, Adele, and Devin Casenhiser
2006    English constructions. In *Handbook of English Linguistics*, Bas Aarts, and April McMahon (eds.), 343–355. Oxford: Blackwell Publishers.
Lambrecht, Knud
1994    *Information Structure and Sentence Form. A Theory of Topic, Focus, and the Mental Representations of Discourse Referents.* Cambridge: Cambridge University Press.
Langacker, Ronald
1987    *Foundations of Cognitive Grammar*, Volume 1, *Theoretical Prerequisites.* Stanford: Stanford University Press.
1990    *Concept, Image, and Symbol. The Cognitive Basis of Grammar.* Berlin/New York: Mouton de Gruyter.
1991    *Foundations of Cognitive Grammar*, Volume 2, *Descriptive Application.* Stanford: Stanford University Press.
1999    *Grammar and Conceptualization.* Berlin/New York: Mouton de Gruyter.
2005a    Construction grammars: Cognitive, radical, and less so. In *Cognitive Linguistics. Internal Dynamics and Interdisciplinary Interaction*, Francisco J. Ruiz de Mendoza Ibáñez, and M. Sandra Peña Cervel (eds.), 101–159. Berlin/New York: Mouton de Gruyter.
2005b    Constructions and constructional meaning. Plenary talk delivered at *New Directions in Cognitive Linguistics*, University of Brighton, 23–25 October 2005.
Matlock, Teenie
2004    Fictive motion as cognitive simulation. *Memory and Cognition* 32: 1389–1400.
Matlock, Teenie, Michael Ramscar, and Lera Boroditsky
2005    The experiential link between spatial and temporal language. *Cognitive Science* 29: 655–664.
Quirk, Randolph, Sidney Greenbaum, Geoffrey Leech, and Jan Svartvik
1995    *A Comprehensive Grammar of the English Language.* London: Longman.
Radford, Andrew
1997    *Syntactic Theory and the Structure of English. A Minimalist Approach.* Cambridge: Cambridge University Press.
Ruiz de Mendoza Ibáñez, Francisco J.
1998    On the nature of blending as a cognitive phenomenon. *Journal of Pragmatics* 30: 259–274.
2002    Construing meaning through conceptual mappings. In *Lengua y Sociedad: Investigaciones Recientes en la Lingüística Aplicada*, Pedro Antonio Fuertes (ed.), 19–38. Valladolid: Universidad de Valladolid.
Ruiz de Mendoza Ibáñez, Francisco J, and M. Sandra Peña Cervel
2005    Conceptual interaction, cognitive operations and projection spaces. In *Cognitive Linguistics. Internal Dynamics and Interdisciplinary Interaction*, Francisco J. Ruiz de Mendoza Ibáñez, and M. Sandra Peña Cervel (eds.), 249–279. Berlin/New York: Mouton de Gruyter.

Sandra, Dominiek, and Sally Rice
  1995   Network analyses of prepositional meaning: Mirroring whose mind –
         the linguist's or the language user's?. *Cognitive Linguistics* 6: 89–130.
Taylor, John R.
  2002   *Cognitive Grammar.* Oxford: Oxford University Press.
Tomasello, Michael
  2003   *Constructing a Language. A Usage-Based Theory of Language Acquisi-*
         *tion.* Harvard: Harvard University Press.
Ungerer, Friedrich, and Hans-Jörg Schmid
  1996   *An Introduction to Cognitive Linguistics.* London: Longman.

# Part two: The conceptual leap

# Three dogmas of embodiment: Cognitive linguistics as a cognitive science

## Tim Rohrer

*Abstract*

Cognitive Linguistics presently suffers from three dogmas. First, we all too often present embodiment as if it were an eliminativist project, requiring that linguists translate their findings into the language of neurons and brain structures and thereby diminishing the role of socio-cultural embodiment. Second, we consider embodiment as if it were something static or fixed, when in fact it is temporally dynamic in ontogenetic, historical and phylogenetic terms. Third, we often confuse embodiment with debates over consciousness. While it is perhaps true that many of Cognitive Linguistics' early findings were the result of phenomenological conscious introspection, the advent of explicitly cross-disciplinary empirical and experimental methods has begun to reshape the field. After tracing the history of the embodiment hypothesis from its origins in conceptual metaphors and related evidence, I propose a broad-based theoretic framework for integrating cross-disciplinary research. The challenges posed by disparate methodologies prompt a reconsideration of how the evidence for embodiment is "converging." I conclude with reflections on what Cognitive Linguistics must do to re-envision itself as one of the cognitive sciences, including identifying some key areas in which we do not yet have enough explicitly cross-methodological projects.

*Keywords*: embodiment; cognitive science; image schemas; eliminativism; development; consciousness

## 1. Introduction

No one would dispute that as academics we run the risk of becoming lost in our thoughts. One of the merits of a proper philosophical education is that we acquire a keen sense of when theorists become so engrossed with their own theories that they lose touch with the chaos of the real world. Or perhaps it is more accurate to note that such theorists do not lose touch with the real world in its entirety, but spend their days exploring the nooks and crannies of a metaphoric monastery built upon the craggy point of their original insight into the real world. Thus Spinoza the lens-grinder constructed a rationalist philosophy replete with optical metaphors for knowledge, metaphysics and ethics. Within linguistics and the philosophy of language, the metaphoric conception of language as a communicative conduit carrying meaning and ideas from speaker to listener (Reddy's (1979) CONDUIT metaphor) has spawned myriad theories divorcing meaning (conceptualized as semantic *content*) from grammar (where the 'underlying' logical and syntactic structure is conceptualized as the *conduit* carrying the semantic content). For example, Chomsky and his followers have constructed theories of nonsense from the insight that even well-formed syntactic constructions do not necessarily carry semantic content, as exemplified by his famous nonsensical sentence 'Colorless green ideas sleep furiously.' Alfred Korzybdski acerbically referred to this general phenomenon of theorists losing touch with the real world as "mistaking the map for the territory" (1948/1972: 34).

Cognitive linguists are not immune to this peril. Although elsewhere I have hailed the return of an awareness of how the body shapes thought and language as an antidote to habits of linguistic abstraction engendered by Chomskyian rationalism and first-generation cognitive science, I am now deeply concerned with what I will call *the three false dogmas of embodiment*. All three of them, as we shall see, rely on overly narrow and non-radical conceptions of embodiment. If we are not careful, the revolution engendered by Cognitive Linguistics is in danger of becoming institutionalized.

## 1.1   The three dogmas

***Embodiment as an eliminative reductionism.*** When I was a graduate student in philosophy, we passed around to each other what we considered a philosophical "howler" of a paper. The paper in question sought to analyze love in terms of symbolic logic. Its end result was a formula that the author proclaimed, without irony, constituted the meaning of the "love" relationship.

To reduce human love to symbolic logic may now seem an obvious absurdity, but I fear we are now running similar risks in Cognitive Linguistics. For example, we hear certain extreme formulations of, for example, Lakoff's Neural Theory of Language, in which it is has been proclaimed that "cognitive linguistics isn't cognitive linguistics if it ignores relevant structure about the brain" (Dodge and Lakoff 2005). In the section entitled "Coda" in that article, Dodge and Lakoff argue that as "linguistic structure reflects brain structure," the underlying brain structure causally "imposes" its image schemas, superpositions, and universal primitives onto language. The obvious implication that many more socio-culturally-minded cognitive linguists draw is that theories of language will be eliminated in favor of theories of how brain structure determines language. Just as the symbolic logicians sought to replace Shakespeare's love sonnets with logical formulae, so do some cognitive linguists run the risk of advocating translating polysemy, syntax and grammatical construals into talk of neural models, neural circuits, axonal firings and parietal-hippocampal networks.

Cognitive linguists are right to question this dogma on both philosophical and substantive grounds. However, oftentimes the reaction to this dogma is a counterproductive iconclasm, in which no shrift is given to evidence of how the brain shapes language. It is equally unpardonable to commit the opposite sin and eliminate our neurophysiological embodiment in favor of our sociocultural embodiment, though I know of no one proclaiming that "cognitive linguistics isn't cognitive linguistics if it ignores relevant facts about the sociocultural context." The right antidote to such extreme formulations is to realize that even brain structures are not isolated, static entities, but are embedded within a nervous system and body that interacts with both physical and sociocultural space. As the American pragmatist philosopher Dewey famously asserted, "to see the organism *in* nature, the nervous system in the organism, the brain in the nervous system, the cortex in the brain is the answer to the problems which haunt philosophy" (Dewey 1925: 198); or, and more appropriately for the present conversation, "haunt cognitive linguistics." In studying language and conceptual structure with the new tools of cognitive neuroscience, we do not necessarily have to engage in an eliminativist reductionism of language to the biophysical. From the perspective of American pragmatism, both the brain and the sociocultural situation have their roles in the interactions which shape language.

***Embodiment as temporally static.*** The second false dogma dovetails neatly with the first. For example, if we aim to offer some insights to linguistics from the study of brain structures, it would help if we understood how brain structures develop and change across time. A brain is fundamentally an organic entity; it grows, matures, changes, suffers injury and recovers, adapts in response to a changing environment; it evolves over generations. It is altogether too facile to take findings about brain structure in right-hand dominant adults and generalize them inappropriately. If we fail to attend to the limitations of the methods and the scope of current brain research, we risk reifying "brain structure" into a static causal force that determines language, rather shaping and motivating it. Brain structure is dynamic; and while it is certainly not infinitely malleable there are important differences between the adult brain and the developing brain, between the adult brain and the aging brain, between the injured brain and the uninjured brain, between brains of left- and right-hand dominant individuals, and so on and so forth. This organic dynamicity has real impact on cognition and language.

When we see the brain and organism in context, we realize that embodiment is not static. We are fundamentally live creatures who are *embodied-in-time*; unlike Athena, we do not spring full-grown from the head of Zeus. As newborns we know no language and have only the barest rudiments of what will eventually become the preconceptual basis for adult language. If in Cognitive Linguistics we hold that semantic structure is largely shaped by preconceptual structures such as image schemas, then we must inquire as to how these image schemas are formed on a developmental timeline and whether they might differ cross-linguistically, however slight a difference that might be. For example, Bowerman and Choi (2003) have shown that while nine-month old Korean- and English-speaking infants can make the same spatial discriminations, at eighteen months their acquisition of language has solidified their spatial categories enough so that they are no longer able to make the discriminations which their language does not. To me this suggests that the developmental course of image schemas is such that their neural instantiations in the brain 'hardens' both with age and exposure to the dominant language of the sociocultural environment. This hypothesis about the neural structure underlying image schemas is further warranted given the evident other differences between early and late language learning experiences in humans, and given what we know from animal research into how different spatial schemas cause different patterns of growth in juvenile versus adult brains.[1] Similarly, languages change across time; every individual speaker is situated within a specific sociocultural and historical context that influences how their metaphors are shaped (Geeraerts and Grondelaers 1995). Thus, there are multiple temporal forces at work, from phylogenetic change to historical language change to learning and other ontogenetic changes.

***Embodiment as consciousness (or as unconscious).*** Having skirted the shoals of an eliminativist Scylla, we must also avoid being engulfed by the Charybdis of consciousness. A standing temptation of academics is to assume that because we can describe and study some mental process, we are (or can be) ordinarily conscious of it. This is in fact not the case. For example, consider how we process sound waves into phonemes. We do not consciously attend to the peaks and valleys of the sound waves at different frequencies, but the fact that we do parse sound waves into phonemes implies that our brains do something very much like that in the auditory neural maps for pitch. However, conscious introspection is almost entirely useless when it comes to determining the sound shape of a phoneme at different frequencies; instead, scientists are forced to rely on sophisticated electronic measuring equipment. Such processes are certainly beneath the level of ordinary conscious awareness, and inaccessible to consciousness without the tools of science.

Nonetheless, Zlatev has recently argued that Lakoff and Johnson's notion of an embodied "Cognitive Unconscious" is seriously mistaken and "conceptually incoherent" (Zlatev in press). He rejects the existence of unconscious mental processes entirely, arguing that every mental process must at least be in principle accessible to conscious introspection. Following Searle (1992), he asserts that if we cannot be aware of a mental process then it is neurophysiological and not mental. However, note that this argument is merely definitional – it simply equates introspective consciousness with all mental processes, a philosophical move which is both trivial and unproductive.

There is more merit to other parts of Zlatev's argument that mental processes are in principle accessible to consciousness, such as those concerning learning and development. To return to the previous example, we are not ordinarily aware of the sound shape that distinguishes one phoneme from another. However when as adults we grapple with hearing a new phoneme while learning a new language, we do become much more conscious of subtle differences in the shape of its sound. We might also become aware that it is easier to learn it if we also try to speak it and associate its sound with the motor movements which produce it. Eventually we will automate this mental process well enough that we can listen and converse in the new language without having to attend to it. Moreover, at some point, as infants we likely had to "consciously" attend to learning each and every phoneme we now have automated – though the infant's "consciousness" indubitably has a very different quality to it than how we would typically construe as "consciousness" in the case of the adult cognition; i.e., as a discursive reflective introspection.[2]

While the philosophical arguments concerning "consciousness" are notoriously interminable, Zlatev is right that embodiment theory must explicate the relationships between at least some of its major theoretical constructs and, as I prefer to designate them, matters of awareness, attention, and feeling. The role of attention in language learning is one example, while another is that the image schemas that underlie conceptual metaphor mappings are construed by Johnson as affect-laden patterns of felt experience – that is, patterns of felt experience of which we can be consciously aware (Johnson 2005, 1987). If we break down the mysterious and ephemeral notion of "consciousness" into its constituent parts (as did the American Pragmatist William James (1900)), we can develop methods to assess when and how it is important to Cognitive Linguistics.

Given this discussion of learning to distinguish phonemes, it should now be clear how the dogmatic assertions about the importance of consciousness (or unconsciousness) to embodiment are intertwined with the dogma that embodiment is temporally static. In his critique, however, Zlatev also points out that banishing the discussion of the various forms of consciousness from Cognitive Linguistics is intertwined with the eliminativist dogma:

> Third, there is a dangerous tendency to underestimate the role of *consciousness* in many – though not all – embodiment theories. There seems to be some sort of fear that in appealing to anything that is irreducible to either biology or behavior, one is bound to fall into the clutches of "Cartesian dualism". The consequence is, however, that such "non-dualistic" approaches run the risk of one form or another of *physico-biological reductionism*, which as pointed out by Itkonen … is deeply misguided. (Zlatev in press: 2)

Obviously, these three dogmas are clearly interwoven. To counter them, we must cultivate a philosophical framework for embodiment that is methodologically pluralistic and dynamically attentive.

## 2.    A brief history of embodiment in Cognitive Linguistics

### 2.1    Origins of the embodiment hypothesis in observations about conceptual metaphors

To understand how these three dogmas of embodiment have emerged as a crisis in Cognitive Linguistics, it is helpful to examine the genealogy of embodiment theory within a single strand of Cognitive Linguistics. Here, I will trace its history in terms of conceptual metaphor theory within cognitive semantics; elsewhere, I have discussed its genealogy in terms of spatial and linguistic frames of reference (Rohrer in press, 2001a). For some time, the conceptual metaphor and embodiment hypotheses were nearly inextricable. Beginning in the late 1970s with a mass of empirical linguistic examples of metaphor, Lakoff and Johnson (1980) discovered that much of the ordinary language we use to characterize a wide variety of experiences is systematically shaped by a relatively small number of metaphors. Their work called into question the traditional distinction between the deeply conventionalized, 'dead' metaphors on one hand and the more creative, literary 'live' metaphors on the other hand. Amassing a large body of examples, they showed that linguistic expressions which were supposed to be 'dead' metaphors are in fact part of larger systematic metaphors which also have very noticeable 'live' metaphorical extensions. They argued that the 'live' metaphorical expressions are the inferential and creative extensions of an underlying metaphor, while the 'dead' metaphorical expressions comprise the core of the metaphor – so well understood that they are hardly noticeable to us as we listen to everyday speech. They dubbed this more systematic notion of metaphor 'conceptual metaphor', both in order to distinguish it from the prior tradition of 'linguistic metaphor' (or 'literary metaphor') and in order to emphasize that conceptual metaphors are a matter of cognition and conceptual structure.

Yet the systematicity of conceptual metaphors was neither their most important nor their most controversial finding. What was even more intriguing was their argument that most conceptual metaphors draw primarily on domains stemming from bodily experience, and that these bodily source domains do the vast majority of the work of structuring more abstract human concepts. In its earliest formulation, the embodiment hypothesis came from a generalization about the directionality of metaphorical projection. Conceptual metaphors tended to characterize the abstract in terms of the concrete:

> First, we have suggested that there is *directionality* in metaphor, that is, we understand one concept in terms of another. Specifically, we tend to structure the less concrete and inherently vaguer concepts (like those for emotions) in terms of more concrete concepts, which are more clearly delineated in our experience. (Lakoff and Johnson 1980: 112)

Lakoff and Johnson (1980: 117–119) identified three sources for these more concrete concepts. They argued these more concrete concepts constitute the 'natural kinds of experience' and are comprised of 'experiential gestalts' more basic than other concepts because they are the natural products of our bodies, our interactions with the physical environment, and our interactions with other people in our culture. Reserving judgment for future research, they also indicated that while some of these natural kinds of experience might be universal, others might very well vary from culture to culture. They explicitly pointed out that they were using the terms 'nature' and 'natural' in a sense which at least encompassed the possibility of cultural variation, and not in the sense of a rigid 'nature–culture' distinction. Lakoff and Johnson concluded this section by arguing that these more concrete concepts can be used in the 'metaphorical definition' of more complex concepts. In short, they argued that these three natural kinds of experience – experience of the body, of the physical environment, *and* of the culture – are what constitute the basic source domains upon which metaphors draw.

## 2.2   Elaborations and extensions of the embodiment hypothesis

Over the ensuing twenty years, the notions of experientialism, embodiment, and a directionality to conceptual metaphor received much scrutiny, generated much controversy, and consequently received much elaboration. More systematic surveys undertaken during the mid-1980s at Berkeley and elsewhere showed that bodily source domains were prevalent not only for the semantics of English, but also for languages as distant from it as Japanese and Mixtec. However, it is equally important to note that the languages *did* vary cross-culturally as to which *particular* bodily source domains were used to understand a given target domain, and with respect to how these patterns were represented linguistically. With respect to historical semantic change, Sweetser (1990) has argued that the direction of such change is motivated by the embodiment hypothesis. For instance, she documented a directionality within Indo-European languages for metaphors such as KNOWING IS SEEING, arguing that the terms which came to be the ordinary ones for abstractions such as knowing were at an earlier time restricted to embodied perceptual capabilities, such as seeing, grasping, hearing, smelling, tasting, and feeling. In a now standard example, she traces the transition of the Indo-European root *\*weid* 'see' through the Greek *eidon* 'to see' and, in its perfective form *oida* 'sight, know', to the English terms *idea*, *wit*, and *witness*, which retain none of their visual sensibility to most native English speakers (Sweetser 1990: 23–48). By observing how a wide range of embodied perceptual terms systematically lose their perceptual connotations as they acquire their intellectual meaning, she proposed that there exists a large-scale temporal constraint on the directionality of semantic change.

In the preface to *The Body in the Mind,* Johnson (1987: xii–xiii) presented six converging bodies of evidence for the embodiment hypothesis understood as a directional constraint on meaning. This list included not only cross-cultural research on metaphor and historical semantic change but also work on prototypes in categorization, the framing of concepts, polysemy, and inferential patterns in metaphor. Near the same time, other research in Cognitive Linguistics (such as Langacker's (1987) Cognitive Grammar) contributed to an increasing focus on the role of the body in shaping linguistic and conceptual structure generally, and not just within a thread of semantic theory. In work that also appeared that same year, Lakoff (1987) characterized the experientialism (or experiential realism) at the core of the embodiment hypothesis as including

> everything that goes to make up the actual or potential experiences of either individual organisms or communities of organisms – not merely perception, motor movement, etc., but especially the internal genetically acquired makeup of the organism and the nature of its interactions in both its physical and social environments. (Lakoff 1987: xv)

Experiential realism, as Lakoff defined it, was to be in direct contrast with the traditional philosophical conception of meaningful thought and reason as the manipulation of symbols that correspond to an objective reality that is independent of the particular kind of embodiment of the organism. By 1987, the embodiment hypothesis had explicitly grown to become much more ambitious in scope than in its more humble origins as a generalization about the directionality of metaphors. Physiology, temporal development, and organism–environment interactions as well as linguistic evidence were explicitly expected to play a role in an increasingly broad theoretical hypothesis which purported to explain an ever larger amount of linguistic phenomena.

## 2.3 Embodiment and image schemas

The enlarging scope of the embodiment hypothesis led to criticisms that its central tenets were underspecified. For example, the idea of embodied 'experiential gestalts' needed further elaboration.[3] Building on work done at Berkeley by Talmy (1985: 293–337, 2000) on the role of force-dynamic patterns in shaping syntactic constructions, Johnson developed a theory of *image schemas.* He defined an image schema as a recurrent pattern, shape or regularity in, or of, our actions, perceptions, and conceptions.

He argued that "these patterns emerge primarily as meaningful structures for us chiefly at the level of our bodily movements through space, our manipulation of objects, and our perceptual interactions" (Johnson 1987: 29). For example, the CONTAINMENT schema structures our regular recurring experiences of putting objects into and taking them out of a bounded area. We can experience this pattern in the tactile modality with physical containers, or we can experience this pattern visually as we track the movement of some object into or out of some bounded area or container. It is particularly important to see that an image schema can also be experienced cross-modally, as when we use the visual modality to guide our tactile and kinesthetic experience when we reach into a container and grasp an object.

Johnson argued that these patterns can then be metaphorically extended to structure nonphysical, nontactile, and nonvisual experiences. In a particularly striking set of examples, he traced many habitual notions of containment we might experience during the course of a typical morning routine: we wake up *out of* a deep sleep, drag ourselves *up out of* bed and *into* the bathroom, where we look *into* the mirror and pull a comb *out from inside* the cabinet. Later that same morning we might wander *into* the kitchen, sit *in* a chair at the breakfast table, and *open up* the newspaper and become lost *in* an article. Some of these experiences are spatial and physical but do not involve the prototypical CONTAINMENT image schema (as in the example of sitting *in* a chair) while some of these experiences draw on purely metaphorical extensions of CONTAINMENT (as in the example of getting lost *in* the newspaper article).

Such image schemas are *preconceptual* embodied structures of meaning in at least two important ways. First, image schemas are developmentally prior to conceptual thinking. Johnson drew on work by the developmental psychiatrist Daniel Stern (1985) and the developmental psychologist Andrew Meltzoff (summarized in Meltzoff 1993). Stern argued that the activation, buildup, and release of emotional intensity is among the earliest and most foundational of our preconceptual experiences:

> For instance, in trying to soothe the infant the parent could say, "There, there, there ...," giving more stress and amplitude on the first part of the word and trailing off towards the end of the word. Alternatively, the parent could silently stroke the baby's back or head with a stroke analogous to the "There, there" sequence, applying more pressure at the onset of the stroke and lightening or trailing it off toward the end ... the infant would experience similar activation contours no matter which soothing technique was performed. (Stern 1985: 58)

As infants we experience these patterns of feeling (image schemas) before we develop a linguistic self, and these image schemas are not unique to any one perceptual modality but have a structure which is shared across them.

Second, Johnson argued that image schemas are preconceptual in that they can underpin the mappings of multiple conceptual metaphors. We can extend – by means of metaphor – these directly emergent experiences to characterize nonspatial experiences, such as falling *into* a depression or getting lost *in* the newspaper (STATES OF MIND ARE PLACES) or being *in* a meeting (TIME IS SPACE). Further, we can project the inference patterns of the CONTAINMENT schema into the metaphorically structured domain. For example, just as we reason that the deeper an object is in a container the harder it will be to get it out, we reason that the deeper someone is in a depression the harder it will be to get them out of their depression. It is important to note that image schemas serve as the preconceptual basis for metaphors in both a developmental and a structural sense. The embodiment hypothesis is thus not only a hypothesis about how image schemas and conceptual metaphors structure adult cognition, but about the ontogenetic acquisition of metaphorical structure as humans develop from infants to adults. Embodiment is not temporally static.

Though calling patterns which are supposed to be cross-modal 'images' may seem to be a little misleading, Johnson fortuitously chose the term 'image schemas' in accordance with burgeoning research in the cognitive sciences on the role of images in our embodied mental conceptualization. In the early 1970s, the psychologists Shepard and Metzler (1971) asked experimental subjects to determine whether a pair of two-dimensional pictures of three-dimensional objects were identical. They discovered that subjects rotated these objects mentally at a fixed speed of approximately 60 degrees each second, suggesting that humans manipulated the images as a whole. That finding was extremely controversial, as the then prevalent view of the mind as a symbol manipulation system favored theories of mind and brain in which perceptual images were decomposed into image-independent propositional representations, much as they would have been represented in the computers of that time (Kosslyn 1980, 1994).

Shepard and Metzler's (1971) original work on visual imagery was one of the key factors that led to a revolution in the cognitive sciences in which the mind and brain are now increasingly understood to be organized in terms of image-like wholes. This revolution has been most dramatically borne out by convergent evidence from cognitive neuroscience (Kosslyn 1994; Kosslyn et al. 1995). In particular, researchers using neuroimaging and neuroanatomical techniques have been able to isolate regions of the cortex which maintain topologically consistent images of (for example) the visual field as perceived, top-down visual imagery, and spatial (i.e., nonvisual, tactile, or kinesthetic) imagery. As the Shepard and Metzler results suggest, humans have topologically mapped neural circuitry for both the visualization and the visual perception of spatial form. Similarly, starting in the 1930s, the neurosurgeon Wilder Penfield and colleagues had shown that the somatosensory and motor regions of the human cerebral cortex topologically map the body's tactile and kinesthetic experience. Such image-like maps are considered to be topological because they preserve the contours of perceptual experience, albeit not in a perfect topography.

Similar topological maps of perceptual experience have been found for the other sensory modalities, such as pitch maps for auditory experience. We now know that these topological maps are refined into more selective maps which respond to higher-order and more selective kinds of contour patterns. Though recent work on grasping schemas in humans and monkeys is promising (Gallese and Lakoff 2005), the current state of cognitive neuroscience stops short of specifying neural maps embodying the exact sets of perceptual contour patterns Johnson identifies as image schemas. This is especially true when image schemas are considered as perceptuolinguistic structures, though several recent experiments comparing linguistic and perceptual stimuli have shown promise (Hauk et al. 2004; Rohrer 2001b). At present, the possible neurophysiological instantiation of image schemas remains an intriguing area for future research (Rohrer 2005). Yet the embodiment hypothesis' proposal of image schemas is still both highly consistent with the known facts about neurophysiology, particularly the ways in which the visual system and other perceptual modalities map perceptual experience, and highly consistent with the kinds of structures we observe in linguistic conceptualizations.

## 2.4    Recent formulations of the embodiment hypothesis

In their recent collaboration in *Philosophy in the Flesh*, Lakoff and Johnson have turned much of their attention away from investigating the socio-cultural dimension of embodiment and toward investigating how the physical and neural substrates of the body shapes language and mind, although they would certainly argue for the importance of continued research on the cultural and social dimensions.[4] Lakoff and Johnson currently formulate the embodiment hypothesis:

The embodied-mind hypothesis therefore radically undercuts the *perception/ conception* distinction. In an embodied mind, it is conceivable that the same neural system engaged in *per*ception (or in bodily movement) plays a central role in *con*ception. That is, it is possible that the very mechanisms responsible for perception, movements, and object manipulation could be responsible for conceptualization and reasoning. (Lakoff and Johnson 1999: 37–38)

In this version of the embodiment hypothesis is that the *same* neural mechanisms which are responsible for 'lower-level' activities like perception and movement are taken to be *essential* to 'higher-level' cognitive abilities, namely to our reasoning and conceptualization. Thus, on their view Lakoff and Johnson argue "that the very properties of concepts *are created* as a result of the way the brain and body are structured and the way they function in interpersonal relations and in the physical world" (1999: 37). The way these properties are created is by means of conceptual metaphors which project cross-domain image-schematic patterns, which in turn are drawn from the more specific structures within visual perception, locomotion, object manipulation, and so on.

In their view, most of the evidence they have gathered earlier is at the 'top levels' of investigation – studies on categorization, metaphorical structuring, historical semantic change, gesture and so on. They argue that what remains to be done is the project of establishing the *specific* neural and physiological bases of image schematic conceptualization. In *Philosophy in the Flesh,* however, they directed their attention primarily to the neurocomputational modeling of language rather than its neurophysiological bases. For example, Regier (1992, 1996) has investigated how spatial relations terms such as *up, down, above,* etc. can be learned by structured connectionist networks that utilize low-level schematizations which have plausible neural analogues in the neuroanatomy of visual perception. Together with related research (Bailey 1997; Narayanan 1997) that approach to the neurocomputational modeling of language eventually came to be known as the Neural Theory of Language (Lakoff and Johnson 1999: 569–583; Feldman and Narayanan 2004).

Another important, if underspecified, facet of the embodiment hypothesis appears *Philosophy in the Flesh* as a new theory of "primary metaphor" (Lakoff and Johnson 1999: 45–59). Primary metaphors are posited as resulting from repeated sensorimotor "primary scenes" in a child's early experience. They are acquired first as conflated linguistic wholes and only later differentiated into source and target domains (Grady and C. Johnson 2002).[5] In older children and adults, primary metaphors are supposedly combined into complex conceptual metaphors via conceptual blending (Grady 2005a, 1997). While the attempt to integrate developmental issues is laudable, there are a number of unresolved questions in the theories of primary metaphor and conflation, including the uncertain and complex relationship between image schemas and primary metaphors – two theoretical constructs that are both supposedly preconceptual and underlie conceptual metaphor mappings (see Grady 2005b: 45–50.). In contrast to the developmental evidence work on image schemas (see summaries in Rohrer 2005: 174–175, Mandler 2005), there is also a dearth of experimental support for both the experiential conflation followed by the emergence of primary metaphors hypothesis and for the notion of primary metaphors as atomic units of meaning that combine into complex conceptual metaphor. Future studies, however, may remedy such deficiencies.

## 2.5  Philosophical foundations of the embodiment hypothesis

In this brief history of the embodiment hypothesis, I have traced the evolution of the embodiment hypothesis from a hypothesis about the grounding of conceptual metaphors to one which has grown increasingly large in scope throughout its dialogue with other branches of cognitive science. This increase in scope has led to the present crisis as to what exactly 'embodiment' means within Cognitive Linguistics.

What we have lacked is a coherent framework which can tie these differing senses of the term together. While Lakoff and Johnson (1999: 112–113) offered a three-tiered proposal with cognitive, neurocomputational, and neurobiological levels of investigation, the usefulness of that proposal is limited by its tight focus on their particular research program, the Neural Theory of Language. Similarly, their broader discussion of the "levels of embodiment" (102–117) is hamstrung by the problematic notion of mental phenomena that are "completely and irrevocably inaccessible" to consciousness with respect to the level they label the "Cognitive Unconscious;" moreover, that failing also cripples their ensuing rejection of eliminativist dogmas in favor of methodological pluralism. In the following section, I argue for adapting a more sophisticated and widely used theoretical framework from the cognitive sciences as an aid in clarifying the full range of current research of Cognitive Linguistics.

## 3. A theoretical framework for doing Cognitive Linguistics as a cognitive science

The first challenge for developing a theoretical framework in which we can address such differing approaches is to propose the adoption of a simple and well-understood organizing criterion. Unfortunately, most previous proposals have generally accorded an ontological status, rather than an epistemological or methodological status, to the organization of their theoretic framework. Most such frameworks postulate "higher" and "lower" levels of cognition in ways which imply that the higher levels may be reduced to operations at the lower levels, ultimately arguing for the elimination of higher-levels of description in favor of lower levels of description (Churchland 1981, 1989). One exception is Posner and Raichle's (1994) schematization of the levels of investigation in cognitive neuroscience, in which the primary emphasis is given to the methodologies used to investigate the phenomena rather than their ontological status. Similarly, Edelman (1992) points out that in the physical sciences, phenomena are operationally grouped in levels according to the physical scale of the methodology that is being used to study the phenomena. Thus the most basic organizing criterion of this theoretic framework is the scale of the relative physical sizes at which we can measure the embodied phenomena which produce the different kinds of socio-cultural, cognitive or neural events to be studied.

In Table 1, physical size is mapped on the y-axis, providing a relative distribution of the "higher to lower" methodological levels of cognitive processes. A general name for each level is indicated by boldface type in the first column. To provide clarification, the next column provides examples of what the relevant physiological structures are at a given physical scale. For example, at the communicative, cultural and social level we study spatial language as it is used between people, and hence the relevant physiological structures are multiple central nervous systems; alternatively, it is possible to measure one individual's (and hence one central nervous system's) performance on a similar set of linguistic tasks. Similarly we can examine, with even more granularity, relative changes in cerebral blood flow to regions of the brain in response to spatial linguistic tasks; or we can construct neurocomputational models of those brain regions. However, Posner and Raichle's key insight is that it is important to consider how the basic inquiry change changes given the different tasks and methods at various levels of investigation. All methodologies have constraints and freedoms which limit or enhance their scope of investigation and define the theoretical constructs that they develop, and these are a product of the physical scale at which the measurement is taking place. The final two columns acknowledge this by specifying some of the relevant theoretic constructs and the various methodologies operative at each level of investigation.

This framework can be used to situate the wide methodological array of studies on various topics of interest to cognitive linguists, such as metaphor, mental imagery, categorization, frames of reference, emotions, and so on. This type of theoretical framework is now fairly common within much of cognitive science, but Cognitive Linguistics has been slow to give explicit attention to the problem of how we are to theoretically situate and reconcile these different levels of investigation (see Table 1 below).

I have included just a single level of cultural and communicative analysis, but by no means should this be taken as indicative of its importance relative to the other levels. Of course, one could argue for a multiplicity of levels embedded within this one, though they might not be clearly differentiated from one another in terms of physical scale. In choosing to include a general level situated at a meter and up on the physical size axis I mean to emphasize only that human beings should be considered not simply in terms of physiological size, but also in terms of the standard scale of their interactional distance in speaking and interacting with one another. At this level of the framework the "physiological structures" column reads "Multiple Central Nervous Systems", but that awkward term is intentionally inadequate so as to emphasize that the physiology is less relevant here – what primarily matters on this level are the social and cultural interactions *between* human beings. Investigations at the cultural level are occasionally given short shrift by some versions of embodied cognitive science, but generally this has been and should remain a strong thrust of future research in Cognitive Linguistics.

Note also that difficult phenomena such as cultural and linguistic norms, or individual consciousness and awareness, are situated at the physical scale at which they are measured and observed, rather than attempting to place them on (or reduce them to) a lower level of investigation. Nonetheless, it is certainly possible and sometimes useful to ask, for example, how long the neural auditory processing of a phonemic slip takes before impacting conscious speech, or how the linguistic norm of forming the English past tense might be performed in a neurocomputational model. However, research in embodied cognitive science should not seek to reduce such phenomena to another level but should instead bridge across these levels in important ways – for example, the linguistic corpora

*Table 1.* Theoretical framework for the embodiment hypothesis in cognitive science as applied to Cognitive Linguistics

| Size (in m) | Physiological Structures | Level of Investigation | Typical Cognitive Linguistics Theory Explanatory Tasks | Sample Operative Theoretical Constructs | Sample Methods of Study |
|---|---|---|---|---|---|
| 1 and up | Multiple central nervous systems | **Communicative and cultural systems** in anthropology, language, science, and philosophy | Uses of widespread cultural metaphors in interpersonal communication; syntactic and semantic change | Complex conceptual metaphor, conceptual blends, disanalogy, subjectification | Linguistic analysis, cross-linguistic typology, discourse analysis, cognitive anthropology |
| .5 to 2 | Central nervous systems | **Performance domain;** Cognitive, conceptual, gestural, and linguistic systems as performed by individual subjects | Understanding metaphors, extending metaphorical inferences to novel cases, facilitation of related information; use of slang; testing choice of syntactic form given extra-linguistic semantic task | Complex conceptual metaphor, conceptual blends, disanalogy, primary metaphor, metaphor mappings, inference generalizations | Verbal report, observational neurology, and psychiatry, cognitive and developmental studies examining reaction time (RT) |
| $10^{-1}$ to $10^{-2}$ | Gross to medium size neural regions (anterior cingulate, parietal lobe, etc.) | **Neural systems** | Activation course in somatosensory, auditory, and visual processing areas when processing conceptual metaphor or multimodal perceptual experiences | Conceptual metaphor mappings, primary metaphor, conceptual blends, disanalogy, image schemas, topological maps | Lesion analysis, neurological dissociations, neuroimaging with fMRI and PET, ERP methods, neurocomputational simulations |
| $10^{-2}$ to $10^{-4}$ | Neural networks, maps and pathways | **Neuroanatomy;** Neural circuitry in maps, pathways, sheets | Neuroanatomical connections from visual, auditory, somatosensory regions to language areas | Image schemas, primary metaphor, topographic maps, convergence zones | Electrocellular recording, anatomical dyes, neurocomputational simulations |
| $10^{-3}$ to $10^{-6}$ | Neurons, cortical columns | **Neurocellular systems;** Cellular and very small intercellular structures | Fine neuroanatomical organisation of particular structures recruited in lang. processing | Orientation-tuning cells; ocular dominance columns | Electrocellular recording, anatomical dyes, neurocomputational simulations |
| Less than $10^{-6}$ | Neuro-transmitters, ion channels, synapses | **Subcellular systems;** Subcellular, molecular and electrophysical | None – beyond theoretical scope | Neurotransmitter, synapse, ion channels | Neuro-pharmacology, neurochemistry, neurophysics |

used to train the neurocomputational model should be based on naturalistic recordings of an actual child's utterances rather than text harvested from internet newsgroups, and so on.

While the table depicting the theoretic framework is designed to give an overview of the relationship between body, brain and culture, this representation is not as illustrative for issues pertaining to evolutionary, developmental and historical time scales, which may be considered at any of these levels. However, this failing is more a limitation of the imagery of a two-dimensional table than of the theoretic framework itself. If we were to add another axis for time perpendicular to the surface plane of the chart, we could imagine this framework as a rectangular solid (Figure 1). Embodiment is not temporally static, and when we strip away the veneer – a finely detailed veneer, to be sure – of synchronic studies, we see that those results are the result of processes of learning and development, and of history and evolution.

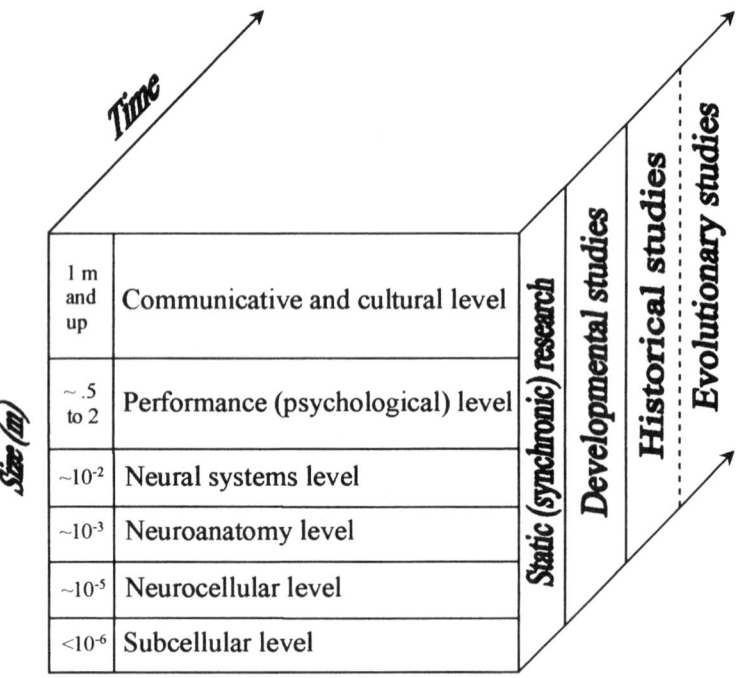

*Figure 1.* The theoretical framework for embodiment considered through time

## 4. Collaborative conclusions: How to exorcise the three dogmas

There can be no doubt that most of the ordinary research tools of Cognitive Linguistics are at the communicative and cultural level of analysis, the level whose undeniable phenomenological components perhaps most lends itself to two standard critiques. First, there is a methodological question about how one is to go about doing the analysis, for example, as to how one knows when a conceptual metaphor is correctly mapped; second, there are legitimate questions as to how empirical such methods are. While the objection that such analyses are not empirical at all can be at least partially rebutted by the argument that the sentences or phrases were empirically gathered from naturalistic contexts, even beginning to answer the first objection is not so easy. The problem is that an appeal as to what counts as a grammatically well-formed sentence, a plausible construal in cognitive grammar, or a correct conceptual metaphor mapping seems to be little more than an introspective gut-check by the practitioners themselves. Of course, one might respond that there is a body of previous work to which a new analysis must either conform, make fine small distinctions from, or challenge and then reorganize satisfactorily. For instance, conceptual metaphors, whether gathered ad hoc (as in Lakoff and Johnson 1980) or systematically gathered from a defined corpus (as in Rohrer 1995), are supposed to yield relatively stable conceptual mappings. However, both in my experience teaching conceptual metaphor analysis in seminars to both advanced students and scholars from other disciplines, and in a careful reading of the conceptual metaphor literature, there appears a wide variety as to how the source and target domains of the same of a conceptual metaphor are named, or as to the exact counterparts or order to the conceptual mappings of the metaphor. In its strongest form, this objection is that such methods are not just non-algebraic, but almost entirely ad-hoc.[6]

Within Cognitive Linguistics I see my colleagues make three types of responses to these metatheoretical critiques. The first is to ignore such criticisms and continue to do the work, using the methodologies as they are, perhaps continually refining them according to the community aesthetic[7] of what counts as a methodological innovation, or perhaps improving them incrementally importing methods from the related social sciences such as inter-coder reliability ratings for corpus analysis, and so forth. A second approach is to confront these questions using a philosophical defense of the importance of sociocultural factors or the irreducibility of consciousness to the methods of Cognitive Linguistics. For example, Zlatev's arguments (in press) have the following philosophical shape: first, language is intrinsically a social behavior for communicating; second, language is intentional, in the sense that every word is a communicative act consciously intended by the speaker to share or convey some experience with (or to) the hearer; third, language must be a triadic communicative system, which is to say that the meanings of its 'signs' are consciously conventional across speakers in a population of $n >= 3$ speakers; ergo, all judgments (by either laypeople or linguists) about whether a sentence is grammatical, or whether the grammar cognitively fits the situation, or whether the term has been used in an appropriate semantic context are intrinsically a conscious act. Other theorists have staked out similar philosophical positions, arguing that it is primarily sociocultural factors of language acquisition that shape spatial relation schemas (for example, Bowerman and Choi 2003; Sinha and Jensen de Lopez 2000), or arguing that the historical context determines metaphor mappings (Geerarts and Grondelaers 1995).

The third response, which I would take to be the standard response of Cognitive Linguistics, is to cite and discuss "converging" bodies of evidence for embodiment from the other cognitive sciences. It is easy to see how such evidence could be "converging" under an eliminativist rubric, because Cognitive Linguistics and the other cognitive sciences would then "converge" on an underlying neurophysiological reality. But methodological pluralism implies that these methodologies are independent and that there is no guarantee that their results can be integrated. If we are not converging on the same ontologically real "material," as eliminative materialism would have it, then "what" are we converging upon? The answer, I think, is a guiding idea or vision: embodiment. Our convergence is more on a set of theoretical assumptions and methodological biases than any findings.

Recent years have witnessed numerous attempts (Hutchins 1995; Lakoff and Johnson 1999; Gibbs 1994; Clark 1998; Fauconnier and Turner 2002) to retell the history of cognitive science so that that an embodied vision of cognitive science can both incorporate past labors and findings and shape new research questions that might bridge the past with the future. While attempts at such grand unifications are laudable, the persuasiveness of the case for convergence likely depends on whether and how accurately the authors have described the evidence gathered outside their own traditions, and whether the conceptual leaps across these traditions are kept suitably small. If not, we are still faced with the possibility that the "convergence" of the evidence will be construed as a myth and the evidence will "turn out to be very heterogeneous" (Zlatev in press: 19), creating unbridgeable conceptual chasms between rival theoretic monasteries.

Yet there is still more that cognitive linguists can do. It is now, more than ever, particularly important for cognitive linguists to reach out to the other cognitive sciences. If we set out to design collaborative research projects that are deliberately cross-methodological, we will no longer be forced to rely on evidence gathered from disparate traditions. We have already begun to see movements in this direction. For example, within psychology, Matlock, Ramscar and Boroditsky have investigated whether spatial metaphors for time alter our inferences about time (2005). Matlock and Richardson (2004) have investigated whether fictive-motion language induces eye-movements. Amorim, Isableu and Jarraya (in press) have shown that adding a cylindrical "head" to the standard Shepard-Metzler cubes used in mental rotation/mental imagery experiments produces both visual and motoric embodiment effects. Within cognitive neuroscience, Coulson and van Petten (2002) have investigated the neural processing of conceptual blends using event-related potentials (ERPs), while Rohrer (2001b) has investigated whether the sensorimotor cortex responds to both literal and metaphoric body-part sentences using both ERPs and functional magnetic resonance imaging (fMRI). But more explicitly cross-methodological efforts are needed, particularly for testing within experimental developmental psychology (see for ideas Mandler 2005) and in primatological studies of sign language use (see for ideas Tomasello, Savage-Rumbaugh and Kruger 1993 and Fouts, Jensvold and Fouts 2002). Only when Cognitive Linguistics takes its hypotheses to the other cognitive sciences and develops collaborative, cross-methodological studies will cognitive linguistics become not just a listening but a speaking member of the family of cognitive sciences.

## Notes

1.  I have in mind several series of studies, but in particular the Knudsen and colleagues studies of juvenile and adult barn owls, some of whom who wore prismatic glasses that distort the visual field in the xy-plane (e.g. 23 degrees to the right) results in an bifurcated neural growth pattern in the cross-modal map of the ICX in their brains. (Knudsen 2002, 1998). To make the connection between this and language more explicit: Just as the juvenile owls who wore glasses in their youth become bi-'visual', so do the bilingual speakers who are

exposed to more than one language from birth are more likely to become more adroit speakers of those languages than those who start off monolingual and acquire a second or third language later in life. It seems likely, then that the many different neural structures underlying second language acquisition also 'grow differently,' particularly when we are talking about distinguishing the subtle sorts of spatial relations differences that underlie using the spatial relations terms perfectly in a second language. For further discussion, see Johnson and Rohrer (in press) and Rohrer (2005).

2.  Infants have what appears to be a near-innate ability to distinguish between the full range of human phonemes on a perceptual basis, but between months 10–12 lose that raw perceptual ability (Bohn 2000: 6–10). Instead, they automate and "zoom in on those contrasts which are functionally relevant (i.e. phonemically distinctive)" in their own peculiar linguistic environment (Kristiansen 2003: 85). Such infant evidence is not only an example of how the categorization of phonemes in the infant mind emerges from the perceptual categorization processes available in the infant brain, but also demonstrates that the infant's mental categorization of phonemes is *neither a result of nor is accessible to the processes of conscious introspection* that Zlatev takes as essential for language. (I wish to thank Gitte Kristiansen and René Dirven for their help in elucidating this point.)

3.  Another source of inspiration that Johnson acknowledges for the idea of image schemas came from the German school of 'gestalt perception.' Many of the notions of pattern completion in visual imagery, of the felt sense of aesthetic organization, as well as pattern completions in auditory imagery and music that contributed to their 'cross-modal' character, were inspired by observations expressed in (for example) Wertheimer (1923).

4.  For example Johnson and Rohrer (in press) discuss the social and cultural dimensions of embodiment in detail, arguing that they are continuous with the physical and neural substrates. Virtually all such attempts to place embodied cognition within an evolutionary context begin with the physical and neural and trace their way up to the social and cultural. This habitual mode of presentation is perhaps a continuing source of the mistaken dogma that embodiment leads to eliminativism.

5.  The conflation hypothesis was arrived at by Christopher Johnson analyzing language acquisition in a well-known corpus of a single child, Shem (Johnson 1997, 1999). Single subject data, while empirical, is of questionable value standing alone. The conflation hypothesis is also at odds with many known facts of the initial development of neural structures; however, it is possible that at a later stage of cognitive development children might find it difficult to differentiate image schematic features which are well-integrated in the underlying cross-modal maps. If found, such evidence would certainly lend credence to Zlatev's (in press, 2005) hypothesis that language socialization is required for image-schematic thought.

6.  In this sense, research in computational modeling such as that of Veale (this vol.) can serve as a useful methodological precision check.

7. By "community aesthetic" I mean the constellation of commitments of the scientific community as it is described by Thomas Kuhn in his 1969 postscript to *The Structure of Scientific Revolutions* (Kuhn 1970).

# References

Amorim, Michel-Ange, Brice Isableu, and Mohammed Jarraya
in press   Embodied spatial transformations: "Body analogy" for the mental rotation. *Journal of Experimental Psychology: General.*
Bailey, David
   1997   When push comes to shove: A computational model of the role of motor control in the acquisition of action verbs. Ph.D. diss., University of California at Berkeley.
Bohn, Ocke-Schwen
   2000   Linguistic relativity in speech perception. An overview of the influence of language experience on the perception of speech sounds from infancy to adulthood. In *Evidence for Linguistic Relativity*, Susanne Niemeier, and René Dirven (eds.), 1–12. Amsterdam: Benjamins.
Bowerman, Melissa, and Soonja Choi
   2003   Space under construction: Language-specific spatial categorization in first language acquisition. In *Language and Mind,* Dedre Gentner, and Susan Goldin-Meadow (eds.), 387–427. Cambridge, Mass.: The MIT Press.
Churchland, Paul
   1981   Eliminative materialism and the propositional attitudes. *Journal of Philosophy* 78: 67–90.
   1989   *A Neurocomputational Perspective: The Nature of Mind and the Structure of Science.* Cambridge, Mass.: The MIT Press.
Clark, Andrew
   1998   *Being There: Putting Brain, Body, and World Together Again.* Cambridge, Mass.: The MIT Press.
Coulson, Seana, and Cynthia Van Petten
   2002   Conceptual integration and metaphor: An event-related potential study. *Memory & Cognition* 30 (6): 958–968.
Dewey, John
   1925   *Experience and Nature.* In *John Dewey, The Later Works, 1925–1953,* vol. 1, Jo Ann Boydston (ed.). Carbondale: Southern Illinois University Press, 1981.
Dodge, Ellen, and George Lakoff
   2005   Image schemas: From linguistic analysis to neural grounding. In *From Perception to Meaning: Image Schemas in Cognitive Linguistics*, Beate Hampe (ed.), 57–91. (Cognitive Linguistics Research 29.) Berlin/New York: Mouton de Gruyter.

Edelman, Gerald M.
1992    *Bright Air, Brilliant Fire: On the Matter of Mind.* New York: Basic
         Books.
Fauconnier, Gilles, and Mark Turner
2002    *The Way We Think: Conceptual Blending and the Mind's Hidden Com-
         plexities.* New York: Basic Books.
Feldman, Jerome, and Srini Narayanan
2004    Embodied meaning in a neural theory of language. *Brain and Language*
         89 (2): 385–392.
Fouts, Roger S., Mary Lee A. Jensvold, and Deborah H. Fouts
2002    Chimpanzee signing: Darwinian realities and Cartesian delusions. In
         *The Cognitive Animal: Empirical and Theoretical Perspectives in Animal
         Cognition*, Bekoff, Marc, Colin Allen, and Gordon M. Burghardt
         (eds.), 285–291. Cambridge, Mass.: The MIT Press.
Gallese, Vittorio, and George Lakoff
2005    The brain's concepts: the role of the sensory-motor system in concep-
         tual knowledge. *Cognitive Neuropsychology* 22: 455–479.
Geeraerts, Dirk, and Stefan Grondelaers
1995    Looking back at anger: Cultural traditions and looking back at anger:
         Cultural traditions and metaphorical patterns. In *Language and the
         Cognitive Construal of the World*, John R.Taylor, and Robert E. Ma-
         cLaury (eds.), 153–179. (Trends in Linguistics Studies and Mono-
         graphs 82.) Berlin/New York: Mouton de Gruyter.
Gibbs, Raymond W.
1994    *The Poetics of Mind: Figurative Thought, Language, and Understanding.*
         Cambridge: Cambridge University Press.
Grady, Joseph E.
1997    THEORIES ARE BUILDINGS revisited. *Cognitive Linguistics* 8:
         267–290.
2005a   Primary metaphors as inputs to conceptual integration. *Journal of
         Pragmatics* 37 (10): 1595–1614.
2005b   Image schemas and perception: Refining a definition. In *From Percep-
         tion to Meaning: Image Schemas in Cognitive Linguistics*, Beate Hampe
         (ed.), 35–55. (Cognitive Linguistics Research 29.) Berlin/New York:
         Mouton de Gruyter.
Grady, Joseph E., and Christopher Johnson
2002    Converging evidence for the notions of 'subscene' and 'primary scene'.
         In *Metaphor and Metonymy in Comparison and Contrast*, René Dirven,
         and Ralf Pörings (eds.), 533–554. Berlin/New York: Mouton de
         Gruyter.
Hauk, Olaf, Ingrid Johnsrude, and Friedemann Pulvermüller
2004    Somatotopic representation of action words in human motor and pre-
         motor cortex. *Neuron* 41: 301–730.
Hutchins, Edwin
1995    *Cognition in the Wild.* Cambridge, Mass.: The MIT Press.

James, William
1900    *Psychology (*American Science Series, Briefer Course). New York: Henry Holt and Company.
Johnson, Christopher R.
1997    The acquisition of the "What's X doing Y" construction. In *Proceedings of the 21st Boston University Conference on Language Development 2*, Somerville, Mass.: Cascadia Press.
1999    Metaphor vs. conflation in the acquisition of polysemy: The case of 'see'. In *Cultural, Psychological and Typological Issues in Cognitive Linguistics. Selected Papers of the Bi-annual ICLA Meeting in Albuquerque, July 1995*, Masako K. Hiraga, Chris Sinha, and Sherman Wilcox (eds.), 155–169. (Current Issues in Linguistic Theory 152.) Amsterdam/Philadelphia: Benjamins.
Johnson, Mark
1987    *The Body in the Mind: The Bodily Basis of Meaning, Imagination, and Reason.* Chicago: University of Chicago Press.
2005    The philosophical significance of image schemas. In *From Perception to Meaning: Image Schemas in Cognitive Linguistics*, Beate Hampe (ed.), 15–34. (Cognitive Linguistics Research 29.) Berlin/New York: Mouton de Gruyter.
Johnson, Mark, and Tim Rohrer
In press.    We are live creatures: Embodiment, American pragmatism, and the cognitive organism. In *Body, Language, and Mind. Vol. 1: Embodiment*, Tom Ziemke, Roslyn Frank, and René Dirven (eds.). Berlin/New York: Mouton de Gruyter.
Knudsen, Eric I.
2002    Instructed learning in the auditory localization pathway of the barn owl. *Nature* 417 (6886): 322–328.
1998    Capacity for plasticity in the adult owl auditory system expanded by juvenile experience. *Science* 279 (5356): 1531–1533.
Korzybdski, Alfred
1948    On structure. In *Selections from Science and Sanity* (1972 ed 7th edition). Lakeville, Illinois: International Non-Aristotlean Publishing.
Kosslyn, Steven
1980    *Image and Mind.* Cambridge, Mass.: Harvard University Press.
1994    *Image and Brain: The Resolution of the Imagery Debate.* Cambridge, Mass.: The MIT Press.
Kosslyn, Stephen, William L. Thompson, Irene J. Kim, and Nathaniel M. Alpert
1995    Topographic representations of mental images in primary visual cortex. *Nature* 378: 496–498.
Kristiansen, Gitte
2003    How to do things with allophones. Linguistic stereotypes as cognitive reference points in social cognition. In *Cognitive Models in Language and Thought. Ideology, Metaphors and Meaning*, René Dirven, Roslyn Frank, and Martin Pütz (eds.), 69–120. (Cognitive Linguistics Research 24.) Berlin/New York: Mouton de Gruyter.

Kuhn, Thomas
1970    *The Structure of Scientific Revolutions*, 2nd edition, enlarged. Chicago: University of Chicago Press.
Lakoff, George
1987    *Women, Fire and Dangerous Things: What Categories Reveal about the Mind.* Chicago: University of Chicago Press.
Lakoff, George, and Mark Johnson
1980    *Metaphors We Live by.* Chicago: University of Chicago Press.
1999    *Philosophy in the Flesh: The Embodied Mind and its Challenges to Western Thought.* Chicago: University of Chicago Press.
Langacker, Ronald W.
1987    *Foundations of Cognitive Grammar. Vol. 1.: Theoretical Prerequisites.* Stanford: Stanford University Press.
1991    *Foundations of Cognitive Grammar. Vol. 2: Descriptive Application.* Stanford: Stanford University Press.
Mandler, Jean
2005    How to build a baby: III. Image schemas and the transition to verbal thought. In *From Perception to Meaning: Image Schemas in Cognitive Linguistics*, Beate Hampe (ed.), 137–164. (Cognitive Linguistics Research 29.) Berlin/New York: Mouton de Gruyter.
Matlock, Teenie, Michael Ramscar, and Lera Boroditsky
2005    The experiential link between spatial and temporal language. *Cognitive Science* 29: 655–664.
Matlock, Teenie, and Daniel Richardson
2004    Do eye movements go with fictive motion? In *Proceedings of the 26th Annual Conference of the Cognitive Science Society*, Kenneth Forbus, Dedre Gentner, and Terry Regier (eds.), Mawhaw, N.J.: Lawrence Erlbaum
Meltzoff, Andrew
1993    Molyneux's babies: Cross-modal perception, imitation and the mind of the preverbal infant. In *Spatial Representation: Problems in Philosophy and Psychology*, Naomi Eilan, Rosaleen McCarthy, and Bil Brewer (eds.), 219–235. Oxford: Blackwell.
Narayanan, Srini
1997    KARMA: Knowledge-based active representations for Metaphor and aspect. MS thesis, University of California at Berkeley.
Posner, Michael I., and Marcus E. Raichle
1997    *Image of Mind.* New York: W. H. Freeman; Scientific American
Reddy, Michael J.
1993    The conduit metaphor: A case of frame conflict in our language about language. In *Metaphor and Thought*, Andrew Ortony (ed.). Cambridge: Cambridge University Press.
Regier, Terry
1992    The acquisition of lexical semantics for spatial terms: A connectionist model of perceptual categorization. Ph.D. dissertation. University of California at Berkeley.

1996      *The Human Semantic Potential: Spatial Language and Constrained Connectionism.* Cambridge, Mass.: The MIT Press.

Rohrer, Tim
1995      The metaphorical logic of (political) rape: The new wor(l)d order. *Metaphor and Symbolic Activity* 10 (2): 115–137.
2001a     Pragmatism, ideology and embodiment: William James and the philosophical foundations of cognitive linguistics. In *Language and Ideology. Volume 1: Theoretical Cognitive Approaches*, René Dirven, Bruce Hawkins, and Esra Sandikcioglu (eds.), 49–81. (Current Issues in Linguistic Theory 204.) Amsterdam/Philadelphia: Benjamins.
2001b     Understanding through the body: fMRI and of ERP studies of metaphoric and literal language. Ms., Paper presented at the 7th International Cognitive Linguistics Association Conference, July 2001.
2005      Image schemata in the brain. In *From Perception to Meaning: Image Schemas in Cognitive Linguistics*, Beate Hampe (ed.), 165–196. (Cognitive Linguistics Research 29.) Berlin/New York: Mouton de Gruyter.
in press. The body in space: Embodiment, experientialism and linguistic conceptualization. In *Body, Language and Mind*, vol. II, Roslyn Frank, Enrique Bernárdez, René Dirven and Tom Ziemke (eds.). Cognitive Linguistics Research. Berlin/New York: Mouton de Gruyter.

Searle, John
1992      *The Rediscovery of the Mind.* Cambridge, Mass.: The MIT Press.

Shepard, Roger N., and Jacqueline Metzler
1971      Mental rotation of three-dimensional objects. *Science* 171: 701–703.

Sinha, Chris, and Kristine Jensen de López
2000      Language, culture, and the embodiment of spatial cognition. *Cognitive Linguistics* 11: 17–41.

Stern, Daniel
1985      *The Interpersonal World of the Infant.* New York: Basic Books.

Sweetser, Eve E.
1990      *From Etymology to Pragmatics: Metaphorical and Cultural Aspects of Semantic Structure.* Cambridge: Cambridge University Press.

Talmy, Leonard
1985      Force dynamics in language and thought. In *Papers from the Twenty-first Regional Meeting of the Chicago Linguistic Society (2): Possession in Causatives and Agentivity*, William H. Eikfont, Paul D. Kroeber, and Karen L. Peterson (eds.). Chicago: Chicago Linguistic Society.
2000a     *Toward a Cognitive Semantics, Vol. I: Concept Structuring Systems.* Cambridge, Mass.: The MIT Press.
2000b     *Toward a Cognitive Semantics, Vol. II: Typology and Process in Concept Structuring.* Cambridge, Mass.: The MIT Press.

Tomasello, Michael, Sue Savage-Rumbaugh, and Ann C. Kruger
1993      Imitative learning of actions on objects by children, chimpanzees, and enculturated chimpanzees. *Child Development* 64 (6): 1688–1705.

Wertheimer, Max
  1923    Untersuchungen zur Lehre von der Gestalt II. *Psycologische Forschung* 4: 301–350. (Translation published in *A Source Book of Gestalt Psychology*, Ellis, W. (ed.) (1938), 71–88). London: Routledge & Kegan Paul).
Zlatev, Jordan
  1997    *Situated Embodiment: Studies in the Emergence of Spatial Meaning.* Stockholm: Gotab Press.
  2003    Polysemy or Generality? Mu. In *Cognitive Approaches to Lexical Semantics*, Hubert Cuyckens, René Dirven, and John Taylor (eds.), 447–494. Berlin/New York: Mouton de Gruyter.
  2005    What's a schema? Bodily mimesis and the grounding of language. In *From Perception to Meaning: Image Schemas in Cognitive Linguistics*, Beate Hampe (ed.), 313–342. (Cognitive Linguistics Research 29.) Berlin/New York: Mouton de Gruyter.
  in press.    Embodiment, language, mimesis In *Body, Language and Mind, vol. 2.* Tom Ziemke, Roslyn Frank, René Dirven (eds.). Berlin/New York: Mouton de Gruyter.

# Metonymy as a usage event [1]

*Klaus-Uwe Panther*

*Abstract*
In this chapter a view of metonymy as an indexical relation between source and target meaning is presented and contrasted with metaphor, which is regarded as a specific kind of iconic relation. It is shown that notions such as 'domain', 'subdomain', 'single domain', and 'separate domains', which have often been used as definitional criteria for distinguishing metonymy from metaphor, are unreliable because they are cover terms for heterogeneous concepts and conceptual relations. Furthermore, it is argued that metonymy is a kind of meaning elaboration whose result is a conceptually prominent target meaning, an integrated whole that contains the backgrounded source meaning and novel meaning components resulting from the process of elaboration. Finally, the role of context in the interpretation of metonymy in usage events is explored in two case studies. A detailed analysis of two contextualized metonymically used expressions, suggests that one important function of metonymy is to provide generic prompts. These serve as inputs for additional pragmatic inferences that flesh out the specifics of the intended utterance meaning.

*Keywords:* conceptual prominence, domain, generic prompt, iconic relation, indexical relation, meaning elaboration, pragmatic inference

## 1. Introduction

The last two decades have seen a remarkable renewed interest in figures of speech, in particular, metaphor and metonymy. The interpretation of metaphor and metonymy has been a major concern in psycholinguistics, pragmatics, and, of course, cognitive linguistics (see Gibbs 1994). In cognitive linguistics the focus of analysis has shifted from the stylistic and embellishing function of metaphor and metonymy in discourse to their role in human thinking and reasoning, and their impact on language structure and language use. The study of language use is of common interest to both pragmatics and cognitive linguistics. In the latter, the analysis of *usage events*, i.e. "actual utterances in their full phonetic detail and contextual understanding" (Langacker 2000: 2), has, in recent years, moved from a mere declaration of intention to a number of full-blown studies based on large corpora (for an overview see Geeraerts 2005). This chapter does not present a corpus-based quantitative analysis of the function of metonymy in usage events, but carries out an in-depth conceptual and pragmatic analysis of a few illustrative examples that involve metonymic reasoning. My aim is to show that metonymic meanings provide generic *prompts* that are fleshed out on the basis of background knowledge (world knowledge), the situation of the utterance and the linguistic context (co-text) in which the metonymic expression occurs. My analysis proceeds from the local, i.e. intra-clausal context, in which the metonymic expression occurs, to the larger discourse and the extralinguistic context.

The method of analysis pursued in this chapter is thus complementary to that of large-scale corpus studies. There are some obvious drawbacks to my methodology – one being that any kind of generalization is highly risky. However, large-scale corpus-based studies also have their disadvantages: the higher the quantity of data to be covered by the analyst, the greater the danger that their conceptual and pragmatic analysis will be somewhat shallow and that important features of the data will be overlooked.

More specifically, the chapter is organized as follows. In section 2, I present my own view of metonymy as a figure of thought and language, and identify some typical properties of metonymy. I share a substantial set of assumptions with other researchers, but I also see some problems with the current use of key notions such as 'domain', 'subdomain', 'single domain', and 'separate domains', which figure prominently as criteria for distinguishing metaphor from metonymy. Rather than defining metaphor and metonymy in terms of the notions 'separate domains' and 'single domain', respectively – which need further clarification – I propose that the difference between metaphor and metonymy resides in the type of semiotic relation between their respective source and target. I contend that metaphor is an *iconic* relation and metonymy an *indexical* relation. This semiotic approach, in the spirit of C. S. Peirce, and more recently Masako Hiraga (1998, 2005) has the advantage that some properties of metonymy follow quite naturally from the premise that it is an indexical relation. I also argue that metonymy is a type of meaning *elaboration*, a term that comes close to, but is not identical with, what Francisco Ruiz de Mendoza calls 'domain expansion' (see e.g. Ruiz de Mendoza Ibáñez and Otal Campo 2002, Ruiz de Mendoza Ibáñez and Peña 2005). Section 2 also addresses some criticism that has been aimed against the approach to metonymy advocated by the present author and Linda L. Thornburg (Haser 2005).

Section 3 presents an in-depth analysis of two metonymies in written discourse. One is an instance of the well-known metonymic principle PLACE FOR EVENT AT PLACE, which provides a prompt that is further elaborated in the discourse context and/or through background knowledge. The second example involves a much richer metonymic (and also metaphoric) structure whose specific meaning is also fleshed out by the discourse context. Section 4 summarizes the results and discusses some questions for further research.

## 2.   Some properties of metonymy

### 2.1. Prototypical metonymy

In this section I argue for a notion of metonymy that is wider than the one usually taken for granted in classical rhetoric. A typical traditional definition of metonymy is found e.g. in the *Oxford English Dictionary* (OED), where it is described as a "figure of speech which consists in substituting for the name of a thing the name of an attribute of it or of something closely related". According to this characterization, metonymy is the result of a substitution of one linguistic sign for another linguistic sign. In addition, at least if one takes the term *thing* literally, the authors of the OED entry seem to imply that metonymy typically, or even exclusively, applies to referential expressions, i.e. noun phrases or proper names referring to "thing-like" entities such as objects, persons, etc. An example from the OED dating back to 1625 is given in (1):

(1)   1625 Gill Sacr. Philos. ii. 156 *Shebet signifies either a staffe, a truncheon, or Scepter, and so by a metonymia it may signifie authority.*

Although SCEPTER FOR AUTHORITY is indeed a universally agreed upon example of metonymy, there is a general consensus among cognitive linguists that metonymy is a much broader conceptual phenomenon than assumed in classical rhetoric (see especially the contributions in Barcelona 2000; Dirven and Pörings 2002). This broader conception of metonymy can be traced backed to at least Roman Jakobson (2002: 42–43), who developed his approach to metaphor and metonymy in the 1950s. Jakobson distinguishes between relations of similarity and relations of contiguity, which manifest themselves in the two dimensions of *meaning* and (syntactic) *position,* respectively. Words that occur in similar positions exemplify what is known as the *paradigmatic* axis of language, whereas words occurring contiguously in a syntactic arrangement exemplify the *syntagmatic* axis. As to similarity and contiguity of meaning, Jakobson reports a psychological test in which children were asked to provide spontaneous verbal responses to the stimulus word *hut*. Some subjects showed a predilection for words that were either similar or opposite in meaning such as *cabin, hovel* (synonyms), *den, burrow* (called metaphors by Jakobson), *palace* (antonym). Other subjects preferred semantically contiguous concepts, as exemplified in words like *thatch, litter*, and *poverty*. According to Jakobson, the former subjects, whose responses were based on similarity (and contrast) manifested a *metaphoric* mode of thinking whereas the latter, whose thinking relied on semantic contiguity, a *metonymic* mode of reasoning.

At first sight, Jakobson's view seems to be at odds with both the rhetorical tradition and cognitive linguistic theories of metonymy. Jakobson relates metonymy to the syntagmatic axis of language, but in cognitive accounts of metonymy it is quite common to regard metonymy as an operation of substitution, i.e. a paradigmatic relation, a view that is reflected in the notation x FOR y, which is commonly used for notating metonymies. However, on closer inspection, Jakobson's conception of metonymy is compatible with the substitution view. The crucial distinction involved here is that between positional similarity/contiguity and semantic similarity/contiguity. In Jakobsonian terms, one could say that metonymy involves *semantic contiguity*, which manifests itself as *positional similarity*. A simple referential metonymy such as *Mary is not in the phone book* substitutes 'Mary's name' (the metonymic target) for the metonymic vehicle *Mary*. The metonymic operation occurs in a specific syntactic position in the sentence and is therefore paradigmatic, but the relation between the metonymic source and its target is one of semantic contiguity.

In principle, Jakobson's conception of metonymy is not restricted to referential metonymy and it is thus quite compatible with cognitive linguistic views of metonymy. However, at least as far as his examples of semantic contiguity are concerned, Jakobson's approach to metonymy is far too unconstrained. Consider e.g. the words that were associatively elicited in the experiment mentioned above from the stimulus word *hut: thatch, litter*, and *poverty*. None of these words seems to be able to be *used* metonymically for 'hut':

(2)    *\*The old man lived in a little thatch/litter/poverty.* (for 'hut')

As pointed out above, the present author views metonymy not only as a referential shift phenomenon, but assumes that metonymic operations are active also on the levels of predication and illocution (see e.g. Panther 2005). In line with other cognitive approaches, especially Radden and Kö-vecses (2006), I regard metonymy as a cognitive operation through which one concept (the source) provides access to another concept (the target). Furthermore, I assume that the target meaning resulting from a meto-nymic shift is an *elaboration* of the source meaning. The metonymic shift can be regarded as a substitution operation, but one in which the source meaning does not vanish but remains part of the conceptual structure of the target meaning.[2] What I regard to be the typical metonymic relation is diagrammed in Figure 1, which is explained in more detail below.

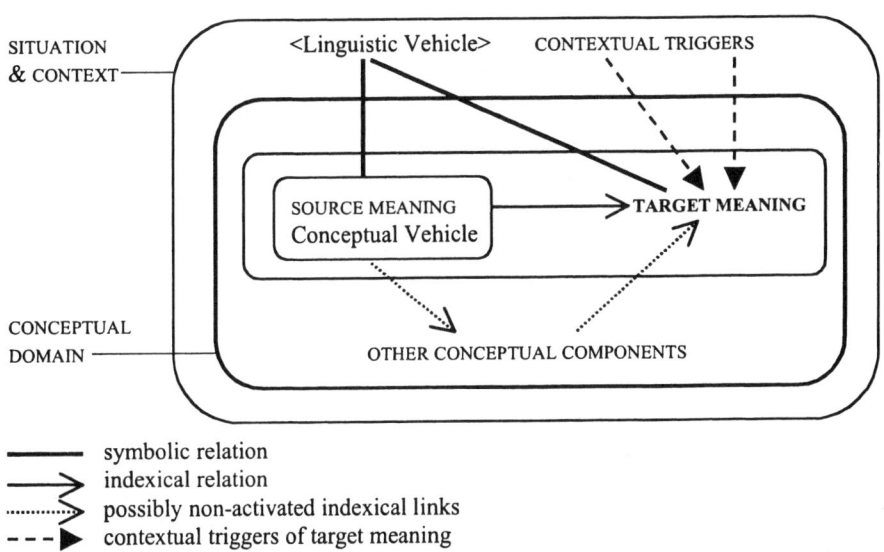

symbolic relation
indexical relation
possibly non-activated indexical links
contextual triggers of target meaning

*Figure 1.* The basic metonymic relation

An adequate analysis of metonymy in usage events must take into account that metonymies are embedded in a larger situational and linguistic con-text.[3] In Figure 1, context (both situational and textual) is indicated by the most inclusive thin-lined rectangle. Discontinuous arrow lines are used to represent the influence of contextual factors on the interpretation of metonymies. Note also the possible influence of 'other conceptual com-ponents', e.g. encyclopedic knowledge, on the interpretation of meto-nymy. That context and encyclopedic background knowledge must play a role in the interpretation of an expression as metonymic is evident from examples like the following:

(3)    *Paul Auster is on the second floor.*

Suppose that Mary is in the New York Public Library and overhears a conversation in which (3) is uttered. Obviously, there are various factors that have an influence on whether Mary interprets (3) metonymically or non-metonymically. First, there is the context of the utterance. If Mary hears a library user ask the person at the circulation desk *Where are Paul Auster's novels?* and the answer is (3), then it is obvious that *Paul Auster* is to be interpreted metonymically as 'Paul Auster's books'. Second, there is the factor of encyclopedic knowledge. If Mary overhears utterance (3) in isolation and does not know who Paul Auster is, she might simply interpret the utterance as stating something about a man called 'Paul Auster'. If however she has a richer knowledge frame about Paul Auster as a novelist, script writer, essayist, etc., i.e., if there are "additional conceptual components" that Mary can activate (see Figure 1), a metonymic interpretation of *Paul Auster* is likely, but – even then – not necessarily enforced. Given that Mary is in a library, and again on the basis of her knowledge about Paul Auster and public libraries, she might infer that Paul Auster, the person, is giving a reading of his latest novel on the second floor. The analysis of utterance (3) thus demonstrates that metonymy interpretation may involve an intricate interplay of contextual factors (including the linguistic context, the situational context, and the world knowledge of the language user).

Returning to Figure 1, the thick-lined rectangle immediately contained within the thin-lined rectangle represents the conceptual domain or frame within which the metonymic operation takes place. For reasons to be clarified below I leave open the question here whether this frame constitutes a "single" domain or whether it contains other domains. In cognitive linguistics, metonymy is often characterized as an operation that occurs within a single domain – in contrast to metaphor, which supposedly involves cross-domain mappings (see e.g. Croft 2002; Ruiz de Mendoza Ibáñez and Otal Campo 2002). Since the difficulties in establishing a set of operational criteria for identifying a "single" domain – in contrast to "separate" domains – are considerable (see section 2.2), I prefer – at least, for the time being – a *semiotic* definition of metonymy, relying on Charles S. Peirce's well-known trichotomy of signs, i.e. symbols, icons, and indices. I assume that conceptual metonymy, and by extension linguistic metonymy, involves an *indexical* relationship. In a linguistic metonymy, a linguistic form, which I call *linguistic vehicle,* denotes a *source meaning.* The relation between linguistic vehicle and source meaning is in general symbolic (indicated by a thick line in Figure 1), i.e. there is no "natural" connection between the form (linguistic vehicle) and its (literal) content. The source meaning, in turn, functions as a *conceptual vehicle* (alternatively, a 'thought vehicle') that provides cognitive access to the *target meaning.*[4] The conceptual vehicle is thus a signifier that *indexically* evokes its signified, i.e. target meaning.[5] The link between source meaning and target meaning can thus be thought of as a semiotic relation, viz. an indexical relation. In the framework adopted here, indexicality is a 'pointing-to' relation between one concept and another concept.[6] In other words, different from the usually *arbitrary* (symbolic) relation between linguistic vehicle and source meaning, the relation between source meaning and target meaning is *motivated.*[7] In Figure 1 the indexical relation between the conceptual vehicle and the target meaning is indicated by an open-headed arrow. As already pointed out above, Figure 1 also encapsulates the idea that the identification of the metonymic target meaning may be dependent on other conceptual components in the conceptual domain. Their potential contribution to the identification of the target meaning is symbolized by dotted-lined arrows. It should be borne in mind that the target conceptually *integrates* the source meaning, allocating it a *backgrounded* status.

Another important property of metonymy graphically represented by means of bold type in Figure 1 is the *conceptual prominence* of the target. In other theories, e.g. Croft (2002), this corresponds roughly to what he calls 'domain highlighting', i.e., an originally backgrounded subdomain within a domain becomes foregrounded through the metonymic operation.[8] The property of conceptual prominence holds for *prototypical* cases of metonymy. Some cases that, in the literature on metonymy, are cited as typical examples of metonymy are consequently classified as more peripheral in my approach:

(4)  *Bush invaded Iraq.*

Sentence (4) is usually regarded as a typical example of referential metonymy of the type CONTROLLER FOR CONTROLLED (cf. Lakoff and Johnson 1980: 38). However, it is clearly a source-prominent metonymy: the target, i.e. troops, air force, etc. that were actively involved in the invasion of Iraq remain indeterminate and backgrounded (see Panther 2005: 371–274 for detailed discussion).

The conception of metonymy presented here is, in some respects, differ-ent from the theories of metonymy developed by researchers such as Antonio Barcelona, William Croft, Francisco Ruiz de Mendoza, Günter Radden and Zoltán Kövecses. It is also, at least partially, at odds with La-koff and Johnson's (1999) approach to metaphor and metonymy (see es-pecially section 2.4 below). To list two differences very briefly:

i. In other theories, metonymy is regarded as linking one subdomain to another subdomain within the same domain (e.g. Barcelona 2002; Croft 2002); as a mapping from a subdomain to its containing matrix domain, or vice versa (e.g. Ruiz de Mendoza Ibáñez and Otal Campo 2002); or as a mapping from part to whole, whole to part, or part to part (Radden and Kövecses 2006). In the present approach, metonymy is regarded as a means of semantic enrichment or elaboration. This means that through a metonymic operation a source concept is ex-panded so that, as a result, the target concept is construed as concep-tually more complex. At the same time, the source concept is an inte-grative part of the target concept.

ii. The approach advocated here assumes that the metonymic relation is *contingent*, i.e. not *any* meaning that is mentally accessible from a cer-tain conceptual reference point gives rise to a metonymic relation. More precisely, I do not regard relations that are conceptually necess-ary as possible metonymies. In other words, mental access of concepts based on semantic entailment and semantic presupposition is not con-sidered to be a mode of metonymic reasoning here.

Contingence as a fundamental property of metonymy has been empha-sized in publications such as Panther and Thornburg (2003) and Panther (2005). The notion of contingence, as used in the above-cited publications, has sometimes been misunderstood. Contingence means simply that the metonymic relation *per se* is *defeasible* or *cancelable* (which distinguishes it from entailment). Contextual factors may however override defeasibil-ity of the metonymic relation and more or less enforce (coerce) a meto-nymic interpretation. For example, in an utterance such as *The bathtub is overflowing*, the noun phrase *the bathtub* is metonymically elaborated into something like 'the water in the bathtub'. The above utterance thus meto-nymically conveys 'The water in the bathtub is overflowing'. This inter-pretation is virtually enforced or *coerced* by the context (here the predi-cate expression *is overflowing*), but this fact does not invalidate the point that the metonymic relation between the source meaning 'bathtub' and the target 'water (in the bathtub)' is incidental, i.e. logically not necessary. No doubt, there is a tight (factual) relation between bathtubs and water in that the primary function of bathtubs is for people to take baths in. Nevertheless, bathtubs can be used for many other purposes. In contrast, the relation between e.g. *broccoli* and *vegetable* is hyponymic and therefore – in the taxonomy of vegetables – necessary by definition. The sentence *They had broccoli with their meal* entails 'They had a vegetable with their meal', but *broccoli* is not a metonym for 'vegetable' (see Bierwiaczonek 2005 for an analogous argument). In this connection, note that for Charles S. Peirce an indexical relation is related to its "object" not by "rational necessitation" but by "blind fact" (see fn. 3). If it is assumed that metonymy is a case of indexicality, the contingence of the metonymic relation follows automatically.

A case that, at first sight, seems to be based on a hyponymic relation between source and target is given by Radden and Kövecses (2006: 11).[9] These authors posit a metonymy MEMBER OF A CATEGORY FOR THE CATEGORY that they claim accounts for uses of *aspirin* for 'pain-relieving tablet'. Obviously, under one construal, the meaning of *aspirin* entails 'pain-relieving tablet'.[10] I agree with Radden and Kövecses that there is a real metonymy here, but it seems that it is not captured by the metonymic principle MEMBER OF A CATEGORY FOR THE CATEGORY.[11] Notice first that the relation between the concepts ASPIRIN and PAIN-RELIEVER is not one of meaning *elaboration*, which I claim is a typical characteristic of metonymy, because the feature PAIN-RELIEVER is already a part of the definition of (one sense of) *aspirin*. The metonymic relation is between ASPIRIN and its *co-hyponyms*, i.e. other pain-relievers (including aspirin itself). The paraphrase given by Radden and Kövecses, viz. '*any* [italics mine, K.-U.P.] pain-relieving tablet', is quite revealing in this respect. It amounts to saying 'aspirin *or* any medication that has the same effect as aspirin'. In other words, what is evoked metonymically is not the superordinate category/class PAIN-RELIEVER, but, via co-hyponymic extension, *any member* of this category/class (see Figure 2 below).

That metonymy is a matter of contingence rather than conceptual necessity is also advocated by Carita Paradis. She contrasts sentences such as (5) with sentences of type (6) (Paradis 2004: 246):

(5)   *The red shirts won the match.*
(6)   *The court had to assume that the statement of claim was true.*

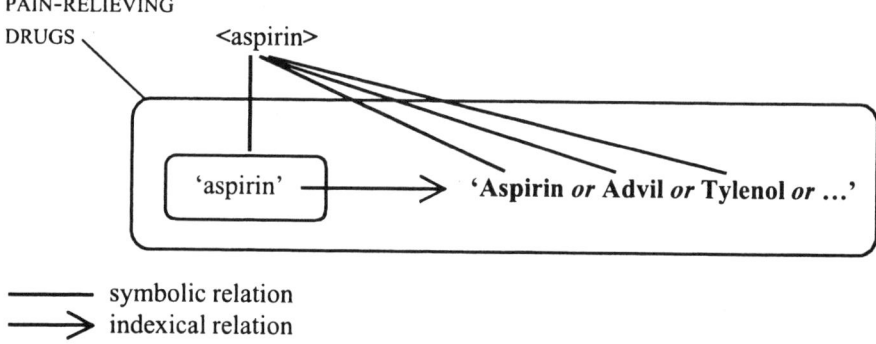

PAIN-RELIEVING DRUGS

<aspirin>

'aspirin' ⟶ 'Aspirin *or* Advil *or* Tylenol *or* ...'

——— symbolic relation
——⟶ indexical relation

*Figure 2.* Metonymic structure of *aspirin*

The noun phrase *the red shirts* in (5) metonymically indexes 'the team wearing the red shirts', but this target meaning is not entailed by the meaning of the linguistic vehicle. In (6), as Paradis points out, the intended target meaning is something like STAFF (i.e. the personnel working in the court), but this meaning is a *facet* of the overall meaning of *court*, the other three facets being ADMINISTRATIVE UNIT, BUILDING, and INTERIOR OUTFIT (251). According to Paradis, individual facets are *entailed* by the overall meaning of a lexical item. This might be too strong a statement, but it is certainly a default assumption (generalized conversational implicature in terms of Levinson 2000) that a court is staffed (with judges and other personnel). However, the same kind of connection does not obtain between the concepts 'red shirts' and 'team wearing red shirts'. The difference between metonymy and facets, as has been pointed out by a number of linguists, is also reflected in grammatical structure. In the case of metonymy, it is usually the target meaning that, because of its conceptual prominence (highlighting), determines grammatical and/or distributional properties of a sentence, whereas a switch from one lexical facet to another within a sentence usually goes unnoticed and is not considered to be anomalous.

(7)   *I listened to some/*a Mozart last Sunday.*
(8)   *The red shirts, who/*which delivered a great game last Saturday, have qualified for the Champions' League.*
(9)   *Put this heavy book back on the shelf; it is rather unreadable.* (Cruse 2000: 114)
(10)  *The court, which is located on Russell Square, has ruled in Mary's favor.*

In (7), *Mozart* is metonymically interpreted as 'music composed by Mozart' and it is interpreted as an abstract SUBSTANCE that determines the choice of *some* over the determiner *a*, which requires a noun with the feature COUNTABLE. Thus the metonymic target determines the grammatical structure of the noun phrase *some Mozart*. Similarly, in (8) it is the conceptual nature of the target 'team wearing red shirts' that determines the selection of the relative pronoun *who*, excluding the choice of *which*. Sentences (9) and (10) are examples of facet shifting. Sentence (9) starts out with the reading of *book* as PHYSICAL OBJECT and, in the second clause, switches to the facet CONTENT. In (10), the overall meaning of *court* is first narrowed down to the facet BUILDING motivating the use of the relative pronoun *which* and then interpreted as STAFF (e.g. 'judge') under the influence of the verb form *has ruled*.

To summarize the main points, I have based my characterization of metonymy on the semiotic notion of indexicality. This is not necessarily incompatible with a definition of metonymy in terms of single domainhood, but it seems extremely difficult to establish criteria that would allow one to distinguish reliably between separate conceptual domains and single conceptual domains. In the case of (8) above, one can view *red shirts* as belonging to the domain of clothing, which is relatable to, but also separate from, the domain of humans (or the narrower domain of athletes). It is difficult to pin down the notions 'single domain' and 'separate domains' in a way that does not seem to be more or less ad hoc. Nevertheless these notions are considered by many scholars to be essential in telling metaphor apart from metonymy. I turn to this problem in more detail in the following section.

## 2.2. Domains and subdomains

As mentioned in section 2.1, standard definitions of metonymy often rely on the notion of 'single domain' or 'domain matrix' within which the metonymic mapping is supposed to operate (see e.g. Radden and Kövecses 2006).[12] More specifically, Francisco Ruiz de Mendoza and his coauthors have forcefully argued in a number of publications (see e.g. Ruiz de Mendoza Ibáñez and Díez Velasco 2002; Ruiz de Mendoza Ibañez and Otal Campo 2002) that metonymy amounts to two kinds of operation: domain expansion (source-in-target metonymy) or domain reduction (target-in-source metonymy). Ruiz de Mendoza and his collaborators reject part-to-part metonymies, claiming that they can be reduced to either domain expansion or domain reduction.

Ruiz de Mendoza's theory is appealing because it reduces proliferation of analytical categories (Occam's razor), but it hinges crucially on some operational criterion for distinguishing domains from subdomains. To my knowledge, to date no scholar has devised a satisfactory working definition. A variety of conceptual relations has been lumped together under the rubric 'subdomain – domain', and vice versa. The following is an incomplete list of such "domain-subdomain" relationships as found in the literature on metonymy. Despite its incompleteness, this list demonstrates that the notions of domain and subdomain are used to refer to distinct conceptual phenomena:

i. Class/set – subclass/subset (hyperonym – hyponym): e.g. *flower* as a hyperonym of *daffodil*.
ii. Class – class member: e.g. *playwrights* with the member *G. B. Shaw.*
iii. Whole – part: e.g. *face – nose, house – room.*
iv. Person – attribute (temporary or permanent): *John – potbelly, Mozart – musical genius.*
v. Location – institution – people working in institution: e.g. *10 Downing Street – British government – staff.*

These few examples suffice to show that domain-subdomain relations are conceptually very diverse. More seriously, often it seems to be a matter of perspective as what to regard as the superordinate domain and what as the subdomain(s), respectively. In (i) the subdomain DAFFODIL is extensionally properly included in the domain FLOWER. Intensionally, however, the definition of *daffodil* requires more attributes than the definition of *flower*. The attribute FLOWER is therefore properly contained in the set of attributes defining the term *daffodil*. From this perspective, one could claim that FLOWER is a conceptual component (subdomain) of DAFFODIL (domain). As to (ii), extensionally, George Bernard Shaw is a member of, i.e. contained in, the class of playwrights. Intensionally, one could regard *Shaw* as a human being with a number of permanent and temporary attributes, one of them being that he was a playwright. In the first case, the concept PLAYWRIGHT (extensionally defined as the class of playwrights) would be the superordinate domain and *Shaw* one of its subdomains; in the second case, *Shaw* would define a superordinate domain, a component of which is the attribute PLAYWRIGHT. Regarding (iii), the relation between *nose* and *face* and *room* and *house*, respectively, is one of part–whole: that is, it is completely different from what is described in (i) and (ii). Neither is the set of noses a subset of the set of faces, nor is the set of rooms a subset of the set of buildings. The relation between noses and faces and rooms and houses, respectively, is not one of class inclusion. Again, it seems to be a matter of perspective that determines what is regarded as the superordinate domain and what as the subdomain. One could argue that a proper understanding of *house* includes some understanding of the concept ROOM, KITCHEN, ATTIC, BASEMENT, etc.; thus *house* would constitute a superordinate domain vis-à-vis *room*. Conversely, one could also argue that *room* requires reference to concepts like HOUSE, BUIDLING, COTTAGE, PALACE and the like, and postulate that ROOM is a superordinate domain from that perspective. The person-attribute relation in (iv) seems to be a clear case, at first sight. Intuitively, one tends to think that an attribute is subordinate to the person that has it. Even if this perspective is the normal one, it does not exclude another perspective where e.g. POTBELLY is a superordinate domain comprising the class of people who display the attribute of having a potbelly. Finally, consider relations such as those exemplified by (v), which also have been claimed to exhibit a domain–subdomain structure. What is the criterion for deciding that LOCATION is the superordinate domain of INSTITUTION, which itself is supposed to be the superordinate domain of PEOPLE (working at the institution)? True, *10 Downing Street*, which refers to a location in London and a house at this location, can metonymically evoke the institution and ultimately the human beings working in the institution, but the same arguments as above again apply: One can see an institution as having as one of its features a location; there is no inherent necessity to view INSTITUTION as being a subdomain of LOCATION, although it can certainly be construed that way.[13]

Croft (2002: 166) seems to offer a viable solution to the problem of distinguishing domains from subdomains. He proposes the following definition for *domain*: "We can […] define a domain as a *semantic structure that functions as the base for at least one concept profile* (typically, many profiles)." The two notions of profile and base (adopted from Langacker 1987) are especially relevant here: According to Croft, a *base* is "the domain immediately presupposed by the profiled concept" (167). Croft calls the base of a profiled concept its 'base domain'. This definition seems, at least in part, to coincide with Ruiz de Mendoza's use of the term matrix domain. Notice that Croft uses the term 'presupposition' to characterize the relation between profile and base. It does not become clear, however, whether he has the notion of *semantic* presupposition in mind; if so, it would render statements about domain structure testable by means of the well-known (internal) negation test for presupposition.[14] But the application of this test leads to unsatisfactory results: For example, the notion ARC is, in Croft's sense, profiled against, or presupposes, the base CIRCLE. However, neither from the proposition *This is an arc* nor from its negation *This is not an arc* follows the proposition *This is a circle*. As another example consider the relations between NOSE, FACE, and HEAD. Does NOSE presuppose FACE, which, in turn, would presuppose HEAD? The (frame-internal) negation test fails here: Neither from *x is a nose* nor from *x is not a nose* does it follow that *x is a face*; analogously, for FACE and HEAD. The presupposition test works somewhat better with taxonomies on condition that negation is restricted to frame- or domain-internal negation: From *This is a rose* the proposition *This is a flower* follows; frame-internal negation (*This is not a rose*) would also imply *This is a flower*. In conclusion, even Croft's attempt at providing a more constrained characterization of the relation between domains and subdomains is inconclusive. Presupposition, as defined in standard semantics, does not provide a sufficient criterion for distinguishing superordinate domains from subordinate domains.

An additional complication results from the fact that Croft – different from e.g. Ruiz de Mendoza – does not propose a characterization of metonymy in terms of domain expansion and domain reduction but in terms of highlighting an originally "secondary" subdomain: "[…] metonymy makes primary a domain that is secondary in the literal meaning" (Croft 2002: 179). This conception of metonymy is not compatible with the idea that metonymy is a domain-subdomain or subdomain-domain relationship.

What counts as a domain and a subdomain might be a matter of perspective or construal on the part of the conceptualizer. Take the example of *french fries*, which is supposedly a subdomain of the domain of customers (see Ruiz de Mendoza Ibáñez and Otal Campo 2002: 132 for an analogous example). I think it is just a matter of perspective to reverse the subdomain–domain relationship in this case. French fries are a specific kind of cooked food (potato sticks fried in oil), often (but not necessarily) served in fast food restaurants to customers who are in a hurry and do not want to spend much time and money on a meal. There is thus a whole knowledge structure concerning french fries and, one could argue that part of this knowledge structure is the concept of customer. From this perspective, FRENCH FRIES constitutes the superordinate domain of RESTAURANT CUSTOMER. There is thus again no clear objective sense that would allow one to distinguish domains from their subdomains.

The preceding discussion should not be interpreted as implying that I argue against the existence of frames, domains, etc., as such. On the contrary, the present author believes that the development of semantic frame theory constitutes a major breakthrough in the history of natural language semantics. My intention has been to point out that the concepts of super- and subordination, with respect to frames or domains, are in need of more precise explication.

For the time being, a semiotically based definition of metonymy (and metaphor) seems preferable to a definition relying on the notions of domain and subdomain.[15] Furthermore, I have proposed that metonymy is an operation of conceptual elaboration. In elaborating a source concept, metonymy relies in general on pre-established inferential patterns. The kind of conceptual realms in which metonymic shifts operate are not necessarily whole cognitive domains (and subdomains) stored in long-term memory, but they might be more like *mental spaces*, i.e. "small conceptual packets constructed as we think and talk, for purposes of local understanding and action" (Fauconnier and Turner 2002: 40). Mental spaces tap portions of frames stored in long-term memory, but it seems implausible that whenever a metonymic operation takes place a whole conceptual frame is activated.

## 2.3. Distinguishing metonymy from metaphor

In cognitive linguistics, metaphor is generally regarded as relating two *separate* conceptual domains via a set of unidirectional mappings from a source domain *into*, or ideally, *onto* a target domain. The general problem with this approach is related to the vagueness of the notion of domain discussed in section 2.2. One difficulty with this definition is that – apart from the most generic conceptual domain, which encompasses all conceptual knowledge – every domain has a superordinate domain and thus two domains will always have at least one domain in common that contains them as proper subdomains. The difficulties arising from the notion of domain are the same for metaphor as for metonymy (see e.g. Barcelona 2002 for insightful discussion).

I propose that reference to "separate domains" should be avoided in a working definition of metaphor. Nothing would speak against the assumption that the source domain and the target domain intersect. For example, an utterance like (11) could be interpreted metaphorically:

(11) *My (pet) tiger is a lion.*

The conceptual frames for *tiger* (target) and *lion* (source) overlap considerably. Still, it is possible to construe a metaphoric sense for (11) where properties of the concept LION are mapped onto tigers. It thus does not seem to be a necessary condition for metaphors that the source domain and the target domain be disjunct. As for metonymy, I suggest a semiotically based conception of metaphor, which is represented in Figure 3. Following Hiraga (1998), I propose that metaphor is based on an *iconic* relation between source meaning and target meaning. The source meaning has some frame or domain structure that is iconically replicated in the target domain. This approach is, to a certain extent, in line with traditional cognitive metaphor theory as advocated by Lakoff and Johnson (1980). The present approach differs from Lakoff and Johnson in that it treats the source meaning of a metaphor, in analogy to metonymy, as a thought vehicle (signifier) for accessing a target meaning (signified). The conception of metaphor as an iconic relationship accords with traditional accounts of metaphor in that it relies on some notion of similarity between source and target. Hiraga (1998) suggests that in metaphor the resemblance between source and target is created rather than given, i.e. even a priori dissimilar domains can be connected through metaphoric mappings. The resemblance in this case is *structural* rather than a "direct" imitation of (perceived) "reality" in the signifier of the linguistic sign, as in onomatopoeia or other kinds of sound symbolism. The structural resemblance is one between the two conceptual frames, the source and the target, as has been demonstrated by Lakoff and Johnson with illuminating examples. The view of metaphor as a special case of iconicity (isomorphism) avoids the pitfalls of having to come up with some criterion for distinguishing single domains from separate domains. Figure 3 diagrams the basic metaphoric relation. Note that the target meaning is printed in bold as in the case of metonymy, indicating that it is conceptually prominent. For convenience of graphic representation, source and target domain are represented as distinct in Figure 3 (see below).

## 2.4. Primary metaphors

Lakoff and Johnson (1999: 45–73), who rely on e.g. Grady (1998), assume the existence of a set of metaphorical primitives that they call 'primary metaphors'. Primary metaphors are supposedly based on experiential correlations, which are originally indistinguishable for the child and become only experientially and conceptually dissociated at a more advanced age. This dissociation is a prerequisite for their development into primary

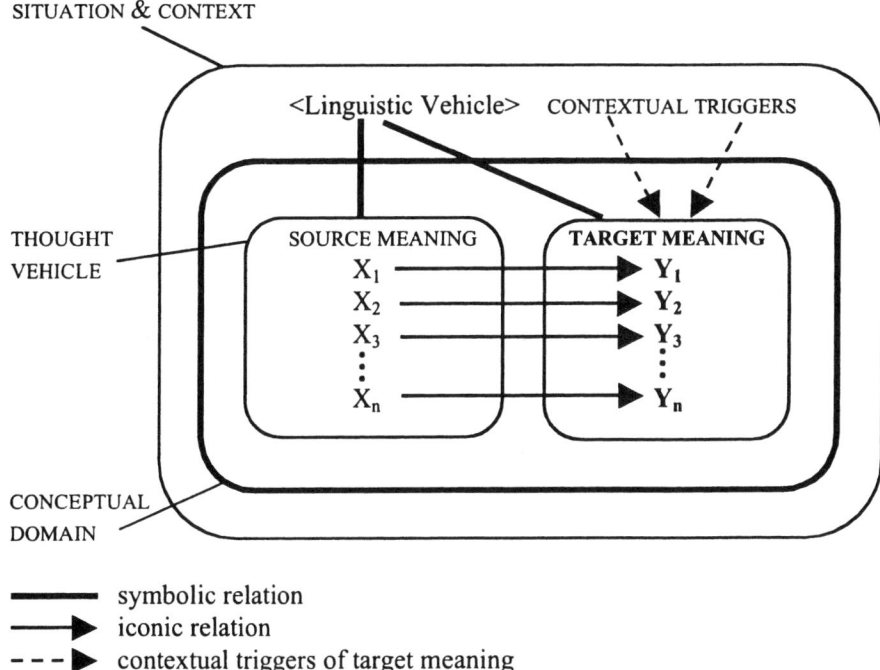

SITUATION & CONTEXT

THOUGHT
VEHICLE

CONCEPTUAL
DOMAIN

━━━━━  symbolic relation
━━━▶  iconic relation
− − −▶  contextual triggers of target meaning

*Figure 3.* The basic metaphoric relation

metaphors. Lakoff and Johnson (1999: 54–55) assume that a primary metaphor

> arises via a neurally instantiated correlation between (1) a sensorimotor operation [...] and (2) subjective experiences or judgment [...]. The conflation of these two is the simultaneous activation of their respective neural networks.

Examples given by Lakoff and Johnson for such primary metaphors are, among others, AFFECTION IS WARMTH, CLOSENESS IS INTIMACY, HAPPY IS UP, STATES ARE LOCATIONS, PURPOSES ARE DESTINATIONS, and KNOWING IS SEEING.[16] In this section, I want to defend the idea that these correlations are first and foremost the experiential basis for conceptual metonymy, which, in turn, may become the basis for the construction of metaphors (see also Radden 2002, who develops a similar argument).

Let us consider the experiential correlation between CLOSENESS and INTIMACY in more detail. Given this correlation, it is not surprising, that people spontaneously infer that two people who are located close to each share a feeling of intimacy (of course, this is a cancelable inference). On the linguistic level this is reflected in utterances such as

(12) *Mary and Peter sat close to each other and watched the sun set behind the mountains.*

From (12) one might spontaneously infer that there is, temporarily at least, a relationship of intimacy between Mary and Peter. This inference is a piece of metonymic reasoning: Peter and Mary's spatial position relative to each other is taken as an index of the intimate feelings they share. The metonymy involved may be called EFFECT FOR CAUSE. All of the properties of metonymy proposed in section 2.1 apply in this example: In particular, there is a tight experiential, and, on the cognitive level, conceptual, connection between source and target and the relation between closeness and intimacy is not necessary, i.e., it is in principle defeasible. One could easily say:

(13) *Mary and Peter sat close to each other that evening, but that does not mean that they like each other.*

In fact, in other situations, spatial closeness of two humans could also be an indication of aggression, intimidation, and the like.

It thus seems that, on the cognitive and semiotic level, the experiential correlation between closeness and intimacy is metonymic rather than metaphoric. What happens when spatial closeness does not apply, as in example (14)?

(14) *Mary and Peter were/felt very close that evening, although she was in America and he was in Europe.*

In (14), the source SPATIAL CLOSENESS of the two participants is not factual. This counterfactuality might be the reason why Lakoff and Johnson would assume that (14) is metaphoric rather than metonymic. In this case, there clearly is no CAUSE-EFFECT relationship between intimacy and spatial proximity, and one could therefore argue that the relationship must be metaphoric. However, the use of *close* in (14) is ultimately motivated by the world knowledge that CLOSENESS is a fairly reliable indicator of INTIMACY. In conclusion then, it appears that the experiential correlations observed by Grady, Lakoff and Johnson, and others, are the basis for metonymy before they are possibly used as metaphorical expressions.

Barcelona (2002: 234–236) discusses some aspects of this important issue with respect to such expressions as (15) and (16):

(15) *She is in the pits.*
(16) *Mike is in low spirits.*

Since Lakoff and Johnson's book *Metaphors We Live By* (1980), cognitive linguists have been used to regarding these as metaphorical sentences based on the conceptual metaphor SAD IS DOWN. The rationale for viewing them as metaphors comes from the assumption that the dimension of verticality (UP vs. DOWN) constitutes a separate conceptual domain from the domains HAPPY and SAD, respectively. But the previous discussion should have made it abundantly clear that this assumption rests on shaky ground. Barcelona (2002: 235) notes quite rightly that, since expressions of sadness are often conveyed through linguistic vehicles that literally denote a vertical downward orientation or location, one could, contrary to Lakoff and Johnson, assume that the dimension VERTICALITY is part of the domain SADNESS. Utterances (10) and (11) would then have a metonymic basis. I believe that Barcelona's conclusion is correct – perhaps *not* because the domain VERTICALITY is a subdomain of the domain SADNESS but because DOWN is experientially related to SAD – as evinced e.g. in drooping shoulders and down-turned corners of the mouth – and the former can therefore be used as a thought vehicle to *indexically* access the latter. There is thus a metonymic basis for these metaphors exemplified by (15) and (16) (see also Radden 2002: 414–416 for the same view).

## 2.5. Metonymy and implicature

The preceding sections have shown that it is not always easy to distinguish metaphor and metonymy and that, for particular linguistic examples, there is not always a consensus whether they constitute metaphors or metonymies. Critics of present-day metaphor and metonymy theory, such as Haser (2005) and Leezenberg (2001), have challenged cognitive linguistics arguing that there is no clear conception of metaphor and metonymy in this framework.

Haser (2005: 17–18) claims that in the cognitive linguistic literature conceptually heterogeneous phenomena have been lumped together as "metonymy". To a certain extent, this is true, as the discussion in section 2.1 has demonstrated. With regard to metonymy, Haser (2005: 18) criticizes Panther and Thornburg (1999: 334) for not properly distinguishing between "meaning something *different* from what is said and meaning something *in addition to* what is said" in their approach to metonymy. Haser points out that, in a case of genuine metonymy, such as the German expression *ein Glas trinken* 'drink a glass', the container (the glass) stands for its liquid contents (water, milk, beer, wine, etc.). Haser claims that Panther and Thornburg classify as metonymies phenomena that do not involve substitution of meaning but rather addition of meaning.

The pragmatic types of metonymy distinguished by Panther and Thornburg are illustrated by the following sentences (see e.g. Panther and Thornburg 2003; Panther 2005; Panther and Thornburg In Press):

(17) *A lot of Ph.D.s have been written about this topic.* (referential: DOCTORAL DEGREE FOR DOCTORAL THESIS)

(18) *The President was clear on the matter.* (predicational: MANNER OF SPEAKING FOR SPEAKING)[17]

(19) *I would like you to close this window.* (illocutionary: WISH FOR REQUEST)

Consider now (20), which Panther and Thornburg regard as inducing a predicational metonymy resulting in the interpretation (21):

(20) *He was able to finish his dissertation.*
(21) *He finished his dissertation.*[18]

Haser (2005: 18) claims that the relation between (20) and (21) is one of addition rather than of substitution so that the almost automatic inference (21) from (20) would not be analyzable as a metonymic relation – contrary to Panther and Thornburg's analysis. Furthermore, Haser (rightly) points out that (21) entails (20). The entailment relation between target and source does, however, according to her, not hold in classical cases of metonymy as in (22), which metonymically evokes (23):

(22) *She is listening to Schubert all day.*
(23) *She is listening to music composed by Schubert all day.*

Obviously, (23) does not entail (22). From this fact Haser concludes that the relation between (22) and (23) is not of the same kind as that between (20) and (21). Haser draws the conclusion that since the relation between (22) and (23) is metonymic, the relation between (20) and (21) cannot be metonymic.

Haser's argumentation is however not stringent. If one wants to establish target-source entailment as a criterion for non-metonymicity, what should be compared is the relation between the denotata of the *nominal* expressions *Schubert* and of its metonymic target 'music composed by Schubert' – not the relation between the two propositions expressed by *sentences* (22) and (23), respectively. The metonymic target 'music composed by Schubert' expresses the underlying proposition 'Schubert composed music'. From this latter proposition the proposition follows that Schubert existed.[19] Thus, the relationship between *was able to finish his dissertation* and 'finished his dissertation' in (20) and (21) is analogous to that between the existential presupposition 'Schubert existed' (following from *Schubert*) and the proposition 'Schubert composed music' (following from *music composed by Schubert*), in (22) and (23), respectively. Just as ability is a prerequisite for action, the existence of a person is a prerequisite for that person to be a composer. Table 1 summarizes these analogies.

*Table 1.* Analogies between referential and predicational metonymy

|  | REFERENTIAL METONYMY | PREDICATIONAL METONYMY |
|---|---|---|
| **Source** ↓ | *Schubert* ↓ | *… was able to finish her dissertation* ↓ |
| **Target** | 'music composed by Schubert' | ' … finished his dissertaton' |
| **Semantic relation:** target – source | From 'Schubert composed music' *it follows that* 'Schubert exists/existed' | From 'X finished his dissertation' *it follows that* 'X was able to finish his dissertation' |

More generally, nobody has ever suggested, to my knowledge, that a metonymic target must not entail its source. Why non-entailment from target to source should be a condition for metonymicity remains unclear. I do not see any reason for introducing such a condition as a defining criterion of metonymy.

Another problem with Haser's approach is her claim that the target of (20), i.e. (21), adds meaning to what is said, whereas in her view a genuine metonymy does not add meaning but substitutes one meaning for another. Consider the expression *drink a glass* again, which everybody regards as a metonymical expression. One condition for employing this metonymy crucially involves the use of a glass; drinking directly from the tap or from one's cupped palms does not count as "drinking a glass". One might object that *drink a bottle (of wine)* does not necessarily, and even not normally, mean that the drinker drinks from a bottle. However, the bottle as a container is still crucially involved, because if somebody drinks directly from the wine barrel, this activity will not count as *drink a bottle* even if the drinker consumes the quantity contained in a bottle. To come back to *drink a glass*, the metonymic meaning can be paraphrased as 'drink (approximately) the quantity of liquid contained in a glass and, most probably, from a glass'. The point is that there is not just substitution of one meaning for another but meaning *elaboration* of the source concept 'glass' (as a container).[20] The source meaning is a conceptual component of the target meaning. This is also what Panther and Thornburg assume for cases of predicational metonymy such as (20) and (21): The source meaning expressed by (20) becomes an integrative part of the target meaning expressed by (21). The metonymic reading induced by (20) can be paraphrased as 'was able to finish his dissertation and actually managed to finish his dissertation'. The meaning component ABILITY is combined with the meaning component SUCCESSFUL ACTION in the metonymic target, but ABILITY becomes a backgrounded meaning component whereas the SUCESSFUL ACTION sense is conceptually prominent.

In conclusion, the problems that Haser has with Panther and Thornburg's metonymy theory are based on a false presumption, viz. that these authors regard "added" meanings as metonymies. Target meanings are not additions, but elaborations of the source meanings, which remain a conceptual part of the target meaning.

Another related point of Haser's critique concerns the relation between metonymy and implicature. Implicature, she seems to assume, is added conceptual material, on top of what is said by the speaker, whereas metonymy is presumably a substitution relation. I believe this to be a fictitious opposition that collapses on closer inspection. Take a standard implicature based on the Gricean maxim of quantity such as SOME +> NOT ALL (as is common, the symbol '+>' is used here to represent the implicature relation). This looks like a case of addition, but the overall (including the implicated) meaning of *some* could alternatively be formulated as meaning elaboration: SOME +> SOME & NOT ALL.[21] Furthermore, the NOT ALL component seems to be a conceptually prominent meaning in most cases whereas the meaning component SOME is more backgrounded (but still activated). Consider the following utterance:

(24) *At midnight, some of the guests left the party.*

In many contexts, in utterances like (24) the meaning that *not all* guests left the party (and probably most did not leave it) is conceptually prominent. The conceptual link between SOME and NOT ALL is by many speakers felt to be so tight that the two meanings are almost indistinguishable. Conceptual tightness of source and target senses is also a property of metonymy.

There are thus some interesting analogies between metonymy and implicature, which have led some scholars to assume that metonymic principles actually underlie many implicatures (see e.g. Barcelona 2003: passim; Ruiz de Mendoza Ibañez and Peña 2005: 274).

## 3.   Metonymy as usage events: two case studies

In this section, I relate the theoretical discussion of metonymy in the previous sections to the more down-to-earth question of how metonymy functions in actual discourse. The section is devoted to the interpretation of two contextualized examples of metonymic usage in written discourse.[22] In the glossary compiled by Larry Gorbet for Langacker's first volume of his pioneering *Foundations of Cognitive Grammar* (1987: 494) a usage event is defined as

> a symbolic expression assembled by a speaker in a particular circumstance for a particular purpose; the pairing of a detailed, context-dependent conceptualization and (in the case of speech) an actual vocalization.

The analysis that ensues considers the particular circumstance of the utterances, their particular purpose and the discourse context in which they are embedded.

### 3.1. What happened at Pearl Harbor?

The first metonymy-in-use example involves an Internet text about a commemoration ceremony (in 1999) of the Japanese attack on Pearl Harbor in 1941, which started World War II in the Pacific. For methodological reasons, I isolate the metonymic sentence to be analyzed looking at it first from a "null-context" perspective, before re-embedding it in a larger discourse context:[23]

(25) *A Pearl Harbor will never happen again.*

The leading question is: What does a metonymic inference *per se* convey? On its own, the noun phrase *Pearl Harbor* in (25) is a straightforward example of the metonymy PLACE FOR EVENT AT PLACE. In terms of generative grammar (25) involves a violation of a selection restriction because the verb phrase *will never happen again* normally selects a subject that denotes an event. Minimally, readers/hearers with no historical knowledge will identify a metonymic interpretation on the basis of their knowledge that Pearl Harbor is a place; the verb phrase, which contains the verb *happen*, will coerce the reading that something happened at that place. The metonymic interpretation 'Something happened at Pearl Harbor' is not more than a *prompt* for further interpretive work. Furthermore, there is also a metonymic inference triggered by the indefinite article *a*: Pearl Harbor is conceptualized as a representative event for a whole class of events with similar properties. Lakoff (1987: 87–88) calls such metonymically based conceptualizations *paragons* (for an in-depth analysis of paragons, see Barcelona 2004). To summarize, (25) metonymically evokes the following propositions:

(26) a. Some event happened at Pearl Harbor.
   b. The event at Pearl Harbor is representative of other events of the same kind.[24]

The full details of the Japanese attack on Pearl Harbor can only be identified on the basis of encyclopedic knowledge, which the historically informed reader might already have at her disposal ("additional conceptual components" in Figure 1 above) or which is provided by the surrounding discourse context. In (27) the discourse context, in which (25) is embedded, is already significantly larger:

(27) "I return each year for this ceremony aboard Taney," said principal speaker VADM Douglas J. Katz, USN(Ret.). "We are here on the eve of the millennium as the greatest, most powerful nation on earth. From World War II until today, we still have the greatest military in the world, but we need to be more alert than ever as we move into the 21st century so that *a Pearl Harbor will never happen again* [italics mine] ... we must never, ever forget."

From (27), at least the following additional inferences about the event that occurred at Pearl Harbor can be drawn:

(28) a. The event at Pearl Harbor was an extremely important event in American history.
   b. The event at Pearl Harbor affected the United States negatively.
   c. The event at Pearl Harbor threatened America's power and potentially America's existence as an independent nation.
   d. What happened at Pearl Harbor was a type of event that should be prevented at all costs in the future.

The above propositions are inferences because there is no *explicit* mention of the importance of the event (28a), its negative consequences (28b), the threat to American power (28c), nor that the type of event should be prevented in the future (28d) (all that is said is "we must never, ever forget"). Not even the name of the country affected by the event is explicitly given but must be inferred on the basis of the encyclopedic knowledge that Pearl Harbor is a port on the island of Hawaii, which, in turn, is part of the territory of the United States.

Finally, consider an even wider discourse context, which provides information that allows additional inferences on some specifics of the Pearl Harbor attack:

(29) Taney (WHEC 37) is the last floating survivor of the 101 warships at Pearl Harbor during Japan's surprise attack. One of seven Treasury Class ships built and commissioned Oct. 24, 1936 as Roger B. Taney, it is named after the former Acting Secretary of Treasury during Andrew Jackson's administration and former Chief Supreme Court Justice. Taney was a native of Maryland and was married to the sister of Francis Scott Key. Now part of the Baltimore Maritime Museum and moored at Baltimore's Inner Harbor, Taney was decommissioned Dec. 7, 1986, and was designated a National Historic Landmark in 1988.

From text (29) more inferences as to *who* and *what* was involved in the Pearl Harbor event can be drawn, which include (30a) and (30b):

(30) a. The event at Pearl Harbor was a (surprise) attack launched by Japan against the U.S.
   b. The Japanese attack led to the destruction of American warships.

Inference (30a) follows from the noun phrase *Japan's surprise attack*, which presupposes that Japan attacked some power (the context and bridging inferences make it clear that the country attacked was the U.S.). The inference in (30b), viz. that 101 American warships were destroyed in the attack, follows from the information that "Taney [...] is the last floating survivor of the 101 warships [...]".

The preceding analysis supports my thesis that metonymies are prompts that induce fairly general inferences, which are in need of further inferential elaboration unless the reader has at her disposal a rich knowledge data-base that enables her to fill in the details on the basis of the metonymy alone. The question remains as to the status of the inferences listed in (28a–d) and (30a–b). Are they metonymic inferences or inferences of a different kind? Some of them are definitely not metonymic as e.g. the presuppositional inference included in (30a); others are very specific and context-driven. Some researchers have treated low-level inferences as metonymic (see Barcelona 2003), but the question as to their cognitive status has to be left open here.

### 3.2. Red hot doorbuster

As a second case study, I discuss in some detail the expression *red hot doorbusters* found in the advertising section of a local American newspaper (see Photo 1 below). This expression exhibits a much more complex conceptual structure than the expression *Pearl Harbor*. There is not only metonymy involved in this case but metaphor as well. The importance of context in the interpretation of a fully specified meaning and the role of metonymy and metaphor as guiding conceptual principles towards a specific interpretation is demonstrated.

A photograph of the advertisement is found below.[25] For heuristic reasons I assume a language user who is not familiar with the word *doorbuster*, i.e. encounters the term for the first time, but recognizes the word as containing the free morphemes *door* (noun), *bust* (verb), and the derivational morpheme *-er*, which has been shown to exhibit a high degree of polysemy (see Panther and Thornburg 2001, 2002) (see Photo 1 below).

What kind of information would help a reader who is not familiar with the expression *doorbuster* to work out the intended meaning 'extremely low prices for desirable products sold for a limited time' or 'desirable products at extremely low prices for a limited sales period'? The interpretative work of the reader is first of all facilitated by the linguistic context, in particular what follows the expression *red hot doorbusters*. The noun phrase *these specials* has as its coreferential antecedent *red hot doorbusters*. The term *special* is well entrenched in English and is found in

*Photo 1.  Red hot doorbusters*

ordinary dictionaries with the meaning 'a lower price than usual for a particular product for a short period of time' (*Longman Dictionary of Contemporary English*, 2003) (LDCE), s.v. *special*). It is actually, for all practical purposes, synonymous with the expression *red hot doorbuster*.
Moreover, the restricted time period of the sale is redundantly conveyed
by the verb phrase *won't last long*.

In what follows, I analyze the meanings of *red hot* and *doorbusters*. Section 3.2.1 contains some reflections on the conceptual structure of *red hot*;
section 3.2.2 analyzes this meaning in conjunction with the metonymic
and metaphoric structure of *doorbusters*.

## 3.2.1.  Red hot

The adjectival expression *red hot* is a well-entrenched lexical item. It has
at its syntactic head *hot*, which is modified by *red*. The compound expression is literally applied to objects or substances such as *poker, metal*,
and *rock*. The attribute *red* denotes the effect of extreme heat; a red hot
object or substance exhibits a glowing or shining red color. However, the

meaning component SHINY RED often gives way to the meaning VERY HOT, i.e. 'extremely high on the heat scale' in utterances like *Be careful with these plates – they're red hot* (LDCE). The target meaning of *red hot* as a modifier of *doorbusters* is – to put things simply – something like 'very desirable'. I contend that this meaning comes about through metonymic elaboration of the source meaning and metaphoric mapping. First, the metonymic elaboration in the source domain is an inference from the modifier *red* to an intensifying meaning 'very, highly, extremely', i.e. an endpoint on a scale of intensity. If something is red hot (visual stimulus), then it is easily inferred to be very hot. Second, *red hot* also suggests, e.g. in the context of *iron poker*, a high degree of salience in terms of visibility. These two metonymically derived meaning components are then metaphorically mapped onto the conceptual entities VERY DESIRABLE and HIGLY SALIENT ON PRICE SCALE, a meaning component that is reinforced by *doorbuster*. The latter actually narrows down HIGHLY SALIENT ON THE PRICE SCALE to the LOW END OF THE PRICE SCALE, i.e. 'inexpensive' and 'affordable'.

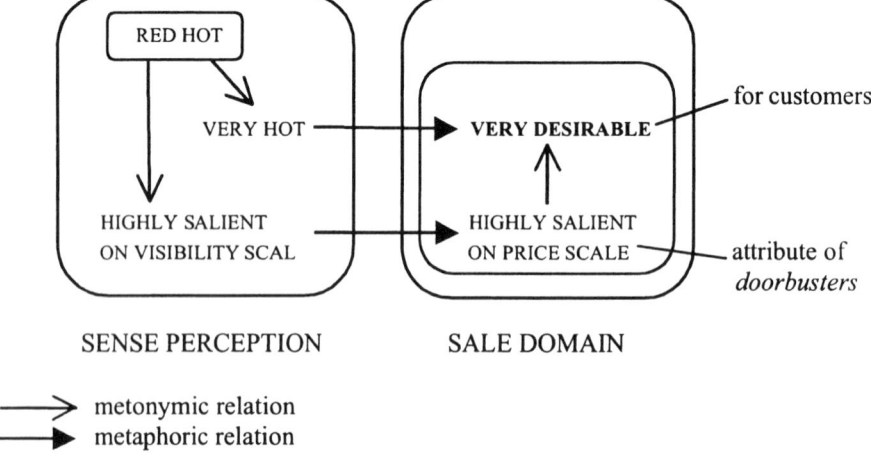

SENSE PERCEPTION          SALE DOMAIN

———▷ metonymic relation
———▶ metaphoric relation

*Figure 4.* The metonymic and metaphoric structure of *red hot (doorbuster)*

The conceptual structure of *red hot (doorbusters)* is diagrammed in Figure 4. At the most general level, there is a metaphoric mapping from the domain of SENSE PERCEPTION to the SALE domain. Both the source and the target domain are inferentially elaborated; it is worth noting that the target domain contains a metonymic inference from CAUSE to EFFECT: the desirability of the sale object is caused by the highly salient feature LOW PRICE.

The EFFECT FOR CAUSE metonymy is necessary in order to reconcile the (target) meanings of *red hot* 'very exciting' and *doorbusters* 'cheap prices for products temporarily on sale'. Cheap prices are not intrinsically "exciting"; they are meant to *cause* excitement in the customer. Thus *doorbuster* has an impact on the conceptual structure of the target domain of its modifier *red hot*.

From a different perspective, which integrates the notion of scale (left implicit in Figure 4), the figurative meaning of *red hot* as a modifier of *doorbuster* can be represented as relating three scales: a heat scale (in the source domain), a desirability scale and a price scale, the latter two inversely and causally related to each other in the target domain.[26] These scales focus on endpoints. In the source domain, the modifier *red* metonymically intensifies the degree of heat encoded in *hot*. The heat scale is metaphorically mapped onto a desirability scale in the target domain. High heat corresponds to high desirability. The base *desire* in *desirability* is here understood as denoting not only a propositional attitude, but also, in the context of frantic consumerism, a strong emotion. Temperature words are quite systematically used in English and other languages to describe emotional states; there is thus a generic metaphor (which itself might be metonymically motivated) for the use of *red hot*. In the target domain, as already noted, there is a remarkable inverse relationship between the desirability scale and the price scale. A high value on the desirability scale corresponds to a low value on the price scale, and vice versa. Moreover, as previously mentioned, the two scales are causally related: desirability is (at least partially) caused by the reduced cost of the sales item and thus a strong incentive for customers to buy a product. This inverse (causal) relationship is indicated by a dotted arrow in Figure 5 (see below).

### 3.2.2. *(Red hot) doorbuster*

In this section the leading question is: How can one make sense of *doorbuster* as a conceptually motivated morphological structure? Let us look at the components (constituent morphemes) of this word and the meanings that are usually assigned to them:

jects/substances and of human emotions. It is clear, however, that other domains are part of this network; I will briefly comment on the domain of food. Expressions such as *red hot pizza* and *red hot baked potato* can be used alongside *piping hot buns, steaming hot apple pie*, etc. Notice that *red*

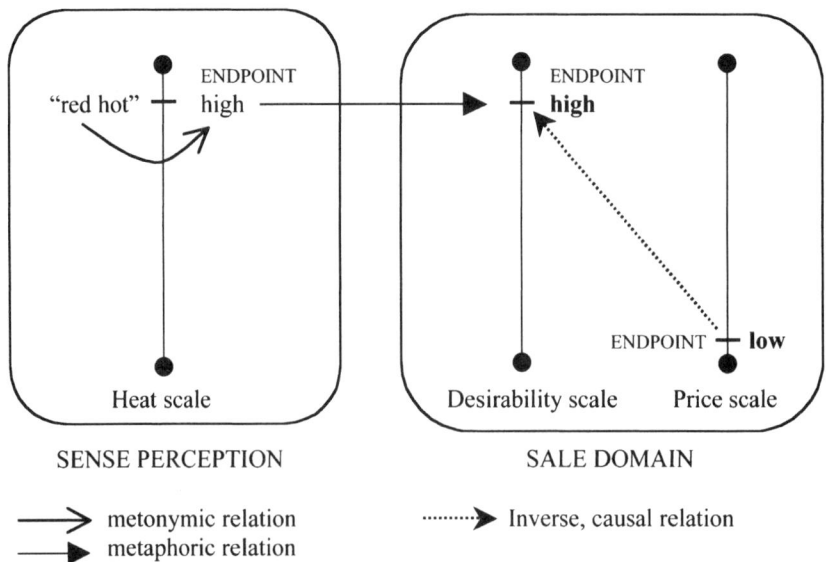

*Figure 5.*  Scalar structure of *red hot (doorbuster)*

(31) a. *door* 'movable panel used to close off an entrance'
     b. *bust* 'burst, break'
     c. *-er* 'person who (professionally or habitually) performs an action'[27]

Taken at face value, these individual meanings would yield the combined or *compositional* meaning:

(32) *doorbuster* 'someone who (professionally or habitually) busts doors'

However, this meaning obviously does not make sense in the given context of a large-scale sale in a department store. Another meaning that would also be possible – given the polysemy of *-er* nominals – is an instrumental meaning: This meaning is actually fairly entrenched: a doorbuster is a tool (sometimes even a firearm) to bust doors. But it is unlikely though perhaps not impossible that the ad is about doorbusters as tools. A third meaning would be an *event* reading as in *Come to our annual doorbuster!*, a meaning that is actually quite plausible. None of these readings is however meant in the present context. The meaning of *doorbuster* that makes most sense in the context is what Panther and Thornburg (2001, 2002) have termed a 'purpose patient' reading. A purpose patient is an object designed or produced for the purpose of being used, consumed, etc. (e.g. *fryer, poster*). But contrary to *fryer* and *poster*, there is only a very indirect relation between the meaning of the base *doorbust-* and its target meaning 'sales items at low prices'. A *fryer* is something to be fried (usually a chicken), a *poster* is something to be posted, but a *doorbuster* is not something to be doorbusted. Nevertheless, "doorbusting" plays a role in the elaborated target meaning (see below). A paraphrase of the meaning of *doorbuster* in the context of the advertisement is something like (33):

(33) *doorbuster* denotes a retail item that has been newly paired with a "special", i.e. temporary, price that is unexpectedly and sufficiently low to motivate consumers to rush to the store, forcefully overcome any obstacle – i.e. burst through (even break down) the doors – to obtain the item while it is available at the new, low price. Doorbuster may also denote the "special" low price itself.

This meaning is not derivable on the basis of the component meanings listed in (31a–c). However, a closer look reveals that (33) contains the content 'busting the door of the store by avid customers' although the busting does not necessarily (or even likely) occur, nor is it intended to occur. The noun *doorbuster* thus has a metaphorical interpretation of "door-busting": The customers behave *like* people who are busting doors in order to achieve a desired goal.[28] What is more, there is a conceptual link between someone who busts a door and the *reason* why this person (metaphorically) busts the door, namely to acquire a highly desirable item that is sold at a reduced price. This link can be inferred in the given context. One can conclude then that the meaning of *doorbuster* is not predictable, but it is not arbitrary either. The base *doorbust* forms the starting point of a metonymic chain that, in conjunction with the meaning of the suffix *-er*, yields a conceptually motivated sense that relates it – albeit in a somewhat indirect fashion – to the constituent morphemes *door, bust,* and *-er*.

To conclude this section, I illustrate in Figure 6 how the meaning of *red hot doorbuster* fits into a larger network of expressions usable with the modifier *red hot*. These expressions belong to different conceptual frames, two of which have been already mentioned: the domains of metallic objects/substances and of human emotions. It is clear, however, that other domains are part of this network; I will briefly comment on the domain of food. Expressions such as *red hot pizza* and *red hot baked potato* can be used alongside *piping hot buns, steaming hot apple pie,* etc. Notice that *red hot pizza* is not as "literal" as *red hot poker* because *red hot pizza* lacks a fiery glow even though it may have just come out of the oven. Furthermore, the modifier *red hot*, combined with a noun denoting food, strongly suggests that the food item has been freshly prepared and should be consumed within a short time period. These attributes are paralleled in the meaning of *red hot doorbuster*: 'freshly (recently) prepared food' corresponds to 'items with new low prices'; 'for immediate consumption' corresponds to 'for immediate purchase'; and in both domains *red hot* is associated with the scalar value 'highly desirable'.

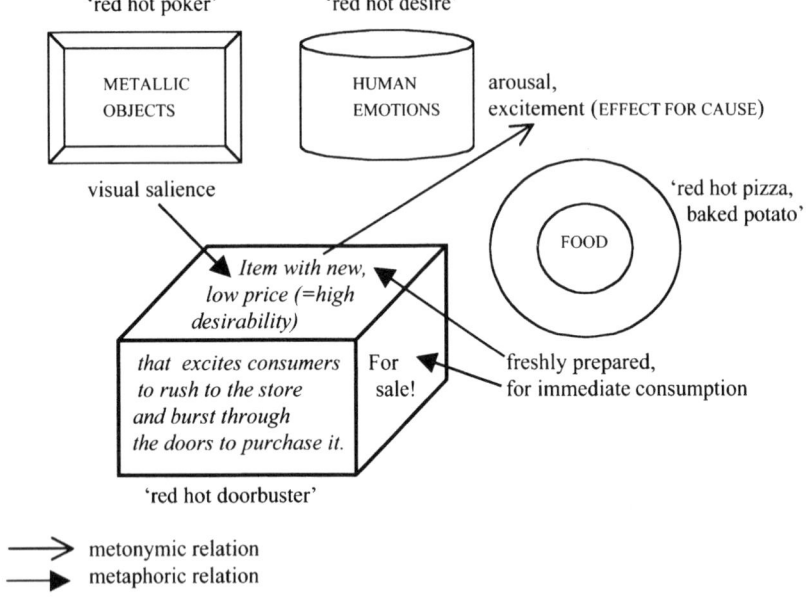

*Figure 6. Red hot doorbuster* and other *red hot* domains

## 4.    Summary and conclusions

In the preceding sections I have defended a view of metonymy that relies on the semiotic relation of indexicality rather than that of single conceptual domain or frame. I have also proposed a semiotic definition of metaphor as a special case of iconicity. The reason for this move is that the notions of domain (or frame), subdomain, single domain, and separate domains are, in my view, notoriously unclear. These notions have however been used by cognitive linguists over and over again to make important conceptual distinctions, in particular of course, as operational criteria to delineate metaphor from metonymy. This is not to challenge the notions of frame or domain as such, but to urge cognitive semanticists to develop more precise criteria for these key concepts.

Another concern of this chapter has been to demonstrate that metonymy accounts for what, to my mind, has been erroneously termed 'primary metaphor'. Given a conception of metaphor as an iconic mapping, i.e. a case of structural resemblance between a source domain and a target domain, it does not make much sense to call (the verbalization of) basic experiential correlations metaphoric. "Primary metaphors" look exactly like the indexical relations that are exploited by metonymy.

A third intention of this chapter has been to defend the view of metonymy advocated here against criticism to the effect that metonymy is a wastebasket category lumping together heterogeneous conceptual phenomena. This view rests on problematic premises of what constitutes "added meanings" in contrast to "substituted meanings". It also erroneously assumes that metonymic targets should not entail their sources.

Finally, I have tried to show, by means of two detailed case studies, how metonymic (and metaphoric) meanings are worked out in context, i.e. how metonymy functions in usage events. The aim has been to demonstrate that discourse context, as discussed in connection with Figure 1, is absolutely crucial in the interpretation of newly encountered expressions like *Pearl Harbor* (as a historic event) and *red hot doorbusters* (as special sale items/prices). Preexisting metonymic principles will guide the hearer or reader in their interpretive efforts, but only the context will allow the hearer to draw the right inferences leading to a sufficiently constrained reading. Knowledge about the semantics of related constructions provides additional input for a plausible interpretation.

## Notes

1.  I am extremely grateful to Linda Thornburg, René Dirven, and Francisco Ruiz for carefully reading the manuscript and making valuable suggestions for improvement. I have tried to heed their advice and have done my best to integrate their suggestions into the final version. This research is associated with Francisco Ruiz de Mendoza's project HUM200405947C0201/FILO (DGI, Spain).
2.  In saying that the source meaning of a metonymy is part of the target meaning, I do not claim that the target meaning necessarily entails or semantically includes the source meaning, although this possibility is not excluded.

3. Cognitive linguists have not contributed much to the elucidation of discourse functions of metonymy (i.e. metonymies in use or as "usage events"). Notable exceptions are Ruiz de Mendoza Ibáñez and Pérez Hernández (2003), who argue that metonymy is part of what is *said* (explicatures), and Barcelona (2003), who proposes an analysis of jokes and anecdotes in terms of metonymic inferences.

4. In Panther and Thornburg (1998), a distinction is made between 'indexical' ('point-to') relations and metonymic relations proper. In the former case, the relation between source and target is relatively loose (conceptually distant); in the latter it is relatively tight (conceptually close). The notion of conceptual distance between source and target is, I believe, a valid one; however, the terms 'point-to' or 'indexical' are somewhat misleading because they suggest that metonymy is not indexical. In this chapter, I assume that all of metonymic reasoning is indexical.

5. Peirce proposes the following definition for *index*: " ... what is an index, or true symptom? It is something which, without any rational necessitation, is forced by blind fact to correspond to its object." ('Telepathy', CP 7.628, 1903) [Source: Bergman and Paavola 2003].

6. Francisco Ruiz de Mendoza (p.c.) argues that the assumption that metonymy is an indexical relation implies that metonymy is an exclusively referential phenomenon, which would contradict my claim that metonymy occurs on the predicational and illocutionary levels as well. I believe that this contradiction does not arise if one assumes that metonymy indexically relates *concepts*, not real-world objects or referents. I have not found any mention of metonymy in Peirce's writings, but Peirce describes metaphor as an iconic relation (more precisely as a 'hypoicon') (see Buchler 1955: 105).

7. For the relevance of motivation in linguistics, see Radden and Panther (2004).

8. I would like to thank Francisco Ruiz de Mendoza for having pointed out to me (p.c.) that in Croft's (2002) approach a metonymic shift involves shifting prominence from a primary domain to a secondary subdomain. For example, an intrinsic feature of *Proust* is that he is a person; a less central feature is his literary work. But it is exactly this latter feature that can be metonymically exploited to refer to 'Proust's work' in sentences like *Paul has read most of Proust* (for a critique of Croft's approach, see Ruiz de Mendoza Ibáñez 2000).

9. I refer here to the latest, as yet unpublished, revision of Radden and Kövecses' (1999) seminal article.

10. Aspirin also has other medical applications, e.g. as a blood-thinner or a preventive medication for heart conditions. Thus aspirin belongs to other taxonomies as well.

11. It also seems that aspirin is not a member of the category of pain relievers, but rather it is a subcategory of the category of pain relievers. In terms of extension, the set of aspirin tablets is a proper subset of the set of pain relievers.

12. A domain can be equated roughly with what other scholars have called *frame* (Fillmore 1982) or *idealized cognitive model* (Lakoff 1987).

13. See e.g. the analysis proposed for *Wall Street* by Ruiz de Mendoza Ibáñez and Díez Velasco (2002: 513) and Ruiz de Mendoza Ibáñez and Otal Campo (2002: 65), where it is assumed that the location *Wall Street* is the matrix domain for an institution, which itself constitutes the matrix domain for people (working in the institution).

14. The kind of negation that is relevant for semantic presupposition is frame-internal negation (see Fillmore 1982).

15. This conclusion supersedes the definition of metonymy provided most recently in Panther (2005) and Panther and Thornburg (2003).

16. As an aside, it should be noted that for some of these examples it is hard to see how they involve a correlation between a sensorimotor operation and subjective experience or judgment. For example, closeness, as a spatial relation, does not seem to be describable as a "sensorimotor operation".

17. This example I have taken from Brdar and Brdar-Szabó (2003: 241). The metonymy where the manner of action stands for the action itself has been explored in some detail from a cross-linguistic perspective by the same authors (Brdar-Szabó and Brdar 2002).

18. I now think that the metonymic relation is better described as obtaining between 'be able to' (source meaning) and 'manage to' (target meaning), but this change is irrelevant to the argument made by Haser.

19. Whether there is a separate relation of semantic presupposition that is distinct from entailment is controversially discussed in the literature. For overviews, see Kempson (1975) and Wilson (1975).

20. Note that *glass* also involves a metonymically exploited relation between substance and container made of substance.

21. The idea that metonymy involves integration of the source meaning into the target meaning has also been put forward by Radden and Kövecses (2006).

22. A usage event comes very close to what in anthropological linguistics is referred to as a *speech event* and in pragmatics as a *speech act*.

23. The text from which examples (25), (27) and (29) are taken is available at: http://www.uscg.mil/reserve/magazine/mag1999/dec1999/Taney.htm. Retrieved May 21, 2006.

24. Note that I analyze *a Pearl Harbor* in way analogous to the case of *aspirin* (Figure 2). The focus is not on the class of events as such but on the any individual event that is like Pearl Harbor in significant respects.

25. By necessity Photo 1 is in black and white. In the original ad the words "red hot doorbusters" are in orange against a red field; the words "4 hours only!" are against a blue field.

26. This alternative analysis as well as Figures 5 and 6 were developed with Linda Thornburg. Much of section 3.2 would not have been possible without her competence as a native speaker of English and her expertise as a linguist. I am grateful to her for inspiring ideas during the writing of this article.

27. This definition is proposed as the basic sense of *-er* nominals in Panther and Thornburg (2001, 2002).

28. Alternatively one might also assume a hyperbolic interpretation, based on a

metonymic shift from a lower value on a behavioral scale, i.e. a relatively civilized way of rushing into a store, to a higher scalar value, i.e. stampede-like behavior that does not shy away from rudeness, aggression and physical force.

# References

Barcelona, Antonio (ed.)
2000    *Metaphor and Metonymy at the Crossroads.* (Topics in English Linguistics 30.) Berlin/New York: Mouton de Gruyter.
Barcelona, Antonio
2002    Clarifying and applying the notions of metaphor and metonymy within cognitive linguistics: an update. In *Metaphor and Metonymy in Comparison and Contrast*, René Dirven, and Ralf Pöhrings (eds.), 207–277. (Cognitive Linguistics Research 20.) Berlin/New York: Mouton de Gruyter.
2003    The case for a metonymic basis for pragmatic inferencing: Evidence from jokes and funny anecdotes. In *Metonymy and Pragmatic Inferencing*, Klaus-Uwe Panther, and Linda L. Thornburg (eds.), 81–102. (Pragmatics & Beyond New Series 113.) Amsterdam/Philadelphia: Benjamins.
2004    Metonymy behind grammar: The motivation of the seemingly "irregular" grammatical behavior of English paragon names. In *Studies in Linguistic Motivation*, Günter Radden, and Klaus-Uwe Panther (eds.), 357–374. (Cognitive Linguistics Research 28.) Berlin/New York: Mouton de Gruyter.
Bergman, Mats, and Sami Paavola (eds.)
2003 ff.    *The Commens Dictionary of Peirce's Terms: Peirce's Terminology in His Own Words.* Helsinki: University of Helsinki. [Available at: http://www.helsinki.fi/science/commens/terms/index2.html. Retrieved April 23, 2006.]
Bierwiaczonek, Bogusław
2005    On the neural and conceptual basis of semantic relations. In *Metonymy–Metaphor Collage*, Elżbieta Górska, and Günter Radden (eds.), 11–36. Warsaw: Warsaw University Press.
Brdar, Mario, and Rita Brdar-Szabó
2003    Metonymic coding of linguistic action in English, Croatian and Hungarian. In *Metonymy and Pragmatic Inferencing*, Klaus-Uwe Panther, and Linda L. Thornburg (eds.), 241–266. (Pragmatics & Beyond New Series 113.) Amsterdam/Philadelphia: Benjamins.
Brdar-Szabó, Rita and Mario Brdar
2002    Manner-for-activity metonymy in cross-linguistic perspective. In *Cognitive Linguistics Today*, Barbara Lewandowska-Tomaszczyk, and K. Turewicz (eds.), 235–257. Frankfort am Main: Peter Lang.
Buchler, Justus (ed.)
1955    *Philosophical Writings of Peirce.* New York: Dover.

Croft, William
2002    The role of domains in the interpretation of metaphors and metonymies. In *Metaphor and Metonymy in Comparison and Contrast*, René Dirven, and Ralf Pöhrings (eds.), 161–205. (Cognitive Linguistics Research 20.) Berlin/New York: Mouton de Gruyter.

Cruse, D. Alan
2000    *Meaning in Language: An Introduction to Semantics and Pragmatics.* Oxford: Oxford University Press.

Dirven, René, and Ralf Pörings (eds.)
2002    *Metaphor and Metonymy in Comparison and Contrast.* (Cognitive Linguistics Research 20). Berlin/New York: Mouton de Gruyter.

Fauconnier, Gilles, and Mark Turner
2002    *The Way We Think: Conceptual Blending and the Mind's Hidden Complexities.* New York: Basic Books.

Fillmore, Charles
1982    Frame semantics. In *Linguistics in the Morning Calm*, The Linguistic Society of Korea (ed.), 111–137. Seoul: Hanshin.

Geeraerts, Dirk
2005    Lectal variation and empirical data in Cognitive Linguistics. In *Cognitive Linguistics: Internal Dynamics and Interdisciplinary Interaction*, Francisco J. Ruiz de Mendoza Ibáñez, and M. Sandra Peña Cervel (eds.), 163–189. (Cognitive Linguistics Research 32.) Berlin/New York: Mouton de Gruyter.

Gibbs, Raymond W., Jr.
1994    *The Poetics of Mind: Figurative Thought, Language, and Understanding.* Cambridge: Cambridge University Press.

Grady, Joseph E.
1998    The conduit metaphor revisited: A reassessment of metaphors for communication. In *Conceptual Structure, Discourse and Language* 2, Jean-Pierre Koenig (ed.), 205–218. Stanford: CSLI.

Haser, Verena
*2005    Metaphor, Metonymy, and Experientialist Philosophy: Challenging Cognitive Semantics.* (Topics in English Linguistics 49.) Berlin/New York: Mouton de Gruyter.

Hiraga, Masako K.
1998    Metaphor-icon link in poetic texts: A cognitive approach to iconicity. *The University of the Open Air* 16: 95–23. [Available at: http://www.con-knet.com/~mmagnus/SSArticles/hiraga/hiraga.html. Retrieved May 26, 2006]

2005    *Metaphor and Iconicity: A Cognitive Approach to Analyzing Texts.* New York: Palgrave Macmillan.

Jakobson, Roman
2002    The metaphoric and metonymic poles. In *Metaphor and Metonymy in Comparison and Contrast*, Dirven, René, and Ralf Pörings (eds.), 41–47. (Cognitive Linguistics Research 20.) Berlin/New York: Mouton de Gruyter.

Kempson, Ruth M.
1975    *Presupposition and the Delimitation of Semantics.* Cambridge: Cambridge University Press.
Lakoff, George
1987    *Women, Fire and Dangerous Things: What Categories Reveal About the Mind.* Chicago: The University of Chicago Press.
Lakoff, George, and Mark Johnson
1980    *Metaphors We Live By.* Chicago: The University of Chicago Press.
1999    *Philosophy in the Flesh: The Embodied Mind and Its Challenge to Western Thought.* New York: Basic Books.
Langacker, Ronald W.
1987    *Foundations of Cognitive Grammar. Volume 1: Theoretical Prerequisites.* Stanford, CA: Stanford University Press.
2000    *Grammar and Conceptualization.* (Cognitive Linguistics Research 14.) Berlin/New York: Mouton de Gruyter.
Leezenberg, Michiel
2001    *Context of Metaphor.* Amsterdam: Elsevier.
Levinson, Stephen C.
2000    *Presumptive Meanings: The Theory of Generalized Conversational Implicature.* Cambridge, MA: MIT Press
Panther, Klaus-Uwe
2005    The role of conceptual metonymy in meaning construction. In *Cognitive Linguistics: Internal Dynamics and Interdisciplinary Interaction,* Francisco J. Ruiz de Mendoza Ibáñez, and M. Sandra Peña Cervel (eds.), 353–386. (Cognitive Linguistics Research 32.) Berlin/New York: Mouton de Gruyter.
Panther, Klaus-Uwe, and Linda L. Thornburg
1998    A cognitive approach to inferencing in conversation. *Journal of Pragmatics* 30: 755–769.
1999    The POTENTIALITY FOR ACTUALITY metonymy in English and Hungarian. In *Metonymy in Language and Thought,* Klaus-Uwe Panther, and Günter Radden (eds.), 333–357. (Human Cognitive Processing 4.) Amsterdam/Philadelphia: Benjamins.
2001    A conceptual analysis of English -*er* nominals. In *Applied Cognitive Linguistics II: Language Pedagogy,* Martin Pütz, Susanne Niemeier, and René Dirven (eds.), 149–200. (Cognitive Linguistic Research 19.2.) Berlin/New York: Mouton de Gruyter.
2002    The roles of metaphor and metonymy in English -*er* nominals. In *Metaphor and Metonymy in Comparison and Contrast,* René Dirven, and Ralf Pörings (eds.), 279–319. (Cognitive Linguistics Research 20.) Berlin/New York: Mouton de Gruyter.
2003    Introduction: On the nature of conceptual metonymy. In *Metonymy and Pragmatic Inferencing,* Klaus-Uwe Panther, and Linda L. Thornburg (eds.), 1–20. (Pragmatics & Beyond New Series 113.) Amsterdam/Philadelphia: Benjamins.

In press   Metonymy (Chapter 10). In *Handbook of Cognitive Linguistics*, Dirk Geeraerts, and Hubert Cuyckens (eds.). Oxford: Oxford University Press.

Paradis, Carita
2004   Where does metonymy stop? Senses, facets, and active zones. *Metaphor and Symbol* 19: 245–264.

Radden, Günter
2002   How metonymic are metaphors? In *Metaphor in Comparison and Contrast*, René Dirven, and Ralf Pörings (eds.), 407–434. (Cognitive Linguistics Research 20.) Berlin/New York: Mouton de Gruyter.

Radden, Günter, and Zoltán Kövecses
1999   Towards a theory of metonymy. In *Metonymy in Language and Thought*, Klaus-Uwe Panther, and Günter Radden (eds.), 17–59. (Human Cognitive Processing 4.) Amsterdam/Philadelphia: Benjamins.
2006   Towards a theory of metonymy. Ms. Hamburg University. [Revised version of Radden and Kövecses (1999)]

Radden, Günter, and Klaus-Uwe Panther (eds.)
2004   *Studies in Linguistic Motivation*. (Cognitive Linguistics Research 28.) Berlin/New York: Mouton de Gruyter.

Ruiz de Mendoza Ibáñez, Francisco J.
2000   The role of mappings and domains in understanding metonymy. In *Metaphor and Metonymy at the Crossroads: A Cognitive Perspective*, Antonio Barcelona (ed.), 109–132. (Topics in English Linguistics 30.) Berlin/New York: Mouton de Gruyter.

Ruiz de Mendoza Ibáñez, Francisco J., and Olga J. Díez Velasco
2002   Patterns of conceptual interaction. In *Metaphor and Metonymy in Comparison and Contrast*, René Dirven, and Ralf Pöhrings (eds.), 489–532 (Cognitive Linguistics Research 20.) Berlin/New York: Mouton de Gruyter.

Ruiz de Mendoza Ibáñez, Francisco J., and José Luis Otal Campo
2002   *Metonymy, Grammar, and Communication*. Granada: Comares.

Ruiz de Mendoza Ibáñez, Francisco J., and Lorena Pérez Hernández
2003   Cognitive operations and pragmatic implication. In *Metonymy and Pragmatic Inferencing*, Klaus-Uwe Panther, and Linda L. Thornburg (eds.), 23–49 (Pragmatics & Beyond New Series 113.) Amsterdam/Philadelphia: Benjamins.

Ruiz de Mendoza Ibáñez, Francisco J., and M. Sandra Peña
2005   Conceptual interaction, cognitive operations, and projection spaces. In *Cognitive Linguistics: Internal Dynamics and Interdisciplinary Interaction*, Francisco J. Ruiz de Mendoza Ibáñez, and M. Sandra Peña Cervel (eds.), 249–280. (Cognitive Linguistics Research 32.) Berlin/New York: Mouton de Gruyter.

Wilson, Deirdre
1975   *Presuppositions and Non-Truth-Conditional Semantics*. London: Academic Press.

# Conceptual blending in thought, rhetoric, and ideology

*Seana Coulson*

*Abstract*
Cultural models are idealized cognitive models of sociocultural phenomena. In this chapter, I suggest that the utility of cultural models lies in the ability of individual culture members to adapt overly simplistic models to our ever-changing social world via conceptual blending, a set of cognitive operations for combining concepts from different domains. A number of rhetorically motivated examples are analyzed to show how speakers use conceptual blending to integrate concepts with different affective valences, often so that the desired course of action is seen as consistent with their audience's value system. Processes of conceptual blending are argued to mediate the exploitation of stable conventional mapping schemes in order to adapt shared cultural models to the idiosyncratic needs of individuals.

*Keywords*: compression; conceptual blending theory; conceptual metaphor theory; cultural models; mental spaces; rhetoric

## 1. Introduction

One key component of ideology is cultural models, or idealized cognitive models of sociocultural phenomena. While these models are widely shared by culture members and figure importantly in reasoning about social issues, they are often inaccurate representations of social reality. They tend to be oversimplified and to apply more readily to some cases than others (see Sweetser 1987). Moreover, speakers can have multiple and, indeed, often contradictory models of the same phenomenon. In this chapter, I suggest that the utility of cultural models lies in the ability of individual culture members to adapt those models to our ever-changing social world via conceptual blending, a set of cognitive operations for combining concepts from different domains. Because blending relies on people's imaginative capacities, it often results in novel concepts and can be used to adapt cultural models to the rhetorical goals of individual members of the culture.

In the first section below, the framework of conceptual blending theory is briefly introduced, and an example of a rhetorically motivated blend is described.

Because conceptual blending theory is motivated by many of the same concerns as conceptual metaphor theory, and because the two theories share a common heritage in cognitive semantics, the relationship between these two frameworks is explored in the section on **Conceptual blending and conceptual metaphor**. This section highlights the interdependence of the two approaches and points to their differing emphasis on the language system versus particular language utterances. Where conceptual metaphor theory is focused on identifying and explaining systematic correspondence in language use across pairs of cognitive domains, conceptual blending theory is aimed at identifying mappings between cognitive models set up to understand particular utterances. Although the latter are considerably more diverse than entrenched mappings studied in conceptual metaphor theory, it is clear that conventional mappings provide speakers with an infrastructure to support the more dynamic and sometimes less principled mappings that underlie the meanings evoked by particular utterances.

This is especially the case in the examples discussed in the section on **Humorous blends**. In this section, I describe the conceptual blending employed in a number of humorous examples including cartoons and jokes. In spite of their jocular nature, the blends in such examples often deal with serious issues and play an important role in the perpetuation and negotiation of cultural models.

However, the role of conceptual blending in the propagation of cultural models is perhaps nowhere more evident than when speakers attempt to persuade one another to adopt a particular viewpoint or to convince them to act in a particular way. A number of different examples of persuasive texts and discourse are analyzed in the section on **Persuasive absurdity** to reveal the spectacular blends that speakers create. The analyses in this section amplify the point raised above that the creative elaboration and accommodation of cultural models relies heavily on conventionalized mapping and blending schemes. Moreover, they suggest that real persuasion depends on the motivational capacity of the cultural models themselves.

In the concluding section, I touch briefly on an issue that is deeply problematic in cognitive linguistics, as it is in all social sciences. That is the relationship between the meaning of sentences and the meaning of utterances, between the standard default meanings explored by linguists and the idiosyncratic meanings speakers derive in situated instances of language use, between public, idealized meaning of cultural models and their private meanings for individual culture members.

## 2. Conceptual blending

Conceptual blending theory offers a general model of meaning construction in which a small set of partially compositional processes operate in analogy, metaphor, counterfactuals, and many other semantic and pragmatic phenomena (Coulson and Oakley 2000, 2006; Fauconnier and Turner 1998, 2002). In this theory, understanding meaning involves the construction of blended cognitive models that include some structure from multiple *input* models, as well as emergent structure that arises through the processes of blending. Discussed at length in Fauconnier and Turner (2002), blending theory describes a set of principles for combining dynamic cognitive models in a network of *mental spaces* (Fauconnier 1994), or partitions of speakers' referential representations.

Mental spaces contain partial representations of the entities and relationships in any given scenario as perceived, imagined, remembered, or otherwise understood by a speaker. Mental spaces (Fauconnier 1994) can be thought of as temporary containers for relevant information about a particular domain. Spaces are structured by *elements* that represent each of the discourse entities, and simple *frames* to represent the relationships that exist between them. Frames are hierarchically structured attribute-value pairs that can either be integrated with perceptual information, or used to activate generic knowledge about people and objects assumed by default. *Cultural models* are a special kind of frame that deals with socially relevant topics. Finally, *mappings* are abstract correspondences between elements and relations in different spaces. For example, in a tale about the life of a butterfly, we might have one mental space to represent a time in the past, and one for the present. We could then posit two elements, **b** in the Past Space, and **b'** in the Present Space. Elements **b** and **b'** would be linked via an identity mapping to represent the fact that they are the same individual. However, the properties of the Past **b** would be those of a caterpillar, while the properties of Present **b'** would be those of a butterfly.

A development of mental space theory, conceptual blending is intended to account for cases in which the content of two or more mental spaces is combined to yield novel inferences. Central to conceptual blending theory is the notion of the *conceptual integration network*, an array of mental spaces in which the processes of conceptual blending unfold. These networks consist of two or more *input spaces* structured by information from discrete cognitive domains, a *generic space* that contains structure common to the inputs, and a *blended space* that contains selected aspects of structure from each input space along with any emergent structure that arises out of the imaginative processes of blending. The first process is called *composition*, and involves the juxtaposition of information from different spaces; *completion*, as in pattern completion, occurs when part of a cognitive model is activated and results in the activation of the rest of the frame. Finally, *elaboration* is an extended version of completion that results from mental simulation, or various sorts of physical and social interaction with the world as construed with blended concepts.

Blending involves the activation of cognitive models in integration networks, the establishment of partial mappings between models in the network's different spaces, and the projection of conceptual structure from space to space. Take, for example, the blended concept of a "snowflake kid", as described in a BreakPoint Online article, published on a pro-life Christian association's website (Morse 2005). Snowflake kids are children conceived through in vitro fertilization and subsequently implanted in unrelated "adoptive" mothers with the help of organizations such as the Snowflake Frozen Embryo Adoption agency. This agency allows infertile couples the opportunity to be implanted with embryos leftover from fertility clinics, and serves to rebut the case of biologists who advocate the use of such embryos for scientific research. Debate over the legitimacy of research with human embryos is quite fierce in the United States due to a lack of consensus over their moral status.

*Table 1.* Spaces in the Snowflake Kid blend

| Snowflake Space | Past Space | Blended Space | Present Space |
|---|---|---|---|
| Snowflake(s) | Embryo(e) | SnowflakeKid(sk) | Kid(k) |
| Frozen(s) | Frozen(e) | Frozen(sk) | |
| Unique(s) | Unique(e) | Unique(sk) | Unique(k) |
| | Organism(e) | Person(sk) | Person(k) |

As described by Coulson and Pascual (2006), the "snowflake kid" concept is a blend with three input spaces, the domain of snowflakes, the past, and the present. Each column in the table below shows the information represented in a mental space in the integration network for "snowflake kid". Corresponding predicates and arguments are listed in the same row, and a blank cell in the table represents the absence of a mapping (see also Broccias, this volume)[1]. The snowflake **s** in the Snowflake Space is linked to the embryo **e** in the Past Space via an analogy mapping, in that both are easily construed as being frozen as well as unique. Further, **e** in the Past Space is linked to the kid **k** in the Present Space by identity. The cognitive model in the blended space derives some of its structure from each of the input spaces.

Part of the rhetorical efficacy of this blend derives from *compression*. Compression is an operation in blending theory by which relationships that obtain between spaces are understood in a single mental model (Fauconnier and Turner 2002). For example, one might use two mental spaces to represent the different properties of an individual at two different points in time, such as that of the caterpillar and butterfly discussed above. Compression is used to construe the situation in a single cognitive model in a blended space. In the snowflake kid blend, for example, the mapping between the embryo **e** in the Past Space and the Kid **k** in the Present Space are compressed in the blend as the two different developmental stages are conflated.

The compression of embryo and child into a single entity in the Blended Space facilitates the application of certain frames that might otherwise be marked due to the ambiguous moral properties of embryos. For example, whereas the personhood of the embryo element in the Past Space is the subject of controversy between two ideological camps, the snowflake kid in the Blended Space is unambiguously a person, having inherited this property from the Present Space. Consequently, the embryo-kid blend affords the possibility of evoking frames (such as murder) whose application in the Past Space is controversial but whose application in the Blended Space is less so due to properties the embryonic snowflake kid has inherited from the kid in the Present Space.

Moreover, at least as described on the BreakPoint website, "Snowflake Kid" does not simply exploit the access principle in mental space theory (Fauconnier 1994), whereby an element in one mental space, i.e. the embryo in the Past Space, is described with language indisputably applicable in another, i.e. the kid in the Present Space. A snowflake kid differs from a normal kid in being frozen and in being extremely small. Further, the framing of a snowflake kid differs quite a bit from the scientific treatment of the microscopic embryos used in scientific research. For example,

Morse (2005) describes the embryos as "tiny humans ... stored in liquid nitrogen tanks," and refers to genetically related frozen embryos as "siblings" who "remain in these frozen orphanages."

## 3.    Conceptual blending and conceptual metaphor

Conceptual blending theory assumes many of the same claims as conceptual metaphor theory, such as the idea that metaphor is a conceptual as well as a linguistic phenomenon, and that it involves the systematic projection of language, imagery, and inferential structure between domains. The two approaches are largely complementary, with similar assumptions about the relationship between language and conceptualization, but with different emphases and foci (see Grady, Oakley, and Coulson 1999). For example, in contrast to the emphasis on conventional metaphors in conceptual metaphor theory, conceptual blending theory is intended to capture spontaneous, real-time processes that can yield short-lived and novel conceptualizations. Further, blending theory reveals connections between the cognitive underpinnings of metaphor and a variety of other linguistic phenomena handled by mental space theory (conditionals, counterfactuals, metonymy, etc.), making it especially amenable to the characterization of rhetorical discourse.

Fauconnier and Turner (2002) propose that metaphoric utterances are represented in conceptual integration networks in which the source and target domain each structure one input space, the generic space represents abstract commonalities in the inputs, and the blended space inherits structure from its inputs as well as containing emergent structure of its own. Rather than emphasizing the extent to which metaphorical utterances instantiate entrenched mappings between source and target domains, conceptual integration networks only represent those cognitive models that are particularly relevant to the mapping supported by the utterances. While mappings in the integration network require knowledge of conceptual metaphors such as those studied by Lakoff and colleagues (e.g. Lakoff and Johnson 1980), blending theory is best suited for representing the joint influence of input domains and the origin of emergent inferences in particular metaphoric utterances.

One motivation for blending theory is the observation that metaphoric expressions often have novel implications that cannot be traced back to either the source or the target domain. For example, "That surgeon is a butcher," customarily connotes the surgeon's incompetence, in spite of the fact that people neither consider surgeons to be typically incompetent, nor do they consider butchers (qua butchers) as inevitably inept at their craft. In blending theory, appreciating this metaphor involves establishing mappings between elements and relations in the source input of butchery and the target input of surgery. As in conceptual metaphor theory, there is a mapping between surgeon and butcher, patient and dead animal, as well as scalpel and cleaver.

However, blending theory also posits the construction of a blended space in which structures from each of these inputs can be integrated. In this example, the blended space inherits the goals of the surgeon and the means and manner of the butcher (Grady, Oakley, and Coulson 1999). The inference that the surgeon is incompetent arises when these structures are integrated to create a hypothetical agent with both characteristics. Behavior that is perfectly appropriate for a butcher whose goal is to slaughter an animal is appalling for the surgeon operating on a live human being. The absurd, hyperbolic nature of the cognitive model in the blended space does not seem to undermine its inferential utility, and may even enhance it (as argued in the section on Persuasive Absurdities). The table below shows the conceptual integration network for "That surgeon is a butcher."

*Table 2.* Mental spaces in Surgeon as Butcher blend

| Surgeon Input Space | Blended Space | Butcher Input Space | Generic Space |
| --- | --- | --- | --- |
| Surgeon(s) | Surgeon(s/b) | Butcher(b) | Agent |
| Patient(p) | Patient(p/a) | Animal(a) | Patient |
| Scalpel(k) | Blade(k/c) | Cleaver(c) | Cutting-Instrument |
| *Goal:* Heal Patient | *Goal:* Heal Patient | *Goal:* Kill Animal | |
| *Means:* Precise Cuts | *Means:* Slashing Cuts | *Means:* Slashing Cuts | |
| | *Emergent Inference:* Incompetent(s/b) | | |

The fact that the inference of incompetence does not originate in the source domain of butchery is further suggested by the existence of other metaphoric uses of *butcher* – such as describing a military official as *the butcher of Srebenica* – that recruit structure and imagery from the butchery domain, but do not connote incompetence. Differences in the implications of the butcher metaphor in the domains of medicine and the military highlight the need for an account of their underlying conceptual origin.

Consequently, blending theory can address the meaning construction in metaphoric expressions that do not employ conventionalized mapping schemes. For example, the italicized portion of this excerpt from an interview with philosopher Daniel Dennet involves a metaphorical blend, "There's not a thing that's magical about a computer. *One of the most brilliant things about a computer is that there's nothing up its sleeve*," (*Edge* 94, November 19, 2001). The input domains here are Computers and Magicians, and the blend involves a hybrid model in which the computer is a magician. However, the connection between these two domains arises purely from the co-text of this example, as there is no conventional COMPUTERS ARE MAGICIANS mapping in English.

Blending can also be used to explain how a number of different kinds of mappings can be combined to explain the meaning of a particular example such as the following (from Grady, Oakley, and Coulson 1999):

> With Trent Lott as the Senate Majority Leader, and Gingrich at the helm in the House, the list to the Right could destabilize the entire Ship of State.

This example involves an elaboration of the conventional Nation-as-Ship metaphor in which the Nation's policies correspond to the ship's course, leadership corresponds to steering the ship, and policy failures correspond to deviations from the ship's course. The Nation-as-Ship metaphor is itself structured by the more abstract event structure metaphor described by Lakoff (1993). The source input is the domain of Ships, which projects an image of a ship on the water, as well as the concept of the helm to the blended space. The target input is the domain of 1996 American politics which projects particular elements, including Trent Lott and Gingrich, to the blend where they are integrated with the sailing scenario.

Grady et al.'s example describes the ship listing to the right. However, in the realistic domain of ships, neither the presence of one individual (Trent Lott) nor the beliefs of the helmsman are likely to cause the ship to list. The logic of this metaphoric utterance comes not from the source input, but rather from the target input in which the Senate Majority Leader and the Speaker of the House can affect national policies and the

overall political orientation of government. Further, the standard association between conservatism and the right as against liberalism and the left
is clearly not based on the ship model, as it is frequently encountered in
other contexts. However, because the scenario in the blend involves spatial motion, the literal notion of rightward movement is integrated with
the other structure in the blend to yield a cognitive model of a ship piloted
by New Gingrich that lists to the right. This example thus demonstrates
that while the linguistic system provides speakers with a set of coherent
mappings between the source and target domains, speakers need not
maintain this coherence in the models set up during the comprehension of
utterances that exploit these conventionalized mappings.

## 4.   Humorous blends

Blending is common in social and political humor and often involves the
projection of people into new contexts where the humorist's point can be
clearly illustrated. Humorous examples highlight the human ability to derive meaningful information from partial, non-systematic correspondences in structure, and even to exploit accidental characteristics of input
frames. As Freud noted, joking provides a relatively safe arena for expressing aggressive, insulting, or otherwise socially unacceptable utterances. Blending and the cognitive abilities that support it are crucial in
this respect by enabling us to frame taboo topics in terms and domains
that are not taboo.

For example, a 1997 cartoon by Chip Bok points up a contrast in then-
President Bill Clinton's alleged penchant for dishonesty and that attributed to his 18th century political counterpart George Washington. On
the left-hand side of the cartoon, George Washington says, "I cannot tell
a lie." Addressing Washington from the right-hand side of the cartoon,
Clinton says, "If everyone's on record denying it you've got no problem."
In some ways, Bok's cartoon is similar to a blend discussed by Fauconnier
and Turner (1996) in which a modern-day philosopher engages in an imagined debate with Immanuel Kant. In the Kant blend, the professor projects Kant into the modern era so that he can get the esteemed German's
reactions to ideas composed after his death.

In Bok's cartoon, however, both Washington's and Clinton's lines were
allegedly uttered by the parties in question. Washington's lines come
straight from the historical record, while Clinton's were attributed to him
by his former mistress, Gennifer Flowers. As for Washington, legend has

it that when he was a boy, he chopped down a cherry tree on his father's farm. When Washington's father discovered what had happened, he went, furiously, to his family and demanded to know who had chopped down the tree. Knowing that he would likely receive a spanking for his efforts, Washington stood up and said, "I cannot tell a lie. It was I who chopped down the cherry tree."

On the other hand, Flowers attributed the remark in the right-hand panel of the cartoon to Clinton in her declaration in the Paula Jones harassment suit against him. Worried about whether people would perceive her relationship to then-Governor Clinton as contributing to her successful career in Arkansas state government, Flowers approached him to discuss whether she should admit to their adulterous affair. Flowers' declaration suggests Clinton told her to deny it, and that he said, "If everyone's on record as denying it, you've got no problem."

The composition of the two men's utterances in the blend results in the activation of a conversation frame and provides a context in which George Washington and Bill Clinton can interact. The mere juxtaposition of the two statements points up a contrast between the two presidents: Washington claimed to be incapable of dishonesty, while Bok portrays Clinton as someone all too willing to lie. Moreover, knowledge that Clinton's remark was originally addressed to Gennifer Flowers allows the reader to set up a mapping between Washington in the blend, and Flowers in the Clinton input. This makes Clinton look bad because it reinforces the idea that he's told people to lie in the past, and, further, it suggests that he would attempt to corrupt someone as upstanding as George Washington.

Moreover, it is only in the blend – where Clinton addresses Washington rather than Flowers – that Clinton's remark can evoke a misunderstanding of Washington's cherry tree. While "I cannot tell a lie," was presumably intended to mean that the guilt Washington would experience from lying precluded him from doing so, Clinton's remark suggests a different interpretation. Rather than guilt over lying, Clinton believes Washington fears reprisal for being caught. By offering Washington advice on how to lie without getting caught, in the cartoon Clinton presents himself as someone likely to behave (and likely to have behaved) in accordance with his own advice. Consequently, it prompts retrospective projections to Clinton's input space, framing denials of the real Clinton's misdeeds as fabricated, and further framing him as untrustworthy. Though the cartoon is probably motivated by the disanalogy between George Washington's reputation for honesty and that of Bill Clinton, the interactive frame set up in the blend provides a context in which unique structure can arise (see Coulson 2003).

Indeed, conceptual blending theory is particularly well-suited for the analysis of persuasive efforts that involve the combination of a number of different kinds of mappings. This is frequently the case in political cartoons which directly represent the contents of a blended space and invite the viewer to unpack it into its inputs. Coulson (2005) describes a cartoon by Blake Carlson that appeared in *The Arizona Republic* in November 2001 – around the time of the American Thanksgiving holiday in which it is customary to have a turkey dinner. In the cartoon, American president George W. Bush stands at the head of a dinner table about to carve a turkey labeled "Afghanistan". Seated at the table are a number of men in turbans with name-cards that read the names of Afghani ethnic groups (e.g. Uzbeks, Tajiks, Pashtuns, Hazara). Carving knife in hand, Bush says "Look, I'm doin' my best here, but there are only two of them. You can't ALL have a drumstick!"

The cartoon presents the viewer with the blend and invites her to unpack the input spaces in the network. The inputs in this case are Thanksgiving dinner and the Taliban overthrow in Afghanistan. Part of understanding this blend involves appreciating the mappings between Dad carving the turkey on Thanksgiving, Bush carving the turkey in the cartoon, and Bush dividing the control of Afghanistan. Children compete over turkey legs in the Thanksgiving input, the Afghanis compete over turkey legs in the blended space, and (many more) Afghanis compete over control of Afghanistan in the Taliban overthrow input. By having a single Afghani metonymically represent each ethnic group (the Uzbeks, Tajiks, etc.), the cartoonist here employs what Fauconnier and Turner (2002) refer to as compression to human scale[2]. In this way complex sociopolitical struggles over land rights are understood (and potentially misunderstood) by analogy to everyday experience with dinner table disputes.

One interesting facet of blending in political cartoons is that some of the actors in the blend play themselves. While some of the mappings between the blend and the Taliban overthrow space involve analogy mappings (between the turkey and Afghanistan), others involve identity mappings (Bush maps to himself). Presumably, by restricting the need to make an analogical inference to one key concept (in this case, competition over a limited resource) and utilizing identity mappings between the actors in the cartoon and the actors in the political arena (i.e. having Bush carve the turkey in the cartoon), the cartoonist facilitates appreciation of the cartoon. Political cartoons and rhetorically motivated discourse prompt us to construct blended cognitive models and, in effective cases of rhetoric, desired inferences are analogically projected from blatantly unrealistic blended cognitive models to the real-world target domain.

Coulson (1996) describes a similar phenomenon in blending in the following joke about a computer virus with some decidedly human qualities:

> Menendez Brothers Virus: Eliminates your files, takes the disk space they previously occupied, and then claims it was a victim of physical and sexual abuse on the part of the files it erased.

While ostensibly a warning about a computer virus, the rhetorical topic of this joke is the trial of Erik and Lyle Menendez. These two California teenagers confessed to the murder of their parents, and subsequently claimed they were only acting in self-defense against parents who had repeatedly abused them. Here the joke refers to elements in a blended space, in order to project structure to one of its inputs.

The inputs include technical knowledge about real computer viruses, and the social knowledge of the Menendez brothers' murder trial. While the initial structuring of the blended space is quite congruent with knowledge about computer viruses, there is some structure projected from the social input with no sensible counterparts in the technical domain. While viruses often delete files, occupy disk space, and even have colorful names, the suggestion that a computer virus could be the victim of physical and/or sexual abuse is patently absurd. The inference that the virus's claim is ridiculous and false gets transferred back to the source domain where it triggers a similar inference for the Menendez Brothers Virus' social counterparts.

Coulson (1996) shows how blending in this joke results in two sorts of alterations of conceptual structure, one momentary and one which is more sustained. First, there is the momentary conceptual integration that enables us to conceptualize an abused computer virus. Moreover, the joke also highlights how this sort of disposable blended concept can reinforce a controversial construal of the social input space. In this case, the controversy involved the agentive construal of the Menendez brothers as conspiring murderers with a phony excuse. Conceptual integration processes allow speakers to construct bizarre, disposable concepts that in turn promote particular construals of their input domains.

## 5. Persuasive absurdity

In fact, the conceptual integration of two scenarios into an absurd scenario in a blended space is a common argumentative tactic. Take the example below, from an actual jury deliberation in a high-profile murder case, videotaped and partly broadcast by an American television station:

> Juror 7: Barbara Davis [victim] doesn't get to come ... when she turns 72 in that casket she doesn't get to come out of that casket.
> Juror 11: Yeah, but there's not a guarantee that technically he'll get out either. [...]
> Juror 13: If she has no chance of getting out of the casket why should he have a chance of getting out of jail?
> Juror 2: Exactly. (JurDel.B., p. 22)

Coulson and Pascual (2006) argue that, in this blend, the victim's casket is construed as a prison from which there is no possibility of release. The disanalogy between the victim's future and the Hypothetical Future of her murderer at age 72 is used to argue for giving the murderer a life sentence. In this blend, the victim has the animate and intentional properties she had in the Past Space, before the crime occurred. Further, in spite of her death, the victim ages in an analogous fashion to the prisoner. However, unlike the prisoner, when the victim turns 72 she does not "get" to come out of the casket. Thus the middle-aged murder victim is construed in the blend as being 72 years old, and actively desiring to get out of her casket. However, she is unable to do so because she is dead.

Unlike the examples in the previous section, the unreal image evoked by this blend was not presented for embellishment or humorous purposes. On the contrary, the aging corpse in Juror 7's blend was used to argue for the appropriateness of a life sentence for the convicted murderer. In spite of the absurdity of the image in the blend, or indeed perhaps because of it, Juror 7's argument is compelling. Interestingly, the speaker's goal in this example was not to draw attention to the absurdities in the blended space, but rather to the inferences and conceptualizations that emerge from it. That is, the speaker is not attempting to argue for the absurdity of a dead individual becoming older and trying to escape from her coffin on the day her murderer is released from prison. Rather, the intended absurdity is the idea of giving a more severe punishment to the victim than to the man who killed her.

Examining other instances of blends produced by speakers under the demands of real-time conversation suggests the comprehension and production of these blends is supported by extensive appeal to conventional cultural, linguistic, and situational knowledge. Oakley and Coulson (under review), for example, analyze the creative blend in the following excerpt from a radio interview with Richard Clarke, former White House Coordinator of counter-terrorism for the Clinton Administration and the George W. Bush Administration. Clarke is deeply critical of the George W. Bush Administration's handling of the "war on terrorism," especially their handling of intelligence leading up to the 9/11 terrorist attacks.

> there's uh, some.. uh dots
> which are meaningless unless you put them together with lots of other dots.
> and,
> I understand what he's say=ing.
> But there are some dots that come out screa=ming at you.
> Uh "do something now about me."

Generically, "to connect the dots" means to understand the relationship between apparently isolated bits of information, and "failure to connect the dots" refers to the failure to do so. However, the expression has a particular conventionalized meaning in the context of the 9/11 terrorist attacks on the World Trade Center in New York City and the Pentagon in Washington, DC, and relates to the American government's failure to predict those attacks. One popular explanation of how 19 hijackers were able to outsmart the collective resources of the FBI (Federal Bureau of Investigation), the CIA (Central Intelligence Agency), and the NSA (National Security Agency) is that while a considerable amount of information relevant to the planned attacks was known to various members of these agencies, it was distributed amongst them such that no single agency had enough information to take preventive action. In this context, "failure to connect the dots" refers to the failure by US intelligence agents to understand the relationship between different facts about individuals with links to terrorist groups.

The "connect the dots" blend co-opts the KNOWING IS SEEING metaphor and applies it to the children's game of Connect the Dots by adding a few new mappings. The most important of these is the mapping between dots and information that is quite simple to establish because a unit of information is often construed as a point. The metaphoric significance of the expression "connect the dots" is bolstered by the fact that there is one entrenched meaning of *connect* that suits the game, and another that suits the epistemic domain. Because the percept corresponds to the knowledge in the KNOWING IS SEEING metaphor, connected dots correspond to known relationships between different pieces of information. In the game, connected dots afford pattern recognition; in the epistemic domain, knowing relationships between different pieces of information allows the inference of new information. Further, because the clarity of the percept maps onto the quality of the knowledge, unconnected dots that yield an unclear percept map onto poor knowledge. Moreover, the unseen pattern in the game maps onto the fact that important information is unknown to the subject of knowing.

The integration network for "connect the dots" involves one input that pertains to the Connect the Dots game, and another that pertains to national security and intelligence. In the blended space, information gleaned by intelligence agents map onto dots on a two-dimensional plane, and the pattern implicit in these dots (structure projected from the Game Space) maps onto terrorist plots in the Intelligence Space. In the blend, it is possible for the intelligence officer to see terrorist activities represented in the dots. The intelligence officer in the blend draws lines between the dots just as the child does in the presentation space. However, while the child sees a pleasing picture in her drawing, the intelligence officer gains a growing understanding of impending terrorist attacks.

In contrast to this culturally supported connect-the-dots blend which is highly coherent and supported by redundant information, Clarke's more creative screaming dots blend is difficult to understand, and especially difficult without supporting context. This difficulty is partially related to the fact that there is no pre-existing domain in which (actual) dots are construed as screaming, and without additional information it is unclear both what conventional mappings could be used to unpack this blend, and what target domain information the screaming dots are meant to evoke.

Oakley and Coulson (under review) speculate that the comprehensibility of this blend in context reflects both its recruitment of an existing blending schema, that of fictive interaction (Pascual 2002), and the way it utilizes a contextually established mapping between dots and intelligence information. Fictive interaction involves the use of frames for the structure of ordinary communicative acts to animate epistemic processes, as for example when a lawyer says that the facts in a case "tell a story". Consequently, knowing that dots map to intelligence information is crucial for understanding the applicability of the fictive interaction schema. Given this information, the manner of interaction conveys a salient inference as the dots in Clarke's blend do not simply speak, they scream. The implication from this screaming dots blend, then, is that the responsible government agencies were ignoring the warning signs.

In fact, the full meaning of Clarke's remarks is not apparent until the succeeding discourse where he points out that the CIA observed a meeting of high-level Al Quaeda operatives where the attendees were assumed to be planning an attack, and that two of these people were known to have entered the United States prior to September 11, 2001. His point is that these facts alone constituted actionable intelligence and thus the analogy to the game of "connect the dots" is not well supported. Because Clarke objects to the very premise of the mappings in the connect-the-dots blend, he explicitly disputes the applicability of the term "connect", recruiting instead the conventionalized fictive interaction blend. While fictive interaction is compatible with Clarke's construal of certain facts as being independently meaningful, it is less compatible with the mapping between facts and dots. Moreover, the impact of additional information about the target domain on the interpretability of the phrase "screaming dots" suggests that what is crucial for the argument is *not* the structure in the blended space, but rather the mappings between blended structures and concepts in the other spaces in the network.

Indeed, analysis of persuasive texts intended to actually change people's behavior ultimately depends on the audience's internalization of the relevant cultural models. For example, Coulson and Oakley (2006) discuss an example of a (real) direct mail advertisement soliciting contributions to a religious organization. The package includes a letter, a prayer page to send with donations, a return envelope for the prayer page, and a purple sealed envelope bearing a message from Jesus Christ. The letter urges its recipient to perform a number of concrete actions in order to show her faith, and be blessed by Jesus. In particular the reader is instructed to:

1. Place the purple sealed envelope under his or her pillow
2. Sleep on this "purple point of contact just like the children of Israel did when God instructed them to do so (Numbers 15:38,39)"
3. Mail back the prayer page with a donation to the Ministry.
4. Open the purple sealed envelope to receive the "purple point of contact blessing."

As one aspect of its persuasive effort, the letter invokes a blend of conceptual structures from cognitive domains associated with organized religion. For example, the letter repeatedly appeals to a metaphoric construal of making a monetary donation as sowing a seed. For example, towards the end of the letter proper, we read:

We believe you are going to sow a seed so God can bless you with a harvest. God said, "Give and it shall be given unto you ..." Luke 6:38. We pray that you will sow $5.00, $10.00, $20.00, or more. Let God lead you. Our prayer is that, by faith, what you sow will start being returned to you before the seventh day of next month, as God sees fit. He knows best how and when to let it begin. Let us pray over this last page and purple sealed word. Let us bow our heads in prayer – shall we?

Comprehension of this passage requires assuming a number of underlying mappings, including sowing a seed and sending a donation, as well as between the harvest and the money that the sender receives in return. Mappings in the network are set up by a conventional metaphoric connection between agriculture and investment, which maps the metamorphosis of a seed into crops for harvest onto the difference between the initial investment and its return. The inputs to the seed-sowing blend thus include one space we might call the Agriculture Space, and another we might call the Material Space. The mapping between the seed and the money is cued explicitly by the statement, "We pray that you will sow $5.00, $10.00 ..." in which the object of "sow" is not a type of seed (as in the Agriculture input), but a unit of currency that originates in the Material input. Linguistic prompts also help the reader identify the mapping between the harvest and the monetary returns, in "Our prayer is that, by faith, what you sow will start being returned to you ..." Since the letter writer will presumably sow money, she can expect money to be returned to her.

The structure in the blend differs from conventional conceptions of agriculture in several ways, especially in its recruitment of structure from a third input which we might dub the Spiritual space. For example, on the prayer page, which the reader sends in with her donation, is written, "I am sowing [followed by a list of potential dollar amounts] as my seed unto the Lord, in faith". Thus unlike real seeds, the seed of $5 is not planted in the earth, and unlike a conventional investment, it has not been used for its purchasing power.

The example here thus involves a prototypical case of conceptual integration in which the blended concept involves partial structure from each of its inputs as well as novel structure of its own. In the context of the blend, the $5 has some of the properties of conventional money (it can be used to buy things) and some of the properties of a seed (it will undergo a transformation). Further, unlike most agricultural endeavors, the relationship between the initial sowing of the seed and the final harvest is not mediated by farming activity. In contrast to default knowledge about managing investments, the transformation from seed to harvest here occurs "by faith". Because it is a seed of faith, the coming harvest depends on receiving a blessing from the Lord. Moreover, receiving the blessing depends on following a particular series of instructions outlined in the letter: mailing in the donation, sleeping on the (enclosed) purple envelope, and opening the purple envelope after sunset on the following day.

Coulson and Oakley (2006) argue that the desired rhetorical effect of this letter depends on the existence of systematic correspondences between the three input spaces displayed in the table. Besides conventional agricultural metaphors for investment (e.g. investments that grow), the letter authors are exploiting conventional agricultural metaphors for spirituality (e.g. spiritual growth). The former play into the reader's greed, while the latter are reminiscent of the Bible and bolster the legitimacy of the religious organization that mailed the letter.[3] The integration of these three domains results in a scenario where the reader can satisfy her greed in a virtuous way. Thus the inputs in this blend are being exploited not only for their inferential possibilities, but also for their sociocultural significance.

*Table 3.* Input spaces in faith sowing blend

| Material Space | Spiritual Space | Agricultural Space |
| --- | --- | --- |
| mail $5 | make an offering | sow a seed |
| sleep on an envelope | commit an act of faith | cultivate a seed |
| receive money | receive blessing | reap harvest |

While the letter clearly establishes the mappings between sending the money, sowing a seed, and making an offering to God, establishing the blend goes further. Without the blend, there is no way that anyone would believe that sending off $5 could result in financial gain. Similarly, the reader will not carry around the purple envelope or sleep on it unless she believes the action will have the spiritual and/or the monetary results implied in the blend. So, to reiterate, anyone who performs the actions described in the letter will do so because they have adopted the blend where mailing $5 *is* sowing a faith seed, sleeping on the envelope *is* an act of faith, and that the ultimate result of these actions will be a monetary blessing from God. Moreover, the difference between someone who does and someone who does not carry out the instructions has little to do with the mappings (presumably anyone can figure out what one is supposed to do and why), and everything to do with integrating and elaborating the structure in the blend until it becomes a motivating frame.

## 6. Conclusion

The examples above show how speakers use conceptual blending to integrate concepts with different affective valences, often so that the desired course of action is seen as consistent with their audience's value system. We have also seen how compression is used to simplify complex causal relationships, both so they can be more readily understood, and so that they can be construed with motivational "human scale" frames. Persuasive discourse in particular demonstrates the fact that our concepts have affective and motivational properties as well as abstract, inferential ones. Moreover, neither is set in stone as speakers frequently employ conceptual blending processes to reconstrue a particular action to alter its inferential, affective, sociocultural, and even spiritual significance.

Be they serious or playful, communicative acts between humans inevitably involve a balancing act between the static, shared set of idealized cultural models and the more dynamic needs of individuals faced with the realities of a social world that is considerably more complex. Because our construals of particular current events derive their social significance from the cultural models they evoke, even humorous framings serve to reinforce the status of those models as interpretive resources, and create social pressure to conform at least somewhat, and in certain restricted circumstances, to the guidelines laid out in those models.

Political jokes and cartoons can thus be seen as part of the larger social negotiation of the proper application of cultural models. By projecting prominent personalities into new contexts, cartoons promote particular construals of events and well-known people. They reinforce the availability of cultural models, and perhaps even police their use. Moreover, in exploiting the fortuitous structure that arises in blended spaces, humorous examples allow us to test the flexibility of our conceptual system, to navigate the space of possible construals, and to explore the radically different social and emotional consequences they can trigger.

However, for all their importance, the frames and cultural models evoked in discourse do not have a deterministic impact on either our behavior or our construals. People construct blends that are likely to be persuasive, given certain assumptions about how frames and cultural models affect behavior. However, the success of such efforts depends on the extent to which the individual accepts the validity of the model both in general and in its particular application. Moreover, people do not respond to each other's rhetorical efforts reflexively, but rather agentively with attempts to reframe evoked models in ways more consistent with their own rhetorical goals (see Coulson 2001 for examples). As Shore (1996: 372) writes, "processes by which cultural models are brought to mind are activities of an active, intentional, and opportunistic intelligence, not a passive recording device."

The difference between blends we act on and those we do not depends as much on the ontology supported by our cultural values and practices as it does on the structural correspondences between the representations in the different domains. For example, the success of rhetorical efforts to reify a blend like sowing a faith seed will depend in a complex way on the character of their appeal to social roles and previously established cultural practices as well as the extent to which the audience has internalized cultural values. While conceptual integration accounts for some of the mental operations necessary to incite action, the roots of action extend beyond the individual's nervous system as conceptual blends are intimately intertwined with human doings. In this sense the reason of conceptual blending is indeed the slave to the "passion" of deeply felt motivational frames.

We have seen throughout how processes of conceptual blending mediate the exploitation of stable conventional mapping schemes and adapt shared cultural models to the idiosyncratic needs of individuals.

## Notes

1. Note that there is no particular theoretical significance to the use of tables as opposed to circles (as in Fauconnier and Turner 2002) to outline conceptual integration networks. They are notational variants. Many people find tables easier to produce and comprehend, however.
2. Conceptual metonymy is a common and theoretically important example of the more general phenomenon of compression (see Fauconnier and Turner 2002). See Barcelona (2003) for a discussion of the role of conceptual metonymy in conceptual blending.
3. Indeed, the New Testament contains several different versions of the parable of the Sower, about a sower who sows seed on a path, rocks, thorns, and good dirt – and only the latter grew into plants that yielded fruit. One of the few parables in the Bible that is actually followed by exegetical notes from Jesus, the parable is typically interpreted as being about Jesus (the Sower), the gospel, or God's message (the seeds), and the inability and/or unwillingness of many people to understand God's message. See Wierzbicka (2001: 257–265) for insightful analysis of this parable. Despite the disanalogies between our letter's appropriation of this metaphor and the parable of the Sower (e.g. Jesus the Sower of God's message is presumably not a good mapping for the sinner this

solicitation is presumably aimed at), the existence of the cultural model by which a willing person can be dramatically transformed by the power of God is crucial for the success of this blend. Thanks to a reviewer for pointing this out.

# References

Barcelona, Antonio
2003    The case for a metonymic basis of pragmatic inferencing. In *Metonymy and Pragmatic Inferencing*, Klaus-Uwe Panther, and Linda L. Thornburg (eds.), 81–104. Amsterdam: Benjamins.
Coulson, Seana
2001    *Semantic Leaps: Frame-shifting and Conceptual Blending in Meaning Construction*. Cambridge: Cambridge University Press.
2003    Reasoning and rhetoric: Conceptual blending in political and religious rhetoric. In *Research and Scholarship in Integration Processes,* Elzbieta Oleksy, and Barbara Lewandowska-Tomaszczyk (eds.), 59–88. Lodz, Poland: Lodz University Press.
2005    What's so funny? Cognitive semantics and jokes. *Cognitive Psychopathology/Psicopatologia Cognitive* 2(3): 67–78.
Coulson, Seana, and Todd Oakley
2000    Blending basics. *Cognitive Linguistics* 11(3): 175–196.
2006    Purple persuasion: Conceptual blending and deliberative rhetoric. In *Cognitive Linguistics: Investigations across Languages, Fields, and Philosophical Boundaries*, June Luchjenbroers (ed.), 47–65. Amsterdam: Benjamins.
Coulson, Seana, and Esther Pascual
2006,    For the sake of argument: Mourning the unborn and reviving the dead
in press    through conceptual blending. *Annual Review of Cognitive Linguistics* 3.
Fauconnier, Gilles
1994    *Mental Spaces: Aspects of Meaning Construction in Natural Language*. Cambridge/New York: Cambridge University Press.
Fauconnier, Gilles, and Mark Turner
1994    Conceptual projection and middle spaces. La Jolla, CA: Cognitive science technical report 9401.
1998    Conceptual integration networks. *Cognitive Science* 2(1): 133–187.
2000    Compression and global insight. In (Special issue: Conceptual Blending, Seana Coulson, and Ted Oakley (guest eds.), *Cognitive Linguistics* 11(3): 283–304.
2002    *The Way We Think: Conceptual Blending and the Mind's Hidden Complexities*. New York: Basic Books.
Grady, Joseph, Todd Oakley, and Seana Coulson
1999    Conceptual blending and metaphor. In *Metaphor in Cognitive Linguistics*, Raymond W. Gibbs, and Gerard J. Steen (eds.), 101–124. Amsterdam/Philadelphia: Benjamins.

Lakoff, George
    1993    The contemporary theory of metaphor. In *Metaphor and Thought*, Or-
            tony, Andrew (ed.), 202–251. Cambridge: Cambridge University Press.
Lakoff, George, and Mark Johnson
    1980    *Metaphors We Live By.* Chicago: University of Chicago Press.
Morse, Anna
    2005    "Snowflake kids: What should we do with frozen embryos?" *Break-
            Point Online*, June 22, 2005.
Oakley, Todd, and Seana Coulson
    under    Connecting the dots: Mental spaces and metaphoric language in dis-
    review   course. In *Mental Spaces Approaches to Discourse and Interaction*,
             Todd Oakley, and Anders Hougaard (eds.). Amsterdam/Philadelphia:
             Benjamins.
Pascual, Esther
    2002    *Imaginary Trialogues: Conceptual Blending and Fictive Interaction in
            Criminal Courts.* Utrecht: LOT Dissertation Series, n. 68.
Shore, Bradd
    1996    *Culture in Mind: Cognition, Culture, and the Problem of Meaning.* Ox-
            ford: Oxford University Press.
Wierzbicka, Anna
    2001    *What Did Jesus Mean? Explaining the Sermon of the Mount and the
            Parables in Simple and Universal Human Concepts.* Oxford/New York:
            Oxford University Press.

# Part three: The psychological basis

# The contested impact of cognitive linguistic research on the psycholinguistics of metaphor understanding

*Raymond W. Gibbs, Jr. and Marcus Perlman*

*Abstract*
The cognitive linguistic revolution has had a major, yet contested, impact on psycholinguistic studies of metaphor understanding. Despite the tremendous success, and increasing popularity of cognitive linguistic work on metaphor, psychologists have been particularly critical of many of the central claims about conceptual metaphor, and its possible implications for theories about conceptual structure and metaphor understanding. Outside of psychology, scholars voice concern about the lack of explicit criteria for identifying conceptual metaphors from a systematic analysis of conventional expressions, how to distinguish one conceptual metaphor from another, and the fact that much cognitive linguist research is not based on the analyses of speech and writing in real cultural contexts. We briefly outline several steps that cognitive linguists can adopt within the context of their research to deal with some of these problems. We then go on to describe recent experimental work from psycholinguistics that partly stems from cognitive linguistic ideas and research, and is, indeed, quite consistent with newer claims about metaphor made in cognitive linguistics. The conclusion provides our impressions of the present state-of-affairs about the application of cognitive linguistics research to psycholinguistic accounts of metaphor understanding.

*Keywords*: psycholinguistics; psychological reality; methodology; experimental re-orientation of CL; conceptual metaphor theory; psycholinguistic critique of introspection; setting up of hypothesis; testing of hypothesis

## 1. Introduction

The cognitive linguistic revolution has had a major, yet contested, impact on psycholinguistic studies of metaphor understanding. Cognitive linguistic studies have demonstrated that metaphor is not just a special linguistic device, perhaps reflecting one-shot mental mappings, but arises from enduring patterns of metaphorical thought, or conceptual metaphor, many of which are grounded in embodied and neural activity. Evidence in favor of conceptual metaphor theory comes from a variety of sources, including systematic patterns of linguistic expressions, novel extensions of conventional metaphors, polysemy, historical development of metaphorical meanings, gesture, nonlinguistic exhibitions (e.g., art), as well as studies in computational modeling of metaphorical inference patterns and psycholinguistic experiments (Lakoff and Johnson 1999). The psycholinguistic data suggest that people (a) appear to possess enduring metaphorical understandings of many abstract concepts, and (b) apply this metaphorical knowledge when making sense of and immediately processing many, but not necessarily all, kinds of conventional and novel metaphoric expressions (Gibbs 1994, 2006).

Despite the tremendous success, and increasing popularity of cognitive linguistic work on metaphor, there are numerous criticisms of this research, both from scholars within and outside of linguistics. Psychologists have been particularly critical of many of the central claims about conceptual metaphor, and its possible implications for theories about conceptual structure and metaphor understanding (Glucksberg 2001; Murphy 1996). Outside of psychology, scholars voice concern about the lack of explicit criteria for identifying conceptual metaphors from a systematic analysis of conventional expressions (Barcelona 2002; Steen 2002), how to distinguish one conceptual metaphor from another, and the fact that much cognitive linguist research, is not based on the analyses of speech and writing in real cultural contexts (but see Deignan 2005; Stefanowitsch 2004).

Our aim in this chapter is to describe some of the important criticisms of cognitive linguistic studies on metaphor. These criticisms are not sufficiently attended to in cognitive linguistic research on metaphor, which ultimately diminishes the impact that this work has for comprehensive, interdisciplinary theories of metaphor use and understanding. We briefly outline several steps that cognitive linguists can adopt within the context of their research to deal with some of these problems. We then go on to describe recent experimental work from psycholinguistics that partly stems from cognitive linguistic ideas and research, and is, indeed, quite consistent with newer claims about metaphor made in cognitive linguistics. The conclusion provides our impressions of the present state-of-affairs about the application of cognitive linguistics research to psycholinguistic accounts of metaphor understanding.

## 2. Problems with Cognitive Linguistic studies

### 2.1 Are linguistic analyses sufficient?

Most of the evidence for conceptual metaphors comes from purely linguistic analyses, and various cognitive psychologists, philosophers and linguists have expressed deep skepticism about these claims on both methodological and theoretical grounds. First, psychologists, in particular, are concerned with the fact that most metaphor analyses come from individual linguists' intuitions without explicit criteria to support these judgments. For instance, Vervaeke and Kennedy (1996) argue that conceptual metaphor theory is unfalsifiable if the only data in its favor is the systematic grouping of metaphors linked by a common theme as identified by an individual linguist, or by linguists inferring single conceptual metaphors from many different texts. Consider, for example, the widely discussed conceptual metaphor ARGUMENT IS WAR (Lakoff and Johnson 1980), which presumably motivates conventional expressions such as "He attacked my argument" and "He defended his position." Lakoff and Johnson list several characteristics of arguments that arise from the mapping of ideas about war onto the target domain of arguments. One participant has a position; the other participant has a different position. Both positions matter because one must surrender for the other to achieve victory. Differences of opinion become a conflict. Both participants plan strategy, marshal their forces, attack the other's claims, defend their own, maneuver to achieve a stronger position, and occasionally retreat before a stronger argument.

But Vervaeke and Kennedy argue that many of these elements and many of the conventional expressions consistent with the ARGUMENT IS WAR conceptual metaphor are also consistent with different possible conceptual metaphors such as ARGUMENT IS CHESS and ARGUMENT IS BOXING (also see Ritchie 2003). The names of some chess pieces suggest a war metaphor (castle, knight), and war is frequently mentioned in the context of athletic and business competition. When terms such as "attack," "defend," or "strategy" appear in discussions of arguments, one cannot be sure whether any particular person will associate these words with chess, boxing, all-out war, or with nothing beyond some highly abstract concept. Other conventional expressions seen as support for ARGUMENT IS WAR such as "He demolished her argument" and "His criticisms were right on target" could just as reasonably be associated with the source domain of BUILDINGS or PLACEMENT (Haser 2005; but see

Grady 1997; Lakoff and Johnson 1999 for how these may be related to an underlying primary metaphor ORGANIZATION IS PHYSICAL STRUC-TURE).

In a similar vein, Haser (2005) notes that the level of generality for the source domain of a conceptual metaphor seems, to her, to be specified in an arbitrary manner. Thus, the ARGUMENT IS WAR metaphor might better be expressed using a more general source domain such as FIGHT, even though this level of abstraction makes it far less clear whether we are still speaking about arguments metaphorically. Many people would feel quite comfortable subcategorizing argument as literally a kind of fight.

Haser does not sufficiently acknowledge how the work on primary metaphors handles some of these problems in specifying the exact level for a source domain in conceptual metaphor theory. But her observations about source domain indeterminacy raise a related issue in that cognitive linguists do not typically explore alternative accounts for their data. For example, Haser (2005) proposes, similar to Murphy (1996), that meta-phorical expressions get extended through a chain of family resemblances. For instance, an expression such as "win an argument" could be linked to other expressions by the domain of GAMES, while it could also be linked to expressions by the domain of WAR. This expression related to WAR could then systematically relate to an extended use of "fortify," which also then links to BUILDINGS, and so on. In this way, Haser claims to account for the wide variety of existing metaphorical expressions about ARGU-MENTS, while eliminating the problematic issue of their indeterminate source domains. Haser contends that her approach is more "theoretically parsimonious" than the cognitive perspective, as well as free from "the-ory-internal contradictions" (Haser 2005: 19–20).

At the very least, linguistic analyses alone are unable to determine what putative conceptual metaphors underlie the use of particular linguistic ex-pressions. As Murphy (1996) advises, metaphorical linguistic patterns might indeed be related to underlying metaphorical conceptual structure; however, there must be *independent* evidence for such structure.

Underlying these criticisms of cognitive linguistic research is the skepti-cism that many scholars have about drawing inferences about the nature of thought from linguistic analyses. In many cases, cognitive linguists assume a direct, or motivated, relationship between systematicity in language with people's underlying cognitive reality, including their unconscious mental representations and brain structures (Dodge and Lakoff 2005). Concepts are talked about in metaphorical language because people think about these ideas metaphorically. At the same time, the complexity of metaphorical meanings are assumed to require equally complex cognitive processes to create or understand by ordinary language users, such as that seen in conceptual blending theory (Fauconnier and Turner 2002). The challenge then for cognitive linguistics is to frame this hypothesis in a falsifiable way, including the ability to test it by language-independent methods in order to reinforce the linguistic evidence (see for example the recent work by Dodge and Lakoff 2005 on a neural theory of metaphor).

## 2.2 What counts as a metaphor?

Some psychologists and linguists argue that many conventional expressions viewed as metaphorical by cognitive linguists are not metaphorical at all, and are treated by ordinary speakers/listeners as literal speech (Glucksberg 2001; Keysar, Shen, Glucksberg and Horton 2000). They suggest that simple expressions like "He was depressed" are entirely literal, and are not motivated by a conceptual metaphor such as SAD IS DOWN. Some empirical evidence suggests that people comprehend many conventional expressions without activating any metaphorical mappings or conceptual metaphors (Keysar et al. 2000).

How does one identify any instance of language as conveying metaphorical meaning? Conceptual metaphor theory lacks an explicit identification procedure capable of reliably identifying metaphorically-used words and expressions in discourse. Various scholars are now working on creating explicit, reliable criteria for doing just this (Barcelona 2002; Dirven 2002; Ruiz de Mendoza 2002; Steen 2002). At the same time, conceptual metaphor theory has no explicit method for identifying conceptual metaphors. How does one determine what constitutes adequate systematicity among linguistic expressions to be able to posit the existence of a conceptual metaphor? The cognitive linguistic logic seems circular. Analysts first examine linguistic expressions, enough so to infer the possible presence of underlying metaphorical mappings, and then test this possibility by referring back to language. But independent, nonlinguistic evidence is needed to break open the language-to-thought-to-language circle. Even if one does find systematicity in a set of expressions, how does one determine the actual source-to-target domain mappings, or metaphorical correspondences? These types of enduring questions are not particular to cognitive linguistics, as generative linguists face the same uncertainties in clearly identifying various syntactical patterns, to take one example.

The failure to provide reliable criteria for identifying metaphoric language and concepts suggests to many scholars that cognitive linguistic claims simply lack empirical support and should not be treated as either psychologically real (Glucksberg 2001; Murphy 1996) or philosophical (Haser 2005) accounts of metaphoric language and thought.

### 2.3    What is metaphor understanding?

Finally, cognitive linguistic discussions of metaphor understanding typically do not distinguish between different aspects of linguistic experience. The claim that conceptual metaphors are "automatically" accessed during language use does not imply that people always compute, or access en bloc, conceptual metaphors when interpreting real speech, especially familiar or conventional language. Similarly, complex blending theory analyses of the meanings associated with different metaphorical constructions do not imply that (a) people necessarily infer all those meaning ordinarily during language processing, or (b) engage in the exact set of blending operations posited by the theory, especially, again, when the expressions being understood are conventional. In general, cognitive linguistics accounts of metaphor typically do not acknowledge the complex ways that language understanding can be characterized, ranging from very fast, unconscious comprehension processes to slower, more reflective, interpretation activities (Gibbs 1994).

### 2.4    Methodological suggestions

There are several ways that cognitive linguistic work on metaphor can be presented in a way to make this research more amenable to empirical validation (adapted from Gibbs in press).

1. Don't rely solely on your own intuitions. Systematically ask others, including nonlinguists, for their judgments, and report the degree of similarity of response.
2. Don't just use made-up examples Examine a large sample of linguistic materials related to the topic or phenomenon of interest. Although individual case studies and the analysis of individual exceptions to broader trends are always interesting and, indeed, often important, determining the extent to which some linguistic phenomenon exists, and its frequency, is critical to establishing the legitimacy of one's intuitions about some aspect of language.
3. Be as concrete as possible about the exact criteria used for classifying some language item as an instance of some larger linguistic or conceptual category. For instance, describe exactly what criteria have been

employed to determine that a particular expression is motivated by one conceptual metaphor, as opposed to another.

4. Acknowledge the context in which linguistic statements appear. Again, cognitive linguistics has a tendency to focus on isolated examples that are either made-up or stripped from their contexts. But just as judgments of grammaticality and semantic anomaly can vary depending on the context in which word strings appear, so too may judgments about matters such as metaphoricity and conventionality alter with the specifics of context.

5. Do not assume that linguistic analyses are isomorphic with individual mental representations. Articulate falsifiable hypotheses about the role of unsconscious conceptual knowledge in language use. Thus, make sure that each speculative possibility mentioned (e.g., a particular blending account of how counterfactuals are understood) can, in principle, shown to be false. By trying to disprove a theory, and failing to do so, this lead to a tentative acceptance of the idea as having a reasonable degree of empirical support.

6. Always specify alternative hypotheses. Most cognitive linguistic proposals do not consider alternatives, which is a special problem when making claims for postulated conceptual entities like image schemas, conceptual metaphors, and the like, as well as hypothetical cognitive processes like conceptual integration.

7. Do not assume that complex meanings require complex mental processes to produce or understand those meanings. People may be able to correctly infer what a linguistic expressions means without having to engage in complex psychological processing because of the familiarity and/or frequency of the individual words and expressions. People may learn and correctly understand the complex meanings of many words and expressions by various means that have little to do with the possible cognitive motivation for such speech within a linguistic community (Langacker 1987). Acknowledge these other forces, such as historical convention, cultural norms, and social context, as relevant reasons for why people speak and understand as they do, and suggest ways of how these factors may even interact with conceptual schemes in explaining realistic linguistic behavior.

Paying close attention to these recommendations would enhance the empirical credibility of cognitive linguistic research on metaphor, at least in the eyes of many cognitive scientists, and likely lead to more experimental studies arising from cognitive linguistic analyses.

## 3.    Embodied metaphor understanding: recent experimental evidence

Our discussion of some criticisms of cognitive linguistic research on metaphor is partly offset by a wide variety of psycholinguistic evidence that supports basic tenets of conceptual metaphor theory. Indeed, many psycholinguistic studies provide evidence suggesting that accessing conceptual metaphors is part of the interpretation and processing of many kinds of metaphorical language (Boroditsky and Ramscar 2002; Gibbs 1994, 2006; Langston 2002), even if there remains much debate within psychology on the merits of this work (Glucksberg 2001; Murphy 1996).

For the most part, psycholinguistic research has followed cognitive linguistic ideas that characterize the activation of conceptual metaphor during metaphor understanding as a purely cognitive process. Thus, understanding the conventional phrase "Our relationship has hit a dead-end street" is partly accomplished through the activation of the conceptual metaphor LIFE IS A JOURNEY in long-term memory. This enduring chunk of metaphorical knowledge has a source domain (e.g., JOURNEY) that is grounded in the pervasive bodily experience, or image-schema, of SOURCE-PATH-GOAL. But the entire process of accessing a specific conceptual metaphor during verbal metaphor understanding is mostly viewed as activating abstract, schematic, disembodied knowledge that is not tied to ongoing bodily action

But there is now an emerging body of empirical work suggesting that understanding what any word or phrase means requires that listeners engage in an experiential/embodied simulation of the described situation (Gallese 2005). Research from cognitive linguistics, known as "simulation semantics," gives a primary role to embodied simulations in drawing appropriate inferences from various metaphorical and non-metaphorical language (Bergen 2005; Feldman and Narayanan 2004; Gallese and Lakoff 2004). For example, concepts are physical objects that can be touched, held on to, juggled, and dropped. When hearing "grasp the concept" listeners engage in, or imagine engaging in, a relevant body action, such as grasping, that facilitates metaphorical construal of the abstract notion of "concept" as a physical entity, such that concepts can be things that are grasped, held on to, dropped, misplaced, chewed on, and so on. In this way, the recruitment of embodied metaphors in some aspects of verbal metaphor understanding is done imaginatively as people recreate what it must be like to engage in similar actions. The remainder of this paper describes various new experimental research, employing rather different methodologies, which provide additional behavioral evidence on embodied simulations in metaphoric language interpretation.

### 3.1  Accessing sensorimotor information in TIME metaphors

Do people rely on sensorimotor information during their interpretation of linguistic metaphor? Research indicates that bodily experience and current bodily positioning also appears to shape the way people respond to questions about the time, which is often characterized by two different versions of the TIME IS SPACE metaphor (e.g., time is moving while the ego is still, and time ix still while the ego is moving). For instance, in one series of studies on metaphorical talk about time, students waiting in line at a café were given the statement "Next Wednesday's meeting has been moved forward two days" and then asked "What day is the meeting that has been rescheduled?" (Boroditsky and Ramscar 2002). Students who were farther along in the line (i.e., who had thus very recently experienced more forward spatial motion) were more likely to say that the meeting had been moved to Friday. Similarly, people riding a train were presented the same ambiguous statement and question about the rescheduled meeting. Passengers who were at the end of their journeys reported that the meeting was moved to Friday significantly more than did people in the middle of their journeys. Although both groups of passengers were experiencing the same physical experience of sitting in a moving train, they thought differently about their journey and consequently responded differently to the rescheduled meeting question. These results demonstrate how ongoing sensorimotor experience has an influence on people's comprehension of metaphorical statements about time.

### 3.2  Imagining metaphorical actions

Consider the phrase "grasp the concept." It is physically impossible to place one's hands on an abstract entity such as a concept, yet people talk as if they do so all the time. Why is this so? One set of studies investigated whether people can form mental images for metaphorical phrases that refer to actions literally impossible to perform, such as "chewing on the idea," "stretch for understanding," and "cough up a secret" (Gibbs, Gould and Andric in press). The idea explored in these experiments was that people's embodied metaphorical conceptualizations of abstract ideas should enable them to imagine the ways that abstract entities may be acted upon. Unlike imagining nonmetaphorical action statements (e.g., "chew on the gum"), where people's images should focus on the procedural characteristics of the concrete actions (i.e., moving their mouths as they chew the gum), people's mental images for metaphorical phrases should show an analogical understanding of how abstract domains, such as ideas or concepts, can be actively structured in terms of embodied source domains (i.e., chewing on something to get more out of it).

The results of a first study showed that when participants were presented specific phrases that were either metaphorical (e.g., "grasp the concept") or nonmetaphorical (e.g., "grasp the branch"), given ten seconds to form a mental image of that action, and asked "What is particularly noticeable in your image?" they gave a wide variety of responses to this question, and these could be roughly divided into two groups. The first set of answers made some specific reference to the participants actually participating in the action. For example, when one participant was given the metaphorical phrase "chew on the idea," she noted, "My jaw goes up and down as I chew." People actually gave far more of these specific references to participating in the action responses for the nonmetaphors (63%) than to the metaphors (29%).

But for the metaphors, people gave significantly more conceptualized description of the action responses (71%) than they did for the nonmetaphors (37%). For instance, when one person was presented with the metaphor "stretch for understanding," he said that the most noticeable thing in his image was "there is much stretching going in both in terms of the ideas being stretched out to see if they are true and me stretching to better see of examine the idea." The participant essentially noted that IDEAS ARE OBJECTS which can be physically inspected, by stretching them out to more effectively examine them, and that UNDERSTANDING IS GRASPING enables the person to extend his or her body to better control the object, and thus better understand it. This response provides an excellent example of how embodied metaphors constrain the mental images people construct when hearing metaphorical action statements.

When participants were next asked, "Why is this concept (e.g., idea) sometimes associated with this action (e.g., chewing)?" they gave two types of responses. The first set of responses focused on providing a concrete explanation of the relevant process or action. For instance, when one participant heard the nonmetaphorical phrase "chew on the gum." she responded with "That is what you do with gum-chew on it." But for the metaphors, people specifically provided an analogous, conceptual explanation as to why some concept was sometimes associated with some action or process. For example, for the metaphorical phrase "chew on the idea," one person said "Chewing is related to a slow methodological activity and it could be related to turning something over in your mind to better understand it." Overall, people gave analogous, conceptual explanations significantly more often to the metaphors (77%) than to the nonmetaphors (36%). This result is as expected, assuming that people's mental images for metaphorical action phrases are constrained by their embodied, metaphorical understandings of the target domains referred to in these expressions (e.g., ideas, concepts, feelings).

A second study more directly explored the possibility that people imagine metaphorical actions by engaging in embodied simulations of the actions referred to in the metaphorical statements. Participants once again heard different metaphorical and nonmetaphorical expressions, formed mental images for these phrases, and then answered a series of questions about their images. In Experiment 2, however, people also participated in one of three enactment conditions in which they first did one of three things: (a) watched the experimenter make a bodily action relevant to the main verb in each statement (e.g., making a stretching motion before forming a mental image for the phrase "stretch for understanding"), (b) watched the experimenter make a relevant bodily action, which they then imitated, before being given ten seconds to form their mental image for a phrase, or (c) watched the experimenter make a relevant bodily action, then imagined themselves doing the same action, before forming a mental image for the phrase. These three experimental treatments were referred to as the watching, imitating, and imagining conditions, respectively.

Analysis of the responses to the conceptual explanations for the metaphors, collapsed across all three enactment conditions, showed that 78% of these referred to additional bodily actions and consequences of these actions related to the main verb in each metaphorical phrase. This proportion was higher than that obtained in Experiment 1 (48%). For example, when one participant was given the phrase "put your finger on the truth" (in the imagine condition), she replied "I guess being able to touch the truth is an important thing, being able to relate to it, being able to actually see that it is a physical thing and can be examined." This evidence reflects the product of the embodied simulation the participant constructed that made this impossible action plausible and meaningful.

The extent to which people ordinarily engage in imagistic processes during online metaphor comprehension is unclear. But the Gibbs et al. studies show that asking people to form explicit mental images for metaphoric and nonmetaphorical language can reveal significant differences in people's intuitions about why these phrases have the specific meanings they do, including the important role of embodied metaphorical thought in constructing simulations of different metaphorical actions. Having people engage in different kinds of bodily action does not interfere with the creation of metaphorical images, but seems to highlight the imaginative reasons for why impossible metaphorical action phrases are meaningful and plausible.

3.3  Bodily movement and metaphor comprehension

In most theories of metaphor understanding, when people read "grasp the concept" they must inhibit the physical meaning of "grasp" to properly infer its abstract, metaphoric meaning (see Glucksberg 2001). Under this view, having people make a grasping motion before reading "grasp the concept" should interfere with their immediate processing of the phrase. Yet one recent set of studies demonstrated this was not true. Wilson and Gibbs (2006) hypothesized that if abstract concepts are indeed understood as items that can be acted upon by the body, then performing a related action should facilitate sensibility judgments for a figurative phrase that mentions this action. For example, if participants first move their arms and hands as if to grasp something, and then read "grasp the concept," they should verify that this phrase is meaningful faster than when they first performed an unrelated body action. Engaging in body movements associated with these phrases should enhance the online simulations that people create to form a metaphorical understanding of abstract notions, such as "concept," even if "concepts" are not things that people can physically grasp.

In fact, a computerized reading-time study showed that participants responded more quickly to the metaphorical phrases that matched the preceding action (e.g., the motor action grasp was followed by "grasp the concept"), than to the phrases that did not match the earlier movement (e.g. the motor action kick was followed by "grasp the concept"). People were also faster in responding to the metaphor phrases having performed a relevant body movement than when they did not move at all. In short, performing an action facilitates understanding of a metaphoric phrase containing that action word. A second study showed that same pattern of bodily priming effects when participants were asked to imagine performing the actions before they made their speeded responses to word strings. This result reveals that real movement is not required to facilitate metaphor comprehension, only that people mentally simulate such action.

Controlled studies demonstrated that these findings were not due to simple lexical associations created from doing or imagining the actions and seeing specific words in the phrases.

Most generally, processing metaphoric meaning is not just a purely cognitive act, but involves some imaginative understanding of the body's role in structuring abstract concepts. People may create embodied simulations of speakers' messages that involve moment-by-moment "what must it be like" processes that make use of ongoing tactile-kinesthetic experiences. These simulations processes operate even when people encounter language that is abstract, or refer to actions that are physically impossible to perform.

## 3.4  Embodied simulations in understanding metaphorical narratives

Consider the following two brief narratives about the development of two different romantic relationships.

Story A
Imagine that you are a single person. A friend sets you up on a blind date. You really like this person and start dating a lot. Your relationship was moving along in a good direction. But then it got even better. The relationship felt like it was the best you ever had. This continues to this day. No matter what happens, the two of you are quite happy together.

Story B
Imagine that you are a single person. A friend sets you up on a blind date. You really like this person and start dating a lot. Your relationship was moving along in a good direction. But then you encountered some difficulties. The relationship did not feel the same as before. This lasted for some time. No matter how hard you two tried, the two of you were not getting along.

Story A and B differ in that A describes a successful relationship, while B describes a relationship that appears to be in trouble. Both stories are similar, however, in conceiving of the relationships as entities that can move along some sort of path (RELATIONSHIPS ARE JOURNEYS), as indicated in the fourth line "Your relationship was moving along in the good direction." Although no other part of the two stories explicitly refers to journeys, the two stories provide different impressions of the "relationship journey." Thus, Story A suggests a smooth, uninterrupted journey that is still progressing, while Story B implies a more difficult, perhaps interrupted, journey that may no longer be progressing.

When college students read the two stories above, they specifically judged the successful metaphorical relationships to be progressing further, moving along in a straighter line and the story participants to be heading more in the same direction than was the case for the unsuccessful metaphorical story (Gibbs 2006b). There is nothing in the metaphorical stories that directly assert anything about the distance, speed, extent, and direction of the relationship "journeys" traveled. All of these inferences were drawn on the basis of people's metaphorical understandings of the stories as referring to RELATIONSHIPS ARE JOURNEYS (with RELA-TIONSHIP ARE VEHICLES TRAVELING ALONG A PATH as a possible more specific instantiation), as suggested by the "Your relationship was moving along in a good direction" statement.

One new set of studies used a new methodology to examine whether people's interpretations of simple narratives, like the above stories, partly rely on their embodied understandings of the metaphors involved (Gibbs 2006b). The hypothesis examined was that people infer the detailed meanings of simple narratives involving conceptual metaphors by imagining their participating in the metaphorical actions explicitly mentioned in these stories. For example, when hearing "moving along in a good direction," listeners imagine engaging in a body action, such as traveling along some path, which facilitates their metaphoric understanding of the abstract, and physically impossible, idea that romantic relationships can move along a path toward some goal. If people imaginatively simulate themselves in the journey, then listening to these different renditions of the RELATIONSHIPS ARE JOURNEYS conceptual metaphor should have different real world embodied effects. To assess this idea, people listened to one of the two above stories, were blindfolded, and then walked along a path toward an object while they thought about the story. People should walk differently when hearing successful and unsuccessful metaphor stories, while these effects should be greatly attenuated after hearing nonmetaphorical narratives that did not suggest a conceptualization of the relationship as a kind of physical journey.

This hypothesis was tested in a novel manner by having participants physically walk toward an object, 40 feet away, after hearing either a successful or unsuccessful story in either the metaphorical or nonmetaphorical condition. Another experimental condition asked participants to simply imagine walking to the object after hearing one of the stories. Analysis of the walking times generally showed that people walked significantly longer for the successful metaphorical stories (15.7 seconds) than for the unsuccessful metaphorical stories (12.8 seconds), but that this difference was not reliable in the nonmetaphorical condition (14.8 and 14.6 seconds). Analysis of the length of walking (in vertical relationship to the target) again showed that people walked further for the successful stories (2 feet 4 inches beyond the object) than for the unsuccessful ones (2 feet 3 inches below the object).

Analysis of the walking times generally showed that people walked significantly longer for the successful metaphorical stories (15.7 seconds) than for the unsuccessful metaphorical stories (12.8 seconds), but that this difference was not reliable in the nonmetaphorical condition (14.8 and 14.6 seconds). Analysis of the length of walking (in vertical relationship to the target) again showed that people walked further for the successful stories (2 feet 4 inches beyond the object) than for the unsuccessful ones (2 feet 3 inches below the object).

Another experimental condition asked participants to simply imagine walking to the object after hearing one of the stories. For the imagined condition, participants were blindfolded, heard a story, but were then instructed to only imagine walking out to the yellow ball as they thought about the story, and to press a stopwatch as soon as they imagined arriving at the ball. The results of the imagine condition showed that people imagined walking longer for the successful metaphor stories (11.4 seconds) than for the unsuccessful metaphoric narratives (9.5 seconds). Unlike the data for the walking condition, where no difference was obtained, people imagined walking longer in the unsuccessful condition (12.5 seconds) than in the successful one (9.5 seconds). The reason for this latter finding is not clear.

These studies suggest that people's interpretation of the stories partly involved creating an embodied simulation, or a reenactment, of the relationship journey alluded to in the different metaphorical narratives. Even though relationships are not physical entities that literally travel along physical paths, people nonetheless conceive of relationships in metaphorical ways, especially when prompted to do so by statements like "Your relationship was moving along in a good direction." This metaphorical conceptualization is not purely abstract, but embodied in the sense that participants imagine themselves moving in the different relationship journeys, perhaps together in a vehicle, which subsequently affected their walking, and imagining of walking, as they thought about the stories.

## 4.  Conclusion

Cognitive linguistic ideas on metaphor understanding have certainly generated a great deal of discussion and experimental research within psycholinguistics. There remain important criticisms of cognitive linguistic methods, and distrust of its theoretical conclusions about metaphorical thought and language use. But it is also clear that much research has been reported which is deeply consistent with aspects of conceptual metaphor theory, especially in regard to newer advances on metaphor understanding as an embodied simulation process. The experimental studies described in this chapter employ a variety of methods to explore various parts of people's immediate comprehension of and intuitions about different metaphoric language. Yet the findings all point to the intriguing idea that interpreting some metaphorical language involves the construction of embodied simulations related to the actions mentioned (e.g., "moving along in a good direction"). This conclusion is consistent with an emerging literature in psycholinguistics on the importance of embodiment in nonmetaphorical linguistic processing (Gibbs 2006a; Pecher and Zwaan 2005). In this way, the application of cognitive linguistic ideas on metaphor are supported by experimental research on language comprehension, more generally.

Despite its success, cognitive linguistic research will continue to be contested by various scholars in different academic disciplines, until it addresses some of its methodological weaknesses, or at least better articulates the methods implicit in much of this work. Psycholinguists should aim to explain systematic metaphor patterns and novel metaphorical extensions, for example, as discovered by cognitive linguists. In this way, psychologists and others must focus more of their attention to the empirical contributions of cognitive linguistic research. But cognitive linguists should also acknowledge the limitations of their own research, as should all scientists, and seek to ground their empirical findings on firmer grounding, especially in the ways that linguistic evidence is gathered, analyzed, and explained in reliable, falsifiable ways.

# References

Barcelona, Antonio
2002    Clarifying and applying the notions of metaphor and metonymy within cognitive linguistics: An update. In *Metaphor and Metonymy in Comparison and Contrast*, René Dirven, and Ralf Pörings (eds.), 207–277. Berlin/New York: Mouton de Gruyter.

Bergen, Benjamin
2005    Mental simulation in literal and figurative language understanding. In *The Literal and Nonliteral in Language and Thought*, Seana Coulson, and Barbara Lewandowska-Tomaszczyk (eds.), 255–280. Frankfurt: Lang.

Boroditsky, Lera, and Michael Ramscar
2002    The roles of body and mind in abstract thought. *Psychological Science* 13: 185–189.

Dirven, René
2002    Metonymy and metaphor: Different mental strategies of conceptualization. In *Metaphor and Metonymy in Comparison and Contrast*, René Dirven, and Ralf Pörings (eds.), 75–112. Berlin/New York: Mouton de Gruyter.

Dodge, Ellen, and George Lakoff
2005    Image schemas: From linguistic analysis to neural grounding. In *From Perception to Meaning: Image Schemas in Cognitive Linguistics*, Beate Hampe (ed.), 57–92. Berlin/New York: Mouton de Gruyter.

Fauconnier, Gilles, and Mark Turner
2002    *The Way We Think. Conceptual Blending and the Mind's Hidden Complexities.* New York: Basic Books.

Gallese, Vittorio
2005    Embodied simulation: From neurons to phenomenal experience. *Phenomenology and the Cognitive Science* 4: 23–48.

Gallese, Vittorio, and George Lakoff
2005    The brain's concepts: The role of the sensory-motor system in conceptual knowledge. *Cognitive Neuropsychology* 22: 455–479.

Gibbs, Raymond W.
1994    *The Poetics of Mind: Figurative Thought, Language, and Understanding.* New York: Cambridge University Press.
2006a   *Embodiment and Cognitive Science.* New York: Cambridge University Press.
2006b   Walking the talk while thinking about the talk: Embodied interpretation of metaphorical narratives. Manuscript submitted for publication.
in press   Introspection and cognitive linguistics: Should we trust our own intuitions? *Annual Review of Cognitive Linguistics.*

Gibbs, Raymond W., Jessica Gould, and Michael Andric
in press   Imagining metaphorical actions: Embodied simulations make the impossible plausible. *Imagination, Cognition, & Personality.*

Glucksberg, Sam
   2001    *Understanding Figurative Language: From Metaphors to Idioms.* New York: Oxford University Press.
Haser, Verena
   2005    *Metaphor, Metonymy, and Experientialist Philosophy: Challenging Cognitive Semantics.* Berlin/New York: Mouton de Gruyter.
Keysar, Boaz, Yeshayahu Shen, Sam Glucksberg, and William S. Horton
   2000    Conventional language: How metaphoric is it? *Journal of Memory and Language* 43: 576–593.
Lakoff, George, and Mark Johnson
   1980    *Metaphors We Live by.* Chicago: University of Chicago Press.
   1999    *Philosophy in the Flesh: The Embodied Mind and its Challenge to Western Thought.* New York: Basic Books.
Langacker, Ronald W.
   1987    *Foundations of Cognitive Grammar.* Vol. 1. *Theoretical perspectives.* Stanford: Stanford University Press.
Langston, William
   2002    Violating orientational metaphors slows reading. *Discourse Processes* 34: 281–310.
Murphy, Gregory
   1996    On metaphoric representations. *Cognitio* 60: 173–204.
Pecher, Diane, and Rolf A. Zwaan (eds.)
   2005    *Grounding Cognition: The Role of Perception and Action in Memory, Language, and Thinking.* New York: Cambridge University Press.
Ritchie, David
   2003    "ARGUMENT IS WAR" – Or is it a game of chess? Multiple meanings in the analysis of implicit metaphors. *Metaphor and Symbol* 18: 125–146.
Ruiz de Mendoza Ibáñez, Francisco J.
   2000    The role of mappings and domains in understanding metonymy. In *Metaphor and Metonymy at the Crossroads: A Cognitive Perspective,* Antonio Barcelona (ed.), 109–132. Berlin/New York: Mouton de Gruyter.
Steen, Gerard J.
   2002    Metaphor identification: A cognitive approach. *Style* 3: 286–417.
Stefanowitsch, Anatol
   2004    Happiness in English and German: A metaphorical-pattern analysis. In *Language, Culture, and Mind,* Michel Achard, and Suzanne Kemmer (eds.), 137–150. Stanford: CSLI Publications.
Vervaeke, John, and John Kennedy
   1996    Metaphor in language and thought: Falsification and multiple meanings. *Metaphor and Symbolic Activity* 11: 273–284.
Wilson, Nicole, and Raymond W. Gibbs
   2006    Real and imagined body movement primes metaphor comprehension. Manuscript submitted for publication.

# X IS LIKE Y: The emergence of similarity mappings in children's early speech and gesture

## Şeyda Özçalışkan and Susan Goldin-Meadow

*Abstract:*

Similarity mapping (e.g., *the butterfly is like a rainbow*) is one of the earliest meta-linguistic abilities children master and is likely to constitute a stepping-stone for the development of analogical and metaphorical mapping abilities. We investigated the initial emergence and later development of this meta-linguistic ability in children's speech and gesture, using longitudinal observations of 40 English-speaking children from ages 1;2 to 2;10. We focused on the construction 'X IS LIKE Y' as the use of the word *like* is one of the earliest signs of similarity mapping ability in young children. Our results showed that children began to produce similarity mappings routinely by age 2;2. They initially conveyed only the source domain of the mapping in their speech and relied on nonverbal modalities (i.e., gesture and communicative context) to convey the target domain. However, with increasing age, children showed a greater tendency to simultaneously convey both the source and target domains of the similarity mapping in their speech. Moreover, the onset of 'X IS LIKE Y' constructions in children's speech was preceded by the onset of gesture-speech combinations expressing similarity relations without the word *like*. Thus, gesture appears to be at the cutting edge of early language development – it both predates and serves as the supporting context for oncoming changes in speech.

*Keywords*: similarity mapping; x is y like construction; acquisition of constructions; early gesture; development of similarity mapping ability; language development; gesture-speech combination; early metaphor

## 1. Statement of the problem and overview of findings

One of the biggest challenges of early language development is learning to articulate correspondences between objects or events based on commonalities in their features or relational structure (e.g., *blue crayon is blue like blue shirt*). In this chapter, we examine the initial emergence and subsequent development of similarity mappings. When tested in an experimental setting, children have been found to understand and produce similarity mappings at preschool age. But children may have the ability to convey

similarity mappings at younger ages. We explore this possibility by looking not only at children's speech but also at their gestures.

Children begin to produce combinations in which gesture conveys different information from speech (*eat* + POINT TO COOKIE) between ages
1;2–1;6, and gesture-speech combinations of this sort index oncoming
changes in speech: Children take the developmental step that allows them
to combine words with gestures to create a sentence-like meaning (e.g.,
*ride* + POINT TO BIKE) several months before they take the step that enables them to combine words with other words to create a sentence (e.g.,
*ride bike*). The question we ask here is whether children use gesture in
combination with speech to convey similarity-based comparisons (*like
ice-cream cone* + POINT TO MUSHROOM; *I go like that over my cup* + ROTATE
FINGER AS IF STIRRING) before they convey these comparisons in speech
(*ice-cream cone is like mushroom; I move my hand like I am stirring*). To explore this question, we use longitudinal observations of 40 typically-de-
veloping children, all raised as monolingual English speakers. The
children were videotaped for 90 minutes in their homes every four months
while interacting with their primary caregivers.

To preview our results, we found that children are able to produce similarity mappings in their spontaneous speech two years earlier than they
produce them in experimental settings. Initially, children convey only the
source domain of the mapping in speech, typically relying on gesture to
convey the target domain. Thus, gesture grounds children's early similarity mappings in the here-and-now. Even more interesting, the onset of
gesture-speech combinations expressing similarity relations without the
word *like* (e.g., *doggie* + POINT TO CAT) heralds the onset of 'X IS LIKE Y'
constructions in the children's speech. In other words, children use the
juxtaposition of gesture and speech to convey a similarity relation before
they use the word *like* to do so. Moreover, gesture-speech combinations
conveying a similarity relation without *like* decline in frequency just when
the 'X IS LIKE Y' construction appears in the children's speech.

Our results place gesture at the cutting edge of early language development – gesture both presages oncoming changes in children's speech and
serves as a forerunner of linguistic advances. At a point when children do
not have the words to express similarity mappings, gesture provides them
with a tool to express such mappings. And by doing so, it acts as a har-
binger of change in the child's developing language system.

## 2.   Children's early uses of similarity mappings

Children spontaneously produce a variety of novel expressions that high-light similarities between objects during the preschool years (Billow 1981; Chukovsky 1968; Carlson and Anisfeld 1969; Elbers 1988; Winner 1979). They use speech to describe a bald man as *having a barefoot head,* a mint candy as *making a draft in the mouth* (Chukovsky 1968), or a spinning top as *wobbling like a snake* (Winner 1979). At these early ages, children also use gesture and speech together to convey similarities between objects (Billow 1981; Elbers 1988; Winner 1979). They point to an upward facing pacifier and call it a *candle,* point to a car-shaped bread crumb and say *car that* (Elbers 1988), hold up a rubber animal next to hair and say *it is going to eat some grass* (Billow 1981), or hold up a horn upside down and turn it in circles while uttering the word *mixer* (Winner 1979).

Experimental work on children's understanding of similarity mappings also points to early onset. Four- to five-year-old children can build simple mappings between two objects based on feature-based similarity (Billow 1975; Epstein and Gamlin 1994; Gardner, Kircher, Winner and Perkins 1975; Mendelsohn, Robinson, Gardner and Winner 1984; Vosniadou and Ortony 1983; Winner, McCarthy and Gardner 1980) and between two events based on action-based similarity (Dent 1984, 1987). For example, when asked to complete the statement, *An eye is like a* ____, children were more likely to choose a similarity-based match (e.g., a button) than an anomalous match (e.g., a fork; Epstein and Gamlin 1994). Similarly, when asked to pick two objects that go together, children were more likely to group a cone-shaped block with a toy rocket-ship which was similar in shape, rather than matching it with another block of a different shape (Winner, McCarthy and Gardner 1980). Five-year-olds could also pro-vide similarity-based interpretations when asked about expressions that involved comparisons between objects such as *her hair is spaghetti, a cloud is like a sponge, or the butterfly is like a rainbow* (Gardner, Kircher, Winner and Perkins 1975; Gentner 1988; Billow 1975; Malgady 1977). For example, they make sense of the statement *a cloud is like a sponge* by say-ing that *both clouds and sponges are round and fluffy* (Gentner 1988), or they complete the statement *he looks as gigantic as ...* by selecting from among multiple choice alternatives an ending that draws on a similarity-based comparison – *he looks as gigantic as a double-decker cone in a baby's hand* (Gardner, Kircher, Winner and Perkins 1975).

Gardner and his colleagues (Gardner, Winner, Bechhofer and Wolf 1978) suggest that the ability to make similarity-based comparisons emerges initially in pretend play contexts in the form of object substitutions (e.g., using a block as if it were a doll). Beginning from age 1;5–2;0, children start verbalizing these object substitutions (e.g., calling the block *a doll*), typically in activity contexts where they are manipulating the objects. Gradually, the physical features of objects become more salient, and children begin to rename objects based on perceptual similarities (e.g., calling a potato chip *a cowboy hat*) roughly between ages 2;0–3;0. And by 3;0 to 4;0, children begin to use appropriate syntactic packaging to make explicit comparisons (e.g., *That pencil looks like a rocket ship*; Gardner et al. 1978).

### 3.   Early similarity mappings provide the stepping-stones for more complex mapping abilities

Children's early ability to make feature-based similarity comparisons is considered to be the initial step in the development of more complex types of mappings (e.g., analogical, metaphorical), mappings that involve not only within domain but also across domain comparisons (Gardner et al. 1978; Gentner 1988; Vosniadou 1987). For example, Gentner and her colleagues (Gentner 1988; Gentner and Rattermann 1990, 1991) propose a shift from mappings based on object commonalities (i.e., similarity matches, e.g., a red apple as similar to a red block) to mappings based on commonalities in relational structure (i.e., analogies, e.g., apple falling from a tree as analogous to book falling from a table). However, under certain conditions, children are able to perform simple cross-domain analogical mappings as early as age four (Gardner 1974; Gentner 1977; Goswami and Brown 1989): they can successfully match pairs of polar adjectives (happy-sad, hard-soft) to pairs of stimuli in various sensory modalities (cold-warm, loud-quiet, light-dark; Gardner 1974), and map spatial relations among human body parts (e.g., nose, knee) onto another concrete object (e.g., they point to the upper middle part of a tree when asked the question *If a tree had a nose where would it be?* Gentner 1977). Children's analogical ability improves over time with their growing grasp of different knowledge domains (Gentner 1988), but these findings clearly show that the basic analogical ability to map familiar domains is already well developed in preschool years.

Furthermore, children also understand metaphorical mappings that are based in familiar domains at around the same age. By age 4;0, they can choose the appropriate meaning for a metaphorical statement that is structured by motion (e.g., *time flies by, ideas run through the mind, sick-*

*ness crawls through the body*) from among forced-choice alternatives, and by age 5;0, they can provide explicit verbal explanations for these metaphorical expressions (e.g., *time crawls by means it goes slowly, ideas slip from the mind means you forget them;* Özçalışkan 2002, 2003, 2005, under review). Thus mappings based on object similarity and simple analogical relations, along with familiar metaphorical mappings, are within the communicative repertoire of the preschool child.

However, not surprisingly, the ability to understand more complex analogical and metaphorical mappings involving less familiar domains (e.g., mapping physical sensations onto psychological traits) or higher order relations (i.e., mapping situations based on common higher order relations, such as the similarity between an apple falling from a tree permitting a cow to reach it and a book falling from a shelf permitting a child to reach it; Gentner and Rattermann 1990) increases with age and achieves adult-like quality somewhere between ages 10;0–14;0 (Asch and Nerlove 1960; Cicone, Gardner and Winner 1981; Gardner et al. 1975; Schechter and Broughton 1991; Winner, Rosentiel and Gardner 1976). But the ability to understand an analogy or metaphor is not determined solely by a child's age; the nature of the conceptual domain also matters (Gentner and Rattermann 1991; Keil 1986). For example, five-year-old children can correctly map animate terms onto cars (e.g., *the car is thirsty*), but have difficulty understanding metaphors that involve mappings between taste terms and people (e.g., *she is a bitter person*; Keil 1986). From this perspective, the development of analogical or metaphorical ability is a learning process that extends well into adulthood and shows different developmental trajectories for different conceptual domains based on one's knowledge of the domain.

## 4. The emergence of similarity mappings in children's early spontaneous communications

The research just reviewed clearly shows that children can form similarity mappings by preschool age when tested in an experimental setting. However, we might find that children are able to convey similarity mappings even earlier if we look at their spontaneous language, particularly when that language is produced along with gesture, simply because a child's initial grasp of an idea is often evident first in gesture. For example, children begin to produce combinations in which gesture conveys different information from speech (*eat* + POINT TO COOKIE) somewhere between ages

1;2–1;6, and gesture-speech combinations of this sort index oncoming changes in their speech. They combine words with gestures to create a sentence-like meaning (e.g., *ride* + POINT TO BIKE) several months before they combine words with other words to create a sentence (e.g., *ride bike*; Capirci, Iverson, Pizzuto and Volterra 1996; Goldin-Meadow and Butcher 2003; Greenfield and Smith 1976; Iverson and Goldin-Meadow 2005; Özçalışkan and Goldin-Meadow 2005a, 2005b). In fact, children routinely produce a number of constructions – argument+argument (*mommy* + POINT TO CUP), predicate + argument (*peg* + MOVE FIST UP AND DOWN AS IF HITTING), and predicate + predicate (*I like it* + MOVE HAND BACK AND FORTH TO MOUTH AS IF EATING) – first in a gesture-speech combination before producing each of these constructions entirely in speech (i.e., *mommy cup; hammer the peg; I like eating it*; Özçalışkan and Goldin-Meadow 2005a, 2006). Thus, a child's ability to convey a construction across gesture and speech serves as an early signal that the child will soon be able to convey the same construction entirely within speech (Özçalışkan and Goldin-Meadow 2005a).

The question we pursue in this chapter is whether children use gesture in combination with speech to convey similarity-based comparisons (*like ice-cream cone* + POINT TO A MUSHROOM CAP; *I go like that over my cup* + ROTATE FINGER IN AIR TO INDICATE STIRRING) before they convey these comparisons in their speech (e.g., *bunny looks like me; the cow is like that cow there*). Our aim is to identify the initial emergence and subsequent development of constructions that convey similarity mappings. We use longitudinal observations of 40 children, all raised as monolingual English speakers in the Chicago area, between ages 1;2 to 2;10. The children were videotaped for 90 minutes in their homes every four months while interacting with their primary caregivers in their everyday routines (see Table 1 for a summary of the sample categorized according to the ethnicity and the income level of the families). All meaningful sounds and communicative gestures were transcribed, and divided into communicative acts.[1] We considered hand movements to be communicative gestures if they were used to convey information to a listener and did not involve direct manipulation of objects (e.g., banging a toy) or a ritualized game (e.g., patty cake). Sounds were considered meaningful words if they were used reliably to refer to specific referents or events; onomatopoeic sounds (e.g., *meow, choo-choo*) and conventionalized evaluative sounds (e.g., *oopsie, uh-oh*) were also included as words. Data were analyzed using ANOVAs, with either one (age) or two (age x domain, age x comparison type) within-subject factors, or chi-squares, as appropriate.

*Table 1.*  The sample of children classified according to ethnicity and family income

| Family income | Parents' ethnicity | | | | | |
|---|---|---|---|---|---|---|
| | *African American* | *Asian* | *Caucasian* | *Hispanic* | *Mixed* | *Total* |
| *Less than $15,000* | 1 | 0 | 1 | 0 | 0 | 2 |
| *$15,000-$34,999* | 2 | 1 | 2 | 2 | 1 | 8 |
| *$35,000-$49,999* | 2 | 0 | 3 | 0 | 1 | 6 |
| *$50,000-$74,999* | 2 | 1 | 6 | 0 | 0 | 9 |
| *$75,000-$99,999* | 1 | 0 | 5 | 1 | 0 | 7 |
| *$100,000 or more* | 0 | 0 | 7 | 0 | 1 | 8 |
| *Total* | 8 | 2 | 24 | 3 | 3 | 40 |

Mixed: two or more ethnic groups

## 5.   Developmental changes in children's overall production of speech and gesture

A broad look at the children's speech showed that they steadily increased their speech production over time. As can be seen in Table 2, children produced more communicative acts containing speech (F(5,170)=84.09, $p<0.001$), more different word types (F(5,170)=174.74, $p<0.001$), and more words overall (i.e., tokens, F(5,170)=95.32, $p<0.001$) with increasing age. There was a significant increase in the number of communicative acts containing speech and word types between ages 1;6 and 1;10 ($p$'s<0.001, Schéffe), and significant increases in all three measures from age 1;10 to 2;2 ($p$'s<0.001, Schéffe). In addition, children continued to increase their word tokens and word types from age 2;2 to 2;6 ($p$'s<0.01, Schéffe). Children's verbal lexicons showed a steep increase from 11 word types and 44 word tokens at age 1;2 to 239 word types and 1741 word tokens at age 2;10, and the majority of the children (37/40) were producing multi-word combinations by age 1;10.

Children also increased their gesture production over time. They produced more communicative acts with gesture (F(5,170)=10.22, $p<0.001$), more gesture tokens (F(5,170)=10.82, $p<0.001$), and more gesture-speech combinations (F(5,170)=34.29, $p<0.001$) with increasing age. There were significant increases in the mean number of communicative acts with gesture and in gesture tokens between ages 1;2 and 1;6 ($p$'s<0.05, Schéffe), and a significant increase in the mean number of gesture-speech combinations between ages 1;6 and 1;10 ($p$<0.01, Schéffe). By 1;2, only half of the children (21/40) were producing gesture-speech combinations, but by 1;6, all but one child were combining gesture with speech. Thus, overall children showed steady increases in their speech and gesture production over time.

Table 2. Summary of children's speech and gesture production[a.]

| | 1;2 | 1;6 | 1;10 | 2;2 | 2;6 | 2;10 |
|---|---|---|---|---|---|---|
| **Speech** [b.] | | | | | | |
| *Mean number of communicative acts containing speech (SD)* | 38 (44) | 157 (125) | 351 (249) | 549 (257) | 608 (234) | 642 (253) |
| *Mean number of word tokens (SD)* | 44 (53) | 179 (142) | 479 (401) | 1054 (658) | 1475 (795) | 1741 (789) |
| *Mean number of word types (SD)* | 11 (12) | 35 (25) | 91 (62) | 162 (79) | 213 (76) | 239 (74) |
| *Percentage of children producing at least one two-word combination* [c.] | 25% (10/40) | 63% (25/40) | 93% (37/40) | 97% (37/38) | 100% (37/37) | 100% (38/38) |
| **Gesture** | | | | | | |
| *Mean number of communicative acts containing gesture (SD)* | 53 (36) | 90 (63) | 117 (73) | 126 (88) | 115 (62) | 105 (59) |
| *Mean number of gesture tokens (SD)* | 54(36) | 91(64) | 119(75) | 131(90) | 123(68) | 112(65) |
| *Mean number of gesture-speech combinations (SD)* | 6(9) | 30(32) | 67(49) | 95(66) | 97(55) | 88(51) |
| *Percentage of children producing at least one gesture-speech combination* | 52% (21/40) | 98% (39/40) | 98% (39/40) | 97% (37/38) | 100% (37/37) | 100% (38/38) |

[a.] SD = standard deviation

[b.] All speech utterances are included in the top part of this table, even those produced with gesture.

[c.] As with most longitudinal designs, we missed a few sessions for some of the children, which led to slight differences in sample size at later data points. Therefore, the total number of children with respect to sample size at each data point is provided in parentheses.

### 6. Developmental changes in children's production of 'X IS LIKE Y' construction in their speech

We focus our analysis on the 'X IS LIKE Y' constructions because the word *like*[2] is one of the earliest signs of similarity mapping ability in young children. Figure 1A shows children's mean production of 'X IS LIKE Y' constructions in speech, and Figure 1B shows the number of children who produced this construction in speech at least once over the six time periods. As the figures illustrate, children did not routinely produce the 'X IS LIKE Y' construction in speech until age 2;2.[3] At 2;2, there were 15 children who produced the construction at a mean frequency of 0.84. Children significantly increased their production of the construction over time (F(5, 170)=6.9, $p<0.001$), showing a reliable increase from age 2;2 ($M=3.24$) to age 2;10 ($M=7.63$; $p<0.005$, Schéffe). The number of children who produced the construction also increased with age. At age 2;2, about 40% of the children used the construction in their speech, but by age 2;10, almost 80% of the children produced at least one instance of the construction in their speech.

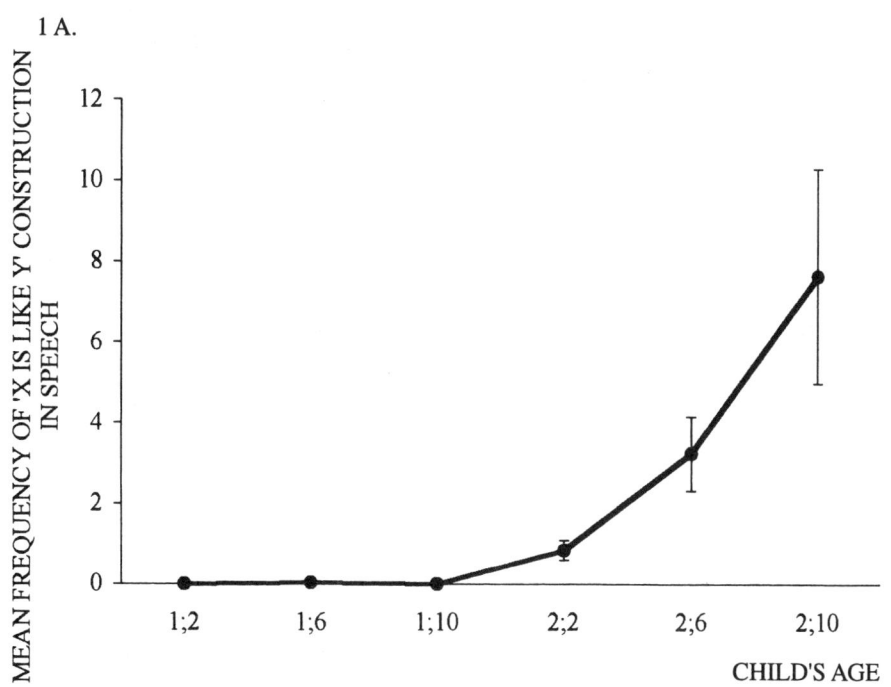

1 A.

1 B.

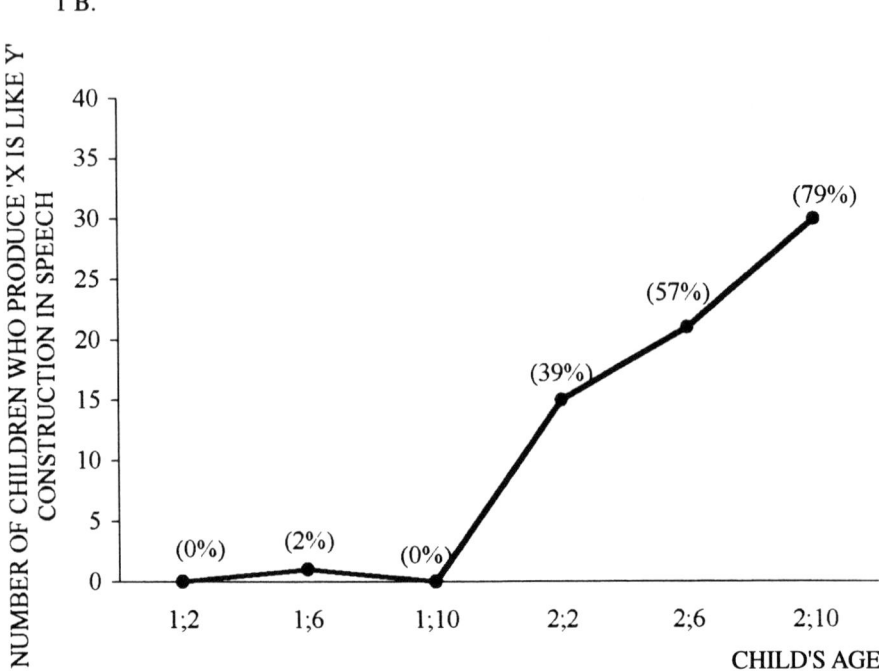

*Figure 1.* Children's mean production of 'X IS LIKE Y' construction in speech (Panel A) and the number of children who produced at least one instance of 'X IS LIKE Y' construction in speech (Panel B; percentage of children is indicated in parenthesis).

The construction 'X IS LIKE Y' involves both a source (Y, e.g., *rainbow* in *Butterfly is like a rainbow*) and a target domain (X, *e.g., butterfly* in *Butterfly is like a rainbow*). Initially children's uses of the construction did not contain both domains. They expressed only one domain (typically the source) and the other (typically the target) could be inferred from context (examples 1–3).

(1)   *Look like a house* + CHILD IS LOOKING AT A CHURCH PAINTING [2;2][4]
       'Church painting looks like a house'
(2)   *Just like potato-head* + CHILD IS PLAYING A COMPUTER GAME SIMILAR TO POTATO-HEAD [2;6]
       'Computer game is like potato-head'

(3)  *Like a mean monster* + CHILD HAS BEEN TALKING ABOUT TORNADOS
[2;10]
'Tornado is like a mean monster'

Thus, children's initial uses of the construction showed an effect of domain type ($F_{(2, 68)}=16.17$, $p<0.0001$). As Figure 2 illustrates, once children began producing the 'X IS LIKE Y' construction, they were significantly more likely to express the source domain on its own than either the target domain on its own ($p<0.0001$, Schéffe) or the source and target domains together ($p<0.03$, Schéffe).

There was also an effect of age in the children's expression of source and target domains ($F_{(5, 170)}=6.77, p<0.0001$), which interacted with domain type ($F_{(10, 340)}=6.88, p<0.0001$). Children increased the number of 'X IS LIKE Y' constructions they produced containing the source domain on its own over time ($F_{(5, 170)} = 8.25$, $p<0.0001$) and the source and target domains together ($F_{(5, 170)} = 4.66$, $p<0.001$), with significant changes from age 2;2 to age 2;10 for both ($p$'s$<0.05$, Schéffe). However, no such developmental trend was observed for the target domain on its own – whenever the children expressed the target domain of a similarity mapping, they also expressed the source domain (see examples 4–6).

(4)  *That one like this one* + CHILD IS HOLDING AN ORNAMENT AND LOOK-
ING AT ANOTHER ORNAMENT IN HER MOTHER'S HAND [2;2]
'Child's ornament is like mother's ornament'
(5)  *Bunny looks like me* + CHILD IS TALKING ABOUT A BUNNY CHAR-
ACTER ON TV [2;6]
'Bunny looks like child'
(6)  *The cow is like that cow there* + CHILD IS TALKING ABOUT THE TWO
COWS IN THE TWO PUZZLES HE IS PLAYING WITH [2;10]
'The cow in one puzzle is like the cow in the other puzzle'

Children also showed developmental changes in the linguistic means they used to express the source and target domains of the 'X IS LIKE Y' construction. As can be seen in Table 3, they predominantly relied on demonstrative (*this, that, these, those*) and personal (*it, he, she, me*) pronouns to express the source domain and reliably increased their use of pronominal references over time ($F_{(5, 170)}=7.95$, $p<0.0001$, $M=0.68$ at age 2;2 vs. $M=4.71$ at age 2;10). They used explicit nouns (e.g., *baby, spider*) or verbs (e.g., *climb, eat*) to express the source domain far less often. Nevertheless, their use of nominal devices also increased reliably

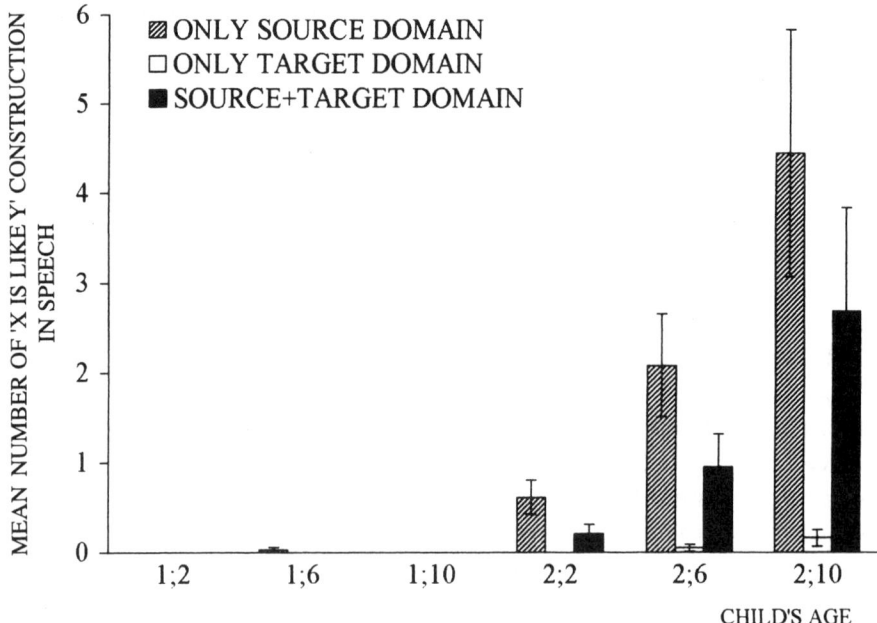

*Figure 2.* Mean number of 'X IS LIKE Y' constructions for which only the source (hatched bars), only the target (gray bars), or both the source and the target domains (black bars) were encoded in speech.

with age (F(5, 170)=4.81, $p$<0.001, $M$=0.16 at age 2;2 vs. $M$=2.42 at age 2;10) (see examples 7–9).

(7) *Looks like it* + CHILD IS COMPARING BINGBONG IN BOOK TO SQUIRREL OUTSIDE [2;2]
   'Bingbong looks like squirrel'
(8) *Just like Dori* + CHILD IS COMPARING HER VOICE TO THAT OF DORI IN MOVIE [2;6]
   'Child's voice like Dori's voice'
(9) *Look like a whale* + CHILD IS LOOKING AT A WHALE PICTURE IN ALBUM [2;10]
   'Whale picture looks like a whale'

The pattern was slightly different for the target domain. Children used both linguistic devices (pronominal and nominal) at roughly equal rates at each age. Their use of nouns and verbs to express the target domain increased reliably over time (F(5, 170)=11.56, *p*<0.0001; *M*=0.08 at age 2;2 vs. *M*=1.42 at age 2;10), but their use of pronominal reference to express the target domain did not (F(5, 170)=1.97, *ns*; *M*=0.13 at age 2;2 vs. *M*=1.39 at age 2;10) (see examples 10–12).

(10) *Do you* **close** *it like this?* + CHILD CLOSES DOOR BY PUSHING IT WITH FOOT [2;6]
  'Do you close door like you close it by pushing it with foot?'
(11) ***Baby*** *like the one at grandma's* + CHILD IS PLAYING WITH A BABY DOLL [2;2]
  'Baby doll is like the baby doll at grandmother's house'
(12) ***Dad*** *is like D and dog* + CHILD IS LEARNING HOW TO SPELL LETTER D [2;10]
  'D in dad is like D in dog'

*Table 3.* Types of linguistic means children used to encode source and target domains of the 'X IS LIKE Y' construction in their speech[a.]

| | 1;2 | 1;6 | 1;10 | 2;2 | 2;6 | 2;10 |
|---|---|---|---|---|---|---|
| **Source domain** | | | | | | |
| *Mean number of source domains that are encoded by a noun or a verb in speech (SD)* | 0 (0) | 0 (0) | 0 (0) | 0.16 (0.55) | 0.89 (2.17) | 2.42 (6.30) |
| *Mean number of source domains that are encoded by a personal or a demonstrative pronoun in speech (SD)* | 0 (0) | 0.03 (0.16) | 0 (0) | 0.68 (1.36) | 2.14 (3.54) | 4.71 (9.32) |
| **Target domain** | | | | | | |
| *Mean number of target domains that are encoded by a noun or a verb in speech (SD)* | 0 (0) | 0 (0) | 0 (0) | 0.08 (0.27) | 0.57 (1.32) | 1.42 (2.23) |
| *Mean number of target domains that are encoded by a personal or a demonstrative pronoun in speech (SD)* | 0 (0) | 0 (0) | 0 (0) | 0.13 (0.53) | 0.43 (1.26) | 1.39 (5.71) |

[a.] SD = standard deviation

In summary, children began to use the 'X IS LIKE Y' construction in their spontaneous speech by age 2;2, a time period much earlier than what has been reported in earlier experimental studies and anecdotal reports. Although their initial uses of the construction typically encoded only the source domain, they showed an increasing tendency to encode both the source and the target domains over time.

## 6.1. Types of 'X IS LIKE Y' constructions in children's speech

Children produced two types of 'X IS LIKE Y' constructions: those involving a comparison of an action to an ongoing action (i.e., *action-based comparison*), and those involving a comparison of an entity (a person or an object) to another entity present in the immediate context (i.e., *feature-based comparison*).

The action-based comparisons typically involved specifying the source action encoded by a demonstrative pronoun (*this, that*) and were actualized in three distinct ways based on the specification of the target domain. In the first and most frequent type of action-based comparison, the source domain was conveyed with a demonstrative pronoun (i.e., *like this/that*) and the target domain could be inferred from context (see examples 13, 14).

(13) *Like this* + CHILD DIPS WASHCLOTH IN WATER AND WIPES HER FACE WITH IT [2;2]
'Wash face like wash it by wiping it with washcloth'
(14) *Like this* + CHILD PRETENDS TO TYPE VERY RAPIDLY ON TOY COMPUTER [2;6]
'Type like type rapidly on keyboard'

In the second type of action-based comparison, the source domain was conveyed by a demonstrative pronoun (*like this/that*) and the target domain was conveyed with a strong verb (e.g., *walk/eat/swim*) (see examples 15–17).

(15) *I want to climb like that* + CHILD ATTEMPTS TO CLIMB UP ON A LADDER [2;2]
'I want to climb like I climb up using a ladder'
(16) *It can run like that* + CHILD MAKES DOLL RUN WITH OUTSTRETCHED LEGS [2;6]
'Doll can run like run by stretching its legs'

(17) *We have to rock her like this* + CHILD ROCKS DOLL GENTLY IN THE TOY
CAR SEAT [2;10]
'We have to rock the doll like rock her gently'

In the third type of action-based comparison, the source domain was conveyed with a demonstrative pronoun (*like this/that*) and the target was conveyed by a bleached verb (*go, do*) (see examples 18–20).

(18) *I go like this* + CHILD HOPS UP AND DOWN LIKE A FROG [2;6]
'I go like I hop like a frog'
(19) *You do it like this* + CHILD PAINTS PICTURE BY STAMPING ON IT [2;6]
'You do the picture like you paint by stamping on it'
(20) *No go like that* + CHILD RIDES BIKE BY WALKING HIS FEET ON THE
SIDES [2;10]
'Go like you ride bike by walking your feet on the sides'

Of the three types of action-based comparisons, the first type in which the target had to be inferred from context was the most frequent and the first to emerge. As Table 4 illustrates, children used the 'like+demonstrative pronoun' construction at age 2;2 ($M=0.42$) and increased their use of this construction over time ($M=2.21$ at age 2;10). 'Like this/that' constructions were followed by 'strong verb+like this' type constructions. Only a few children produced this construction at age 2;2 ($M=0.05$) but these constructions became more frequent at age 2;6 ($M=0.46$) and by age 2;10, half of the children were using the 'strong verb+like this' construction ($M=1.08$). The 'bleached verb + like this/that' type constructions emerged later. Children did not begin to use bleached verbs to express the target domain until age 2;6 and then only 8 of the 40 children used this construction ($M=0.97$). Children remained relatively stable in their use of bleached verbs to mark the target domain through age 2;10 ($M=0.68$).

*Table 4.* Mean number of different types of action-based comparisons in children's speech[a].

| | 1;2 | 1;6 | 1;10 | 2;2 | 2;6 | 2;10 |
|---|---|---|---|---|---|---|
| ∅ + *like this (SD)* | 0 (0) | 0.03 (0.16) | 0 (0) | 0.42 (1.0) | 0.76 (1.4) | 2.21 (3.06) |
| *Strong verb + like this (SD)* | 0 (0) | 0 (0) | 0 (0) | 0.05 (0.23) | 0.46 (0.99) | 1.08 (1.38) |
| *Bleached verb + like this (SD)* | 0 (0) | 0 (0) | 0 (0) | 0 (0) | 0.97 (2.61) | 0.68 (1.36) |

[a.] SD = standard deviation, ∅ = no mention of target domain

The feature-based comparisons highlighted similarities in perceptual features (e.g., shape, size, color) between two entities. The most typical linguistic construction for feature-based comparisons consisted of a noun encoding the source domain without any mention in speech of the target domain; the verb *look* often accompanied these constructions (see examples 1–3, repeated below).

(1)  *Look like a house* + CHILD IS LOOKING AT A CHURCH PAINTING [2;2]
     'Church painting looks like a house'
(2)  *Just like potato-head* + CHILD IS PLAYING A COMPUTER GAME SIMILAR
     TO POTATO-HEAD [2;6]
     'Computer game is like potato-head'
(3)  *Like a mean monster* + CHILD HAS BEEN TALKING ABOUT TORNADOS
     [2;10]
     'Tornado is like a mean monster'

In the second type of feature-based comparison, both the source and target domains were encoded in a noun or a pronoun, frequently accompanied by the verb *look*. Interestingly, most of these feature-based comparisons highlighted the general appearance of the two objects, without specifying the exact basis of the comparison, as can be seen in examples 21-to-23.

(21)  *That looks like Scooby* + CHILD IS LOOKING AT A DOG PICTURE [2;2]
      'Dog picture looks like Scooby the dog'
(22)  *It looks like a skirt* + CHILD IS HOLDING HER UNDERSKIRT [2;6]
      'Underskirt looks like a skirt'
(23)  *I want to make a boat like that one* + CHILD HAS BEEN BUILDING BOATS
      WITH BLOCKS [2;10]
      'I want to make a boat like my previous boat'

There were, however, a few feature-based comparisons, which specified the basis of comparison between the two objects. The two dimensions that were explicitly mentioned were color (examples 24–25) and size (example 26).

(24)  *It is like blue like this one* + CHILD POINTS TO BLUE SCRIBBLE WHILE
      PLAYING WITH A BLUE TOY [2;6]
      'Blue toy is blue like the blue scribble'
(25)  *It is brown like my hair* + CHILD IS DRAWING WITH A BROWN CRAYON
      [2;10]
      'Brown crayon is brown like child's brown hair'

(26) *It is big like that* + CHILD IS MAKING CHURCHES OF DIFFERENT SIZES
WITH BLOCKS [2;10]
'Church A is big like church B'

The children were also able to highlight these dimensions using contextual cues (see examples 27–28 for color, example 29 for size, and examples 30–31 for shape).

(27) *Like the man with the yellow hat* + CHILD IS PLAYING WITH YELLOW
TRIANGLE [2;10]
'Yellow triangle is yellow like the man with the yellow hat'
(28) *And this one is like this* + CHILD COMPARES GREEN CRAYON TO GREEN
STRIPE ON HIS SHIRT [2;10]
'Green crayon is green like green stripes'
(29) *Like this* + CHILD PINCHES FINGERS TO PRODUCE THE ICONIC GES-
TURE OF SMALL [2;10]
'Size of ponytail is small like the size of my finger'
(30) *Like a tunnel* + CHILD HOLDS HAND IN THE SHAPE OF AN ELONGATED
HOLLOW OBJECT [2;10]
'Child's hand is elongated like a tunnel'
(31) *Like a circle* + CHILD IS PLAYING WITH LETTER O [2;10]
'Letter O is circular like a circle'

Children's production of action-based and feature-based comparisons showed a main effect of age ($F(5, 170)=6.96$, $p<0.001$), but no effect of comparison type ($F(1, 34)=0.63$, *ns*) and no interaction ($F(5, 170)=0.39$, *ns*). As can be seen in Figure 3, children reliably increased their production of both action-based ($F(5, 170)=16.49$, $p<0.0001$) and feature-based comparisons ($F(5, 170)=2.78$, $p<0.05$) over time, with significant changes occurring between ages 2;2 and 2;10 ($p$'s$< 0.001$, Schéffe). However, their production of action-based and feature-based comparisons was comparable at each age.

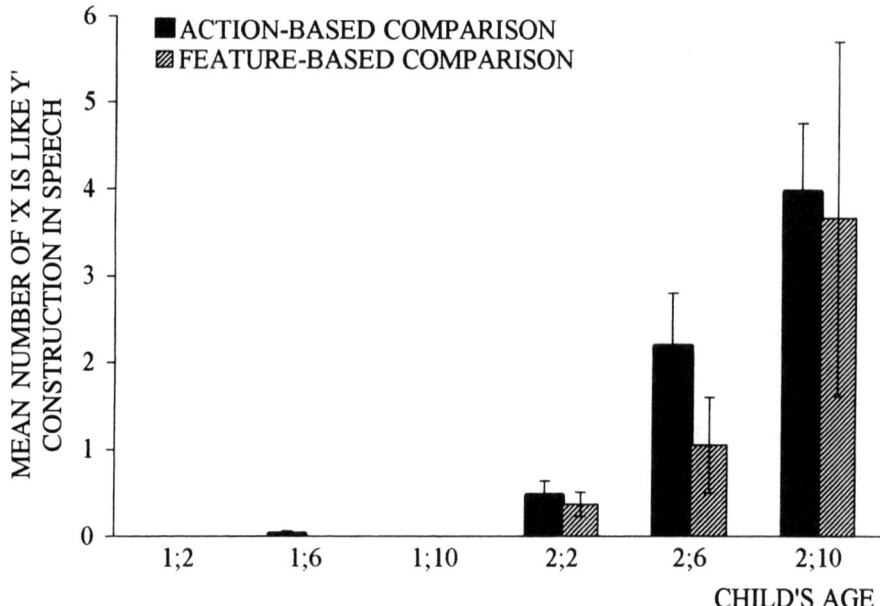

*Figure 3.* Mean number of 'X IS LIKE Y' constructions that involve action-based comparisons (black bars) or feature-based comparisons (hatched bars).

To summarize thus far, children produced two types of 'X IS LIKE Y' constructions in their speech – those comparing two actions, and those comparing two objects. They used each type of comparison at roughly equal rates, and their production of each type increased with age. Note that the children in our study produced 'X IS LIKE Y' constructions in their spontaneous speech earlier than children have been reported to produce or understand these constructions in experimental settings. One of the reasons for this early appearance of the construction may be that there was typically a great deal of contextual support for these constructions. Children relied on a variety of non-verbal tools to specify both their action- and feature-based comparisons. As can be seen in Table 5, across the different ages, 80 to100% of action-based comparisons were accompanied by an ongoing action that specified the source domain (see examples 13–20), and 40 to 70% of feature-based comparisons were accompanied by a present object that clarified either the source or the target domain (see examples 21–23). Thus, children's initial uses of the 'X IS LIKE Y' construction were highly context-dependent, typically accompanied by an ongoing action, visible object, or gesture. In the next sections, we focus on one of these non-verbal devices, namely gesture, asking whether gestures play a role in helping children to convey the 'X IS LIKE Y' construction before they can convey it entirely in speech.

*Table 5.* Number of action-based comparisons that are accompanied by an ongoing action and number of feature-based comparisons that are accompanied by a present object[a.]

| | 1;2 | 1;6 | 1;10 | 2;2 | 2;6 | 2;10 |
|---|---|---|---|---|---|---|
| *Number of action-based comparison that are accompanied by an action specifying the source domain* | 0 | 1 (100%) | 0 | 17 (94%) | 63 (78%) | 126 (83%) |
| *Number of action-based comparison that are accompanied by an action specifying the target domain* | 0 | 0 | 0 | 0 | 2 (2%) | 9 (6%) |
| *Total number of action-based comparisons* | 0 | 1 | 0 | 18 | 81 | 151 |
| *Number of feature-based comparison that are accompanied by a present object specifying the source domain* | 0 | 0 | 0 | 7 (50%) | 15 (38%) | 61(44%) |
| *Number of feature-based comparison that are accompanied by a present object specifying the target domain* | 0 | 0 | 0 | 10 (70%) | 28 (72%) | 96 (69%) |
| *Total number of feature-based comparisons* | 0 | 0 | 0 | 14 | 39 | 139 |

[a.] Percentages of action-based or feature-based comparisons that are accompanied by an action or an object are provided in parenthesis. For action-based comparison percentages were computed by dividing the total number of action-based comparisons that are accompanied by an action by the total number of action-based comparisons. For feature-based comparisons, percentages were computed by dividing the total number of feature-based comparisons that are accompanied by a present object by the total number of feature-based comparisons.

## 7.    Children's use of gesture in their 'X IS LIKE Y' constructions

We begin by asking how often children used gesture (as opposed to other non-verbal cues) to specify either the target or the source domain in an 'X IS LIKE Y' construction. Figure 4A shows children's mean production of gesture in 'X IS LIKE Y' constructions and Figure 4B shows the number of children who produced gesture in these constructions over the six time periods. As the figures illustrate, gesture was used in 'X IS LIKE Y' constructions as soon as children began producing these construction in speech, that is, at age 2;2. The number of times the children used gesture in the 'X IS LIKE Y' construction increased steadily over time ($F(5, 170)=4.61$, $p<0.001$), as did the number of children who used gesture. Four children used gesture in these constructions at age 2;2 ($M=0.16$);[5] at 2;6, one third of the children (N=12/37) used gesture in at least one instance of the construction ($M=0.62$); and by age 2;10, almost half of the children (N=17/38) used gesture in the construction ($M=1.21$). Thus, gesture was used more and more often in the 'X IS LIKE Y' constructions over time.

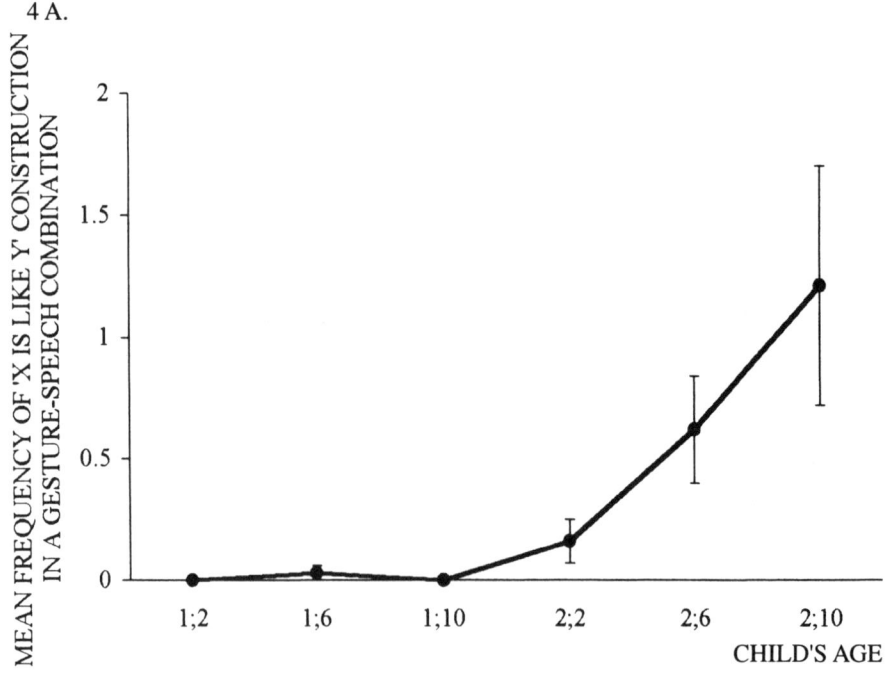

4 A.

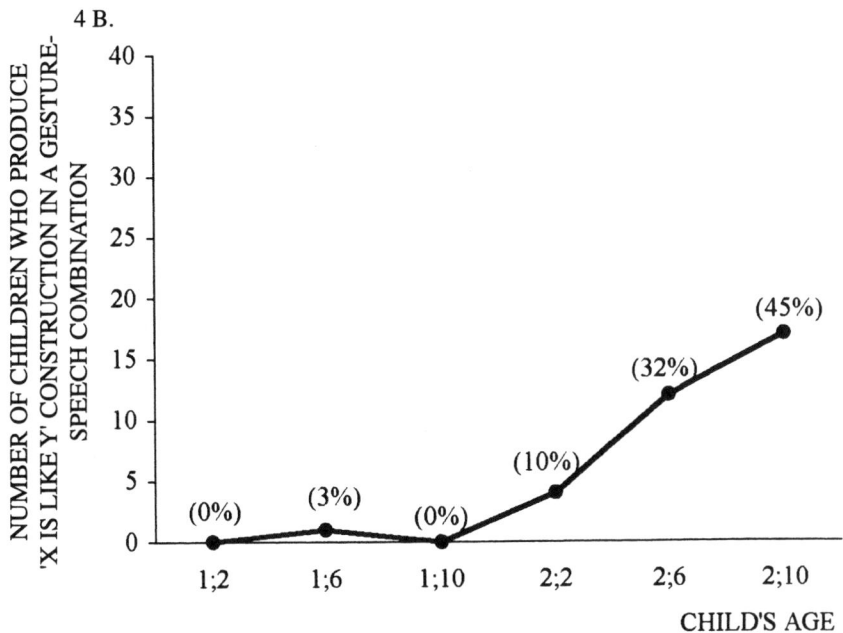

*Figure 4.*  Children's mean production of 'X IS LIKE Y' construction in their gesture-speech combinations (Panel A) and the number of children who
produced at least one instance of 'X IS LIKE Y' construction in a gesture-speech combination (Panel B).

Gesture served two functions in children's 'X IS LIKE Y' constructions.
First and most often, gesture clarified a source or a target domain that
was conveyed by a pronominal in speech. Second, gesture conveyed a
source or a target domain that was not conveyed in speech at all.

In terms of clarifying a pronominal reference in speech, pointing gestures were used to specify the entity in either the target domain (see
examples 32–34) or the source domain (see examples 35–36) and iconic
gestures were used to specify the action in the source domain (see
examples 37–41).

(32) *This like earl grey* + CHILD POINTS TO CUP OF COFFEE [2;2]
'Coffee is like earl grey tea'
(33) *Those are like strawberries but they are not strawberries* + CHILD
POINTS AT TOY TOMATOES [2;6]
'Toy tomatoes are like strawberries but they are not strawberries'

(34) *Is that look like grandpa Johndeer?* + CHILD POINTS AT TRACTOR PIC-
     TURE [2;6]
     'Does the tractor picture look like grandpa's Johndeer tractor?'
(35) *Shelley has sticky tape just like this one* + CHILD POINTS AT STICKY
     TAPE ON DESK [2;10]
     'Shelley has sticky tape just like the sticky tape on desk'
(36) *I can hug a baby like this one* + CHILD POINTS AT BABY MOUSE IN BOOK
     [2;6]
     'I can hug a baby like the baby mouse in book'
(37) *I eat like this* + CHILD PERFORMS THE ICONIC GESTURE OF EATING
     WITH FIST BY MOVING FIST BACK AND FORTH TO MOUTH [2;2]
     'I eat like I eat with my fist'
(38) *Like this* + CHILD PERFORMS THE ICONIC GESTURE OF PLAYING THE
     ACCORDION BY MOVING ARMS INWARD AND OUTWARD [2;6]
     'I play the accordion like I play it in a particular style'
(39) *Give it to me like this* + CHILD PERFORMS THE ICONIC GESTURE OF
     PUTTING PRETEND NECKLACE ON NECK BY HOLDING TWO PINCHED
     FINGERS IN AIR [2;6]
     'Give the necklace to me like you put it around my neck'
(40) *I go like that over my cup* + CHILD PERFORMS THE ICONIC GESTURE OF
     DROPPING SOMETHING INTO THE CUP BY OPENING A CLOSED FIST IN
     AIR (iconic) [2;10]
     'I go like I drop something into my cup'
(41) *Knocked over like this* + CHILD PERFORMS THE ICONIC GESTURE OF
     SWAYING BY MOVING ARM OUTWARD FORCEFULLY (iconic) [2;10]
     'I knocked it over like I knocked it over by swaying it'

In terms of specifying a source or a target domain that was *not* encoded in
speech, pointing gestures were used to convey the entity in the target domain that was not mentioned in speech (examples 42–45) and iconic gestures were used to convey the action in the source domain that was not
mentioned in speech (example 46).[6]

(42) *Like ice-cream cone* + CHILD POINTS TO MUSHROOM [2;2]
     'Mushroom is like ice-cream cone'
(43) *Like a sun* + CHILD POINTS TO CIRCULAR OBJECT ON TV [2;10]
     'Object on TV is like a sun'
(44) *Like a sheep* + CHILD POINTS TO SHEEP PICTURE [2;10]
     'Sheep picture is like a sheep'

(45) *Like a square* + CHILD POINTS TO BLOCK STRUCTURE [2;10]
'Block structure is like a square'
(46) *You do it like* + CHILD PERFORMS THE ICONIC GESTURE OF THROWING
BY MOVING HER HAND FORWARD FORCEFULLY [2;6]
'You do it like you throw it forcefully'

## 8. Does gesture pave the way for 'X IS LIKE Y' constructions?

As examples 32 to 45 illustrate, gesture was often used to convey a target or a source domain in an 'X IS LIKE Y' construction that was not specified in speech. The question we turn to next is whether gesture served as a precursor, signaling the onset of the 'X IS LIKE Y' construction in speech, as has been found with respect to a number of other linguistic constructions (Özçalışkan and Goldin-Meadow 2005a, 2006). In other words, did children use gesture and speech together to highlight a comparison between objects *before* they were able to produce the word *like*? The short answer to this question is *yes* (see also Özçalışkan and Goldin-Meadow, under review).

We found a number of gesture-speech combinations in which the relation between the object conveyed in gesture and the object conveyed in speech was similarity. For example, the child points at a cat and says *doggie*. An utterance of this sort might be an error on the child's part. Alternatively, the utterance could reflect the child's intent to highlight dimensions of similarity between the cat and the dog (e.g., four-legged, furry). Gesture-speech combinations of this sort might constitute the child's earliest efforts in similarity mapping and, accordingly, might serve as a stepping-stone for the onset of 'X IS LIKE Y' constructions in their speech (i.e., *a dog is like a cat*). If so, we would expect the emergence of gesture-speech combinations that highlight the similarity between two objects to precede the appearance of the 'X IS LIKE Y' constructions in children's speech. Moreover, we would expect children to produce fewer gesture-speech combinations of this sort once they have begun to use 'X IS LIKE Y' constructions routinely in their speech.

The children in our study produced many gesture-speech combinations in which the object conveyed in gesture and the object conveyed in speech were similar in overall appearance, shape, or color (see examples 47–61). These utterances thus resembled the types of comparisons found in the children's early 'X IS LIKE Y' constructions, with the exception that they did not contain the word *like*.

(47) *Dog* + CHILD POINTS TO SQUIRREL [1;2]
(48) *Juice* + CHILD POINTS TO MILK [1;2]
(49) *Mommy* + CHILD POINTS TO FEMALE EXPERIMENTER [1;6]
(50) *Car* + CHILD POINTS TO TRUCK [1;6]
(51) *A butterfly* + CHILD POINTS TO BOW TIE [1;10]
(52) *Boot* + CHILD POINTS TO SOCK [1;10]
(53) *Donkey* + CHILD POINTS TO HORSE [1;10]
(54) *Raining* + CHILD POINTS TO SNOW FALL [2;2]
(55) *Purple* + CHILD POINTS TO BLUE BLOCK [2;2]
(56) *He has the moon* + CHILD POINTS TO WHITE HAIR ON NOAH'S HEAD [2;2]
(57) *They have a penis* + CHILD POINTS TO PIG'S TAIL [2;6]
(58) *A square* + CHILD HOLDS UP A DIAMOND SHAPE [2;6]
(59) *More sugar* + CHILD POINTS TO FLOUR [2;10]
(60) *Every whale loves a bubble bath* + CHILD POINTS TO OCEAN WITH WAVES [2;10]
(61) *I think these are cats* + CHILD POINTS TO FOX [2;10]

As can be seen in Figure 5 (see below), the frequency of children's gesture-speech combinations expressing similarity relations without the word *like* changed significantly over time (F(5, 170)= 3.45, $p<0.01$), increasing from age 1;2 ($M=0.40$) to age 1;6 ($M=2.23$). Children's production of these combinations remained relatively unchanged between ages 1;6 and 2;6, but began to decline thereafter. Importantly, the decline at age 2;6 co-incided with an increase in 'X IS LIKE Y' constructions. Thus, the children became less likely to produce gesture-speech combinations expressing similarity relations without the word *like* at just the point when they began producing similarity-based mappings in appropriate syntactic packaging (i.e., with the word *like*).

Consistent with the hypothesis that gesture is playing a bootstrapping role in the emergence of 'X IS LIKE Y' constructions, the onset of gesture-speech combinations expressing similarity relations without the word *like* routinely preceded the onset of 'X IS LIKE Y' constructions in speech. Of the 40 children in our sample, 29 (73%) produced a gesture-speech combination of this sort before producing an 'X IS LIKE Y' construction in speech, compared to only one child who displayed the opposite pattern (29 vs. 1, $X^2(1) = 38.88$, $p<0.001$). Of the remaining 10 children, 5 produced gesture-speech combinations of this sort but had not yet produced the 'X IS LIKE Y' construction in speech; we expect these children to produce 'X IS LIKE Y' in speech in subsequent sessions. The remaining 5

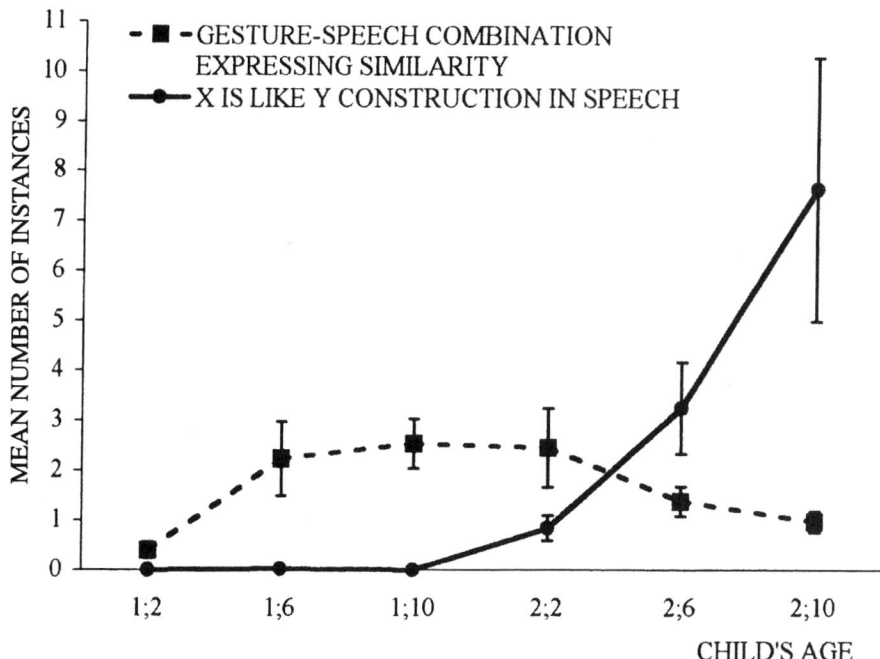

*Figure 5.* Mean number of gesture-speech combinations expressing similarity (dotted line) and mean number of 'X IS LIKE Y' constructions in speech (straight line).

children produced their first gesture-speech combination expressing a similarity relation without the word *like* and their first 'X IS LIKE Y' construction in speech during the same observation session; it is likely that we missed the onset time for the constructions in these children, possibly due to the relatively long time interval between observations (~4 months). As a result, the data for these 5 children neither support nor refute our predictions. Thus, 34 (97%) of the 35 relevant children in our sample first produced a gesture-speech combination expressing a similarity mapping without the word *like*, compared to 1 (2%) who first produced the 'X IS LIKE Y' construction in speech. Thus, gesture-speech combinations expressing a similarity relation clearly preceded the 'X IS LIKE Y' construction in speech, signaling a child's readiness to make similarity-based mappings in appropriate syntactic packaging.

## 9.  Conclusion

In the process of learning a language children have to learn not only to map a word onto a particular referent or an event (e.g., calling a red block *a red block*) but also to articulate correspondences between objects or events based on commonalities in their features or relational structure (e.g., *a red block is red like a red crayon*). In this chapter, we examined the beginnings of this mapping ability in a sample of English-speaking children from ages 1;2 to 2;10, as indexed by their use of the 'X IS LIKE Y' construction. Our analysis showed an early onset of the 'X IS LIKE Y' construction. Children began to produce the construction in their spontaneous speech routinely by age 2;2 – two years earlier than they have been found to produce such similarity mappings in experimental settings. However, these early uses of the 'X IS LIKE Y' construction were highly constrained. First, the source and target domains of the mapping were typically bound by the here-and-now, involving objects that were present in the immediate environment or actions that were often being executed by the child. Second, the linguistic forms that the children used to describe either domain were context dependent. Children typically used pronominal references to encode the source and/or the target domain and relied on non-verbal cues (i.e., ongoing action, gesture) to clarify these references. Thus, at the early ages, speech provided a skeletal structure for the 'X IS LIKE Y' construction and children relied on non-verbal means to flesh out this structure.

Children produced two types of 'X IS LIKE Y' constructions, those involving comparison of an object to another object (i.e., feature-based comparison) and those involving comparison of an action to an ongoing action (i.e., action-based comparison). In line with earlier work (Gentner and Rattermann 1991), children's initial feature-based comparisons were typically holistic and global, involving mappings based on overall appearance of objects (e.g., *pizza picture looks like pizza*) rather than particular aspects or dimensions of the objects (e.g., *blue scribble is blue like a blue stripe*). Similarity mappings in which the children made it clear which part or dimension of the objects they were highlighting were infrequent in our data. Indeed, in most instances, the dimension of similarity had to be inferred from non-verbal cues and other aspects of context. Moreover, all instances of the 'X IS LIKE Y' construction involved similarity mappings, rather than more complex types of mappings (e.g., analogical, metaphorical), providing further support for the hypothesis that similarity mappings between objects act as precursors to more complex mapping types (Gentner 1988; Vosniadou 1987).

However, unlike earlier work, a large portion of the 'X IS LIKE Y' constructions the children in our study produced involved action-based comparisons, which functioned in slightly different ways from feature-based comparisons. Action-based comparisons provided children with a linguistic frame that they could use to specify an action for which they lacked a lexical item. The children framed the action-based comparison in general terms, using phrases such as *like this* or *go like this* and then acting out or gesturing the specific action they intended to convey (e.g., CLIMB UP A LADDER; MOVE HAND FORWARD FORCEFULLY TO INDICATE THROW-ING). Interestingly, even in cases where the children produced a strong verb to encode the action (e.g., *I run/eat ... like this ...*), they often produced an action or a gesture to provide a more detailed rendition of the action specified by the verb (e.g., MAKE DOLL RUN RAPIDLY WITH OUT-STRETCHED LEGS; PERFORM THE ICONIC GESTURE OF MOVING FIST BACK AND FORTH TO MOUTH TO CONVEY EATING WITH FIST).

This type of framing is not unique to similarity mappings and is commonly observed in metaphorical types of mappings at later ages. As shown in earlier work (Özçalışkan 2003, under review), when 3- and 4-year-old children are asked to provide verbal explanations for different types of metaphorical mappings (e.g., *How does time fly? What does it mean when ideas escape from your mind?*), they typically produce a *like this/that* construction in speech and act out whole body gestures to further specify the source domain (*Like this* + CHILD CRAWLS ON FLOOR TO INDICATE HOURS CRAWLING BY; *Like that* + CHILD MOVES ARMS UP AND DOWN TO INDICATE IDEAS FLYING BY). This type of response typically disappears by age 5;0 when children begin to produce more elaborate verbal descriptions, along with semantically well-integrated gestures (e.g., *time drips by means it goes really slowly like that* + CHILD MOVES FINGER DOWNWARD WITH SMALL PAUSES LIKE DRIPPING WATER; Özçalışkan 2002, under review). Thus, the particular way children framed action-based comparisons in our study might be their initial step on the way to verbally more elaborate 'X IS LIKE Y' constructions. Moreover, gesture and bodily action might be signaling the child's readiness to take the next step towards more complete linguistic constructions.

Indeed, as shown in this paper, gesture played two important roles in children's production of 'X IS LIKE Y' constructions. First, gesture served as the supporting context for children's early 'X IS LIKE Y' constructions. Children initially expressed either the target or the source domains of the similarity mapping, and used gesture to convey the other domain. Even in cases where children expressed both of the domains in speech, they typically used demonstrative pronouns to do so. In these cases, gesture clarified the object or action to which the source or target domain was being compared. Thus, gesture grounded children's early similarity mappings in the here-and-now, making those mappings much easier to understand.

Second, the onset of gesture-speech combinations expressing a similarity relation without the word *like* heralded the onset of 'X IS LIKE Y' constructions. The vast majority of the children in our study used the juxtaposition of gesture and speech to convey a similarity relation well before they seemed able to make the similarity mapping explicit with the word *like*. The children's gesture-speech combinations without the word *like* highlighted similarities between objects and events based on attributes of shape, size, or movement (cf. Clark 1973), and thus set the stage for the 'X IS LIKE Y' constructions that the children were about to produce. Importantly, the children's gesture-speech combinations conveying a similarity relation without *like* not only showed a rapid increase at age 1;6–a time point where we also observed rapid changes in lexicon (as has been found in previous observations, e.g., Gershkoff-Stowe & Smith, 1997) – they also showed a marked decline at just the moment that the 'X IS LIKE Y' construction appeared in the children's speech. Furthermore, the gesture-speech constructions conveyed similarity mappings based on shape, size, color, movement, all of which became dimensions of comparison in early 'X IS LIKE Y' constructions. Gesture-speech combinations expressing a similarity relation without *like* thus constituted the children's first attempts to build similarity mappings. But once the job was done – that is, once the child was able to produce the 'X IS LIKE Y' construction in speech – gesture-speech combinations of this sort disappeared.

In summary, our findings place gesture at the cutting edge of early language development. Gesture both preceded and served as the supporting context for oncoming changes in children' speech. Children in our study not only produced 'X IS LIKE Y' constructions in their speech at an earlier age than reported in previous research, but even this onset age seemed to underestimate children's abilities – children were able to use gesture and speech together to express similarity mappings without the word *like* well before they produced their first 'X IS LIKE Y' construction. Thus, at a point when children did not have the spoken language skills to express similarity mappings explicitly, gesture offered them an easy-to-use tool to convey such meanings. And the use of this tool is likely to have served as a stepping-stone for learning to convey similarity mappings entirely in speech.

## Acknowledgements

We thank Kristi Schoendube, Jason Voigt, Becky Free, and Laura Schneidman for their administrative, technical and coding support, and the project research assistants, Karyn Brasky, Elaine Croft, Kristin Duboc, Jennifer Griffin, Carrie Meanwell, Erica Mellum, Molly Nikolas, Jana Oberholtzer, Lillia Rissman, Becky Seibel, Kevin Uttich, and Julie Wallman for their help in collecting and transcribing the data. The research presented in this paper was supported by grant #PO1 HD406–05 to Goldin-Meadow.

## Notes

1. Communicative acts are words or gestures, alone or in combination, which were preceded and followed by a pause, a change in conversational turn, or a change in intonational pattern.
2. The word *like* in children's speech became polysemous at age 2;2, functioning as a verb in some instances (e.g., *I like ice-cream*) and as a comparative marker in others (e.g., *ice-cream cone is like mushroom*). Beginning at age 2;6, a few children occasionally used *like* as a discourse marker. In this paper, we focus exclusively on the uses of *like* as a comparative marker.
3. The only exception was one child who produced one instance of such a construction at age 1;6.
4. Speech is provided in italics and any nonverbal information (e.g., gesture, communicative context) is given in small caps; the age of each child is indicated in brackets. Each example is followed by a gloss that approximates what the child is intending to convey in his/her communication.
5. The only exception was one child who produced one instance of the construction in a gesture-speech combination at age 1;6; this was the same child who also produced one instance of the construction in speech at age 1;6.
6. Children also produced several gesture-speech combinations that drew on a similarity-based comparison by using linguistic devices other than the word *like*. In these instances, gesture encoded the target domain of the mapping, and speech conveyed information about the source domain (e.g., *It is chocolate–kind of chocolate* + CHILD HOLDS UP BROWN MARKER; *Color is an apple* + CHILD POINTS TO A GREEN BALLOON THAT LOOKS LIKE A GREEN APPLE). We first observed such instances at age 2;6, after the onset of the 'X IS LIKE Y' construction in children's speech.

# References

Asch, Solomon E., and Harriet Nerlove
  1960    The development of double function terms in children. In *Perspectives in Psychological Theory*, Bernard Kaplan, and Seymour Wapner (eds.), 47–60. New York: International Universities Press, Inc.
Billow, Richard M.
  1975    A cognitive developmental study of metaphor comprehension. *Developmental Psychology* 11(4): 415–423.
  1981    Observing spontaneous metaphor in children. *Journal of Experimental Child Psychology* 31: 430–445.
Capirci, Olga, Jana M.Iverson, Elena Pizzuto, and Virginia Volterra
  1996    Gestures and words during the transition to two-word speech. *Journal of Child Language* 23: 645–673.
Chukovsky, Kornei
  1968    *From Two to Five*. Berkeley: University of California Press.
Carlson, Patricia, and Mosche Anisfeld
  1969    Some observations on the linguistic competence of a two-year-old child. *Child Development* 40: 565–575.
Cicone, Michael, Howard Gardner, and Ellen Winner
  1981    Understanding the psychology in psychological metaphors. *Journal of Child Language* 8: 213–216.
Clark, Eve V.
  1973    What is in a word? On the child's acquisition of semantics in his first language. In *Cognitive Development and the Acquisition of Language*, Timothy E. Moore (ed.), 65–110. New York: Academic Press.
Dent, Cathy H.
  1984    The developmental importance of motion information in perceiving and describing metaphoric similarity. *Child Development* 55: 1607–1613.
  1987    Developmental studies of perception and metaphor: The twain shall meet. *Metaphor and Symbolic Activity* 2 (1): 53–71.
Elbers, Loekie
  1988    New names from old words: Related aspects of children's metaphors and word compounds. *Journal of Child Language* 15: 591–617.
Epstein, Ruth L., and Peter J. Gamlin
  1994    Young children's comprehension of simple and complex metaphors presented in pictures and words. *Metaphor and Symbolic Activity* 9 (3): 179–191.
Gardner, Howard
  1974    Metaphor and modalities: How children project polar adjectives onto diverse domains. *Child Development* 45: 84–91.
Gardner, Howard, Mary Kircher, Ellen Winner, and David Perkins
  1975    Children's metaphoric productions and preferences. *Journal of Child Language* 2: 125–141.

Gardner, Howard, Ellen Winner, Robin Bechhofer, and Dennie Wolf
1978    The development of figurative language. In *Children's Language: Volume I*, Katherine Nelson (ed.), 1–38. New York: Gardner Press.

Gentner, Dedre
1977    Children's performance on a spatial analogies task. *Child Development* 48: 1034–1039.
1988    Metaphor as structure mapping: The relational shift. *Child Development* 59: 47–59.

Gentner, Dedre, and Mary J. Rattermann
1990    Deep thinking in children: The case for knowledge change in analogical development. *Behavioral and Brain Sciences* 21 (6): 837–838.
1991    Language and the career of similarity. In *Perspectives on Language and Thought: Interrelations in Development*, Susan A. Gelman, and James P. Byrnes (eds.), 225–277. New York, Cambridge University Press.

Gershkoff-Stowe, Lisa, and Linda B. Smith
1997    A curvilinear trend in naming errors as a function of early vocabulary growth. *Cognitive Psychology* 34: 37–71.

Goldin-Meadow, Susan, and Cynthia Butcher
2003    Pointing toward two word speech in young children. In *Pointing: Where Language, Culture, and Cognition Meet,* Sotaro Kita (ed.), 85–107. Mahwah, N.J.: Lawrence Erlbaum.

Goswami, Usha, and Ann L. Brown
1989    Melting chocolate and melting snowmen: Analogical reasoning and casual relations. *Cognition* 35: 69–95.

Greenfield, Patricia M., and Joshua H. Smith
1976    *The Structure of Communication in Early Language Development*. New York: Academic Press.

Iverson, Jana M., Olga Capirci, and Cristina M. Caselli
1994    From communication to language in two modalities. *Cognitive Development* 9: 23–43.

Iverson, Jana M., and Susan Goldin-Meadow
2005    Gesture paves the way for language development. *Psychological Science* 16: 368–371.

Keil, Frank C.
1987 Conceptual domains and the acquisition of metaphor. *Cognitive Development* 1: 73–96.

Malgady, Robert G.
1977    Children's interpretation and appreciation of similes. *Child Development* 48: 1734–1738.

Mendelsohn, Eve, Susan Robinson, Howard Gardner, and Ellen Winner
1984    Are preschooler's renamings intentional category violations? *Developmental Psychology* 20 (2): 187–192.

Özçalışkan, Şeyda
2002    Metaphors we move by: A crosslinguistic-developmental analysis of metaphorical motion events in English and Turkish. Ph. D. diss., Department of Psychology University of California, Berkeley, CA.

2003    Children's developing understanding of metaphors about the mind. In *Proceedings of the 27th Boston University Conference on Language Development,* Barbara Beachley, Amanda Brown, and Francis Conlin (eds.), 541–552. Somerville, MA: Cascadilla Press.

2005    On learning to draw the distinction between physical and metaphorical motion: Is metaphor an early emerging cognitive and linguistic capacity? *Journal of Child Language* 32 (2): 291–318.

under    Metaphors we move by: Children's developing understanding of meta-
review    phorical motion in typologically distinct languages.

Özçalışkan, Şeyda, and Susan Goldin-Meadow

2005a    Gesture is at the cutting edge of early language development. *Cognition* 96 (3): B101–B113.

2005b    Do mothers lead their children by the hand? *Journal of Child Language* 32 (3): 481–505.

2006    Role of gesture in children's early constructions. In *The Acquisition of Constructions,* Eve V. Clark, and Barbara Kelly (eds.), 31–58. Stanford, CA: CSLI Publications.

under    Learning to build similarity mappings in gesture and speech with and
review    without a language model.

Schecter, Barbara, and John Broughton

1991    Developmental relationships between psychological metaphors and concepts of life and consciousness. *Metaphor and Symbolic Activity* 6 (2): 119–143.

Vosniadou, Stella

1987    Contextual and linguistic factors in children's comprehension of non-literal language. *Metaphor and Symbolic Activity* 2 (1): 1–11.

Vosniadou, Stella, and Andrew Ortony

1983    The emergence of the literal-metaphorical-anomolous distinction in young children. *Child Development* 54: 154–161.

Winner, Ellen

1979    New names for old things: The emergence of metaphoric language. *Journal of Child Language* 6: 469–491.

Winner, Ellen, Margaret McCarthy, and Howard Gardner

1980    The ontogenesis of metaphor. In *Cognition and Figurative Language,* Richard P. Honeck and Robert Hoffman (eds.), 341–361. Hillsdale, N.J.: Lawrence Erlbaum.

Winner, Ellen, Anne K. Rosenstiel, and Howard Gardner

1976    The development of metaphoric understanding. *Developmental Psychology* 12: 289–297.

# Part four: Go, tell it on the mountain

# Energy through fusion at last: Synergies in cognitive anthropology and cognitive linguistics

*Gary B. Palmer*[1]

*Abstract*
In language and culture research, one often finds cognitive linguists and cognitive anthropologists working on the same problems. This chapter reviews a few topics to which both cognitive linguists and cognitive anthropologists have made significant research contributions. These topics are (1) Language as culture, (2) Disentangling psychological unity from cultural diversity: The case of experiential language, (3) Distributed knowledge versus consensus in language communities; (4) Complex categories, (4.1) Reduplication as a complex category, (4.2) Noun classifiers as complex categories, (5) The new relativity in spatial orientation, and (6) The origins of language.

*Keywords*: language and culture; cultural variation; cultural distribution; psychological unity; categorization; complex category; classifier system; reduplication; origin of language

A topic such as the one assigned – Cognitive Anthropology and Cognitive Linguistics: How can One Enrich the Other? – provides a fine occasion to apply prototype semantics, because cognitive linguistics and cognitive anthropology are complex categories lacking clear boundaries. We may lack clear disciplinary definition because we lack consensus on definitions of cognition or because we enjoy a somewhat haphazard cross-disciplinary mixing of ideas through the usual academic channels of conferences, seminars, and publications. If this were not enough to dissolve boundaries, there are also cross-currents: Our cooperative field of academic discourse draws the participation of other linguists (e.g. typologists), other anthropologists (e.g. linguistic anthropology), and scholars from other disciplines in the sciences (e.g. cognitive psychology, neurophysiology, computer science), the humanities (e.g. philosophy, English, American Studies), and various applied fields in language education. Most researchers would agree that the interdisciplinary exchange has been intellectually stimulating and productive. Within the larger field of activity defined by the sum of these exchanges, one often finds cognitive linguists and cognitive anthropologists working on the same problems. A review of their findings shows that they have made significant contributions and conducted fruitful dialogues, which have been supported and joined by the many others who explore the nexus of language, and culture and cognition. This chapter reviews a few of the topics of mutual interest.

In section (1) *Language as culture*, it is argued that linguistic categories are predominantly cultural even while they are constrained by biology and universal physical experiences. Section (2) *Disentangling psychological unity from cultural diversity* examines this important cultural issue as it applies to language, in part by comparing the Tagalog and English models of cognitive process. Section (3) *Distributed knowledge versus consensus in language communities* examines the linguistic side of another important and related cultural issue. The two issues intersect because distributed knowledge is the primary form of cultural diversity within language communities, however they may be understood and defined, and because arguments for consensus may be based on assumptions of psychological unity. Section (4) *Complex categories*, shows that a cultural perspective on language helps to explain two widespread and important grammatical phenomena: reduplication and systems of noun classifiers. Subsection (4.1) *Reduplication as a complex category*, describes Nahuatl reduplication as a complex category in both its phonology and its semantics. In (4.2) *Noun classifiers as complex categories*, I argue from Shona data that each classifier in a system of classifiers is a polycentric linguistic category based on multiple interconnected cultural scenarios. Similar arguments are applied to the language of spatial orientation, which is discussed in (5) *The new relativity in spatial orientation*. This section revisits the question of psychological unity and proposes a general framework of cognitive maps useful for cross-linguistic, *ergo* cross-cultural, descriptions of the semantics of spatial orientation. In (6) *The origins of language*, cognitive linguistic and cultural theory are combined to argue that human language originated in the ceremonials of *Homo heidelbergensis*, an immediate precursor to our own species. Section (7) presents conclusions.

## 1.   Language as culture

Language emerges within culture both historically and developmentally. We may take this statement for granted and still fail to see its implications for research. It means that categories based on even the most fundamental physical experiences are shaped and filtered by cultural practices and artifacts. For example, our experience of gravity is shaped by the degree to which our culture causes us to assume restful or strenuous postures, walk in easy or difficult terrain, and move heavy or light objects. Our experience of temperature is influenced by shelter, clothing, and activities in local topographies. Northern fishermen and equatorial farmers experience very different ranges of ambient temperatures and mediate them using different sorts of shelter, clothing, and technologies for heating and cooling. Similar considerations apply to the whole spectrum of our sensory experience, including our perception of phonology, which is often overlooked in discussions of cultural relativity (Trabant 2000, Bohn 2000). Even very basic physical categories of the developing infant, such as "inside" and "under" vary radically according to *prelinguistic* directed experience with common household utensils (Sinha and Jensen de López 2000). Cultural institutions and artifacts of all sorts come into concerted play in language development and the transmission of language to successive generations. The importance of the culture concept to the common enterprise of cognitive linguistics and cognitive anthropology has been explicitly recognized at least since 1987 (Lakoff and Kövecses 1987), and since emphasized by Geeraerts and Grondelaers (1995), Langacker (1994), D'Andrade (1995a), and Palmer (1996). The concept has been the basis of sessions at the meeting of the International Cognitive Linguistics Association and the Conferences on Language, Culture, and Mind.[2]

Cognitive linguistics would be easier if all categories and image-schemas were innate or emergent, embodied in some simple way, and elemental, but in fact most are woven into the web of cultural patterns. Image-schemas become enmeshed in elaborate cultural models and take meaning from their cultural loci. Life may be a journey in many or all cultures, but a path schema is one thing in an urban shopping mall and another in a furrowed field. In Polynesia, elemental schemas such as *up/down, male/female*, and *light/dark* become enmeshed with more obviously cultural notions, such as *seaward/inward, sacred/profane*, and *clean/dirty* (Keesing 1997; Shore 1996). The conceptual metaphors of political parties in the U.S. may come from the family (Lakoff 2002), but the families in question are not universal in their structure and ideology; they are culturally North American. Cognitive linguists could focus on just those categories that are demonstrably innate or "emergent" from basic experiences that are shared by all mankind (Lakoff and Johnson 1980: 81; Johnson 2005), but in doing so, they might overlook a great deal of interesting grammar. It appears that the bulk of grammar consists of phonological and semantic categories that are specific to their language communities (Croft 2001). One outcome of this perspective is the growing interest in the relation of within-community phonological variation to socio-cultural schemas, scenarios and categories (Kristiansen 2003; see also, Dirven 2005 on the cognitive sociolinguistic strand of cognitive linguistics and its use of cultural models).

Considering these same facts from the perspective of cognitive anthropology, one concludes that grammar must be a rich source of information about cultural schemas. In the United States, this realization came to academic anthropology through the writings of Franz Boas, who in 1911 treated grammatical constructions as expressions of selected partial images arising from ethnic psychologies (Boas 1966 [1911]: 39, 59). In this, he was influenced by "19th Century Humboldtians," especially Heymann Steinthal and Wilhelm von Humboldt (1972 [1836]) (The quoted phrase is from Koerner [2000: 6]; see also Trabant 2000). Boas wrote that "in each language only a part of the complete concept that we have in mind is expressed, and ... each language has a peculiar tendency to select this or that aspect of the mental image which is conveyed by the expression of the thought" (1966 [1911]: 39). Boas's linguistic relativity was subsequently taken up by Sapir (1949 [1921]), Whorf (1956), Lee (1959), Friedrich (1971, 1979), and others (See discussion in Palmer 1996: 10–18). Lucy's (1992 a,b) recent examination and test of the Whorfian hypothesis represent a continuation of the tradition in American anthropology. Whorf's thinking on linguistic relativism has been reconstructed by cognitive linguist Lee (1996).[3]

The relativistic approach introduced above is one of two predominant approaches to cognitive anthropology in the U.S. The second is *ethnoscience*, a subfield that emerged in the 1960s. Its proponents study cultural categories, cultural logic, and what natives must know in order to act appropriately within their own cultures, including those of Western societies.[4] One line of investigation in ethnoscience looks at how relatively well-ordered terminological domains such as kinship are spanned by small sets of semantic features, components, or dimensions, such as the dimensions of sex, generation, and lineality, that would permit the arrangement of terms in a tabular componential analysis (Goodenough 1965) or taxonomic tree (Kay 1966). Whether such dimensions have the status of native categories or are merely analytical constructs invented by researchers has been a major issue in ethnoscience (Schneider 1965). This concern with psychological reality can also be found in cognitive linguistics, as in the study by Sandra and Rice (1995) of polysemy in spatial prepositions. Researchers also seek to apply Western symbolic logic to understand the cultural logic governing usages of terms (Lounsbury 1964).[5] Another line of investigation in ethnoscience searches for linguistic universals in systems of basic color terms and in classifications of plants and animals (Berlin and Kay 1969; Berlin 1992; Brown 1984). A third line of investigation elicits language data to determine the extent of cultural consensus in a population of speakers, with some researchers finding extensive consensus (Romney 1999), while others find significant variation (Borofsky 1994). These issues will be taken up in more detail in section (2). Although the ethnoscience approaches may seem less immediately applicable to the problems of cognitive linguistics than Whorfian relativism, there are potential applications and common problems here, too, as will become evident in Section (2).

## 2.   Disentangling psychological unity from cultural diversity: The case of experiential language

Having made the case for a broad, inclusive field of cultural linguistics in the previous section, I will admit to overstating the freedom of cultural forms from biological and environmental constraints. Innate cognitive abilities and universal experiences play important roles in supporting and constraining the myriad categories of thought and language (Langacker 1994). Human cognition has evolved *for* language and cultural variation, not independently nor in opposition to them.[6] On the list of good candidates for innate image-schemas one finds horizontal and vertical orientations of viewed objects, color foci, small numbers, animacy, possession of bodily parts, and a template for the human face, which enables us to recognize thousands of faces, though each may be viewed only briefly (Ehrsson 2004; Haxby et al. 2001; Gordon 2004). Johnson (2005) listed several image-schemas, but he seems not to regard these simply as innate structures. Instead, they are seen as properties of bodily experience in the environment: "image schemas are not to be understood either as merely 'mental' or merely 'bodily,' but rather as contours of what Dewey (1925) called the 'body-mind'". Johnson mentioned the schemas CONTAINER, RIGHT and LEFT, FRONT and BACK, NEAR and FAR, HORIZON, CENTER-PE-RIPHERY, COMPULSION, ATTRACTION, BLOCKAGE OF MOVEMENT, VERTI-CALITY, RECTILINEAR MOTION, SOURCE-PATH-GOAL, and SCALARITY.

In spatial cognition, Langacker (2002: 139) has proposed several basic notions expected to "figure prominently" in the locative systems of all languages. These are "separation, inclusion, proximity, line, surface, source-path-goal." Other concepts proposed by Langacker for describing constructions in general include "profiling, trajector/landmark alignment, correspondence, elaboration, and profile determinance" (2002: 158). Similarity mapping must also be listed as one of the innate or essential cognitive abilities that support language (Özçalışkan and Goldin-Meadow: this volume). Derivative from these are the universal tendency to create new concepts from blends of existing concepts and the ability to profile conceptual metaphors and metonymies (Fauconnier and Turner 2002; Lakoff and Johnson 1980; Dirven and Pörings 2002; Panther and Thornburg in press). There is also a substantial subgroup of cognitive linguists who accept Wierzbicka's still controversial proposal of a Natural Semantic Metalanguage consisting of some 60 universal and irreducible semantic primes that can be used to explicate the meaning of any non-prime term in any language (Wierzbicka 1996; Goddard 2002).

The term *psychological unity* needs to be used with qualification, because it may refer either to innate inherited categories or to "emergent" categories and motivations, which arise from common universal experiences of the physical world (Lakoff and Johnson 1980: 81). The collection of analytic concepts listed above refers to innate cognitive abilities or candidates for that status (Johnson's image-schemas excepted), that support human language and confer a degree of psychological and linguistic unity on humankind. Definitions can be found in Langacker (1987, 2000) and Lakoff (1987) or in textbooks such as Ungerer and Schmid (1996), Foley (1997), and Dirven and Verspoor (2004).

In calling attention to the importance of selection of partial images for representation in grammar, Boas anticipated by three quarters of a century the notion of construal that was later elaborated so productively in cognitive linguistics as one of the innate cognitive abilities that supports human language. Compare Langacker's statement that "every language evolves vast inventories of constructions each of which embodies a particular way of construing certain kinds of situations" (2002: 139). But where Boas was making a point about the uniqueness of each language deriving from its ethnic psychology (i.e. culture), Langacker emphasizes that basic cognitive abilities such as construal are universal aspects of a "common human potential" (Langacker 2002: 139). Thus we have the apparent paradox in which universal cognitive abilities underpin global linguistic diversity. But this paradox is easily resolved. The biological substrate includes universal cognitive abilities that register and participate in certain physiological processes, such as general bodily arousal. It also contributes a share of cognitive diversity, though just how much and of what kind is a controversial and largely unstudied topic. Experience, history, and tradition motivate and sustain cultural and linguistic diversity and a significant share of uniformity. Since both biology and culture are sources of both uniformity and diversity, there is no lack of interesting work for analysts.

In their analyses of language data, cognitive linguists and anthropologists must often try to sort out the innate from the emergent and the emergent from the culturally determined. Langacker has commented on the complexity of the problem:

> Any new experience then draws upon a combination of innate abilities and established mental structures from all previous strata, so that it becomes rather pointless (if not impossible) to fully disentangle the innate from the learned, the pre-cultural from the cultural, the linguistic from the non-linguistic. (Langacker 1994: 51)

Langacker is no doubt correct to doubt the possibility of full disentanglement, but the position holds a potential contradiction, since he himself has done as much as anyone to call attention to the importance of innate cognitive abilities in constraining the variety of grammatical constructions. To recognize such abilities and base a theory of language on them is to intimate that some disentangling has been done. Furthermore, the growing body of interesting new analyses based on the principles of cognitive linguistics suggest that the effort has achieved a measure of success.

In cognitive anthropology, the problem of identifying innate categories has been defined most clearly in cross-linguistic studies of basic color terms, the main point of reference being Berlin and Kay (1969), who proposed an evolutionary sequence in color naming and universal constraints on the naming of colors. A limitation on these findings is that they apply only to basic color terms, which are usually only a small percentage of color terms found in any language. Conklin (1964) showed how the full range of color terms incorporates other dimensions in addition to the color spectrum, dimensions such as moisture and temperature, or as I encountered in a Salish language, the texture of the underside of a leaf. Using the notion of construal from cognitive linguistics, MacLaury (1992) proposed that cross-linguistic variations in the extensions of color terms reflect differences in the construal of color fields. He argued that color categorization is analogous to spatial orientation, so that people are able to determine their position in color space by adopting a particular point of view or vantage point. Wierzbicka (1990) seeks the origin of color terms in the projection of innate foci of color perception onto common experiences of sky, land, the sun, fire and blood, an approach which resembles the broader theory of Alverson (1991: 112) who would derive schemas from the *primal scene* of "the dial, orbit, or trajectory of sun and moon, whose light is both a point and a sweep or array; ... cloud cover; ... altitude; ... courses of movement/travel through the trajectory; ... barriers to sensory or locomotor access; and ... behavior of entities occupying this scene." While one normally thinks of Wierzbicka's essentialist approach as diametrically opposed to the Lakoff and Johnson (1980) concept of image-schemas as emergent categories, if Wierzbicka's primes are actually derived from experience in the world, then the two approaches have something important in common. It appears from the diversity of conclusions in these studies that neither the causes of variations nor of universals in color terms are well established.[7]

The language of emotion is a second domain in which much work has been motivated by the issue of psychological unity versus cultural variation (Kövecses and Palmer 1999; Kövecses, Palmer, and Dirven 2002). Kövecses (2000, 2005) has aimed at discovering conceptual universals that motivate metaphors of emotions, especially the emotions of anger and love. He has found that English, Hungarian, Chinese, and Japanese all have the container metaphor as the ontological basis for their talk about anger (2000: 146). In this model, human bodies are containers of anger, which is conceptualized as a heated substance in a closed container. The explanation offered by Kövecses for uniformity in these four languages and others, is that people everywhere experience the same physiological responses to the causes of anger (2000: 156). A major component of this response is a rise in blood pressure, which motivates the image of a pressurized container. Kövecses (2000: 159) generalized that it is conceptual metonymies (the physiological correlates of anger) that motivate conceptual metaphors of emotion. This explanation fits the emergent/embodied explanation of category formation and psychological unity.

Kövecses is not fixated on language universals. He asked *"How can we construct a comprehensive theory that can account for both the universality and the variation in our use of metaphor?"* (Kövecses 2005: 3, emphasis in original) He explains variation as the expression of cultural models and in fact he was one of the first to introduce cultural models into cognitive linguistics (Lakoff and Kövecses 1987). For example, he accepted the view of Geeraerts and Grondelaers (1995) that the Euro-American concept of anger comes from the classical-medieval notion of the *four humors*. He observed that the Japanese concept of anger involves keeping the real, true self (*honne*) hidden in the body container (*hara* 'stomach/bowels') by exercising self control. The Chinese concept of anger involves the rise of *qi*, energy that flows through the body, which upsets the desired balance of *yin* and *yang* postulated by Chinese philosophy and medicine. Cross-linguistic variations in choices of specific metaphors for anger derive from these differing cultural models (Kövecses 2005: 234–235). Support for cultural influences on these metaphors is provided by Yu (1998).

Closely related to the problem of emotion language is the problem of language about thinking. I will refer to the language of emotion and thought together as *experiential language*. The two domains of experience are so closely entwined in English that one might conclude that the field is thoroughly culturally structured (Damasio 1994). Many terms have both emotional and nonemotional meanings. To see how this semantic conflation manifests linguistically, it may help to consider a few examples such as the Tagalog definitions in (1–4) from Palmer (2003a). Emphasis has been added to the translations:

(1) *Ang akala ay    isang    pag-iisip na binabase sa pakiramdam …*
SPC[8] idea INV one-LG thinking LG based DR feeling
'*Akalà* is a way of thinking based on a feeling …'

(2) *Ang batid ay isang pag-iisip na may kahalong pakiramdam.*
SPC know INV one-LG thinking LG EX combined-LG feeling
'*Batid* is a thinking combined with feeling.'

(3) *Ang intensyón ay pag-iisip at pakiramdam*
SPC intention INV thinking and feeling
*bago nagpaplano ng isang bagay.*
before planning GN one-LG thing
'**An intention is thinking and feeling before planning of a thing.**'

(4) *Ang nahihirapan ay maaaring mangyari sa damdamin, pag-iisip, o' pisikal*
SPC hardship INV possibly event DR emotion thoughts or physical
*kapag nabibigatan ang isang tao sa kanyang ginagawa*
if weighed.down SPC one-LG person DR his do.(x)
*o' nararamdaman.*
or feel.(x)
'***Nahihirapan* is possibly an event in the emotions, thoughts, or physical [being] if a person is weighed down by what he does or feels.**'

The examples show that concepts that one can translate as *idea, know, intention*, and *hardship*, are all defined in Tagalog to predicate a combination of 'thinking' and 'feeling' (*pagisip* and *pakiramdam/damdamin*). Lee (2003) reported a similar mixing of thinking and feeling in the mental models of her English test subjects:

Analytical thought is conceived as paradigmatically active, definable, and separable from other internal behavior. By contrast, feelings and other kinds of thinking, especially contemplative activity, seem less easily definable and separable from each other ... A strong negative/positive polarity generated from within the feelings/emotions range provides an alternative axis of organization in some personal models, penetrating what has more traditionally been regarded as the domain of thought (2003: 247).

Proponents of the Natural Semantic Metalanguage would doubtless find the distinction between thinking and feeling and the occurrence of many mixed categories in English and Tagalog to be as they predicted, because THINK and FEEL are two of the irreducible semantic primes included in the theory: "The innate and universal theory of mind includes the ... major constituents: THINK, KNOW, WANT, and FEEL" (Wierzbicka 1996: 48). Emotion concepts are defined as patterns of thinking:[9]

The semantic structure of most emotion concepts, then, can be represented as follows:

X feels something
sometimes a person thinks something like this
...
...
...
...
because of this, this person feels something
X feels something like this
(Wierzbicka 1996: 182)

But, it would be no surprise to find that many, or even all, cultures recognize and lexicalize two regions on a gradient that extends from mental events that are accompanied by intense physiological arousal (emotions) to those with relatively little physiological arousal (thoughts). Damasio (1994: xiv; cited in Lee 2003: 247) has argued on evolutionary grounds that reason is more effective under the governance of emotion and feeling. This would not necessarily imply that the distinction between thought and emotion is sufficiently clear and discrete in any language to qualify the two terms as lexical primitives, but it may be true that the two concepts, however delineated, are necessary to the explication of other concepts, as required by NSM theory (Goddard 2002: 6). Just as likely, this is another instance of complex categories that needs further description and analysis.

Putting aside the issue of whether the distinction between thinking and feeling is universally discretely defined, there is the related question of whether cultures and languages vary in their models of experiential processes. The following quote from Palmer (2003a: 271) illustrates one such model:

> Roy D'Andrade (1987, 1995[a]) has discovered what he calls "a major direction of causation" in English as follows: action > perception > thought (> feeling) > wish > intention > action. Feelings may be bypassed, so that wishes result directly from thoughts (1995[a]: 162). Feelings may also stimulate expressive reflex acts such as sneezing, smiling, and crying. [Brackets added.]

D'Andrade presented the model with a number of qualifications concerning the order of elements in the process, but let us assume that the model is sufficiently well-defined to enable cross-linguistic comparison. Analysis of a sample of Tagalog statements about causation yields the findings summarized as follows:

> Thoughts or thinking are most likely to arise from effort or from other thoughts, but they may also result from states or feelings. The fact that thoughts arise from effort follows from the common notion that the mind and thinking are used. Thought may produce action or further thought, but seldom is it said to produce feelings. Thought and feeling are not tightly linked in these expressions. To the extent that they are, the direction of causation often runs in the opposite direction from D'Andrade's model for English. The definitions contain no instance of perception motivating thought.
>
> In these expressions, feelings result most commonly from actions, events, states and changes of state, and from other feelings, not, as in English, from thoughts and perceptions. Feelings typically produce bodily responses, actions, thoughts, and other feelings. It is as though two stages in the English model were omitted from Tagalog (Palmer 2003a: 274).

Where D'Andrade's model for English has six stages, the Tagalog model seems to require only three, with one path running through thought, the other through feeling. Action and perception lead to thought in English, and then on to wishes, intentions, and further actions. In Tagalog, action and several other kinds of mental experience lead to either thought or feeling, and then on to more thoughts or more feelings, or actions and bodily responses. Both models have a potential pathway with action at both the initiation and the completion of the scenario. The Tagalog model can be related to traditional philosophy of mind and body in which the thoughts pertain to outward conscious being (*malay*), while feelings are inner events (*niloloob*). There is little causal interaction between the two domains. Both respond to events outside the person and lead to actions directed outside the person.

The Tagalog model of experiential process was arrived at by applying standard methods of ethnoscience and anthropology combined with concepts from cognitive linguistics: Native language question frames were used to elicit definitions which were found to fit standard analytical frameworks – in this case, a taxonomy and a process model; and published ethnographic documentation was reviewed in search of cultural schemas and scenarios that would help to explain the models (See Palmer 2003a for references).

To summarize, it may be the case that thought and feeling or emotion are semantic universals, as claimed by Wierzbicka. Nevertheless, thought and feeling must always be embedded in cultural scenarios that mix the two domains (Lutz 1988). Lexical domains of experience profile elements and construals of such mixed socio-cultural models. Case studies from a wider sample of languages would be welcome, as would further comparative studies such as that of Fortesque (2001). The next section looks at the issue of how much consensus or diversity may exist within a language community in the cultural schemas and scenarios that constitute the semantic pole of grammar.

## 3.  Distributed knowledge versus consensus in language communities

Language is cultural and cultural knowledge is located in individual minds,[10] but it is also learned from others and shared. This raises the question of how much of cultural knowledge must be shared within a language community. How much consensus is required? Does culture inhere in the sharing and continuity through generations, or is it the way that we organize the knowledge of a diverse population of individuals, each of whom holds a few pieces of the puzzle? Wallace (1961: 22, 109, 123) characterized these two opposed ways of understanding culture as the *replication of uniformity* versus *the organization of diversity*. He argued convincingly that culture is characterized more by the organization of diversity than by the replication of uniformity. In fact, he asserted that "human societies may characteristically *require* the non-sharing of certain cognitive maps among participants in a variety of institutional arrangements" (1961: 35). Wallace's bias is echoed in the work of Borofsky (1994) and Sharifian (forthcoming). Citing several studies that

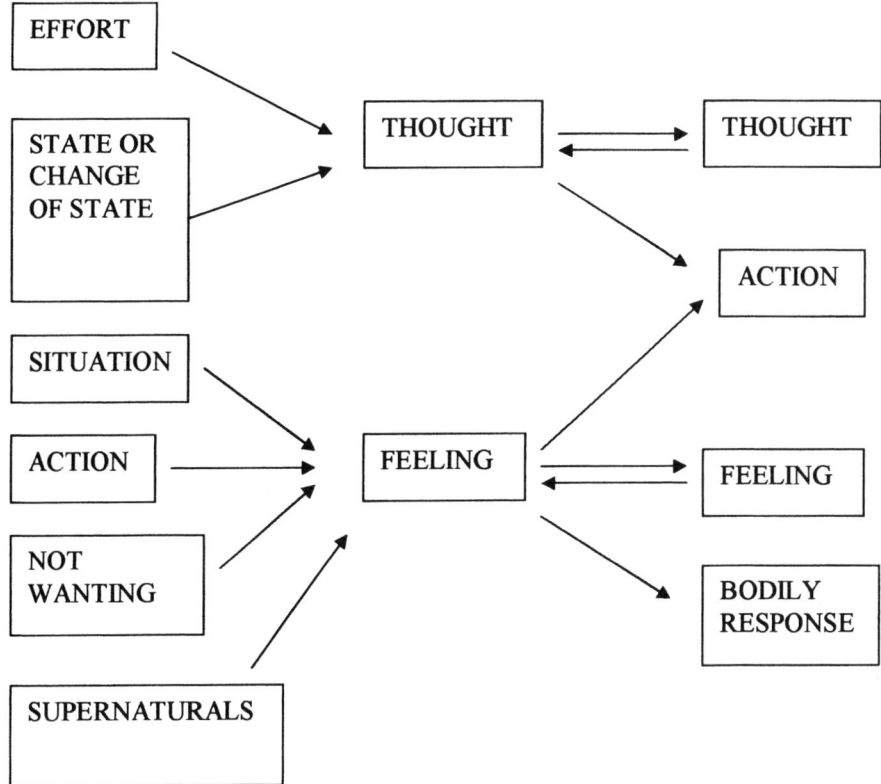

*Figure 1.* Causal sequences in Tagalog experiential statements. (Palmer 2003: 274)

find diversity in community values and classifications, Borofsky concluded:

> Look as one will through all this literature on intracommunity diversity – and it is rather extensive – there is, however, little mention of people not interacting effectively with one another. How do we make sense of this? What knowledge is being shared in what ways? (1994: 331)

Borofsky proposed that knowledge in a language community exists on a continuum from highly structured and widely shared, to fluid, context oriented, and apparently diverse. He suggested that some apparent diversity might be explained by the inappropriateness of researchers' questions to the lives of study subjects.

Sharifian (forthcoming), regards language as *emergent cultural cognition* that integrates knowledge, which is distributed heterogeneously across the minds of a language community. The emergent system is dynamic and adaptive. He cites similar views of the anthropologists Keesing (1987), Borofsky (1994), and Kronenfeld (2002), as well as Hutchins's (1994) view that cultural knowledge and process are also to be found outside the mind in material artefacts such as a ship's navigational instruments. As an instance of distributed knowledge, Sharifian cited high variation in the acceptability of a set of sentences in Persian (Sharifian and Lofti 2003). It is anticipated that further studies will explore the difficult problem of how such diverse linguistic understandings are integrated by the Persian language. Cognitive linguists can study the sharing and integration of both sound and meaning within language communities, bringing new perspectives to the old topics of, for example, gender differences, honorifics, and within-community sociolinguistic variation (Kristiansen 2003).

Returning briefly to the research problem introduced by Hutchins – cognition embodied in cultural artefacts – I would suggest that cognitive linguists narrow this field of study by applying their toolkit to the language usages embedded in particular domains of artefacts and often inscribed upon them. I am thinking of such exotic and commonplace domains as ritual paraphernalia, navigational instruments, computers, construction tools and materials, facial makeup, cooking utensils, and personal equipment for sports.

One might think that these researchers had settled the issue in favor of diversity and distributed knowledge within language communities. After all, anytime there is economic specialization, there must be corresponding diversity in knowledge and language, and most societies have some specialization. But other researchers in cognitive anthropology and psychology find it important to consider and measure the degree of cultural consensus. For example, Kronenfeld (2000: 210) concluded that "the 'thought' language shapes will be collective, not individual," but in Kronenfeld (2002) he argued for diversity. López et al. (1997: 253–254) reasoned that "knowledge associated with core domains of human cognition, such as folk biology, spreads within a population in rapid, extensive and lasting fashion owing to an affinity of such knowledge with basic (possibly innate) cognitive dispositions." By way of contrast, knowledge from specialized domains of activity is shared among kinsmen or other social groups. These researchers evaluate degree of consensus with a statistical model called the *cultural consensus model*, which is a type of factor analysis developed by A. Kimball Romney and others (Romney, Weller and

Batchelder 1986; Romney, Batchelder and Weller 1987; Romney, Moore and Rusch 1997; Romney and Moore 1998; Romney 1999). The model involves testing a population with true-false, multiple choice, or fill-in-the-blank formats, creating a matrix of scores for every subject and item, and calculating the eigenvalues of the matrix. A clearly dominant eigenvalue (i.e. factor) is taken as evidence of cultural consensus.[11] But even Romney and his associates are shifting their studies of cultural consensus in the direction of analyzing distributed knowledge and the organization of diversity. He cited recent studies that have used the model to study "intercultural phenomena" and "complicated intracultural variations" (1999: 107). He noted that "the most useful and prototypical example" of cultural knowledge is provided by language.

Still unexamined is the problem of exactly how language integrates diversity of knowledge within a community. One might begin by requiring that an utterance that profiles some construal of a complex scenario evokes an intended construal in the listener. The speaker need not predict all the associations in the mind of her interlocutor, but she will very likely have some idea of how her words will be interpreted. The interlocutor may then proceed to share knowledge or to act on knowledge not possessed by the speaker. The theory of complex categories can establish the language-specific pathways of association that may be evoked by particular grammatical forms. It reveals how an ostensibly simple prefix may invoke entire domains of culture and place interlocutors in a common frame of reference.

## 4. Complex categories

A good way to approach complexity in language is to begin with Langacker's (1987: 58) notion of a symbolic unit of language as a phonological unit linked to a semantic unit. The phonological unit might be a speaker's concept, more or less concrete or abstract, of the sound of a morpheme, a word, or a phrase structure. The semantic unit could be an elementary concept or some construal of a complex situation. To say that they are linked suggests that the sound may evoke the thought, or the thought the sound. There may be variants of the semantic unit that are linked to the same phonological unit. This is a precise way of describing polysemy or roughly speaking, what Geeraerts and Grondelaers (2004) have called *semasiology*, which in traditional grammar would be called homonymy. It may also be the case that a single semantic unit is linked to a variety of phonological units. Geeraerts and Grondelaers refer to this structure as *onomasiology*, which begins with the notion of synonymy, but is also extended to cover antonymy and words related in a *lexical field*. This broad notion of onomasiology corresponds to what cognitive anthropologists typically refer to as a lexical or semantic domain.

## 4.1 Reduplication[12] as a complex category

Given Langacker's idea of the linguistic symbol, it is not hard to imagine quite complex combinations of phonological and semantic units that form networks of meaning and phonology. One such network, the system of grammatical reduplication in Nahuatl, has been set out in great detail by Tuggy (2003), yet he would not claim that his analysis is exhaustive. Figure 2 shows Tuggy's representation of the symbolic network, which is characterized not by tidy hierarchical or productive rules readily available to a deductively minded speaker, but rather by numbers of irregular phonological forms associated with other forms by similarity. Two phonological prototypes (1. a, e, indicated with bold rectangles) are linked to semantic units characterized by different levels of prototypicality and schematicity. Neither the phonological space nor the semantic space is clearly demarcated, but there are discernable fields. On the left side of the semantic space, most tightly linked to the consonant-vowel reduplication form CV[CV ...], are found various kinds of repetition, which are associated with replication, spatial distribution, the progressive aspect, and intensity. At least some of these notions are probably universally associated with grammatical reduplication. On the right side of the diagram, most tightly linked to the form CVh[CV ...] there is a sub-network of concepts that reflect evaluations: legitimacy, good, bad, willful, social approval/ disapproval, and difference. These concepts, too, are very commonly, if not universally, found in the semantic space of reduplication morphology.

I would attribute the substantial number of evaluative terms to the metonymic thinking process called *subjectification* (Langacker 1990). Terms used repeatedly in a certain context take on as part of their meaning the emotions and perspectives of speakers and observers. The process involves metonymy because the emotions and perspectives belong to the evocative scene along with other components, and because terms for other components of the scene (such as repetitive noise) evolve semantically to include the associated emotion (such as irritation) in their conventional meaning. It is the reduplication which evokes the scenario-based emotions and evaluations in the interpretation (Compare Kristiansen

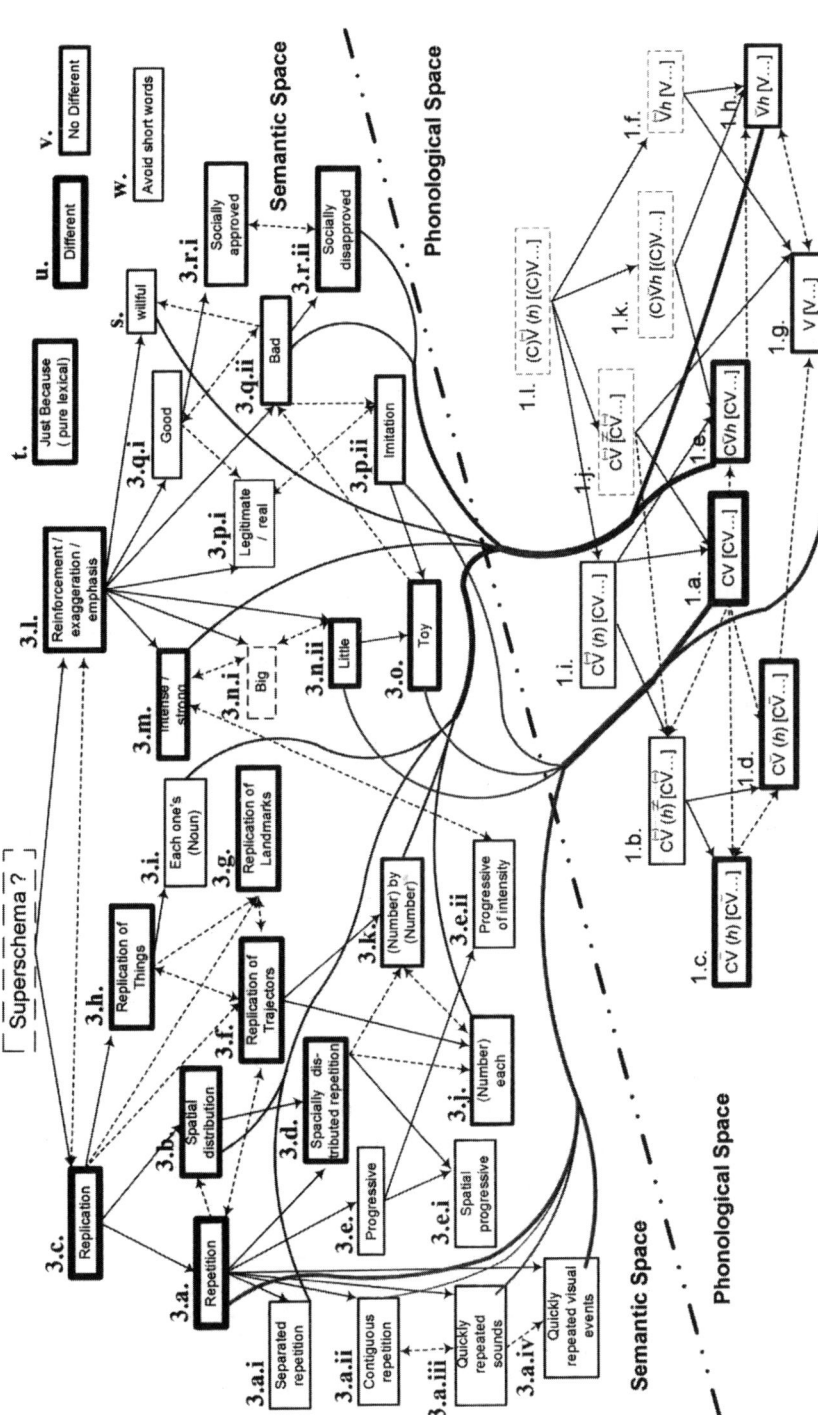

*Figure 2.* Nahuatl reduplication construction (Tuggy 2003:104)

2003). With repeated usages, responses and perceptions of the observer move gradually from offstage to onstage. Additional examples of evaluative complexes have been described. Palmer, Rader and Clarito (forthcoming) found that a subset of lexemes using the Tagalog prefix *ka-*, which they analyzed as a *metonymic partial*, expresses evaluations in forms that reduplicate roots. A set of lexemes using the agent-focus prefix *mag-* also has reduplicative forms that express distributives, repetition, and intensity (Palmer 2003b). Occhi (1999) has analyzed the intricate reduplication grammar of Japanese *gitaigo* mimetics of emotion. Very much as with Tuggy's network analysis of reduplication in Nahuatl, Occhi observed that "metonymic and metamorphic extensions among sense modalities (e.g. *kan kan*), as well as between semantically similar lexemes with different [high (H) and low (L)] pitch patterns (e.g. *ira ira* LHHH and HLLL), result in fuzzy categorization" (1999: 166) [material in brackets added].

How might this relate to the integration of diversity? As reduplications cue the listener to evaluative, intensive, or distributive interpretations of lexemes, interlocutors can harmonize evaluations without exchanging much specific information. They may seek a consensus of attitudes while maintaining substantial diversity of knowledge.

## 4.2   Noun classifiers as complex categories

Analyzing classifier systems requires an analyst to put in play many of the principles of cognitive grammar in combination with ethnographic data. The most important feature of classifier systems is that a class may have not just one central category or image, but a small set of them related to one another by metonymies as illustrated in the schematic presentation in Figure 3. These categories are typically scenarios of various kinds: a common domestic activity, an important ritual complex, or a tribal myth such as the myth of the sun and moon that figures into the *balan* class of Djirbal (Lakoff 1987). The central categories can also be thought of as cultural models. Some terms in a class are related by metonymy or function to the cluster of scenarios that constitute the central categories of the class. That is, they name objects that play significant roles in the scenarios. In the Shona (Bantu) class 3/4, a *pestle* is a kind of *pole*, which is a *long thin thing*. It is used daily in pulverizing *mealie* (various kinds) and in crushing the *leaves* of *trees* and other *medicinal plants*. *Prayers* are directed to the *ancestors*, who control *rain* and the growth of medicinal plants and grain. *Witchcraft* is crushing. Every one of the items in these central scenarios requires the noun class prefix *mu-/mi-* (sg./pl.) together

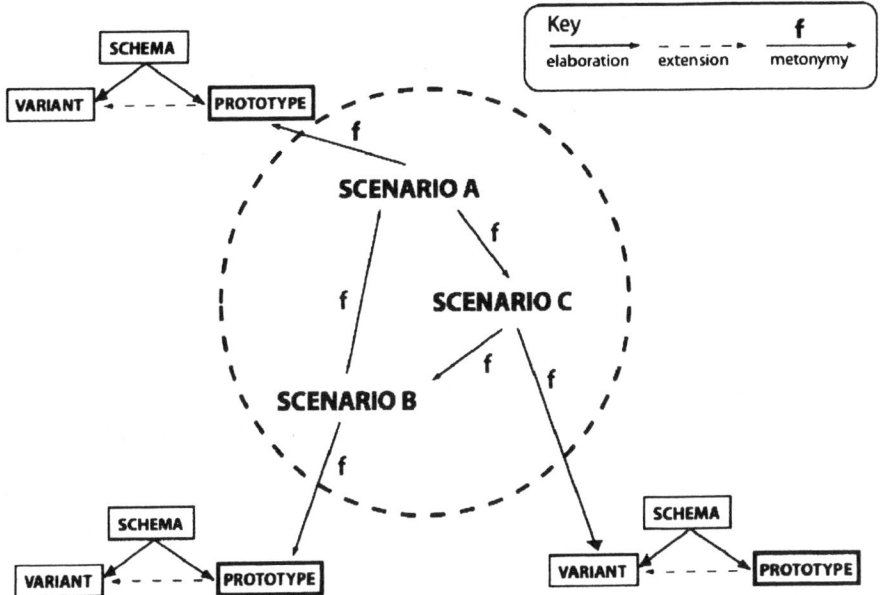

*Figure 3.* Schematic of polycentric category as proposed by Palmer and Woodman (1999). From Palmer, Gary B. 2006. When does cognitive linguistics become cultutal? Case Studies in Tagalog Voice and Shona Noun Classifiers. In: June Luchjenbroers (ed.), *Cognitive Linguistics Investigations across Languages, Fields, and Philosophical Bounderies.* Amsterdam/ Philadelphia: John Benjamins.
With kind permission by John Benjamins Publishing Company, Amsterdam/Philadelphia. www.benjamins.com

with concordial morphology on verbs, adjectives, and locatives. Other terms of the class are related to these and to one another by metonymy or similarity (including metaphor). The pole makes a *repetitive sound,* and repetitive sounds are often *irritating sounds.* Repetition and crushing both beget multiplicities and crushing produces scattering. One such scattered multiplicity, *molting* of feathers, provides the root for *language* and various *ways of speaking,* which also qualify as repetitive sounds. Some terms are clearly examples of subjectification, as with terms predicating irritation and foolishness (because these originally belong to the subjective experience of speakers and listeners and evolve to become part of the objective or onstage meaning), while others are clearly end point transformations of path or long-thin-thing schemas (*end of path, end of axe/hoe blade, last time*) (Palmer and Woodman 1999).

As in Tuggy's study of Nahuatl reduplication, the symbolic sub-network (lexical domain) of a Shona classifier obeys no clear rules of taxonomy or deduction. There is no necessary set of features that a nominal must possess to belong to the class. It must only have a direct or indirect semantic connection to one of the central scenarios of the language and culture. The salient connection of a nominal to a semantic domain of related scenarios qualifies it for the special grammatical treatment given to its class. The concordial forms constitute the phonological pole of the classifier as a complex category. The semantic pole is the class sub-network of central categories and their satellites.[13] Whole classes may also manifest oppositions *vis a vis* one another, such as *earth/sky* or *male/female, giving moisture/accepting moisture.* The oppositions are harder to isolate from the noise of the semantic sub-networks, but they appear more clearly when the central scenarios have been delineated.

How might the theory of classifiers as complex categories contribute to our understanding of the consensus problem? To the extent that classifiers cue evaluations, they would function similarly to evaluative reduplications, but that is only a part of their semantic content, which has more to do with central cultural scenarios. Classifiers clearly function to evoke large frames of reference, domains of experience, or what were formerly referred to as *cultural themes.* The use of classifiers increases the accessibility of related knowledge (as culturally defined). They may, for example, direct the recall of specific events that fit the frame of reference. Each interlocutor in a verbal exchange may choose to share her own partial knowledge of the evoked domain or domain related events and thereby contribute to knowledge consensus in the community or, without sharing information, she may choose to act as intended by her interlocutor or to act constructively in that domain. In the latter case, unshared knowledge of the interlocutors is integrated for community purposes. Of course, she may choose to neither share nor act, or to act disfunctionally, in which cases there is no net gain to either consensus or the integration of diversity. Similar reasoning may apply to the figurative usages of spatial language which were brought to our attention so forcefully by Lakoff and Johnson (1980).

## 5.    The new relativity in spatial orientation

The language of spatial orientation has long fascinated cognitive anthropologists and linguists (Bühler, K. 1982 [1934]; Hallowell 1955; Friedrich 1971; Haugen 1969; Basso 1984; Hunn 1990; Haviland 1993, 1996; Senft 1997). This domain of language can reveal how people conceptualize their surroundings, make their way from one place to another, and direct one another to places. It can reveal how they think about the relative positions of objects and the manipulation of objects. The concepts of cognitive linguistics, particularly *figure/ground* alignment (or Langacker's *trajector/landmark* alignment) and Langacker's concept of the *search domain* have found extensive application and they have been particularly helpful in enabling enlightening comparisons of spatial language (Talmy 1983, 2005; Brugman 1983, 1988; Lakoff 1987; Casad 1988, 1993; Casad and Langacker 1985; Heine 1997; Levinson 1996a, b, 1997; Ogawa and Palmer 1999; Occhi, Palmer and Ogawa 1993).

In an important chapter summarizing research results from Max Planck Institute for Psycholinguistics at Nijmegen, Levinson (1996b) concluded that the language of spatial orientation is characterized by a high degree of relativity. He found no universal coordinate systems nor any universal grammatical patterns beyond the very abstract notion of figure and ground orientation conventionalized in clause structure. Even such seemingly basic and inescapable notions as *left/right* are not universally recognized and evidently not necessary to spatial orientation. Languages vary in the degree to which they profile and elaborate figures, grounds, and the relations that connect them, and they vary in the sorts of spatial information they include in each of these. For example, a positional adjective in Tzeltal Mayan includes information on the shape of the figure – whether it is a container with a mouth that is wider than any other part, or that has an upright cylindrical body, or that has a narrow neck. They vary in the extent to which they lexicalize orientations in intervening space itself as opposed to contact with various parts of grounds. They vary according to whether spatial language is ego-centric and deictic (relating to the bodily orientations of persons in the speaking situation), which gives directions such as *left/right*, or whether it is based on absolute orientations, which gives directions such as *uphill/downhill* or *north/south*). The Guugu Yimithirr give directions only in absolute terms. Guugu Yimithirr spatial language relates to a cultural model that constrains orientation even in the absence of speech. This has been demonstrated with clever experiments in which subjects are shown a set of objects in a certain relation, the objects are rearranged in their absence, and then they are asked to restore the objects to the original positions. Dutch subjects consistently restore them to their original positions relative to the left or right of the subject. The Guugu Yimithirr restore them to their original positions relative to north/south or east/west.

Contra Levinson, Talmy (2005) proposed a universal "fundamental system of spatial schemas" that constrain the semantics of *closed-class forms* such as spatial prepositions, noun affixes, and verb satellites. In his framework, scenes segment into Figure, Ground, and Secondary Reference Object. Components of scenes may have zero, one, two, or four dimensions (i.e. they may be a point, line, plane, or volume). Schemas have number: one, two, between two, among, or amidst. Figures and Grounds may be stationary or moving. Pathways may be bounded or unbounded. Motions or locations may be rectilinear or radial. Regions of one, two, or three dimensional space may be compact or diffuse. Volumes may be vacant, solid, liquid, or (possibly) fire, a category that occurs in Atsugewi, in which "–*caw* specifies motion into a fire." Other schemas pertain to relations between components of scenes, force dynamics, and cognitive/affective states. Relations among components include relative orientation (parallel, perpendicular, and oblique), degree of remove, and degree of dispersion (sparse or dense). Degree of remove includes contact (coincidence and adjacency) and non-contact (proximal, medial, distal). Other categories in his framework are not listed here because they seem more arguable. Talmy does not argue that these schemas are innate – only that they are universal and basic. Perhaps a few are innate while others are emergent.

From the various findings of both universalists and relativists, one can infer that, cross-linguistically, space may be thought of as a complex field of stationary or moving figures and grounds which may be conceptualized as having shapes and content, inherent spatial orientations (front, back, etc.), as having parts (head, arm, buttocks, etc.), or as having positions and postures (upright, bunched together) and mutual orientations (parallel, perpendicular). Entities in the spatial field may be conceptualized at varying degrees of concreteness or schematicity. Figures and grounds relate to one another by being located at some orientation in space, or in some degree of contiguity, which may involve localized or distributed contact with various types of adhesion (Ogawa and Palmer 1999). Conventional spatial constructions in any particular language may (or may not) profile any of these in various combinations. Even languages from the same language family, such as English and German, may use quite different principles in giving directions or explaining spatial events (Carroll

1997). Talmy's contraints on the closed-class forms may apply, but systematic cross-linguistic comparisons will be needed to establish their validity and universality.

Palmer (in press) presents a framework suitable for capturing the relativity of spatial orientation. The framework distinguishes two kinds of cognitive maps involved in orientation: *object maps* and *view maps*. View maps, the most interesting from a linguistic standpoint, are cognitive models of the field of view of speakers or other participants. Their substantive conceptual content is primarily relational with inherent abstract figures and grounds. Complex orientational predications, such as "The ball is to the right of the tree" are based on *focus chains* embedded in view maps (Langacker 2000). Focus chains are connected instances of trajector/landmark relations. In the example sentence, the owner of the view map, whether speaker or other participant in the discourse, could only be known from context.

Object maps are cognitive models of the spatial qualities of things, such as the shape of a vase or the parts of an automobile. Utterances that imply certain orientations of the bodies of speakers and participants or of the speech situation itself, are termed *deictic*. Large scale orientations, such as cardinal directions, uphill/downhill, upstream/downstream, and inland/ocean are qualities of *macro-maps*, which differ from ordinary object maps only in existing on a grander scale and consequently having greater stability and availability for reference. It is only in this sense that they are "absolute". Given this framework, one would expect different languages and cultures to assign orientational qualities to objects of sizes varying from parts of the body, whether human or animal, at the small end of the scale, to landforms, rivers, the prevailing weather patterns, and the cosmos including its supernatural terrain, at the large end of the scale. Some, like the Guugu Yimithirr, may use only a single macro-map, but it is probably more typical for spatial language to recruit multiple types of maps.

The Belhare of Eastern Nepal have four kinds of orientational maps, which have been labeled *ecomorphic, personmorphic, geomorphic, and physiomorphic* (Bickel 1997). Bickel (2000: 178) has argued strongly for the mutual influence of grammar and cultural practices:

Indeed, ... the distinction between various readings of 'UP' and 'DOWN' in language is recapitulated almost to perfection in cultural practices: the difference between hill-based (geomorphic) or verticality-based uses of linguistic morphemes, for instance, exactly parallels the difference between the practices mentioned above and another set of practices which are performed along vertical, sky-ward trajectories. Trajectories of the latter sort are found, for instance, in architectural elevations of religious buildings or in upward gestures as symbols of gratitude. They are culturally most dense in the notion of 'raising one's soul' (*samet phokma*) in shamanist curing rituals. Shock and certain illnesses can cause one's soul to fall down, and without the necessary remedies, to get lost. All curing of such maladies and conditions is centered around invoking an upward trajectory.

Bickel's argument is explicitly based upon the Whorfian theory that grammar is related to habitual thought and behavior. It resembles Lakoff's (1987) argument that Djirbal classifiers relate to domains of experience, i.e. the myth of the sun and the moon and my own, discussed above, that the central categories in Shona noun classifiers are cultural scenarios of domestic life and ritual practices. In my approach, cultural scenarios are defined as schematizations of social actions and events (Palmer 1996). Bickel offered this general statement of his theory:

> The relationship between language and culture thus turns from a relationship between modes of expression into a relationship between the semantic constraints imposed by a specific linguistic category and the *habitus* of socio-cultural practice within which language use is embedded. Together, the boundaries of linguistic signs that segment experience, and the *habitus* that schematizes practice, channel and guide cognition into a heightened attention to specific experiences and actions. (Bickel 2000: 165)

Bickel's observations suggest again that a large domain of grammar is recruited to cue and sustain central cultural/cognitive frames of reference. The many observations by linguists and social anthropologists of the interpenetration of spatial, ritual, and social categories become explainable in terms of this function. To the extent that the linguistic correlation of domain structures is shared in the community of speakers, consensus is fostered, but structural correlation also enables the harmonization of actions while leaving much knowledge in the community uncommunicated and unshared. The problem for the linguist is to discover, through elicitation and ethnography, the relations between figurative usages of spatial expressions, which evoke scenarios and evaluations, and their actual social contexts. Like reduplications and classifiers, closed class spatial terms acquire affective or evaluative connotations (Lakoff and Johnson 1980; Talmy 2005).

Given the extreme degree of interesting variation evident in the spatial grammar of the few languages that have been studied and the thousands of languages remaining, it is hoped that cognitive linguists and cognitive anthropologists will continue to explore the topic using the conceptual tools of cognitive grammar together with the experimental procedures developed at the Max Planck Institute for Psycholinguistics at Nijmegen and ethnographic methods (Haviland 1993, 1996; Shore 1996). These recent studies have shown that the universalism of cognitive grammar combines with the rehabilitated relativity of cognitive anthropology and with ethnographic field methods in a very effective research program. Now, in the last substantive section, we turn from the development of theory to its application to a longstanding topic of compelling interest: the problem of the origins of human language.

## 6. The origins of language

Cognitive anthropologists have long sought to explain how early humans or pre-humans evolved the capacity for language. This is a topic to which cognitive linguistics have begun to contribute. In addition to the general repertoire of concepts from cognitive linguistics listed above, *intersubjectivity* and *mimesis* (made possible by mirror neurons) have figured prominently in speculations on language origins (Tomasello 1999; Donald 1991; Arbib 2005; Zlatev 2002, n.d., Sinha 2004).[14] If all or some of these cognitive processes are important in language, they must have been so in language evolution. In particular, one can ask how symbols gained sufficient salience to be remembered, shared, and used repeatedly. This is also to ask how their phonological and semantic components gained relative salience in association with one another over those of competing forms and notions. One may also ask whether the universal cognitive features of language, such as complex categories, were present in pre-humans; and since the phonologies of language are themselves systems of categories, one may ask whether precursor phonologies may be identified in pre-humans.

A variety of situations have been proposed as providing the conditions that fostered human proto-language.[15] Some of these are song (Jespersen 1922; Livingstone (1973), call-blending and play (Hockett and Ascher 1964; Knight 1998), gesture communication (Hewes 1973, 1994; Yao 1989; Armstrong, Stokoe and Wilcox 1995; King 1996), mothering (Wong 2004; Falk 2004), social grooming and gossip (Dunbar 1998; Power 1998), mating rituals (Deacon 1997), proto-ceremonials (Palmer et al., n.d.), and culture itself by attaining a critical point of complexity and integration (Wallace 1969; Bickerton 1998; Li 2002 a,b), thus favoring recombinance (Talmy in press), or by freeing early speakers from natural selection and neurological constraints operating against speech (Deacon 1997: 408). All of these theories and doubtless others have received serious consideration (See also, Johannson 2005).

It may be that human language was over-determined and all of these circumstances played their roles. But one or more of them may have been more influential than the others. One may have provided the motivation together with the opportunity for linking simple verbalizations to concepts to form proto-linguistic symbols. The same set of circumstances may have fostered learning, sharing, repeated use, and entrenching of proto-linguistic symbols and their eventual elaboration into language. In Palmer et al. (n.d.), we proposed that pre-humans had already developed effective cognitive maps for spatial orientation and ordered schemas supporting the skills of tool-making and foraging. It was proposed that they had complex categories based on conceptual metonymies (functional associations within scenes and scenarios) and similarities, or even conceptual metaphors, such as MATING IS HUNTING, a theme common in hunter-gatherer myth and ceremonial (Biesele 1993). Given these substantial cognitive abilities, the introduction of linguistic symbols would have given them an effective way to communicate their cognitive models of the natural world and their own communities, share them with others, reinforce them, and pass them down over the generations as folk wisdom. Because language is a human universal, one must conclude that it was an adaptive skill from its inception. Verbal skills were favored by both natural and sexual selection and proto-human speakers of proto-languages developed increasingly effective adaptations *vis a vis* pre-humans.

Palmer et al. (n.d.) proposed that human speech originated with an African population of *Homo heidelbergensis*, a descendant of *Homo erectus* that lived in the Middle Pleistocene between 800Kya and 130Kya (Klein 1989). Evidence from fossil skeletons suggests that the vocal apparatus needed for speech was in place by about 300K ya. There is evidence for a lengthening of the vocal tract and its evolution towards the modern right-angle shape with increased thoracic control over air pressures behind the glottis (Nishimura, et al. 2003; Ross, et al., 2004). Apparently the capacity for human language phonology was emerging.

We proposed that the cognitive capabilities of *H. heidelbergensis* were basically similar to those of modern humans in that *heidelbergensis* was a cultural being, capable of semantic construction, conceptual metaphor, conceptual metonymy, conceptual blending, complex orientation, and iconic sound symbolism. These conceptual figures acted on the salient scenarios and cultural models formed in daily activities of foraging trips, seasonal cycles of migration, childbirth, childcare, real and mock captures, and narrow escapes from predators. Salient images deriving from these activities were presented to audiences in ceremonials consisting of mimetic performances with dance, music, and vocalizations that created a forcing environment for language genesis. Highly iconic vocalizations of performers and audience responses were mapped to mimetic imagery by something akin to fast mapping that we see in language development in children (Nelson 1996). Ceremonial mimesis also motivated the narrative combination of proto-symbols in constructions and their entrenchment and standardization through repetition and mimicry.

Enhanced intersubjectivity involving joint attention frames, intention reading, and conceptual role substitutions was a key to symbol genesis. Intersubjectivity was also supported by ceremonial contexts. Performers and audiences shared joint attention frames and understood performances to have communicative intentions. The first linguistic constructions grammaticalized[16] to produce proto-morphology, and consequently, proto-grammar, at which point, selection for recombinance became possible (Talmy 2004). Speech and song enhanced the effectiveness and status of skillful and dominant performers, so that sexual selection favored the genes of good speakers and singers. Symbols generated first in other activities, such as child care, grooming, tool making, and hunting, could be brought to ceremonials, shared more widely, and standardized.

Thus, cognitive linguistics provides a new perspective on the emergence of language. But applying the new perspective requires supporting information derived from archaeological research into proto-human cultures and comparative studies of the vocalizations, proto-cultures, and cognition of primates.

## 7.  Conclusions

Cognitive linguists and cognitive anthropologists have a common field of interest in language and culture, a field of interest which they share with scholars from many disciplines in the sciences, humanities, and the applied field of language education. Among the enduring problems they have studied in relation to language are its cultural nature, its subjection to universal psychological and experiential constraints, the degree to which it requires consensus and organizes diversity, the complexity of its categories, its relativity in the domain of spatial orientation, and its origins. The shared cognitive perspective is helping to disentangle some of the biological, experiential, and cultural dimensions of language. A cognitive linguistic model of experiential process in Tagalog was compared to D'Andrade's model for English, revealing fundamental similarities and differences between the two languages and cultures. In both languages, thoughts are distinguished from emotions and feelings, but the theories of cognitive process differ. It seems incontrovertible that language communities manifest a high degree of diversity, but the problem of how diversity is balanced with consensus needs further clarification and research. Clues to how grammars participate in the integration of diversity in community knowledge are found in studies of complex categories and the language of spatial orientation. Rapid advances in the theory of complex categories are leading to useful descriptions of grammatical domains such as reduplication and classifier systems. Classifier systems narrow the focus of discourse by cueing common frames of reference that may intentionally evoke recall of specific events. The amazing relativity of spatial language can be described with a new framework consisting of cognitive maps, including object maps and viewer maps, which contain focus chains. Conventional spatial expressions may, like classifiers, evoke larger sociocultural frames of reference. Finally, it is proposed that verbal symbols and proto-language originated with *Homo heidelbergensis* in the forcing environment of proto-ceremonials consisting of mimetic presentations of salient cultural and natural scenarios. This theory of language origins is supported by cognitive theory, archaeology, and paleontology.

Cognitive linguistics is proving its value by producing insightful applications to the descriptions, analyses, and comparisons of both western and non-western languages (e.g. Casad and Palmer 2003). Its value has been seen by a number of linguistic and/or cognitive anthropologists.[17] I have found in my own research involving three non-Indo-European language families (Salishan, Western Austronesian, and Bantu) that a version of cognitive linguistics that emphasizes the cultural origins of linguistic categories enables cross-linguistic comparisons and insights into both grammar and world view that were unavailable to other paradigms in anthropology or linguistics. Conversely, it appears from the vantage point of anthropology that cognitive linguists could do more to incorporate the frameworks of cognitive anthropology, such as those of ethnoscience, and they could make more use of ethnography to discover cultural schemas and scenarios, especially those that have non-linguistic as well as linguistic expressions, for these will provide additional evidence for proposed cognitive linguistic models.

# Notes

1. Gary B. Palmer is Professor Emeritus at the University of Nevada, Las Vegas. The author thanks Ed Shoben for his comments on the manuscript.
2. I am indebted to Gitte Kristiansen for pointing out the use of the culture concept in Lakoff and Kövecses (1987) and for reminding me of recent conference sessions which all reflect a growing interest in culture or language-internal variation: Language, Culture, and Cognition: An International Conference on Cognitive Linguistics, Catholic University of Portugal-Braga, July 16–18, 2003; Session on Lectal Variation and Conceptualisation, International Cognitive Linguistics Association Conference, Seoul, Korea, July 17–22, 2005; Language, Culture and Mind: Integrating Perspectives and Methodologies in the Study of Language, University of Portsmouth, July18–20, 2004, and Paris July 17–20, 2006.
3. At the occasion of the 100th anniversary of Humboldt's death several symposia revived the popularity of linguistic relativity. An example is the 26th International LAUD Symposium, Humboldt and Whorf Revisited: Universal and Culture-Specific Conceptualizations in Grammar and Lexis, Mülheim/Ruhr, April 1–4, 1998. See Niemeier and Dirven (2000).
4. Keesing (1987: 369) listed as synonyms *ethnoscience, ethnographic semantics,* and *the new ethnography.* One also sees the term *ethnosemantics.* I am unaware of any clear boundaries between ethnosemantics and ethnoscience. Ethnoscience has been harshly criticized (e.g. Keesing 1987), but its methods and assumptions are not hard to find in recent work, such as that of López et al. (1997).
5. For canonical examples of componential and taxonomic analysis, see Tyler (1969) and Casson (1981). For a recent example, see Kronenfeld (1996). For discussions of cultural logic in terminological systems, see Lakoff (1987: 24) and Palmer (1996: 98–99) on what Lakoff called *generative categories.* For an excellent extended presentation of the theoretical framework of ethnoscience, see D'Andrade (1995a). See also, Colby (1996).
6. "Human cognition is built for culture, and thus built for enculturated variation" (Levinson 1996b: 177).
7. For further discussion of color terms, including both basic and non-basic terms and refinements to the theory based on more recent research, see Palmer (1996: 80–88) and Foley (1997: 150–165).
8. DR: directional; EX: existential; GN: genitive; INV: inverse; LG: ligatur; SPC: specific.
9. I am indebted to René Dirven for calling this to my attention.
10. Any knowledge existing outside of human minds, say in books or other artefacts, can not function as knowledge without the existence of human minds that comprehend the design of the artefactual knowledge.
11. Matrices and their eigenvalues fall under the topic of linear algebra. The formal mathematical derivation of the model appears in Batchelder and Romney (1988), but this in turn is premised on derivations of supporting formulas found in other sources. I am grateful to Roy Ogawa for leading me through the linear algebra.

12. Reduplication: "A term in MORPHOLOGY for a process of repetition whereby the form of a *prefix/suffix* reflects certain phonological characteristics of the root" (Crystal 1980: 293).

13. More in the spirit of cognitive grammar, one can think of a Bantu classifier not as a mere prefix, but as an abstract clause construction consisting of abstract nominals (the classifying prefixes and morphology of function words) of one or more classes awaiting instantiation with appropriate nouns, verb stems, locatives, and demonstratives. This nominal clause construction would have links to a similarly dependent abstract verb phrase consisting of tense and aspect morphemes and slots for nominals. It is really the combination of the two that would require instantiation. The final utterance involves the meshing of at least three entities: (1) the abstract nominal construction; (2) the abstract verbal construction; and (3) the substantive noun and verb stems.

14. Donald (1991: 168) defined *mimetic skill* or *mimesis* as "the ability to produce conscious, self-initiated, representational acts that are intentional but not linguistic." Mimesis is "rooted in kinematic imagination" and "the ability to model the whole body, including its voluntary action systems" (1991: 49). He included in the concept of mimesis "tones of voice, facial expressions, eye movements, manual signs and gestures, postural attitudes, [and] patterned whole-body movements of various sorts" (1991: 169). I disagree with Donald's restriction of mimesis to non-linguistic acts. I think we should entertain the subtle notion that mimesis of phonology occurred at the origins of language and continues in language development and other performative contexts.

15. I use the term *proto-language* to profile the incipient phase of human language, which I theorize had linguistic qualities such as phonology, prosody, figure-ground relations, conceptual metonymy, and grammar in general, but lacked complexity compared to the languages of *Homo sapiens*. Of course, some proto-language or proto-languages would also be proto- in the sense of being ancient parent languages to known languages.

16. On *grammaticalization*, see Heine (1997) and Hopper and Traugott (1993). In part, it is the evolutionary process whereby constructions involving verbs and nouns and other forms may contract into fewer lexemes, undergo subjectification, lose features of substantive meaning, and eventually become function words, such as prepositions or auxiliary verbs. Something much more rudimentary must have occurred in proto-language.

17. I am thinking of Hoyt Alverson, Balthazar Bickel, Penelope Brown, Eve Danziger, Roy D'Andrade, John C. Haviland, the late Roger Keesing, David Kronenfeld, John Lucy, the late Robert MacLaury, Debra Occhi, Stephen Levinson and myself, but there are certainly others. I apologize to any of the living members of this group who would not wish to be included, as I did not consult them. While cognitive linguists have sought to understand the role of cognitive universals in language, anthropology has swung toward radical cultural relativism. Not surprisingly, at least two cognitive anthropologists have opposed the trend in print (D'Andrade 1995b; Keesing 1987, 1992).

# References

Alverson, Hoyt
1991    Metaphor and experience: looking over the notion of image-schema. In *Beyond Metaphor: The Theory of Tropes in Anthropology*, James W. Fernandez (ed.), 94–117. Stanford: Stanford University Press.

Arbib, Michael
2005    From monkey-like action recognition to human language: An evolutionary framework for neurolinguistics. *Behavioral and Brain Sciences* 28 (2): 105–124.

Armstrong, David F., William C. Stokoe, and Sherman E. Wilcox
1995    *Gesture and the Nature of Language*. Cambridge: Cambridge University Press.

Bachelder, William H., and A. Kimball Romney
1988    Test theory without an answer key. *Psychometrika* 53: 71–92.

Basso, Keith H.
1984    "Stalking with stories": names, places and moral narratives among the Western Apache. In *Text, Play and Story*, Edward M. Bruner (ed.), 19–55. Washington, D.C.: American Ethnological Society. Reprinted in Keith H. Basso, 1990, 99–137.

Berlin, Brent
1992    *Ethnobiological Classification: Principles of Categorization of Plants and Animals in Traditional Societies*. Princeton: Princeton University Press.

Berlin, Brent, and Paul Kay
1969    *Basic Color Terms: Their Universality and Evolution*. Berkeley: University of California Press.

Bickel, Balthazar
1997    Spatial operations in deixis, cognition, and culture: where to orient oneself in Belhare. In *Language and Conceptualization*, Jan Nuyts, and Eric Pederson (eds.), 46–83. Cambridge: Cambridge University Press.
2000    Grammar and social practice: On the role of "culture" in linguistic relativity. In *Evidence for Linguistic Relativity*, Susanne Niemeier, and René Dirven (eds.), 161–191. Amsterdam/Philadelphia: Benjamins.

Bickerton, Derek
1998    Catastrophic evolution: The case for a single step from protolanguage to full language. In *Approaches to the Evolution of Language: Social and Cognitive Bases*, James R. Hurford, Michael Studdert-Kennedy, and Chris Knight (eds.), 341–358. Cambridge: Cambridge University Press.

Biesele, Megan
1998    *Women Like Meat: The Folklore and Foraging Ideology of the Kalahari Jul'Hoan*. Johannesburg, South Africa: Witwatersrand University Press / Bloomington: Indiana University Press.

Boas, Franz
1966    [1911] *Introduction to the Handbook of American Indian Languages*. Lincoln: University of Nebraska Press.

Bohn, Ocke-Schwen
2000    Linguistic relativity in speech perception: An overview of the influence of language experience on the perception of speech sounds from infancy to adulthood. In *Evidence for Linguistic Relativity*, Susanne Niemeier, and René Dirven (eds.), 1–28. Amsterdam/Philadelphia: Benjamins.

Borofsky, Robert
1994    On the knowledge and knowing of cultural activities. In *Assessing Cultural Anthropology*, Robert Borofsky (ed.), 331–348. New York: McGraw-Hill.

Brown, Cecil H.
1984    *Language and Living Things: Uniformities in Folk Classification and Naming*. New Brunswick, N.J.: Rutgers University Press.

Brugman, Claudia
1983    The use of body-part terms as locatives in Chalcatongo Mixtec. In *Survey of California and Other Indian Languages*, Alice Schlichter, Wallace Chafe, and Leanne Hinton (eds.), 235–290. Studies in Mesoamerican Linguistics. Report no. 4. Berkeley: Survey of California and Other Indian Languages.

1988    *The Story of Over: Polysemy, Semantics, and Structure of the Lexicon.* New York: Garland Publishing.

Bühler, Karl
1982    [1934] The deictic field of language and deictic words. Reprinted in *Speech, Place and Action,* Robert J. Jarvella, and Wolfgang Klein (eds.), 9–30. Chichester: John Wiley & Sons.

Carroll, Mary
1997    Changing places in English and German: language-specific preferences in the conceptualization of spatial relations. In *Language and Conceptualization,* Jan Nuyts, and Eric Pederson (eds.), 137–161. Cambridge: Cambridge University Press.

Casad, Eugene
1988    Conventionalization of Cora locationals. In *Topics in Cognitive Linguistics,* Brygida Rudzka-Ostyn (ed.), 345–378. Amsterdam/Philadelphia: Benjamins.

1993    "Locations," "paths," and the Cora verb. In *Conceptualizations and Mental Processing in Language,* Richard A. Geiger, and Brygida Rudzka-Ostyn (eds.), 593–645. Berlin/New York: Mouton de Gruyter.

Casad, Eugene, and Ronald Langacker
1985    "Inside" and "outside" in Cora grammar. *International Journal of American Linguistics* 51: 247–281.

Casad, Eugene, and Gary B. Palmer (eds.)
2003    *Cognitive Linguistics and Non-Indo-European Languages.* Berlin/New York: Mouton de Gruyter.

Casson, Ronald W. (ed.)
1981    *Language, Culture and Cognition: Anthropological Perspectives.* New York: Macmillan.

Colby, Benjamin N.
1996   Cognitive Anthropology. *In Encyclopedia of Cultural Anthropology,* Volume 1, David Levinson, and Melvin Ember (eds.), 209–215. New York: Henry Holt and Company.
Conklin, Harold
1964   Hanunóo color categories. In *Language in Culture and Society: A Reader in Linguistics and Anthropology,* Dell Hymes (ed.), 189–192. New York: Harper and Row.
Croft, William
2001   *Radical Construction Grammar: Syntactic Theory in Typological Perspective.* Oxford/New York: Oxford University Press.
Crystal, David
1980   *A Dictionary of Linguistics and Phonetics.* 3rd Ed. Oxford: Basil Blackwell.
Damasio, Antonio R.
1994   *Descartes' Error: Emotion, Reason and the Human Brain.* London: Macmillan.
D'Andrade, Roy G.
1987   A folk model of the mind. In *Cultural Models in Language and Thought,* Dorothy Holland, and Naomi Quinn (eds.), 112–148. Cambridge: Cambridge University Press.
1995a  *The Development of Cognitive Anthropology.* Cambridge: Cambridge University Press.
1995b  Moral Models in Anthropology. *Current Anthropology* 36 (3): 399–408.
Deacon, Terrence W.
1997   *The Symbolic Species: The Co-Evolution of Language and the Brain.* New York/London: W. Norton & Company.
Dewey, John
1958   [1925] Reprint. *Experience and Nature.* New York: Dover Publications. Original edition, Chicago/ London: Open Court, 1925. Cited in Johnson (2006).
Dirven, René
2005   Major strands in cognitive linguistics. In *Cognitive Linguistics. Internal Dynamics and Interdisciplinary Interaction,* Francisco J. Ruiz de Mendoza Ibañez, and M. Sandra Pena Cervel (eds.), 17–68. CLR 32. Berlin/New York: Mouton de Gruyter.
Dirven, René and Ralf Pörings (eds.)
2002   *Metaphor and Metonymy in Comparison and Contrast,.* Berlin/New York: Mouton de Gruyter.
Dirven, René, and Marjolijn Verspoor (eds.)
2004   *Cognitive Exploration of Language and Linguistics. Second Revised Edition.* (Cognitive Linguistics in Practice 1). Amsterdam/Philadelphia: Benjamins.
Donald, Merlin
1991   *Origins of the Modern Mind: Three Stages in the Evolution of Culture and Cognition.* Cambridge, Mass.: Harvard University Press.

Dunbar, Robin
1998    Theory of mind and the evolution of language. In *Approaches to the Evolution of Language: Social and Cognitive Bases,* James R. Hurford, Michael Studdert-Kennedy, and Chris Knight (eds.), 92–110. Cambridge: Cambridge University Press.

Enfield, Nick J. (ed.)
2002    *Ethnosyntax: Explorations in Grammar and Culture.* Oxford: Oxford University Press.

Ehrsson, H. Henrik, Charles Spence, and Richard E. Passingham
2004    That's my hand! Activity in premotor cortex reflects feeling of ownership of a limb. *Science* 305: 875–877.

Falk, Dean
2004    Prelinguistic evolution in early hominins: Whence motherese? *Behavioral and Brain Sciences* 27: 491–541.

Fauconnier, Gilles, and Mark Turner
2002    *The Way We Think: Conceptual Blending and the Mind's Hidden Complexities.* New York: Basic Books.

Foley, William A.
1997    *Anthropological Linguistics: An Introduction.* Oxford: Blackwell.

Friedrich, Paul
1979    *Language, Context, and Imagination.* Stanford: Stanford University Press.
1971    *The Tarascan Suffixes of Locative Space.* Bloomington: Indiana University / The Hague: Mouton & Co.

Geeraerts, Dirk, and Stefan Grondelaers
1995    Looking back at anger: Cultural traditions and metaphorical patterns. In *Language and the Cognitive Construal of the World,* John R. Taylor, and Robert E. MacLaury (eds.). 153–179. Berlin/New York: Mouton de Gruyter.
2004    What's in a word: Lexicology. In *Cognitive Exploration of Language and Linguistics. Second Revised Edition,* René Dirven and Marjolijn Verspoor (eds.), (Cognitive Linguistics in Practice 1), 25–50. Amsterdam/Philadelphia: Benjamins.

Goddard, Cliff
2002    The search for the shared semantic core of all languages. In *Meaning and Universal Grammar Theory and Empirical Findings,* Cliff Goddard, and Anna Wierzbicka (eds.), 5–40. Volume I. Amsterdam/Philadelphia: Benjamins.
2003    Thinking across languages and cultures: Six dimensions of variation. *Cognitive Linguistics* 14 (2): 109–139.

Goodenough, Ward H.
1965    Yankee kinship terminology: A problem in componential analysis. *American Anthropologist* 67/5, pt. 2, (Special Publication): 259–287. Reprinted in *Cognitive Anthropology,* Stephen A. Tyler (ed.), 255–288. New York: Holt, Rinehart & Winston, 1969.

Gordon, Peter
2004    Numerical cognition without words: Evidence from Amazonia. *Science* 306: 496–499.
Hallowell, A. Irving
1955    Ch. 9, Cultural factors in spatial orientation. *Culture and Experience,* 184–202. New York: Schocken Books.
Haviland, John C.
1993    Anchoring, iconicity, and orientation in Guugu Yimithirr pointing gestures. *Journal of Linguistic Anthropology* 3(1): 3–45.
1996    Projections, transpositions, and relativity. In *Rethinking Linguistic Relativity,* John J. Gumperz, and Stephen C. Levinson (eds.), 271–323. Cambridge: Cambridge University Press.
Haugen, Einer
1969    The semantics of Icelandic orientation. In *Cognitive Anthropology,* Stephen A. Tyler (ed.), 330–342. New York: Holt, Rinehart, and Winston.
Haxby, James V., M. Ida Gobbini, Maura L. Furey, Alumit Ishai, Jennifer L. Schouten, and Pietro Pietrini
2001    Distributed and overlapping representations of faces and objects in ventral temporal cortex. *Science* 293: 2425–2430.
Heine, Bernd
1997    *Cognitive Foundations of Grammar.* Oxford: Oxford University Press.
Hewes, Gordon
1973    Primate communication and the gestural origin of language. *Current Anthropology* 14: 5–24.
1994    The gestural origin of language and new neurological data. *Studies in Language Origins* 3: 293–307.
Hockett, Charles F., and Robert Ascher
1964    The human revolution. *Current Anthropology* 5:133–47.
Hopper, Paul, and Elizabeth Traugott
1993    *Grammaticalization.* Cambridge: Cambridge University Press.
Humboldt, Wilhelm von
1972    [1836] translated by George C. Buck, and Frithjof A. Raven. *Linguistic Variability and Intellectual Development.* Philadelphia: University of Pennsylvania Press (Orig. 1836. *Über die Verschiedenheit des menschlichen Sprachbaus und ihren Einfluss auf die geistige Entwicklung des Menschengeschlechts.* Berlin: Royal Academy).
Hunn, Eugene
1990    *Nch'i-wána, "the big river": Mid-Columbia Indians and their land / Eugene S. Hunn with James Selam and family.* Seattle: University of Washington Press.
Hutchins, Edwin
1996    *Cognition in the Wild.* Cambridge, Mass./London: The MIT Press.
Jespersen, Otto
1922    *Language: Its Nature, Development, and Origin.* London: George Allen & Unwin Ltd/New York: Henry Holt and Company.

Johansson, Sverker
2005    *Origins of Language: Constraints on Hypotheses.* Amsterdam/Philadelphia: Benjamins.
Johnson, Mark
2006    The philosophical significance of image-schemas. In *From Perception to Meaning: Image Schemas in Cognitive Linguistics,* Hampe, Beate (in cooperation with Joseph E. Grady) (ed.). (Cognitive Linguistics Research 29). Berlin/New York: Mouton de Gruyter.
Kay, Paul
1966    Comment on "Ethnographic semantics: A preliminary survey." *Current Anthropology* 7 (1): 20–23. Reprinted in *Cognitive Anthropology,* Stephen A. Tyler (ed.), 78–92. New York: Holt, Rinehart & Winston, 1969.
Keesing, Roger
1987    Models "folk" and "cultural": Paradigms regained. In *Cultural Models in Language and Thought,* Dorothy Holland, and Naomi Quinn (eds.), 369–393. Cambridge: Cambridge University Press.
1992    Anthropology and linguistics. In *Thirty Years of Linguistic Evolution: Studies in Honor of René Dirven on the Occasion of His Sixtieth Birthday,* Martin Pütz (ed.), 593–609. Philadelphia: Benjamins.
1997    Constructing space in Kwaio (Solomon Islands). In *Referring to Space: Studies in Austronesian and Papuan Languages,* Gunter Senft (ed.), 127–141. Oxford: Clarendon Press.
King, Barbara J.
1996    Syntax and language origins. *Language and Communication* 16 (2):193–203.
Klein, Richard G.
1989    *The Human Career: Human Biological and Cultural Origins,* 2nd ed. Chicago: University of Chicago Press.
Knight, Chris
1998    Ritual/speech coevolution: A solution to the problem of deception. In *Appraoches to the Evolution of Language,* James R. Hurford, Michael Studdert-Kennedy, and Chris Knight (eds.), 68–91. Cambridge: Cambridge University Press.
Koerner, E. F. Konrad
2000    Towards a 'full pedigree' of the 'Sapir-Whorf hypothesis': From Locke to Lucy. In *Explorations in Linguistic Relativity,* Martin Pütz, and Marjolijn Verspoor (eds.), 1–24. Amsterdam/Philadelphia: Benjamins.
Kövecses, Zoltán
2000    *Metaphor and Emotion: Language, Culture, and Body in Human Feeling.* Cambridge: Cambridge University Press.
2005    *Metaphor in Culture: Universality and Variation.* Cambridge: Cambridge University Press.
Kövecses, Zoltán, and Gary B. Palmer
1999    Language and emotion concepts: What experientialists and social constructionists have in common. In *Languages of Sentiment,* Gary B.

Palmer, and Debra J. Occhi (eds.), 237–262. Amsterdam/Philadelphia: Benjamins.
Kövecses, Zoltán, Gary B. Palmer, and René Dirven
2002   Language and emotion: The interplay of conceptualization with physiology and culture. In *Metaphor and Metonymy in Comparison and Contrast*, René Dirven, and Ralf Pörings (eds.), 133–160. Berlin/New York: Mouton de Gruyter
Kristiansen, Gitte
2003   How to do things with allophones. Linguistic stereotypes as referece points in social cognition. In *Cognitive Models in Language and Thought. Ideology, Metaphors and Meanings*, René Dirven, Roslyn Frank, and Martin Pütz (eds.), 69–120. CLR 24. Berlin/New York: Mouton de Gruyter.
Kronenfeld, David B.
1996   *Plastic Glasses and Church Fathers: Semantic Extension from the Ethnoscience Tradition*. Oxford: Oxford University Press.
2000   Language and thought: Collective tools for individual use. In *Explorations in Linguistic Relativity*, Martin Pütz, and Marjolijn Verspoor (eds.), 197–224. Amsterdam/Philadelphia: Benjamins.
2002   Culture and society: The role of distributed cognition. In: *Cybernetics and Systems* Vol.1, Robert Trappl (ed.), 430–431. Vienna: Austrian Society for Cybernetic Studies.
Lakoff, George
1987   *Women, Fire, and Dangerous Things: What Categories Reveal About the Mind*. Chicago: University of Chicago Press.
2002   *Moral Politics: How Liberals and Conservatives Think*. Chicago: University of Chicago Press.
Lakoff, George, and Mark Johnson
1980   *Metaphors We Live By*. Chicago: The University of Chicago Press.
Lakoff, George, and Zoltán Kövecses
1987   The cognitive model of anger in American English. In *Cultural Models in Language and Thought*, Dorothy Holland, and Naomi Quinn (eds.), 195–221. Cambridge: Cambridge University. Press.
Langacker, Ronald W.
1987   *Foundations of Cognitive Grammar, Vol. I. Theoretical Prerequisites*. Stanford: Stanford University Press.
1990   Subjectification. *Cognitive Linguistics* 1: 5–38.
1994   Culture, cognition, and grammar. In *Language Contact and Language Conflict*, Martin Pütz (ed.), 25–53. Amsterdam/Philadelphia: Benjamins.
2000   *Grammar and Conceptualization*. Berlin/New York: Mouton de Gruyter.
2002   A study in unified diversity: English and Mixtec locatives. In *Ethnosyntax: Explorations in grammar and culture*, Nick J. Enfield (ed.), 138–161. Oxford: Oxford University Press.
Lee, Dorothy
1959   *Freedom and Culture*. Englewood Cliffs, N.J.: Prentice-Hall.

Lee, Penny
1996    *The Whorf Theory Complex: A Critical Reconstruction.* Amsterdam/
New York: Benjamins.
2003    Feeling of the mind in talk about thinking in English. *Cognitive Linguistics* 14/2,3: 221–249.

Levinson, Stephen C.
1996a   Frames of reference and Molyneux's question: Crosslinguistic evidence.
In *Language and Space,* Paul Bloom Mary A.Peterson, Lyn Nadel, and
Merril Garrett (eds.), 109–170. Cambridge, MA: The MIT Press.
1996b   Relativity in spatial conception and description. In *Rethinking Linguistic Relativity,* John J. Gumperz, and Stephen C. Levinson (eds.),
177–202. Cambridge: Cambridge University Press.
1997    From outer to inner space: Linguistic categories and non-linguistic
thinking. In *Language and Conceptualization,* Jan Nuyts, and Eric Peterson (eds.), 13–45. Cambridge: Cambridge University Press.

Li, Charles N.
2002a   Some issues concerning the origin of language. In *Complex Sentences in
Grammar and Discourse,* Joan Bybee, and Michael Noonan (eds.),
203–221. Amsterdam/Philadelphia: Benjamins.
2002b   Missing links, issues and hypotheses in the evolutionary origin of language. In *The Evolution of Language out of Pre-language,* Talmy Givón,
and Bertram F. Malle (eds.), 83–106. Amsterdam/Philadelphia: Benjamins.

Livingstone, Frank B.
1973    Did the Australopithecines sing? *Current Anthropology* 14 (1–2): 25–29.

Lounsbury, Floyd
1964    A formal account of the Crow- and Omaha-type kinship terminologies.
In *Explorations in Cultural Anthropology,* W. H. Goodenough (ed.),
351–394. New York: McGraw-Hill. Reprinted in *Cognitive Anthropology,* Stephen A. Tyler (ed), 212–254. New York: Holt, Rinehart & Winston, 1969.

López, Alejandro, Scott Atran, and Edward E. Smith
1997    The tree of life: Universal and cultural features of folkbiological taxonomies and inductions. *Cognitive Psychology* 32: 251–295.

Lucy, John
1992a   *Language Diversity and Thought: A Reformulation of the Linguistic
Relativity Hypothesis.* Cambridge: Cambridge University Press.
1992b   *Grammatical Categories and Cognition: A Case Study of the Linguistic
Relativity Hypothesis.* Cambridge: Cambridge University Press.

Lutz, Catherine A.
1988    *Unnatural Emotions: Everyday Sentiments on a Micronesian Atoll and
their Challenge to WesternTtheory.* Chicago: University of Chicago Press.

MacLaury, Robert E.
1992    From brightness to hue: An explanatory model of color-category evolution. *Current Anthropology* 33: 137–186.

Marwick, Ben
2003    Pleistocene exchange networks as evidence for the evolution of language. *Cambridge Archaeological Journal* 13 (1): 67–81.
Mathews, Holly F.
1987    Intracultural variation in beliefs about gender in a Mexican community. *American Behavioral Scientist* 31: 219–233.
Nelson, Katherine
1996    *Language in Cognitive Development: The Emergence of the Mediated Mind*. Cambridge: Cambridge University Press.
Niemeier, Susanne, and René Dirven (eds.)
2000    *Evidence for Linguistic Relativity*. Amsterdam/Philadelphia: Benjamins.
Nishimura, Takeshi, Akichika Mikami, Juri Suzuki, and Tetsuro Matsuzawa
2003    Descent of the larynx in chimpanzee infants. *PNAS* 100 (12): 6930–6933.
Nuyts, Jan, and Eric Pederson (eds.)
1997    *Language and Conceptualization*. Cambridge: Cambridge University Press.
Occhi, Debra J.
1999    Sounds of the heart and mind. In *Languages of Sentiment: Cultural Constructions Of Emotional Substrates,* Gary B. Palmer, and Debra J. Occhi (eds.), 151–170. Amsterdam/Philadelphia: Benjamins.
Occhi, Debra J, Gary B. Palmer, and Roy H. Ogawa
1993    Like Hair, or Trees: Semantic Analysis of the Coeur d'Alene Prefix *ne'* 'amidst'. In *Proceedings of the 1993 Annual Meeting of the Society for the Study of the Indigenous Languages of the Americas, July 2–4, 1993, and the Hokan-Sioux Conference, July 3, 1993, Columbus, Ohio. Report 8,* Margaret Langdon (ed.), 40–58. Survey of California and Other Indian Languages. Berkeley, CA: Berkeley Linguistics Department.
Ogawa, Roy H., and Gary B. Palmer
1999    Langacker Semantics for Three Coeur d'Alene Prefixes Glossed as 'On'. In *Issues in Cognitive Linguistics,* Leon de Stadler, and Christopher Eyrich (eds.), 165–224. Berlin/NewYork: Mouton de Gruyter,.
Palmer, Gary B.
1996    *Toward a Theory of Cultural Linguistics*. Austin: University of Texas Press.
2003a    Talking about thinking in Tagalog. *Cognitive Linguistics* 14 (2): 251–280.
2003b    The Tagalog prefix category *PAG-*: Metonymy, polysemy, and voice. In *Cognitive Linguistics and Non-Indo-European Languages,* Gene Casad, and Gary B. Palmer (eds.), 193–221. Berlin/New York: Mouton de Gruyter.
In press    Cognitive Linguistics and Anthropological Linguistics, Chapter 40. In *Handbook of Cognitive Linguistics,* Dirk Geeraerts, and Hubert Cuyckens (eds.). Oxford: Oxford University Press.
Palmer, Gary B. and Claudia Woodman
1999    Ontological Classifiers as Polycentric Categories, as Seen in Shona Class 3 Nouns. In *Explorations in Linguistic Relativity,* Martin Pütz,

and Marjolijn Verspoor (eds.), 225–249. Amsterdam/Philadelphia: Benjamins.

Palmer, Gary, Jeffrey Parkin, Elizabeth Harmon, and Jennifer Thompson.
n.d     The song cycles of *heidelbergensis*: Cultural linguistics at the origins of language. A paper presented to the conference on Language, Culture and Mind, Portsmouth, July 18–20, 2004. Unpublished ms. in possession of the author.

Palmer, Gary, Russell Rader, and Art Clarito
In press     The metonymic basis of a semantic 'partial': Tagalog lexical constructions with *ka-*. In *Metonymy*, Klaus-Uwe Panther, and Linda Thornburg (eds.). Amsterdam/Philadelphia: Benjamins.

Panther, Klaus-Uwe and Linda Thornburg (eds.)
In press     *Metonymy*. Amsterdam/Philadelphia: Benjamins.

Power, Camilla
1998     Old wives' tales: The gossip hypothesis and the reliability of cheap signals. In *Approaches to the Evolution of Language: Social and Cognitive Bases,* James R. Hurford, Michael Studdert-Kennedy, and Chris Knight (eds.), 111–129. Cambridge: Cambridge University Press.

Romney, A. Kimball
1999     Cultural Consensus as a Statistical Model. *Current Anthropology* 40: 103–115.

Romney, A. Kimball and Carmella C. Moore
1998     Toward a Theory of Culture as Shared Cognitive Structures. *Ethos* 36 (3): 314–337.

Romney, A. Kimball, William H. Batchelder, and Susan Weller
1987     Recent applications of cultural consensus theory. *American Behavioral Scientist* 31 (2): 163–177.

Romney, A. Kimball, Carmella C. Moore, and Craig D. Rusch
1997     Cultural universals: Measuring the semantic structure of emotion terms in English and Japanese. *Proceedings of the National Academy of Sciences of the United States of America* 94((10): 5489–5494.

Romney, A. Kimball, Susan Weller, and William H. Bachelder
1986     Culture as consensus: A theory of culture and informant accuracy. *American Anthropologist*, New Series, 88 (2): 313–338.

Ross, Callum F., Maciej Henneberg, Mathew J. Ravosa, and Simon Richard
2004     Curvilinear, geometric and phylogenetic modeling of basicranial flexion: Is it adaptive, is it constrained? *Journal of Human Evolution* 46: 185–213.

Sandra, Dominiek, and Sally Rice
1995     Network analyses of prepositional meaning: Mirroring whose mind – the linguist's or the language user's? *Cognitive Linguistics* 6: 89–130.

Sapir, Edward
1949[1921]*Language*. New York: Harcourt, Brace and World.

Schneider, David M
1965     American kin terms and terms for kinsmen: A critique of Goodenough's componential analysis of Yankee kinship terminology. *Ameri-*

*can Anthropologist* 67/5, pt. 2, (Special Publication): 288–308] Reprinted in *Cognitive Anthropology*, Stephen A. Tyler (ed.), 288–311. New York: Holt, Rinehart & Winston, 1969.

Senft, Gunter, (ed.)
1997   *Referring to Space: Studies in Austronesian and Papuan Languages.* Oxford: Clarendon Press:.

Sharifian, Farzad
In press   Distributed, emergent cultural cognition, conceptualisation, and language. In *Body, Language, and Mind ( Vol. 2): Sociocultural Situatedness*, Roslyn M. Frank, René Dirven, Tom Ziemke, and Enrique Bernárdez (eds.). Berlin/New York: Mouton de Gruyter.

Sharifian, Farzad, and Ahmad R. Lofti
2003   "Rices" and "Waters": The mass/count distinction in Modern Persian. *Anthropological Linguistics* 45(2): 226–244.

Shore, Bradd
1996   *Culture in Mind: Cognition, Culture, and the Problem of Meaning.* Oxford: Oxford University Press.

Sinha, Chris
2004   The evolution of language from signals to symbols to system. In *Evolution of Communication Systems: A Comparative Approach*, D. Kimbrough Oller, and Ulrike Griegbel (eds.), 217–236. (Vienna Series in Theoretical Biology). Cambridge, Mass. The MIT Press.

Sinha, Chris, and Kristine Jensen de López
2000   Language, culture and the embodiment of spatial cognition. *Cognitive Linguistics* 11(1): 17–41.

Talmy, Leonard
1983   How language structures space. In *Spatial Orientation: Theory, Research and Application*, Herbert L. Pick, and Linda P. Acredolo (eds.), 225–320. New York: Plenum Press.
2005   The fundamental system of spatial schemas in language. In *From Perception to Meaning: Image Schemas in Cognitive Linguistics*, Beate Hampe (in cooperation with Joseph E. Grady) (ed.), 199–234. Berlin/New York: Mouton de Gruyter.
In press   Recombinance in the evolution of language. In *Proceedings of the 39th Annual Meeting of the Chicago Linguistic Society: The Panels*, Jonathon E. Cihlar, David Kaiser, Irene Kimbara, and Amy Franklin (eds.). Chicago: Chicago Linguistic Society.

Tomasello, Michael
1999   *The Cultural Origins of Human Cognition.* Cambridge, MA: Harvard University Press.

Trabant, Jürgen
2000   How relativistic are Humboldt's "Weltansichten"? In *Explorations in Linguistic Relativity*, Martin Pütz, and Marjolijn Verspoor (eds.), 25–44. Amsterdam/Philadelphia: John Benjamins.

Tuggy, David
  2003    Reduplication in Nahuatl: Iconicities and paradoxes. In *Cognitive Linguistics and Non-Indo-European Languages,* Eugene H. Casad, and Gary B. Palmer (eds.), 91–133. Berlin/New York: Mouton de Gruyter.
Tyler, Stephen A. (ed.)
  1969    *Cognitive Anthropology.* New York: Holt, Rinehart and Winston.
Ungerer, Friedrich, and Hans-Jörg Schmid
  1996    *An Introduction to Cognitive Linguistics.* London/New York: Longman.
Wallace, Anthony F. C
  1961    *Culture and Personality.* New York: Random House.
Whorf, Benjamin
  1956    *Language, Thought and Reality: Selected Writings of Benjamin Lee Whorf.* John B. Carroll (ed.), Cambridge, MA: The M.I.T. Press.
Wierzbicka, Anna
  1990    The meaning of color terms: Semantics, culture, and cognition. *Cognitive Linguistics* 1: 99–150.
  1996    *Semantics: Primes and Universals.* New York: Oxford University Press.
Wong, Kate
  2004    Baby talk beginnings: Infant pacification may have led to the origin of language. *Scientific American* 291 (1): 30.
Yao, Shunchiu
  1989    Moulded gestures and guided syntax: Scenario of a linguistic breakthrough. In *Studies in Language Origins, Volume 1,* Jan Wind, Edward G. Pulleyblank, Eric de Grolier, and Bernard H. Bichakjian (eds.), 34–42. Amsterdam/Philadelphia: John Benjamins.
Yu, Ning
  1998    *The Contemporary Theory of Metaphor. A Perspective from Chinese.* Amsterdam/Philadelphia: Benjamins.
Zlatev, Jordan
  2002    Mimesis: The "missing link" between signals and symbols in phylogeny and ontology? In *Mimesis, Sign and Language Evolution,* Anneli Pajunen (ed.), Publications in General Linguistics 3, University of Turku, Finland.
  n.d    Embodiment, language, and mimesis. Unpublished ms. in possession of the author.

# Cognitive linguistic applications in second or foreign language instruction: rationale, proposals, and evaluation

*Frank Boers and Seth Lindstromberg*

*Abstract*

In this chapter we examine the contributions that Cognitive Linguistics (CL) can make to second or foreign language teaching. A lot of CL premises are found to be fully compatible with those of modern strands of education-oriented applied linguistics. However, the CL feature that seems to have the greatest potential as a source for complementing current language pedagogy is its quest for linguistic motivation, i.e. for explainable meaning-meaning connections (e.g. polysemy), meaning-form connections (e.g. iconicity) and form-form connections (e.g. alliteration). Presenting segments of language as motivated is likely to be beneficial for learners as it may enhance comprehension, retention, cultural awareness and positive affect. We survey the calls that have been made for the introduction of CL insights in language teaching and evaluate the empirical evidence of the pedagogical effectiveness of CL approaches. Although most controlled experiments reported so far have tended to be small-scale, taken collectively they are beginning to constitute a fairly robust body of evidence in favour of CL-inspired pedagogy. It needs to be acknowledged, however, that the evidence collected so far is largely confined to the pedagogical exploitation of figurative thought, and this mostly with regard to polysemous words (especially prepositions and particles) and idiomatic expressions. We conclude by proposing an agenda for future research.

*Keywords*: applied linguistics; second/foreign language pedagogy; linguistic motivation; figurative thought; empirical evidence

## 1. Cognitive linguistics meets applied linguistics

### 1.1. General relevance of CL for language pedagogy

Insights from cognitive linguistics (CL) have been taken up by education-oriented applied linguistics at a surprisingly slow pace given that at least six beliefs held by cognitive linguists could serve as meeting points:

1. Language is an integral part of cognition as a whole, rather than a separate and unique faculty (Langacker 1987). From this it follows that language learning is likely to benefit from the application of established, relatively general theories of cognitive processing. especially those which concern memory. These include *dual coding theory* (Clark and Paivio 1991; Paivio 1971, 1986), which holds that association through figurative thought of verbal information with a mental image facilitates recall, and *trace theory*, which holds that repetition of encounters with a given linguistic instantiation strongly tends to entrench its traces in memory (Baddeley 1990; Cohen, Eysenck and LeVoi 1986; Squire and Kandel 2000).

   In applied linguistics (AL), explicit discussions of dual coding and trace theory do not abound but they are widely assumed. Stevick (1986) offers an early and still perhaps the most explicit account of applications of both theories in L2 pedagogy.

2. In a dynamic usage-based model of language (Langacker 1988, 2000; Tomasello 2000), there is no innate language-acquisition faculty which leads to essentially the same results in L1 acquisition (being most importantly the acquisition of syntax and phonology) regardless of whether input is very rich or rather impoverished and imbalanced. Instead, acquisition is markedly influenced throughout early childhood and beyond by quantity and quality of input. Frequency of encounter is key – if a language user encounters a linguistic unit often enough, it eventually becomes a standard item in the learner's linguistic inventory. Concomitant with such learning is the formation in the mind of an over-arching schema which can be said to 'sanction' its instantiations. At the level of groups of language users, frequency of occurrence of understood linguistic forms (be they morphemes, words, phrases or patterns) determines the likelihood of their becoming 'entrenched' in a language community's linguistic repertoire.

   A number of applied linguists have adopted a usage-based model of language (e.g. Ellis 1998, 2005; Skehan 1998), along with the explicit belief that the frequency of expressions and patterns in input has an effect on acquisition in L2, as evidenced by features of inter-language (e.g. Ellis 2002).

3. The grammar-lexis dichotomy at the heart of both structural and generative linguistics is rejected. Instead, language is viewed as a non-dichotomous, structured inventory of conventional symbolic units of varying complexity (Langacker 1987, 1991). This new conception of

language as a continuum of meaningful forms has led to a rapid increase in research into semi-fixed multiword expressions (e.g. idioms), which had hitherto received the attention of relatively few linguists (e.g. Makkai 1972) owing to the dubious legitimacy of these forms within the then widely accepted lexis-grammar dichotomy.

No doubt in part thanks to fruitful computer-aided corpus studies (e.g. Sinclair 1991), a growing number of applied linguists have become active in the study of collocation in general and of multiword units in particular (e.g. Howarth 1998; Nattinger and DeCarrico 1992; Pawley and Syder 1983; Schmitt 2004; Wray 2002), with the contribution of such units to oral fluency being a topic of particular interest (e.g. Boers, Eyckmans, Kappel, Stengers and Demecheleer Forthcoming; Oppenheim 2000; Segalowitz 2000).

4. The distinction between linguistic, or 'dictionary', meaning (the theoretical ideal of which is word meanings that are equivalent to necessary and sufficient conditions) and wider, 'encyclopaedic' meaning is a fallacy (Haiman 1980; Langacker 1987). Rather, words – and patterns too – are conceived of as nodes in elaborate semantic networks such that activation of one node (by a usage event) may trigger the activation of many other nodes in the network. Put simply, words and other constructions in the mental lexicon carry many more associations (ranging from the culturally shared to the idiosyncratic) than earlier theory allowed.

In AL, this view corresponds to language instruction that aims at:
a) 'depth' (in addition to 'breadth') of linguistic knowledge (e.g. Read 2004; Vermeer 2001)
b) an enhanced general language awareness on the part of the language learner (e.g. James and Garrett 1995)
c) pedagogical exploration of the inter-subjectivity of 'personal' word meanings (e.g. Morgan and Rinvolucri 2004: 118).

5. Figuration (especially metaphor and metonymy) plays an immense role in the semantics of natural languages and in patterns of thought (Gibbs 1994; Johnson 1987; Lakoff 1987; Lakoff and Johnson 1980).

The view that metaphor is of major importance in everyday usage also began to make headway in AL during the late 1980s. Low (1988) seems to have been one of the first (at least in English) to offer a to-do list. Additional AL work on metaphor, up to the end of the 1990s, is excellently and extensively surveyed in Cameron and Low (1999). Classroom or self-study materials combining the recent interests in multiword units in general and figurative expressions in particular have finally begun to appear, too (e.g. Flower 2002; Lazar 2003; Wright 2002), but not yet with an outspoken CL perspective. Concern with metaphor is the element of CL which has had the most (albeit still minor) impact in L2 pedagogy, so far (see section 4 below).

6. Semantics is a matter of conceptualisation – of how *particular* language users construe the world anthropocentrically, subjectively, and often under the influence of culture-specific preferences (Lakoff 1987; Langacker 1987). Thus, a single event or state of affairs can be construed or encoded in various ways. Importantly, languages differ with regard to (degrees of) preference for some construals over others, with the result that certain ones have become (more or less) conventionalised. One example is the distinction between 'satellite-framed' languages and 'verb-framed' languages in the construal of motion events (Talmy 1985; Slobin 2000). Put simply, the former (e.g. English) show a preference for expressing the manner of motion in the main verb itself and the path of motion by means of a satellite such as a particle (e.g. *He staggered into the restaurant*). The latter (e.g. French) show a preference for expressing the path in the main verb and the manner (if at all) by means of an adverbial-type of constituent (e.g. *Il est entré d'un pas chancelant*). Cadierno (2004) shows how this relative preference for framing motion events in language learners' L1 is likely to be transferred to their expression of motion events in a target language whose native speakers may well display a different preference. One of the possible applications of cognitive linguists is to help learners appreciate such cross-lingual variations in construal (e.g. Cadierno and Lund 2004), for example by exploring their connection with culture (e.g. Goddard 2000; Lakoff 1987; Palmer 1996; Niemeier and Dirven 2000). An example here is the exploration of cultural differences in metaphor (e.g. Kövecses 2005).

In AL, after some decades of only scattered interest, there has been a conspicuous renewal of interest in language instruction with a robust cross-lingual and cross-cultural component intended to raise language awareness and cultural awareness (e.g. Byram 1997; Kramsch 1993). This revival includes an interest in cross-lingual and cross-cultural comparisons of metaphor (e.g. Boers and Littlemore 2003) and, more particularly, in how to foster L2 learners' 'metaphoric competence' (e.g. Littlemore 2001a) so as, in turn, to foster L2 'conceptual fluency' (Danesi 1995).

Given just these points of contact (and we are likely to have overlooked others) it should not be surprising that mutually enriching research has already been carried out in both CL and education-oriented AL. Still, as we suggested at the very outset of this introduction, there is plenty of scope for advancement.

## 1.2. The notion of motivation in cognitive linguistics

So far, we have focused on areas of common ground, but now it is time to consider key elements of CL which are under-appreciated both in AL and in fields which AL may serve (e.g. language pedagogy and materials design) – namely the element of categorisation by prototype and the related concept of (semantic) *motivation*. As to the latter, something in language is 'motivated' when it is neither arbitrary nor (fully) predictable either (Lakoff 1987: 346). While the majority of applied linguists will claim, for example, that the form-meaning connections in language are arbitrary (e.g. Lewis 1997: 17–19) – with the exception, perhaps, of onomatopoeic words – cognitive linguists, building on their view that language is a reflection of general cognitive processes, will consider it their task to look for (retrospective) explanations for form-meaning connections in language. Any finding that portions of natural language are motivated rather than arbitrary should be taken as a cordial invitation for educational linguists to investigate the pedagogical potential of presenting linguistic phenomena as motivated in contexts of second or foreign language learning.

Radden and Panther (2004) propose a taxonomy of linguistic motivation which turns on whether a process of motivation involves (1) meaning-meaning connections, (2) form-form connections, or (3) form-meaning connections.

### 1.2.1. Meaning – meaning connections

The majority of CL investigations of motivation pertain to meaning-meaning relations which is to say – in terms from Langacker (1987) – that they focus on the semantic poles of symbolic units. (This is also the focus of the great majority of applications of CL in foreign language pedagogy; see sections 1.4 and 2 below). These investigations include studies of polysemy, where peripheral senses of a word are found to be extended from a central or prototypical sense via image-schema transformations or via metonymy and metaphor. Prepositions (including particles of phrasal verbs), typically being highly polysemous, have often served as showcase objects of CL semantic analysis (e.g. Brugman 1981; Dewell 1994; Evans and Tyler 2004; Lindner 1981; Tyler and Evans 2003). By identifying the core spatial sense of a preposition it becomes possible to motivate (i.e. retrospectively explain) particular occurrences and types of occurrence (or non-occurrence) of its less central spatial senses and its figurative senses. For example, a comparison of the radial networks of the near-synonyms *under* and *below* (Boers 1996), shows that the central spatial sense of the former allows for contact between the trajectory and the landmark (e.g. *The love letters under my pillow*) while the central spatial sense of *below* describes a relation of separation or distance (e.g. *People talking below my window* and *Basel, also on the Rhine, is below Schaffhausen*). Because of our experience with objects that are attached to one another, the possible contact relation in *under* allows for an image-schema transformation that gives rise to a rotated sense (e.g. *The shirt under his jacket was drenched*). Because of its separation relation, *below* does not have this rotated meaning extension. Metaphorically, interpersonal relationships are conceived as contact relations (e.g. *Are you still in touch with any of your schoolmates?*). Consequently, *under* is a likely candidate to describe hierarchical interpersonal relationships involving interaction (e.g. *She served under Clinton*), while *below* is not (e.g. *?She served below Clinton?*). Another near-synonym, *underneath*, prototypically describes contact relations, too (typically where the TR is completely covered by the LM), which also helps motivate its derived rotated sense (e.g. *The shirt underneath his jacket*). However, because of the 'covering' relationship, this preposition is an unlikely candidate for describing figurative interpersonal interaction (e.g. *?She served underneath Clinton?*). Finally, the fourth near-synonym in the set, *beneath*, provides an example of *ecological* motivation (Lakoff 1987: 487; Taylor 2004) in which linguistic units strive to occupy their own niche in a network. Originally, *beneath* was used in the sense that *below* is now used in (i.e., prototypically to describe spatial relations where the trajectory is lower than the landmark and separated from it). Over time, however, *beneath* started to invade the territory of *under*, and *below* was drafted in to express the general 'lower than' relation. *Beneath* was then relegated to its own niche, describing vertical relations in formal and literary registers.

As a source of information for L2 instruction, some cognitive linguists have maintained that it is useful to compare the meaning networks of prepositions (and other spatial lexis) across languages (e.g. Rudzka-Ostyn 1983; Taylor 1988), as this may alert learners to both the benefits and the pitfalls of L1 transfer.

While a great deal of early cognitive semantic work focuses on polysemy displayed by prepositions and particles, lexical items from other word classes have also been given cognitive semantic treatment in recent years (e.g. da Silva 2003; Tuggy 2003). In addition, a number of linguists have argued that linguistic phenomena on the (outdated) borderline between lexis and grammar, such as modal verbs and other 'grammaticalised' words, can be motivated by tracing the grammaticalised form to its prototypical lexical meaning (e.g. Fisher 1999; Lehti-Eklund 2003; Sweetser 1990).

Still with respect to meaning-meaning connections, a second fashionable type of cognitive semantic case study focuses on figurative idioms. Idioms, which structural and generative linguists have traditionally treated as semantically arbitrary and non-decomposable, have been shown by cognitive semanticists to be linguistic instantiations of overarching conceptual metaphors (CMs) or conceptual metonymies (Lakoff and Johnson 1980), which are grounded in physical or social experience. For example, idiomatic expressions such as *He reached his boiling point* and *She flipped her lid* are instantiations of the CM ANGER IS A HOT FLUID IN A CONTAINER (Kövecses 1986). Apart from everyday idiomatic language, conceptual metaphor theory (CMT) has also been applied to the analysis of conventional figurative expressions in a panoply of text genres of various specialised target domains, such as economics (e.g. Boers 1999; Jäkel 2003, Chung 2003a, 2003b, Herrera 2000, 2003, Koller 2000, 2003, 2004, White 1999, 2003), architecture (Caballero 2003a, 2006), medicine (Salager-Meyer 1990), politics (Charteris-Black 2004, Chilton 1987, 1993, 1995, 1996, 3002, 2004, 2005, Cienki 2004, Lakoff 2002, Morgan 1997, 2000, Musolff 1996, 2000, Rohrer 2000, Schäffner 1995, 1996), and language teaching (see Low 2003, for a survey of the latter).

Although it is acknowledged that the correspondence of idioms to their CMs is sometimes far from self-evident, quantitative studies of the instantiations of given CMs have pointed to cross-linguistic or cross-cultural variation in the popularity of congruent metaphors and metonymies (Boers 2003; Charteris-Black 2003; Deignan 2003).

While the CM approach to idioms tends to look at idioms from a synchronic perspective, other cognitive semantic investigations take a more diachronic approach. Boers and Stengers (forthcoming), for example, motivate the semantics of idioms by tracing them back to their historical-cultural-etymological origins. This exercise allows for a matching of idioms with quite specific source domains (e.g. matching *Win hands down* with the source domain of horse racing) and this in turn allows for cross-linguistic comparisons at a more detailed level. The level of specificity at which the semantics of idioms is motivated (i.e., at the level of general CMs or at the level of more precise origins) may also prove relevant in contexts of language instruction, since dual coding in the learner's mind is likely to be facilitated by presenting the learner with precise, rich images (Boers 2004).

### 1.2.2. Form – form connections

Motivation can also pertain to form-form relations (i.e. at the phonological poles of symbolic units). Radden and Panther (2004) do not provide any examples, and this is clearly an under-explored category. We suggest it includes rhyme as well as two types of less heavy phonological repetition, alliteration and assonance. These patterns have been found to motivate the precise lexical selection in a large number of compounds (e.g. *pickpocket* and *playmate*) and multiword units (e.g. *publish or perish* and *drunk as a skunk*) (Boers and Stengers, forthcoming; Lindstromberg and Boers 2005a).

### 1.2.3. Form – meaning relations

This category pertains to connections between the phonological and the semantic poles of symbolic units. These are motivations as to why certain linguistic forms have a given meaning or why certain meanings are expressed by means of a given form. In this category of motivation belong phenomena such as:
- *imitative iconicity* (e.g. onomatopoeia) and *diagrammatic iconicity* (e.g. the fact that simple grammatical forms typically represent basic concepts while complex forms typically represent complex concepts in line with the 'more-form-is-more-meaning' principle) (Taylor 2002: 46);
- instances of the 'sameness-of-form, sameness-of-meaning' principle, as in *phonesthemes* – which are sound sequences that have associated meanings – such as /sp/ which, as an onset, occurs in a striking number of English words of negative connotation (e.g. *spam, spit, spew, spite, spleen* and *spoil*) (Radden and Panther 2004: 18).
  The 'sameness-of-form, sameness-of-meaning' principle also applies at the higher, schematic level of grammatical constructions, where each grammatical schema (or template) is semantically distinct from others in the language's repertoire. A major concern of cognitive linguists has indeed been to reveal the meaningful nature of grammar. In particular, cog-

nitive grammarians consider grammatical constructions to be symbolic, just like lexical items, and thus meaningful too. In CL theory, grammatical constructions are motivated more abstractly in that they reflect language users' choices of construal, that is, their choices of how to conceptualise a given situation or event (i.e., with one rather than another of the patterns conventionally available in their language). The challenge for L2 learners in this respect is to appreciate cross-linguistic variation in the preference for a given kind of construal. Such variation leads to L1 interference which, in turn, is an important source of errors, even in the case of congruent constructions or congruent forms. For example, many more nominal concepts are conventionally construed as unbounded in English than in French, which may lead French-speaking students to erroneously treat English uncountable nouns as countable (as they are in their L1) and thus talk about *informations and *researches in English. One of the most interesting challenges for CL is to find (cultural) motivations behind the particularly strong conventionalisation of certain construals and thus the factors promoting deep entrenchment of grammatical phenomena which express those construals in any given language (Niemeier 2004).

## 1.3. The pedagogical potential of motivation in second or foreign language instruction

If important segments of language are motivated rather than arbitrary – and this clearly seems to be the case – then opportunities for insightful L2 learning (as opposed to learning by rote, or blind memorisation) must be considerably more numerous, and perhaps also more varied, than has been generally realised.

Firstly, we may hypothesise that presenting elements of the L2 as motivated can help learners reach a deeper understanding of these elements, since the process of helping learners to see motivation typically involves highlighting connotations and activation of semantic networks. For example, motivating the meaning of the idiom *jump the gun* by revealing its original context of use (i.e. that of a contender in a running contest who leaves the blocks before the starting pistol has been fired) may help a learner better appreciate the evaluative meaning of the expression, especially if that learner (like the first author of this chapter) initially mistakenly associated the expression with the brave act of attempting to get hold of the weapon of a person who is holding you at gun point. It may also help the learner to connect the unfamiliar expression to idioms that he or she may already have mastered and that are also derived from the same source domain. One such expression, to remain with the case of athletics, could be *quick off the mark*. Relating new words to already acquired knowledge is believed to foster learning (e.g. Sökmen 1997).

Secondly, we may hypothesise that motivating L2 phenomena can be beneficial to retention. Thinking about the motivation for a given meaning-meaning, form-form or form-meaning connection is an example of what in AL literature is called *elaboration* (e.g. Barcroft 2002). *Semantic* elaboration refers performance of a mental operation with regard to the *meaning* of words or constructions; *structural* elaboration refers to performance of a mental operation with regard to the *form* of words or constructions. Elaboration is known to foster learning as it involves processing information at a relatively "deep" level, which according to 'levels-of-processing' theory (Cermak and Craik 1979) increases the likelihood of the information being retained in memory. One type of deep-level processing is exemplified by dual coding (see above, section 1, point 1). Since many types of linguistic motivation rely heavily on figurative thought (i.e. metaphor and metonymy), learners are likely to reap the benefits of dual coding when that motivation is revealed to them. Dual coding is likely to take place in, for example, the teaching of figurative idioms such as *jump the gun,* if the learner is encouraged to associate the idiom with the concrete scene of its original literal use (i.e. an image of the scene in the form of schematic visual and motoric images). Dual coding is also likely to occur when drawings or pictorials are used to represent the meaning of words (e.g. drawings of the TR-LM configurations of a preposition) and constructions (e.g. a time-line to contrast the scope of different tenses). As is well known, the use of pictorial representations is also common practice in CL.

Thirdly, we may hypothesise that showing segments of the L2 to be motivated can contribute to a heightened pragmatic and cultural awareness on the part of learners. Recognition of CMs, for example, may help learners comprehend texts in general and recognise persuasive rhetoric in particular. The ability to identify the source domains behind sets of idioms may help students recognise (historically) culturally salient fields of experience through confrontation, for example, with (a) the large number of sailing, card-playing, horse-racing and hunting idioms in English; (b) the large number of idioms derived from religion in Spanish; (c) the large number of food-related idioms in French; and so on.

Finally, an awareness that a second or foreign language need not be learned entirely via a long and daunting road of blind memorisation must be an encouraging thought to learners who recognise that large segments of the target language actually 'make sense'. This encouragement can lead to positive affect, which is obviously beneficial to longer-term learning behaviour (Arnold 1999)

## 1.4. Perception of CL in periodicals for teachers

Despite its pedagogical potential, CL has left surprisingly few traces in periodicals for teachers, so far. Looking back to the 1980s, Lindstromberg (1991a) found very few examples of any applications of CL in TESOL. The new survey we carried out for the purpose of this chapter[1] suggests that the intervening years have seen relatively little increase in the influence of CL on day-to-day L2 pedagogy, with the sole exception of a few traces we found of CMT, a strand of CL dating from Lakoff and Johnson (1980).

A particularly stark example of CL's unimpressive impact on TESOL is provided by the popular-academic *TESL-EJ*, which seems not to have had a single article on any aspect of CL, including CMT, since its founding in 1997 (and, of all places, it is hosted at Berkeley, the base camp of CMT!). *ELT Journal*, a similarly popular-academic journal for teachers, has featured only a few articles explicitly drawing on CMT (Boers and Demecheleer 2001; Deignan, Gabrys and Solska 1997) or CMT plus versions of prototype theory (Boers and Demecheleer 1998; Lindstromberg 1996). The more popularising periodicals that we have looked at provide a few additional examples, such as Hannan (1998), a two-page account of the semantics of *up* and *down* in phrasal verbs, and Ponterotto (1994), Baker (1998) and Rundell (2002), three very short articles recommending Lakoff and Johnson (1980).

Of all the for-teachers periodicals we looked at, the eclectic online journal *Humanising Language Teaching* has profiled CMT most often: Boers and Lindstromberg 2006; Holme 2001; Lindstromberg 2001b,c,d, 2002; Lindstromberg and Boers 2005; Littlemore 2001b, 2004a, 2005; Stengers, Eyckmans, Horemans and Boers 2004; Rundell 2001, 2005a.

Compared to the situation in general-English teaching, CMT is slightly better represented in periodicals devoted to the teaching of English for specific purposes (ESP) (e.g. Caballero 2003b; Lindstromberg 1991b), especially in the fields of English for business and economics, where the figurative nature of a vast number of (more or less) 'technical' terms can be revealed by tracing the terms (e.g. *cashflow, human capital, fledgling companies, elastic demand*) back to their literal origins and/or by grouping them under common CMs (e.g. Boers 2000a; Charteris-Black 2000; Charteris-Black and Ennis 2001; Charteris-Black and Musolff 2003; Little-more 2002; White 2003). For example, *a chronic deficit, an arthritic mar-ket, the economy is recovering, we need to slim down our labour force, the right economic remedy, we'll have to amputate loss-making departments,* etc. could be grouped under the CM ECONOMICS IS HEALTH CARE. Like-wise, *a flourishing firm, pruning expenses, a branch of our company,* etc. could be grouped under ECONOMICS IS GARDENING. Having students cat-egorise figuratively used words or expressions under such 'metaphor themes' or 'source domains' is believed to facilitate retention both via the likelihood of dual coding occurring (i.e. the likelihood of an association between the words and a mental image) and via the likelihood of 'deep' processing occurring (i.e. the likelihood of cognitive effort being invested in the categorising task). Empirical support for such beliefs in the peda-gogic effectiveness of CL-inspired treatments is surveyed in section 2.

Finally, a particularly important source of information for teachers and learners is that of learner's dictionaries. Lindstromberg (2001), taking *on* as a case study on how prepositions were treated in UK published mono-lingual learner's dictionaries, provides a stark example of the scant impact of CL in pedagogy-oriented lexicography at his time of writing. None of the dictionaries under examination was found to consistently present senses in the order of likely relatedness or provided any hints at the moti-vated nature of the polysemy, despite the fact that by 1997 there was avail-able a relatively jargon-free CL-influenced depiction of more or less the entire contemporary system of English spatial prepositions (Lindstrom-berg 1997), which was addressed to ESOL teachers, translators and lexi-cographers. Fortunately, it seems the tide may now slowly be turning; as evidenced by Rundell (2005b), a dictionary of phrasal verbs which has plainly taken CMT (and prototype theory) into account in its 'semantic maps' of the meanings of individual prepositions.

## 2.  CL proposals for language instruction and their effectiveness

In this – core – section of the chapter, we shall survey in more detail some of the proposals for second or foreign language instruction that have been put forward by cognitive linguists in recent years. The rationale behind CL-inspired language pedagogy was outlined by several scholars (focus-ing on various segments of language) in Pütz, Niemeier and Dirven (2001a, 2001b) and in Achard and Niemeier (2004). Crucially, we shall here survey the available evidence of the surplus effectiveness of the proposed applications in comparison with other instructional methods. Most space will be devoted to publications that describe relatively concrete applications of CL in language instruction and/or experiments to measure the effect of CL-inspired pedagogy.

## 2.1 CL approaches to polysemy

A great many CL case studies reveal the interrelatedness of the different senses of high frequency words with multifarious usages. For teachers, lexicographers, and materials writers, a treatment of such words as cases of monosemy and homonymy is unhelpful. Treating such words as monosemes would mean looking for an overarching meaning that is capable of operating in all instances of use, and such a definition is likely to be so abstract as to defy characterization. The pedagogical disadvantage of this is that abstract meanings are known to be hard to learn, all else being equal. On the other hand, treating such words as homonyms, i.e. telling learners that such and such a word has distinct senses which happen to be homophonic and homographic, would ignore the pedagogical potential of creating meaningful associations between senses. And yet, portrayals of homonymy 'by omission' (i.e. by giving no information about links of polysemy) abound in both course books and learner's dictionaries (Lindstromberg 1999, 2001a).

The basic intention behind a CL approach to teaching a polysemous word is to make the learner aware both of the word's central (or 'core' or 'prototypical') sense and of how additional senses of the word are extended from this central sense (sometimes via intermediate meaning extensions). A meaning extension, or a chain of them, can simply be pointed out and explained to learners. Alternatively, learners may be spurred to a higher degree of involvement by proceeding as follows:

1. Encourage learners to hypothesise on their own (or in pairs/groups) about the semantic motivation of a target use – i.e. about the semantic relation of the use-at-hand to a known core sense or to a sense which is at least nearer the core on an extension chain, and then …
2. Provide learners with the means to corroborate (or falsify) their hypotheses.

Meaning extensions from the central sense can be literal, although figurative (especially metaphoric and metonymic) extensions are very common; in short, motivation of meaning extensions very often requires figurative thought.

*2.1.1. Prepositions and phrasal verbs*

As mentioned above, particles in English phrasal verbs, and prepositions generally, have been a favourite object of CL research into polysemy. In TESOL circles, on the other hand, prepositions have tended to be dealt with in a cursory fashion owing no doubt to their reputation for being unsystematic, hard to teach, and extremely hard to learn. (We cannot say how true this is of functionally analogous morpho-lexical elements in a wide range of other target languages.) In fact, it is symptomatic of this view of prepositions that ones which occur in English phrasal verbs have typically not been recognised as such – as the term *particle* suggests.

Unsurprisingly, FLT-oriented cognitive linguists have sought to fill this educational niche, with Rudzka-Ostyn being an early example. She helped pioneer the inclusion of CL presentations of prepositions (including so-called particles) in FLT course materials (e.g. Rudzka-Ostyn, Ostyn, Godin and Degreef 1991). Her efforts to implement CL in vocabulary teaching would eventually culminate in a home study book which targets more than 1,000 English phrasal verbs (Rudzka-Ostyn 2003). Illustrations of how prepositions and phrasal verbs can be treated in CL-inspired language pedagogy are Dirven (2001), and Tyler and Evans (2004), who propose a step-by-step presentation of meaning extensions from the core sense of various prepositions and particles. We may exemplify this step-by-step approach by means of the preposition *beyond*: from (a) *We cannot recover our ball; it's beyond the neighbour's hedge* (literal) via (b) *Her recent behaviour is beyond my understanding* (metaphor) to (c) *The use of English prepositions is still beyond me* (metaphor + metonymy). Even senses that at first sight appear to be hard to motivate may be embraceable along such lines. For example, Lindstromberg (1996) proposes a staged approach to teaching the various senses of the highly multi-faceted preposition *on*, including a characterization of its sense in *My car died on me* through verbal and pictorial explication of the metaphor MISFORTUNES ARE BURDENS.

Let us now turn to experiments that were conducted to measure the effectiveness of CL-inspired instruction of prepositions and phrasal verbs.

In an experiment with the participation of 73 French-speaking students of English, Boers and Demecheleer (1998) showed that students were more likely[2] to correctly interpret various figurative senses of *beyond* (e.g. *This theory is beyond me*) in the context of a reading comprehension task, if they had been presented with a definition of the core spatial sense that helps motivate the metaphorical extensions, i.e. a definition that emphasises that *beyond* implies some distance between the TR and the LM, a feature which makes *beyond* a likely candidate to instantiate the metaphor ABSTRACT INACCESSIBILITY IS DISTANCE. Moreover, although these students had been given only this core spatial sense of *beyond*, they significantly outperformed their peers who had been given access to complete dictionary definitions including explanations of the figurative senses.

Kövecses and Szabó (1996, revisited in Kövecses 2001) focused on English phrasal verbs with *up* and *down*. In the experimental condition, 15 Hungarian students were asked to study ten phrasal verbs accompanied by CL explanations that raised the students' awareness of the conceptual metaphors (henceforward: CMs) underlying the given phrasal verbs (MORE IS UP, HAPPY IS UP, etc). Under the control condition, another 15 Hungarian students were asked to study the same phrasal verbs accompanied by L1 translations. In an immediate post-test (a gap-filling exercise) the experimental students outperformed the control students by almost 9%. The immediate post-test also targeted ten more *up / down* phrasal verbs that had not been included in the instruction stage and, interestingly, the experimental students outperformed their control peers by almost 25% on these items, which suggests that the experimental students managed to transfer the acquired knowledge of the chosen CMs to their interpretation of instantiations they had not previously studied.

One of the experiments reported by Boers (2000b) focused on phrasal verbs instantiating a wider range of CMs (including, VISIBLE IS OUT, e.g. *find out, turn out*; VISIBLE IS UP, e.g. *look it up, show up*, etc). In the experimental condition, 39 French-speaking students were asked to study a list of 26 phrasal verbs that were grouped under various CMs and accompanied by a synonym. In the control group, another 35 French-speaking students were asked to study the same phrasal verbs listed alphabetically and accompanied by more elaborate explanations (e.g. several synonyms) copied from a well-known grammar book. In an immediate post-test (a text-based gap-filling exercise) that targeted ten of the phrasal verbs studied, the experimental students outperformed their control peers significantly. The post-test also targeted ten more phrasal verbs that were not included in the list the students had been asked to study. Unlike Kövecses and Szabó's (1996) set-up, these extra items did not instantiate the same CMs as the phrasal verbs studied. Students' post-test scores on this sub-set of the gaps showed no difference between the experimental and the control group. In other words, these results show no evidence of any transfer strategy beyond the CMs that experimental students were made conscious of.

The finding by both Kövecses and Szabó (1996) and Boers (2000b) that a presentation of phrasal verbs in terms of CMs is measurably beneficial to – at least short-term – retention is certainly encouraging, although it does not pinpoint whether the benefits are due to figurative thought (i.e. mental imagery resulting in dual coding) or simply to the fact that organised vocabulary is easier to learn than random lists (e.g. Schmitt 1997; Sökmen 1997), and CMs can indeed help organise vocabulary. We acknowledge too, that the findings do not guarantee that the whole category of prepositions and phrasal verbs lends itself well to the proposed strategy. Neither do the results imply that CL analyses of prepositional polysemy can be copied straight into course materials or lesson plans. CL-inspired pedagogues and materials writers would need to take at least the following points into consideration:

1. There are several aspects of prepositional polysemy which cognitive linguists tend to disagree about, e.g. what, in a given case, the prototype is; how many distinct senses/schemas there are; how these relate to the prototype; and how they relate to each other. Rice (1996, 2003) and Sandra and Rice (1995) report psycholinguistic evidence of structured polysemy, but *not* at the level of the multiple fine-grained distinctions among senses that some cognitive linguists have been wont to propose. Rice and Sandra (*op. cit.*) therefore caution that purely introspective linguistic analysis may result in portrayals of semantic networks that may be lacking in inter-subjectivity. Even if semantic networks of polysemes are streamlined for teaching purposes (e.g. Evans and Tyler, forthcoming), full agreement may not be realistically achievable, given that an individual's language resources are usage-based. From a learner's perspective, however, the benefits of presentation of meaning extensions as motivated may well depend on the perceived plausibility of the motivations.

2. Not all explicated motivation is equally likely to facilitate learning. Sometimes the motivation of meaning extensions is pretty straightforward, but at other times it may be quite abstract and may even come across to learners as far-fetched. In a small-scale experiment, Condon and Kelly (2002) used an early manuscript of a chapter to be included in Rudzka-Ostyn (2003) to teach 19 university students (the experimental group) phrasal verbs with *out* (e.g. *break out, pick out, rule out, check out, set out, stand out*). A control group (14 students) was taught the same phrasal verbs along the lines of the treatment in *Collins Cobuild Phrasal Verb Wordbook* (Goodale 1998). In a post-test measuring

students' recollection of the meaning of the phrasal verbs taught, experimental students did better than the control students, but *only* on the phrasal verbs whose motivation had been straightforward and concrete enough to be illustrated with a drawing during the instruction stage.

3. If they are to be embraced by the teaching community, applications of CL must be learner-friendly and adapted to the target audience. For one thing, CL-inspired materials writers may need to modify their jargon and refrain from using terms such as 'trajector'. More importantly, they may need to keep in mind that relatively few L2 learners are inclined to engage in the kind of prolonged and intensive semantic analyses that linguists find so fascinating. An informal study by Kurtyka (2001) found that Rudzka-Ostyn's (2003) materials for teaching and learning phrasal verbs were evaluated quite positively by a group of Polish EFL teachers, but they also reported that students at relatively low levels of proficiency felt the materials were too demanding.

4. The perceived relevance of explicit instruction of the multiple senses of prepositions may be undermined by the fact that most prepositions are high-frequency items that can be acquired incidentally, in a rough and ready fashion, given ample enough exposure to the target language. Also, intermediate and advanced students are often already familiar with the meanings of the prepositions taught, especially if cognates are available in the students' L1. Lowie and Verspoor (2004) report an experiment the results of which show significant effects of both frequency of occurrence and cognates in students' mastery of prepositions. Beginning learners will tend to rely on L1 cognates, but as learners progress and experience more exposure to L2, the frequency effect tends to gain in power and overrides the cognate-effect. However, many languages have no straightforward counterparts of prepositions at all, let alone cognates. And even across such moderately related languages as French and English, misunderstandings about prepositions can persist at extremely high levels of proficiency (Coppieters 1987).

## 2.1.2. *Beyond prepositions and phrasal verbs*

The presentation of polysemous words in terms of meaning extensions from a central or prototypical sense has been applied to other classes of expressions than prepositions, typically by motivating the metaphoric/ metonymic connections between the literal sense of a word and its figurative extensions (e.g. MacLennan 1994; Scott 1994). Segments of language that might traditionally be treated under 'grammar' in course books have been analysed as cases of teachable polysemy, too.

Lindstromberg (1991c) demonstrates that a very wide range of usages of *get* (which is generally considered in TESOL circles to be chaotically idiomatic) can be interpreted as extensions from the sense seen in *The cat got a mouse*, where *get* foregrounds result and backgrounds manner.

Littlemore and Low (2006), building on work by Sweetser (1990), Dirven and Taylor (1994) and Traugott and Dasher (2002), suggest that in theory the ideal sequence in acquiring modal verbs would be to move from the deontic senses (e.g. *Helen must come home by ten*) to the epistemic senses (e.g. *Helen must be home by now*).

Athanasiadou (2004) analyses the meaning extensions of the discourse connectors *when, as long as, as soon as, as, since* and *while*. She shows that by precisely defining the core temporal senses of these items, it becomes possible to motivate why certain non-temporal senses have developed. For example, *while* prototypically describes simultaneity, whereas *since* prototypically describes posteriority. This helps motivate why the latter has developed a non-temporal sense of 'reason' (e.g. *Since it was Sunday, he slept in*), while the former has not.

The effectiveness of CL-inspired instruction of various kinds of polysemous lexis was measured in the following studies:

One of the experiments reported in Boers (2000b), conducted with the participation of 73 French-speaking students taking a course in business English, aimed at helping learners expand their range of expression to describe upward and downward trends. The participants were given a rather elaborate vocabulary list containing words such as *soar, skyrocket, plunge, dive, slide* and *peak*. In the experimental condition students were encouraged to try to categorise the words by source domains such as aircraft, diving and mountaineering, i.e. they were encouraged to process the vocabulary through imagery. In the control condition students were encouraged to categorise the words along a cline from descriptors of slow to fast upward or downward change. This set-up was meant to trigger the investment of a similar amount of cognitive effort under both conditions so that any observed difference in learning effect could be ascribed to the more explicit use of imagery in the experimental condition. In an immediate post-test, the students were asked to write a short essay based on a couple of graphs (about unemployment rates). Counts of the number of different up-down lemmas used in the collected essays revealed that the experimental students used a significantly wider range than their control peers, which again suggests that making learners aware of the literal senses behind figuratively used polysemes facilitates vocabulary retention. However, when the same students were given a similar task one year later, the experimental group did not do any better than the control group anymore (Boers 2004).

In an experiment with the participation of 78 Dutch-speaking students of English, Verspoor and Lowie (2003) first confronted experimental group learners with the core senses of polysememes in order to test their ability to interpret and remember more peripheral senses in the radial network. The researchers chose 18 polysemous words whose core sense had given rise to a meaning extension that is still relatively close to the core sense, but also had given rise to a meaning extension occupying a more peripheral position in the network. Experimental students were asked to 'guess' the meaning of the core sense before attempting to figure out the relatively closely connected meaning extension. Control students were first asked to guess the meaning of the more peripheral sense of the word before tackling the less peripheral one. Experimental students were found to be significantly more likely to correctly interpret the relatively closely connected meaning extension and also to remember its exact meaning in a delayed post-test (after two weeks).

Csábi (2004) reports an experiment set up to measure the pedagogic effect of explicit CL explanations of the semantic networks of the English verbs *hold* and *keep*. Participants were 52 Hungarian secondary school pupils. The experimental group was told that the core meaning of *hold* involves an agent's hand (as in *She held the purse in her right hand*). Meaning extensions were explained via conceptual metonymies and metaphors such as THE HAND FOR CONTROL and POSSESSING IS HOLDING (e.g. *The terrorists held them hostage* and *He did not hold the right certificate*). They were told that the core meaning of *keep* implies a durative state of possession (as in *You can keep the change*), but without implying the use of hands. The durative component was then used to explain other uses of *keep* as in *Earn enough to keep a family* and *Keep that dog out of my study.* In addition to verbal explanations, the experimental condition involved some pictorial support, e.g. the teacher illustrating core senses by miming or by drawing on the blackboard. The control group was presented with the same examples of *hold* and *keep*, but these were explained by means of translations into Hungarian. An immediate post-test and a delayed post-test (one day after instruction) in which students were asked to fill in gaps with either *hold* or *keep* showed that the experimental students were significantly more likely to make the right choice of lemma. These results suggest that even fairly abstract motivations of meaning extensions can be beneficial to learners. The better performance by the experimental students may partly be due to the extra cognitive effort they invested in comprehending the examples on the basis of the motivations, which presumably involved deeper processing than going over the translations. It may also partly be due to the pictorial support of the explanations, which was absent in the control condition.

To evaluate the effects of visual, and possibly motoric, support, Lindstromberg and Boers (2005b) conducted an experiment focusing on 24 manner-of-movement verbs (e.g. *hobble, stagger, teeter, veer, saunter, slump, flit*). In the experimental condition, students took turns miming the verbs so that their peers could guess what verb was being acted out. In the control condition, students explained the meaning of the verbs verbally so that their peers could guess what verb was being explained. An immediate post-test (a gap-filling exercise) targeting the verbs used in their literal senses revealed that the experimental students were significantly more likely to recollect them. In a delayed post-test, the students were presented with the same verbs used in their figurative senses accompanied by an L1 translation, which was deliberately kept fairly vague (e.g. it did not hint at the level of hostility in *He hurled insults at his girlfriend*, or at the incidental nature of *He stumbled on a crucial piece of evidence*). Students were asked to evaluate the proposed translations. The results show that students who had watched each other mime the literal senses of the verbs were significantly more likely to spot the lack of precision in the translations of the metaphorical uses of the verbs. Students were especially likely to correctly question the translations of the verbs they had acted out themselves. The significantly better scores under the 'miming' condition in the post-test that was administered to measure students' recollection of literal uses of the verbs, suggests a strong mnemonic effect of dual coding. The significantly better scores in the test that was administered to measure in-depth comprehension of the figurative uses of the verbs, suggests that students are often capable of transferring their enhanced comprehension of core senses onto their appreciation of metaphorical extensions from those core senses, which confirms the results of the Verspoor and Lowie (2003) study.

## 2.2. CL approaches to idioms

Idioms are traditionally described as 'dead' metaphors, the idea being that they have become so standardised that few people are normally aware of their figurative nature. Cognitive linguists, however, have shown that the imagery behind an idiom can easily be resuscitated either by enhancing people's awareness of the underlying CMs or by tracing the idiom back to its original, literal context (e.g., Gibbs 1994). Lazar (1996) is an early call for promoting metaphor awareness in teaching and learning figurative expressions (though not yet from a CL perspective at the time), and Lazar (2003) is possibly the first EFL exercise book with a strong focus on raising awareness of metaphor.

Boers and Lindstromberg (2006) propose classroom activities whereby students (in accordance with research results, see below) first hypothesise about the origin of an idiom and then try to work out its figurative meaning on the basis of that original use. This 'problem-solving' task is meant to engage students in deep processing; additionally, the aim is to foster dual coding by asking volunteers to mime or draw the literal senses of the idioms. Littlemore and Low (2006) describe a variety of more incidental classroom interactions in which students who encounter an unfamiliar figurative expression gradually figure out its meaning via the teacher's hints at relevant associations with the literal, sometimes culture-specific, origin of the expression.

Empirical evidence of the usefulness of CM as a categorising principle behind sets of figurative idioms comes from a number of different sources.

Boers (2000b) reports an experiment with 118 Dutch-speaking secondary school pupils who were presented with a list of 18 expressions (borrowed from Kövecses 1986) such as *She blew up at me, Her comments added fuel to the fire* and *Don't bite my head off.* In the experimental condition, these expressions were grouped under headings referring to CMs, i.e. ANGER IS A HOT FLUID IN A CONTAINER, ANGER IS FIRE and ANGRY PEOPLE ARE DANGEROUS ANIMALS. In the control condition, the same lexis was organised under functional headings, referring to whether the expressions were used to describe sudden anger, a slow build-up of anger, or angry personalities. This was done to ensure the same degree of organisation of the input under both conditions. In an immediate post-test (a text-based gap-filling exercise targeting ten of the expressions), the experimental group outperformed the control group significantly. However, the data also hint at the possibility that an enhanced awareness of congruent CMs may lead to a greater inclination for L1-to-L2 transfer, and thus also to a greater risk of erroneous L1 transfer at the level of linguistic form (e.g. *add *oil to the fire* and *don't bite my *nose off*).

Learners are typically wary of using idioms in their target language (Irujo 1993). In this connection, Deignan, Gabrys and Solska (1997) propose cross-linguistic comparisons of figurative idioms (English and

Polish, in their case) to help students appreciate conventional figurative language. Their proposed exercises are meant to help students recognise congruent CMs, but also to alert students to the risks of L1-to-L2 transfer at the linguistic (formal) level. However, and hugely intriguingly, in investigating degrees of learner willingness to transfer literal and metaphorical L1 locutions into L2, Kellerman (1978) found that Dutch learners were particularly sceptical about the transferrability into English of Dutch expressions involving *non*-prototypical senses of *breken* (= *'break'*) almost regardless of whether these expressions were literal or metaphorical.

Skoufaki (2005), inspired by Cacciari (1993) evaluates the likelihood of L2 learners identifying CMs autonomously when they are asked to interpret unfamiliar idioms (see also Bortfeld 2002, 2003). She asked 40 Greek students to hypothesise about the meaning of ten English idioms and to describe their line of reasoning. Only a minute proportion of the responses revealed any spontaneous use of CM as a means of figuring out idiomatic meaning. This suggests that, unless learners are first given explicit instruction about CMs of hypothesised relevance, a CM treatment of idioms is unlikely to be very effective in contexts of learner autonomy. A programme of explicit metaphor instruction is put forward by Li (2002), who describes a series of experiments with the participation of a total of 394 Chinese students of English. In the experimental conditions, students engaged in teacher-led discussions about CM, conscious application of the knowledge of CMs to the interpretation of figurative expressions, and the deliberate use of pictorials for mnemonic support. The experimental students consistently scored significantly better in post-tests measuring recall of the expressions than their control peers, who had not received explicit guidelines for learning the input language. It was just when the target items were VP idioms that the experimental condition and the control condition did not differ significantly but this may be due to the relative formal complexity of multiword phrases such as idioms. The variable that the experimental students were probably engaged more intensely (and for longer) with the materials than their control peers is likely to have advantaged the former group, but the overall performance by the experimental students nevertheless indicates that explicit instruction around CMs can lead to considerable learner gain.

While the above studies focus on CMs as motivation and categorising principle behind sets of idioms, Boers (2001) reports an experiment set up to measure the mnemonic effect of tracing idioms back to their original, literal contexts, without resorting to overarching CMs. 54 Dutch-speaking students were asked to look up the meaning of ten English idioms they did not yet know (e.g. *pass the baton* and *a dummy run*). The experimental students were given the supplementary task of writing down a hypothesis about the origin of each idiom, while the control students were asked to invent a communicative situation in which each idiom could be used. It was assumed both tasks would involve a comparable investment of cognitive effort (i.e. comparable levels of 'deep' processing), but it was hoped as well that the hypothesising about the literal origin of an idiom would call up a picture of a concrete scene in the learner's mind, resulting in dual coding (e.g. associating *pass the baton* with the scene of a relay race). In an immediate post-test targeting the idioms in a gap-filling exercise, the experimental students significantly outperformed their control peers, which may be indicative of the mnemonic power of dual coding. In a delayed post-test (after a week) in which students were asked to explain the meaning of the ten idioms, the experimental group again did significantly better.

Encouraged by the mnemonic effect observed in the Boers (2001) study, Boers, Demecheleer and Eyckmans (2004a) and Boers, Eyckmans and Stengers (Forthcoming) conducted a series of larger-scale experiments with the aid of an on-line programme of exercises they developed to help Dutch-speaking students comprehend and remember a total of 400 English idioms (see also Stengers, Eyckmans, Horemans and Boers 2004). In this programme, each idiom is presented to the students in three types of exercises: a multiple-choice exercise (the 'origin' exercise) where the student is asked to tick the right source domain of the idiom (e.g. "What domain of experience do you think the expression *To be on the ropes* comes from? Sports, food or sailing?"), a multiple-choice exercise (the 'meaning' exercise) where the student is asked to tick the right dictionary-like definition of the idiom, and finally a gap-filling exercise where the student is invited to fill in (a keyword of) the idiom inserted in a suggestive context. After each exercise the student is given feedback with the correct answer. In the case of the 'origin' exercise, the feedback gives a brief explanation of the literal, historical-cultural-etymological origin of the idiom, which is meant to help the student associate the expression with a concrete scene (for example an association of *To be on the ropes* with the scene of boxing where one fighter is in trouble). Boers, Demecheleer and Eyckmans (2004a) found that students who had had access to the 'origin' exercises but not the 'meaning' exercises were significantly more likely to be able to reproduce the idioms in the gap-filling exercise than their colleagues who had had access to the 'meaning' exercises but not the 'origin' exercises. In a second experiment they found that apart from a couple of exceptions (see below) the mnemonic effect of giving explanations about the literal origins of idioms was just as strong for opaque idioms (defined here as idioms whose source domain the student was unable to guess, e.g. the source domain of card games behind *To follow suit*) as for transparent idioms (e.g. *To break ranks*). These results too offer strong support for the dual coding hypothesis. In a third experiment, Boers, Eyckmans and Stengers (Forthcoming) found that this mnemonic effect was optimised significantly by giving students the 'origin' exercise before the 'meaning' exercise, so that they could use the newly acquired knowledge of the literal sense of the idiom to figure out its figurative sense. We hypothesise that this optimal sequence of events adds deeper processing to the learning process (in the form of insightful problem-solving rather than blind guessing in the 'meaning' exercise). The finding that students are significantly more likely to identify the correct dictionary-like definition in the 'meaning' exercise after they have been told about the literal origin of the idioms shows that these idioms became motivated for L2 learners too. In addition, interviews with the students suggest that the high scores obtained under this approach contribute to positive affect and thus to willingness to continue learning.

Boers and Demecheleer (2001) report a small-scale experiment the results of which suggest that cross-cultural variation in the salience of (congruent) source domains for metaphor can impact learners' ability to interpret idioms, and that therefore learners' comprehension of idioms could benefit additionally from cultural knowledge (in its widest sense). More conclusive evidence of the effect of cultural variables on learners' ability to comprehend and also remember L2 idioms is offered by Boers, Demecheleer and Eyckmans (2004b). In a retrospective analysis of a large databank of students' scores on on-line English idiom exercises (see above), it was found that idioms derived from rather culture-specific source domains (such as cricket and horse-racing) were significantly harder for Dutch-speaking students to interpret and remember. The lack of familiarity with a given source domain may obviously reduce the likelihood of dual coding taking place in the learner's mind (if a verbal explanation fails to call up a mental picture in the first place).

All the above-mentioned studies examine the pedagogic potential of motivating the relations between literal and figurative senses through imagery. This type of motivation may help learners comprehend and remember idioms. What it cannot do, however, is motivate the precise lexical make-up of idioms. Boers and Lindstromberg (2005b) and Boers and Stengers (forthcoming) investigate the *phonological* motivation behind the lexical selection in idioms. It appears that in the process of standardising word combinations, the phonological properties of one word may determine the choice of another. Hand counts in idiom dictionaries reveal, for example, that the lexical selection in up to 20% of English idioms may be influenced by the appeal of alliteration and/or rhyme (e.g. *from pillar to post, through thick and thin, go with the flow*). A retrospective analysis of the performance of several generations of students in on-line exercises targeting 400 English idioms (see above) shows that idioms with alliterating word combinations are significantly more likely to be retained than idioms without apparent phonological appeal. Moreover, this effect is observed even though the instructional programme was set up to draw the students' attention to imagery rather than sounds, i.e. it was set up to stimulate *semantic* elaboration (via the 'etymological' feedback) in the students' minds rather than *structural* (or, more precisely, *phonological*) elaboration. By occasionally raising learners' awareness of catchy sound patterns, the mnemonic effect of alliteration can be enhanced significantly (Boers and Lindstromberg 2005b). With a view to optimising the memorability of catchy sound patterns, Lindstromberg and Boers (2005a) propose various classroom activities that go beyond mere noticing and which can target not just idioms but compounds and collocations as well. It is clear, though, that we are only just beginning to appreciate the potential scope of phonological (and phonetic) motivation in natural language and in language pedagogy.

## 2.3. CL approaches to constructions

Although within CL there are various opinions on the nature of 'constructions' (see Goldberg 1995, Croft 2001, Langacker 2005), it is correct to say that CL treats grammatical constructions on a par with lexis, in the sense that, like words, constructions are symbolic units comprising a semantic and a phonological pole. The difference is that constructions are more schematic than words and may more clearly function as overarching templates sanctioning a greater variety of lexically elaborated instantiations. Dirven (1989), Hüllen (1992), Langacker (2001), Meex and Mortelmans (2002), Taylor (1993), Turewicz (2000) are among those who have conjectured that this treatment of grammatical constructions as meaningful makes CL an appealing source for the design of a pedagogical grammar.

A speaker's choice of a given construction to present a state of affairs reflects the speaker's construal of that state of affairs. However, languages obviously differ with respect to the kinds of constructions that are available for purposes of construal and with respect to the relative 'coverage' by congruent (or equivalent) constructions. For example, French does not have the progressive tenses that English does. Conversely, English does not have the subjunctive tenses that French does. Some applied cognitive linguists (e.g. Meex and Mortelmans 2002; Niemeier 2004) have outlined contrastive approaches to pedagogical grammar as a way to make learners aware of the conceptualisations in L2 that differ from their L1. An additional way of helping learners get a grip on L2 grammar is to point out cases of the operation of the same cognitive principle in different segments of the language. For example, the bounded versus unbounded categorisation of things (resulting in the grammatical distinction between countable and uncountable nouns) also applies to actions, resulting in the grammatical distinction between simple and progressive tenses in English (Dirven 1989).

Much of the pedagogic appeal of cognitive grammar lies in its treatment of constructions as usage-based. Like words, constructions are subject to processes of elaboration and schematisation. Through usage events, constructions may develop meanings and uses that do not correspond completely with their prototypical meaning or usage. However, if the novel use occurs frequently enough to become entrenched, it will eventually be fully sanctioned by an adapted, overarching schema (Langacker 1987). Several cognitive linguists (e.g. Hüllen 1992; Langacker 2001) have called for grammar teaching whose first stage is attempting to heighten awareness of the prototypical usage of each target construction (e.g. a tense) and whose later stages involve showing how other usages derive from the prototype. This cognitive sequence from typical to special cases is certainly not a new idea in grammar teaching (as a quick glance through best-selling grammar books will reveal). The novelty lies in the presentation of non-prototypical uses of a given construction not as 'exceptions to the rule', but rather as motivated extensions from the prototype. Thus, to a far greater extent than has been true of other approaches, CL-inspired pedagogy has been conceived to help learners see that the L2 is informed by principles that make sense and are useful to know because they facilitate learning. There is, additionally, an emphasis on (i) the language user's needs to construe and produce L2 discourse, (ii) the manner in which these needs are met by the available repertoire of L2 constructions, and (iii) the fact that under certain conditions that repertoire can be stretched and adapted (Taylor 1993). For example, many so-called uncountable nouns in English can become countable if the language user decides to reinterpret concepts that are conventionally construed as unbounded and construe them as bounded (and thus countable) instead (e.g. *behaviours*).

The cognitive sequence from-prototype-to-extensions does not necessarily imply that cognitive grammarians endorse explicit, sequential teaching of discrete grammar points. According to Achard (2004), the conception of grammatical constructions as radial categories organised around a deeply entrenched prototype (i.e. one that is frequent, physically grounded, and/or early-learned) and slightly less entrenched (e.g. less frequent) peripheral uses is perfectly compatible with relatively un-programmed inductive grammar acquisition as proposed, for example, by Natural Approach theorists (Krashen and Terrell 1983; see, however, critique of Krashen in Taylor 1993) and by Prabhu's (1987) early version of Task-Based Learning. The idea here is that through exposure to large amounts of input, learners tend most often and/or most perceptually saliently to encounter uses that correspond to the prototype, while they will encounter the less typical instantiations less often (and/or less saliently) and automatically consider these as more peripheral cases. At the same time, the confrontation with atypical instances can be used to raise students' appreciation of the way native speakers bend the 'grammar-book rules' in order to present the way they construe a given state of affairs. In a similar vein, the use of authentic materials for grammar acquisition instead of discrete-point grammar teaching is favoured by Grundy (2004), who uses the figure-ground notion from CL to demonstrate how important context (the ground) is in learners' comprehension and intake (of segments) of the target language.

The case-studies used to back up the above-mentioned proposals for a pedagogical cognitive grammar are a bit too complex to be summed up in this survey chapter. For easy exemplification we therefore turn to Littlemore and Low (2006), who give straightforward examples of figurative thinking behind grammatical choices. One of these examples is the use, in academic writing, of tenses to make references which may reflect authors' evaluation of the work that they are referring to by creating either a sense of proximity or a sense of distance. For example, the present tense in *Smith (1998) suggests that* ... reflects closer mental proximity (and thus more agreement) than the past tense in *Smith (1998) suggested that* ... Another example is the choice of the demonstrative *this* (rather than *that* or the indefinite article) in joke openings like *There was this English-man* ..., which creates closer proximity between the listener and the protagonist in the created mental space.

The above survey shows that a considerable number of appealing proposals for CL-inspired pedagogical grammar have been put forward in recent years. It is unfortunate, however, that – to our knowledge at least – no reports have yet been published of any empirical studies conducted to assess the pedagogical effectiveness of CL-inspired treatments in comparison with other, traditional instruction of L2 grammar.

## 2.4. CL approaches to reading comprehension

Reading research is a very vast research area in psycholinguistics and applied linguistics. The contribution that CL can offer to it will typically investigate the potential role of figurative language present in texts as a potential facilitator (or obstacle) in the comprehension process. Sometimes texts are structured around a recurring metaphor theme, i.e. an overarching CM that helps lend rhetorical coherence and – through its linguistic instantiations – lexical cohesion to a text. Allbritton, McKoon and Gerrig (1995) conducted a series of experiments in which respondents were asked to read texts, some of which were structured around an overarching metaphor and some of which were not. The respondents were then presented with small segments from the texts and asked if they could remember encountering these in the reading task. The segments taken from the texts with a recurring metaphor theme turned out significantly more likely to be recognised than those taken from other text fragments. In other words, the presence of an overarching CM facilitates readers' (receptive) recollection of words or phrases they come across in a given text. While this kind of recollection can only be an indirect measure of a reader's comprehension of a text, it can nevertheless be indicative of the extent to which intake has taken place. If recurring metaphor themes facilitate this intake, then their presence could be exploited when reading texts in a second or foreign language, too. The only prerequisite seems to be that the language learners need to be able to recognise the CM, and to do that they need to be able to recognise at least a couple of its linguistic instantiations in the text. Again, some CM instruction may be useful, but to our knowledge there have been no reports of controlled experiments set up to measure the effect of CM instruction on learners' intake of CM-structured texts.

An area in reading comprehension where metaphor awareness may be especially useful to readers is when metaphors are used as a persuasive or manipulative device, as in political rhetoric. Experiments have shown that the CMs used by authors to frame problems and dilemmas can have a profound impact on readers' thought patterns (Boers 1997; Robins and Mayer 2000) because the experiential 'logic' associated with the source domain of the metaphors tends to be preserved in the way the metaphor frames the target domain under discussion. Littlemore (2004b) describes an experiment that shows the benefits of CM instruction on EAP (English for Academic Purposes) students' ability to critically analyse and question metaphorically framed discourse. Students who had received explicit CM instruction were much more likely than their peers to question the validity of the metaphors used by an author and to expose the impartial author stance.

In in-depth reading comprehension, one of the crucial skills is the ability to recognise the position the author holds with regard to the subject matter. Boers (2000a) tried to measure the effect of enhanced metaphor awareness on this ability, but did so without resorting to explicit instruction about CMs. Instead, experimental students were merely made aware of the original, literal usage of the figurative lexis they were encountering in their (specialised) reading. In an experiment 85 French-speaking university students taking a course in ESP (business and economics) were asked to read a newspaper-style article about (fictitious) trade talks. The text contained figuratively used lexis (e.g. *Some governments are still bailing out firms* and *They are reluctant to wean their industries off state support*) that hinted at the author's scepticism about state subsidies. The text was accompanied by a glossary. For control students, the entries gave synonyms adapted to the context of the text. For example, *bailing out* was explained as "giving state subsidies" and *weaning off* was explained as "making independent". For experimental students, only the literal, original meaning was revealed. For example, *Bailing out* was explained as "trying to keep a sinking boat afloat by throwing out water out with a bucket" and *Weaning off* was explained as "gradually stopping breastfeeding a baby". After reading the text, students were asked whether they thought the author was in favour of, against or undecided about giving prolonged state subsidies to companies in trouble. The experimental students were significantly more likely than their peers to recognise the author's opinion. They reported they felt the author was against giving prolonged state subsidies, since bailing out a boat can only be a temporary solution and since breastfeeding cannot go on indefinitely either.

So, it seems that activities that raise learners' awareness of CM as well as activities that simply resuscitate the literal origins of figurative lexis can at least occasionally be beneficial for (aspects of) reading comprehension.

## 2.5. CL approaches to raising cultural awareness

The impact of cross-cultural differences on learners' comprehension and retention of figurative expressions has already been mentioned in section 5.2. Additional evidence is provided by Littlemore (2003), who demonstrated that Bangladeshi students studying at a British university often misinterpreted the figurative discourse used by their British lecturers. The evaluative stance reflected in the lecturers' choice of metaphors turned out to be especially difficult for some foreign students to grasp because the connotations associated with a given source or target domain varied across the two cultures. For example, the metaphor *the machinery of government* was meant by a British lecturer to convey a negative value judgement about government, but his Bangladeshi students did not perceive that negative connotations of machinery were mapped onto government apparently because their culture tends to hold government in higher regard than the British culture does. Littlemore (2002, 2004) proposes classroom activities for helping students develop metaphor interpretation strategies and capacities, among which cultural awareness is included.

Deignan (2003) and Boers and Stengers (forthcoming) explore the diachronic connection between culture and language communities' idiom repertoires. Cultures show variation in their degree of 'preoccupation' with certain experiential domains because of geographical, historical or cultural reasons, and this variation is reflected in the extent to which those experiential domains have 'generated' figurative idioms. Boers, Eyckmans and Stengers (Forthcoming) argue that pointing out the source domains of idioms that students encounter helps instil an appreciation of the cultural dimension of language. In addition, they offer empirical evidence that knowledge of the source domain of idioms can help students make educated guesses about the likelihood of given idioms being typical of informal or formal registers. For example, in comparison with some other domains, such as warfare, the domain of games and sports has generated significantly more idioms that are signalled in the *Oxford Idiom Dictionary* (Speake 1999) as 'informal', and learners have been shown to intuitively evaluate 'games' and 'sports' idioms as more 'playful' and more likely to be used in informal contexts than, for example, 'war' idioms.

Niemeier (2004) calls for an instructional programme that makes students aware of the culture-relatedness of language. This objective fits in nicely with recent trends in language pedagogy that have re-introduced objectives of language awareness (e.g. James and Garrett 1995) and cultural awareness (e.g. Byram 1997; Kramsch 1993). Ways of working to-

wards this objective include cross-cultural comparisons of CMs and metonymies, and cross-cultural comparisons of the prototypical members of
categories and the inclusion vs. exclusion of 'peripheral' members to those
categories.

Goddard (2004) even proposes classroom use of 'semantic primes' and
'cultural scripts' (e.g. Wierzbicka 1996, 1997) to raise students' awareness
of subtle cross-cultural differences in the connotations of congruent concepts. For example, he claims that the concept 'freedom' in British English
seems constrained by the idea that one's free actions should not be bad for
others. This cultural constraint could help motivate a whole panoply of
'tentative' phrases, such as *Would you mind ...?*) which have so far been
relegated to folk wisdom about the oddly 'polite' nature of English discourse.

Neither Niemeier (2004) nor Goddard (2004) offer any empirical evidence for the pedagogical effectiveness of their proposed classroom activities, but students who invest cognitive effort in them can certainly be
expected to engage in deep processing and associative thinking, which is
bound to be beneficial for learning.

## 3. Evaluation: A research agenda

As shown by the above survey, proposals for CL-inspired second or
foreign language instruction have proliferated in the past fifteen years.
Some of the proposals have been rather vague as to the exact implementation of the CL insights in terms of materials design or precise classroom
activities. Some of the others have offered more concrete suggestions, but
are lacking in the provision of empirical evidence of any surplus pedagogical effectiveness in comparison with already established teaching
methods. In our survey, we have given most attention to studies that do
provide such empirical evidence (preferably via controlled experiments).
Although these studies have tended to be small-scale, taken collectively
they are beginning to constitute a fairly robust body of evidence in favour
of CL-inspired language pedagogy. Still, a great deal of work remains to
be done to (a) expand the scope of linguistic motivation, (b) measure the
impact of learner-connected variables on its pedagogic effectiveness, and
(c) fine-tune its implementations with a view to maximising the pedagogic
benefits.

## 3.1. Expanding the scope of motivation

The majority of the proposed pedagogical applications of CL exploit motivated meaning-meaning connections (e.g. between a prototypical sense and its extended literal and figurative senses). Many more segments of language could be explored to find out if they could be subsumed under the category of motivated meaning-meaning connections. Other categories of motivation have received comparatively little attention in pedagogy-oriented CL so far, although they carry considerable pedagogic potential as well.

Under the category of form-form connections, for example, belongs lexical selection in compounds, multiword units and collocations that may be motivated by sound patterns (such as alliteration, assonance and rhythm) and by ease of articulation. A possible pedagogical advantage of addressing motivated form-form connections is accommodation of learning styles that tend not to favour imagery (see below). Another advantage may be expansion of the scope of motivation to include non-figurative phrases. For example, phonological motivation may help explain why:

– *seek* seems to invite noun collocates that either start with /s/ (*solace, solitude, solution, satisfaction*) or nearly do (*asylum*)
– *do* (which normally profiles the activity itself) is selected in some collocations where one could expect *make* (which normally profiles the product or result of the activity), such as *do damage, do a degree, do a doctorate*.

Another under-explored category in CL-inspired language pedagogy is that of motivated form-meaning connections, where, for example, a speaker's choice to use 'more form than necessary' in itself carries meaning (e.g. distancing oneself from the content as in long-winded tentative statements, such as "It is not inconceivable that X might possibly be Y", or in polite requests, such as "I was wondering if you would mind doing some cleaning") (Littlemore and Low 2006).

Identifying more cases of linguistic motivation is but the first step. The next step is to measure to what extent revealing these kinds of motivation is beneficial to language learners in terms of comprehension, retention and socio-linguistic competence.

## 3.2. Measuring learner-related variables

While most of the empirical studies surveyed above provide evidence of the effectiveness of CL-inspired instruction in general, detailed reading of the reports nevertheless reveals that the results are often mixed at the level of individual learners. Not all CL-inspired pedagogy seems to yield equally encouraging learner gain for all individual students. Learner-related variables include levels of proficiency and aptitude. The great majority of the world's second or foreign language learners are non-language specialists who may not be intrinsically interested in unravelling the motivated nature of given L2 segments unless the benefits for learning of this activity are sufficiently transparent. After all, what L2 pedagogy is meant to do is facilitate and speed up acquisition. While non-language-specialist learners may still appreciate the usefulness of CL-style explanations and activities when it comes to fairly straightforward and concrete types of motivation, they may fail to see the relevance of investing time and cognitive effort in contemplating more abstract (and in their view possibly 'far-fetched') types of motivation. In the worst-case scenario, negative affect due to a lack of face-validity of the instructional method may even short-circuit the benefits of deep processing which the method is meant to stimulate (e.g. Stengers, Eyckmans, Horemans and Boers 2004).

Another important learner-related variable that may influence the effectiveness of a given CL-inspired instructional method is the student's cognitive-style profile (Kurtyka 2001; Littlemore 2001a). We cannot go into detail here about the panoply of cognitive styles that have been identified in the literature (for an overview, see, e.g. Riding and Rayner 1998). Nor are we able to say much about the various proposed correlations between cognitive style profiles and the way individuals tend to process metaphor (Boers and Littlemore 2000) beyond mentioning the distinction between 'high imagers' (people who show a preference for thinking in mental pictures) and 'low imagers' (people who show a preference for thinking in words) (Katz 1983). Experiments set up to measure likely retention of idioms via dual coding show that high imagers tend to benefit significantly more from explanations about the origins or literal usage of the idioms than low imagers do (Boers, Eyckmans and Stengers 2005). Much CL-inspired language instruction encourages 'figurative thinking', but not all learners seem equally responsive. On the other hand, low imagers have been found to be more open than high imagers to the mnemonic effect of phonological motivation (alliteration and rhyme). Expanding the scope of motivation beyond figuration may thus offer the possibility of catering for learners whose cognitive style profiles are less in tune with recognition of CMs and metonymies.

## 3.3. Fine-tuning the implementations

As shown, a number of experiments have measured the general pedagogical effectiveness of CL-inspired language instruction in comparison with other, more traditional methods of instruction. However, CL-inspired language pedagogy can take various forms and can contain various elements that each contribute to learning. We feel that applied cognitive linguistics is now mature enough to start comparing the relative effectiveness of those different forms of CL-inspired instruction and to start pin-pointing precisely what elements in the approach are especially beneficial with regard to specific learning objectives (e.g. objectives of comprehension, retention of meaning, recollection of form, and socio-linguistic competence).

For example, controlled experiments may help evaluate the usefulness and feasibility of learners' independent hypothesising about the source domains or CMs behind the figurative expressions they encounter, before receiving corroboration or falsification from the teacher or course materials. On the one hand, independent hypothesising is expected to stimulate deep processing. On the other hand, frequent falsification may result in negative affect.

Controlled experiments may also help evaluate the usefulness of pictorial representations of meaning, for example pictures illustrating the literal, original sense of idioms (as in Kövecses, Tóth and Babarci 1996). For example, the meaning of *A carrot-and-stick method* may be illustrated by the picture of a donkey with a carrot dangling before it and a stick behind it. Pictures may be expected to facilitate dual coding and may thus help students remember the meaning of idioms. On the other hand, they may distract students from the precise lexical make-up and morphological form of the expressions so that chances of accurate reproduction of the idiom may become compromised. In other words, pictures may contribute to semantic elaboration, but they may be counter-productive when it comes to structural elaboration (Stengers, Boers and Eyckmans 2005).

Finally, it needs to be mentioned that most of the experiments surveyed above measure short-term learning effects, under 'controlled' conditions, and that most of the proposals for implementation focus on relatively small segments of the target language (e.g. a set of prepositions or phrasal verbs, a series of idioms, a couple of modal verbs). Concerted efforts now need to be made to integrate the various research insights and pedagogical proposals on a larger scale, in authentic language teaching settings, and in coherent curricula.

This research agenda is addressed in two collective volumes, one by Boers and Lindstromberg, eds. (Forthcoming) that focuses on vocabulary and phraseology instruction, and one by De Knop, De Rijcker, Meex and Mortelmans, eds. (Forthcoming) that concentrates on pedagogical grammar, both to appear in the present book series, *Applications of Cognitive Linguistics.*

## Notes

1.  With respect to CL in the L2 classroom, our impressions stem from:
    (a) our necessarily limited base of contacts with other teachers (e.g. colleagues, participants on training courses and workshops, and teachers we meet at TESOL and AL conferences);
    (b) our inevitably lacunae'd acquaintance with published classroom and study materials (mostly for English as a target language); and
    (c) our screening of the following periodicals for teachers, which we class as:
        (i) popular-academic: *ELT Journal* (UK) and *TESL-EJ* (US)
        (ii) popularising: *Forum* (USA), *English Teaching Professional* (UK) and *Modern English Teacher* (UK); and
        (iii) mixed: *Humanising Language Teaching* (UK).
2.  Throughout this chapter, the term *significant* is used to refer to statistical significance, i.e. with p-values smaller than .05. Actually, in most of the instances where we have used the term in connection with the surveyed experiments, significance levels at $p < .01$ or at $p < .001$ were obtained.

## References

Achard, Michel
    2004    Grammatical instruction in the Natural Approach: a Cognitive Grammar view. In *Cognitive Linguistics, Second Language Acquisition, and Foreign Language Teaching*, Michel Achard, and Susanne Niemeier (eds.), 165–194. (Studies on Language Acquisition 18.) Berlin/New York: Mouton de Gruyter
Achard, Michel, and Susanne Niemeier (eds.)
    2004    *Cognitive Linguistics, Second Language Acquisition, and Foreign Language Teaching.* (Studies on Language Acquisition 18.) Berlin/New York: Mouton de Gruyter.
Allbritton, David W., Gail McKoon, and Richard Gerrig
    1995    Metaphor-based schemas and text representations: making connections through conceptual metaphors. *Journal of Experimental Psychology: Learning, Memory and Cognition* 21: 612–625.

Arnold, Jane
  1999    *Affect in Language Learning.* Cambridge: Cambridge University Press.
Athanasiadou, Angeliki
  2004    Teaching temporal connectors and their non-temporal extensions. In
          *Cognitive Linguistics, Second Language Acquisition, and Foreign Lan-*
          *guage Teaching*, Michel Achard, and Susanne Niemeier (eds.), 195–210.
          (Studies on Language Acquisition 18.) Berlin/New York: Mouton de
          Gruyter
Baddeley, Alan
  1990    *Human Memory: Theory and Practice.* Needham Heights, MA: Allyn
          and Bacon.
Baker, Judith
  1998    Metaphor. *English Teaching Professional* 7: 13–14.
Barcroft, Joe
  2002    Semantic and structural elaboration in L2 lexical acquisition. *Lan-*
          *guage Learning* 52: 323–363.
Boers, Frank
  1996    *Spatial Prepositions and Metaphor: A Cognitive Semantic Journey along*
          *the UP-DOWN and the FRONT-BACK Dimensions.* Tübingen: Gunter Narr
          Verlag.
  1997    No pain, no gain in a free-market: A test for cognitive semantics?
          *Metaphor and Symbol* 12: 231–241.
  1999    When a bodily source domain becomes prominent: the joy of counting
          metaphors in the socio-economic domain. In *Metaphor in Cognitive Lin-*
          *guistics*, Raymond W. Gibbs, and Gerard J. Steen (eds.), 47–56. (Current
          Issues in Linguistic Theory 175.) Amsterdam/Philadelphia: Benjamins.
  2000a   Enhancing metaphoric awareness in specialised reading. *English for*
          *Specific Purposes* 19: 137–147.
  2000b   Metaphor awareness and vocabulary retention. *Applied Linguistics* 21:
          553–571.
  2001    Remembering figurative idioms by hypothesising about their origin.
          *Prospect* 16: 35–43.
  2003    Applied linguistics perspectives on cross-cultural variation in concep-
          tual metaphor. *Metaphor and Symbol* 18: 231–238.
  2004    Expanding learners' vocabulary through metaphor awareness: What
          expansion, what learners, what vocabulary? In *Cognitive Linguistics,*
          *Second Language Acquisition, and Foreign Language Teaching*, Michael
          Achard, and Susanne Niemeier (eds.), 211–234. (Studies on Language
          Acquisition 18.) Berlin/New York: Mouton de Gruyter.
Boers, Frank, and Murielle Demecheleer
  1998    A cognitive semantic approach to teaching prepositions. *English Lan-*
          *guage Teaching Journal* 53: 197–204.
  2001    Measuring the impact of cross-cultural differences on learners' com-
          prehension of imageable idioms. *English Language Teaching Journal* 55:
          255–262.

Boers, Frank, and Seth Lindstromberg
2005 Finding ways to make phrase-learning feasible: the mnemonic effect of alliteration. *System* 33: 225–238.
2006 Means of mass memorisation of multiword expressions, part two: the power of images. *Humanising Language Teaching* 8 www.hltmag.co.uk
Boers, Frank, and Seth Lindstromberg (eds.)
forthcoming *Not So Arbitrary: Cognitive Linguistic Approaches to Teaching Vocabulary and Phraseology.* (Applications of Cognitive Linguistics.) Berlin/New York: Mouton de Gruyter.
Boers, Frank, and Jeannette Littlemore
2000 Cognitive style variables in participants' explanations of conceptual metaphors. *Metaphor and Symbol* 15: 177–187.
Boers, Frank, and Jeannette Littlemore (eds.)
2003 *Cross-cultural Differences in Conceptual Metaphor: Applied Linguistics Perspectives.* Special Issue of *Metaphor and Symbol.* Mahwah, New Jersey/London: Lawrence Erlbaum Associates.
Boers, Frank, and Hélène Stengers
forthcoming Adding sound to the picture: An exercise in motivating the lexical composition of metaphorical idioms in English, Spanish and Dutch. In *Confronting Metaphor in Use: An Applied Linguistic Approach*, Lynne Cameron, Maria Sophia Zanotto, and Marilda C. Cavalcanti (eds.), Amsterdam/Philadelphia: Benjamins.
Boers, Frank, Murielle Demecheleer, and June Eyckmans
2004a Etymological elaboration as a strategy for learning figurative idioms. In *Vocabulary in a Second Language: Selection, Acquisition and Testing,* Paul Bogaards, and Batia Laufer. (eds.), 53–78. Amsterdam/Philadelphia: Benjamins.
2004b Cultural variation as a variable in comprehending and remembering figurative idioms. *European Journal of English Studies* 8: 375–388.
Boers, Frank, June Eyckmans, and Hélène Stengers
2005 Means of 'motivating' multiword units: Measuring the mnemonic effects. Paper presented at *EUROSLA 15*, Dubrovnik, Croatia: The University of Zagreb.
Forthcoming Presenting figurative idioms with a touch of etymology: more than mere mnemonics? *Language Teaching Research* 10 (4).
Boers, Frank, June Eyckmans, Jenny Kappel, Hélène Stengers, and Murielle Demecheleer
Forthcoming Formulaic sequences and perceived oral proficiency: Putting a lexical approach to the test. *Language Teaching Research* 10 (3).
Bortfeld, Heather
2002 What native and non-native speakers' images for idioms tell us about figurative language. In *Advances in Psychology: Bilingual Sentence Processing*, Roberto Heredia and Jeanette Altarriba (eds.), 275–295. North Holland: Elsevier Press.
2003 Comprehending idioms cross-linguistically. *Experimental Psychology* 50: 217–230.

Brugman, Claudia
1981    Story of *Over*. M.A. thesis. University of California, Berkeley.
Byram, Michael
1997    *Teaching and Assessing Intercultural Communicative Competence.* Clevedon: Multilingual Matters.
Caballero, Rosario
2003a   Metaphor and genre: The presence and role of metaphor in the building review. *Applied Linguistics* 24: 145–167.
2003b   How to talk shop through metaphor: Bringing metaphor research into the classroom. *English for Specific Purposes* 22: 177–194.
2006    *Re-Viewing Space: Figurative Language in Architects' Assessment of Built Space.* (Applications of Cognitive Linguistics 2.) Berlin/New York: Mouton de Gruyter.
Cacciari, Cristina
1993    The place of idioms in a literal and metaphorical world. In *Idioms: Processing, Structure, and Interpretation*, Cristina Cacciari, and Patrizia Tabossi (eds.), 27–56. Hillsdale, NJ: Erlbaum.
Cadierno, Teresa
2004    Expressing motion events in a second language: A cognitive typological approach. In *Cognitive Linguistics, Second Language Acquisition, and Foreign Language Teaching*, Michael Achard, and Susanne Niemeier (eds.), 13–49. (Studies on Language Acquisition 18.) Berlin/New York: Mouton de Gruyter
Cadierno, Teresa, and Karen Lund
2004    Cognitive linguistics and second language acquisition: Motion events in a typological framework. In *Form-Meaning Connections in Second Language Acquisition*, Bill VanPatten, Jessica Williams, Susanne Rott, and Mark Overstreet (eds.), 139–154. Hillsdale, N.J.: Lawrence Erlbaum.
Cameron, Lynne, and Graham Low
1999    Metaphor. State of the art survey. *Language Teaching* 32: 77–96.
Cermak, Laird S., and Fergus I. M. Craik
1979    *Levels of Processing in Human Memory.* Hillsdale, N.J.: Lawrence Erlbaum.
Charteris-Black, Jonathan
2000    Metaphor and vocabulary teaching in ESP economics. *English for Specific Purposes* 19: 149–65.
2004    *Politicians and Rhetoric: Persuasive Power of Metaphor.* Basingstoke, U.K.: Palgrave MacMillan.
Charteris-Black, Jonathan, and Timothy Ennis
2001    A comparative study of metaphor in Spanish and English financial reporting. *English for Specific Purposes* 20: 249–66.
Charteris-Black, Jonathan, and Andreas Musolff
2003    'Battered hero' or 'innocent victim'? A comparative study of metaphors for euro trading in British and German financial reporting. *English for Specific Purposes* 22: 153–176.

Chilton, Paul
1987    Metaphor, euphemism and the militarization of language. *Current Research on Peace and Violence* 10: 7–17.
1996    *Security Metaphors. Cold War Discourse from Containment to Common House.* New York: Peter Lang.
2002    Do something! Conceptualising responses to the attacks of 11 September 2001. *Journal of Language and Politics* 1: 181–195.
2004    *Analysing Political Discourse: Theory and Practice.* London/New York: Routledge (Taylor and Francis).
2005    Manipulation, memes and metaphors: The case of 'Mein Kampf'. In *Perspectives on Manipulation and Ideologies: Theoretical Aspect*, Louis de Saussure and Peter Schulz (eds.), Amsterdam/Philadelphia: Benjamins.
Chilton, Paul, and Mikhail Ilyin
1993    Metaphor in political discourse: The case of the 'Common European House'. *Discourse and Society* 4: 7–31.
Chilton, Paul, and George Lakoff
1995    Foreign policy by metaphor. In *Language and Peace*, Christina Schäffner, and Anita. L. Wenden (eds.), 37–59. Dartmouth, U.K.: Aldershot.
Chung, Siaw Fong, Kathleen Ahrens, and Chu-Ren Huang
2003    ECONOMY IS A TRANSPORTATION DEVICE: Contrastive representation of source domain knowledge in English and Chinese. *Proceedings of the Special Session of UONLP, 2003 International Conference on Natural Language Processing and Knowledge Engineering (NLP-KE), Beijing.* Taipei: Association for Computational Linguistics and Chinese Language Processing.
2003    ECONOMY IS A PERSON: A Chinese-English corpora- and ontological-based comparison using the conceptual mapping model. *Proceedings of the 15th ROCLING Conference, Tsing-Hwa University, Taiwan of China.* Taipei: Association for Computational Linguistics and Chinese Language Processing.
Cienki, Alan J.
2004    Bush's and Gore's language and gestures in the 2000 US presidential debates: A test case for two models of metaphors. *Journal of Language and Politics* 3: 409–440.
Clark, James M., and Allan Paivio
1991    Dual coding theory and education. *Educational Psychology Review* 3: 233–262.
Cohen, Gillian, Michael W. Eysenck, and Martin E. LeVoi
1986    *Memory: A Cognitive Approach.* Milton Keynes: Open University Press.
Condon, Nora, and Peter Kelly
2002    Does cognitive linguistics have anything to offer English language learners in their efforts to master phrasal verbs? *ITL Review of Applied Linguistics* 137/138: 205–231.

Coppieters, René
1987    Competence differences between native and near-native speakers. *Language* 63 (3): 544–73.
Croft, William
2001    *Radical Construction Grammar: Syntactic Theory from a Typological Perspective.* Oxford: Oxford University Press.
Csabí, Szilvia
2004    A cognitive linguistic view of polysemy in English and its implications for teaching. In *Cognitive Linguistics, Second Language Acquisition, and Foreign Language Teaching*, Michel Achard, and Susanne Niemeier (eds.), 233–256. (Studies on Language Acquisition 18.) Berlin/New York: Mouton de Gruyter.
Danesi, Marcel
1995    Learning and teaching languages: the role of 'conceptual fluency'. *International Journal of Applied Linguistics* 5: 3–20.
Da Silva, Augusto Soares
2003    Image schemas and category coherence: The case of the Portuguese verb *deixar*. In *Cognitive Approaches to Lexical Semantics*, Hubert Cuyckens, René Dirven, and John R. Taylor (eds.), 281–322. (Cognitive Linguistics Research 23.) Berlin/New York: Mouton de Gruyter.
De Knop, Sabine, Antoon De Rijcker, Birgitta Meex, and Tanja Mortelmans (eds.)
in preparation *Pedagogical Grammar.* (Applications of Cognitive Linguistics.) Berlin/New York: Mouton de Gruyter.
Deignan, Alice
2003    Metaphorical expressions and culture: An indirect link. *Metaphor and Symbol* 18: 255–271.
Deignan, Alice, Danuta Gabrys, and Agnieszka Solska
1997    Teaching English metaphors using cross-linguistic awareness-raising activities. *ELT Journal* 51: 352–360.
Dewell, Robert
1994    *Over* again: Image-schema transformations in semantic analysis. *Cognitive Linguistics* 5: 451–80.
Dirven, René
1989    Cognitive linguistics and pedagogic grammar. In *Linguistic Theorizing and Grammar Writing,* Gerhard Leitner, and Gottfried Graustein (eds.), 56–75. Tübingen: Max Niemeyer.
2001    English phrasal verbs: Theory and didactic application. In *Applied Cognitive Linguistics II: Language Pedagogy*, Martin Pütz, Susanne Niemeier, and René Dirven (eds.), 3–27. (Cognitive Linguistics Research 19b.) Berlin/NewYork: Mouton de Gruyter.
Dirven, René, and John R. Taylor
1994    English modality: A cognitive-didactic approach. In *Perspectives on English. Studies in Honour of Professor Emma Vorlat,* Keith Carlon, Kristin Davidse, and Brygida Rudzka-Ostyn (eds.). 542–556. Leuven/Paris: Peeters.

Ellis, Nick
1998    Emergentism, connectionism and language learning. *Language Learning* 48: 631–664.
2002    Frequency effects in language processing. A review with implications for theories of implicit and explicit language acquisition. *Studies in Second Language Acquisition* 24: 143–188.
Eubanks, Philip
2000    *A War of Words in the Discourse of Trade: The Rhetorical Constitution of Metaphor.* Carbondale, Ill.: Southern Illinois University Press.
Evans, Vyvyan, and Andrea Tyler
2004    Spatial experience, lexical structure and motivation: the case of *in*. In *Studies in Linguistic Motivation*, Günter Radden, and Klaus-Uwe Panther (eds.), 157–192. (Cognitive Linguistics Research 28.) Berlin/ New York: Mouton de Gruyter:
forthcoming Applying cognitive linguistics to pedagogical grammar: The English prepositions of verticality. *The Brazilian Journal of Applied Linguistics.*
Fisher, Olga
1999    On the role played by iconicity in grammaticalisation processes. In *Form Miming Meaning: Iconicity in Language and Literature*, Max Nänny, and Olga Fisher (eds.), Amsterdam/Philadelphia: Benjamins.
Flower, John
2002    *Phrasal Verb Organiser.* Boston, MA: Thomson Heinle.
Gibbs, Raymond W.
1994    *The Poetics of Mind: Figurative Thought, Language and Understanding.* Cambridge: Cambridge University Press
Goddard, Cliff
2000    Communicative style and cultural values: cultural scripts of Malay (*Bahasa Melayu*). *Anthropological Linguistics* 42: 81–106.
2004    'Cultural scripts': A new medium for ethnographic instruction. In *Cognitive Linguistics, Second Language Acquisition, and Foreign Language Teaching*, Michael Achard, and Susanne Niemeier (eds.), 143–163. (Studies on Language Acquisition 18.) Berlin/New York: Mouton de Gruyter.
Goldberg, Adele E.
1995    *Constructions: A Construction Grammar Approach to Argument Structure.* Chicago: University of Chicago Press.
Goodale, Malcolm
1998    *Collins Cobuild Phrasal Verb Workbook.* London: Harper Collins Publishers.
Gries, Stefan Th., and Stefanie Wulff
2005    Do foreign language learners also have constructions?: Evidence from priming, sorting, and corpora. In *Annual Review of Cognitive Linguistics 3*, Ruiz de Mendoza, Francisco. J. (ed.), 182–200. Amsterdam/ Philadelphia: Benjamins.

Grundy, Peter
2004    The figure / ground Gestalt and language teaching methodology. In *Cognitive Linguistics, Second Language Acquisition, and Foreign Language Teaching*, Michel Achard, and Susanne Niemeier (eds.), 119–142. (Studies on Language Acquisition 18.) Berlin/New York: Mouton de Gruyter.

Haiman, John
1980    Dictionaries and encyclopaedias. *Lingua* 50: 329–57.

Hannan, Peter
1998    Particles and gravity: Phrasal verbs with *up* and *down*. *Modern English Teacher* 7: 21–27.

Herrera, Honesto, and Michael White
2000    Cognitive linguistics and the language learning process: A case from economics. *Estudios Ingleses de la Universidad Complutense* 8: 55–78.
2002    Business is war or the language of takeovers. In *Pragmatica y Analisis del Discurso. Panorama Actual de la Linguistica Aplicada: Conocimiento, Procesamiento y Uso del Lenguaje, vol. 1*, Mercedes Fornés Guardia., Juan Manuel Molina Valero, and Lorena Perez Hernandez (eds.), 231–239. Rioja, Spain: Universidad de la Rioja.

Holme, Randal
2001    Metaphor, language learning, and affect. *Humanising Language Teaching* 3. www.hltmag.co.uk. Pilgrims.

Howarth, Peter
1998    Phraseology and second language proficiency. *Applied Linguistics* 19: 22–44.

Hüllen, Werner
1992    Kognitive Linguistik – Eine Möglichkeit für den Grammatikunterricht. Ein neuer Vorschlag zur Lösung eines alten Problems. In *Grammatica vivat. Konzepte, Beschreibungen und Analysen zum Thema 'Fremdsprachengrammatik'. In memoriam Hartmut Kleineidam*, Alberto Barrera-Vidal, Manfred Raupach, and Ekkehard Zöfgen (eds.), 15–30. Tübingen: Gunter Narr.

Hunston, Susan
2002    *Corpora in Applied Linguistics*. Cambridge: Cambridge University Press

Irujo, Suzanne
1993    Steering clear: Avoidance in the production of idioms. *International Review of Applied Linguistics* 31: 205–219.

Jäkel, Olaf
2003    Motion metaphorized in the economic domain. In *Motivation in Language (Studies in Honor of Günter Radden)*, Hubert Cuyckens, Thomas Berg, René Dirven, and Klaus-Uwe Panther (eds.), 297–318. Amsterdam/Philadelphia: Benjamins.

James, Carl, and Peter Garrett (eds.)
1995    *Language Awareness in the Classroom*. London: Longman.

Johnson, Mark
1987   *The Body in the Mind: the Bodily Basis of Meaning, Imagination, and Reason.* Chicago/London: University of Chicago Press.
Katz, Albert N.
1983   What does it mean to be a high imager? In *Imagery, Memory and Cognition*, John C. Yuille (ed.), 39–63. Hillsdale, N.J.: Lawrence Erlbaum.
Kellerman, Eric
1978   Giving learners a break: Native language intuitions, a source of predictions about transferability. *Working Papers on Bilingualism*, 15: 59–92.
Koller, Veronika
2002   "A Shotgun Wedding": Co-occurrence of war and marriage metaphors in mergers and acquisitions discourse. *Metaphor and Symbol* 17: 179–203.
2003   Metaphor clusters, metaphor chains: Analyzing the multifunctionality of metaphor in text. *metaphorik (electronic journal)* 5/2003.
2004   Businesswomen and war metaphors: "Possessive, jealous and pugnacious"? *Journal of Sociolinguistics* 8: 3–23.
Kövecses, Zoltán
1986   *Metaphors of Anger, Pride and Love: A Lexical Approach to the Study of Concepts.* Amsterdam/Philadelphia: Benjamins.
2001   A cognitive linguistic view of learning idioms in an FLT context. In *Applied Cognitive Linguistics II: Language Pedagogy*, Martin Pütz, Susanne Niemeier, and René Dirven (eds.), 87–115. (Cognitive Linguistics Research 19b.) Berlin/New York: Mouton de Gruyter.
2005   *Metaphor in Culture: Universality and Variation.* Cambridge: Cambridge University Press.
Kövecses, Zoltán and Peter Szabó
1996   Idioms: A view from Cognitive Semantics. *Applied Linguistics* 17: 326–355.
Kövecses, Zoltán, Mariann Tóth, and Bulcsú Babarci
1996   *A Picture Dictionary of English Idioms.* Budapest: Eötvös University Press.
Kramsch, Claire
1993   *Context and Culture in Language Teaching.* Oxford: Oxford University Press.
Krashen, Stephen D., and Tracy D. Terrell
1983   *The Natural Approach: Language Acquisition in the Classroom.* Hayward, CA: Alemany Press.
Kurtyka, Andrzej
2001   Teaching phrasal verbs: a cognitive approach. In *Applied Cognitive Linguistics II: Language Pedagogy*, Martin Pütz, Susanne Niemeier, and René Dirven (eds.), 29–54. (Cognitive Linguistics Research 19b.) Berlin/New York: Mouton de Gruyter.
Lakoff, George
1987   *Women, Fire and Dangerous Things: What Categories Reveal about the Mind.* Chicago/London: University of Chicago Press.

2002    *Moral Politics: How Liberals and Conservatives Think (2nd edition)*. Chicago: University of Chicago Press.

Lakoff, George, and Mark Johnson

1980    *Metaphors We Live By*. Chicago/London: University of Chicago Press.

Langacker, Ronald W.

1987    *Foundations of Cognitive Grammar, Volume 1: Theoretical Prerequisites*. Stanford: Stanford University Press.

1988    A usage-based model. In *Topics in Cognitive Linguistics*, Brygida Rudzka-Ostyn (ed.), 127–161. Amsterdam/Philadelphia: Benjamins.

1991    *Foundations of Cognitive Grammar, Volume 2: Descriptive Applications*. Stanford: Stanford University Press.

2000    A dynamic usage-based model. In *Usage Based Models of Language*, Michael Barlow, and Suzanne Kemmer (eds.), 1–63. Stanford: CSLI.

2001    Cognitive linguistics, language pedagogy, and the English present tense. In *Applied Cognitive Linguistics I: Theory and Language Acquisition*, Martin Pütz, Susanne Niemeier, and René Dirven (eds.), 3–39. (Cognitive Linguistics Research 19a.) Berlin/New York: Mouton de Gruyter.

2005    Constructions and constructional meaning. Ms. San Diego, University of California.

Lazar, Gillian

1996    Using figurative language to expand students' vocabulary. *ELT Journal* 50: 43–51.

2003    *Meaning and Metaphor: Activities to Practise Figurative Language*. Cambridge: Cambridge University Press.

Lehti-Eklund, Hanna

2003    The grammaticalization of *alltsa* and *saledes*: two Swedish conjuncts revisited. In *Cognitive Approaches to Lexical Semantics*, Hubert Cuyckens, René Dirven, and John R. Taylor (eds.), 123–162. (Cognitive Linguistics Research 23.) Berlin/New York: Mouton de Gruyter.

Lewis, Michael

1997    *Implementing the Lexical Approach*. Hove, UK: LTP.

Li, F. Thomas

2002    The acquisition of metaphorical expressions, idioms, and proverbs by Chinese learners of English: A conceptual metaphor and image schema-based approach. Ph.D. diss., Chinese University of Hong Kong.

Lindner, Susan

1981    *A lexico-semantic analysis of English Verb-particle constructions with UP and OUT*. Ph.D. diss., University of California at San Diego.

Lindstromberg, Seth

1991a   Metaphor and ESP: A ghost in the machine? *English for Specific Purposes* 10: 207–25

1991b   *Get*: Not many meanings. *IRAL* 29: 285–301.

1996    Prepositions: meaning and method. *ELT Journal* 50: 225–236.

1997    *English Prepositions Explained*. Amsterdam/Philadelphia: Benjamins.

1999    Spatial prepositions in three U.K. published general English courses. *Folio* 5: 19–23.

2001a   Preposition entries in UK monolingual learner's dictionaries: Problems and possible solutions. *Applied Linguistics* 22: 79–103.

2001b   Total Physical Response for teaching metaphorical language. *Humanising Language Teaching* 3. www.hltmag.co.uk. Pilgrims.

2001c   Are prepositions really incredibly idiomatic? *Humanising Language Teaching* 3. www.hltmag.co.uk. Pilgrims.

2001d   More about spatial prepositions. *Humanising Language Teaching* 3. www.hltmag.co.uk. Pilgrims.

2002    Sailing expressions. *Humanising Language Teaching* 4. www.hltmag.co. uk. Pilgrims.

Lindstromberg, Seth, and Frank Boers

2005a   Means of mass memorisation of multiword expressions, part one: the power of sounds. *Humanising Language Teaching* 7. www.hltmag.co.uk Pilgrims.

2005b   From movement to metaphor with manner-of-movement verbs. *Applied Linguistics* 26: 241–261.

Littlemore, Jeannette

2001a   Metaphoric competence: a language learning strength of students with a holistic cognitive style? *TESOL Quarterly* 35: 459–491.

2001b   Metaphorical intelligence and foreign language learning. *Humanising Language Teaching* 3. www.hltmag.co.uk. Pilgrims.

2002    Developing metaphor interpretation strategies for students of economics: a case study. *Les Cahier de L'APLIUT* 22: 40–60.

2003    The effect of cultural background on metaphor interpretation. *Metaphor and Symbol* 18: 273–288.

2004a   The misinterpretation of metaphors by international students at a British university: Examples, implications, and possible remedies. *Humanising Language Teaching* 6. www.hltmag.co.uk. Pilgrims.

2004b   Conceptual metaphor as a vehicle for promoting critical thinking skills amongst international students. In *Directions for the Future: Directions in English for Academic Purposes* , Leslie E. Sheldon (ed.), 43–50. Oxford: Peter Lang:

2005    Using corpora to discover figurative extensions of word meaning in the language classroom. *Humanising Language Teaching* 7 www.hltmag.co. uk. Pilgrims.

Littlemore, Jeannette, and Graham Low

2006    *Figurative Thinking and Foreign Language Learning*. Basingstoke, U.K.: Palgrave MacMillan

Low, Graham

1988    On teaching metaphor. *Applied Linguistics* 9: 125–147.

2003    Validating metaphoric models in applied linguistics. *Metaphor and Symbol* 18: 239–254.

Lowie, Wander, and Marjolijn Verspoor
2004    Input versus transfer? The role of frequency and similarity in the ac-
        quisition of L2 prepositions. In *Cognitive Linguistics, Second Language
        Acquisition, and Foreign Language Teaching*, Michael Achard, and Sus-
        anne Niemeier (eds.), 77–94. (Studies on Language Acquisition 18.)
        Berlin/New York: Mouton de Gruyter
MacLennan, Carol H.G.
1994    Metaphors and prototypes in the teaching and learning of grammar
        and vocabulary. *IRAL* 32: 97–110.
Makkai, Adam
1972    *Idiom Structure in English*. The Hague: Mouton.
Meex, Birgitta, and Tanja Mortelmans
2002    Grammatik und Kognition. Deutsch anders gedacht (Grammar and
        cognition: Thinking differently about German (LLBA)). *Germani-
        stische Mitteilungen* 56: 48–66.
Morgan, John, and Mario Rinvolucri
2004    *Vocabulary*. Oxford: Oxford University Press.
Morgan, Pamela S.
1997    Self-presentation in a speech of Newt Gingrich. *Pragmatics* 7: 275–308.
2000    The semantics of an impeachment. In *Language and Ideology. Vol-
        ume II: Descriptive Cognitive Approaches*, René Dirven, Roslyn Frank,
        and Cornelia Ilie (eds.), 77–106. Amsterdam/Philadelphia: Benjamins.
Musolff, Andreas, Christina Schäffner, and Michael Townson (eds.)
1996    *Conceiving of Europe – Unity in Diversity*. Aldershot, U.K.: Dartmouth.
2000    Political imagery of Europe: A house without exit doors? *Journal of
        Multilingual and Multicultural Development* 21: 216–229.
Nattinger, James R., and Jeanette S. DeCarrico
1992    *Lexical Phrases and Language Teaching*. Oxford: Oxford University
        Press.
Niemeier, Susanne
2004    Linguistic and cultural relativity: reconsidered for the foreign language
        classroom. In *Cognitive Linguistics, Second Language Acquisition, and
        Foreign Language Teaching*, Michael Achard and Susanne Niemeier
        (eds.), 95–118. (Studies on Language Acquisition 18.) Berlin/New
        York: Mouton de Gruyter
Niemeier, Susanne, and René Dirven (eds.)
2000    *Evidence for Linguistic Relativity*. Amsterdam/Philadelphia: Benjamins.
Oppenheim, Nancy
2000    The importance of recurrent sequences for non-native speaker fluency
        and cognition. In *Perspectives on Fluency*, Heidi Riggenbach (ed.),
        220–240. Ann Arbor: University of Michigan Press.
Paivio, Alan
1971    *Imagery and Verbal Processes*. New York: Holt, Rinehart & Winston.
1986    *Mental Representations: A Dual Coding Approach*. New York: Oxford
        University Press.

Palmer, Gary
1996    *Toward a Theory of Cultural Linguistics.* Austin: Texas University Press.
Pawley, Andrew, and Frances H. Syder
1983    Two puzzles for linguistic theory: native-like selection and native-like fluency. In *Language and Communication*, Jack C. Richards, and Richard W. Schmidt (eds.), 191–225. London: Longman.
Ponterotto, Diane
1994    Metaphors we can learn by: how insights from cognitive linguistic research can improve the teaching/learning of figurative language. *Forum* 32: 2–7.
Prabhu, Nagore S.
1987    *Second Language Pedagogy.* Oxford: Oxford University Press.
Pütz, Martin, Susanne Niemeier, and René Dirven (eds.)
2001a   *Applied Cognitive Linguistics I: Theory and Language Acquisition.* Berlin/New York: Mouton de Gruyter.
2001b   *Applied Cognitive Linguistics II: Language Pedagogy.* (Cognitive Linguistics Research 19b.) Berlin/New York: Mouton de Gruyter.
Radden, Günter, and Klaus-Uwe Panther
2004    Introduction: reflections on motivation. In *Studies in Linguistic Motivation*, Günter Radden, and Klaus-Uwe Panther (eds.), 1–46. (Cognitive Linguistics Research 28.) Berlin/New York: Mouton de Gruyter:
Radden, Günter, and Klaus-Uwe Panther (eds.)
2004    *Studies in Linguistic Motivation.* (Cognitive Linguistics Research 28.) Berlin/New York: Mouton de Gruyter:
Read, John
2004    Plumbing the depths: how should the construct of vocabulary knowledge be defined? In *Vocabulary in a Second Language: Selection, Acquisition and Testing*, Paul Bogaards, and Batia Laufer (eds.), 209–228. Amsterdam/Philadelphia: Benjamins.
Rice, Sally
1996    Prepositional prototypes. In *The Construal of Space in Language and Thought*, Martin Pütz, and René Dirven (eds.), 135–165. (Cognitive Linguistics Research 8.) Berlin/New York: Mouton de Gruyter.
2003    Growth of a lexical network: Nine English prepositions in acquisition. In *Cognitive Approaches to Lexical Semantics.* Hubert Cuyckens, René Dirven, and John R. Taylor (eds.), 243–260. (Cognitive Linguistics Research 23.) Berlin/New York: Mouton de Gruyter
Riding, Richard, and Stephen Rayner
1998    *Cognitive Styles and Learning Strategies: Understanding Style Differences in Learning and Behaviour.* London: David Fulton Publishers Ltd.
Riggenbach, Heidi (ed.)
2000    *Perspectives on Fluency.* Ann Arbor: University of Michigan Press.
Robins, Shani, and Richard E. Mayer
2000    The metaphorical framing effect: metaphorical reasoning about text-based dilemmas. *Discourse Processes* 30(1): 57–86.

Rohrer, Tim
1995    The metaphorical logic of (political) rape: The new wor(l)d order. *Metaphor and Symbolic Activity* 10: 115–137.

Rudzka-Ostyn, Brygida
1983    Cognitive Grammar and the structure of Dutch *uit* and Polish *wy*. Trier: LAUT (Linguistics Agency of the University of Trier) Series A 109.
2003    *Word Power: Phrasal Verbs and Compounds. A Cognitive Approach*. Berlin/New York: Mouton de Gruyter.

Rudzka-Ostyn, Brygida, Paul Ostyn, Pierre Godin, and Francis Degreef
1991    *Woordkunst. Une Synthèse Cognitive et Communicative du Lexique de Base du Néerlandais*. Brussels: Plantyn.

Rundell, Michael
2001    Cats, conversations, and metaphor. *Humanising Language Teaching*, 3. www.hltmag.co.uk. Pilgrims.
2002    Metaphorically speaking. *English Teaching Professional* 23: 21.
2005a    Why are phrasal verbs so difficult? *Humanising Language Teaching*, 7. www.hltmag.co.uk. Pilgrims.

Rundell, Michael (ed.)
2005b    *Macmillan Phrasal Verbs Plus*. Hampshire: Macmillan.

Salager-Meyer, Francoise
1990    Metaphors in medical English prose: A comparative study with French and Spanish. *English for Specific Purposes* 9: 145–59.

Sandra, Dominiek, and Sally Rice
1995    Network analyses of prepositional meaning: Mirroring whose mind – the linguist's or the language user's? *Cognitive Linguistics* 6: 89–130.

Schäffner, Christina
1991    Zur Rolle von Metaphern für die Interpretation der aussersprachlichen Wirklichkeit. *Folia Linguistica* 25: 75–90.
1995    Metapher als Bezeichnungsübertragung?. In *Wort und Wortschatz: Beiträge zur Lexikologie*, Inge Pohl, and Horst Ehrhardt (eds.), 175–184. Tubingen: Max Niemeyer.
1996    Building a European house? Or at two speeds into a dead end? Metaphors in the debate on the United Europe. In *Conceiving of Europe – Unity in Diversity*, Andreas Musolff, Christina Schäffner, and Michael Townson (eds.), 31–59. Aldershot, U.K.: Dartmouth.

Schmitt, Norbert
1997    Vocabulary learning strategies. In *Vocabulary: Description, Acquisition and Pedagogy*, Norbert Schmitt, and Michael McCarthy (eds.), 199–236. Cambridge: Cambridge University Press.

Schmitt, Norbert (ed.)
2004    *Formulaic Sequences: Acquisition, Processing and Use*. Amsterdam/ Philadelphia: Benjamins.

Scott, Mike
1994    Metaphors and language awareness. In *Reflections on Language Learning*, Leila Barbara, and Mike Scott (eds.), 89–104. Clevedon, U.K.: Multilingual Matters.

Segalowitz, Norman
2000    Automaticity and attentional skill in fluent performance. In *Perspectives on Fluency,* Heidi Riggenbach (ed.), 200–219. Ann Arbor: University of Michigan Press.
Sinclair, John
1991    *Corpus, Concordance, Collocation.* Oxford: Oxford University Press.
Skehan, Peter
1998    *A Cognitive Approach to Language Learning.* Oxford: Oxford University Press.
Skoufaki, Sophia
2005    Use of conceptual metaphors: A strategy for the guessing of an idiom's meaning? In *Selected Papers on Theoretical and Applied Linguistics from the 16th International Symposium, April 11–13, 2003,* Marina Mattheoudakis, and Angeliki Psaltou-Joycey (eds.), 542–556. Thessaloniki: Aristotle University of Thessaloniki.
Sökmen, Anita J.
1997    Current trends in teaching second language vocabulary. In *Vocabulary: Description, Acquisition and Pedagogy,* Norbert Schmitt, and M. McCarthy (eds.), 237–257. Cambridge: Cambridge University Press.
Speake, Jennifer (ed.)
1999    *Oxford Dictionary of Idioms.* Oxford: Oxford University Press.
Squire, Larry R., and Eric R. Kandel
2000    *Memory: From Mind to Molecules.* New York: Scientific American Library.
Stengers, Hélène, June Eyckmans, Arnout Horemans, and Frank Boers
2004    Idiom Teacher: Problems in designing a CALL package. *Humanising Language Teaching* 6. www.hltmag.co.uk. Pilgrims.
Stengers, Hélène, Frank Boers, and June Eyckmans
2005    Putting memory theories to the test with an on-line instrument for teaching idioms. Paper presented at *The many faces of phraseology conference,* Louvain-la-Neuve, Belgium: Université Catholique de Louvain-la-Neuve.
Stevick, Earl
1986    *Images and Options in the Language Classroom.* Cambridge: Cambridge University Press.
Sweetser, Eve
1990    *From Etymology to Pragmatics: Metaphorical and Cultural Aspects of Semantic Structure.* Cambridge: Cambridge University Press.
Taylor, John R.
1988    Contrasting prepositional categories: English and Italian. In *Topics in Cognitive Linguistics,* Brygida Ruzdka-Ostyn (ed.), 299–326. Amsterdam/Philadelphia: Benjamins.
1993    Some pedagogical implications of cognitive linguistics. In *Conceptualizations and Mental Processing in Language. A Selection of Papers from the First International Cognitive Linguistics Conference in Duisburg,*

*1989*, Richard A. Geiger, and Brygida. Rudzka-Ostyn (eds.), 201–223. Berlin/New York: Mouton de Gruyter.

2002     *Cognitive Grammar.* Oxford: Oxford University Press.

2004     The ecology of constructions. In *Studies in Linguistic Motivation*, Günter Radden, and Klaus-Uwe Panther (eds.), 49–74. (Cognitive Linguistics Research 28.) Berlin/New York: Mouton de Gruyter

Tomasello, Michael

2000     Do young children have adult syntactic competence? *Cognition* 74: 209–253.

Traugott, Elisabeth, and Richard Dasher

2002     *Regularity in Semantic Change.* Cambridge: Cambridge University Press

Tuggy, David

2003     The Nawatl verb *kisa*: a case study in polysemy. In *Cognitive Approaches to Lexical Semantics.*, Hubert Cuyckens, René Dirven, and JohnR. Taylor (eds.), 323–362. (Cognitive Linguistics Research 23.) Berlin/New York: Mouton de Gruyter.

Turewicz, Kamila

2000     *Applicability of Cognitive Grammar as a Foundation of Pedagogical/Reference Grammar.* Lódz: Wydawnictwo Uniwersytetu Lodzkiego.

Tyler, Andrea, and Vyvyan Evans

2003     *The Semantics of English Prepositions: Spatial, Embodied Meaning and Cognition.* Cambridge: Cambridge University Press.

2004     Applying cognitive linguistics to pedagogical grammar: the case of *over*. In *Cognitive Linguistics, Second Language Acquisition, and Foreign Language Teaching*, Michael Achard, and Susanne Niemeier (eds.), 257–280. (Studies on Language Acquisition 18.) Berlin/New York: Mouton de Gruyter

Vermeer, Anne

2001     Breadth and depth of vocabulary in relation to L1/L2 acquisition and frequency of input. *Applied Psycholinguistics* 22: 217–234.

Verspoor, Marjolijn, and Wander Lowie

2003     Making sense of polysemous words. *Language Learning* 53: 547–586.

Wierzbicka, Anna

1996     *Semantics, Primes and Universals.* Oxford: Oxford University Press.

1997     *Understanding Cultures through their Keywords.* Oxford: Oxford University Press.

White, Michael

1999     The Bundesbank and the making of an economic press story. *Anglistik und Englischunterricht* 62: 107–128.

2003     Metaphor and economics: The case of growth. *English for Specific Purposes* 22: 131–151.

White, Michael, and Honesto Herrera

2003     Metaphor and ideology in the press coverage of telecom corporate consolidations. In *Cognitive Models in Language and Thought: Ideologies,*

*Metaphors, and Meanings*, René Dirven, Roslyn Frank, and Martin Pütz (eds.), 277–323. Berlin/New York: Mouton de Gruyter

Wray, Alison
2002    *Formulaic Language and the Lexicon*. Cambridge: Cambridge University Press

Wright, Jon
2002    *The Idioms Organiser*. Boston: Thomson Heinle.

# Part five: Verbal and beyond: Vision and imagination

# Visual communication: Signed language and cognition

## Terry Janzen

*Abstract*

Signed languages are articulated with gestures of the hands and face in an articulation space that is visible to the addressee. In many ways, signed languages and spoken languages pattern similarly, although the phonemic material of each is rather obviously radically different. Evidence has been mounting in cognitive linguistic research that while human, embodied conceptual structures and domains are expressed in linguistic structure across both spoken and signed languages, the articulation system of signed language enables a higher level of iconic relationship between the conceptual world and linguistic expression. This plays out in numerous ways, including the appearance of iconic relationships at all levels of grammar and discourse, in metonymic and metaphoric relationships, and in so-called simultaneous constructions that include body partitioning, in which various parts of the signer's body represent different entities simultaneously, and the expression of shifting points of view in discourse. In signed languages, visible articulation is particularly suited to the mapping between conceptual structure and linguistic expression because in both action schemas and visible attributes, visual imagery is highly salient, and the hands and bodies of signers are well-suited to reflecting this imagery iconically.

*Keywords*: signed language; gesture; iconicity; metaphor; simultaneity; visible articulation

## 1. Introduction[1]

Signed languages are the primary languages of Deaf communities around the world. They are primary in the sense that they are not alternate means of representing spoken language, but evolve within the community of users without much regard to the spoken language of the surrounding "hearing" community. The first linguistic research on American Sign Language (ASL) appeared in the mid-twentieth century, describing the signs that Deaf people were making as full-fledged linguistic units rather than holistic, unprincipled gestures as once assumed. William Stokoe and his colleagues (Stokoe 1960; Stokoe, Casterline and Croneberg 1965) demonstrated that signs were built along organizing principles in ways not so different from the words of spoken languages. In the years that followed, linguists investigating signed languages sought to show that despite not having sound-based phonemic systems, they were indeed languages. In some cases this notion has been met with skepticism, but the more we have learned about both signed and spoken languages structurally, functionally, and with regard to their representation of cognitive domains, the clearer it has become that signed languages are no less complex linguistic systems, even though they are entirely visual. It means that language has more than one articulation option, and this has drawn the attention of cognitive linguists interested in how conceptual structure maps onto linguistic structure.

This chapter highlights some of the current research and findings in the area of cognitive linguistics and signed languages. In section 2 we look at what visual perception of language means for an articulation system, which forms the basis for the discussion in the remaining sections. Some aspects of the relation between gesture and signs are explored in section 3, in particular a discontinuous versus a continuous view of these domains. In section 4 the many facets of iconic representation are discussed, including a proposal for cognitive iconicity grounded in the theory of cognitive grammar. A brief discussion of metaphor and metonymy takes up section 5, and in section 6, simultaneous constructions in the grammars of signed languages are examined along with body partitioning and blended spaces and as well the embodied expression of point of view. A brief conclusion is given in section 7.

## 2.  Visible articulation

In the late 1950s and early 1960s William Stokoe presented evidence that, far from being holistic, non-linguistic gestures, the signs that Deaf people articulated with their hands and used with each other patterned in ways analogous to the words of spoken languages (Stokoe 1960; Stokoe, Casterline and Croneberg 1965). Of particular relevance was the analysis of individual signs as resulting from the combination of definable elements that belonged to a restricted number of categories, those of handshapes, locations (i.e., points of contact or positions in space), and movement types. These were thought to combine in arbitrary ways in much the same way as do the arbitrary sounds that together make up spoken words. Over the next number of years much effort was subsequently expended producing evidence that not only did individual signs conform to the organizing principles of linguistic material, despite the obvious difference in means of articulation, but so too did constructions larger than the word. Phrase structure and sentence-level organization were thought to pattern no differently from that of spoken languages. At the level of articulation, however, differences between signed and spoken languages are profound.

A second crucial difference is that signed languages are seen and not heard. The reception of linguistic structure visually has numerous consequences for those structures, some specifics of which are the subject of this chapter, for example various iconic structures (section 4 below), structures with multiple, simultaneously articulated elements (section 6), and body partitioning and perspective coding constructions (section 6.1). In the absence of the ability to perceive language as sound, Deaf communities worldwide have developed signed languages that are not substitutes for spoken languages, that is, they are not visual versions of spoken languages but have evolved to take advantage of the complementary properties of both vision and the physiology of the human body (Armstrong, Stokoe and Wilcox 1995). One advantage of vision over hearing for language reception is that many aspects of a visual stimulus such as a motor action can be perceived simultaneously without compromising the perception of the signal as a whole. As a non-linguistic example, when we watch someone jump to catch a ball, we can see (among other things) the person's legs bend and then extend to propel him into the air, the arms reaching toward the ball, and the ball arching toward the person all as simultaneous actions, and we create an action schema for what the combined set of actions mean. In a visible linguistic sequence, we may see a person's two hands, each having a distinct, albeit changing shape configuration, moving independently through space, perhaps colliding, along with some particular facial gestures and intentionally directed eye gaze. The ability to manipulate parts of the body simultaneously in this way and to perceive and process visible components in such combinations has a profound effect on how linguistic constructions can be composed. For several decades researchers have maintained that the most significant differences between signed and spoken languages are found at the phonetic level whereas at higher levels of organization the differences all but disappear (Brentari 1998). However, we are now seeing evidence that highly complex morphological and syntactic constructions may also show some unique patterning unlike what is attested for spoken languages (cf. Meier 2002). One major consequence of the features of signed language articulation combined with visual perception is that semantic categories can at times be much more gradient than is the case for spoken language (Talmy 2003, 2006). Talmy suggests that this is what takes place within the classifier systems of signed languages, where the hands as objects move about the signer's articulation space as representations of objects and their relationships in some actual space.

Describing the linguistic system of a signed language has not been without its problems. Stokoe and his colleagues (1965) delineated categories of phonemic units[2] that were understood to be finite sets of meaningless parts – handshapes, locations, and movements – that combined to create meaningful words, as duality of patterning has always maintained is the case in spoken language. But more recent work (e.g., Brentari 1998; Liddell 1984, 2003; Liddell and Johnson 1989) has suggested that these fairly simple categories are not entirely comparable to the phonemes of spoken languages. Rather, some elements such as handshape and location are better understood as features of timing units and, in certain cases, movement features are often transitional and epiphenomenal. The distinction between what is gestural and what is linguistic can be difficult to determine; locations that are not contact points on the body have been argued to be gestural rather than purely linguistic (Liddell 2003). At higher levels of grammar, descriptive problems also arise. For example, in complex morphological forms each hand may contribute a meaningful unit distinct from the other, and further, meaning bearing facial gestures may co-occur. It is usually the case that such facial gestures constitute bound morphology (Janzen 2004b; Wilcox 2004a), but how such morphology is structurally bound to the "root" articulated by the hands is unclear. A further difficulty arises when each of the two hands articulates a different root, such as in classifier-based verb complexes. In many such cases, the two hands refer to two distinct entities involved together in some event, for example as agent and patient nominals, but whether they should be considered as separate morphological units or as parts of a larger, single complex is uncertain (Janzen, to appear).

Visible articulation means that the hands and body form signs that symbolize concepts in the human mind. As we will see in the discussion below, a visual orientation to one's world of experience, which includes experiencing linguistic form, allows for the signer to map the conceptualization of events and space onto a visible articulation space. It should be no surprise, then, that the potential for iconic relationships is high: what is conceptualized in the mind and what is symbolized in articulation can be closely aligned. Wilcox (2004a) notes that the hands as physical objects in space can be manipulated by the signer to reflect features of objects and actions in the conceptualized world. The physiology of the hand also lends itself to iconic mapping: closed fists are dense, bulky objects while flat hands have wide, flat surfaces, etc. (see Wilcox 2004a for discussion of the hand as an object; see also Talmy 2003, 2006; Taub 2001). So too, the hand can move along paths through space like many objects do. Thus if signed language users co-opt this visually oriented articulation system, they make use of what these articulators do best. This is both unremarkable and remarkable. It is unremarkable because what else might we expect? And yet it is remarkable in that it exemplifies humans' creativity and ingenuity in producing language despite the unavailability of auditory perception.

Signed languages would be sufficiently of interest if these iconic mappings formed the extent of the relationship between the conceptualized world and a signer's symbolic representation of it in language structure, but as a number of cognitivist studies have uncovered, such iconic underpinnings appear to be the basis of highly abstract metaphoric and metonymic expressions, discussed in some detail in section 5 below. Metaphorically we see, for example, the visual dimension of space, not just referred to in arbitrary terms as we've come to expect in spoken language, but physically "demonstrated" in the signer's visible articulation space as the source domain for concepts of time. Space is portioned out, that is, to stand for similarly apportioned time. In a visual articulation system, language users can "look at" time just as they look at space.

## 3. From gesture to sign

The relationship between gesture and signs can be approached from several angles. In evolutionary terms it has been argued that gesture has played a crucial role in the development of all language (e.g., Armstrong, Stokoe and Wilcox 1995; Corballis 2002; Wilcox 2002). Regarding the relationship between gesture and speech, there is evidence that the two are an integrated system (Kendon 2004; McNeill 1992), which begs the question of whether a similar integration is possible for gesture and signed languages. Emmorey (1999) argues that it is clear that signers do gesture, but because the medium is the same (hands, generally), gestures and linguistic material do not occur simultaneously. Sandler (2006) shows that in Israeli Sign Language a modality "switch" takes place: because the hands are occupied with linguistic expression, gestures are simultaneously found on the mouth.

3.1. Continuous and discontinuous views on gesture and sign

One of the most critical concerns regarding the question of sign and gesture integration is whether the two are seen as fundamentally different or not, in other words, from a discontinuous or continuous point of view. In a discontinuous view, what is gesture is not sign, and what is sign is not gesture, a principle fundamental to both Emmorey's (1999) and Sandler's (2006) work. A hallmark study along this view is Singleton, Goldin-Meadow, and McNeill (1995) which claims a discontinuity between gestures that occur with speech and those that occur in the absence of speech, the second of which can rapidly become more language-like when compared to actual signed language material. This does not mean, however, that gesture and lexical material cannot be produced together in a single stream. Sandler's claim of reversed modality suggests the potential for an equally simultaneous production of language and gesture. Liddell (2003) argues that the location parameter of third person indexical pronouns is gestural rather than linguistic, by which he means that in a single sign, certain elements are definable in the phonology and others are not. In Liddell's analysis of pronouns the gestural component and linguistic component are combined in a single item. Liddell's reasoning is that in ASL pronouns are realized as points, with the extended index finger either pointing toward an existing item in the signer's real space, or to a conceptually positioned item in an imaginary space, what Liddell refers to as either "surrogate space" or "token space". In surrogate space, for example, an absent referent is conceptualized as occupying a space near the signer as a life-size entity that can be pointed to, described, etc. The structure of the indexical pronoun is in part linguistic: the hand configuration and movement features of the sign can be specified and constrained, but the location feature cannot be. A pronoun in ASL can move toward any location point in the entire articulation space depending on either the actual location or conceptualized location of the referent, so location must remain unspecified for the pronoun, and is in this sense necessarily gestural.

Studies that view gesture and signed language from a continuous perspective are less inclined to maintain a divide between what is gestural and what is linguistic. Here the interesting question regards how gestural and linguistic material coincide and perhaps even overlap. Because the medium is much the same, what is gestural may *also be* linguistic. Wilcox (2004b) takes the view, based on gestural accounts of phonology (following Browman and Goldstein 1989) and the notion that pragmatically, words are also gestures (Janney 1999), that to attempt to distinguish between what is gesture and what is within a signed language system does not lead us in the right direction. Continuous accounts (e.g., Armstrong, Stokoe and Wilcox 1995; Janzen and Shaffer 2002; Wilcox 2002, 2004b) suggest generally that what originates as gestural eventually regularizes and conventionalizes as lexical or grammatical items (cf. Haiman 1994) but that the transition from gesture to language is not abrupt. In grammaticization terms, overlap may occur, so that different senses and functions of an item co-occur in usage simultaneously (Hopper 1991). In the case of the development of signs and grammatical morphemes in a signed language, this overlap may mean that an item that has been regularized into the linguistic system may still be present as a gesture. To cite one example, Janzen (1998a, 1999) and Janzen and Shaffer (2002) propose that both yes/no question and topic marking morphology in ASL developed out of a more generalized questioning gesture that includes a facial expression with the eyebrows raised. While this facial feature is required by the grammar in these constructions, it is the case that raising the eyebrows as a questioning gesture occurs frequently for both hearing and Deaf people in North America and elsewhere.

## 4.   Iconic signs and iconic structure

A striking feature of words in signed languages is that many are iconic in form. It would be a mistake, however, to assume that signed languages are emblematic. Iconicity in signed language does not mean that the relation between form and meaning is transparent. Klima and Bellugi (1979) show for ASL, and Pizzuto and Volterra (2000) for Italian Sign Language, that non-signers are not very good at guessing meanings even of highly iconic forms. Iconicity in signed languages has been described at virtually every level of grammar. At a level that is normally understood as phonological, that is, where we find meaningless units which combine to form morphological units, there are features that are undeniably iconic, which has caused uncertainties as to whether some aspects of signs should be categorized as phonemic or even sub-phonemic features on one hand, or meaning-bearing morphemes on the other. Classifier constructions in signed languages have long allowed for meaningful single handshapes, for example a single upright extended index finger as a "person" classifier, which van der Hulst and Mills (1996) argue is unproblematic because such a unit can be morphological in classifier environments but phonetic in others, akin to /s/ in English where it is phonetic in *stop* but morphological in *tops*. But even in lexical items in ASL we find handshapes that are quite obviously iconic, and thus they bring a certain amount of meaning to the composite word. The verb MEET, for example, uses extended upright index fingers, and the noun BOOK has two flat /B/ handshapes that iconically represent the flatness of book pages. Janzen (1998b) suggests that in the verb UNDERSTAND, which involves a handshape change from a closed fist (/S/) to an extended index finger (/1/), the initial closed fist handshape metaphorically represents a "closed" state of not (yet) understanding and the final extended index finger handshape represents the realized state of subsequently having understood. Note that Wilcox (2000) describes numerous instances in which an idea or thought is metaphorically represented by a /1/ handshape.

Iconicity abounds at higher levels as well. Morphological categories associated with verbs are often tightly bound to verb forms, such as aspect and agreement morphemes that alter the movement path and the beginning and endpoint locations of the path respectively. At the sentence level, ASL and many other signed languages use topic-comment constructions that iconically represent known information first, new information second (Ingram 1978; Janzen 1998a). Shaffer (2004) demonstrates that modal verbs are positioned pre-verbally when their scope is just the action coded by the verb, and clause-final when the entire proposition is under their scope. Even at the discourse level, Winston (1995) for example shows that space is used iconically as a visual representation of items being compared even if the items are highly abstract concepts, and Sallandre (2006) reports that in French Sign Language (LSF) narratives, the iconic use of space serves an organizing function for the narrative events because three-dimensional articulation space "preserves" a three-dimensional real-world event. In fact, the iconic representation of spatial elements has been described in some detail, for example in Emmorey (2002) for ASL and in Engberg-Pedersen (1993) for Danish Sign Language. Talmy (2003, 2006) lists some thirty spatial categories that may be represented in the linguistic structure of signed languages, many of which are combinable in, for example, classifier constructions. Talmy concludes that the iconicity available in a signed language in terms of how space is represented in linguistic form is much greater than for spoken language because there is virtually no way to represent space structurally with the vocal apparatus.

Taub (2001) gives an inventory of iconic categories in ASL that includes, in part, form-meaning relationships in shape (i.e., a handshape or the path that the hand takes represents the shape of a referent), movements, locations as representing locations in mental spaces, size, number, and temporal ordering. Taub defines iconicity as "not an objective relationship between image and referent; rather, it is a relationship between our mental models of image and referent" (Taub 2001: 19) and as "the existence of a structure-preserving mapping between mental models of linguistic form and meaning" (2001: 23). Such relationships are largely motivated by our embodied human experiences. Taub claims that references (or sources) in iconic structures are much more abundant in the visual, as opposed to auditory, modality of signed language, leading to an abundance of iconic structures in these languages as opposed to spoken languages: "Thus, users of a visual/gestural language will be able to draw on a far wider range of sensory images than will users of aural/oral languages. A much greater percentage of the language's concepts have the potential for iconic representation" (2001: 61). In comparing the prevalence of iconic structures in signed versus spoken languages, Taub says that it is "a consequence of the fact that most phenomena do not have a characteristic noise to be used in motivating a linguistic form [in spoken languages]" (2001: 3). I would suggest, however, that it is not so much a characteristic noise but that, in our observation of, or interaction with, an object or event, it is the *saliency* of a sound associated with the item that might spark a linguistic string naming the item to be iconic. As sound salience increases for spoken language users, imagic iconicity (Haiman 1980) emerges. Taub uses the example of *crash*, suggesting that the forceful impact of one object on another is one concept that has a characteristic sound, and thus we choose (in English) an iconic word that resembles this characteristic sound. But here we might say that the sound of such physical impact is highly salient (but not "characteristic") in our experience of the event. Saliency in this respect is scalar: the more salient a sound is to our experience, the more likely it is that we might choose an iconic symbol for it.

Much about our embodied experience in the world is visual, thus we might say that visual aspects of what we experience are often highly salient. So for a language with visible articulation, the visual imaging that translates into iconic structure takes two general forms: action schemas and visible attributes. But once again, this can extend to highly abstract notions metaphorically (cf. Johnson 1987 on "image schemas"). Fictive motion, for example, refers to expressions that represent a movement in the conceptual domain where none actually exists in the real world (Wilcox 2003). Wilcox describes such expressions in signed language where a movement is iconically associated with a source domain that does not itself move. The ASL sign ALWAYS has a large circular movement path that represents, according to Wilcox, un-ending or imperfective time. Wilcox also cites Shaffer's (2002) analysis of CAN'T in ASL, which she describes as articulated action on one hand that encounters a stationary barrier articulated by the other. Of interest is that these examples have an iconic property that relates linguistic form to conceptualized form and not real-world form because no real-world form exists.

## 4.1. Cognitive iconicity

Wilcox (2004a) proposes a novel view of iconicity, referred to as "cognitive iconicity", which Wilcox defines "not as a relation between the form of a sign and what it refers to in the real world, but as a relation between two conceptual spaces. Cognitive iconicity is a distance relation between the phonological and semantic poles of symbolic structures" (2004a: 122). In much of language, the phonological pole and semantic pole of symbolic structure, both conceptual entities, reside in very different regions of conceptual space. When this is the case, the linguistic item has no formal resemblance to its meaning. However, if the two poles are in close proximity, it means that the conceptualizer construes the two as largely similar in some iconic way. Wilcox uses the example of the ASL sign SLOW, which can be tempered to mean VERY-SLOW. The phonological pole for SLOW includes a slowly articulated path movement, but for VERY-SLOW, the movement increases in speed and intensity so as to quickly reach its final ending point. Items such as this have long been considered examples of a general principle of historical change from iconic to arbitrary in the lexicon of signed language (Frishberg 1975) in which the iconicity seen in the lexical word is submerged when it appears in a grammatical structure (Klima and Bellugi 1979), but Wilcox argues that while certain iconic properties may submerge when individual items are inserted into grammatical constructions, others emerge. For VERY-SLOW, the increased intensity in the movement iconically represents the conceptualized notion of intensity which may be applied to a host of adverbs and adjectives. The difference between SLOW and VERY-SLOW is a difference in what is profiled, either slowness or the intensity of the attribute. The super-imposition of pervasive iconic structures has also been noted in French Sign Language and are central to Sallandre and Cuxac's (2002) theory of the organization of signed language grammar.

## 5. Metaphor and metonymy

Until very recently, metaphoric and metonymic expressions were not thought to be particularly common in signed languages. Not, at least, until several cognitively oriented ideas came to the forefront regarding aspects of both spoken and signed language. Works such as Lakoff and Johnson (1980) and Sweetser (1990) opened the door to considering metaphor in everyday speech, and researchers such as Boyes Braem (1981) began to see the benefit in considering iconicity as regularized in signed language. As Phyllis Wilcox (2000) suggests, the shroud of iconicity that threatened to expose signed language as something less than real language was being shed. Both Wilcox (2000) and Taub (2001) seek to chart the many metaphorical domains that have been uncovered in ASL, showing that metaphorical mapping is shared across language modalities.

In her detailed description of metaphor and metonymy that arises in the everyday signing of an uneducated ASL signer, P. Wilcox (2004) demonstrates that these features are not just "poetic", but are used everywhere in the course of human interaction. Wilcox's signer tells of his regrets at being miseducated, thought to be of low mental ability, and yet Wilcox finds his discourse to be rife with metaphors and metonyms. As one rather complex example, the signer conceives of his mind as a computer, with efficient input and output ability. In keeping with visual imagery mapped onto a visible articulation system, the signer maps components of the imagined computer in the space around his own head so that the two (the computer/his head) occupy the same space. Thus aspects of the mind and of the computer combine into a conceptualized blended space. Metonymic items abound here as well: a flat hand projected out from the forehead represents the paper output of a printer; a gestural key turned at the forehead stands in for the process of opening the mind. The relation between iconicity and metaphor is clear in visibly articulated language. The motor action of grasping something physically and grasping something mentally is virtually the same, although the spatial dimension may differ. Iconically, grasping something mental such as a thought or idea means that the action is most likely going to be oriented toward the head.

## 6.    Simultaneity in articulation: the uniqueness of signed language

As mentioned above, signed language users have at their disposal a set of articulators that produce linguistic structure for reception in the visual domain. For some time it has been clear that even though the human body is symmetrical in having two arms and hands, signers do not always do exactly the same thing on both hands together. Some signs, for example, use only one hand. Others use two, in which case the hands may or may not produce the same motor sequence. If both hands move, structural complexity increases depending on what each hand is doing. When each hand does something different, there are constraints on what is possible. In most cases, the constraints apply to the non-dominant hand. If both hands move, for example, the movement and handshape must be identical; if one hand acts on the other, the stationary hand may have a different handshape from that on the hand that moves, but the allowable handshapes form a limited set of about seven "basic" handshapes (Battison 1978). At least, this constraint is imposed when both hands participate in the articulation of single lexical items.

Recently it has been observed that signers are able to produce complexes in which each hand simultaneously contributes something semantically different to the construction, which may turn out to be one of the most sharply distinguishing features between signed and spoken languages. Research on simultaneous constructions has just begun. Instances of such usage have been described along with some attempts to categorize the construction types, but it is not yet clear what constraints on complexity might exist. It appears, however, that simultaneous constructions also represent complex iconic mapping: they are complex structures that symbolize complex events (e.g., about more than one entity or event) and their simultaneous nature iconically represents simultaneously occurring events.

Based on work by Miller (1994), Leeson and Saeed (2004) examine simultaneous constructions in Irish Sign Language (ISL). They find examples in ISL discourse where two lexical items are signed simultaneously, where one lexical item is preserved by retaining a handshape required for that item while something new is signed on the other hand, where a topic is signed and a remnant handshape remains on one hand while a comment is then signed on the other (this may be a further instance of the type listed just previously; Liddell 2003 refers to these remnants as "buoys"), where a locative position for some entity is articulated on one hand while a second locative is iterated on the other, and where a listing strategy is used on one hand (usually the non-dominant hand). All in all, Leeson and Saeed conclude that what these simultaneous construction strategies have in common is that the dominant hand marks foregrounded information while the non-dominant hand marks backgrounded information.

### 6.1. Blended spaces, body partitioning and the expression of point of view

In many types of simultaneously articulated constructions, different parts of the signer's body represent different entities which are described as participating together in a single event. This is the position of Dudis (2004a, 2004b), who terms what is taking place in the signer's articulation as "body partitioning". Dudis shows that in addition to the two hands being able to depict two distinct entities, the face may also participate. In one example from Dudis (2004a: 235) in which a librarian glares at a library patron, the signer's body depicts the patron while the signer's right hand forms the verb STARE-AT, signifying the librarian's gaze toward the patron. But in addition to this, the signer's facial gestures further depict the librarian's expression, while his eye gaze depicts the patron looking back at the librarian by being directed toward the verb articulated on the right hand. The combined result constitutes a blended space conceptually for the signer and addressee and demonstrates the complexity possible within a simultaneously articulated construction. This further suggests that such constructions may be constrained in part by the ability of humans to view and assimilate multiple aspects of visual images cognitively, and when the mode of expression allows it, to articulate this complexity in an iconically simultaneous manner.

The expression of point of view in verb complexes in ASL is similarly complex and exemplifies an iconic relationship between how the signer construes a scene and the use of space. In such cases (Janzen 2004a, 2005, to appear) the signer's own vantage point coincides with some entity's perspective on a scene which may or may not be her own. In one type of construction, the signer mentally rotates her conceptualized space so that others' perspectives align with her own stance and view of the scene, whereas what has typically been described in the literature is the case where the signer shifts in her physical space to align her body with the spatially located position of some other referent. In a mentally rotated space, every point of reference also "rotates". In the narratives that are described in Janzen (2004a, 2005) the signer enacts the utterances and actions of two interacting referents positioned opposite one another and rotates the entire conceptualized space, inviting the addressee to view the scene from one referent's perspective and then the other. The result is that the signer maintains two spaces mentally: each is an arrangement of entities from one of the referent's vantage points. In order to keep track of the signer's spatial referencing, the addressee must understand which viewed space is being referred to at each moment in the discourse.


## 7.  Conclusion

In this discussion I have outlined several aspects of signed language expression that exemplify the visual nature of its articulation and reception. Early descriptions of signed languages concentrated on their organizational similarities with spoken languages, but clearly there are important differences to examine. These differences neither detract from the reality that signed languages are complex linguistic systems nor make them anomalous. Rather, we can learn much about human conceptual organization through the study of signed language because the mapping between conceptual space and articulation space is so often expressly iconic. A cognitively oriented approach to research on signed languages allows us to learn much about human conceptual structures.

What might be future directions for cognitive linguistic research on signed language? Most certainly we are experiencing a resurgence of analyses of iconic relationships between conceptual and linguistic structure, but with the "shroud" lifting, as Phyllis Wilcox so eloquently puts it, perhaps we have yet to see through the veil. Signed languages seem to be the epitome of embodied language: physical and visual – surely there is more to discover here. As well, we have begun to uncover the gestural roots of both lexicon and grammar in signed languages. The gesture-language interface that Wilcox (2002) speaks of is particularly interesting when the medium for both gesture and language is the same. Cognitive linguistics embraces rather than rejects the connection between language and gesture, and so we might expect further enlightening work in this regard. Finally, vision is taking an increasingly prominent role in the description of language structure and language usage altogether. In light of this, language that is purely of a visual nature has much to offer our understanding of the embodied experience of interactions with each other, our environments, and our linguistic expression of that experience.

## Notes

1. There are many colleagues with whom I have had helpful discussions on cognitive linguistics and signed language, but in particular, I am indebted to Sherman Wilcox and Barbara Shaffer for their insights, without which this chapter could not have been written. Any errors, of course, remain my own.
2. Stokoe et al. (1965) refer to these categories as "aspects" and to "cheremes" as opposed to phonemes. Phonologists since Stokoe, however, have tended to retain terminology more widely used in the discipline of phonology.

## References

Armstrong, David F., William C. Stokoe, and Sherman E. Wilcox
1995     *Gesture and the Nature of Language.* Cambridge: Cambridge University Press.
Battison, Robbin
1978     *Lexical Borrowing in American Sign Language.* Silver Spring, MD: Linstok Press.
Brentari, Diane
1998     *A Prosodic Model of Sign Language Phonology.* Cambridge, MA: MIT Press.
Browman, Catherine P., and Louis Goldstein
1989     Articulatory gestures as phonological units. *Phonology* 6: 201–251.
Boyes Braem, Penny
1981     Features of the handshape in American Sign Language. Ph.D. diss., University of California, Berkeley.
Corballis, Michael C.
2002     *From Hand to Mouth: The Origins of Language.* Princeton/Oxford: Princeton University Press.
Dudis, Paul G.
2004a    Body partitioning and real-space blends. *Cognitive Linguistics* 15(2): 223–238.
2004b    Depiction of events in ASL: Conceptual integration of temporal components. Ph.D. diss., University of California, Berkeley.
Emmorey, Karen
1999     Do signers gesture? In *Gesture, Speech, and Sign,* Lynn Messing, and Ruth Campbell (eds.), 133–159. New York: Oxford University Press.
2002     *Language, Cognition, and the Brain: Insights from Sign Language Research.* Mahwah, NJ: Lawrence Erlbaum.
Engberg-Pedersen, Elisabeth
1993     *Space in Danish Sign Language: The Semantics and Morphosyntax of the Use of Space in a Visual Language.* Hamburg: Signum-Verlag.
Frishberg, Nancy
1975     Arbitrariness and iconicity: Historical change in American Sign Language. *Language* 51: 676–710.

Haiman, John
1980    The iconicity of grammar: Isomorphism and motivation. *Language* 56: 514–540.
1994    Ritualization and the development of language. In *Perspectives on Grammaticalization*, William Pagliuca (ed.), 3–28. Amsterdam/Philadelphia: Benjamins.

Hopper, Paul J.
1991    On some principles of grammaticization. In *Approaches to Grammaticalization: Volume 1, Focus on Theoretical and Methodological Issues*, Elizabeth C. Traugott, and Bernd Heine (eds.), 17–35. Amsterdam/ Philadelphia: Benjamins.

Hulst, Harry van der, and Anne Mills
1996    Introduction. Issues in sign linguistics: Phonetics, phonology and morpho-syntax. In *Sign Linguistics: Phonetics, phonology and Morpho-syntax*, Harry van der Hults, and Anne Mills (eds.), *Lingua* (special issue) 98 (1–3): 3–17.

Ingram, Robert M.
1978    Theme, rheme, topic, and comment in the syntax of American Sign Language. *Sign Language Studies* 20: 193–218.

Janney, Richard W.
1999    Words as gestures. *Journal of Pragmatics* 31: 953–972.

Janzen, Terry
1998a   Topicality in ASL: Information ordering, constituent structure, and the function of topic marking. Ph.D. diss., University of New Mexico, Albuquerque, NM.
1998b   Multi-level iconic relationships in American Sign Language grammar. In *Proceedings of the first High Desert Linguistics Society conference, April 3–4, 1998*, Catie Berkenfield, Dawn Nordquist, and Angus Grieve-Smith (eds.), Vol. 1, 159–172. Albuquerque, NM: High Desert Linguistics Society.
1999    The grammaticization of topics in American Sign Language. *Studies in Language* 23 (2): 271–306.
2004a   Space rotation, perspective shift, and verb morphology in ASL. *Cognitive Linguistics* 15 (2): 149–174.
2004b   The expression of grammatical categories in signed languages. Rome, Italy. Lingue verbali e lingue dei segni: Confronti di strutture, construtti e metodologie (Verbal and Signed Languages: Comparing Structures, Constructs and Methodologies). International Colloquium, Università Roma Tre, October 4 – 5, 2004.
2005    Perspective Shift Reflected in the Signer's Use of Space. CDS/CLCS Monograph Number 1. Dublin: Centre for Deaf Studies, University of Dublin, Trinity College.
to appear    Perspective shifts in ASL narratives: The problem of clause structure. In *Language in the Context of Use: Usage-Based Approaches to Language and Language Learning. Selected Papers from Georgetown University*

*Roundtable on Languages and Linguistics 2003,* Andrea Tyler, Yiyoung Kim, and Mari Takada (eds.). Berlin/New York: Mouton de Gruyter.

Janzen, Terry, and Barbara Shaffer
2002 Gesture as the substrate in the process of ASL grammaticization. In *Modality and Structure in Signed and Spoken Languages,* Richard Meier, Kearsy Cormier, and David Quinto-Pozos (eds.), 199–223. Cambridge: Cambridge University Press.

Johnson, Mark
1987 *The Body in the Mind: The Bodily Basis of Meaning, Imagination and Reason.* Chicago: Chicago University Press.

Kendon, Adam
2004 *Gesture: Visible Action as Utterance.* Cambridge: Cambridge University Press.

Klima, Edward S., and Ursula Bellugi
1979 *The Signs of Language.* Cambridge, MA: Harvard University Press.

Lakoff, George, and Mark Johnson
1980 *Metaphors We Live By.* Chicago: The University of Chicago Press.

Leeson, Lorraine, and John I. Saeed
2004 Windowing of attention in simultaneous constructions in Irish Sign Language (ISL). In *Proceedings of the Fifth Annual High Desert Linguistics Society Conference, November 1–2, 2002, University of New Mexico,* Terry Cameron, Christopher Shank, and Keri Holley (eds.), 1–17. Albuquerque, NM: High Desert Linguistics Society.

Liddell, Scott K.
1984 THINK and BELIEVE: Sequentiality in American Sign Language signs. *Language* 60 (2): 372–399.
2003 *Grammar, Gesture, and Meaning in American Sign Language.* Cambridge: Cambridge University Press.

Liddell, Scott K., and Robert E. Johnson
1989 American Sign Language: The phonological base. *Sign Language Studies* 64: 195–277.

McNeill, David
1992 *Hand and Mind: What Gestures Reveal About Thought.* Chicago: The University of Chicago Press.

Meier, Richard P.
2002 Why different, why the same? Explaining effects and non-effects of modality upon linguistic structure in sign and speech. In *Modality and Structure in Signed and Spoken Languages,* Richard P. Meier, Kearsy Cormier, and David Quinto-Pozos (eds.), 1–25. Cambridge: Cambridge University Press.

Miller, Christopher
1994 Simultaneous constructions in Quebec Sign Language. In *Word Order Issues in Sign Language, Working Papers,* Mary Brennan, and Graham H. Turner (eds.), 89–112. Durham: International Sign Linguistics Association.

Pizzuto, Elena, and Virginia Volterra
2000    Iconicity and transparency in sign languages: A cross-linguistic cross-cultural view. In *The Signs of Language Revisited: An Anthology to Honor Ursula Bellugi and Edward Klima*, Karen Emmorey, and Harlan Lane (eds.), 261–286. Mahwah, NJ: Lawrence Erlbaum.
Sallandre, Marie-Anne
2006    Iconicity and space in French Sign Language. In *Space in Languages: Linguistic Systems and Cognitive Categories*, Maya Hickmann, and Stéphane Robert (eds.), 239–255. Amsterdam/Philadelphia: Benjamins.
Sallandre, Marie-Anne, and Christian Cuxac
2002    Iconicity in sign language: A theoretical and methodological point of view. In *Gesture and Sign Language in Human-Computer Interaction. International Gesture Workshop, GW 2001, London, UK, April 18–20, 2001 Proceedings*, Ipke Wachsmuth, and Timo Sowa (eds.), 173–180. Berlin: Springer.
Sandler, Wendy
2006    Iconic mouth gestures in Israeli Sign Language. Paper presented at the Linguistic Society of America 2006 Annual Meeting, Albuquerque, NM, January 5–8.
Shaffer, Barbara
2002    CAN'T: The negation of modal notions in ASL. *Sign Language Studies* 3 (1): 34–53.
2004    Information ordering and speaker subjectivity: Modality in ASL. *Cognitive Linguistics* 15 (2): 175–195.
Singleton, Jenny L., Susan Goldin-Meadow, and David McNeill
1995    The cataclysmic break between gesticulation and sign: Evidence against a unified continuum of gestural communication. In *Language, Gesture, and Space*, Karen Emmorey, and Judy S. Reilly (eds.), 287–311. Hillsdale, NJ: Lawrence Erlbaum.
Stokoe, William C.
1960    *Sign Language Structure: An Outline of the Visual Communication System of the American Deaf*. Studies in Language Occasional Papers, no. 8. Buffalo, NY: University of Buffalo. [Reprint: 1993. Silver Spring, MD: Linstok Press]
Stokoe, William C., Dorothy C. Casterline, and Carl G. Croneberg
1965    *A Dictionary of American Sign Language on Linguistic Principles*. Washington, DC: Gallaudet College Press.
Sweetser, Eve
1990    *From Etymology to Pragmatics: Metaphorical and Cultural Aspects of Semantic Structure*. Cambridge: Cambridge University Press.
Talmy, Leonard
2003    The representation of spatial structure in spoken and signed language: A neural model. *Language and Linguistics* 4: 207–250.
2006    The representation of spatial structure in spoken and signed language.

In *Space in Languages: Linguistic Systems and Cognitive Categories,* Maya Hickmann, and Stéphane Robert (eds.), 207–238. Amsterdam/ Philadelphia: Benjamins.

Taub, Sarah F.
2001   *Language from the Body: Iconicity and Metaphor in American Sign Language.* Cambridge: Cambridge University Press.

Wilcox, Phyllis Perrin
2000   *Metaphor in American Sign Language.* Washington, DC: Gallaudet University Press.
2004   A cognitive key: Metonymic and metaphorical mappings in ASL. *Cognitive Linguistics* 15 (2), 197–222.

Wilcox, Sherman E.
2002   The gesture-language interface: Evidence from signed languages. In *Progress in Sign Language Research: In Honor of Siegmund Prillwitz/ Fortschritte in der Gebärdensprachforschung: Festschrift für Siegmund Prillwitz,* Rolf Schulmeister, and Heimo Reinitzer (eds.), 63–81. Hamburg: Signum-Verlag.
2003   Fictive Motion, Manner of Motion, and Cognitive Iconicity: Data from American Sign Language. Paper presented at the Eighth International Cognitive Linguistics Conference, Logroño, Spain, July 20 – 25, 2003.
2004a   Cognitive iconicity: Conceptual spaces, meaning, and gesture in signed language. *Cognitive Linguistics* 15 (2): 119–147.
2004b   Gesture and language: Cross-linguistic and historical data from signed languages. *Gesture* 4 (1): 43–73.

Winston, Elizabeth A.
1995   Spatial mapping in comparative discourse frames. In *Language, Gesture, and Space,* Karen Emmorey, and Judy S. Reilly (eds.), 87–114. Hillsdale, NJ: Lawrence Erlbaum.

# Non-verbal and multimodal metaphor in a cognitivist framework: Agendas for research

## Charles Forceville

*Abstract*

Conceptual metaphor theory (CMT) has over the past 25 years amply sought to underpin the claim that humans' pervasive use of verbal metaphor reflects the fact that they think largely metaphorically. If this tenet of CMT is correct, metaphor should manifest itself not just in language but also via other modes of communication, such as pictures, music, sounds, and gestures. However, non-verbal and multimodal metaphor have been far less extensively studied than their verbal sisters. The present article provides a review of work done in this area, focusing on a number of issues that require further research. These issues include the proposal to distinguish between monomodal and multimodal metaphor; reflections on the difference between structural and creative metaphor; the question of how verbalizations of non-verbal or conceptual metaphors may affect their possible interpretation; thoughts as to how similarity between target and source is created; and suggestions about the importance of genre for the construal and interpretation of metaphor.

*Keywords*: Monomodal and multimodal metaphor; pictorial metaphor; structural versus creative metaphor; similarity in metaphor; genre.

## 1. Introduction

Andrew Ortony's edited volume *Metaphor and Thought* (1979) and Lakoff and Johnson's monograph *Metaphors We Live By* (1980) were milestone publications in the sense that they marked the switch from research into metaphor as a primarily verbal to a predominantly conceptual phenomenon. The "conceptual metaphor theory" (CMT), as the Lakoffian-Johnsonian model is habitually referred to, has been a very productive one (e.g., Gibbs 1994; Johnson 1987, 1993; Kövecses 1986, 2000, 2002; Lakoff 1987, 1993; Lakoff and Johnson 1999, 2003; Lakoff and Turner 1989; Sweetser 1990; Turner 1996). A key notion in this theory is that "the mind is inherently embodied, reason is shaped by the body" (Lakoff and Johnson 1999: 5; Chapter 3). Very briefly, what this means is the following. Human beings find phenomena they can see, hear, feel, taste and/or smell easier to understand and categorize than phenomena they cannot. It is perceptibility that makes the former phenomena concrete, and the lack of it that makes the latter abstract. In order to master abstract concepts, humans systematically comprehend them in terms of concrete concepts. Thus abstract concepts such as LIFE, TIME, and EMOTIONS are systematically understood in terms of concrete phenomena. LIFE is understood as A JOURNEY (*He's without* direction *in his life*; *I'm* at a crossroads *in my life*) – but also, for instance, as A STORY (*Tell me the* story *of your life*; *Life's ... a* tale told *by an idiot ...*). TIME is comprehended in terms of SPATIAL MOTION (*The time for action* has arrived; *Time is* flying *by*; *He* passed *the time happily*). Emotions are typically represented by drawing on the domain of FORCES. (*I was* overwhelmed; *I was* swept off *my feet*; examples from Kövecses 2000; Lakoff 1993; Lakoff and Johnson 1980). Conceptualisations of many phenomena, CMT proposes, have deeply entrenched metaphorical forms, in which the metaphor's target (topic, tenor) is abstract and its source (vehicle, base) is concrete. A metaphor's interpretation boils down to the "mapping" of pertinent features from the source to the target; a mapping that in the case of entrenched metaphors such as the above occurs automatically. Since "concreteness" is apprehended perceptually, metaphorical source domains are strongly rooted in the functioning of the human body. Metaphorical reasoning is thus governed by the "arch" metaphor MIND IS BODY (Lakoff and Johnson 1999: 249). A more recent development rooted in CMT is "blending theory" (Fauconnier and Turner 2002). Rather than postulating a target and a source domain, it presents two (or more) "input spaces." The input spaces have both shared and unique characteristics, and it is this combination that allows for the construal of a so-called "blended space." Blending theory is a, mainly descriptive, model claiming to be superior to metaphor theory in being able to account for *ad hoc* forms of creativity, metaphorical and otherwise. Hitherto it cannot quite convince (for a critical review, see Forceville 2004a), but new work, taking into account pragmatic rhetorical factors, is promising (see Coulson and Pascual, in press; Terkourafi and Petrakis, under review).

CMT has inspired conferences (e.g., those organized by the International Cognitive Linguistics Association, and the Researching and Applying Metaphor [RaAM] association), journals (e.g., *Metaphor and Symbol*, *Cognitive Linguistics*), as well as empirical research (for references see Gibbs 1994; Lakoff and Johnson 1999: 587–88). Its importance is evident: if CMT is basically correct, it provides crucial insights into what, thanks to embodiment, lays claim to being universal in human cognition, and what is rooted in, or shapes, (sub)cultural differences.

However, CMT is restricted in at least the following very important dimension. Even though Lakoff and Johnson's (1980: 5) characterization of metaphor's essence as "understanding and experiencing one kind of thing in terms of another" emphatically avoids the word "verbal" or "linguistic," the validity of CMT's claims about the existence of conceptual metaphors depends almost exclusively on the patterns detectable in *verbal* metaphors. This entails two dangers: in the first place, there is the risk of a vicious circle: "cognitive linguistic research suffers from circular reasoning in that it starts with an analysis of language to infer something about the mind and body which in turn motivates different aspects of linguistic structure and behavior" (Gibbs and Colston 1995: 354; see also Cienki 1998). Clearly, to further validate the idea that metaphors are *expressed by language*, as opposed to the idea that they *are necessarily linguistic in nature*, it is imperative to demonstrate that, and how, they can occur non-verbally and multimodally as well as purely verbally. Secondly, an exclusive or predominant concentration on verbal manifestations of metaphor runs the risk of blinding researchers to aspects of metaphor that may typically occur in non-verbal and multimodal representations only. This latter awareness, of course, exemplifies a more general principle. Ever since Marshall McLuhan's "the medium is the message" (McLuhan 1964: 24 *et passim*), it is a truism that as soon as one changes the medium via which a message (including both its factual and emotive aspects) is conveyed, the content of this message is changed as well (see also Bolter and Grusin 1999). Each medium – here defined as a material carrier and transmitter of information – communicates via one or more signalling systems. The medium of non-illustrated books, for instance, exclusively draws on the mode of written language; radio relies on the modes of spoken language, non-verbal sound, and music; advertising billboards on written language and visuals; and post-silent film on visuals, written language, spoken language, non-verbal sound, and music. If, as is argued here, each of these signalling systems (which will henceforward be called "modes") can cue, independently or in combination, metaphorical targets as well as metaphorical sources, a full-blown theory of metaphor cannot be based on its verbal manifestations alone, since this may result in a biased view of what constitutes metaphor.

In this article I will sketch how adopting the view that metaphors can assume non-verbal and multimodal appearances can and should guide the research of a new generation of metaphor scholars. I will do so partly by bringing to bear multimodal perspectives on issues already familiar from research by language-oriented metaphor scholars, and partly by discussing issues that have either been neglected by such researchers or are simply not pertinent to purely verbal metaphors. The paper should be seen as a map of mostly uncharted territory, with only a few details inked in, much of it reporting theory-driven analyses and informed speculation awaiting empirical testing. Multimodal metaphor researchers have a vast amount of work to look forward to.

## 2.    Multimodality versus monomodality

In order to distinguish multimodal metaphor from monomodal metaphor, it should first be further clarified what is meant by "mode." This is no easy task, because what is labelled a mode here is a complex of various factors. As a first approximation, let us say that a mode is a sign system interpretable because of a specific perception process. Acceptance of this approach would link modes one-on-one to the five senses, so that we would arrive at the following list: (1) the pictorial or visual mode; (2) the aural or sonic mode; (3) the olfactory mode; (4) the gustatory mode; and (5) the tactile mode. However, this is too crude a categorization. For instance, the sonic mode under this description lumps together spoken language, music, and non-verbal sound. Similarly, both written language and gestures would have to be part and parcel of the visual, since one cannot hear, smell, taste, or touch either conventionally written language or gestures (although a blind person feels Braille language and, by touch, perceives certain gestures – for instance those of a statue). If justice is to be done to these distinctions (between images and gestures, between spoken and written language, between spoken language, sounds, and music), other factors need to be taken into account, such as the manner of production (e.g., printed versus Braille letters in relief on paper; signs made with parts of the body versus signs whose use is governed by the grammar and vocabulary rules of a natural language). There are other problematic issues. For instance, what is music and what "mere" sound may differ from one culture, or period, to another. Similarly, it is impossible to assess objectively where music shades off into sound effect. And is "typeface" to be considered an element of writing, of visuals, or of both? In short, it is at this stage impossible to give either a satisfactory definition of "mode," or compile an exhaustive list of modes. However, this is no obstacle for postulating that there are different modes and that these include, at least, the following: (1) pictorial signs; (2) written signs; (3) spoken signs; (4) gestures; (5) sounds; (6) music (7) smells; (8) tastes; (9) touch. We can now provisionally define monomodal metaphors as metaphors whose target and source are exclusively or predominantly rendered in one mode. The prototypical monomodal metaphor is the verbal specimen that until recently was identical with "metaphor" *tout court*, and which has yielded thousands of studies (de Knop et al. 2005; Shibles 1971; Van Noppen et al. 1985; Van Noppen and Hols 1990). A type of monomodal metaphor that has more recently become the subject of sustained research is pictorial or visual metaphor.[1]

An early discussion of metaphor in pictures is Kennedy (1982). This perception psychologist takes "metaphor" in the all-encompassing sense of what literary scholars call a "trope" or a "figure of speech" (and which Tversky 2001 calls "figures of depiction") and identifies some 25 types, including for instance "metonymy," "hendiadys," and "litotes." Kennedy's attempts to describe an extensive catalogue of "figures of depiction" using the tenor/vehicle distinction that Richards (1965) specifically coined for "metaphor" are sometimes strained. There are other problems. It is a matter for debate whether the names he selects for his examples are always necessarily the best ones, and each trope is illustrated with one or two examples only, making generalizations difficult (the same problem also adheres to Durand 1987). This having been said, Kennedy makes a number of points that are illuminating for a theory of pictorial/visual-metaphor-in-the-narrow-sense. In the first place he argues that for a phenomenon to be labelled a visual metaphor it should be understandable as an intended violation of codes of representation, rather than as being due to carelessness or error. Secondly, Kennedy emphasizes that target and source are, in principle, irreversible, which ensures that what he labels metaphor remains commensurate with a generally accepted criterion in theories of verbal metaphor. Thirdly, Kennedy introduces the helpful notion of "runes": the kind of non-iconic signs used profusely in comics and cartoons to indicate speed, pain, surprise, happiness, anger and many other phenomena by means of straight or squiggly lines, stars, bubbles etc. surrounding characters or moving objects (see also Smith 1996). In later work, Kennedy elaborates on his theoretical work in various experiments. Kennedy (1993) reports, among other things, how congenitally blind children metaphorically draw a spinning wheel.

Whittock (1990) describes cinematographic metaphor. While his numerous examples are subsumed under ten subtypes, and thus are less wide-ranging than those by Kennedy, they still go beyond metaphor-in-the-narrow-sense, including for instance metonymy and synecdoche. Whittock is criticized by Carroll (1994) for failing to take into account what the latter considers the most typical variety of visual or cinematographic metaphor, the visual hybrid (see also Carroll 1996). Carroll, unlike Kennedy and Whittock, moreover argues that visual metaphors differ from verbal ones in often allowing for reversal of target and source. In Forceville (2002a), expanding on earlier work (Forceville 1988, 1994, 1995, 1996, 2000), I in turn question Carroll's choice for visual hybrids as "core filmic metaphor" (Carroll 1996: 218) as well as his proposal for the typical reversibility of target and source in visual metaphors. My argument rests on the claim that Carroll is biased by his exclusive reliance on examples rooted in Surrealist art. My own model, largely developed with respect to advertising representations (but see Forceville 1988) and based on Black's (1979) interaction theory of metaphor (see also Gineste et al. 2000; Indurkhya 1991, 1992), centres on the answerability of the following three questions: Which are the two terms of the pictorial metaphor?; which is the target and which is the source?; and which is/are the features that is/are mapped from source to target? The last question pertains to the metaphor's interpretation: in principle all elements metonymically associated (by a whole community or by a single individual) with the source domain qualify as potential candidates for a mapping. The crucial issue what is actually mapped by a specific addressee in a specific situation is governed by the relevance principle as developed by Sperber and Wilson (1995). (For more discussion of the role of metonymy in metaphor, see various contributions in Dirven and Pörings 2002; for the pertinence of Relevance Theory to the interpretation of pictorial metaphors, see Forceville 1996, chapters 5 and 6.) In this model, Carroll's examples would rank as one of three (Forceville 2002b) or four (Forceville 2005a, forthcoming a) subtypes of monomodal metaphor. It is to be noted that the distinction between two of these types – metaphor and simile – is also made by Kaplan (1990, 1992; see also Rozik 1994, 1998).

By contrast to monomodal metaphors, multimodal metaphors are metaphors whose target and source are each represented exclusively or predominantly in different modes. The qualification "exclusively or predominantly" is necessary because non-verbal metaphors often have targets and/or sources that are cued in more than one mode simultaneously. To give a fictive example: imagine somebody wants to cue, for whatever reason, the metaphor CAT IS ELEPHANT pictorially in an animation film. She could do this for instance by depicting the cat with a trunk-like snout and large flapping ears; by showing the cat with a canopy on its back in which a typical Indian elephant rider is seated; by juxtaposing cat and elephant in the same salient pose; or by letting the cat behave (for instance: move) in an elephant-like manner. These variants would constitute monomodal metaphors of the pictorial kind, featuring hybrid, contextual, simile, and integrated subtypes respectively (see Forceville 1996, 2002b, 2005a) – and of course these subtypes could be combined. Now imagine the producer wishes to cue the same metaphor multimodally. She could for instance have the cat make a trumpeting sound or have another cat shout "elephant!" to the first one (note that this is not a case of synaesthesia, since there is no conflation of the two domains). In these cases the source domain ELEPHANT would be triggered in two modes (sound and language, respectively) that are different from the target (visuals). By this token, the metaphor would be truly multimodal. But, as in the case of the visual mode alone, the producer would of course not have to *choose* between any of these modes: she could depict the cat with a trunk-like snout and large ears *and* have it trumpet, *and* have another cat shout "elephant!" In this case, the source is cued in three modes simultaneously, only one of these (namely: the visual) exemplifying the same mode as the target. In such a case I propose to label the metaphor multimodal. Of course the metonymy cueing the source domain in itself is often chosen for its specific connotations. Both tusks and a trunk trigger ELEPHANT, but the former connotes, among other things, aggressiveness, whiteness, costliness and the latter among other things flexibility, sensitivity, and "instrument-to-spray-water-or-sand-with." For examples, as well as more discussion of, multimodal metaphors involving (moving) images, see Forceville (1999a, 2003, 2004b, 2005b, forthcoming a, b). There is also a growing literature on multimodal metaphors involving language and gestures (Cienki 1998; McNeill 1992; Müller 2004), in which the gesture-modality cues the source rather than the target domain (McNeill 2005: 45).

### 3. Structural versus creative metaphor

Lakoff and Turner (1989) have argued that not only metaphors occurring in everyday verbal communication can be traced back to conceptual metaphors, but also those in artistic texts, specifically poetry. Particularly when poems thematize abstract concepts such as life and death, they cannot but draw on the same conceptual metaphors that permeate non-artistic language. Thus Lakoff and Turner cite, and richly illustrate, many passages featuring LIFE and TIME as metaphorical targets (LIFE IS A JOUR-

NEY, LIFE IS A PLAY, LIFE IS BONDAGE, LIFE IS A BURDEN; TIME IS A THIEF, TIME IS A MOVER, TIME IS A DEVOURER) concluding that "although human imagination is strong, empowering us to make and understand even bizarre connections, there are relatively few basic metaphors for life and death that abide as part of our culture" (1989: 26). They acknowledge that the art and craft of good poets resides in finding fresh, original verbal formulations for these conceptual metaphors, and that these formulations resonate both with the rest of the poem and with the extra-textual knowledge of the reader. I take it that Lakoff and Turner allow that this, in turn, may result in temporary readjustments of the basic level conceptual metaphors, and thus that they would agree that the linguistic level of the metaphor is not a mere *illustration* or *exemplification* of the pre-existing basic conceptual level. But not all verbal metaphors in poetry, as Lakoff and Turner acknowledge, reflect basic conceptual metaphors. While conventional metaphors can be expressed either in common or in idiosyncratic language, "modes of thought that are not themselves conventional cannot be expressed in conventional language" (1989: 26) and hence require idiosyncratic language. (If I understand her correctly, Renate Bartsch would probably object to the label "conceptual metaphor" for the metaphorical schema that underlies such novel metaphors. She stipulates that a phenomenon deserves the name of "concept" only if it has a stable interpretation in a community, and hence must *by definition* have been "linguistically explicated" (Bartsch 2003: 50). A stable interpretation requires that the community agrees on the phenomenon's characteristic features and these, in turn, reveal themselves in the true predications that can be used for it. Novel metaphors focus attention on non-characteristic features and therefore, in Bartsch' reasoning, cannot (yet) have the status of being "conceptual.") Often, the border between conventional metaphors and idiosyncratic ones is difficult to draw, not least because conventional metaphors may have idiosyncratic extensions. Lakoff and Turner thus admit that not all poetic metaphors are conventional ones, but the bulk of their examples and discussions pertain to the latter. This is unsurprising, since their aim is to show that poetic metaphors normally tap into conventional ways of thinking ("great poets can speak to us because they use the modes of thought we all possess," Lakoff and Turner 1989: xi).

Nonetheless Lakoff and Turner's account raises some questions. In the first place, it is not clear how representative their chosen examples are of poetic metaphors in general. While they convincingly show that structural metaphors pervade poetry, the relative distribution of metaphors may depend on time and place: older poetry, or non-Western poetry, may feature

more, or less, instances of a given metaphor. Gevaert (2001), basing herself on corpus-based data, questions for instance the embodied, "time-
less" status of ANGER IS HEAT claimed for conceptualisations of anger in
Lakoff (1987). She demonstrates, among other things, that in the Old
English period SWELLING was a much more important source domain in
ANGER metaphors than HEAT, and speculates that the latter's growing
popularity in more recent periods may well be due to the humoral theory
that dominated mediaeval times; that is, to cultural no less than embodied
knowledge (see also Gevaert 2005). Moreover, a systematic, corpus-based
analysis might reveal that many poetic metaphors are not so easily amenable to conventional ones. Numerous poetic metaphors may simply not
have abstract concepts such as LIFE, DEATH, TIME, PURPOSE as their target
domain. As pointed out by Grady, they may more often be "resemblance
metaphors" than, possibly (near)universal, "correlation metaphors"
(Grady 1999). This would not invalidate Lakoff and Turner's impressive
findings, but their one-sided emphasis on correlation and generic-level
metaphors[2] in poetry may inadvertently lead to an uncritical acceptance
of the view that most poetic metaphors are of this kind.

One important difference between conventional and idiosyncratic
metaphors is that the interpretation of the latter is, by definition, far less
governed by entrenched, pre-existing correspondences between the schematic structures in target and source. It is only by downplaying this difference that Lakoff and Turner can say that "the preservation of generic-
level structure is, we believe, at the heart of metaphorical imagination,
whether poetic or ordinary" (1989: 83; for critical accounts of this view
see also Stockwell 1999; Crisp 2003).

Secondly, we should not forget that a metaphor can also conceptualize
the concrete in terms of the concrete. Lakoff and Turner, to be fair, are
aware of this. They discuss at some length the Elizabethan notion of the
"Great Chain of Being" (see e.g., Tillyard 1976), which endorsed the idea
of "natural" hierarchies within various types of creatures – angels, humans, birds, mammals, etc. – and state that "the GREAT CHAIN METAPHOR
can apply to a target domain *at the same level* on the Great Chain as the
source domain" (Lakoff and Turner 1989: 179, emphasis in original). Put
differently, metaphors may have targets as well as sources that are directly
accessible to the senses. But given that CMT puts great emphasis on metaphor's role in conceptualising the abstract in terms of the concrete, this
possibility receives rather scant attention, while CONCRETE IS CONCRETE
metaphors are particularly relevant once we leave the realm of the purely
verbal. In the case of monomodal metaphors of the pictorial variety, both

target and source are depicted. In advertising, metaphorical targets usually coincide with promoted products and, unsurprisingly, are depicted – and hence are necessarily concrete: a beer brand is depicted as a wine; an elegant watch as a butterfly, a close-fitting bathing suit as a dolphin's tight and supple skin (examples from Forceville 1996). The same holds for metaphors in feature films (Forceville 2005b; Whittock 1990). In short, to what extent monomodal metaphors of the non-verbal variety and multimodal metaphors are amenable to the correlation metaphors that are the centre of attention in CMT is an empirical question. Some of them no doubt do; for instance, the personification of commodities is a very familiar marketing strategy, and ties in with CMT views (Lakoff and Turner 1989: 72). But many pictorial and multimodal metaphors are of the OBJECT A IS OBJECT B TYPE. Traditional CMT has not much to say about these. Even Lakoff and Turner's (1989) invocation of the Great Chain metaphor is only of limited use here, since it depends on typological hierarchies that may be subverted, or simply be irrelevant, in creative metaphors, many of which function in contexts creating highly specific, *ad hoc* metaphorical resemblances (see Black 1979).

There is a third aspect in which CMT has a one-sided emphasis. As discussed above, the typical source domain's concreteness has in CMT been traditionally connected to the notion of "embodiment." The embodied nature of source domains emphasizes their physical nature: it is human physical interaction with the world that familiarizes humans with it to such an extent that the resulting knowledge structures can in turn be mapped onto abstract concepts. Knowledge about source domains is not simply a matter of embodiment, however, but also of cultural connotations, as Lakoff and Turner (1989: 66) acknowledge. More recent studies have demonstrated in a variety of ways how the structure of source domains – and the salient (and hence: easily mappable) elements in it – is influenced by culture (Gibbs and Steen 1999; Kövecses 2005; Shore 1996; Yu 1998). Indeed, the cultural connotations that are metonymically related to a source domain are often more important for potential mappings to a target than its embodied aspects. In a Dutch commercial promoting a Gazelle bicycle in terms of a dressage horse the embodied mapping of "riding a horse" to "riding a bicycle" is less important for the interpretation of the metaphor than the mapping of the cultural connotations from the dressage horse's owner, champion Anky van Grunsven, to the prospective buyer and user of the bike. Similarly, while advertising a high-tech Senseo coffee machine in terms of a motorbike certainly has embodied aspects, the subcultural connotations associated with motorbike-riding evoked by Steppenwolf's "Born to be wild," audible on the commercial's soundtrack, are at least as important in the mapping (Forceville 2004b, forthcoming b; Forceville et al. in preparation). The relevant "similarity" that is created between target and source pertains to these connotations more than to anything else. The examples bear out Bartsch' observation that in metaphor "the role of similarity is not restricted to the identity of internal properties of objects and situations, rather similarity also is due to identity of external contiguity relationships between objects, between situations, and it is due to relationships of objects and situations with emotional attitudes, desires, and behavioural dispositions of people" (Bartsch 2003: 52). Indeed, it might be ventured that "a single, embodied correspondence between target and source is enough to trigger a wide range of further 'cultural' correspondences between target and source, and hence of inferences about the target" (Forceville et al., forthcoming). The old adage that a picture tells more than a thousand words should not blind us to the fact that pictures and other multimodal representations seldom communicate automatically or self-evidently. As in verbal metaphors, it is connotations rather than denotations of source domains that get mapped in metaphors, and these may substantially differ from one (sub)cultural group to another (see e.g., Maalej 2001). Even when non-verbal metaphors verge toward the conventional, as in comics representations of ANGER (Eerden 2004; Forceville 2005c; see Simons 1995 for multimodal instantiations of structural metaphor in pre-election TV spots promoting political parties), it may well be the case that, as in their verbal counterparts (see Kövecses 1986, 2000, 2005), there is cultural variation (cf. Shinohara and Matsunaka 2003).

The three issues briefly mentioned above ("metaphors frequently have concrete rather than abstract targets"; "many metaphors with idiosyncratic surface manifestations do not reflect correlation metaphors"; "what gets mapped from source to target domains are often cultural, not embodied, features") are thrown in relief when the study of purely verbal metaphors gives way to that of non-verbal and multimodal metaphors. That is, generalizing observations on metaphor based on the systematic investigation of verbal specimens need to be considered afresh by testing these observations in metaphors occurring in other modes.

### 4. The verbalization of non-verbal metaphor and the nature of "similarity"

We have seen that within the CMT paradigm, most surface metaphors should be amenable to a pre-existing conceptual A IS B format. Inevitably, in order to discuss the metaphor, this A and B must be *named*, i.e., rendered in language. It is by no means a foregone conclusion, of course, that the "language of thought" is actually a verbal language. The convention to verbalize the image-schematic structures underlying surface metaphors by using SMALL CAPITALS – useful inasmuch as this facilitates analysing them – may disguise a number of consequences that seem to me more problematic in the discussion of representations that are not (exclusively) verbal ones than of purely verbal ones. One of these consequences is that it is the analyst's responsibility to find an adequate or acceptable verbal rendering of the metaphor's underlying image-schematic level, but such a verbalization, even though used as a convenient shorthand, is never neutral. The design of the Senseo coffee machine suggests the posture of somebody bending over and modestly offering something (i.e., a cup) on a plate. But should this awareness result in the verbalization COFFEE MACHINE IS SERVANT, or is COFFEE MACHINE IS BUTLER more appropriate? Although "servant" and "butler" share many features, they also differ: "butler" is more specific, and may in some people (but not in others) evoke connotations of Britishness and standards of service that "servant" does not. As a result, the mappings suggested by the two verbalizations may differ. Bartsch might conclude that this very inability to agree on a single verbalization of the source domain that is shared within a community shows that the source has no conceptual status, and reflects a "quasi-concept" at best (Bartsch 2003: 50). However, to the extent that there is a community that recognizes the source as cueing a serving person, the source admits predicates understood as "true" in the community (such as "is there to serve the user," "obeys your requests," and "is almost always available"). In a visually literate society, a vast number of endlessly repeated and recycled images (such as famous paintings, photographs, film shots, flags, logos, animation characters) evoke specific phenomena and events in a clichéd, shorthand manner widely shared within a community, and hence arguably aspire to conceptual status. But this speculation leads us far beyond the concerns of the present chapter and deserves in-depth reflection elsewhere.

Another consequence is that verbalization of a non-verbal metaphor is necessarily a conscious action, and a fairly unusual one at that. It is only the scholar writing an academic paper who, to be able to discuss a multi-modal metaphor, needs to resort to GAZELLE BICYCLE IS VAN GRUNSVEN DRESSAGE HORSE; the metaphor is not verbalized in this form in the commercial, and it is an open question whether the construal of a non-verbal metaphor requires its verbalization by the audience. The question can be reformulated as follows: does comprehension of a non-verbal or multimodal metaphor imply that recipients "mentally" verbalize the metaphor? It is an important question, but difficult to test empirically.

Since non-verbal modes of communicating by definition do not have the "is" or "is like" in order to signal a metaphorical identity relation between two entities belonging, in the given context, to different categories, one issue that deserves attention is by what stylistic means the similarity is triggered. Of course this holds for verbal metaphors that do not have the paradigmatic A IS (LIKE) B format as well (cf. Brooke-Rose 1958; Goatly 1997). But whatever means are chosen in this latter case, the cues are themselves of a verbal nature. In non-verbal and multimodal metaphors, the signals that cue metaphorical similarity between two phenomena are different, and bound to differ depending on the mode(s) in which the metaphorical terms are represented. Here are some possibilities that are deployed in isolation or in combination:

*Perceptual resemblance.* This can only function as a trigger in the case of monomodal metaphors: only a visual representation can perceptually resemble another visual representation; only a sound can perceptually resemble another sound. In the case of visual resemblance, there is a range of choices: two things can resemble one another because they have the same size, colour, position, posture, texture, materiality, etc. Note that the resemblance need not reside in the "things" themselves, but may surface in their manner of representation: they may for instance be photographed from the same unusual angle, or filmed with the same unusual camera movement.

*Filling a schematic slot unexpectedly.* Placing a thing in a certain context may strongly, even inescapably, evoke a different kind of thing, namely the thing for which the given context is the natural or conventional place. Put differently, we encounter deviations from typical *gestalts* or schemas. For example, when in a musical environment a violin case contains a monkey wrench, this suggests the metaphor MONKEY WRENCH IS VIOLIN (OR V.V.).

*Simultaneous cueing.* If two things are signalled in different modes, metaphorical identification is achieved by saliently representing target and source at the same time. For instance a kiss could be accompanied by the sound of a car crash, of a vacuum cleaner, or of the clunking of chains, to cue metaphorical mappings of, say, disaster, dreary domestic routine, and imprisonment, respectively. Alternatively, in a variant on the previous mechanism, two disparate things can be linked because of an unexpected filling of a slot, as when a photograph of a kiss has the caption "imprisonment."

## 5.  The influence of genre

Human beings in most cases appear to construe a text automatically, very quickly, and probably largely subconsciously as belonging to one genre rather than to another. Anecdotal support for this claim is the experience of channel-surfing: seasoned TV watchers guess in a split second what kind of programme they surf into (and decide at once whether they want to spend time with it). Another illustration for the claim is the very funny, self-reflexive trailer for the film *Comedian* (http://www.geocities.com/tvtranscripts/misc/comedian.htm). A man, Jack, sits in a booth in a sound studio to record the voice-over for the trailer, but as soon as he has said a few words he is impatiently interrupted by the director:

Jack:       "In a world where laughter was king ..."
Director:  No "in a world," Jack ...
Jack:       What do you mean, "No 'in a world'"?
Director:  It's not that kind of movie.
Jack:       Oh ... OK ... "In a land that ..."
Director:  No "in a land" either ...
Jack:       "In the time ..."
Director:  No, I don't think so.

In a rapid exchange Jack makes one abortive attempt after another – "One man ..."; "When your life is no longer your own ..."; "When everything you know is wrong ..."; "In an outpost ..."; "On the edge of space ..." – only to be cut short by the director straightaway. For present purposes the point to be made is that, to an audience with expertise in the area of film, the few words uttered by Jack suffice to cue an entire genre. Finally, Hayward (1994) offers empirically attested support for the claim that people are able to decide very fast to what genre a text belongs. Hayward found that almost 80% of experimental subjects, given randomly selected passages of history or fiction writing, recognized the genre of the work even on the basis of very short passages (5 to 15 words).

The genre within which a text (in whatever medium) is presented, or the genre to which it is attributed, determines and constrains its possible interpretations to an extent that is difficult to overestimate (see Altman 1999; Charteris-Black 2004; Forceville 1999b, 2005d; Steen 1994; Zwaan 1993 for discussion). For this reason, it is important to study how genre has an impact on the production and interpretation of metaphors (monomodal and multimodal alike). In advertising, for instance, the targets of metaphors often coincide with the product promoted (Forceville 1996). This is to be expected: an advertisement or commercial predicates something about a product, brand, or service, and this neatly and naturally fits the metaphor's TARGET IS SOURCE format. Moreover, the features mapped from source to target are positive ones (unless the metaphor is used to disqualify a competitor's brand, in which case the mapped features are typically negative). But in feature films, there is no phenomenon that in a similar, "natural," way qualifies as a metaphorical target. Metaphors in artistic narratives pertain to phenomena that, for whatever reason, are deemed salient by their producers. These phenomena can be protagonists, but also objects. The mapped features will often be less clear-cut, and may have a richer "aligned structure" (Gentner and Loewenstein 2002), than those in advertising.

Metaphors in artistic representations may also differ in other respects from those in commercial messages. For instance, while in commercials there will seldom be a question what is target and what is source in a metaphor, an artistic narrative may give rise to two different construals of a metaphor: both A IS B and B IS A are appropriate. (While Carroll 1994, 1996 calls such metaphors "reversible," I prefer to say that, in the given context, both the metaphors A IS B and B IS A are pertinent, in order to retain the notion that target and source in a metaphor are, in principle, irreversible.) Commensurate with this, metaphors in artistic contexts presumably allow for greater freedom of interpretation than do metaphors in commercials (cf. also Shen 1995).

Another parameter that deserves further research is whether any of the subtypes of pictorial metaphor or of the manifold varieties of multimodal metaphor can be systematically related to certain text genres. For instance, it seems that commercial advertising seldom makes use of the hybrid variety of pictorial metaphors (in Forceville 1996 these were called MP2s). Again, this makes sense: if metaphorical targets typically coincide with products, advertisers would want their product portrayed in their entirety, and not in a manner that might evoke connotations of incompleteness or mutilation. Hybridizing it with a metaphorical source domain would not fit this goal. By contrast, in animation films, or science fiction films, no such problem arises.

Finally, it would be worthwhile to investigate whether in the case of multimodal metaphors there are any systematic correlations between textual genres and the modes in which a target and source are represented. In advertisements, the visual mode is typically used for representing the target – and this may well be true for different genres as well. But perhaps alternative patterns in the choice of mode for the source domain are detectable in different types of texts, while this may also change over time *within* a genre.

## 6.   Concluding remarks

Researching multimodal metaphor, in short, is a natural next step in the further development of metaphor studies – a development in which theoretical reflection will have to go hand in hand with empirical testing. If creative and conventional metaphor are key factors in human thinking, and if human thinking is reflected in more than verbal manifestations alone, investigating multimodal metaphor is highly worthy of extensive scholarly effort. Given its long disciplinary tradition, the robust insights of metaphor scholarship can in turn fruitfully feed into the budding field of multimodality in general (Kress and Van Leeuwen 1996, 2001; Ventola et al. 2004). Genres to be investigated include advertising (Forceville 1996, 2003, forthcoming a; McQuarrie and Mick 2003; Phillips 2003; Wiggin and Miller 2003), political cartoons (El Refaie 2003), film (Forceville 1999a, 2005b; Rohdin 2003; Whittock 1990), oral speech accompanied by gestures (Cienki 1998; McNeill 1992, 2005; Müller 2004), design (Cupchik 2003; Van Rompay 2005). And inasmuch as multimodal representations (in the form of advertising, videoclips, games, TV-formats, mainstream films, animation) travel faster and more easily across the world than verbal ones, examining their metaphorical manifestations will help focus on what remains stable and what changes in cross-cultural communication. Furthermore, such work may provide the starting point for how other tropes besides metaphor can assume multimodal appearances (e.g., metonymy, irony, hyperbole, oxymoron, see Gibbs 1993; Kennedy 1982; Teng and Sun 2002). Here the analysis of multimodal metaphor ties in with the study of rhetoric. In a global society in which media are increasingly used, or abused, as mouthpieces for the views of powerful factions (politicians, industry, tycoons, religious leaders), the critical analysis of the tools of persuasive discourse in the broadest sense constitutes an excellent interface between research in academia and its possible usefulness in the world beyond its walls.

On virtually all of the issues discussed in this article, Forceville and Urios-Aparisi (in preparation) will provide new insights.

## Acknowledgments

I am indebted to Francisco Ruiz de Mendoza and René Dirven for comments and suggestions on earlier drafts of this article.

## Notes

1. The topic of metaphor and music also has inspired studies over the past few years, but for lack of expertise in this area I will not dwell on these. For references, see Johnson and Larson 2003; see also Cook 1998, Zbikowski 2002, Thorau 2003, and Spitzer 2004 – the last one rather difficult for laymen.
2. Lakoff and Turner describe generic-level metaphors as metaphors which are minimally specific in two senses: "they do not have fixed source and target domains, and they do not have fixed lists of entities specified in the mapping" (1989: 81). They introduce the term using the example of the EVENTS ARE ACTIONS metaphor which they contrast with LIFE IS A JOURNEY, one of its specific-level instantiations.

## References

Altman, Rick
1999    *Film/Genre*. London: British Film Institute.
Bartsch, Renate
2003    Generating polysemy: Metaphor and metonymy. In *Metaphor and Metonymy in Comparison and Contrast*, René Dirven, and Ralf Pörings (eds.), 49–74. Berlin/New York: Mouton de Gruyter.
Black, Max
1979    More about metaphor. In *Metaphor and Thought*, Andrew Ortony (ed.), 19–43. Cambridge: Cambridge University Press.
Bolter, Jay David, and Richard Grusin
1999    *Remediation: Understanding New Media*. Cambridge MA: MIT Press.
Brooke-Rose, Christine
1958    *A Grammar of Metaphor*. London: Secker and Warburg.

Carroll, Noel
1994    Visual metaphor. In *Aspects of Metaphor,* Jaakko Hintikka (ed.), 189–218. Dordrecht: Kluwer.
1996    A note on film metaphor. In *Theorizing the Moving Image,* 212–223. Cambridge: Cambridge University Press.
Charteris-Black, Jonathan
2004    *Corpus Approaches to Critical Metaphor Analysis.* London: Palgrave/ MacMillan.
Cienki, Alan
1998    Metaphoric gestures and some of their relations to verbal metaphoric expressions. In *Discourse and Cognition: Bridging the Gap,* Jean Pierre Koenig (ed.), 189–204. Stanford, CA: Center for the Study of Language and Information.
Cook, Nicholas
1998    *Analyzing Musical Multimedia.* Oxford: Clarendon.
Coulson, Seana, and Esther Pascual
In press    For the sake of argument: Mourning the unborn and reviving the dead through conceptual blending. *Annual Review of Cognitive Linguistics* 4.
Crisp, Peter
2003    Conceptual metaphor and its expression. In *Cognitive Poetics in Practice,* Joanna Gavins, and Gerard Steen (eds.), 99–113. London/New York: Routledge.
Cupchik, Gerald D.
2003    The "interanimation" of worlds: Creative metaphors in art and design. *The Design Journal* 6 (2): 14–28.
Dirven, René, and Ralf Pörings (eds.)
2002    *Metaphor and Metonymy in Comparison and Contrast.* Berlin/New York: Mouton de Gruyter.
Durand, Jacques
1987    Rhetorical figures in the advertising image. In *Marketing and Semiotics: New Directions in the Study of Signs for Sale,* Jean Umiker-Sebeok (ed.), 295–318. Berlin/New York: Mouton de Gruyter.
Eerden, Bart
2004    *Liefde en Woede: De Metaforische Verbeelding van Emoties in ASTERIX.* [Love and anger: the metaphorical visualization of emotions in ASTERIX.] MA diss., University of Amsterdam, The Netherlands.
El Refaie, Elisabeth
2003    Understanding visual metaphors: The example of newspaper cartoons. *Visual Communication* 2 (1): 75–95.
Fauconnier, Gilles, and Mark Turner
2002    *The Way We Think: Conceptual Blending and the Mind's Hidden Complexities.* New York: Basic Books.
Forceville, Charles
1988    The case for pictorial metaphor: René Magritte and other Surrealists.

In *Vestnik IMS 9*, Aleš Erjavec (ed.), 150–160. Ljubljana: Inštitut za Marksistične Študije [Slovenia].

1994 Pictorial metaphor in advertisements. *Metaphor and Symbolic Activity* 9 (1): 1–29.

1995 (A)symmetry in metaphor: The importance of extended context. *Poetics Today* 16: 677–708.

1996 *Pictorial Metaphor in Advertising*. London/New York: Routledge.

1999a The metaphor COLIN IS A CHILD in Ian McEwan's, Harold Pinter's, and Paul Schrader's *The Comfort of Strangers*. *Metaphor and Symbol* 14: 179–98.

1999b Art or ad? The effect of genre-attribution on the interpretation of images. *Siegener Periodicum zur Internationalen Empirische Literaturwissenschaft [SPIEL]* 18 (2): 279–300.

2000 Compasses, beauty queens and other PCs: Pictorial metaphors in computer advertisements. *Hermes, Journal of Linguistics* 24: 31–55.

2002a The identification of target and source in pictorial metaphors. *Journal of Pragmatics* 34: 1–14.

2002b Further thoughts on delimitating pictorial metaphor. *Theoria et Historia Scientiarum* 6: 213–27 [Torún, Poland].

2003 Bildliche und multimodale Metaphern in Werbespots [Trans. from English by Dagmar Schmauks] *Zeitschrift für Semiotik* 25: 39–60.

2004a Review of Fauconnier and Turner (2002). *Metaphor and Symbol* 19: 83–89.

2004b The role of non-verbal sound and music in multimodal metaphor. In *Words in their Places: A Festschrift for J. Lachlan Mackenzie*, Henk Aertsen, Mike Hannay, and Rod Lyall (eds.), 65–78. Amsterdam: Faculty of Arts, VU Amsterdam.

2005a When is something a pictorial metaphor? [Lecture 2 in eight-lecture *Course on Pictorial and Multimodal metaphor*] http://www.chass.utoronto.ca/epc/srb/cyber/cforcevilleout.html

2005b Cognitive linguistics and multimodal metaphor. In *Bildwissenschaft: Zwischen Reflektion und Anwendung*, Klaus Sachs-Hombach (ed.), 264–284. Cologne: Von Halem.

2005c Visual representations of the Idealized Cognitive Model of anger in the Asterix album *La Zizanie*. *Journal of Pragmatics* 37: 69–88.

2005d Addressing an audience: time, place, and genre in Peter Van Straaten's calendar cartoons. *Humor: International Journal of Humor Research* 18 (3): 247–278.

Forthc. a Multimodal metaphor in ten Dutch TV commercials. *Public Journal of Semiotics*. http://semiotics.ca/

Forthc. b Metaphors in pictures and multimodal representations. In *The Cambridge Handbook of Metaphor and Thought*, Ray Gibbs (ed.), Cambridge: Cambridge University Press.

Forceville, Charles, Paul Hekkert, and Ed Tan
Forthc. The adaptive value of metaphors. In *Heuristiken der Literaturwissen-*

*schaft. Einladung zu disziplinexternen Perspektiven auf Literatur*, Uta Klein, Katja Mellmann, and Steffanie Metzger (eds.), 167–188. Paderborn: Mentis.

Forceville, Charles, Gerry Cupchik, and Michelle Hilscher
In prep.　The interpretation of multimodal metaphors in Dutch commercials by Dutch and Canadian subjects [provisional title].

Forceville, Charles, and Eduardo Urios-Aparisi (eds.)
In prep.　*Multimodal Metaphor* [provisional title]. Berlin/New York: Mouton De Gruyter.

Gentner, Dedre, and Jeffrey Loewenstein
2002　Relational language and relational thought. In *Language, Literacy, and Cognitive Development*, Eric Amsel, and James P. Byrnes (eds.), 87–120. Mahwah, NJ: Erlbaum.

Gevaert, Caroline
2001　Anger in Old and Middle English: a "hot" topic? *Belgian Essays on Language and Literature*, 89–101.
2005　The anger is heat question: detecting cultural influence on the conceptualisation of anger through diachronic corpus analysis. In *Perspectives on Variation*, Nicole Delbecque, Johan van der Auwera, and Dirk Geeraerts (eds.), 195–208. Berlin/New York: Mouton de Gruyter.

Gibbs, Raymond W., Jr.
1993　Process and products in making sense of tropes. In *Metaphor and Thought*, Andrew Ortony (ed.), 2nd edition, 252–276. Cambridge: Cambridge University Press.
1994　*The Poetics of the Mind: Figurative Thought, Language, and Understanding*. Cambridge: Cambridge University Press.

Gibbs, Raymond W., Jr., and Gerard J. Steen (eds.)
1999　*Metaphor in Cognitive Linguistics*. Amsterdam/Philadelphia: John Benjamins.

Gibbs, Raymond W., Jr., and Herbert L. Colston
1995　The cognitive psychological reality of image schemas and their transformations. *Cognitive Linguistics* 6: 347–378.

Gineste, Marie-Dominique, Bipin Indurkhya, and Véronique Scart
2000　Emergence of features in metaphor comprehension. *Metaphor and Symbol* 15: 117–135.

Goatly, Andrew
1997　*The Language of Metaphors*. London/New York: Routledge.

Grady, Joseph
1999　A typology of motivation for conceptual metaphor: correlation vs. resemblance. In *Metaphor in Cognitive Linguistics*, Raymond W. Gibbs, Jr., and Gerard J. Steen (eds.), 79–100. Amsterdam/Philadelphia: Benjamins.

Hayward, Malcolm
1994　Genre recognition of history and fiction. *Poetics* 22: 409–421.

Indurkhya, Bipin
1991    Modes of metaphor. *Metaphor and Symbolic Activity* 6: 1–27.
1992    *Metaphor and Cognition: An Interactionist Approach.* Dordrecht: Kluwer.
Johnson, Mark
1987    *The Body in the Mind: The Bodily Basis of Meaning, Imagination and Reason.* Chicago: University of Chicago Press.
1993    *Moral Imagination: Implications of Cognitive Science for Ethics.* Chicago: University of Chicago Press.
Johnson, Mark, and Steve Larson
2003    "Something in the way she moves" – metaphors of musical motion. *Metaphor and Symbol* 18: 63–84.
Kaplan, Stuart J.
1990    Visual metaphors in the representation of communication technology. *Critical Studies in Mass Communication* 7: 37–47.
1992    A conceptual analysis of form and content in visual metaphors. *Communication* 13: 197–209.
Kennedy, John M.
1982    Metaphor in pictures. *Perception* 11: 589–605.
1993    *Drawing & the Blind: Pictures to Touch.* New Haven/London: Yale University Press.
Knop, Sabine de, René Dirven, Ning Yu, and Birgit Smieja (eds.)
2005    *Bibliography of Metaphor and Metonymy.* Amsterdam/Philadelphia: Benjamins. Available electronically only at: http://www.benjamins.com/online/met
Kövecses, Zoltán
1986    *Metaphors of Anger, Pride and Love.* Amsterdam/Philadelphia: Benjamins.
2000    *Metaphor and Emotion: Language, Culture, and Body in Human Feeling.* Cambridge: Cambridge University Press.
2002    *Metaphor: A Practical Introduction.* Oxford: Oxford University Press.
2005    *Metaphor in Culture: Universality and Variation.* Cambridge: Cambridge University Press.
Kress, Gunther, and Theo van Leeuwen
1996    *Reading Images: The Grammar of Visual Design.* London/New York: Routledge.
2001    *Multimodal Discourse: The Modes and Media of Contemporary Communication.* London: Edward Arnold.
Lakoff, George
1987    *Women, Fire and Dangerous Things: What Categories Reveal about the Mind.* Chicago: University of Chicago Press.
1993    The contemporary theory of metaphor. In *Metaphor and Thought* (2nd edition), Andrew Ortony (ed.), 202–251. Cambridge: Cambridge University Press.
Lakoff, George, and Mark Johnson
1980    *Metaphors We Live By.* Chicago: University of Chicago Press.

1999    *Philosophy in the Flesh: The Embodied Mind and its Challenge to Western Thought.* New York: Basic Books.
2003    Afterword, 2003. In *Metaphors We Live By*, 243–276. Chicago: University of Chicago Press.

Lakoff, George, and Mark Turner
1989    *More Than Cool Reason: A Field Guide to Poetic Metaphor.* Chicago: University of Chicago Press.

Maalej, Zouhair
2001    Processing pictorial metaphor in advertising: A cross-cultural perspective. *Academic Research* 1: 19–42 [Sfax, Tunisia].

McLuhan, Marshall
1964    The medium is the message. In *Understanding Media: The Extensions of Man* (2nd edition), 23–35. New York: McGraw-Hill.

McNeill, David
1992    *Hand and Mind: What Gestures Reveal about Thought.* Chicago: University of Chicago Press.
2005    *Gesture and Thought.* Chicago: University of Chicago Press.

McQuarrie, Edward F., and David Glen Mick
2003    The contribution of semiotic and rhetorical perspectives to the explanation of visual persuasion in advertising. In *Persuasive Imagery: A Consumer Response Perspective*, Linda M. Scott, and Rajeev Batra (eds.), 191–221. Mahwah, NJ/London: Lawrence Erlbaum.

Müller, Cornelia
2004    *Metaphors, Dead and Alive, Sleeping and Waking: A Cognitive Approach to Metaphors in Language Use.* Habilitationsschrift, Freie Universität Berlin, Germany.

Ortony, Andrew (ed.)
1979    *Metaphor and Thought.* Cambridge: Cambridge University Press.

Phillips, Barbara J.
2003    Understanding visual metaphor. In *Persuasive Imagery: A Consumer Response Perspective*, Linda M. Scott, and Rajeev Batra (eds.), 297–310. Mahwah, NJ: Lawrence Erlbaum.

Richards, Ivor Armstrong
1965 [1936]    *The Philosophy of Rhetoric.* New York: Oxford University Press.

Rohdin, Mats
2003    Summary in English. In *Vildsvinet I Filmens Trädgård: Metaforbegreppet inom Filmteorin* [The wild boar in the garden of film: The concept of metaphor in film theory], 318–329. PhD diss., Stockholm: Edita Norstedts Tryckeri AB.

Rompay, Thomas van
2005    *Expressions: Embodiment in the Experience of Design.* PhD diss., Technische Universiteit Delft, The Netherlands.

Rozik, Eli
1994    Pictorial metaphor. *Kodikas/Code* 17: 203–218.
1998    Ellipsis and the surface structures of verbal and nonverbal metaphor. *Semiotica* 119: 77–103.

Shen, Yeshayahu
1995    Cognitive constraints on directionality in the semantic structure of poetic vs. non-poetic metaphors. *Poetics* 23: 255–274.
Shibles, Warren A.
1971    *Metaphor: An Annotated Bibliography and History.* Whitewater, WI: The Language Press.
Shinohara, Kazuko, and Yoshihiro Matsunaka
2003    An analysis of Japanese emotion metaphors. *Kotoba to Ningen: Journal of Yokohama Linguistic Circle* 4: 1–18.
Shore, Bradd
1996    *Culture in Mind: Cognition, Culture, and the Problem of Meaning.* New York: Oxford University Press.
Simons, Jan
1995    *Film, Language, and Conceptual Structures: Thinking Film in the Age of Cognitivism.* Ph.D. diss., University of Amsterdam, The Netherlands.
Smith, Ken
1996    Laughing at the way we see: The role of visual organizing principles in cartoon humor. *Humor: International Journal of Humor Research* 9: 19–38.
Sperber, Dan, and Deirdre Wilson
1995    *Relevance: Communication and Cognition* (2nd edition). Oxford: Basil Blackwell.
Spitzer, Michael
2004    *Metaphor and Musical Thought.* Chicago/London: University of Chicago Press.
Steen, Gerard J.
1994    *Understanding Metaphor in Literature: An Empirical Approach.* London: Longman.
Stockwell, Peter J.
1999    The inflexibility of invariance. *Language & Literature* (8) 2: 125–42.
Sweetser, Eve E.
1990    *From Etymology to Pragmatics: Metaphorical and Cultural Aspects of Semantic Structure.* Cambridge: Cambridge University Press.
Teng, Norman Y., and Sewen Sun
2002    Grouping, simile, and oxymoron in pictures: A design-based cognitive approach. *Metaphor and Symbol* 17: 295–316.
Terkourafi, Marina, and Stefanos Petrakis
Under rev.  A critical look at the desktop metaphor 25 years on.
Thorau, Christian
2003    Metapher und Variation: Referenztheoretische Grundlagen musikalischer Metaphorizität. *Zeitschrift für Semiotik* 25: 109–124.
Tillyard, Eustace M.W.
1976 [1943]  *The Elizabethan World Picture.* Harmondsworth: Penguin.
Turner, Mark
1996    *The Literary Mind.* New York/Oxford: Oxford University Press.

Tversky, Barbara
    2001    Spatial schemas in depictions. In *Spatial Schemas and Abstract Thought*, Merideth Gattis (ed.), 79–112. Cambridge, MA: MIT Press/ Bradford book.
Van Noppen, Jean-Pierre, Sabine de Knop, and René Jongen (eds.)
    1985    *Metaphor: A Bibliography of Post-1970 Publications*. Amsterdam/Philadelphia: Benjamins.
Van Noppen, Jean-Pierre, and Edith Hols (eds.)
    1990    *Metaphor II: A Classified Bibliography of Publications From 1985– 1990*. Amsterdam/Philadelphia: Benjamins.
Ventola, Eija, Cassily Charles, and Martin Kaltenbacher
    2004    *Perspectives on Multimodality*. Amsterdam/Philadelphia: Benjamins.
Whittock, Trevor
    1990    *Metaphor and Film*. Cambridge: Cambridge University Press.
Wiggin, Amy A., and Christine M. Miller
    2003    "Uncle Sam wants you!" Exploring verbal-visual juxtapositions in television advertising. In *Persuasive Imagery: A Consumer Response Perspective*, Linda M. Scott, and Rajeev Batra (eds.), 267–295. Mahwah, NJ: Lawrence Erlbaum.
Yu, Ning
    1998    *The Contemporary Theory of Metaphor: A Perspective from Chinese*. Amsterdam/Philadelphia: Benjamins.
Zbikowski, Lawrence M.
    2002    *Conceptualizing Music: Cognitive Structure, Theory, and Analysis*. Oxford: Oxford University Press.
Zwaan, Rolf
    1993    *Aspects of Literary Comprehension: A Cognitive Approach*. Amsterdam/Philadelphia: Benjamins.

# The fall of the wall between literary studies and linguistics: Cognitive poetics

*Margaret H. Freeman*

*Abstract*

This paper explores how cognitive poetics may serve as a bridge between literary studies and linguistics. Because cognitive poetics studies the cognitive processes that constrain literary response and poetic structure, it provides a theoretical cognitive basis for literary intuition. At the same time, by exploring the iconic functions that create literature as the semblance of felt life, cognitive poetics contributes to our understanding of the embodied mind. The effect of what I call "poetic iconicity" is to create sensations, feelings, and images in language that enable the mind to encounter them as phenomenally real. The paper draws upon Susanne K. Langer's (1953, 1967) theory of art, Charles Sanders Peirce's (1955[1940]) theory of the sign, Ellen Spolsky's (1993) theory of literature bridging the gap caused by the mind's modularity, Elaine Scarry's (1999) theory of images in the mind, and the cognitive-semiotic notions of blending, deixis, negative polarity, and schema theory to show how Robert Frost manipulates the fictive and factive planes in his poem, "Mending Wall," to create a poetic iconicity of feeling that leads literary critics to their various interpretations of the poem. It concludes by arguing that both literary studies and cognitive linguistics are complementary ways of showing how a literary text extends natural language use in order to bridge the gap between mind and world.

*Keywords*: Cognitive poetics; iconicity; blending; schema; deixis; negative polarity; Robert Frost

## 1. Introduction: Brief sketch of literary and linguistic relations

Over thirty years ago, George Steiner (1970) explored the history of "the language revolution" in literary studies from its development at the turn of the twentieth century. In his chapter on linguistics and poetics, he comments on "the arrogant absurdity" of those who deem themselves qualified in the art of literary study and yet who are totally ignorant of what linguistics contributes to the knowledge of language (p.150). One could just as well say that linguistics as practiced in the twentieth century was just as arrogantly oblivious of the literary text (but see Jakobson1987 for a notable exception). When the editors of this volume invited me to contribute this chapter on the "fall of the wall between literary studies and linguistics" as they put it, I had no doubt that they had in mind, in Steiner's phrase, the "mutually suspicious" attitudes of both literary critics and linguists to each others' work that still exist in academic departments today (Henkel 1996). Whether "the cognitive revolution" that has replaced "the language revolution" at the turn of the twenty-first century can succeed where its predecessor has so obviously failed remains to be seen. In this short essay, I will attempt to outline what I see in cognitive poetics that might suggest a means for better understanding between linguistics and literary studies.

Twentieth century linguists, especially Noam Chomsky and his followers, scorned what they called "mere performance" in their aim to produce a theoretical account of linguistic competence. Cognitive linguists, to the contrary, as the other chapters in this volume show, adopt an encyclopedic view of language and attempt a scientific account of natural language in use. As a result, they have shown increasing awareness of how literary texts might provide a productive source of data for investigation. They have not yet, however, generally recognized the contribution that the accumulated knowledge of literary studies might make to their own research agenda. Likewise, literary critics have been dismissive of linguistic approaches to literature, cognitive or otherwise, either because such approaches fail to account for what the critics consider significant or because the "scientific" apparatus simply recasts in technical jargon what they have said, and said more clearly.

More intense collaboration between linguistics and literary studies could be mutually beneficial. Literary studies has developed over centuries an expertise in reading and analyzing texts which, in the process, has led to the recognition and better understanding of such phenomena as point of view, perspective, narrative, tone, foregrounding, implied author, and so on. It has also developed expertise in relating imaginary worlds to the real contextual worlds of author and reader. Cognitive linguistics, for its part, has developed theories of such phenomena as deixis, figure-ground, fictive motion, mental space mappings, and so on, that parallel literary discoveries. It is no surprise, therefore, that many literary critics find cognitive linguistic applications to literary texts merely "jargonizing" what they already know, and cognitive linguists find literary readings ad hoc and impressionistic. The paralleling of terminology between the two fields is, however, deceptive. Whereas literary critics focus on illuminating the language of the text, cognitive linguists focus on illuminating the language of the embodied mind. This is where cognitive poetics comes in.

## 2. Cognitive poetics

In linking the processes of language in literary text construction and interpretation to the processes of language in the workings of the human mind, cognitive poetics provides a bridge between the two fields.

### 2.1 Brief history

Cognitive Poetics developed over the past twenty years or so from several different strands. Reuven Tsur (1983) was the first to use the term to describe his theoretical and methodological approach to poetry, drawing from studies in psychology, neuro-anatomy, and literary criticism. Another strand developed almost a decade later in Tabakowska's (1993) work in applying Langacker's (1987, 1991) studies in cognitive grammar to poetic translation. Meanwhile, Lakoff and Johnson's (1980) work in conceptual metaphor theory led to Lakoff and Turner's (1989) *More than Cool Reason: A Field Guide to Poetic Metaphor*, from which another strand more closely linked to metaphor theory developed. This strand broadened into further studies as a result of Fauconnier and Turner's (1994, 2002) work in conceptual integration theory, or "blending," as it is more commonly known. Yet another strand emerged from a more general interest in the relation of cognition as reflected in the multidisciplinary approaches of cognitive science to literary studies (Crane and Richardson 1999). Meanwhile, work in cognitive narratology (Emmott 1997; Fludernik 1993), text-world theory (Werth 1999; Gavins 2005), and cognitive stylistics (Semino and Culpeper 2002) expanded the role of cognitive poetics to include other theoretical perspectives and all literary texts.

### 2.2 What is cognitive poetics?

As a result of these different strands, cognitive poetics embraces a broad array of theoretical and methodological approaches. Tsur (1992) defines cognitive poetics as an exploration of how cognitive processes shape and constrain literary response and poetic structure. As Elena Semino (personal correspondence) notes:

Cognitive poetics therefore combines the detailed analysis of linguistic choices and patterns in texts with a systematic consideration of the mental processes and representations that are involved in the process of interpretation. Within cognitive poetics, literary reading is assumed to involve the same mental processes and representations that are involved in comprehension generally. However, special attention is paid to linguistic creativity and its interpretation, since creativity is a central part of the literary experience (even though it is not an exclusively literary phenomenon).

More broadly, Ellen Spolsky (personal correspondence) defines cognitive poetics as "an anti-idealist, anti-platonist enterprise" that entails the following assumptions: 1) the embodiment of the mind-brain constrains what humans can do; 2) human works, including works of art, are attempts to push the boundaries of what can be controlled, known, understood; 3) any study of cognitive issues in a specific work of art must be historically grounded. Thus, cognitive poetics includes not just interpretation from the reader's perspective, but creativity and cultural-historical knowledge of the writer too.

At its best, cognitive poetics is Janus-faced: looking both toward the text and toward the mind. In so doing, it offers the possibilities of developing both a true theory of literature and contributing to a theory of mind. In my own work, I take the position that the study of literature, as part of the broader study of all the arts, contains two elements crucial to the study of mind: the role of feeling and the role of mimesis. As Susanne K. Langer (1953, 1967), the American philosopher, has extensively argued, art is the "semblance of felt life." Studies of mimesis, or iconicity as it has come to be known, and studies of feeling, or the sensory-emotive element in all reasoning, are relative newcomers to the field of linguistics. It is in these areas that literary studies have most to offer cognitive linguistics. Many cognitive researchers have spoken to the question of what cognitive approaches to literature might offer linguistics and literary studies (see, for example, Crane 2001, A. Richardson 2000, Schauber and Spolsky 1986, Spolsky 1993, Turner 1991). I therefore decided to take a literary text appropriate to the theme of this essay – Robert Frost's "Mending Wall" – and set myself the challenge of attempting to identify at least some of the ways in which cognitive poetics says "something new" in literary studies about the text as well as saying "something different" in linguistics. Frost's poem is an appropriate choice, not only because of its subject matter, but because it is one of the most anthologized and analyzed poems in modern literature. Although the choice of one poem necessarily restricts areas of interest to cognitive poetics that might be studied, I hope that such a cognitive poetics application will realize the spirit of this series in applied linguistics and give some sense of the work in cognitive poetics to date.[1]

### 3. A case study in cognitive poetics: Robert Frost's "Mending Wall"

"Mending Wall" might seem an odd choice for a case study on a chapter devoted to the fall of a wall. However, as I hope to show in the ensuing analysis, Frost's poem reveals, as he said himself, that man is both "a wall builder and a wall toppler. He makes boundaries and he breaks boundaries. That's man" (quoted in Cook 1974: 82–83). This human characteristic reflects man as part of nature. Frost notes elsewhere: "Nature within her inmost self divides / To trouble men with having to take sides."[2] Although Frost's poem ostensibly appears to be about two men taking opposing sides, a close analysis reveals a somewhat different purpose, as several critics have noticed: the value of opening up the imagination. In this way, the gaps in the physical wall become identified with gaps in nature, gaps in the human mind (Spolsky 1993). In seeing the emergent meaning of the poem as a blend between the physical story of the two neighbors as they go about mending their boundary wall and the imaginative story of the work of the human mind, one can also see the poem iconically invoking images of boundary walls from the reader's own experience which is then mapped onto the narrative, thus making the language of the poem become phenomenally real, to create, in Langer's words, the semblance of felt life. How this works is what I hope to show in the rest of this essay.

### 3.1 Poetry as iconicity

Poetic iconicity is one way of explaining why poetry cannot be successfully paraphrased. As Frost would invariably remark in response to a question as to what he meant by a poem, "What do you want me to do, say it again in different and less good words?" (quoted in Raab 1996). "It" is not simply "meaning", it is the poem itself. According to Charles Sanders Peirce (1955[1940]), every word is a symbol that may or may not have an icon or index function. A poem that is true to the experience of felt life is mimetically representing that experience by evoking a mental image of it. Mimesis, literary or so-called "exophoric" iconicity, is the principle of form miming meaning, language miming the world. But poems are also mostly self-referential, displaying instances of "endophoric" iconicity, with form miming form (Nöth 2001).

The effect of poetic iconicity is to create sensations, feelings, and images in language that enable the mind to encounter them as phenomenally real. In this way, poetic iconicity bridges the "gap" between mind and world. This gap takes on different forms and arises from different causes depending on the perspective taken. In neurological theory, the gap occurs because the mind is modular, receiving and processing multiple sense impressions in discrete areas of the brain (Aleksander 2005; Modell 2003; Velmans 2002). In cognitive theory, the gap is caused, as Spolsky (1993: 2) explains, by the "inevitable asymmetry and incompleteness of mental representation" through the idealization that occurs as the result of the mind's modularity (Lakoff and Johnson 1999). In philosophical theory, the gap is described in terms of the lack of connection between mind and world. In linguistic theory, the gap arises from underdetermination; that is, the phono-morphemic syntactic system of language does not of itself generate meaning. One should not consider this gap to be a flaw in human nature. Rather, it is the means by which we are able to think at all, to reason, to hypothesize, to consider counterfactual possibilities, to respond emotionally and ethically to situations we find ourselves in, and so on. It accounts for our ability to anticipate, accept, and encourage change. Fundamentally, it enables creativity. When Spolsky (1993: 2) says that the "mind itself can hurt you into poetry," she is suggesting that "innovation in literary systems can be understood as evidence of the mind's responses to incompatible representations" created by the gap (ibid. p.7).[3] Poetic iconicity, as I define the term, is the means by which poetry both exploits and bridges this gap.

Because of its subject matter and the fact that it is a poem, Frost's "Mending Wall" becomes a prototypical exemplum of the poetic iconicity I am talking about (see Appendix for complete text). Across the relatively long history of human culture, tension exists between conservancy of conventionalized strategies that preserve the relationships of intermodular activity and the multiple flexibility of change needed for the mind to adapt to the challenges of new stimuli in producing unconventional relationships. This tension is reflected in Frost's poem.[4] It is the poet-speaker who distinguishes between the "gaps" caused by human agency in the work of the hunters and the "gaps" made by "something" no one can see or hear. It is the farmer-neighbor who holds on to the traditional attitudes of his cultural forebears. Frost's poem suggests that imaginative creativity occurs when writers probe beyond the outward appearance of things to explore their significance and "meaning." When linguistic forms are brought into mimetic correspondence with this act of imaginative creativity, iconicity results. This, I believe, is the ideal poets attempt to achieve: the breaking down of the conventionally arbitrary barrier between form and essence in order to bridge the gap between stimuli (sensory, emotional) and conceptualization, to access as far as possible what Merleau-Ponty (1962, 1968) calls precategorial experience and Tsur (1992, 2002) "lowly differentiation," the blurring of distinct categories and forms to capture that which cannot be directly perceived, what Peirce (1955[1940]) calls "suchness," anything immediately but not directly perceived.

## 3.2  Blending and beyond: Knowledge domains in "Mending Wall"

The phenomenological world of the semiotic base space represented in Frost's "Mending Wall" is that of two adjacent New England farms.[5] It includes both knowledge of New England farming practices as well as cultural knowledge of classical mythology. Critics, for example, tend to note that although the poet-speaker seems to be sympathetic, if not outright to identify, with the "something that doesn't love a wall," it is he who repairs the gaps made by hunters and who initiates the cooperative wall-mending ritual each spring. This is not a puzzling feature of authorial intention as some have supposed. According to legal property rights, there is no such thing as a boundary wall that is owned in common. Historically, if a wall has been built equally on both sides of a property boundary, the principle of *medium filum* applies: the abutting property owners own up to the middle line of the wall and share a "common interest" in the wall as a whole.[6] According to a recent Scottish report on Boundary Walls, "Common interest imposes both a restraint and a positive obligation. The restraint is that each owner must take care not to disturb the stability of the wall as a whole. The positive obligation is that each must maintain his own part of the wall."[7] As one would expect, the poet repairs his own walls when the hunters dismantle them. We are told that his farmer-neighbor lives "beyond the hill." This deictic projection distances the farmer from the wall in question both visually and spatially. It would be natural and appropriate, then, for the poet to initiate the information that gaps have appeared. Finally, we are told that the poet owns an apple orchard that abuts the farmer's pine forest. New England stone walls that can be seen today in the woods indicate that the land was once farmed or used for pasture. No one builds walls in pine woods, since there is no "need" for such walls. Walls, however, are crucial for apple orchards, to keep out cows and other animals. It is, therefore, more in the interest of the poet than the farmer to maintain this particular wall.

The situation of the semiotic base space describes the activity of the two neighbors who set out in the spring to repair a boundary wall between their properties. The poem is narrated by one of the two neighbors, so that we are presented with a discourse situation in which the narrator is also a character in his own story. The farmer is meeting his obligation to maintain his side of the wall out of his belief that "good fences make good neighbors." Here is a man who practices what Ferdinand Tönnies (1957 [1887]) has called *Gemeinschaft* and acts upon his beliefs.[8] And those beliefs are even further emphasized and reinforced by the fact that there is no longer any real need for the wall that divides apple and pine trees. Had there been a real need for the wall, the significance of the farmer's gesture would have been somewhat lessened. That significance, as George Monteiro (1988:126–129) has shown us, is deeply embedded in two historical, cultural domains: the existence of a Spanish proverbial saying (*una pared entre dos vezinos guarda mas (haze durar) la amistad*) which goes back "at least to the Middle Ages" and was recorded by Emerson in his journal of 1832 as "A wall between both, best preserves friendship"; and the myth of the god of boundaries, named *Terminus* by the Romans, who celebrated a *Terminalia* festival each year on February 23 (in early spring) when "neighbors on either side of any boundary gathered around the landmark" to offer sacrifice to the god and celebrate with a feast. The poem, Monteiro believes, is moving toward this mythological link in the speaker's description of his neighbor at the end of the poem as "an old-stone savage armed" who "moves in darkness." The occurrence of magical elements such as "spell' and the notion of "Elves" in the poem conjures up the mysteries of pre-scientific knowledge that is reflected in the myth as well as in the unconscious elements of the human mind.

### 3.3  Metaphor and mimesis

One curious thing about Frost's poem is that its central metaphor is expressed so simply and its meaning is so transparent that we tend not to see it as a metaphor at all. This occurs in line 24: "He is all pine and I am apple orchard." By identifying the two characters in the poem with their land, Frost is doing two things: he is establishing the two sides of the actual boundary wall that is the subject of the poem and at the same time he is making that wall a mental representation. So one can see the presentation space as being the actual, factive story of two men repairing a boundary wall in springtime, and the reference space as being the virtual, fictive story of the operations of the mind (Fig. 1). The balanced shifts between the factive (indexical) to the fictive (virtual) create the image in the mind, so that the fictive lies within the factive, the factive within the fictive. In

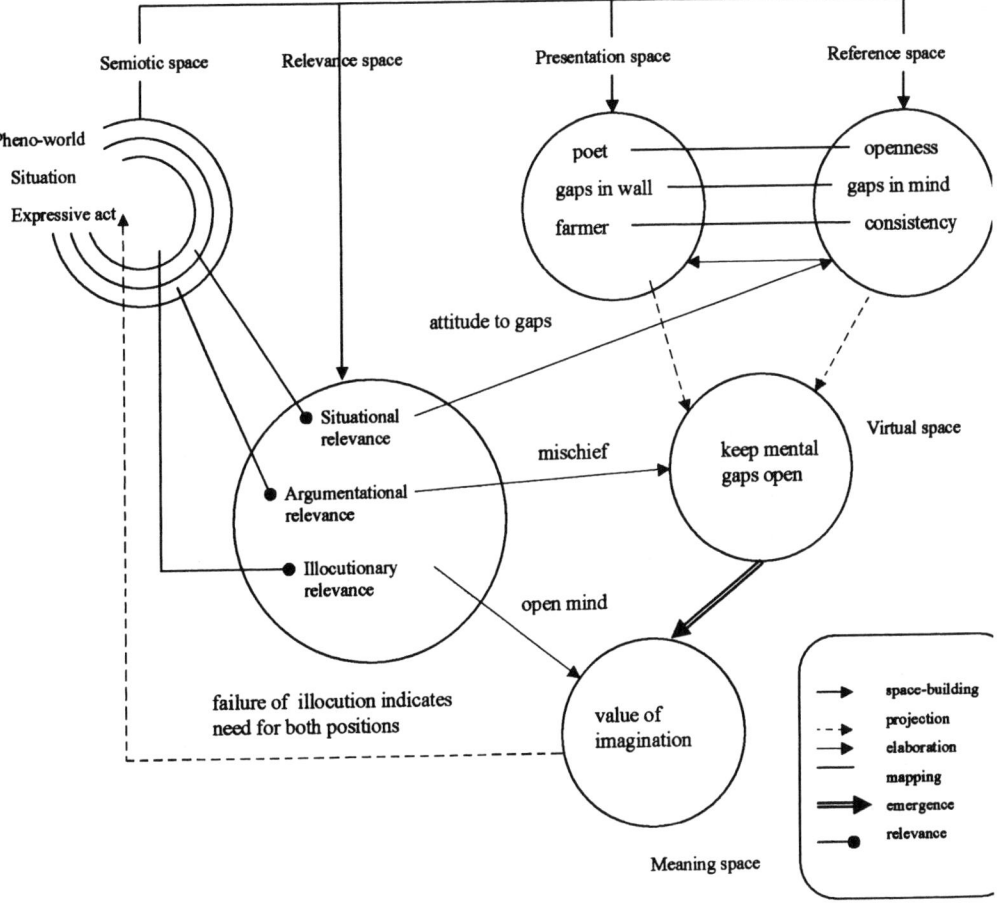

*Figure 1.* The cognitive-semiotic blend in "Mending Wall" (based on Brandt and Brandt 2005: 239)

the blend, the poet represents the creative, open-ended operations of the mind; the farmer, the mind's need for coherence and continuity. The meaning that emerges from this blend is the value that is being attached to the poem's topic, that is, the gaps in the wall/mind.

The bringing together of the gaps in the physical world of Frost's poem and the mental world of his imagination occurs through a particular characteristic of mental representations. Frank Lentricchia's (1975) study of the "landscapes of the self" in "Mending Wall" reflects Elaine Scarry's (1999) argument that references to the rarefied and intangible facilitate the creation of images in the mind. He argues that not naming what it is that causes walls to fall enables Frost "to manipulate intransigent fact into the world of the mind where all things are pliable" (p.104). In making "fiction" about how the wall developed gaps, the poet is inviting the farmer to accompany him, "to take a journey in the mind."[9] Thus, the poem becomes a paeon to the "play spirit of imagination." For the cognitive linguist, the question becomes how Frost makes language work to make us think the poem is about minds as well as about walls.

As Scarry (1999) has shown, poetry sets up a mimesis of making and a mimesis of motion. Right from the outset, Frost introduces the idea of a (solid) wall by referring to something immaterial, "rarefied" in Scarry's terms. This "something" is unseen, unheard. It "makes gaps" which are themselves the absenting of materiality. This, Scarry suggests, is what enables us to take an image more easily into the mind.[10] The image itself – the wall – is then immediately made to move through the technique of introducing light, with some force spilling its boulders into the sun. The sudden addition into the scene of rabbits and dogs as natural living organisms helps to reinforce the mental image of motion as the hunters subtract the stones from the fictive wall we have been invited to imagine. Similarly, Frost's introduction of the seemingly inappropriate images of the fallen boulders as "loaves" – associating them with plant life and relative insubstantiality compared with stones – and "so nearly balls" – associating them with a shape and a size easy to handle and pick up – enables Frost to create the image of movement and precarious balance as the neighbors "wear [their] fingers rough with handling them" as they "set the wall." Having created these mental images of the activity of wall mending, Frost has prepared the way for his speaker to "put a notion in his [neighbor's] head" as he has put mental images into ours. The "notion" challenges the need for a physical barrier. It asks the reasons why and, in wondering what might cause walls to fall, invokes the assumption of invisible natural forces and the resulting inevitability of change. It expresses the human ability to cognize, to imagine the existence of things neither seen nor heard, to acknowledge and accept the idea of change. It is no surprise, then, that many critics identify the imaginative thoughts of the poet-speaker with those of Frost and think the poem is about "modes of thought, about language, perhaps even about poetry itself" (Kemp 1979: 24) or that the wall is "a mental wall ... as well as a physical one" (Holland 1988: 25).

### 3.4  Macrostructure of "Mending Wall": the BALANCE schema

Frost's poem moves from the idea of an invisible force breaking down walls in the first line of the poem to the idea of fences being necessary for social harmony in the last, from, in Frost's own words, "Something there is that doesn't love a wall" to "Something there is that does."[11] The poem iconically reflects this movement in its structure and choice of language. Two major cognitive processes are at work: our awareness of phenomena not directly presented to our senses (phenomenologically called "appresentation" and psychologically, "inferential apperception"); and the need for consistency in categorization and coherence (what Tsur (1992, 2002) calls "cognitive stability," and Turner and Pöppel (1980) "procrustean" and "synthetic"). These are brought into imaginative contrast through the interrelated devices of deixis, negative polarity, and the BALANCE schema.[12]

The poem's macrostructure iconically reflects the structure of the dry stone wall that is its subject (Fig. 2). First, the exact center of the poem occurs in line 23: "There where it is we do not need the wall." The line is set off from the first 22 lines by a colon, and is set off from the next 22 lines by another colon, which makes it serve almost as a ratio between the two parts of the poem, acting as a pivot, balancing the two halves. It has both indexical deixis – "there where it is" – and negation – the wall exists, but we don't need it. And the reason we don't need it is immediately provided by the metaphor we've already noticed: because of who the two men are. That Frost creates an identity mapping between pine trees and the farmer, and apple trees and the poet is no accident. Unlike pine trees, apple trees blossom in spring. I am reminded of Emily Dickinson's poem, "This is a Blossom of / the Brain."

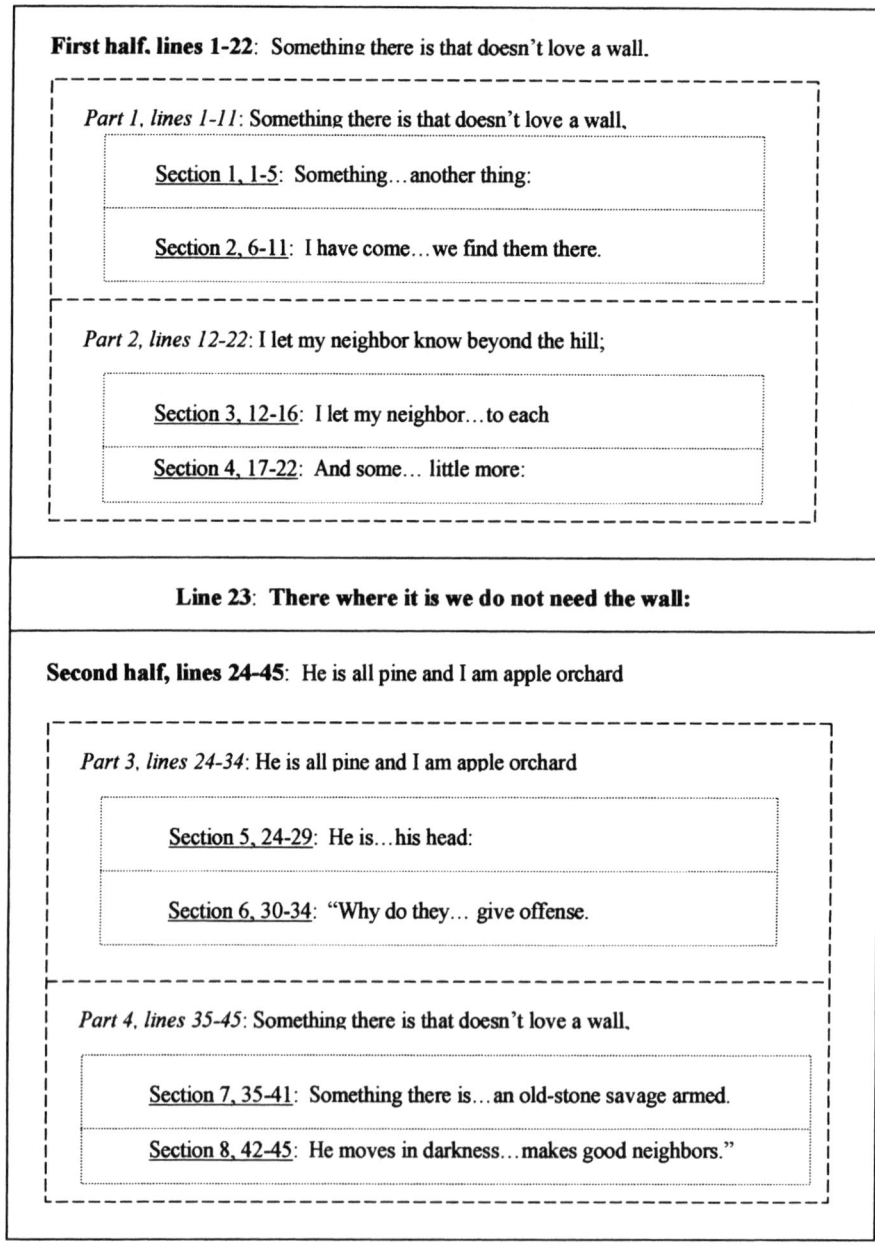

*Figure 2.* The structure of "Mending Wall"

On either side of this wall that we don't need but that divides the two halves of the poem, each set of 22 lines falls into two parallel parts, marked by syntactic openings and closures and lexical patterns and repetitions. These are the building blocks on which the wall/poem is constructed. The first and last parts of the poem serve to frame the two inside parts. The first part (lines 1–11) introduces the idea of the "Something there is that doesn't love a wall," and the last part (lines 35–45) begins with the same line and ends the poem with the idea that "Good fences make good neighbors." The interior parts deal with the interaction of the two neighbors. Part 2 (lines 12–22) describes the collaborative process they adopt to mend the wall. Part 3 (lines 24–34) contrasts the thoughts of the poet with that of the farmer over the reasons for mending the wall. If this were not enough, each of these parts divides into two sections of five and six lines apiece, creating a chiasmic pattern or mirror image across the dividing line. In the first half, the section divisions are 5 lines followed by 6; in the second half, the section divisions are 6 lines followed by 5. These wall/poem components, though, are not so perfectly constructed as they seem. The 19 sentences of the poem (marked by end punctuation) sometimes cut across these parts and sections and occur irregularly both in position and number within them. Those familiar with New England dry stone walls, created over two hundred years ago, will know that they are not at all uniform in appearance. They are made up of irregular-sized and irregular-shaped boulders that seem to balance precariously on one another, a method called "random rubble" in the dry-stone-wall making trade. It is these irregularities that enable the frost heaving that occurs when ice forms and melts to "spill the upper boulders in the sun." The BALANCE schema of the poem is therefore not a static one. It is a dynamic process of ongoing annual activity that the neighbors must undertake to maintain their wall, just as the mind must be engaged in continual activity to create coherency and consistency from multiple and inchoate experience, to achieve cognitive stability, to make sense out of things.

This iconic macrostructure creates a structural blend of wall and poem, so that in the blend what is true of one is true of the other. Just as the wall is embodied in the poem, the poem is embodied in the wall. What happens as a result is that the gaps in the wall become gaps in the mind. And the poem becomes a way of responding to and dealing with those gaps. The techniques we use, linguistic or literary, to articulate and explore these gaps are all salient and valid ways to understand them. The poet calls the object of their mending a wall, the farmer calls it a fence. This is not arbitrary naming. The meaning network of the word *wall* encompasses more than the word *fence*. A fence forms a barrier to divide one space from another. A wall not only has this function but also may be constructed as a shelter and a refuge (it is used in this way by the rabbits in the first part of the poem). As the literary critic Lawrence Raab (1996) has noted, "mending fences" is an idiom for restoring communication and harmony. He writes: "The repetition of *between* [in lines 14 and 15] should give us pause and remind us of its two equally common meanings: *between* as separation, as in 'something's come between us,' and *between* as what might be shared and held in common, as in 'a secret between two people' or 'a bond between friends.' The wall divides but it also connects, if you look at it that way." Looking at language "that way" is what literature does. It opens up the possibilities created by the gaps between our conceptualizations and our experiences of the world.


3.5   Mind in the wall and the wall in mind: Deixis and negative polarity

Mental representations occur on two planes – the virtual or fictive and the actual or factive – depending on whether they are generalized and unspecified or individualized and particularized (Langacker 2005). That is, conceptualizations may be construed as generalized abstractions or as specific representations, depending on whether reference is being made to an imagined or virtual situation (fictive) or an actual one (factive). This distinction is created in the poem by the two cognitive processes of deixis and negative polarity.

Deixis is of two kinds: the kind that introduces something into the fictive plane ("existential") and the kind that points out something in the factive plane ("indexical"). The first notable use of deixis in the poem is the existential "there" of the first line: "Something there is that doesn't love a wall." It introduces the unpresentable, that which cannot be seen or heard by the embodied senses, thus invoking the cognitive process of the imagining of "things unseen." The indefinite article, "a wall" indicates that the wall exists in a virtual mental space or plane; that is, it is a generalized mental conception, not a reference to an actual wall. Part 1 is framed by the movement from the existential "there" of line 1 to the indexical "there" at the end of line 11, which serves to introduce the actual physical wall that the neighbors will mend. A similar movement occurs in the plural form of the word "gaps" in line 4 on the virtual plane and in the definite article of "the gaps" in line 9 on the actual plane. Once deictic "there" has placed the gaps in physical space, the means has been opened up for "the wall" on the actual plane to be introduced in the second section (lines 12–16).

The second section establishes the cognitive stability of the factive action of wall construction, reflected in the balance achieved by end-stopped, regularly metered lines and the repetition of equivalent phrases – *set the wall / keep the wall; between us / between us; to each / to each* – as the neighbors "walk the line." However, the negative polarities that have been running through part 1 (*doesn't love, gaps, not one, but, no one*) surface in the very next section (lines 17–22) with the limited polarities of not-quite expressions (*so nearly, just another, little more*) that make balance precarious and prepare for the indexical repetition "there where it is" in line 23, introducing the idea that the wall is, after all, not needed, and yet is expressed in the line which serves as the boundary dividing the two halves of the poem. Once this boundary wall has been presented, it again loses its deictic specificity in all the references on the other side: the general "fences" of the farmer's comment and the hypothetical fictive musings of the poet as he thinks of why he would build "a wall," preparing for the repetition of the first line, "Something there is that doesn't love a wall" at the beginning of the last part (line 35).

Deictic and negative polarity terms contrasting conceptions in the mind (virtual-fictive) and representations of objects in the world (actual-factive) are tossed through the poem like the "loaves" and "balls" of line 17 (Fig. 3). The existential "there-where" of lines 1 and 7 is repeated in the deictic "there-where" of lines 11 and 19 that prepares for the deictic "there where" of the pivot line 23. On the other side of the pivot, "there" occurs at the end of the two word phrases in the existential "where there" and deictic "here there" of line 31, creating another kind of chiasmus with the phrases on the other side. These deictic alternations culminate in the final existential-indexical contrast of the last part of the poem in the repetition of "Something there is" (line 35) and "I see him there" (line 38), which parallels the move from fictive to factive in the first part. This existential-indexical alternation balances the fictive and the factive. It embodies the actions of the mind as phenomenally real.

Fictive-factive alternation also occurs across two different kinds of negative polarity: the kind that establishes a subtraction from positive existence, as in "not one stone on a stone" (line 7), and the kind that results in the opening up of possibilities beyond the physical, as in "No one has seen ... or heard" (line 10). In the first kind of negation, an element created in the fictive plane is cancelled out in the actual plane. In the second, only a portion of possible elements in the fictive part is cancelled,

*Line 23*: There where[a] it is we do not[c] need the wall:[a]

..... there[i] ..... doesn't[c] ..... a wall,[i]            He ........ I ...............
...............................                                My ....... never ..........
...............................                                ...........his......I......him.
....... gaps[i] ..................                             He only ......... fences[i] .........
...............another thing[a]                                ............. me, ....... I ...........
I ..............................                               ...... I ....... his ..........
Where[i]..... not one[c]..................                     ...................................
...............................                                Where there[i]..........here there[a] ........
...............................                                no[c] ........
.................. The gaps[a] I.......                         ....I..... a wall[i] .....................
No one[o] .......... them ..............                        ......... I ............................
them ............                                              ........................................
..................we ...... them there[a]                      ............. I ........................
I.............................the hill[a]                       ........there ........ doesn't[c] love a wall[i]
...............we ........... the line[a]                       ............ I .............. him,
......... the wall[a] ....us ..............                     ...... not[o] ...... exactly, ....... I'd ........
We ......... the wall[a] ......us ...we ....                    He ........... himself. I ...... him there[a]
......... the boulders[a] ..............                        ........................................
........ some .............. some so                           ........................................
nearly[o] ............                                         ........................................
We...........................                                  He .................................. me,
......where[a]...............our............                    Not[o] .......... only[o] ....................
We ......our ...........................                        He ....... not[c] .......... his .............
..... just another[o] .....................                     ........ he ...........................
........................... little more[o]                     He ............ fences[i] .................

[i] fictive     [a] factive     [c] closed     [o] open

Figure 3. Deixis and negative polarity in "Mending Wall"

thus leaving open the possibility of the rest being actualized. These two kinds of polarities are repeated in the second half of the poem with the contrasts between the subtraction of "no cows" (line 31) and the opening up of possibilities in "not elves" (line 37) and their chiasmic reversal in "Not of woods only" (line 42) and "He will not go behind" (line 43). In other words, what the poem is doing is oscillating between the fictive and factive planes as the poet plays with ideas of balancing the imagined and the real, the possible and the actual.

## 3.6    Balancing deixis and negation in the poem/wall, poet/farmer, mind/ world

The making of such balance occurs also in the self-referential, endophoric iconic functions at the lexical as well as the structural level.The verb *make* occurs in parallel usage. It is used three times in the first half of the poem to indicate the destructive force creating gaps in the wall and three times in the second half to indicate the constructive force creating social harmony (good neighbors). It is also used to make repair (line 6) and to make balance (line 18). Making repair occurs in the context of the destruction of a wall by seen and heard forces (the hunters). Making balance occurs in the context of the destruction of a wall by unseen and unheard forces (a something that doesn't love walls). This distinction is reinforced by the invocation of a "spell" in the act of balancing, which, both semantically in its meaning and phonetically in its relation to the "spills" of line 3, suggests something magical, beyond the known world, as opposed to the merely physical routine of repairing a wall broken by hunters. This contrast is mimetically paralleled in the language and structure of the two sections of part 1. Section 1 begins with "something" (invisible, unheard) and ends with "another thing" (seen and heard). The "something" has three verbs in section 1: *sends, spills, makes*; the "another thing" also three in section 2: *have left, would have, please*. Note the difference between these sets of verbs: that which is unseen, fictive, has immediate causal agency: *sends, spills, makes gaps*. The work of the hunters, factive, doesn't: *have left, would have, to please*. This contrast gives greater valence to the fictive which accords with the poem's illocutionary force (see note 5): the importance of the imagination.

    The balanced oppositions of negation and deixis are reinforced by deictic pronoun use. In the first half, as the two neighbors work together to rebuild the wall, all references to them occur by means of the first person plural forms: *we, us, our*. In the second half, where the poet tries to create flexibility and change in the farmer's thinking, there are no *we*'s, *us*'s, or *our*'s; only *he* and *I*, *me* and *him*, *his* and *my*. The neighbors, once joined in collaborative work to mend the wall, are now forced apart by the central line querying the need for a wall at all, just as the wall once whole developed gaps. Parts 3 and 4 also provide a kind of balance between themselves. Part 3 (lines 24–34) begins with repeated alternations of "he" and "I" forms and ends in the fourfold repetition of "I" as the speaker questions the reasons for wall building; part 4 (lines 35–45) begins with alternations of "I" and "he" forms and ends in the fourfold repetition of "he" forms as the neighbor reiterates his belief. The "I" repetitions at the end of part 3 question the use of a wall as a barrier, ending in the echo of "fence" in "offense" (line 34).

At the graphemic level, too, the repetition of the letter *l* in *wall, swell, spills, hill, fallen, balls, spell, wall, all, tell, walling (in and out), will, well,* reflects the two sides of the barrier.[13] The word "spring" occurs twice, one on each side of the pivot line in the center of the poem, and is related to mending and mischief respectively, another kind of balance between cognitive stability and opening up the mind to alternative possibilities. Finally, the opposition of "sun" (line 3) and "darkness" (line 41) on either side points to the idea of openness and illumination created by gaps and the idea of closed conservancy that nevertheless signifies in the poet's mind something beyond the physical pine woods and "shade of trees."

## 4.    Conclusion: Literature, linguistics, and cognitive poetics

Robert Graves (1963) was the first critic to identify the possible pun Frost is playing with in not naming the "frost" that causes walls to heave, which serves to identify the poet-speaker with unseen forces that upset solidity and disrupt order. However, Mark Richardson (1997: 141) is surely right in enlarging the idea to include "the vernal mischief of spring and its insubordinations."[14] The creation through deixis of identification between the factive and the fictive, between the physical gaps in the actual wall and the mental gaps of the mind in its reception of multiple and overlapping information, is paralleled by the identification of the volcanic nature of the unseen forces (that spew out the boulders to cause gaps in the actual wall) with the "Spring" that "is the mischief" in the mind of the poet-speaker that wants to create a similar unsettled disturbance in the mind of his farmer-neighbor, to open up his mind to the recognition of mental gaps in the articulation of knowledge and feeling. The poet is thus kicking against the obligation of restraint in undermining stability of wall and feeling. Spring mischief leads him to "wonder" if he "could put a notion" in the farmer's head. Literary critics (e.g., Lentricchia 1975, Kemp 1979) are divided over whether the poet actually utters the words that follow (lines 30–36). However, these are the climactic words of the poem. They bring the thoughts of the poet (fictive) into communication (factive) with the farmer, and thus make the "mischief" of making gaps phenomenally real. They point to the possible answer the farmer might give, the "Elves" reflecting his cultural mythological heritage, and the answer he does in fact give, the reiteration of "Good fences make good neighbors." In the end, the only direct speech acts in the poem are four in number, all indicated by quotation marks: the joint admonition to the stones to "Stay where you are until our backs are turned" (line 19) that both poet and farmer participate in, the poet's questions (lines 30–36), and the repetition of the proverb, "Good fences make good neighbors" (lines 28 and 46) uttered by the farmer. It is noteworthy that in all these cases, it is inanimate objects (stones and fences) that are ascribed agency. Frost's restatement of the Spanish proverb ascribes more causal agency in the act of making than either the proverb or Emerson's translation of it do. It is this "making," this construction of the fictive in the factive that creates the poem's iconicity, and explains why Frost saw himself in both characters.[15] It is people that make good fences (factive), but it is fences that make good people (fictive).

Cognitive poetics, I suggest, is in essence an exploration into poetic iconicity, as I am defining the term. It links the literary text to the cognitive processes of the human mind, and provides a theoretical cognitive linguistic basis for literary intuition. That's what makes it different from purely linguistic or literary approaches. It does not replace these approaches; rather, it shows how they evidence ways in which a literary text bridges the gap between mind and world. It is for this reason, I believe, that cognitive poetics can contribute to both the scientific and the humanistic enterprise. It does not try to transform humanistic enquiry into a science. Nor does it presume that scientific enquiry could replace humanistic enquiry as an adequate way to account for artistic creativity. As it "walks the line" between the two, it defines the boundary that both separates and joins the two endeavors.

## Appendix

### MENDING WALL
**Robert Frost**

1   Something there is that doesn't love a wall,
2   That sends the frozen-ground-swell under it,
3   And spills the upper boulders in the sun,
4   And makes gaps even two can pass abreast.
5   The work of hunters is another thing:
6   I have come after them and made repair
7   Where they have left not one stone on a stone,

8    But they would have the rabbit out of hiding,
9    To please the yelping dogs. The gaps I mean,
10   No one has seen them made or heard them made,
11   But at spring mending-time we find them there.
12   I let my neighbor know beyond the hill;
13   And on a day we meet to walk the line
14   And set the wall between us once again.
15   We keep the wall between us as we go.
16   To each the boulders that have fallen to each.
17   And some are loaves and some so nearly balls
18   We have to use a spell to make them balance:
19   "Stay where you are until our backs are turned!"
20   We wear our fingers rough with handling them.
21   Oh, just another kind of out-door game,
22   One on a side. It comes to little more:
23   There where it is we do not need the wall:
24   He is all pine and I am apple orchard.
25   My apple trees will never get across
26   And eat the cones under his pines, I tell him.
27   He only says, "Good fences make good neighbors."
28   Spring is the mischief in me, and I wonder
29   If I could put a notion in his head:
30   "Why do they make good neighbors? Isn't it
31   Where there are cows? But here there are no cows.
32   Before I built a wall I'd ask to know
33   What I was walling in or walling out,
34   And to whom I was like to give offense.
35   Something there is that doesn't love a wall,
36   That wants it down." I could say "Elves" to him,
37   But it's not elves exactly, and I'd rather
38   He said it for himself. I see him there
39   Bringing a stone grasped firmly by the top
40   In each hand, like an old-stone savage armed.
41   He moves in darkness as it seems to me,
42   Not of woods only and the shade of trees.
43   He will not go behind his father's saying,
44   And he likes having thought of it so well
45   He says again, "Good fences make good neighbors."

*North of Boston.* New York: Henry Holt & Co. 1915.

## Acknowledgments

I am grateful to Christina Ljungberg, Claiborne Rice, and the editors of this volume for helpful suggestions to the ideas broached in this essay. I trust that issues of theory and interpretation that emerge as a result will contribute to further discussions in the field.

## Notes

1. See Gavins and Steen (2003) and Stockwell (2002) for introductory texts in cognitive poetics. There are many cognitive poetics articles appearing in various journals, such as *Poetics Today, Style, Language and Literature, Journal of English Linguistics,* all of which have published special issues on cognitive approaches to literature. See also Hogan (2003). For a survey of recent work in the field, see Freeman (in press). The following websites contain other bibliographic sources: cognitive approaches to literature at http://www.ucs.louisiana.edu/~cxr1086/coglit/; blending at http://markturner.org/; iconicity in language and literature at http://home.hum.uva.nl/iconicity/; textworld theory at http://www.sheffield.ac.uk/textworldtheory/; art and cognition at http://www.interdisciplines.org/artcog; literature, cognition, and the brain at http://cogweb.ucla.edu/.
2. Robert Frost. "FROM IRON: Tools and Weapons. To Ahmed S. Bokhari." As James Reston noted in *The New York Times* for October 27, 1957: "The United Nations, disturbed by Mr. Frost's opposition, suggested to him recently that he might like to write a poem celebrating the ideal of the interdependence of the nations. Sweden had given the U. N. a huge chunk of solid iron, and somebody thought that this should be built into the U. N. building as a symbol of nature's strength and unity. Frost was not interested. Iron, he said, could be used to strengthen the U. N. building, or it could be used for weapons of war. That was the way with nature, he said: always confronting mankind with decisions. So he rejected the invitation with a couplet ..." http://www.frostfriends.org/FFL/Periodicals/reston-nyt.html. Accessed March 21, 2006. I am grateful to Nick Fleck for drawing my attention to this couplet.
3. Spolsky's line is an adaptation of W. H. Auden's line, "mad Ireland hurt you into poetry" in his poem, "In Memory of W. B. Yeats."
4. The speaker of the poem is not Frost but the poem's persona. However, the ability of the speaker in contrast to his neighbor to see the difference between the gaps made by seen and unseen forces and recognize their significance marks him as a poet. I shall therefore refer to the two characters as the poet and the farmer.
5. Here, I am following Per Aage Brandt's (2004) modification and elaboration of Fauconnier and Turner's (2002) blending model. Blending accounts for how new information can emerge from old through the projection from given

input spaces into a new space, called the blend. Brandt adds a "semiotic base space" which includes the phenomenological world, or "pheno-world" for short, the situation in which communication occurs, and the actual semiosis of the discourse, including the participants and what is being communicated. The input spaces of the blend are renamed as Presentation and Reference spaces. Instead of the generic space in the original model, Brandt substitutes a "relevance space" from which situational, argumentational, and illocutional relevance triggers activity at various points in the development of meaning.

6. Scott Sylvester (New England forester), personal communication.

7. Report on Boundary Walls. Scottish Law Commission No. 163. Printed 25th March, 1998. (584 Edinburgh: The Stationery Office) p. 2. New England followed common law practice in establishing the metes and bounds of property, and the wording of the Scottish report (though not part of English common law) reflects New England practices.

8. Tönnies (1957: 223) distinguished between *Gemeinschaft* (community) and *Gesellschaft* (society) as follows: "There is a contrast between a social order which – being based upon consensus of wills – rests on harmony and is developed and ennobled by folkways, mores, and religion, and an order which – being based upon a union of rational wills – rests on convention and agreement, is safeguarded by political legislation, and finds its ideological justification in public opinion."

9. The first poem, "The Pasture," in Frost's *North of Boston* immediately preceding "Mending Wall," is just such an invitation.

10. Scarry's theory is suggestive, even if there is as yet little empirical evidence that the mind entertains insubstantiality more readily than solidity. Limitations of space and exigencies of presentation prevent me from documenting all the cognitive science research that supports this and subsequent claims throughout this paper. I refer readers to Scarry's book and my other reference citations for further cognitive literature on the topics raised.

11. Lawrence Raab (1996) recounts Frost's reaction to the Russians making use of his poem to defend the construction of the Berlin Wall by dropping the first line. Frost wonders how they "got the poem started" and said he could have done better for them by saying: "Something there is that doesn't love a wall / Something there is that does." It is noteworthy that Frost continues: "Why didn't I say that? I didn't mean that. I meant to leave that until later in the poem." Why he meant to leave it until later results I think from the poem's iconicity.

12. Johnson (1987: 29) defines a schema as "a recurrent pattern, shape, and regularity in, or of, [the] ongoing ordering activities" of our actions, perceptions, and conceptions. See Johnson (1987: 18–30) for a detailed discussion of how this use of the term *schema* differs from earlier uses in cognitive science. Examples of schema are PATH, CONTAINMENT, CHANGE, and the one I am referring to here: BALANCE. For a discussion on how schemas can illuminate a poet's poetics, see Freeman (2002).

13. I am grateful to Christina Ljungberg for pointing out the phonetic repetition

of the [l] sound in the poem. A full cognitive-phonetic analysis of the poem would show other iconic functions at work, but would lengthen what is already a long paper on a short poem.

14. It is rather the melting of the frost that causes subsidence and imbalance, as the *Encyclopedia Britannica*'s entry on *frost* notes: "Frost action, the freezing and thawing of moisture in the ground, has long been known to seriously disrupt and destroy structures in both polar and temperate latitudes. In the winter the freezing of ground moisture produces upward displacement of the ground (frost heaving), and in the summer excessive moisture in the ground brought in during the freezing operation causes loss of bearing strength."

15. Norman Holland (1988: 26) quotes Frost's comments on the poem as follows: "Maybe I was both fellows in the poem". *Interviews with Robert Frost*, ed. Edward Connery Lathem (New York: Holt, Rinehart and Winston 1966) 257.

# References

Aleksander, Igor
　2005　*The World in My Mind, My Mind in the World: Key Mechanisms of Consciousness in People, Animals and Machines.* Exeter, UK: Imprint Academic.

Brandt, Line, and Per Aage Brandt
　2005　Making sense of a blend: A cognitive-semiotic approach to metaphor. *Annual Review of Cognitive Linguistics* 3: 216–249.

Brandt, Per Aage
　2004　*Spaces, Domains and Meaning: Essays in Cognitive Semiotics.* European Semiotics Series No 4. Bern: Peter Lang.

Cook, Reginald L.
　1974　*Robert Frost: A Living Voice.* Amherst, MA: University of Massachusetts Press.

Crane, Mary Thomas
　2001　*Shakespeare's Brain: Reading with Cognitive Theory.* Princeton, NJ: Princeton University Press.

Crane, Mary Thomas, and Alan Richardson
　1999　Literary studies and cognitive science: Toward a new interdisciplinarity. *Mosaic* 32: 123–140.

Emmott, Catherine
　1997　*Narrative Comprehension: A Discourse Perspective.* Oxford: Clarendon Press.

Fauconnier, Gilles, and Mark Turner
　1994　*Conceptual Projection and Middle Spaces.* San Diego: University of California, Department of Science Technical Report 9401 (available on – line at markturner.org/blending).

　2002　*The Way We Think: Conceptual Blending and the Mind's Hidden Complexities.* New York: Basic Books.

Fludernik, Monika
1993    *The Fictions of Language and the Languages of Fiction*. London/New York: Routledge.

Freeman, Margaret H.
2002    Momentary stays, exploding forces: A cognitive linguistic approach to the poetics of Emily Dickinson and Robert Frost. *Journal of English Linguistics* 30 (1): 73–90.
In press.  Cognitive linguistic approaches to literary studies: State of the art in cognitive poetics. In *Handbook of Cognitive Linguistics*, Dirk Geeraerts, and Hubert Cuyckens (eds.). Oxford: Oxford University Press.

Frost, Robert
1915    Mending Walls. In *North of Boston*. New York: Henry Holt and Co.

Gavins, Joanna
2005    Text world theory in literary practice. In *Cognition in Literary Interpretation and Practice*, Bo Pettersson, Merja Polvinen, and Harri Veivo (eds.), 89–104. Helsinki: University of Helsinki Press.

Gavins, Joanna, and Gerard Steen (eds.)
2003    *Cognitive Poetics in Practice*. London/New York: Routledge.

Graves, Robert
1963    Introduction to *Selected Poems of Robert Frost*, ix – xiv. New York: Holt, Rinehart and Winston.

Henkel, Jacqueline
1996    *Language of Criticism: Linguistic Models and Literary Theory*. Ithaca, NY: Cornell University Press.

Hogan, Patrick Colm
2003    *Cognitive Science, Literature, and the Arts: A Guide for Humanists*. New York/London: Routledge.

Holland, Norman
1988    *The Brain of Robert Frost: A Cognitive Approach to Literature*. New York/London: Routledge.

Jakobson, Roman
1987    *Language in Literature*. Cambridge, MA and London: The Belknap Press of Harvard University Press.

Johnson, Mark
1987    *The Body in the Mind: The Bodily Basis of Meaning, Imagination, and Reason*. Chicago/London: The University of Chicago Press.

Kemp, John C.
1979    *Robert Frost and New England: The Poet as Regionalist*. Princeton, NJ: Princeton University Press.

Lakoff, George, and Mark Johnson
1980    *Metaphors We Live By*. Chicago/London: The University of Chicago Press.
1999    *Philosophy in the Flesh*. New York: Basic Books.

Lakoff, George, and Mark Turner
1989    *More than Cool Reason: A Field Guide to Poetic Metaphor*. Chicago/London: The University of Chicago Press.

Langacker, Ronald W.
1987   *Foundations of Cognitive Grammar. Vol I: Theoretical Perspectives.*
       Stanford: Stanford University Press.
1991   *Foundations of Cognitive Grammar. Vol II: Descriptive Application.*
       Stanford: Stanford University Press.
2005   Dynamicity, fictivity, and scanning: The imaginative basis of logic and
       linguistic meaning. In *Grounding Cognition: The Role of Perception and
       Action in Memory, Language, and Thinking*, Diane Pecher, and Rolf A.
       Zwaan (eds.), 164–197. Cambridge: Cambridge University Press.
Langer, Susanne K.
1953   *Feeling and Form: A Theory of Art.* New York: Charles Scribner's.
1967   *Mind: An Essay on Human Feeling.* Baltimore: The Johns Hopkins
       Press.
Lentricchia, Frank
1975   *Robert Frost: Modern Poetics and the Landscapes of Self.* Durham, NC:
       Duke University Press.
Merleau-Ponty, Maurice
1962   *Phenomenology of Perception*, C. Smith (tr.). London: Routledge and
       Kegan Paul.
1968   *The Visible and the Invisible*, Claude Lefort (ed.), Alphonso Lingis (tr.).
       Evanston: Northwestern University Press.
Modell, Arnold H.
2003   *Imagination and the Meaningful Brain.* Cambridge, MA: The MIT
       Press.
Monteiro, George
1988   *Robert Frost and the New England Renaissance.* Lexington, KY: The
       University Press of Kentucky.
Nöth, Winfried
2001   Semiotic foundations of iconicity. In *The Motivated Sign*, Max Nänny,
       and Olga Fischer (eds.), 17–29. Amsterdam: Benjamins.
Peirce, Charles Sanders
1955   *Philosophical Writings of Peirce*, Justus Buchler (ed.). New York: Dover.
Raab, Lawrence
1996   *Touchstone: American Poets on a Favorite Poem*, Robert Pack and Jay
       Parini (eds.). Hanover: University Press of New England. http://www.
       english.uiuc.edu/maps/poets/a–f/frost/wall.htm. Accessed April 15,
       2006.
Richardson, Alan
2000   Rethinking romantic incest: Human universals, literary representation,
       and the biology of mind. *New Literary History* 31(3): 553–572.
Richardson, Mark
1997   *The Ordeal of Robert Frost: The Poet and His Poetics.* Urbana: Univer-
       sity of Illinois.
Scarry, Elaine
1999   *Dreaming by the Book.* Princeton, NJ: Princeton University Press.

Schauber, Ellen, and Ellen Spolsky
1986    *The Bounds of Interpretation: Linguistic Theory and the Literary Text.*
        Stanford: Stanford University Press.
Semino, Elena, and Jonathan Culpeper (eds.)
2002    *Cognitive Stylistics: Language and Cognition in Text Analysis.* Amster-
        dam: Benjamins.
Spolsky, Ellen
1993    *Gaps in Nature: Literary Interpretation and the Modular Mind.* Albany:
        State University of NewYork Press.
Steiner, George
1970    *Extraterritorial: Papers on Literature and the Language Revolution.*
        New York: Atheneum.
Stockwell, Peter
2002    *Cognitive Poetics: An Introduction.* London: Routledge.
Tabakowska, Elzbieta
1993    *Cognitive Linguistics and Poetics of Translation.* Tübingen: Gunter
        Narr Verlag.
Tönnies, Ferdinand
1957    *Community and Society: Gemeinschaft und Gesellschaft*, Charles P.
        Loomis (ed. and tr.), 223–231. Ann Arbor: The Michigan State Uni-
        versity Press. http://www2.pfeiffer.edu/~lridener/courses/GEMEIN.
        HTML Accessed March 18, 2006.
Tsur, Reuven
1983    *What Is Cognitive Poetics.* Tel Aviv: The Katz Research Institute for
        Hebrew Literature.
1992    *Toward a Theory of Cognitive Poetics.* Amsterdam: North Holland.
2002    *On the Shore of Nothingness: A Study in Cognitive Poetics.* Exeter, UK:
        Imprint Academic.
Turner Frederick, and Ernst Pöppel
1980    The neural lyre: Poetic meter, the brain, and time. *Poetry* 135: 224.
Turner, Mark
1991    *Reading Minds: The Study of English in the Age of Cognitive Science.*
        Princeton, NJ: Princeton University Press.
Velmans, Max
2002    How could conscious experiences affect brains? *Journal of Conscious-
        ness Studies, Special Issue* 9 (11): 3–95.
Werth, Paul
1999    *Text Worlds: Representing Conceptual Space in Discourse.* London:
        Longman.

# Part six: Virtual reality as a new experience

# Artificial intelligence, figurative language and cognitive linguistics

## John A. Barnden

*Abstract*
This chapter addresses not the internal nature of the field of Cognitive Linguistics but rather its relationship to another domain, Artificial Intelligence. One important vein in AI research on metaphor is to use ideas drawn from or similar to the notion of conceptual metaphor in Cognitive Linguistics, although another important vein has been to seek to account for (some) metaphor understanding from scratch without any prior knowledge of particular mappings. AI can contribute to Cognitive Linguistics by attempting to construct computationally detailed models of structures and process drawn from or similar to those proposed more abstractly in Cognitive Linguistics. The computational model construction can confirm the viability of a proposal but can also reveal new problems and issues, or put existing ones into sharper relief. A case in point is the problem of the nature of domains and consequent problems in conceptions of the nature of metaphor and metonymy. In the author's approach to metaphor, which is briefly sketched, mappings between domains are replaced by mappings between metaphorical pretence and reality.

*Keywords*: metaphor; metonymy; conceptual domains; artificial intelligence; computational models

## 1. Introduction

In this chapter I do not try to describe the geography of Cognitive Linguistics (henceforth CL) as a whole or of some internal region of it, but rather to suggest the shape of the boundary between it and one other discipline, namely Artificial Intelligence. I do this partly by discussing how my own work on figurative language has drawn from CL and in turn offers potential contributions to the development of CL. I also briefly survey some other work in AI on figurative language and comment on some of the relationships to CL. The chapter deals primarily with metaphor, with some mention of metonymy, and does not attempt to address other forms of figurative language. A more detailed discussion of various AI projects on metaphor – and of how AI can contribute to the study of

metaphor as part of its contribution to the study of cognition in general –
can be found in Barnden (in press, a).

My own general impression of how AI researchers regard utterance
generation and understanding *by humans* is that it is tightly bound up
with the rest of human cognition – the crucial tenet of CL (in my understanding of that discipline). This doesn't mean that any one sub-thesis,
such as that syntactic form is determined fundamentally by cognitive
structures/functions, let alone that any particular detailed technical proposal about an aspect of language, would necessarily be believed by a
given type of AI researcher. But it does mean that to the extent that AI researchers concern themselves with the principles underlying *human* language use they would (I would estimate) tend to find CL relatively con-
genial, compared to other forms of linguistics. Also, there is a common
interest between CL and many areas of AI in deep cognitive representational structures and processing mechanisms, as opposed to just the description and manipulation of surface phenomena.

In considering these matters we meet the important question of what the
aims of AI are. AI has at least three distinguishable – though related and
mutually combinable – aims. In describing the aims I will use the deliberately vague and inclusive term "computational things" to mean computational *principles, computationally-detailed theories,* or – but by no means
necessarily – *running computational systems.* The possible abstractness if
not abstruseness of a "computational thing" here is fundamental to understanding the nature of AI, and in fact Computer Science in general, and is
often not understood (even within the field!). "Computational" is itself a
difficult term but will mean here something to do with processing information to create new or differently formed information, using in turn
"information" in the broadest possible sense. "Computation" cheerfully
embraces both traditional forms of symbol processing and such things as
connectionist, neural and molecular processing, and allows for webs of
processing that fundamentally include processes in the surrounding world
as well as within the organism itself. Well then, to the aims of AI.

First there is an "Engineering" aim, concerned with devising computational things in pursuit of the production of useful artefacts that are arguably intelligent in some pragmatically useful sense of that term, without
necessarily having any structural/processual similarity to biological
minds/brains. Then there is a "Psychological" aim, concerned with devising computational things that provide a basis for possible testable accounts of cognition in biological minds/brains. Finally, there is a "Gen-
eral/Philosophical" aim, concerned with devising computational things

that serve as or suggest possible accounts of cognition *in general* – whether it be in human-made artefacts, in naturally-occurring organisms, or in cognizing organisms yet to be discovered – and/or that illuminate *philosophical issues* such as the nature of mind, language and society. It would be respectable to try to split the third aim into a General Cognition aim and a Philosophical aim, but the question of whether there *is* any useful general sense of the word "cognition" going beyond the collection of known forms of biological cognition is itself a deep philosophical issue.

On top of this multiplicity of aims, the word "intelligence" is usually taken very broadly in AI, to cover not only pure rational thought but also almost anything that could come under the heading of "cognition," "perception," "learning," "language use," "emotion," "consciousness" and so forth. Thus, the name "artificial intelligence" has always been somewhat of a *nom de plume*, with both words in the name each acting merely impressionistically.

I said the aims are interrelated and combinable. Indeed, they are often inextricably combined in a given piece of research. An individual researcher may by him or herself have more than one of the aims (without necessarily making this clear), and in any case developments by different researchers in pursuit of different aims can happen to bolster each other.

Now, even an Engineering-AI artefact may need to understand language as produced by *people,* whether the discourse is directed at the artefact itself or at other people, and may need to generate utterances for human consumption. So, even the pursuit of Engineering AI, when language-using, may derive benefit from models of how people use language, and how language is connected to the rest of cognition, and therefore derive benefit from advances in CL. This is partly from the completely general point, not peculiar to language processing, that the structures and algorithms used in an Engineering-AI system can be borrowed from Psychology and from Psychological AI, even though the researcher concerned is not aiming at constructing a psychologically realistic model. But it is also partly from the additional point that in order for a person or AI system (a) to understand people's utterances or (b) to address utterances at people, it may be useful to understand something about what underlies those people's (a) creation of utterances or (b) understanding of utterances, respectively. So, an AI system may need to be a (folk) psychologist to roughly the extent that people need to be, even if the AI system is computationally very different from a person.

To be sure, there is currently a strong fashion in the natural language processing arena in Engineering AI to seek to process language using statistical or related techniques that do not rest on considerations of the principles underlying human language, on any attempt to reason about how human speakers or hearers understand process language, or even on any derivation of meanings of utterances. Such approaches, which I will call "human-free" here for ease of reference, have met with considerable practical success, and incidentally raise interesting issues for Psychological and General/Philosophical AI. Nevertheless that still leaves a good body of work in AI, whether with the Engineering aim or another aim, that does concern itself with the principles of language, human cognition behind language, and meaning of language.

It should also be realized that a researcher pursuing a human-free approach for a particular purpose does not necessarily make strong claims that the approach can achieve more than a certain, adequate-for-purpose level of success, and may agree that for different purposes – whether of the Engineering, Psychological or General/Philosophical types – the approach would be inadequate, and may therefore in regard to those other purposes be prepared to be friendly to insights from fields such as CL and Psychology.

Given these introductory comments, we will now move to looking briefly at AI research on metaphor (and to some extent metonymy) in general, in relation to CL concerns. After that we will consider the particular case of the "ATT-Meta" approach and system for metaphor processing developed in my own project, as a particular case study of CL-influenced work in AI. Then we will briefly look at a few potential issues or challenges that that work raises in relation to CL, notably with regard to the distinction between metaphor and metonymy.

## 2.    Metaphor and metonymy in AI, and connections to CL

Metaphor has long been an interest within AI. Salient amongst the earliest work is that of Carbonell (1980, 1982), Russell (1976), Weiner (1984), Wilks (1978) and Winston (1979). Other more recent work includes Asher and Lascarides (1995), Fass (1997), Hobbs (1990, 1992), Indurkhya (1991, 1992), Lytinen, Burridge, and Kirtner (1992), Martin (1990), Narayanan (1997, 1999), Norvig (1989), Veale and Keane (1992), Veale (1998), Way (1991) and Weber (1989), and the work on my own project (cited below), all of which address the problem of understanding metaphorical utterances. There has also been statistical work on uncovering metaphoricity in corpora (e.g. Mason 2004). As for metonymy, research includes that of

Fass (1997), Hobbs (1990, 1992) and Lytinen, Burridge, and Kirtner (1992) again, and also Lapata and Lascarides (2003), Markert and Hahn (2002), Markert and Nissim (2003) and Stallard (1987, 1993). Also, much work on polysemy involves metonymy at least implicitly given that often polysemy is driven relatively straightforwardly by metonymic connections (see, for example, Fass 1997, on the work of Pustejovsky – see, e.g., Pustejovsky 1995). See Fass (1997), Martin (1996) and Russell (1986) for more comprehensive reviews of work on figurative language in AI. Also, see Barnden (in press, a) for more extensive description than is possible here of the work of Wilks, Fass, Martin, Hobbs, Veale and Narayanan, and see Barnden (in press, b) for additional comments on Wilks's work.

In spite of this long history in AI, metaphor has only ever been a minority interest in the field, and to some extent this is true of metonymy as well. The minority status of metaphor in AI is no doubt for complex historical reasons. The message from CL and elsewhere that metaphor is fundamental to and prevalent in ordinary language has not had the effect on AI it should have had, despite the point being perfectly evident even in the earliest AI work mentioned above, and being explicitly plugged by, for instance, Carbonell. It is also surprising in view of the international prominence within AI of such figures as Carbonell, Hobbs and Wilks. There has remained some tendency, despite the evidence, to view metaphor as an outlying, postponable phenomenon, but perhaps more importantly the field has happened to concentrate on other particular problems of language such as anaphor resolution and ordinary word-sense disambiguation (ordinary in the sense of not paying explicit attention to the role of metaphor or metonymy in polysemy). The field, perhaps through familiarity more than rational evaluation, has tended to regard such problems as intrinsically easier and more tractable than those of metaphor and metonymy.

However, metaphor is becoming an increasingly looming obstacle for (even) Engineering AI, as attempts are made to bring better automated human-language processing into commercial products, to develop ever more advanced computer interfaces and virtual reality systems, to develop automated understanding and production of emotional expression given that this is often conveyed explicitly or implicitly by metaphor (Delfino and Manca 2005; Emanatian 1995; Fainsilber and Ortony 1987; Fussell and Moss 1998; Kövecses 2000; Thomas 1969; Yu 1995), and also to develop systems that can understand or produce gesture and sign language, given that these forms of communication have strong metaphorical aspects (McNeil 1992; P. Wilcox 2004; S. Wilcox 2004; Woll 1985). It is to be hoped that the continued "humanization" of Computer Science via the development of more human-sensitive interfaces will see a greater attention to matters such as metaphor. Metaphor has actually long been an important issue in HCI (human-computer interaction) systems, cf. the now-prevalent "desktop metaphor." However, there has been division of opinion about the wisdom or otherwise of consciously including metaphorical considerations in interface design, and concern about the possibly misleading qualities of metaphor (for a discussion see Blackwell, in press).

As for links to CL, much of the AI work mentioned above on metaphor has explicitly drawn upon the idea that a language user knows a set of commonly used conceptual metaphors. For example, Russell (1986) addresses conceptual metaphors concerning mind such as CONCEPT AS OBJECT, and Martin's system is based on having a knowledge base of conceptual metaphors (Martin's work has mainly considered conceptual metaphors such as PROCESS AS CONTAINER that are relevant to understanding and generating metaphorical language about computer processes and systems). Narayanan's work (1997, 1999) is closely based on Lakoff's conceptual metaphor theory, and in its application to the domain of economics has been based on knowledge of conceptual metaphors such as ACTING IS MOVING, OBSTACLES ARE DIFFICULTIES, and FAILING IS FALLING. My own work, described below, is loosely inspired by conceptual metaphor theory and rests on an understander knowing mappings that are reminiscent of those forming conceptual metaphors; more precisely, they are reminiscent of the primary metaphor mappings of Grady (2002). One arm of Hobbs's approach to metaphor also makes use of known mappings that are tantamount to conceptual metaphor maps.

On the other hand, the work of Wilks, Fass and Veale has dealt with the question of finding metaphorical mappings from scratch, rather than enaging in language understanding on the basis of known metaphorical mappings (and Fass's account is descended from Wilks's, while also adding a treatment of metonymy). Such work is therefore a useful foil to the work of Hobbs, Martin, etc., and to my own work. Nevertheless, to my knowledge there is nothing in the approaches of Wilks, etc. that is not in principle combinable with Hobbs, etc. There is surely room both for knowing some mappings in advance of understanding a sentence and for working out new mappings while understanding the sentence, and in different ways Hobbs, Martin and Veale address both matters. My own view, based partly on the analysis of poetic metaphor in Lakoff and Turner

(1989), is that entirely novel metaphor – metaphor that rests *entirely* or even *mainly* on not-yet-known mappings – is quite rare in real discourse, so that map-discovery from scratch is best thought of ultimately as providing "top-ups" to approaches that rest more on known mappings.

It should also be mentioned that, while Martin's new-mapping discovery has the intent of extending already known conceptual metaphors, the new-mapping discovery in Wilks, Fass and Hobbs does not have the intent of extending or creating conceptual metaphors of long-term significance, but rather with creating some metaphorical maps that happen to work for the current utterance but that do not necessarily have systematic significance for other utterances and would thus not necessarily qualify as being (parts of) conceptual metaphors.

Work on metonymy in AI is often akin to accounts of metonymy in CL that rest on known, common metonymic patterns such as ARTIST FOR ART PRODUCT, to take an instance from Fass's case. Fass's work is interesting also in combining a treatment of metaphor and a treatment of metonymy, and allowing for sentence interpretations that chain together a metaphor mapping with one or more metonymic steps. From the CL point of view there is perhaps a disparity between the metaphor account in resting not at all on known metaphorical mappings and the metonymy account in resting entirely on known metonymic patterns. The reader's attention is also drawn to the Metallel system of Iverson and Helmreich (1992), which compared to Fass's system (called *meta5*), from which it is descended, combines metaphor and metonymy more flexibly, and deals more flexibly with each individually. Hobbs's work also smoothly integrates metonymy and metaphor, though here the metonymic processing does not rely on a set of known metonymic patterns but rather on finding metonymic relationships ad hoc during discourse interpretation, in a way that is driven by the needs raised by trying to understand the particular discourse at hand.

So far our allusion to metaphor research within CL have been focussed on the more Lakovian accounts rather than the other main account, namely "blending" (Fauconnier and Turner 1998). Some AI researchers have explicitly addressed the question of how blending might be implemented, notably Veale and O'Donoghue (2000) and Pereira (in press), and the "pretence cocoons" in my own work on metaphor as described below can be seen as a type of blend space.

Insofar as accounts of metaphor in CL rest on collections of mappings and therefore on (generally) complex analogies between source domains and target domains, there is a match with AI in that AI has a long history of research on analogy and analogy-based reasoning (ABR), as witnessed by the survey of Hall (1989). In particular, a main, and very applications-orientated, branch of analogy research in AI has been so-called case-based reasoning (CBR) (see, e.g., Kolodner 1993). (Caveat: many researchers see a distinction between ABR and CBR in that the former is commonly held to be "between-domain" and the latter being "within-domain." However, I find this distinction suspect, an issue that will resurface in Section 5 in looking at the difference between metaphor and metonymy.)

Most work on analogy has been conducted without reference to metaphor, because the work has largely been about problem solving rather than language understanding. Nevertheless, we can make the following general observation. Analogy is considered by many in AI to be a central facet of human cognition and an important thing to include in intelligent artefacts. Thus, indirectly, AI can be said to be in the right frame of mind to agree with of the CL notion that metaphor is fundamentally a matter of cognition and only secondarily of language. Certainly, the AI research into metaphor that has adopted a conceptual-metaphor basis appears to be entirely compatible with allowing that the knowledge structures and reasoning processes involved are part of general cognition, not set aside just for language processing.

By contrast, one can have less confidence that the CL notion that *metonymy* is fundamentally a cognitive as opposed to linguistic matter (e.g., Lakoff 1987) is taken on board in AI research. It depends on what metonymy being cognitive amounts to. Certainly, in the metonymy treatment of Hobbs, for example, metonymic linkages pop out of general processing used during language understanding, where that general processing would also be available in other forms of reasoning (Hobbs views language understanding as a case of abductive reasoning). However, this is different from saying that metonymy has, say, an important role in the explicit structuring of concepts, as it can have in Idealized Cognitive Models in CL (Lakoff 1987). In Hobbs' account, the inferencing that amounts to establishing metonymic links during language understanding would just be unremarkable inference steps when performed within general reasoning, so that it would in the latter case be artificial to label them as "metonymy." Overall, it is fair to say that AI work to date has been focussed on metonymy as a matter of the reference of linguistic strings, albeit that the metonymic steps in such reference are based on deep cognitive connections that are not necessarily specialized for language.

## 3. ATT-Meta, map-transcendence and pretence

With colleagues I have developed an approach and related computer program, called ATT-Meta, for performing a type of reasoning that is arguably often necessary for metaphor interpretation. The approach is described in, for instance, Barnden (1998, 2001a); Barnden, Glasbey, Lee and Wallington (2004); Barnden, Helmreich, Iverson and Stein (1994, 1996); Barnden and Lee (1999, 2001); Lee and Barnden (2001a). The implemented ATT-Meta program is only a reasoning system and does not take linguistic strings as input, but takes, rather, logical forms derived from sentences by initial processing. For now the reader can take these logical forms to encode the literal meanings of the sentences, but we will refine this point below.

The metaphorical utterances of main interest in the ATT-Meta project are those that are conceptually related to known conceptual metaphors but that transcend them by involving source-domain elements not directly handled by the mappings in those metaphors. In ATT-Meta parlance these utterances are *map-transcending*. For instance, to take a modified version of an example from Hobbs (1990), consider the sentence "[the computer program variable] N leaps from 1 to 100." Suppose the understander only knows a *physically-leap* lexical sense for the verb "leap" but does not know a mapping for that sense into the target domain of variables and values, even though he/she/it does know a mapping from, say, *spatially-at* to *have-as-value*. Thus, the sentence is map-transcending in using a *physically-leap* concept that is related to the mappable concept *spatially-at* but that is not itself mapped. Similarly, to take an example from Martin (1990), if an understander knows a metaphorical mapping from *physically-in* to *using-a-process* but has no mapping for *physically-enter*, then the sentence "How do I enter [the computer program] Emacs?" is map-transcending.

Clearly, map-transcendence is a fuzzy concept that is relative to particular understanders and to particular conceptual metaphors the understander knows, and to our intuitive perceptions as to what is conceptually related to what (e.g., physically-leaping to being-spatially-at). Nevertheless, it is a useful intuitive characterization of a phenomenon that lies along a broad sector of the spectrum between completely conventional metaphorical phraseology on the one hand and, on the other hand, entirely novel metaphor where no relevant mapping is known at all.

Map-transcendence is strongly related to the phenomenon of "unused" parts of the source domain as discussed in Lakoff and Johnson (1980).

However, we prefer to avoid that term because it may wrongly suggest that the parts in question have *never* been used. Far from it: it is in principle possible even that a given understander has *often* met sentences of the form "*variable* leaps from *value1* to *value2*" without happening to bother to develop a mapping from *physically-leap* to something in the target domain.

ATT-Meta is based on rules encapsulating known metaphorical correspondences, such as between *physically-at* and *has-as-value*, and on an integrated inferential framework which, in particular, allows arbitrarily rich source-domain reasoning to connect map-transcending sentence components to source-domain concepts that can be mapped by known mappings. In this respect, ATT-Meta's approach is similar to one strand of Hobbs's approach to metaphor. Both approaches can infer that a variable N *has value* 100 from any sentence couched in spatial terms that implies that N is *physically-at* 100, as long as the systems have the necessary knowledge about physical space to infer that N is physically-at 100 from the sentence. The inference can be arbitrarily indirect and complex in principle. To make the point, a vivid example would be a sentence such as "N meandered along a circuitous route towards 100 but didn't complete the journey until after M fell to 0." This implies, among other things, that N (at some point) had value 100.

However, there is a fundamental difference of approach, as well as many technical differences of representation and reasoning, between ATT-Meta and Hobbs's scheme. The fundamental difference is that ATT-Meta avoids placing internal propositions such as *N is physically-at 100*, which are not statements about reality, on a par with statements such as *N has value 100*, which are. Hobbs's approach does maintain them on a par: there is nothing in his internal representation to say that the former proposition is merely a metaphorical pretence or fiction.

Instead, ATT-Meta creates a special computational "mental space" in which such propositions and inference arising from them are kept aside from propositions and reasoning about reality. We call this space a *metaphorical pretence cocoon*. Thus, the internal proposition *N physically-leaps from 1 to 100* arising directly from the sentence "N leaps from 1 to 100" is placed in the cocoon, and an inference result that (say) *N is spatially-at 100 afterwards*, together with the inference chain itself, lies within the cocoon. A metaphorical mapping rule that takes *spatially-at* to *has-as-value* can then give the result that, in reality, N has value 100 afterwards as one aspect of the meaning of the utterance.

By clearly marking some propositions as being pretences, the use of a cocoon ensures that the system is not misled by the propositions directly derived from metaphorical utterances, that is, propositions like *N physically-leaps from 1 to 100*. This isn't perhaps a practical problem in this particular example, but notice that in the case of "McEnroe killed Connors," which could be taken literally in principle, the understander needs to be clear that the directly-derived proposition *McEnroe biologically-killed Connors* is not a statement about reality.

But, in addition, we do not want to allow the knowledge that McEnroe definitely did not biologically-kill Connors in reality to defeat the pretend information that McEnroe did biologically-kill Connors. Thus, pretence cocoons prevent pretences from infecting reality but, equally, protect the integrity of pretences.

The use of cocoons has another benefit. Lee and Barnden (2001a) studied mixed metaphor of various types, and showed how ATT-Meta deals with them. The main distinction studied was between serial mixing (commonly called chaining), where A is viewed as B and B is viewed as C, and parallel mixing, where A is used simultaneously as B and as C. (See also Wilks, Barnden and Wang 1991.) Serial mixing is viewed as having the B material in a cocoon directly embedded in the reality space, whereas the C material as in a cocoon embedded within the B cocoon. Thus, there is a pretence within a pretence. In parallel mixing, on the other hand, the B and C material is either combined in a single cocoon or is in two separate cocoons both directly embedded within the reality space. Thus, we have two pretences either side by side or blended with each other. There are unresolved issues about how to decide between these two possibilities, but in any case different dispositions of pretence cocoons allow important differences between types of mixing of metaphor to be reflected in the processing.

We have indicated that what is initially inserted in the pretence cocoon in the case of "N leaps from 1 to 100" is the proposition *N physically-leaps from 1 to 100*, and what is inserted in the case of "McEnroe killed Connors" is *McEnroe biologically-killed Connors*. This reflects a general assumption in the ATT-Meta approach that what is inserted in the cocoon is a "direct" meaning of the metaphorical sentence (or of some metaphorical sentence-component such as a clause). A direct meaning is a logical form derived compositionally from the "direct" senses of lexical units in sentences. A direct sense is just any sense listed for the lexical unit in the understander's lexicon, so that it is directly accessible from the lexical unit. In particular, we have been assuming that the verbs "leap" and "kill" have as direct senses the concepts of *physically-leap* and *biologically-kill* respectively.

Clearly, a given lexical unit could actually have more than one direct sense, and indeed some of the direct senses could be metaphorical or special in some other way. We simply embrace such possibilities, saying that if, for instance, "leap" had something like *change-value* as a direct sense, then "N leaps from 1 to 100" could be understood without use of the inferential pretence mechanism outlined above (although in principle the mechanism could still be redundantly used alongside).

Equally, a direct sense may be figurative in some way but nevertheless still lead to the construction of a proposition in the pretence cocoon. For instance, suppose the word "star" has *astronomical-star* and *prominent-movie-actor* as its only direct senses in the understander's lexicon, and that we regard the latter as a figurative sense. Then one way of understanding "Mike is a star of the department" would proceed via the pretence mechanism, using the proposition that *Mike is a prominent movie actor in the department* in the cocoon.

Thus, in the ATT-Meta approach, the pretence mechanism is potentially useful whenever there is the potential for direct meanings of sentence to lead by within-pretence reasoning to within-pretence propositions that can be mapped by known mapping rules. It is irrelevant whether the direct meaning is dubbed as "literal" or not. We may or may not wish to regard *physically-leap* as a literal sense of "leap" and *prominent-movie-actor* as a literal sense of "star", but such terminological decisions have no bearing in themselves on whether the pretence mechanism could be fruitful.

Another fundamental reason for not relying on a notion of literal meaning arises from serial mixing (A as B as C). In such a case, some of the phrasing in the utterance refers to the C domain, and this can cause material to arise in the B domain by C-to-B transfer. Therefore, B-to-A transfers may be working on non-literal material derived by transfer from C. For this reason alone, it is misguided to think of metaphorical mapping as necessarily a matter of transforming literal meanings. The consequences of this point have hardly been explored in metaphor research, whether within CL or elsewhere.

Insofar as direct meanings of sentences *can* often be regarded as literal meanings, ATT-Meta is in the class of systems that rely on constructing a literal meaning first (not necessarily from a whole sentence, but perhaps from a component such as a prepositional phrase or clause) – or at least before the final metaphorical meaning is constructed. Still, there is no reliance on *rejecting* that literal meaning before proceeding to metaphorical processing.

Before proceeding further in this description of ATT-Meta we also must explain that its reasoning is entirely query-directed. Query-directed reasoning – more usually called goal-directed reasoning – is a powerful technique much used in AI (see, e.g., Russell and Norvig 2002). In this form of reasoning, the process of reasoning starts with a query – an externally supplied or internally arising question as to whether something holds. Queries are compared to known propositions and/or used to generate further queries by some means. In a rule-based system as ATT-Meta, queries are compared to the result parts of rules, and then new queries arise from the condition parts. For example, in the case of a rule that says if someone is a student then he or she is presumably poor, a query as to whether John is poor would give rise to a subquery as to whether John is a student.

The system's metaphor-based reasoning is thoroughly integrated into a general-purpose, query-directed, rule-based framework for uncertain reasoning using qualitative uncertainty measures. ATT-Meta's reasoning both in source-domain terms and in target-domain terms is generally uncertain. Rules and propositions are annotated with qualitative certainty levels. There is a heuristic conflict-resolution mechanism that attempts to adjudicate between conflicting lines of reasoning, by considering their relative specificity.

Both ATT-Meta's long-term knowledge of individual domains and its knowledge of conceptual metaphors is couched in terms of IF-THEN inference rules. For instance, one crucial rule about the domain of physical objects and space can be glossed in English as follows:

IF a physical object is not physically accessible to a person to some degree D
   THEN presumably the person cannot physically operate on the object to degree D.

The "presumably" annotation makes this rule a default rule: even if the rule's condition is established with complete certainty, the system only takes the result of the rule as a default (a working assumption). The rule also illustrates that ATT-Meta can handle gradedness with which states of affairs can hold. There is a small set of qualitative degrees going from "very low" up to "absolute."

We are now ready to look in more detail at an example. Consider:

In the far reaches of her mind, Anne believed that Kyle was having an affair.

This is slightly adapted from a real-discourse example (Gross 1994). We assume ATT-Meta is given knowledge of mappings that could be considered to be involved in the conceptual metaphors of MIND AS PHYSICAL SPACE and IDEAS AS PHYSICAL OBJECTS. We also assume, for the sake of example, that "far reaches" only has a spatial sense for the system and that the notion is not mapped to the mental domain by any conceptual metaphor known to the system. The most important mapping known to ATT-Meta is the following, and is part of ATT-Meta's knowledge of IDEAS AS PHYSICAL OBJECTS:

> degree of (in)ability of an agent's conscious self to operate physically on an idea that is a physical object, *in the pretence cocoon*, corresponds to degree of (in)ability of the agent to operate in a conscious mental way on the idea, *in the reality space.*

A given metaphorical mapping link such as this is implicit in a set of *transfer rules* that we will not detail here.

In the example as we run it using the ATT-Meta system, the system is given an initial target-domain query (IQ) that is, roughly speaking, of the form *To what exact degree is Anne able to consciously operate mentally on the idea that Kyle had an affair?* In Barnden and Lee (2001) we justify this a reasonable query that could arise out of the surrounding context. The query is *reverse-transferred* from target terms to source terms via the above mapping to become a query of form *To what degree is Anne's conscious self able to operate physically on the idea?*

ATT-Meta can then reason that that degree of physical operability is very low, using the source-domain information gleaned from the mention of "far reaches" in the utterance and from common-sense knowledge about physical spaces and objects. Once this very low degree is established in the source domain, it is forward-transferred via the mapping to give a very low degree of conscious mental operability as the answer to the initial query (IQ). The program's reasoning for this example is treated in more detail in Barnden and Lee (2001). A variety of other examples are also treated in that report and Barnden (2001c), Barnden *et al.* (2002) and Lee and Barnden (2001b), and Barnden (2001b) discusses the theoretical application to some further examples.

We must note a largely unimplemented aspect of the ATT-Meta approach: "view-neutral mapping adjuncts" (VNMAs) (Barnden and Lee 2001; Barnden *et al.* 2003). With partial inspiration from Carbonell (1982)'s AI work on metaphor, we view certain aspects of source domain information such as attitudes, value judgments, beliefs, functions, rates, gradedness, uncertainty and event structure to carry over to the target domain. The transfer is by default only, so the results can be overridden by other information about the target. As examples of VNMAs, we have the following:

- We assume that the ordering of events and their qualitative rates and durations carry over by default, whatever the nature of the particular metaphorical mapping being used, thus avoiding the need for individual mapping rules to deal with them.
- If an agent A in the pretence has an attitude X (mental or emotional) to a proposition P, and *if* A and P correspond, respectively, to an agent B and a proposition Q in reality, then B has attitude X to Q.
- As for gradedness, if a property P in a pretence corresponds to a property Q in reality, then a degree of holding of P should map to the same degree of holding of Q.

We have produced an experimental implementation that handles rates and durations as VNMAs, but much work remains to be done on other VNMAs. In particular, gradedness is currently handled directly in individual rules – notice the degrees in the metaphorical correspondence used above. In place of this handling we would like to have, instead, simpler mapping rules that do not mention degree, relying on a separate, general mechanism for the degree transfer.

## 4. E-drama and metaphor

I am also engaged in a related research project that draws upon the ATT-Meta research. I mention this project to show another case of how CL can not only affect theoretical research in AI but can also affect work that is immensely practical. The project is looking at the metaphorical expression of affect (emotion, value judgments, etc.) and at the automated detection of affect in utterances, in the context of an "e-drama" system that supports virtual dramatic improvisation by users (actors) sitting at computer terminals (Zhang, Barnden and Hendley 2005). The initial system on which the project is based was provided by one of our industrial partners, Hi8us Midlands Ltd. Improvisations can be on any topic, but the system has in particular been used for improvisations concerning school bullying and embarrassing illnesses such as Crohn's Disease. The actors improvise within a loose scenario, which for instance specifies that a particular character is a bully and another particular character is the bully victim. However, actors are free to improvise creatively, and in fact do things such as starting to bully the bully; or someone who is meant to be a friend of the victim may turn against him/her.

The affect detection is mainly towards providing an automated assistant to the human director who monitors the unfolding improvisation. The director can intervene by sending advice messages to the actors or by introducing a bit-part character into the improvisation in order to stir things up. Since one reason for directorial intervention is that the affective quality of the improvisation could be improved upon (e.g., the emotions expressed are neither appropriate to the provided scenario nor indicative of a creative novel direction), an important ability of an automated assistant is to detect affect expressed in the characters' speeches (which are entirely textual, and shown in text bubbles above the characters on the computer screens).

In fact, the affect detection mechanisms we have developed have not yet (at the time of writing) been used directly in an assistant, but instead in an automated actor program that can operate a bit-part character – with the intent that such a character be introduced on the discretion of the director, and thus indirectly help the director in his/her job. The actor program does not do full understanding of utterances of other characters (which would in any case be beyond the state of the art in AI), but does a certain amount of complex syntactic and semantic processing in order to try to detect some emotions, emotional emphases, and value judgments. As part of this, we are developing methods for limited sorts of metaphor analysis, and are also using the metaphor examples that freely arise in the e-dramatic improvisation genre as a fertile ground for testing our metaphor theories and suggesting new theoretically interesting examples and phenomena.

As mentioned above, the metaphorical description of emotional states (or behaviour) is common. Two illustrations are "He nearly exploded" and "Joy ran through me." Such examples describe emotional states directly (perhaps without naming them). We are concerned to have some basic handling at least of this phenomenon. Examples we have encountered in e-drama improvisations include the conventional metaphorical phraseology italicized in "It's *a struggle*," "It's *on my mind* 24/7" and "Listen, *don't keep it in*, if you need to talk I'm all ears." (These linguistic strings are sanitized versions of the originals encountered, which include mobile-phone-style textese, spelling errors, etc.)

However, affect is also often conveyed more indirectly via metaphor, as in "His room is a cess-pit": affect (such as disgust) associated with a source item (cess-pit) gets carried over to the corresponding target item (the room). This is because of one of the view-neutral mapping adjuncts (VNMAs) mentioned in Section 3. Examples of this phenomenon that we have encountered in e-drama include "It's *a struggle*" (again), "you buy [your clothes] at the *rag market*" and "Whatever, you piece of *dirt.*" Note that the "struggle" case was also included as a direct description of an emotional state above, in that some internal process is being likened structurally to a struggle. However, this of itself doesn't convey a negative value-judgment about that emotional state: it is our negative value judgment of physical struggles that gives the effect that the described emotional state is negatively valued.

As in most discourse, metaphorical phraseology in our genre tends to be of conventional form, the extreme being stock fixed phrases such as "sit on the fence." Such phrases can be stored in a lexicon and directly recognized. Our intended approach to affective metaphor handling in the project is partly to look for stock phraseology and straightforward variants of it, and partly to use a simple version of the more open-ended, reasoning-based techniques taken from the ATT-Meta approach. As an example of stock phrase handling, insults in e-drama are often metaphorical, especially the case of animal insults ("you stupid cow," "you dog"). We currently use simple pattern-matching rules in our implemented affect-detection to deal with some animal insults, but aim to have a more general (if still simplistic) treatment based on value judgments that people make of animals, in cases where an animal that is not covered by the rules is mentioned.

Interestingly for us, it is common for stock phraseology to be modified in a way that defeats a lexicon-based approach and raises the need for some knowledge-based reasoning. For example, a Google search found the following variant of the "on the fence" stock phrase: "It will put them on a shaky fence between protecting their copyrights and technology terrorists." Such cases would benefit from the reasoning capabilities of ATT-Meta. Similarly, some e-drama transcript examples of metaphor have gone in an open-ended way beyond conventional wording even though based on familiar metaphorical conceptions – in other words have been "map-transcending" in the sense defined in Section 3. Such examples include: "I think the mirror breaks all the time you look in it," "you're looking in the mirror right now, but you probably can't see yourself with all the cracks," "do you even have any brains to think about that one!" and "I'm trying very hard but there's too much stuff blocking my head up."

One particular phenomenon of theoretical and practical interest is that physical size is often metaphorically used to emphasize evaluations, as in "you are a big bully", "you're a big idiot," and "You're just a little bully." "Big bully" expresses strong disapproval and "little bully" can express contempt, although "little" can also convey sympathy or be used as an endearment. Such examples are not only important in practice but also theoretically challenging, especially as the physical size mentioned can in some cases be intended literally as well as metaphorically.

We have encountered surprisingly creative uses of metaphor in e-drama. For example, in the school-bullying scenario, Mayid is portrayed as having already insulted Lisa by calling her a "pizza" (short for "pizza-face"). This figurative insult was given a theoretically intriguing, creatively metaphorical elaboration in one improvisation, where Mayid said "I'll knock your topping off, Lisa."

## 5.    Further remarks on ATT-Meta and CL

While ATT-Meta draws strongly on general notions concerning conceptual metaphor, there are a number of observations we need to make. First, the ATT-Meta approach makes no use of the notion of image schemata or the notion that conceptual metaphors arise from embodied experience (Lakoff 1987). The approach is not inconsistent with these notions, but it is agnostic as to their validity. In particular, we fully embrace metaphor where the source subject-matter is more abstract and presumably less "embodied" than the target subject-matter.

Next, it is worth noting that ATT-Meta's mapping rules (the transfer rules) are more akin in their extent of general purpose-ness and fundamentality to the primary metaphorical mappings that Grady (2002) proposes than they are to the original types of conceptual metaphorical mapping, such as the mapping between lovers and travellers in the LOVE AS JOURNEY conceptual metaphor. For example, the mapping we used in the Anne/Kyle example Section 3 was one between PHYSICAL OPERATION (on ideas viewed as physical objects) and MENTAL OPERATION. PHYSICAL OPERATION and MENTAL OPERATION here are extremely general notions, and the mapping between them can underlie many different specific metaphorical views such as IDEAS AS ANIMATE BEINGS, MIND AS MACHINE and so forth.

Relatedly, in ATT-Meta there is no bundling of individual mappings together to form the larger complexes that conceptual metaphors are thought of as being. For example, as well as the PHYSICAL-OPER-ATION/MENTAL-OPERATION mapping already discussed, in our work on mental metaphor we have incorporated mappings such as: a mapping between an idea (viewed as a physical entity) being PHYSICALLY LO-CATED in the mind and the agent MENTALLY ENTERTAINING the idea; and a mapping between PART OF A MIND BELIEVING something X and the WHOLE MIND HAVING A *TENDENCY* TO BELIEVE X. (This is used in sentences such as "Part of me thinks she's wrong.") In work on non-mental metaphor we have incorporated mappings such as one be-tween POSSESSING a disease considered as a physical object and SUF-FERING the disease. These mappings are not regarded as mere compo-nents of more complex metaphorical schemata such as, say, IDEAS AS PHYSICAL OBJECTS, in the case of the PHYSICAL-OPERATION/MEN-TAL-OPERATION mapping. We may use the term "IDEAS AS PHYSI-CAL OBJECTS" for convenience in discussion, but it does not correspond to anything real in our approach and system: only individual mappings such as as the ones listed exist. In addition, the mappings are freely com-binable in the understanding of a given utterance. For instance, a sentence which both conceives of someone's mind as a physical space *and* the ideas in it as physical objects can be addressed by using both the PHYSICAL-OPERATION/MENTAL-OPERATION mapping and the PHYSICALLY-LOCATED/MENTALLY-ENTERTAINING mapping. There is no need to postulate the existence (as an identifiable entity in the system) of a con-ceptual metaphor that bundles these two mappings together. This is con-venient, because not all metaphor that involves the view of MIND AS A PHYSICAL SPACE also involves the view of IDEAS AS PHYSICAL OB-JECTS, and not all metaphor that involves the view of IDEAS AS PHYSI-CAL OBJECTS also involves the view of MIND AS PHYSICAL SPACE. At the same time, the combinability does allow the very common cases when these two views are indeed combined to be dealt with readily.

Our Grady-like deconstruction of original-style conceptual metaphors into more basic and general mappings is accompanied by the postulation of the general mapping principles that we have dubbed "view-neutral mapping adjuncts" (see Section 3). These are powerful tools in the decon-struction, as they make redundant many of the component mappings that tend to be postulated in conceptual metaphor theory. For instance, in using the view of LOVE AS A JOURNEY, the VNMA that maps DIFFI-CULTY between the source and the target gives the effect that a physical

obstacle to the journey causes difficulty for the progress of the love relationship, because it causes difficulty for the physical journey. There is no
need to have a specific mapping between journey difficulties and relationship difficulties, cf. the correspondence between difficulties in a love relationship and impediments to travel in Lakoff (1993: 207).

The importance of this factoring out of many aspects of conceptual
metaphors into VNMAs is magnified when one realizes that discussions in
the literature on conceptual metaphor often tend to leave some assumed
mapping abilities purely tacit, without any specific explanation. For
example, in the discussion of "We're driving in the fast lane on the freeway
of love" in Lakoff (1993), it is said that the excitement the imaginary
travellers experience in travelling fast transfers to the target to become excitement of the lovers. But no mapping is provided that relates emotions on
the source side to emotions on the target side – there is simply a tacit assumption that the emotion transfers. By postulating explicit VNMAs we
are attempting to bring such tacit assumptions out into the open and make
them into theoretically interesting aspects of metaphor in their own right.
This move also has the benefit of raising the need to explicitly consider exceptions to VNMAs, e.g. exceptions to the general rule that emotions of
source agents map over to emotions of corresponding target agents.

In conceptual metaphor theory, metaphor is generally viewed as mapping between two "domains." In contrast, the ATT-Meta approach does
not rely on domain distinctions, even theoretically, let alone enshrine
them in some way in the implemented system. Although in this article we
generally adopt the common practice of saying that metaphor transfers
information from a source domain to a target domain, this purely for purposes of intuitive exposition, and the ATT-Meta approach has a different
technical stance: metaphor is a matter of transferring from a *pretence* to
*reality* (or to a surrounding pretence, in the case of serial mixing). Notice
that in the mapping rules as described in Section 3, reference is made to
pretence and reality, not to domains. It does not matter what domains the
information used in the pretence comes from, and this means that it does
not matter how we may intuitively circumscribe the source and target domains in the metaphor. In particular, it does not matter how close, difficult to distinguish, or overlapping those domains are. In practice, it will
often be the case that we can theoretically identify a source domain in
which the direct meaning of the sentence lies, and that inferences from this
meaning also lie within that domain. However, this has no bearing on the
course of processing, and the reasoning within the pretence is not limited
by any consideration of domains.

Some other authors, in CL and elsewhere, have questioned the usefulness of the domain notion or the degree of distinctness that is required between the two domains in a metaphor. See, e.g., Cameron (1999), Kittay (1989) and several chapters in Dirven and Pörings (2002). I have found in working on the ATT-Meta approach that the detail and clarity required for well-founded computational implementation to be a major factor in coming to doubt the usefulness of the concept of "domain," or related concepts such as idealized cognitive models, as a source of constraints in characterizing metaphor (and metonymy) or as a real aspect of metaphorical processing. In trying to make decisions about what domains particular pieces of knowledge should be assigned to, in a way that respects the idea that metaphor maps between different domains, I came to realize what a hopeless and arbitrary task it was.

The nature of some of the other AI approaches to metaphor mentioned above also throws doubt on the usefulness of the notion of domains. For instance, although Hobbs does believe that metaphor is a matter of mapping between qualitatively disparate domains, this stance has no operational effect in his approach. In Narayanan's work, domains do play an operational role, but he does not note the difficulties arising from a major degree of overlap between the domains that he presents as if they were entirely separate (for more discussion, see Barnden, in press, a).

It is certainly quite common for the two sides of a metaphor to involve qualitatively very different subject matters. But, equally, the two sides of a metaphor can be arbitrarily close in their qualitative nature. Metaphors such as "Jules Verne is the H.G. Wells of France" have source and target domains that are broadly similar in subject matter. For an example with even less qualitative distance between the two sides, one's neighbour's teenage children can act as a metaphor for one's own: if one has a daughter Jenny and the neighbours have a son Jonathan who behaves similarly to Jenny, then one could say "Jenny is our family's Jonathan." Of course, it is open to someone to say that the Jenny family is qualitatively different from the Jonathan family, and that they are therefore different domains, but this is post-hoc rationalization with no operational significance.

Despite the closeness between target and source in the Jenny/Jonathan example, the metaphorical utterance appears quite apt to the present author. If this impression is shared with other language users, it may appear to conflict with the the evidence adduced by Tourangeau and Sternberg (1982) that, within limits, the greater the conceptual distance between source and target the more apt the metaphor. However, note that the linguistic form of the metaphorical utterance and the presence of context are important factors. The simple equation "Jenny is Jonathan" without much context might well not be judged as apt.

It is quite possible to maintain a fiction that domains are useful in characterizing metaphor or analysing metaphorical processing as long as one only deals schematically with some isolated examples, and does not try to come up with a unified and processually detailed approach to metaphor that can work on a wide variety of metaphors on the basis of the same overall knowledge base. This is not to say qualitative differences between the two sides of a metaphor are not interesting: the amount of difference can potentially affect aptness, vividness, persuasiveness, perceived indirectness or politeness, etc.

Finally, the virtual abandonment of domains as a genuine operational or explanatory construct in metaphor leads to heightened difficulty in distinguishing metaphor from metonymy, given some tendency in CL to view metaphor as operating between domains and metonymy within domains. In recent work (Barnden 2005) I have begun to develop a view of metaphor and metonymy as merely being vague notions that serve only a heuristic role in thinking about language, that the real phenomena lie at a more detailed level of description, and that the differences between what is commonly classed as metaphor and what is commonly classed as metonymy is a matter of differences on a sizable set of dimensions (which form the more detailed level of description). It is these dimensions that have reality, not metaphor and metonymy in themselves. The dimensions include such matters as the degree of conceptual distance between the source and target items in a metaphor or metonymy, the degrees to which similarity and contiguity are involved, and the degree to which the connection(s) between source item(s) and target items(s) are themselves part of the message conveyed. In the imaginary N-dimensional space spanned by these and other dimensions, metaphor and metonymy form fuzzy clouds that have no firm borders and that potentially overlap, and when attention is confined to only one dimension it can be very hard to draw any firm distinction between metaphor and metonymy; so the multi-dimensionality is important in itself in distinguishing between metaphor and metonymy.

The developing analysis is in much the same spirit as the proposals of CL authors such as Radden (2002) who put metaphor and metonymy at different points on a linear spectrum of phenomena, except that we have taken the idea further and replaced an individual spectrum by a multitude of spectra (the mentioned dimensions), and made each individual spectrum less clearcut in terms of the placing of metaphor and metonymy along it. The developing account is also analogous to the analysis by Peirsman and Geeraerts (in press) of metonymy into various dimensions concerned with the type and degree of source-target contiguity involved. Their analysis appears compatible to ours, in that our single contiguity dimension could be replaced by the multiple contiguity-related dimensions that they propose.

## 6. Conclusion

We have seen that one important vein in AI research on metaphor is to use ideas drawn from or similar to the notion of conceptual metaphor in CL. This vein is mined by, for example, Hobbs, Martin, Narayanan and me. However, another important vein has been to seek to account for (some) metaphor understanding from scratch without any prior knowledge of particular mappings (e.g., Fass, Hobbs, Veale). Equally, in AI research on metonymy, use has been made both of knowledge of common metonymic patterns (Fass, Markert), and of the approach of finding metonymic linkages from scratch in analysing a sentence (Hobbs).

AI can contribute to CL by attempting to construct computationally detailed models of structures and process drawn from or similar to those proposed more abstractly in CL. The computational model construction can confirm the viability of a proposal but can also reveal new problems and issues, or put existing ones into sharper relief. A case in point is the problem of the nature of domains and their involvement in conceptions of the nature of metaphor and metonymy.

### Acknowledgments

This chapter draws on research supported by current grant EP/C538943/1 and previous grant GR/M64208 from the Engineering and Physical Sciences Research Council (EPSRC) of the UK. The e-drama research draws also from grant RES-328–25–0009 from the Economic and Social Research Council (ESRC) of the UK, under the "PACCIT" programme funded by the EPSRC, ESRC and DTI (UK government's Department of Trade and Industry). I am grateful to the industrial partners on that grant (Hi8us Midlands Ltd, Maverick TV Ltd, and BT), and to my colleagues in the metaphor and e-drama research groups in my department.

## References

Asher, Nicholas, and Lascarides, Alex
1995    Metaphor in discourse. In *Proceedings of the AAAI Spring Symposium Series: Representation and Acquisition of Lexical Knowledge: Polysemy, Ambiguity and Generativity*, 3–7. Stanford, CA.

Barnden, John
1998    Combining uncertain belief reasoning and uncertain metaphor-based reasoning. In *Proceedings of the Twentieth Annual Meeting of the Cognitive Science Society*, Morton A. Gernsbacher, and Sharon J. Derry (eds.), 114–119. Mahwah, NJ: Lawrence Erlbaum.
2001a   Uncertainty and conflict handling in the ATT-Meta context-based system for metaphorical reasoning. In *Proceedings of the Third International Conference on Modeling and Using Context*, Varol Akman, Paolo Bouquet, Rich Thomason, and Roger A. Young (eds.), 15–29. Lecture Notes in Artificial Intelligence, Vol. 2116. Berlin: Springer-Verlag.
2001b   Application of the ATT-Meta metaphor-understanding approach to selected examples from Goatly. *Technical Report CSRP–01–01*, School of Computer Science, The University of Birmingham.
2001c   Application of the ATT-Meta metaphor-understanding approach to various examples in the ATT-Meta project databank. *Technical Report CSRP–01–02*, School of Computer Science, The University of Birmingham.
2005    Metaphor and metonymy: Escaping the domination of domains. Talk delivered at *New Directions in Cognitive Linguistics: First UK Cognitive Linguistics Conference*, University of Sussex, Brighton, U.K., October 2005.
In press a   Metaphor and artificial intelligence: Why they matter to each other. In *Cambridge Handbook of Metaphor and Thought*, Ray W. Gibbs, Jr. (ed.). Cambridge, MA: Cambridge University Press.
In press b   Metaphor, semantic preferences and context-sensitivity. *Words and Intelligence. Vol. 1: A Festschrift for Yorik Wilks*, C. Brewster, M. Stevenson (eds.). Berlin: Springer-Verlag.

Barnden, John, Sheila Glasbey, Mark Lee, and Alan Wallington
2002    Application of the ATT-Meta metaphor-understanding system to examples of the metaphorical view of TEACHERS AS MIDWIVES. *Technical Report CSRP–02–10*, School of Computer Science, The University of Birmingham.
2003    Domain-transcending mappings in a system for metaphorical reasoning. In *Conference Companion to the 10th Conference of the European Chapter of the Association for Computational Linguistics* (EACL 2003), 57–61. Association for Computational Linguistics.
2004    Varieties and directions of inter-domain influence in metaphor. *Metaphor and Symbol* 19 (1): 1–30.

Barnden, John, Stephen Helmreich, Eric Iverson, and Gees Stein
1994    An integrated implementation of simulative, uncertain and metaphorical reasoning about mental states. In *Principles of Knowledge Representation and Reasoning: Proceedings of the Fourth International Conference,* Jon Doyle, Erik Sandewall, and Pietro Torasso (eds.), 27–38. San Mateo, CA: Morgan Kaufmann.
1996    Artificial intelligence and metaphors of mind: within-vehicle reasoning and its benefits. *Metaphor and Symbolic Activity* 11 (2): 101–123.
Barnden, John, and Mark Lee
1999    An implemented context system that combines belief reasoning, metaphor-based reasoning and uncertainty handling. In *Second International and Interdisciplinary Conference on Modeling and Using Context,* Paolo Bouquet, Patrick Brezillon, and Luciano Serafini (eds.), 28–41. (Lecture Notes in Artificial Intelligence, 1688.) Berlin: Springer-Verlag.
2001    Understanding usages of conceptual metaphors: An approach and artificial intelligence system. *Technical Report CSRP–01–05,* School of Computer Science, University of Birmingham.
Blackwell, Alan
In press    The reification of metaphor as a design tool. In *ACM Transactions on Computer-Human Interaction.*
Cameron, Lynne
1999    Operationalising 'metaphor' for applied linguistic research. In *Researching and Applying Metaphor,* Lynn Cameron, and Graham Low (eds.), 1–28. Cambridge: Cambridge University Press.
Carbonell, Jaime
1980    Metaphor – a key to extensible semantic analysis. In *Proceedings of the 18th Annual Meeting of the Association for Computational Linguistics,* 17–21.
Croft, William
1982    Metaphor: an inescapable phenomenon in natural-language comprehension. In *Strategies for Natural Language Processing,* Wendy Lehnert, and Martin Ringle (eds.), 415–434. Hillsdale, NJ: Lawrence Erlbaum.
Delfino, Manuela, and Stefania Manca
2005    Figurative language expressing emotion and motivation in a web based learning environment. In *Proceedings of the Symposium on Agents that Want and Like: Motivational and Emotional Roots of Cognition and Action,* 37–40. AISB'05 Convention, University of Hertfordshire, UK, April 2005. Brighton, UK: Society for the Study of Artificial Intelligence and Simulation of Behaviour.
Dirven, René, and Ralf Pörings (eds.)
2002    *Metaphor and Metonymy in Comparison and Contrast.* Berlin/New York: Mouton de Gruyter.
Emanatian, Michele
1995    Metaphor and the experience of emotion: the value of cross-cultural perspectives. *Metaphor and Symbolic Activity* 10 (3): 163–182.

Fainsilber, Lynn, and Andrew Ortony
1987    Metaphorical uses of language in the expression of emotions. *Metaphor and Symbolic Activity* 2 (4): 239–250.
Fass, Dan
1997    *Processing Metaphor and Metonymy.* Greenwich, Connecticut: Ablex.
Fauconnier, Gilles, and Mark Turner
1998    Conceptual integration networks. *Cognitive Science* 22 (2): 133–187.
Fussell, Susan, and Mallie Moss
1998    Figurative language in descriptions of emotional states. In *Social and Cognitive Approaches to Interpersonal Communication*, Susan Fussell, and Roger J. Kreuz (eds.), Mahwah, N. J.: Lawrence Erlbaum.
Grady, Joseph
2002    THEORIES ARE BUILDINGS revisited. *Cognitive Linguistics* 8 (4): 267–290.
Gross, Linden
1994    Facing up to the dreadful dangers of denial. *Cosmopolitan* (USA edition) 216 (3): 190–193.
Hall, Rogers
1989    Computational approaches to analogical reasoning: a comparative analysis. *Artificial Intelligence* 39: 39–120.
Hobbs, Jerry
1990    *Literature and Cognition.* (CSLI Lecture Notes 21). Stanford, CA: CSLI Publications.
1992    Metaphor and abduction. In *Communication from an Artificial Intelligence Perspective: Theoretical and Applied Issues*, Andrew Ortony, Jon Slack, and Oliveiro Stock (eds.), 35–58. Berlin: Springer-Verlag.
Indurkhya, Bipin
1991    Modes of metaphor. *Metaphor and Symbolic Activity* 6 (1): 1–27.
1992    *Metaphor and cognition: An Interactionist Approach.* Dordrecht: Kluwer.
Iverson, Eric, and Stephen Helmreich
1992    Metallel: an integrated approach to non-literal phrase interpretation. *Computational Intelligence* 8 (3): 477–493.
Kittay, Eva
1989    *Metaphor: Its Cognitive Force and Linguistic Structure.* Oxford: Clarendon Press.
Kolodner, Janet
1993    *Case-Based Reasoning.* San Mateo, CA: Morgan Kaufmann.
Kövecses, Zoltán
2000    *Metaphor and Emotion: Language, Culture, and Body in Human Feeling.* Cambridge: Cambridge University Press.
Lakoff, George
1987    *Women, Fire and Dangerous Things. What Categories Reveal about the Mind.* Chicago: University of Chicago Press.
1993    The contemporary theory of metaphor. In *Metaphor and Thought*, 2nd

ed., Andrew Ortony (ed.), 202–251. Cambridge: Cambridge University Press.

Lakoff, George, and Mark Johnson
1980    *Metaphors We Live By*. Chicago: University of Chicago Press.

Lakoff, George, and Mark Turner
1989    *More Than Cool Reason: A Field Guide to Poetic Metaphor*. Chicago: University of Chicago Press.

Lapata, Mirella, and Alex Lascarides
2003    A probabilistic account of logical metonymy. In *Computational Linguistics* 29 (2): 261–315.

Lee, Mark, and John Barnden
2001a   Reasoning about mixed metaphors with an implemented AI system. *Metaphor and Symbol* 16 (1&2): 29–42.
2001b   Mental metaphors from the Master Metaphor List: Empirical examples and the application of the ATT-Meta system. *Technical Report CSRP-01-03*. School of Computer Science, The University of Birmingham.

Lytinen, Steven, Robert Burridge, and Jeffrey Kirtner
1992    The role of literal meaning in the comprehension of non-literal constructions. *Computational Intelligence* 8 (3): 416–432.

Markert, Katja, and Udo Hahn
2002    Understanding metonymies in discourse. *Artificial Intelligence* 135:145–198.

Markert, Katja, and Malvina Nissim
2003    Corpus-based metonymy analysis. *Metaphor and Symbol* 18 (3): 175–188.

Martin, James
1990    *A Computational Model of Metaphor Interpretation*. San Diego, CA: Academic Press.
1996    Computational approaches to figurative language. *Metaphor and Symbolic Activity* 11 (1): 85–100.
2000    Representing UNIX domain metaphors. *Artificial Intelligence Review* 14 (4–5): 377–401.

Mason, Zachary
2004    CorMet: A computational, corpus-based conventional metaphor extraction system. *Computational Linguistics* 30 (1): 23–44.

McNeil, David
1992    *Hand and Mind: What Gestures Reveal about Thought*. Chicago: University of Chicago Press.

Narayanan, Srini
1997    KARMA: Knowledge-based action representations for metaphor and aspect. Ph.D. diss., Computer Science Division, EECS Department, University of California, Berkeley.
1999    Moving right along: A computational model of metaphoric reasoning about events. *Proceedings of the National Conference on Artificial Intelligence* (AAAI '99), 121–128. AAAI Press.

Norvig, Peter
1989    Marker passing as a weak method of text inferencing. *Cognitive Science* 13 (4): 569–620.
Peirsman, Yves, and Dirk Geeraerts
In press    Metonymy as a prototypical category. *Cognitive Linguistics.*
Pereira, Francisco
In press    *Creativity and Artificial Intelligence: A Conceptual Blending Approach.* Berlin/New York: Mouton de Gruyter.
Pustejovsky, James
1995    *The Generative Lexicon.* Cambridge, MA: MIT Press.
Radden, Günter
2002    How metonymic are metaphors? In *Metaphor and Metonymy in Comparison and Contrast*, René Dirven, and Ralf Pörings (eds.), 407–434. Berlin/New York: Mouton de Gruyter.
Russell, Sylvia Weber
1976    Computer understanding of metaphorically used verbs. *American Journal of Computational Linguistics* 2: 15–28.
1986    Information and experience in metaphor: a perspective from computer analysis. *Metaphor and Symbolic Activity* 1 (4): 227–270.
Russell, Stuart, and Peter Norvig
2002    *Artificial intelligence: A Modern Approach.* Englewood Cliffs, NJ: Prentice-Hall.
Stallard, David
1987    The logical analysis of lexical ambiguity. In *Proceedings of the 25th Annual Meeting of the Association for Computational Linguistics*, 179–185, Stanford, CA: Stanford University.
1993    Two kinds of metonymy. In *Proceedings of the 31st Annual Meeting of the Association for Computational Linguistics*, 87–94. Ohio: Ohio State University.
Thomas, Owen
1969    *Metaphor and Related Subjects.* New York: Random House.
Tourangeau, Roger, and Robert Sternberg
1982    Understanding and appreciating metaphors. *Cognition* 11: 203–244.
Veale, Tony
1988    'Just in Time' analogical mapping, an iterative-deepening approach to structure-mapping. In *Proceedings of the Thirteenth European Conference on Artificial Intelligence* (ECAI'98). John Wiley.
Veale, Tony, and Mark Keane
1992    Conceptual scaffolding: a spatially founded meaning representation for metaphor comprehension. *Computational Intelligence* 8 (3): 494–519.
Veale, Tony, and Diarmuid O'Donoghue
2000    Computation and blending. *Cognitive Linguistics* 11 (3): 253–281.
Way, Eileen
1991    *Knowledge Representation and Metaphor.* Dordrecht: Kluwer.

Weber, Susan
1989 Figurative adjective-noun interpretation in a structured connectionist network. In *Proceedings of the Eleventh Annual Conference of the Cognitive Science Society*, 204–211. Hillsdale, NJ: Lawrence Erlbaum.

Weiner, Judith
1984 A knowledge representation approach to understanding metaphors. *Computational Linguistics* 10 (1): 1–14.

Wilcox, Phyllis
2004 A cognitive key: Metonymic and metaphorical mappings in ASL. *Cognitive Linguistics* 15 (2): 197–222.

Wilcox, Sherman
2004 Cognitive iconicity: Conceptual spaces, meaning, and gesture in signed language. *Cognitive Linguistics* 15 (2): 119–147.

Wilks, Yorick
1978 Making preferences more active. *Artificial Intelligence* 11: 197–223.

Wilks, Yorick, John Barnden, and Jin Wang
1991 Your metaphor or mine: belief ascription and metaphor interpretation. In *Proceedings of the 12th International Joint Conference on Artificial Intelligence*, 945–950. San Mateo: Morgan Kaufmann.

Winston, Patrick
1979 Learning by creating and justifying transfer frames. In Patrick Winston and Richard Brown (eds.), *Artificial Intelligence: An MIT Perspective, Vol. 1*, 347–374. Cambridge, MA.: MIT Press.

Woll, Bencie
1985 Visual imagery and metaphor in British Sign Language. In Wolf Paprotté and René Dirven (eds.), *The Ubiquity of Metaphor: Metaphor in Language and Thought*, 601–628. Amsterdam/Philadelphia: Benjamins.

Yu, Ning
1995 Metaphorical expressions of anger and happiness in English and Chinese. *Metaphor and Symbolic Activity* 10 (2): 59–92.

Zhang, Li, John Barnden, and Robert Hendley
2005 Affect detection and metaphor in e-drama: The first stage. In *Proceedings of the Workshop on Narrative Learning Environments*, 12th International Conference on Artificial Intelligence in Education (AIED-2005), Amsterdam.

# Computability as a test on linguistics theories

## Tony Veale

*Abstract*
Scientific theories are more than purely formal constructs, but linguistic artefacts that often rely on the rhetorical qualities of language to give their claims additional resonance and argumentative force. This reliance of theory upon language is even greater in those theoretical domains whose main concern is language itself, leading to a sometimes convenient blurring of content and form. Though Cognitive Linguistics has consistently revealed metaphor to be a fundamental building block in the development of complex conceptualizations, Cognitive Linguistic theories often exploit metaphor as an allusive place-holder when more formal clarity is demanded. Nonetheless, in this paper we argue that one such metaphor – the MIND-AS-COMPUTER metaphor that underlies the enterprises of Artificial Intelligence and Cognitive Science – can yield precisely the kind of formal clarity that is required by the most suggestive or radical of theories in Cognitive Linguistics. An exploration of how this metaphor informs the computational realization of cognitive theories will allow us to illuminate the often wide gap that exists between the descriptive suggestiveness of a linguistic theory and its actual computational sufficiency.

*Keywords*: Computability, Tractability; Mind As Computer; Verbal Humour; Blending; Radical Construction Grammar

## 1. Introduction

In seeking mechanical insight into the workings of the mind, researchers of different eras have, unsurprisingly, drawn inspiration from the dominant artefacts of the age. Consequently, the mind have variously been described as a wax tablet, a book, a library of books, a grain mill, a clock, a steam engine, an internal combustion engine and even a telephone exchange. This evolution of MIND AS MECHANISM metaphors has reached it zenith with the metaphor that underlies modern Cognitive Science, that of MIND AS COMPUTER (e.g., see Gardner 1985; Jackendoff 1987). But as useful as this metaphor has proven in Cognitive Science and its sibling fields (such as Artificial Intelligence), one might be forgiven for some scepticism as to its ultimate suitability as a model of mind. As older metaphors, such as the mind as grain mill, have passed their use-by date, is it not likely that the mind as computer metaphor will one day be superseded by another, more apropos model of cognition?

A strong rebuttal to this scepticism is to be found in the extreme generality of the modern computer, which is much more than a mere calculating machine but a universal computing device in itself. This universality implies that any realizable computing device can itself be simulated by a general purpose computer. Such a computer is a physical instantiation of a Turing machine, an abstract mathematical device on which every function that can naturally be considered computable *can* be computed (see Turing 1936). As such, if one is inclined to see the actions of the mind in terms of information processing, as Cognitive Science demonstrates we must, then the mind as computer metaphor has no expiry date. By information processing we mean, of course, more than the manipulation of electronic data, but include also the construction and manipulation of mental representations that have computational correlates in the form of strings, frames, records, trees, graphs and networks (see Veale and O'Donoghue 2000). This general belief in the mind as computer metaphor has been dubbed the *hypothesis of computational sufficiency* by Ray Jackendoff, who makes the following bold claim:

> Every phenomenological distinction is caused by/supported by/projected from a corresponding computational distinction. Jackendoff (1987: 24).

Jackendoff exhorts us to reason at the level of computational rather than phenomenological (or rhetorical) distinctions, for only the former is conducive to an explanatory account of the phenomenon under consideration. As an example, consider an analogical theory of car mechanics: a car travelling at 59 miles per hour is within the speed limit, but a slight acceleration to 60 miles per hour may cause it to break the law. This discontinuity at the social level (between legal and illegal) is not in the least reflected at the mechanical level of the car, which maintains the same engine throughout. To understand the engine then, we must focus only on those distinctions that directly arise from its architectural design and operational limits.

Given this perceived dependence of cognition on computation, it follows that the theoretical foundations of Computer Science, which place fundamental limitations on the actions of universal computing devices, should be of equal significance to any theory that views the workings of cognition from an information processing perspective (e.g. see Veale et al.

1996), and especially so to any linguistic theory that posits complex abstract machinery to capture the intricacies of natural language phenomena. Consider Chomsky's (1957) transformational grammar (TG), which models language as a multi-strata phenomenon in which complex transformations mediate between an unseen deep-structure representation and a visible surface form. The fact that TG approaches to language are often misunderstood as theories of language generation is due only in part to the ambiguity inherent in Chomsky's notion of linguistic *generativity*, for the fact is, TG-based models are more computationally felicitous when viewed as theories of language generation. The burdensome complexity of TG for parsing purposes is demonstrated, for example, by Plath's (1973) transformational parser, which requires an additional layer of transformational inverses to apply TG in reverse to an initial surface structure, and requires a complex sanity-checking mechanism (based on the forward application of TG transformations to the derived deep-structure) to additionally ensure that these inverses are always applied in a truly reversible manner. Just as it much easier to break a teacup than to properly re-assemble its broken parts, some theories can be seen as inherently directional from a computational perspective.

In this paper we shall explore the pertinence of a computational perspective to theories in Cognitive Linguistics by focussing on three specific theories of language use. The first two model creative linguistic phenomena, while the third represents a rather extreme example of the construction-based approach to language study. Since creativity is an area of study where one intuitively expects to find the least amount of formal substance, these first two models – Attardo and Raskin's *General Theory of Verbal Humour* or GTVH (1991) and Fauconnier and Turner's theory of *Conceptual Integration Networks* (1998, 2002) – therefore allow us to explore the often wide gap between descriptive suggestiveness and true computational sufficiency. This notion of sufficiency cuts directly to the computational core of a theory, and allows us to consider distinct theories for distinct phenomena as comparable if they ultimately hinge upon the same computational distinctions. This notion of computational equivalence – a corollary of sorts of computational sufficiency – allows us to consider the computational feasibility of Radical Construction Grammar, not in terms of its own software realization but in terms of a comparable computationally-precise theory of language translation that has been implemented on a large scale.

The rest of the paper assumes the following outline: in section two we provide capsule descriptions of the three linguistic theories that fuel the arguments to come; in section three we then consider three desirable features of scientific theories – falsifiability, explanatory power and formal specificity – before considering, in section four, the desirable properties that one additionally seeks from a computational perspective – computational specificity, efficiency and tractability. In section five we explore theoretical and engineering aspects of computational feasibility. We conclude in section six with a discussion of theories as linguistic artefacts, showing how a computational perspective can look beyond the rhetorical layers of a theory to its core.

## 2.    Three models of language processing

Before considering the role of computationalism in linguistic theorization, we first consider a broad overview of the three particular models on which the substance of our arguments will be focussed.

### 2.1. The general theory of verbal humour

Attardo and Raskin's GTVH, which currently dominates humour research, is a juxtapositional theory of humour that is a modular reworking of Raskin's (1985) Semantic Script Theory of Humour (or SSTH). Like the SSTH, the GTVH views a joke as a narrative that is compatible with multiple scripts, one of which will at first appear primary until the punch-line contrives a *incongruity* that must be resolved (see Ritchie 2003; Veale 2004). Resolution is achieved, either partially or fully, by a special logical mechanism that analyses the nature of the mismatch between the primary script and the text, before switching the thrust of interpretation from this script to another. For instance, it is suggested that an LM called *false-analogy* is central to jokes whose humour derives from ill-judged comparisons, as in the old joke where a mad scientist builds a rocket to the sun but plans to embark at night to avoid being cremated. Here a false analogy is created between the sun and a light-bulb, suggesting that when the sun is not shining it is not "turned on", and hence, not hot. Different LMs may be employed in different jokes, bringing a distinctive logical flavour to each. More recently, Attardo *et al.* (2002) enumerate a variety of different logical mechanisms (27 in all) and offer a new, graph-theoretic account of script representation that now sees scripts as arbitrarily complex symbolic structures to which juxtapositional processes like subgraph isomorphism can be applied. GTVH scripts can now accommodate not just the semantic structure of events, but the phonological structure of words. For example, Attardo *et al.* (ibid) argue that the pun in the mathematical book title *The joy of sets* is resolved by structure-mapping two phonological "script" graphs, *[s, e, tz]* and *[s, e, ks]*.

## 2.2. Conceptual integration networks or blending theory

Our second model of interest is Fauconnier and Turner's (1998, 2002) theory of conceptual integration networks, more popularly called *blending theory*. Like the GTVH, blending theory offers a juxtapositional account of creative language use, one in which multiple mental spaces (called *inputs*) are integrated to generate a new mental space, the *blend space*, that contains a selective projection of the inputs which is formed subject to a variety of interacting optimality principles. This new space, which is connected to, but independent from, the original input spaces, is invoked to explain the emergent properties of many compositional structures, from metaphors to noun compounds to jokes. When relations between elements of different input spaces are projected into a blended space, they may become compressed through a process of metonymic tightening. Thus, a similarity relation outside the blended space may become an identity relation within the blended space. Coulson (2000) has used blending theory to offer a theory of humour, called *frame shifting*, that is in many respects similar to the *script-switching* view of the GTVH. Though some attempts have been made to realize blending theory in computational form (e.g. see Veale and O'Donoghue 2000), such implementations are necessarily incomplete and require a loose, almost metaphorical reading of the theory's principal mechanisms.

## 2.3. Radical Construction Grammar

Our third model is Croft's (2001) Radical Construction Grammar, which, as its name suggests, is a theory whose simplifying assumptions pose a radical challenge to key elements of linguistic orthodoxy. Like other construction grammars, RCG gives a central position to the role of the construction, a mapping between form and meaning that can be almost entirely substantive (as in the case of idioms) or entirely parameterized (as in the case of grammatical schemata). RCG thus obliterates the traditional distinction between lexicon and grammar, as constructions may lie anywhere along a lexico-syntactic continuum. As in other variants of construction grammar (e.g. see Goldberg 2003), the purpose of constructions in RCG is to break down the traditional barrier between form and meaning by directly motivating issues of form in semantic and pragmatic terms. But RCG is radical in suggesting that conventional formal categories like S, V and NP are not universal building blocks for grammar rules or constructions. Indeed, RCG is radical to the point of claiming that such categories are not even language-specific, but are merely specific to the constructions that contain them. This pitches conventional linguistic orthodoxy on its head, for since these categories serve a local rather than general role with no absolute meaning, one cannot derive the meaning of a construction from the categories it contains; rather, RCG claims that the meaning of these categories is instead inferred from the constructions in which they appear.

## 3.    Desirable properties of scientific theories

To be truly scientific, a theory should make sufficiently strong claims that are open to rebuttal by experimentation or direct observation. This principle, most famously reduced to the single term *falsifiability* (e.g. see Popper 1959), is tightly woven into the practice of modern day linguistics wherever the inner processes of language impinge on superficial form (consider the linguist's frequent appeal to verification via native speaker intuitions). In Cognitive Linguistics, with its emphasis on conceptual structure, such opportunities for surface-level falsification can be altogether less frequent. Bell (2002), for example, has questioned whether Fauconnier and Turner's (1998, 2002) theory of conceptual blending exposes enough of its workings to external observation at the textual level to be falsifiable. Falsification, then, is just one of several properties one should desire of a linguistic theory, and in lieu of observation-based falsification, one must look to other indicators of a theory's soundness. The first of these is explanatory power, which separates theories with a post-hoc descriptive utility from those that exhibit genuine causal insight into the workings of a particular mechanism. The second is formal specificity, which separates those theories whose attractiveness is largely rhetorical from those that exhibit an unadorned logical clarity.

### 3.1. Explanatory power

In linguistic terms, the difference between an explanatory theory and a descriptive theory is much like the difference between a metaphor and a simile: a good metaphor reveals the deep causal structure beneath a domain (e.g., *the Earth is an electron buzzing around its nucleus, the sun*) while a good simile is only superficially revealing (e.g., *the Earth is like a football*). Are the GTVH and blending theories merely similes for the superficial workings of our creative use of words, or do they capture real cognitive mechanisms at work? The GTVH does not explain why a text that is compatible with two overlapping but incongruous scripts should be considered humorous, but merely claims that successful jokes appear to exhibit this property. In specifying 27 different logical mechanisms of humour (and leaving the door open for more to come), Attardo et al. (2002) appear to be engaged in what the physicist Ernest Rutherford dismissed as a form of science more akin to "stamp-collecting" than physics. Likewise, in attempting to "explain too much" (see Bell 2002; Gibbs 2000), one can argue that conceptual blending theory trivializes its subject matter: is every compositional mental structure to be seen as a blend (albeit, in many cases, a bad or sub-optimal blend)? Are we to take as a blend any conceptual structure whose composition can be described by blending theory, or should we require a more restrictive definition? Unfortunately, there seems little in the formal apparatus of the theory itself to satisfactorily answer these questions.

A descriptive theory can afford to be agnostic as to the specific processes that yield the description for a given phenomenon, even when competing accounts of these processes are available. An explanatory theory, in contrast, should commit to just one account, and moreover, should offer reasons as to why this account is not simply the "official" account, but a truly superior account in light of the available facts and data. Conceptual blending is a mechanism that, when run *forward* from its inputs, attempts to explain how a complex conceptual product is created, and when run *backward* from an integrated product, attempts to explain how this product is comprehended. Since conceptual blending provides a very detailed account of how creative products are comprehended, it is tempting to believe that the theory also explains how such products are created. However, one can easily imagine other, simpler and more computationally felicitous accounts, of how such conceptual products are created.

Consider the complex ideas "drive-by shooting" and "date-rape", two apparently archetypal products of conceptual blending in action. The linguistic form of "date-rape" directs us to comprehend the concept as an integration of two scenarios ("date" and "rape") that necessitates a tight mapping of participants (e.g., suitor = rapist, target-of-affection = victim), as does the linguistic form of "drive-by-shooting" (e.g., driver/passenger = shooter, pedestrian = victim). Each also gives rise to emergent inferences: drive-by shootings are faster but less accurate forms of attack, and typically involve higher rates of collateral damage; date-rape is typically harder to prosecute, and may not even be acknowledged as rape by its perpetrator. From a generation perspective, however, it is surely more intuitive to think of each not as an explicit integration of distinct ideas, but as a simple deviation from a single prototype. Date-rape represents a subversion of the prototypical dating scenario (or script) in which consent for sexual activity has been edited out, thereby resulting in a scenario that more resembles the rape scenario. Likewise, a drive-by shooting can be seen as an edited version of a prototypical "hit", in which the attacker does not leave (or even stop) his car. This single-input subversion account can also be used to explain the mechanics of many jokes. For instance, an industrial-drowning script can be subverted into a form that resembles (and thus recalls) a swimming-pool script, either by editing-out the tragic conclusion (though this is unlikely to result in humour) or by editing-*in* some elements that suggest the tragic event was a pleasurable one.[1] Each of these examples demonstrate that complex products with emergent features can be constructed from a single input structure by assuming a simple form of internal editing. We should be wary then of cognitive just-so stories: we cannot conclude from the fact that "date-rape" and "drive-by-shooting" (or, for that matter, "house-boat", "sofa-bed", or any number of classic blends and jokes) *can* be described as an integration of multiple input structures, that they *should* be so described. Ultimately, explanatory force arises not from apparent possibility, but from apparent necessity. We consider how computational concerns might provide this necessity in section 4.2.

### 3.2. Formal specificity

Though formalization can seem a dry affair, it is a necessary step if a theory is to achieve unambiguous clarity, particularly so if the entities to which it is ontologically committed are to be specified in a way that neither relies on metaphor or unarticulated intuition. A theory of creativity, for instance, must be capable of formally separating those processes and artefacts that are deserving of the label "creative" from those that are not. Similarly, a theory of humour must be capable of unambiguously defining a joke. As we have argued, a theory of conceptual blending must likewise be capable of defining what kinds of construct constitute a blend, and more importantly, what constructs do not constitute a blend. The classical approach to such formalization is the use of necessary and sufficient feature sets. For instance, Raskin (1985) claims that two features are individually necessary and jointly sufficient for a text to constitute a joke: the joke must be partially compatible with at least two scripts (the criterion of "script overlap") and these scripts must be opposed to each other in a particular way (the criterion of "script opposition"). Neither script overlap alone (e.g., as found between dentist and doctor scripts) or script opposition alone (e.g., as found in baptism/life and funeral/death scripts) is sufficient in this view to produce humour.

Necessary and sufficient features have long been rejected by cognitivists as a model of human category structure, as they lead to brittle and simplistic structures that are easily invalidated by real world examples. To a researcher in Cognitive Linguistics, it may therefore seem unrealistic to build a theory around such features, since theories are categories too and we would like our theories, like our categories, to be robust in the face of real world data. For instance, it is commonly held outside Cognitive Linguistics that semantic anomaly is a necessary feature of metaphors (e.g. see Fass 1988). However, this claim is easily refuted by metaphors like *my lawyer is my bodyguard* and *my mechanic is a magician*. Likewise, it is commonly held, even by cognitivists, that incongruity is a necessary feature of humour (see Ritchie 2003 for a review), while Veale (2004) argues that incongruity is merely a by-product of a listener's desire to opportunistically seek humour in a text when socially licensed to do so. Nonetheless, though the anomaly theory is unattractive as a theory of metaphor on aesthetic grounds, inasmuch as it tends to over-simplify the phenomenon, it's bold claims are very attractive in Popperian terms. Likewise, incongruity theories of humour are unattractive to some researchers (such as Veale 2004) for similar reasons, inasmuch as they deny the listener a collaborative role in humour construction, yet they too are attractive for so readily courting falsification. From a scientific perspective then, a lack of robustness in the face of real data can be seen as a desirable by-product of the bold claims made by necessary and sufficient feature definitions, since bold claims are more easily falsified than weak ones. This scientific perspective has a valuable engineering corollary: since necessity and sufficiency more easily translate into computational form (e.g., as an exhaustive collection of set-theoretic conditionals) than the equivalent system of potentially incomplete family resemblances, a theory formalized in this classical way can automatically be applied to a much larger corpus of potentially falsifying data.

## 4.    Computational realization of scientific theories

From a computational perspective, two further properties are desirable in a theory. Firstly, the theory must be specific enough to allow a computational realization to be constructed, which in turn requires that the theory is shorn of any linguistic ambiguity or vagueness, either by the theorist (which is the most desirable case) or, ultimately, by the programmer (via the much less desirable case of theoretical "interpretation"). Secondly, this computational implementation must be tractable, which is to say, it must exhibit desirable run-time performance that is in line with human performance on the same inputs. We now consider each of these properties in greater depth.

### 4.1. Computational specificity

Once sufficiently formalized, a theory can be recast in a computational form. This transformation requires that the entities of concern to the theory are sufficiently defined as to suggest adequate data representations for a computer to operate upon, and that the processes of concern to the theory are sufficiently defined (in terms of chronology, inputs and outputs) to be expressed algorithmically. There are good engineering reasons for realizing a cognitive theory computationally, not least the A.I. goal of imbuing software systems with some semblance of human intelligence. But there are strong scientific reasons also, not least the opportunity for large scale automated testing of the theory that a software realization would enable. For instance, a semantic theory for the interpretation of noun-noun phrases could, if implemented in software, be applied to all of the noun-noun phrases in a machine-readable dictionary, or better yet, to all of the noun-noun phrases in WordNet, a large-scale hierarchical database of English terms and their meanings (see Miller 1995). Suppose such a theory makes the simplifying claim that the meaning of non-idiomatic noun-noun compound is only rarely a specialization of the modifier term (e.g., *a rat-catcher* is a kind of person, not a kind of rat). A large-scale analysis of WordNet entries would reveal that the exceptions to this view – such as *sofa-bed, boy-scout* and *lady-friend* – are simply too numerous to discount as rare occurrences.

In fact, the very act of computationally implementing a cognitive theory is itself an extreme test of the formal specificity of the theory and the extent to which it can support itself without the aid of human interpretation. For inasmuch as computers lack the ability to process metaphorical or vague, suggestive language, they are immune to the seductive qualities of language that can otherwise bewitch humans. Computational specificity requires that every step and every data element of a process must be explicitly defined, so to the extent that a software realization requires a programmer to make certain guesses or fudges – e.g., by using random selection of candidates when a theory simply assumes that the best selection is made in a given context – then the underlying theory must also be seen to be damagingly fudged.

Computational specificity also requires a theory to explicitly quantify the thresholds that implicitly govern its application. For instance, how much inter-script similarity should the GTVH consider a sufficient overlap to support humour? How many optimality constraints can a juxtaposition of two mental spaces violate before the juxtaposition is discarded as a failed blend (as opposed to, say, a poor blend). While such questions can go largely unanswered at the pre-computational level, they cannot remain so in any software realization that demands raw numbers, or at the very least, workable heuristics, with which to make these decisions.

## 4.2. Computational efficiency

When multiple accounts can be offered for the same phenomenon, how should one choose between them? For example, how can one reliably choose one account of conceptual creativity, such as the single-input subversion account described earlier (in the context of the concepts *date-rape* and *drive-by shooting*), over another, such as the multiple-input integration account favoured by blending theory or the comparable multiple-script resolution account advanced by the GTVH? Computationalism does not provide a complete answer, but it can decisively boost the explanatory status of a given account by showing it to be more efficient than its competitors. This argument can be seen as a computational extension of Occam's razor, which might be stated thus: computational entities, such as representations, constraints and processes, should not by multiplied without cause, so that theories that presuppose the least number of such entities are to be preferred to the extent that they can account for the same data. This makes good explanatory sense, for one because it reflects our intuition that the brain, while not always optimal, is nonetheless thrifty in its use of valuable processing resources, and secondly (though no less important) because it requires a theorist to strongly motivate the use of entities which are shown to be superfluous in a simpler competing account. In fact, this perspective often reveals such entities to be post-hoc rationalizations whose only purpose is to "save" a theory from under- or over-generation (e.g. see Bell 2002).

The multiple-input account offered by blending theory is inefficient as a theory of creative conceptualization not because of the need to computationally process these inputs (though this is a non-trivial factor, as we shall discuss in section 5), but because of the computational effort needed to actually populate these input spaces. Though blending theory has been criticized for attempting to explain too much (Bell 2002), in this key respect it does not attempt to explain enough. Despite the fact that blending theory is typically employed to describe creative linguistic activities, from jokes to poetic allusions to brainteasers and clever advertisements, the creativity *per se* is assumed to happen off stage, before blending even begins, for it is the idea of the combination, rather than its principled execution, that constitutes the creative insight. Consider a gastronomic example: it is the decision to combine duck with orange, rather than the act of executing the combination (e.g., by covering the duck with orange sauce) that exemplifies the culinary creativity of *duck a l'orange*. For the single-input subversion account, the relevant search space is defined as the set of possible edits of the given input structure, which can be explored in a highly constrained and controlled manner (such as hill-climbing). However, since it is not at all clear that the optimality principles that guide the construction of a blended space can be applied in reverse to determine the ideal contents of the input spaces, one must thus assume that a computational realization of blending theory must engage in a broad-horizon search of all possible partner concepts if it is to populate these spaces. Compare this situation with that faced by the GTVH, whose creative search space is confined to just those script pairings that exhibit a sharing of structure and some explicit opposition of elements. The relative computational inefficiency of blending theory, born of an inherent computational insufficiency, suggests that the theory offers a descriptive account of creativity that is not yet a genuinely explanatory one.

### 4.3. Computational tractability

Even if sufficiently formalized to be computationally realized, a cognitive theory meets one final hurdle. It is well known in Computer Science that problems that are solvable in principle (and thus realizable in software) may nonetheless prove unsolvable in practical terms. The distinction is akin to that between competence and performance that is commonly made in linguistics (see Chomsky 1957): computational specificity reflects the ability to encode a theory as abstract software (competence), while computational tractability reflects the ability to run this software on a specific instantiation of a universal computing device and obtain the desired outputs in a reasonable amount of time (performance). Problems are considered "intractable" if they cannot be coded in such a way as to allow them to be solved for a wide range of inputs without making unrealistic assumptions about time or resources. As the reader will detect from the judicious use of the words *reasonable* and *unrealistic*, intractability is very much a practical notion that depends both on the patience of the user and the quantity of resources (such as memory, disk-size, etc.) that is available, though generally speaking, the problems of most interest in Computer Science are such that no earthly amount of either can make an optimal solution viable. Our point in this paper is that many of the problems of most interest to Cognitive Linguists, such as the optimal selection of a subset of objects or the mapping of two structured representations, correspond, in computational terms, to these very same problems.

From a tractability perspective, solutions (i.e., computationally realized theories) can be segmented into two broad categories. Polynomial-time solutions are those whose time complexity can be given as a formula of variables raised to constant powers; for instance, a naïve sorting program for a list of $n$ elements may require $n^2$ steps and take a corresponding amount of time, denoted $O(n^2)$, to finish. In contrast, exponential-time solutions are those whose time complexity is given by a formula of terms raised to variable powers; for instance, a naïve algorithm for choosing an optimal selection from $n$ elements may require a consideration of $2^n$ different combinations, and so take $O(2^n)$ time to finish (see Garey and Johnson 1979).

Problems that can be solved with a polynomial-time solution belong to a class of problems that computer scientists denote as P. For example, the class P includes many theories of syntactic processing via phrase-structure rules, since in general a grammar can be used to validate a sentence of n words in $n^3$ steps or less. However, most of the interesting problems (and thus theories) in Cognitive Science and Artificial Intelligence appear to require an exponential-time solution, at least if one seeks an optimal solution. Many such problems could be solved in polynomial time if realized on a computer capable of pursuing an unlimited number of processing pathways in parallel, so that it could always execute both branches of every conditional statement simultaneously. Such a non-deterministic machine is of course physically impossible, but theoretically useful nonetheless. Computer scientists denote the class of problems that can be solved in polynomial time on such a machine as NP, for non-deterministic polynomial. Though it is tempting to simply read NP as meaning "non-polynomial", the question of whether P = NP remains amongst the most important, and elusive, of any question in theoretical Computer Science.

The hardest known problems in NP are dubbed NP-Hard.[2] One such problem is the travelling salesman problem (or TSP), in which one must select the shortest tour route among a set of *n* cities (which would seem to necessitate a consideration of *n!* different tours). To prove that a problem is NP-Hard, one must reduce a known NP-Hard problem to the given problem, to demonstrate that when solving this particular problem, one is in effect solving an NP-problem like TSP in another guise. Computational complexity is thus a relative (perhaps even parasitic) notion; if one were to find an optimal polynomial-time solution for TSP, the set NP would collapse into P, such that all NP problems would be solvable in principle in polynomial time. Since this is highly unlikely to happen, complexity classes like P and NP are extremely useful to computationalists and cognitivists alike: if a cognitive theory is sufficiently specific to indicate NP-hardness, one must anticipate either limited application of the theory (to very small problem instances) or that a sub-optimal variation of the theory is implemented by the brain.[3]

## 5.    Computational feasibility and complexity

The more daring or radical a theory, the greater the challenge it can pose to our sensibilities about what is and is not feasible in practice. But once again, the substance of this challenge is to be found not in the novelty of the theory or the sparsity of its assumptions, but in the computational feasibility of the processes that it entertains. Certain commonplace abilities and processes, such as the ability to pair off like with like from two different collections, are so familiar as to suggest no computational challenge whatsoever. Nonetheless, such mapping abilities are presupposed by any conceptual output that is the product of structural matching, from the integrated spaces of metaphors and blends, to the overlapping scripts of the GTVH, and the overlapping semantic maps of radical construction grammar (RCG). Viewed in abstract terms, these abilities become recognizably more complex as one moves from the limited demands of toy examples to the scale often demanded by real-world data.

## 5.1. Feasibility by proxy: Radical Construction Grammar

Though Croft (2001) considers RCG to be "disarmingly simple" in its theoretical claims, one might ask whether the same can be said of its implied computational claims, namely, that one can implement an algorithmic model of language by eschewing long-standing linguistic orthodoxies like distinct lexicons and rules, or grammar-wide formal categories. The issue then is not so much whether RCG can be efficiently realized but whether it can be computationally realized at all. It may be that RCG is too disarmingly simple to provide the computational sufficiency required for a practical implementation. While there exist some computational proofs-of-concept for other varieties of construction grammar, such as embodied construction grammar (see Bergen and Chang 2005; Bryant 2003), there are none, to our knowledge, that demonstrate the large-scale computational feasibility of RCG's most radical claims.

Nonetheless, large-scale computational systems have been successfully created and deployed for a linguistic model that is, from the perspective of computational sufficiency, remarkably similar to RCG. Within the paradigm of *example-based machine translation* or EBMT (e.g. see Carl and Way 2003), researchers also dispense with traditional linguistic assumptions about the absoluteness of formal categories and the hard distinction between lexicon and grammar. Instead, EBMT exploits a database of construction-like exemplars which map fragments of a source language like English onto corresponding fragments of a target languages like Japanese and German. Translations for a given text are then produced, quilt-like, by combining the appropriate translation fragments as provided by these exemplars. EBMT exemplars are not hand-coded, but are typically derived from existing parallel corpora such as the multilingual product manuals that international corporations produce in abundance. Like RCG, EBMT strives toward a radical view of language processing that jettisons as much linguistic convention as possible, not because of a fundamental distaste for orthodoxy, but because of the onerous knowledge-engineering demands and resulting brittleness that comes from the need to develop and maintain hand-crafted grammars and lexicons.

The exemplars of EBMT exhibit many of the key properties of constructions in RCG. Since exemplars range in size from single lexemes to entire sentences, they collectively constitute both the lexicon of the system and its implicit grammar. Likewise, EBMT systems like Veale and Way's *Gaijin* (see Carl and Way 2003) support schematic exemplars that serve the role of abstracted grammar rules. And like RCG, EBMT does not attempt to cluster exemplars into families of mappings that exhibit the same deep-structural form. Rather, each exemplar is treated as an island, and no generalization is formed, for example, from active and passive variations of the same textual proposition. Furthermore, because exemplars are typically derived via automated statistical alignment techniques from bilingual corpora, the same exemplars can be extracted many times over, thus providing a basis for considering some exemplars as providing more prototypical translations than others.

While EBMT exemplars are mappings from form to form, rather than form to meaning, their structure (as again judged from the viewpoint of computational sufficiency) is comparable. Indeed, in no sense do form-to-form mappings underestimate the difficulties of dealing with form-to-meaning mappings. Exemplars that are semantically compatible at a propositional level are frequently incompatible at a form level, due to disagreements in number, case, grammatical role or register. This problem, denoted *boundary friction*, means that EBMT exemplars can be extremely sensitive to the ways they are combined. Since EBMT strives toward a linguistics-lite theory of translation, most systems tackle boundary friction with statistical or corpus methods, such as establishing the validity or otherwise of possible translation candidates by determining which candidate occurs most often on the world-wide-web.

To the extent that RCG can also be seen as a rules-lite approach to language, RCG and EMBT are sufficiently similar to ultimately imagine a role for the semantic maps of RCG in the detection and elimination of boundary friction, for EBMT and RCG do attempt to model comparable issues of language use in comparable ways. As such, the engineering practicality of EBMT as a model of machine translation strongly supports the computational feasibility of RCG as a linguistic theory.

## 5.2. Complexity Theory in action

As we have seen, both the GTVH and blending theory rely crucially on a cognitive mechanism capable of mapping two arbitrarily complex mental structures. In the case of the GTVH, this mapping determines the extent of script overlap, where scripts are now mathematically conceived in graph-theoretic terms (see Attardo et al. 2002). In the case of blending theory, such mappings are central to the identification of correspondences between input spaces (see Veale and O'Donoghue 2000). Several analyses have been made of the complexity of the structure mapping process required for analogical reasoning, and so by extension, conceptual blending and script-based joke analysis (see Falkenhainer et al. 1989; Forbus and Oblinger 1990; Winston 1982). Nonetheless, though structure-mapping is intuitively NP-Hard, none of these analyses have the status of a proof. In this section, we present our own proof and a subsequent analysis to highlight some of the important properties of structure-mapping.

Structure-mapping between two structured representations (essentially graphs) proceeds by first identifying obvious partial mappings between sub-structures of each representation. These partial mappings are then combined to create successively larger mappings until a maximal partial mapping is generated; such mappings are maximal in the sense that no other elements can be added without violating the 1-to-1 isomorphism of the mapping. Though some metaphors and blends may involve many-to-one correspondences, as in the blend "one-man-band" (which maps every position in a band onto the same musician), most analogical mappings are intelligible by virtue of being isomorphic (e.g. see Falkenhainer et al. 1989; Veale and Keane 1997). The goal of structure-mapping is to find the largest maximal partial mapping that is possible between both conceptual representations. In an ideal situation, every element of each representation is mapped in such a mapping; in other situations, the largest partial mapping represents a "best match" of the available knowledge structures.

Defining structure-mapping in graph-theoretic terms allows us to identify the problem as a rewording of the known NP-Complete problem LCS, or Largest Common Sub-Graph (see Garey and Johnson 1979):

*Analogical Mapping (AM): Given the directed and arc-labelled graphs $S = (SV, SA)$ and $T = (TV, TA)$ which represent, respectively, the source and target domains of the analogy, we ask, do there exist subsets $SA'$ $SA$, $TA'$ $TA$, $SV'$ $SV$, $TV'$ $TV$, with $|SV'| = |TV'|$ and $|SA'| = |TA'|$ $K$ such that the sub-graphs $S' = (SV', SA')$ and $T' = (TV', TA')$ are isomorphic? Two graphs $S'$ and $T'$ are isomorphic if there exists a function f: $S'$ $T'$ such that $<v_i, v_k> S'$ iff $<f(v_i), f(v_k)> T'$.*

However, since LCS is a decision problem (returning true or false, rather than actual structure), it does not provide us with a particularly useful low-level picture of the computation performed during structure-mapping, which is centred around the aggregation and combination of partial mappings. The following NP-Hard problem 3DM (see again Garey and Johnson 1979) yields a clearer picture:

***Unique 3-Dimensional Matching (3DM):*** *Given a set M of points in 3-D space, i.e., $M \subseteq X \times Y \times Z$, where X, Y and Z are disjoint sets of integers and $|X|=|Y|=|Z|=q$, find the largest set $M' \subseteq M$ such that no two elements of M' agree in any co-ordinate.*

We can recast structure-mapping in terms of 3DM quite easily, if the set of points in three-dimensional space is seen as the set of possible cross-domain correspondences between source and target structures. Partial mappings will thus be aggregates of these points, such that the largest maximal partial mapping will correspond to the largest set $M'$ of non-overlapping points. A detailed reduction of 3DM to structure-mapping, and thus, a complete proof of the NP-hardness of the latter, can be found in Veale and Keane (1997).

## 5.3. Ramifications

Such a proof of NP-hardness imposes a number of very real constraints on cognitive theories that are predicated on an ability to generate systematic mappings between arbitrarily complex structures. First, these theories cannot assume an optimal mapping, unless they can demonstrate that the structures involved will always possess a simplicity bordering on the trivial (as is not the case for either the GTVH or blending theory). Second, computational specificity demands that the nature of any sub-optimal mapping scheme be reflected at the theory level, for Veale and Keane (1997) demonstrate that the effectiveness of any sub-optimal mapping scheme is intimately bound up in the nature of the representations on which it is used. In the case of the GTVH, for instance, this suggests that scripts not be viewed as arbitrary graph structures after all; recall that this arbitrariness was introduced in Attardo et al. (2002) to allow script-overlap to encompass both narrative similarity for jokes and phonological similarity for puns. Generally speaking, the more highly constrained a representation, the more highly constrained and delimited will be the search space derived from this representation. Thus, a more constrained script representation (like that originally assumed by Raskin, 1985) may lead to a polynomial-time mapping algorithm more akin to the efficient, top-down unification of feature structures. Indeed, we see efficient unification of this kind at work in computationally realized models of construction grammar, such as the implementation of Embodied Construction Grammar (or ECG) described in Bryant (2003) and Bergen and Chang (2005).

## 6.   Concluding remarks

Language can be a bewitching medium in which to theorize, for one can easily seduced be into assuming a clear understanding of a given concept simply because one knows how to use the corresponding words. Much of the later philosophy of Wittgenstein (e.g. see Wittgenstein 1958, 1979) is characterized by an attempt to reveal this seductive power for what it is, as when he argues – counter to our linguistic intuitions on the matter – that there is no coherent concept of Knowledge behind the word *know*.[4] Many of the problems that hinder the true understanding of a scientific phenomenon are, in essence, problems of language, for theories are linguistic artefacts in their own right. One must separate out the rhetorical devices used by a theory to gain widespread acceptance from the ontological commitments that the theory makes to specific entities and processes. For instance, a theory that makes reference to the notion of a *domain* might make an ontological commitment to a particular cognitive structure, or might simply use the term as a rhetorical shorthand. Since rhetorical and ontological commitments are often tightly entwined in the persuasive exposition of a theory, these are best separated by a computationalist perspective that appeals to Jackendoff's notion of computational sufficiency: only those claims of a cognitive theory that are mirrored by a corresponding computational distinction should be considered as having a potentially explanatory value.

   This separation is easier if a theory makes few rhetorical commitments, or in the case of Radical Construction Grammar, the theory makes what amount to *negative* ontological commitments. For instance, RCG explicitly denies the existence of universal syntactic categories, and even denies that such categories have language-wide scope. But to make this minimalism possible, RCG makes a *positive* ontological commitment to the existence of semantic maps in a shared conceptual space.

   The rhetorical qualities of a term often colour its theoretical function. Consider again the term *script*, which denotes the ontological core of Attardo and Raskin's general theory of humour. Raskin (1985) originally employs the term in the sense popularized by the work of Schank and Abelson (1977), that is, to denote a schematic structure that imposes a sequential, causal ordering on a narrative and which reflects a single top-down interpretation of events based on an abstracted distillation of relevant episodic memories. Because of the cinematic connotations of the word, one is intuitively directed to view a cognitive script as a film script, one that provides a narrative sequence of actions for a set of actors to perform, albeit for mundane actions like visiting the doctor, eating at a restaurant or being the victim of a mugger. However, this is not the interpretation of the term favoured by a computational reading of the SSTH and GTVH, as evident from attempts to realize these theories in software. In Raskin (1996), a script is taken to mean a conventional frame structure, much like the frames of conceptual blending theory, one supposes, or the unification structures used to represent constructions in Bryant's (2003) implementation of construction grammar. Raskin's frames thus comprise a collection of labelled slots, denoting event roles, into which semantic fillers may be placed. But in Attardo et al. (2002), a script is revised to mean little more than a generalized graph structure (that now presupposes an NP-hard mapping problem rather than a polynomial time unification process). With this generalization, the GTVH moves further from the conventional cinematic interpretation of a script toward a completely neutral symbolic representation. The term script, however, remains, to suggest that the GTVH still views humour as a by-product of our cognitive faculty for reasoning about events and their social consequences. How else can a social phenomenon like humour arise out of an abstract operation over graphs? But however suggestive the term script, the underlying computational distinction needed to support this suggestion is now absent, and we conclude that the explanatory power of the GTVH is diminished as a result.

The GTVH and blending theory serve as interesting case studies of cognitive theorizing for yet another reason: each represents a separate evolution of Koestler's (1964) influential theory of Bisociation, in which creativity is said to arise at the juncture of orthogonal mental *matrices*. Both theories embody different solutions to the issues of specificity that vex Koestler's original theory, which arise for the most part from Koestler's lack of a suitably concrete vocabulary with which he might express his claims. The computationalist influence on the cognitive sciences has since – through its emphasis on specific well-formed representations and processes – allowed theories like blending and the GTVH to surmount these descriptive difficulties. We now possess a rich vocabulary of frames, scripts, schemata and mappings that each suggest largely the same notion, more or less, as we move from Cognitive Linguistics to Cognitive Science to Artificial Intelligence and Computer Science. As we have seen, however, there is still a substantial difference between, on one hand, the rhetorical suggestiveness of such terms, and on the other, their precise theoretical meaning as seen from the perspective of computational sufficiency. The ongoing importance of the computationalist perspective is to ensure that these terms are always understood from the latter, formally-precise, perspective. Only then can cognitive theories be judged and evaluated on their fundamentals, that is, on those aspects that arise directly from computational distinctions, rather than on the suggestive linguistic penumbras that surround them.

## Notes

1. Such a subversion is evident in the following joke: "A worker at the Guinness beer factory drowns tragically one day after falling into a giant vat of Guinness. A manager is dispatched to inform the unfortunate man's wife. 'Did he die quickly?', she asks the manager. 'No', he replies, 'in fact, he got out twice to use the toilet'".
2. For "decision problems", which are those that diagnose a given set of inputs to return a simple true or false, the corresponding class of hardest problems is called NP-Complete.
3. There is a third option, which is to assume that the brain is, in fact, a non-deterministic machine (exploiting, say, some oddity of quantum mechanical physics) or that it does not operate on Turing-compatible computational principles. Though possible in principle, this option is still largely the stuff of science fiction.
4. "One is often bewitched by a word. For example, by the word 'know'" (from Wittgenstein 1979)

## References

Attardo, Salvatore, and Victor Raskin
  1991    Script theory revis(it)ed: joke similarity and joke representational model. *Humor: International Journal of Humor Research* 4 (3): 293–347.
Attardo, Salvatore, Christian F. Hempelmann, and Sara Di Maio
  2002    Script oppositions and logical mechanisms: Modeling incongruities and their resolutions. *Humor: International Journal of Humor Research* 15 (1): 3–46.
Bell, Philip
  2002    Blending linguistics and cognition: a methodological critique. In *Odense Working Papers in Language and Communication* 23, Anders Hougaard, and Stefan Nordahl (eds.), 163–180. Syddansk University, Denmark.
Bergen, Benjamin, and Nancy Chang
  2005    Embodied construction grammar in simulation-based language understanding. In *Construction Grammars: Cognitive Grounding and Theoretical Extensions,* Jan-Ola Östman, and Miriam Fried (eds.), 147–190. Amsterdam: Benjamins.
Bryant, John
  2003    Constructional analysis. M.A. diss., University of California, Berkeley.

Carl, Michael, and Andy Way (eds.)
2003    *Recent Advances in Example-based Machine Translation.* (Text, Speech and Language Technology 21.) Berlin: Springer-Verlag.

Chomsky, Noam
1957    *Syntactic Structures.* The Hague: Mouton.

Coulson, Seana
2000    *Semantic Leaps: Frame-shifting and Conceptual Blending in Meaning Construction.* New York/Cambridge: Cambridge University Press.

Croft, William A.
2001    *Radical Construction Grammar; Syntactic Theory in Typological Perspective.* Oxford: Oxford University Press.

Falkenhainer, Brian, Kenneth D. Forbus, and Dedre Gentner
1989    Structure-mapping engine: algorithm and examples. *Artificial Intelligence* 41: 1–63.

Fass, Dan
1988    An account of coherence, semantic relations, metonymy, and lexical ambiguity resolution. In *Lexical Ambiguity Resolution: Perspectives from Psycholinguistics, Neuropsychology and Artificial Intelligence,* Steven I. Small, Garrison W. Cottrell, and Mark K. Tanenhaus (eds.), 151–178. San Mateo, CA: Morgan Kaufman.

Fauconnier, Gilles, and Mark Turner
1998    Conceptual integration networks. *Cognitive Science,* 22 (2): 133–187.
2002    *The Way We Think.* New York: Basic Books.

Forbus, Kenneth D., and Daniel Oblinger
1990    Making SME pragmatic and greedy. In *Proceedings of the Twelfth Annual Meeting of the Cognitive Science Society.* 61–68. Hillsdale, N. J.: Lawrence Erlbaum.

Gardner, Howard
1985    *The Mind's New Science.* New York: Basic Books.

Garey, Michael R., and David S. Johnson
1979    *Computers and Intractability: A Guide to the Theory of NP-Completeness.* San Francisco: W.H. Freeman.

Gibbs, Ray
2000    Making good psychology out of blending theory. *Cognitive Linguistics* 11 (3): 347–358.

Goldberg, Adele
2003    Constructions: a new theoretical approach to language. *TRENDS in Cognitive Sciences,* 7 (5): 219–224.

Jackendoff, Ray
1987    *Consciousness and the Computational Mind.* Cambridge, Mass.: MIT Press.

Koestler, Arthur
1964    *The Act of Creation.* New York: Macmillan.

Miller, George
1995    WordNet: A lexical database for English. *Communications of the ACM,* 38 (11): 39–41.

Plath, William J.
1973    Transformational grammar and transformational parsing in the RE-
        QUEST system. In *Proceedings of the Fifth International Conference on
        Computational Linguistics*, 585–610. Pisa, Italy.

Popper, Karl
1959    *The Logic of Scientific Discovery*. New York: Basic Books.

Raskin, Victor
1985    *Semantic Mechanisms of Humor*. Dordrecht: D. Reidel.
1996    Computer Implementation of the General Theory of Verbal Humor. In
        *The International Workshop on Computational Humour: Proceedings of
        the Twelfth Twente Workshop on Language Technology*, Jan Hulstijn,
        and Anton Nijholt (eds.), 9–20. (Series TWTL 12.) Enschede: UT Ser-
        vice Centrum.

Ritchie, Graeme
2003    *The Linguistic Analysis of Jokes*. London: Routledge.

Schank, Roger C., and Richard P. Abelson
1977    *Scripts, Plans, Goals and Understanding*. New York: Wiley.

Turing, Alan M.
1936    On computable numbers, with an application to the Entscheidung-
        sproblem. In *The Collected Works of Alan Turing*. Vol. 4, Robin O.
        Gandy, and C. E. Michael Yates (eds.). Amsterdam: North Holland.

Veale, Tony
2004    Incongruity in humor: root-cause or epiphenomenon? *Humor: Inter-
        national Journal of Humor Research* (Festschrift for Victor Raskin) 17
        (4): 410–428.

Veale, Tony, and Mark T. Keane
1997    The competence of sub-optimal structure mapping on 'hard' analogies.
        In *Proceedings of the Fifteenth International Conference on Artificial In-
        telligence*, Nagoya, Japan: 232–327. San Mateo, CA.: Morgan Kauf-
        mann.

Veale, Tony, and Diarmuid O'Donoghue
2000    Computation and blending. *Cognitive Linguistics*, 11 (3): 252–281.

Veale, Tony, Diarmuid O'Donoghue, and Mark T. Keane
1996    Computability as a limiting cognitive constraint: complexity concerns
        in metaphor comprehension. In *Cognitive Linguistics: Cultural, Psy-
        chological and Typological Issues*, Masako Hiraga, Chris Sinha, and
        Sherman Wilcox (eds.), 129–155. Amsterdam/Philadelphia: Benjamins

Winston, Patrick H.
1982    Learning new principles from precedents and exercises. *Artificial Intel-
        ligence* 19: 321–350.

Wittgenstein, Ludwig
1958    *Philosophical Investigations*. (Translated by G.E.M. Anscombe). Lon-
        don: Basil Blackwell.
1979    *On Certainty* (Translated by D. Paul and G.E.M. Anscombe). London:
        Basil Blackwell.

# Author index

# Subject index